AutoCAD® 2013 &
AutoCAD LT® 2013
BIBLE

AutoCAD® 2013 & AutoCAD LT® 2013
BIBLE

Ellen Finkelstein

WILEY

John Wiley & Sons, Inc.

AutoCAD® 2013 & AutoCAD LT® 2013 Bible

Published by
John Wiley & Sons, Inc.
10475 Crosspoint Boulevard
Indianapolis, IN 46256
www.wiley.com

Copyright © 2012 by John Wiley & Sons, Inc., Indianapolis, Indiana

Published by John Wiley & Sons, Inc., Indianapolis, Indiana

Published simultaneously in Canada

ISBN: 978-1-118-32829-3

Manufactured in the United States of America

10 9 8 7 6 5 4 3 2 1

For general information on our other products and services or to obtain technical support, please contact our Customer Care Department within the U.S. at (877) 762-2974, outside the U.S. at (317) 572-3993 or fax (317) 572-4002.

Library of Congress Control Number: 2012940033

To MMY, for teaching me that there's more to life than meets the eye and that the deeper levels of life are the most intelligent, powerful, and blissful.

About the Author

Ellen Finkelstein learned AutoCAD in Israel, where she always got to pore over the manual because it was in English. After returning to the United States, she started consulting and teaching AutoCAD as well as other computer programs, including Microsoft Word, Excel, and PowerPoint. She has also taught courses on website creation and Internet marketing. Her website, www.ellenfinkelstein.com, contains tips and techniques for AutoCAD, PowerPoint, and presenting, and she publishes the AutoCAD Tips Blog and the AutoCAD Tips Newsletter. Ellen has written extensively on AutoCAD, including articles for Autodesk's website and features for AutoCAD's Help system. Ellen's first book was AutoCAD For Dummies Quick Reference. Since then, she has written books on PowerPoint, OpenOffice.org (OpenOffice.org For Dummies), Flash (including Flash CS5 For Dummies), and web technologies (Syndicating Web Sites with RSS Feeds For Dummies). You're holding the thirteenth edition (wow!) of this book, which previously appeared for AutoCAD releases 14, 2000, 2002, 2004, 2005, 2006, 2007, 2008, 2009, 2010, 2011, and 2012.

Credits

Senior Acquisitions Editor
Stephanie McComb

Project Editor
Jade L. Williams

Technical Editors
Lee Ambrosius
Melanie Perry

Copy Editor
Marylouise Wiack

Editorial Director
Robyn Siesky

Business Manager
Amy Knies

Senior Marketing Manager
Sandy Smith

**Vice President and Executive Group
Publisher**
Richard Swadley

Vice President and Executive Publisher
Barry Pruett

Senior Project Coordinator
Kristie Rees

Graphics and Production Specialists
Sennett Vaughan Johnson
Jennifer Mayberry

Proofreading
Evelyn Wellborn

Indexing
BIM Indexing & Proofreading Services

Vertical Websites Production Manager
Richard Graves

Contents at a Glance

Bonus Chapters on the Companion Website

Contents

Contents

Contents

Contents

Contents

Contents

Contents

Contents

Contents

Contents

Contents

Acknowledgments

I would like to offer special thanks to Stephanie McComb, my acquisitions editor, who was very supportive throughout the writing of this book.

A huge thank-you goes to Jade Williams, whose extensive organizing power kept the book on track. Jade kept up with a seemingly infinite number of versions of text documents and images, coordinating the writing, editing, and production of the entire book. She's been doing it for years, an amazing accomplishment!

My thanks to Lee Ambrosius (`www.hyperpics.com`), the highly knowledgeable technical editor for most of the book. Lee's comments improved the book throughout. In addition, Lee also took on about one-half of the chapters to update; his expert help made this huge project a lot easier. Melanie Perry did the technical editing for Lee's chapters. They are both AutoCAD authorities and you, the reader, benefit.

Thanks to Jennifer Adams for helping me with some of the edits required for each update. I also thank Marylouise Wiack for her precise editing of this very technical book, and all of the people at Wiley who helped with the production of this book and its companion website.

I also want to express my great appreciation to the members of Autodesk's beta and product teams who were very supportive throughout the beta period. Many people contributed drawings and software for this book. I'd like to thank all of them. They have helped to make this the most comprehensive book on AutoCAD and AutoCAD LT available.

Finally, I would like to thank my husband, Evan, who helped out around the house while I was writing, writing, and writing. Without his support, I could not have completed this book.

Introduction

Welcome to the *AutoCAD 2013 & AutoCAD LT 2013 Bible*. Whether you use AutoCAD or AutoCAD LT, you'll find complete explanations of all the powerful features that you need to know about to design and draw anything. This book is intended to be your comprehensive guide to both the AutoCAD and AutoCAD LT programs.

This book covers every significant AutoCAD and AutoCAD LT feature. If you're a beginning user, you'll find everything you need to start out; if you're already using AutoCAD or AutoCAD LT regularly, the book covers advanced material as well. Although you can use this book as a tutorial if you're just starting out or learning a new set of features, it also provides a solid reference base to come back to again and again. The short tutorials on almost every topic will quickly have you creating professional-level drawings.

For the first time, we have moved a significant amount of content onto the companion website. In fact, you'll find about 500 pages there, including 15 bonus chapters and several addenda. The companion website also includes downloads with the drawings for the exercises, the results of those exercises, a link to the trial version of both AutoCAD 2013 and AutoCAD LT 2013, and add-in programs (which are for AutoCAD only). This book plus the downloads on the companion website contain all that you need to make full use of either program.

AutoCAD 2013 offers a range of new features, including an updated command line; a way to store, open, and even edit drawings online (AutoCAD 360); expanded features for 2D documentation and layout of 3D drawings; a preview of choices you make in the Properties palette; and many small additions to improve your efficiency in both 2D and 3D drawings. Autodesk also offers a new feature, Autodesk Cloud, for online storage.

Is This Book for You?

The *AutoCAD 2013 & AutoCAD LT 2013 Bible* covers all of the essential features of AutoCAD and AutoCAD LT and includes clear, real-life examples and tutorials that you can adapt to your needs.

Although I fully cover the basics, I have also included material on the many advanced features, such as AutoLISP, 3D modeling, rendering, and customization. (Most of the advanced features apply to AutoCAD only and are available as bonus chapters on the companion website.) The following categories should help you decide whether this book is for you.

If you are a new AutoCAD or AutoCAD LT user

If you are new to AutoCAD or AutoCAD LT, the *AutoCAD 2013 & AutoCAD LT 2013 Bible* guides you through all that you need to know to start drawing effectively, whatever your field. Just start at the beginning.

If you are upgrading to AutoCAD 2013 or AutoCAD LT 2013

This book highlights all of the new features and helps you to make the upgrade transition as seamless as possible. Look for the New Feature icons.

If you are switching from another CAD program

You already know what CAD is all about. This book clearly explains the AutoCAD and AutoCAD LT way of drawing the models that you have already been drawing. In addition, you'll find a great deal of essential information about transferring files and data from other formats.

How This Book Is Organized

This book is divided into five parts and includes a companion website.

Part I: Introducing AutoCAD and AutoCAD LT Basics

Part I provides the background information that you need to start drawing. It starts with a "quick tour" that has you drawing right away and then covers how to start a drawing, use commands, specify coordinates, and set up a drawing.

Part II: Drawing in Two Dimensions

Part II covers all of the commands and procedures for drawing and editing in two dimensions. In addition, I discuss how to control the drawing process with layers, zooming, and panning. This part also includes information about dimensioning, plotting, and printing. An addendum on the companion website provides supplemental content on parametric constraints, groups, and selection filters.

Part III: Working with Data

Part III covers many ways to organize and share data, including using blocks, attributes, and external references. An addendum on the companion website covers extracting attribute data.

Part IV: Drawing in Three Dimensions

Part IV explains everything that you need to know to draw in three dimensions. A bonus chapter on the companion website discusses how to present 3D drawings using shading and rendering techniques; it's an Adobe PDF file.

Part V: Appendixes

Part V provides additional information for AutoCAD and AutoCAD LT users. Appendix A covers additional resources for AutoCAD and AutoCAD LT users. Appendix B explains what you'll find on the companion website. Bonus Chapter 15, which was an appendix in the previous edition, gives instructions for installing and configuring AutoCAD and AutoCAD LT; you'll find it on the companion website in PDF format.

The companion website

By now, you're probably wondering how to find the companion website, since I've mentioned it so many times. The companion website contains all of the drawings that you need to do the exercises in this book. These drawings are a great resource to help you learn using real-world examples. Look for the Drawings download. In addition, the website includes the drawings that result after you finish an exercise or tutorial. In this way, you can check whether you have done an exercise correctly; you'll find these drawings in the Result download.

In addition, the companion website contains 15 bonus chapters, several addenda (pieces of chapters), a few video tutorials, and a list of AutoCAD resources.

NOTE
You can download the current 30-day trial of AutoCAD from www.autodesk.com/autocad-trial. For AutoCAD LT, go to www.autodesk.com/autocadlt-trial.

Appendix B contains a list of everything on the companion website.

You can find all this extra material in two places:

- The publisher, Wiley, maintains the official companion website at www.wiley.com/go/autocad2013bible.
- I have the same content on my website. The only difference is that, when you sign up for my free AutoCAD Tips Newsletter, you'll get a free ebook, "25 Productivity Tips Every AutoCAD User Should Know," additional video tutorials, and a collection of software for AutoCAD. Just go to www.ellenfinkelstein.com/autocadbible/.

How to Use This Book

You can use this book in two ways: as a tutorial and learning tool, or as a reference.

As a tutorial

The overall organization of the book goes from simple to complex, and each chapter has several step-by-step exercises. This enables you to use the book as a tutorial, from beginning to end. You can always go back and redo any exercise when you need to refresh your memory on a particular feature. I've taught AutoCAD using this book and it makes a great textbook!

For newcomers to AutoCAD or AutoCAD LT, Parts I (AutoCAD and AutoCAD LT Basics) and II (Drawing in Two Dimensions) are essential. After that, you can refer to chapters that interest you. Parts III (Working with Data) and Bonus Chapters 3 through 5 are also useful for beginners. Intermediate users will probably be familiar with most of the material in Part I and will be more likely to skip around, looking for the specific topics that they need. However, don't forget that many new features are introduced in Part I. Enough material appears in this book to bring intermediate users up to an advanced level.

I have designed this book to be comprehensive and to include every significant feature of AutoCAD and AutoCAD LT. Therefore, do not be concerned if some of the material seems too advanced. It will be there when you are ready for it.

As a reference

The *AutoCAD 2013 & AutoCAD LT 2013 Bible* is organized as a reference that you can use whenever you are stuck, or when you try to do something for the first time. Each chapter covers a topic completely, making it easy to find what you're looking for. You can do each Steps exercise (with a few exceptions) on its own without doing the other exercises in the chapter. You can easily look up a topic and complete a related exercise without having to go through the entire chapter. A complete index at the back of the book can also help you to find features and topics.

Using the Kindle version

The *AutoCAD 2013 & AutoCAD LT 2013 Bible* is available in a Kindle version. As with the printed book, you need to access the drawings from the companion website. (The two available URLs are listed earlier in this introduction.)

Doing the Exercises

I recommend that you do the exercises from the beginning. These earlier exercises include important instructions that may affect your system later. For example, one of the first exercises is to create a new folder to hold the drawings for other exercises. This folder keeps your exercise drawings separate from other drawings that have been created in your office. However, most exercises stand on their own so that you can go back and do only the exercises that you need.

AutoCAD is a very customizable program. AutoCAD LT can also be customized in many ways, although to a lesser extent. This book assumes that you are working with the default setup. However, a number of changes may have been made to your system that could result in the user interface and drawings appearing or even functioning differently from those shown in this book. If you installed AutoCAD or AutoCAD LT yourself and made some adjustments, you know what changes you have made. However, if you are using a computer that was set up by someone else, it may help to talk to that person first, to see what changes he or she made.

In addition, as you work through some of the exercises in this book, you will make certain changes in the program's setup. Most of these are minor changes that any user would make while drawing. For safety, Cautions and Tips accompany all changes that could have serious consequences, such as customizing the menu. For example, when customizing the menu, you will be instructed to copy the menu file under a new name, and you will then work with the new menu file, not the original one. Nevertheless, if you are working on a network or sharing your computer with someone else, it is important to consult with others who may be affected by the changes that you make.

 You can create your own configuration to help ensure that certain changes that you make will not affect others. Instructions for doing this appear in Bonus Chapter 15 under the heading "Creating Multiple Configurations."

The exercises in the *AutoCAD 2013 & AutoCAD LT 2013 Bible* have been carefully checked by a technical editor to ensure accuracy. However, we cannot anticipate all situations, due to either varying hardware and software configurations or customization. If you have a problem with an exercise, contact me at the e-mail address listed at the end of this Introduction so that I can correct the problem in the book's next edition. I will also try to give you the information that you need to complete the exercise.

Conventions Used in This Book

Given all the ways in which you can execute a command in AutoCAD and AutoCAD LT, you'll find it useful to read this section, which describes this book's typographical conventions. You will find this section helpful for doing the step-by-step exercises as well.

Using commands

AutoCAD and AutoCAD LT offer workspaces (covered fully in Bonus Chapter 15) that provide very different ways of executing commands. The default workspace, Drafting & Annotation, uses the ribbon and Application menu, whereas the Classic workspace uses more traditional menus and toolbars. I use the default workspace (or the 3D Modeling workspace for 3D drawing in AutoCAD) throughout the book. All workspaces offer a command line, where you can execute a command by entering its name.

When I explain how to execute a command, I give the instructions for doing so on the ribbon. In addition, I almost always provide the name of the command so that you can enter it on the command line.

The ribbon created a quandary for me, because I know that some people, especially those upgrading from earlier releases, don't use it; instead, they will prefer to use the Classic workspace with its familiar menus and toolbars. However, I felt that explaining how to execute each command in three ways (the ribbon, the menu/toolbar, and the command line) would be awkward, perhaps confusing, and space consuming.

So what should you do if you are using this book with the Classic workspace? In many cases, especially if you're upgrading, you'll already know where to find familiar commands. For new commands, it's easy to find their location in the Classic workspace by going to the Help system. Follow these steps:

1. Type the name of the command on the command line or in the Dynamic Input box.
2. Press F1 to open the Help window of Autodesk Exchange.
3. Look at the top of the right-hand pane, where you'll find instructions for all the available methods of executing the command.

When referring to the ribbon, I might say, "Choose Home tab⇨Draw panel⇨Line," which means to click the Home tab if it's not already displayed, look for the Draw control panel, and click the Line button in that panel. If you're not sure which button to click, hover the mouse cursor over a button to see its tooltip, which provides more information. You can expand many control panels by clicking their title at the bottom of the ribbon; if a command is on the expanded section, I indicate that in the instruction.

A few of the ribbon panels have drop-down menus, which are equivalent to sub-menus. Therefore, to indicate which button to click, I may need to tell you to choose View tab⇨Navigation panel⇨Zoom drop-down menu⇨Zoom Extents. Although I haven't found a good alternative, this is not completely satisfactory for two reasons. First, it's a mouthful! Second, the drop-down menus' names do not appear, making it hard to know which is the Zoom drop-down menu. However, in most cases, the button icon will make it obvious which drop-down menu I'm talking about.

To indicate that you should choose a command from the Application menu, for example, I say, "Choose Application Button⇨Save," which means that you should click the Application Button at the upper-left corner of the application window (which opens the Application menu), and then click the Save item.

Every command also has a command name that you can type on the command line, which appears at the bottom of your screen. Command names are shown in capital letters, as in CIRCLE. AutoLISP functions (which apply to AutoCAD only) are shown in small capital letters, as in COMMAND.

Figures

In order to create clear, legible figures, I have used a white background in AutoCAD. However, many people use a black or dark gray drawing area. In Bonus Chapter 15, I explain how to change this color. As you read through the book, you should be aware that you may see on your screen a negative image of what I show in the figures — a dark background and light-colored objects. Once you get used to this difference, you'll easily recognize what you see in the figures.

In AutoCAD, the 3D environment further changes what you see on your screen. The default 3D background is gray. Again, I have sometimes changed the background color to white (in most cases) for the purpose of creating a clear figure.

Prompts, your input, and instructions

In the step-by-step exercises, most instructions are presented in the same font and style that you are reading now. However, when I reproduce the command line, the prompts appear in a `nonproportional font`. Other instructions (such as *"Type the first coordinate"*) are shown in italic. In any context, input that you need to type appears in **bold**.

The Dynamic Input feature shows prompts near your cursor, but additional options only appear if you click the down arrow on your keyboard. To make clear all of the available options, I use the command line format of prompts.

I often refer to specific elements in a drawing. References to these elements appear in the text as numbers in circles, such as ❶, ❷, ❸, and so on. (In chapter addenda, you'll just see the number in bold.) You'll find the corresponding number in the figure to which the text refers.

Mouse and keyboard terms

A mouse can have two or more buttons. Many users like using a mouse with at least three buttons, because you can customize the buttons to suit your needs. However, because many mice have only two buttons, I assume only two plus a wheel. The left mouse button is used to choose commands and toolbar buttons and to pick points in your drawing. For this reason, it is sometimes called the *pick button*. The right button usually opens a shortcut menu.

The time-sensitive right-clicking feature enables you to use the right button either to open a shortcut menu or as the equivalent of pressing Enter. Because this feature is not on by default, I do not assume that you have turned it on. I use the term *right-click* when you need to access a shortcut menu. If you have time-sensitive right-clicking turned on, you need to hold down the right mouse button for more than 250 milliseconds (by default) to display the shortcut menu. See Chapter 3 and Bonus Chapter 15 for more details.

Introduction

If I say one of the following

- Choose Application Button⇨Options
- Choose Home tab⇨Draw control panel⇨Line
- Select the circle in your drawing

it means you need to use the left button on your mouse.

When I say to press Enter, it means that you need to press the key that is marked Enter, Return, or ↵ on your keyboard. Often I use the bent arrow symbol (↵) that you see on your Enter key to indicate that you should press Enter.

I also use the mouse terms listed in the following table.

Mouse Terms

Term	Description
Cursor	The shape on your screen that shows you where the mouse is pointed. It can take a number of forms, such as crosshairs, a pickbox, or an arrow. It is also known as the mouse pointer.
Pickbox	A type of cursor consisting of a small box, used to select drawing objects.
Crosshairs	A type of cursor consisting of intersecting lines, sometimes with a pickbox at their center.
Pick	Point to a drawing object and click the left mouse button.
Click	Press the left mouse button once and release it.
Double-click	Press the left mouse button twice in rapid succession.
Click and drag	Click the left mouse button and hold it down while you move the mouse, dragging an object on your screen with it.
Choose	Click a ribbon item, menu item, toolbar button, or dialog box item. You can sometimes choose an item using the keyboard, as well. I also use this word when you need to choose a command option, which you can do by choosing from a shortcut menu with a mouse, as well as by typing the option's abbreviation on the keyboard.
Right-click	Press the right mouse button once and release it. If you have turned on time-sensitive right-clicking, hold the right mouse button for at least 250 milliseconds (by default) before releasing it.
Shift and click	While holding down the Shift key, press the left mouse button once and release it.
Shift and right-click	While holding down the Shift key, press the right mouse button once and release it.
Shift and mouse wheel	Press the Shift key and hold down the mouse wheel, using it like a button.
Select	Highlight an object in a drawing by picking it or by using another object selection method, or highlight text in a dialog box or text document.

What the Icons Mean

The *AutoCAD 2013 & AutoCAD LT 2013 Bible* is liberally sprinkled with icons — symbols in the left margin that call your attention to noteworthy points.

AUTOCAD ONLY

This icon means that the feature that I am discussing is not available in AutoCAD LT.

CAUTION

The Caution icon means that you should pay special attention to the information or instructions because you could cause a problem otherwise.

 Cross-reference arrows refer you to a related topic elsewhere in the book. Because you may not read this book straight through from cover to cover, you can use cross-references to quickly find just the information you need.

NEW FEATURE

The New Feature icon means that a feature is new to AutoCAD 2013 or AutoCAD LT 2013 or has been significantly changed.

NOTE

A Note icon alerts you to some important point that requires special attention, or additional information that may be helpful.

ON THE WEB

The On the Web icon highlights references to related material on the companion website.

TIP

A Tip shows you a way to accomplish a task more efficiently or quickly. You'll find plenty of practical advice here.

Other Information

This book assumes that you know the basics of Windows, although the instructions that you'll read here are usually detailed enough to get you through any task.

The *AutoCAD 2013 & AutoCAD LT 2013* Bible covers AutoCAD 2013 and AutoCAD LT 2013. However, most of the information also applies to the 2012 release of both programs. I have used AutoCAD in Windows 7, but almost everything also applies to Windows Vista, although some of the screens will look different. If you are using AutoCAD LT 2013, again, some of the screens will look different. Where there is a significant difference between AutoCAD and AutoCAD LT, I explain the difference.

Contacting the Author

I would be happy to hear any comments that you have about this book. The best way to contact me is by e-mail at ellen@ellenfinkelstein.com. You can also use the United States Postal Service (a.k.a. snail mail) and write to me in care of Wiley. Please note that I can't provide technical support for my readers. I have my own website at www.ellenfinkelstein.com that contains information on my books, errata (at www.ellenfinkelstein.com/autoCAD.html#errata), and AutoCAD, including many AutoCAD tips. I invite you to sign up there for my free AutoCAD Tips Newsletter, so that you can continue the learning process. Go to www.ellenfinkelstein.com/acad_submit.html.

Part I

Introducing AutoCAD and AutoCAD LT Basics

Drawing a Window

L earning AutoCAD or AutoCAD LT is a bit like trying to decide which came first — the chicken or the egg. On one hand, you need to know the basics before you can start drawing. On the other hand, understanding the basics can be very difficult if you haven't had the experience of drawing something. In this Quick Start chapter, you resolve this problem by drawing, dimensioning, and printing a simple window in AutoCAD or AutoCAD LT.

This Quick Start chapter is meant for beginners. You get the feel of AutoCAD's precision drawing tools and experience how to build a drawing. The AutoCAD/AutoCAD LT interface is very customizable. Note that the instructions for the exercise in this chapter assume that no one has made major changes to the default settings.

> **NOTE**
> When you start AutoCAD 2013 for the very first time, the Migrate Custom Settings dialog box may appear, asking you to migrate your custom settings from a previous release of AutoCAD. By default, the Welcome Screen opens each time you open AutoCAD; just click the Close button to close it.

> **NOTE**
> In Chapter 1, I provide instructions for creating a special `AutoCAD Bible` folder for all the exercises in this book. If you want to create this folder now, do so and save the drawing in the folder.

> **ON THE WEB**
> The file used in this exercise on drawing a window, `abqs-a.dwt`, is a template available from the Drawings download on the companion website. This download is in zipped format, so you need to unzip the file before doing this exercise (as well as others in this book).You can find the location of the companion website in the Introduction to this book.

1. Double-click the AutoCAD or AutoCAD LT icon on your desktop to start the program.

    You see a new drawing. (If you are prompted for a template, skip to Step 2, third sentence.)

2. Choose Application Button ⇨ New. (The Application Button is the red A at the upper-left corner of your screen.) The Select Template dialog box opens. Navigate to the folder where you unzipped the Drawings download from this book's companion website, choose `abqs-a.dwt`, and click Open. You see a blank drawing. (I explain more about templates and opening drawings in Chapter 2.)

> **CAUTION**
> Don't use the default drawing. You need to open this template, available from the companion website, for the rest of the exercise to work properly.

3. To save the drawing and give it a name, choose Application Button ⇨ Save. In the Save Drawing As dialog box, use the Save In drop-down list to navigate to any convenient folder, such as the `My Documents` (or `Documents`) folder or the `AutoCAD Bible` folder you created. Type **abqs-01** in the File Name text box and click Save. (I go into more detail about saving a drawing in Chapter 1.)

4. To free up the drawing area, close any windows or palettes that are open by clicking their Close (X) button, so that your screen looks like Figure QS.1. I've changed the background color to white, but yours will probably be dark gray or black.

> **NOTE**
> This chapter assumes that you're using the default Drafting & Annotation Workspace. If the Drafting & Annotation workspace isn't shown in the drop-down list located in the upper-left corner of your screen, click the Workspace drop-down arrow and choose Drafting & Annotation.

FIGURE QS.1

The AutoCAD screen, as shown while drawing a rectangle (see Step 6)

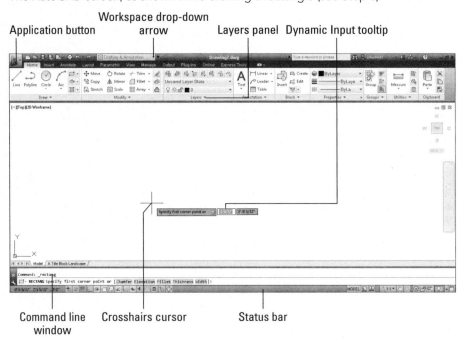

5. At the top of the screen, you see a tabbed area filled with buttons, called the *Ribbon*, which contains the Layers *panel* (section) on the Home tab, as shown in Figure QS.1. From the Layer drop-down list in the Layers panel, click the down arrow and choose WINDOW, as shown in Figure QS.2. (Layers help you organize the objects in your drawing; I cover them in detail in Chapter 11.) Anything you draw will now be on the WINDOW layer. (If you don't see the WINDOW layer, you may not have started with the `abqs-a.dwt` template. This template contains the layers that you need to use.)

FIGURE QS.2

Choose the WINDOW layer from the list of layers.

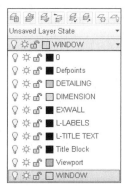

 6. With your left mouse button (also called the *pick button*), choose Home tab⇨Draw panel⇨ Rectangle/Polygon drop-down menu⇨Rectangle. (Using the Ribbon is only one way to give AutoCAD and AutoCAD LT commands. I explain other ways in Chapter 3. You can find more about drawing lines and rectangles in Chapter 6.)

Move your mouse so that the cursor is in the main drawing area. Your screen should look like Figure QS.1. If you don't see the tooltip bar — also called the Dynamic Input tooltip — near the cursor, then click the Dynamic Input button on the status bar at the bottom of your screen.

7. Follow these prompts to draw a rectangle that is 44" wide and 80" high.

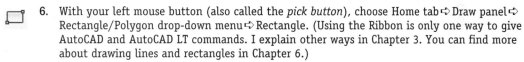
```
Specify first corner point or [Chamfer/Elevation/Fillet/Thickness/Width]:
    0,0 ↵
Specify other corner point or [Area/Dimensions/Rotation]: 44,80 ↵
```

> **NOTE**
> In an architectural drawing using Imperial units, distances are assumed to be in inches, so you don't need to specify a unit (although you can if you want).

Notice that the text that you type appears next to the cursor in the Dynamic Input tooltip. When you press Enter, the text that you typed is echoed in the Command Line window at the bottom of the screen.

8. To create a second rectangle inside the first one, choose Home tab⇨Modify panel⇨Offset. (I cover this and other editing commands in Chapters 9 and 10.) Follow these prompts:

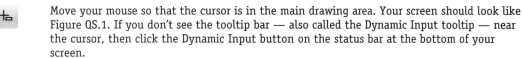
```
Specify offset distance or [Through/Erase/Layer] <Through>: 4 ↵
Select object to offset or [Exit/Undo] <Exit>: Click the rectangle's edge
    to select it.
Specify point on side to offset or [Exit/Multiple/Undo] <Exit>: Click
    anywhere inside the rectangle.
Select object to offset or [Exit/Undo] <Exit>: ↵
```

9. You can draw from geometric points on objects such as endpoints and midpoints. (I explain how to specify coordinate points in Chapter 4.) To draw a line between the midpoints of the inner rectangle, choose Home tab ⇨ Draw panel ⇨ Line, and follow these prompts:

```
Specify first point: Press and hold the Shift key and right-click. From
    the shortcut menu that opens, choose Midpoint. Place the cursor near
    the midpoint of the left side of the inner rectangle. When you see a
    triangle and the Midpoint tooltip, click.
Specify next point or [Undo]: Press and hold the Shift key and right-
    click. From the shortcut menu that opens, choose Midpoint. This time,
    place the cursor near the midpoint of the right side of the inner
    rectangle. When you see the Midpoint tooltip and triangle, click.
Specify next point or [Undo]: ↵
```

Your drawing should now look like Figure QS.3. (Your window should be green.)

FIGURE QS.3

The beginning of a window

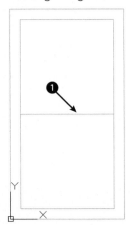

10. You will now draw a temporary construction line to help you find a starting point for the pane in the top of the window. Again, choose Home tab ⇨ Draw panel ⇨ Line. Follow these prompts:

```
Specify first point: Press Shift and right-click. Choose Endpoint from
    the shortcut menu. Pick the left endpoint of the last line you drew
    at ❶ in Figure QS.3.
Specify next point or [Undo]: 4,4 ↵. (This notation specifies that the
    endpoint of the line is 4 units above and to the right of the first
    point. Chapter 4 explains more about specifying coordinates in this
    manner.)
Specify next point or [Undo]: ↵
```

11. Again, choose Home tab ⇨ Draw panel ⇨ Rectangle/Polygon drop-down menu ⇨ Rectangle. Follow these prompts:

```
Specify first corner point or [Chamfer/Elevation/Fillet/Thickness/Width]:
    Press Shift and right-click. Choose Endpoint and pick the final
    endpoint of the diagonal line you just drew.
Specify other corner point or [Area/Dimensions/Rotation]: 2'4",2'4" ↵
```

 12. Choose Home tab ⇨ Modify panel ⇨ Erase. At the Select objects: prompt, click the short, diagonal construction line that you drew in Step 10. The Select objects: prompt appears again. Press Enter to end the command. (Chapter 9 explains the ERASE command as well as other simple editing commands.)

 13. Click the Ortho Mode button on the status bar at the bottom of the drawing area if it is not already selected (blue). The Ortho feature constrains drawing to right angles — either horizontal or vertical. (You can find more about Ortho Mode in Chapter 4.)

14. To finish the bottom of the window, choose Home tab ⇨ Draw panel ⇨ Line. Follow these prompts:

```
Specify first point: 8",3'4" ↵
Specify next point or [Undo]: Move the mouse cursor down from the start
    point of the line. You see a temporary drag line. Then type the
    following length of the line. 2'8-7/16 ↵
```

```
Specify next point or [Undo]: Move the cursor horizontally to the right
    and type 28 ↵.
Specify next point or [Close/Undo]: Now try entering the distance using
    decimal notation, rather than feet and inches. Move the cursor up and
    type 32.4375 ↵
Specify next point or [Close/Undo]: ↵
```

15. To draw shutters, first change the layer. Choose Home tab ⇨ Layers panel, click the Layer drop-down list, and choose EXWALL.

16. Choose Home tab ⇨ Draw panel ⇨ Line. Follow the prompts:

    Specify first point: *Press Shift and right-click. Choose Endpoint from*
        the shortcut menu. Click the upper-left corner of the window.
    Specify next point or [Undo]: *Move the cursor to the left. Type* **1'6"** ↵
    Specify next point or [Undo]: *Move the cursor down. Type* **6'8"** ↵
    Specify next point or [Close/Undo]: *Type* **#0,0** ↵. *(The pound sign ensures*
        that your line goes to 0,0 no matter where you are.)
    Specify next point or [Close/Undo]: ↵

17. To draw the opposite shutter, you'll mirror the first shutter that you just drew. (I cover the MIRROR command and many other editing commands in Chapter 10.) Choose Home tab ⇨ Modify panel ⇨ Mirror, and follow these prompts:

    Select objects: *Click the three lines that make up the shutter.*
    Select objects: ↵
    Specify first point of mirror line: *Press Shift and right-click. Choose*
        Midpoint from the shortcut menu.
    Place the cursor near the middle of the top horizontal line of the
        window. Click when you see the triangle and Midpoint tooltip.
    Specify second point of mirror line: *(The Ortho Mode button should still*
        be blue. If it isn't, click it.) Move the cursor downward and pick
        any point.
    Erase source objects? [Yes/No] <N>: ↵

    The window should look like Figure QS.4.

18. To add a dimension to the bottom of the window, you should first change the layer. Choose Home tab ⇨ Layers panel ⇨ Layer drop-down list, and choose DIMENSION. (Chapters 14 and 15 explain how to create and format all types of dimensions.)

FIGURE QS.4

The completed window

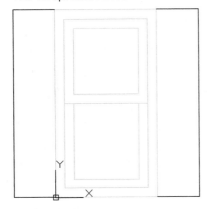

19. To place the dimension, choose Home tab ⇨ Annotation panel, and click the Dimension drop-down menu. Choose Linear from the list of dimension types. Follow the prompts.

```
Specify first extension line origin or <select object>: ↵ (Pressing Enter
    lets you select an object to dimension.)
Select object to dimension: Pick the bottom horizontal line of the window
    (the bottom of the rectangle).
Specify dimension line location or [Mtext/Text/Angle/Horizontal/Vertical/
    Rotated]: Move the cursor down until the dimension is nicely spaced
    below the window. Click to place the dimension line.
```

> **NOTE**
> If you don't have enough room to place the dimension below the window, type pan and press Enter. Click and drag upward a bit. Press the Esc key to end panning.

20. Click Save on the Quick Access Toolbar at the upper-left corner of the window to save your work.

21. To prepare for printing, click the A Title Block-Landscape tab just above the Command line, on the left. (If you don't see a tab, click the A title Block-Landscape button, which is the second button from the left in the right-hand group of buttons on the status bar at the bottom of your screen.) You then see the window inside a titleblock and border, as shown in Figure QS.5. This titleblock and border come with the template to help you easily prepare the drawing for printing. (Chapter 17 explains how to lay out and print/plot a drawing.)

FIGURE QS.5

The window with a titleblock as it appears on the Layout tab.

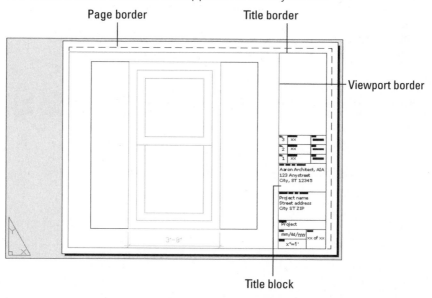

22. To set the scale for printing, click the magenta viewport border (labeled in Figure QS.5). Choose View tab ⇨ Palettes panel ⇨ Properties. In the Properties palette's Misc. section, click the Standard Scale item. (To see this item, you may have to scroll down in the Properties palette or enlarge it by dragging on its bottom and right edges. If the palette collapses to a thin bar, pass your cursor over the bar to expand it.) Click the down arrow that appears to the right of this item and check that the scale is set to 1" = 1'-0". Click the Close button at the top of the Properties palette. (I explain more about scales in Chapter 5.)

23. If the window and its dimension are not centered in the viewport window, double-click inside the viewport border. Then choose View tab ⇨ Navigate 2D panel ⇨ Pan. Click and drag as necessary to center the window in the viewport. Press Esc to exit Pan mode. Double-click outside the viewport border to return to the layout.

24. To add some text to the titleblock, you need to zoom in. (I explain zooming in more detail in Chapter 8.) Choose View tab ⇨ Navigate 2D panel ⇨ Zoom drop-down menu (the bottom button in the panel) ⇨ Window. At the first prompt, click slightly above and to the left of the words Project Name. At the next prompt, click slightly below and to the right of the words City ST ZIP.

    These words should now appear very large in the drawing area. They are already placed and formatted, so all you need to do is replace them. (I explain all about how to create and edit text in Chapter 13.)

25. Click the `Project name` text. Then right-click and choose Mtext Edit from the menu that appears. A Text Editor tab appears. A ruler also appears, as shown in Figure QS.6.

FIGURE QS.6

Editing text for a drawing

26. Select the text by dragging from the upper-left corner to the lower-right corner. Type the following:

    Double-hung window ↵

    2010 Coral Lane ↵

    Anytown, IA 12345

    Click the Close Text Editor button at the right end of the Text Editor tab to close the In-Place Text Editor.

27. To return to your previous view, choose View tab⇨Navigate 2D panel⇨Back.

28. Click Save on the Quick Access Toolbar to save your drawing.

29. You're ready to print your drawing! Depending on your setup, either you can print directly to your printer, or if you have a plotter available, you can use that. (The layout is set up to fit on an 8 1/2-x-11-inch or A-size sheet of paper.) Choose Plot on the Quick Access Toolbar. The Plot dialog box opens. (I cover printing and plotting in Chapter 17. Bonus Chapter 15 explains how to configure a printer or plotter.)

30. In the Printer/Plotter section of the Plot dialog box, click the Name drop-down list and choose the printer or plotter that you want to use. In the Plot Area section, make sure that the What To Plot drop-down list reads Layout; if not, choose Layout from the list.

31. Click the Preview button to open the preview window. You should see the window and its titleblock laid out, as shown in Figure QS.7.

FIGURE QS.7

Viewing the window in Preview mode

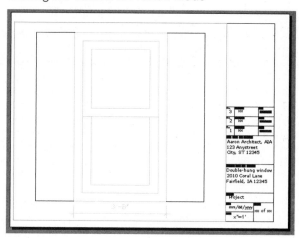

Help! My Drawing Doesn't Look Like the Figure

If your drawing doesn't look like the image shown in Figure QS.7, there could be several reasons. To fix the problem, try one of the following solutions:

- You may have made a mistake when creating the drawing. Start over and follow the prompts again.

- You may not have opened the correct template. Be sure to use the template from the Drawings download on the *AutoCAD 2013 and AutoCAD LT 2013 Bible* companion website, as explained in Step 2 of the preceding exercise. Then follow the prompts again.

- If your drawing still seems wrong, go to the companion website and download the finished file from the Results download. Unzip this file. Choose Application Menu ⇨ Open and use the Open dialog box to find abqs-01.dwg. This drawing contains the end result of the exercise. Try to find the difference between this drawing and yours. You can also open abqs-01.dwg and print or plot it.

One of the preceding options should solve your problem.

NOTE

If things don't seem right, click the Close Preview Window button and review the previous steps to see if you can find the problem. Also, see the sidebar, "Help! My drawing doesn't look like the figure."

  32. Make sure that your printer or plotter has an 81/2-x-11-inch or A-size sheet of paper, and click the Plot button on the Preview window's toolbar. Congratulations — you've just created and printed your first drawing!

33. Click the Close button at the upper-right corner of the AutoCAD application window to close both AutoCAD and the drawing. Click Yes to save your changes.

ON THE WEB

If you're still having problems with the exercise, view QS-Drawing_a_Window.avi, a video of the exercise, available from the Videos download on the companion website.

Summary

In this exercise, you practiced many of the skills that you need to use AutoCAD or AutoCAD LT effectively. Most of your work in AutoCAD or AutoCAD LT builds on these basic skills. The rest of the chapters in this book explain these procedures in more detail as well as many features not covered in this Quick Start exercise.

Starting to Draw

I n this chapter, I explain the essentials that you need to start drawing. After a little background, I discuss the basics of the screen that you see when you open AutoCAD or AutoCAD LT, and how to use it. If you've never used AutoCAD before, do the "Quick Start: Drawing a Window" chapter first.

AutoCAD and its younger sister, AutoCAD LT, are both created by Autodesk. Together they are the most widely used technical drawing programs anywhere. According to Autodesk, CAD stands for *computer-aided design,* but it can also stand for computer-aided *drafting* or *drawing.*

The first version of AutoCAD, running under DOS, came out in 1982. At the time, most other technical drawing programs ran on high-end workstations or even mainframes. AutoCAD LT was introduced in 1993, as a less expensive alternative to AutoCAD, for people who don't need all of AutoCAD's advanced features.

Exploring AutoCAD's Advantages

AutoCAD's success has been attributed to its famous *open architecture* — the flexibility that the end user has to customize the program by using source code files in plain text (ASCII) format — and programming languages (such as AutoLISP, VB.NET, C#, and C++).

As a result, AutoCAD is an extremely flexible drafting program, applicable to all fields. AutoCAD's support for languages other than English, including those using other alphabets, is unparalleled, making AutoCAD highly popular abroad. As a result, AutoCAD is used in all disciplines and in more than 150 countries.

Through a high level of technical innovation and expertise, Autodesk has created a program with advanced features and capabilities, including 3D surface and solid modeling and visualization, access to external databases, intelligent dimensioning, importing and exporting of other file formats, Internet support, and much more.

Comparing AutoCAD and AutoCAD LT

AutoCAD LT's advantages are its lower cost and its compatibility with AutoCAD. The programming code that is used to create AutoCAD LT is a subset of the code used in AutoCAD. Here are the major differences between AutoCAD and AutoCAD LT:

- AutoCAD includes features that enable CAD managers to hold drawings to certain standards, such as for layer names and text styles. AutoCAD LT doesn't contain these features.
- AutoCAD LT is not as customizable as AutoCAD, which is both programmable and fully customizable. It also doesn't include the Action Recorder.
- AutoCAD LT includes minimal options for 3D; AutoCAD includes a full-featured 3D capability, including visual styles and 3D rendering.
- AutoCAD LT is deployable on a network but does not have AutoCAD's network license management feature that includes reporting and flexible licensing.
- AutoCAD LT does not come with Express Tools, a set of additional routines that ship with AutoCAD.
- AutoCAD LT does not include parametric constraints, which allow you to constrain the relationships among objects, but you can use the parametric constraints that are in a drawing that was created with AutoCAD.

Some of the other differences are only in the user interface, so you can accomplish the same task but the procedure is slightly different.

Starting AutoCAD and AutoCAD LT

This section starts a quick tour of AutoCAD and AutoCAD LT. The first step is to start the program.

ON THE WEB

You can download a 30-day trial version of the current version of AutoCAD at www.autodesk.com/autocad-trial and AutoCAD LT at www.autodesk.com/autocadlt-trial.

This book covers AutoCAD 2013 and AutoCAD LT 2013 running on Windows XP Home/Professional, Windows Vista, or Windows 7. (The figures were taken in Windows 7.) Every computer is set up somewhat differently, so you may need to adjust the following steps slightly. If you didn't install the software yourself and are unfamiliar with the folders (also called *directories*) on your computer, get help from someone who is familiar with your computer system.

NOTE

AutoCAD is available for the Mac OS; this book doesn't cover it, but you can find out more and get a free trial from the Autodesk website. Go to www.autodesk.com/autocadformac to learn more.

 If you need information on installing AutoCAD or AutoCAD LT, see Bonus Chapter 15. Bonus Chapter 15 also covers configuring the software and printers or plotters.

By default, installing AutoCAD or AutoCAD LT places a shortcut on your desktop. You can double-click one of the shortcuts to launch the program that is installed on your machine, or use the Windows Start menu to choose one of the following:

- **For AutoCAD.** Start ➪ (All) Programs ➪ Autodesk ➪ AutoCAD 2013 – English ➪ AutoCAD 2013 – English (or as appropriate for your language)
- **For AutoCAD LT.** Start ➪ (All) Programs ➪ Autodesk ➪ AutoCAD LT 2013 – English ➪ AutoCAD LT 2013 – English (or as appropriate for your language)

> **NOTE**
>
> When you first open AutoCAD or AutoCAD LT, the Welcome window appears, providing access to recently opened drawings, related applications for purchase, training, tips, and more. To close the window, click its Close button. If you don't want to see this window when you open AutoCAD, uncheck the Display at Startup check box in the lower-left corner of the window. To display the Welcome window at any time, click the drop-down menu attached to the Help button on the right side of the title bar (see Figure 1.1).

Creating a New Drawing

After you launch AutoCAD or AutoCAD LT, it automatically opens a new drawing named `Drawing1.dwg`. You can see the drawing name on the title bar. You can start drawing immediately. In Chapter 2, I explain how to start a drawing based on a template and how to open an existing drawing.

STEPS: Starting AutoCAD or AutoCAD LT

1. Click Start on the Windows task bar at the bottom of your screen.
2. Choose one of the following:
   - **For AutoCAD.** Start ➪ (All) Programs ➪ Autodesk ➪ AutoCAD 2013 – English ➪ AutoCAD 2013 – English
   - **For AutoCAD LT.** Start ➪ (All) Programs ➪ Autodesk ➪ AutoCAD LT 2013 – English ➪ AutoCAD LT 2013 – English

   You see a blank drawing named `Drawing1.dwg`.

If you are continuing with this chapter, keep this drawing open. I cover exiting from AutoCAD and AutoCAD LT later in this chapter.

Using the AutoCAD and AutoCAD LT Interface

AutoCAD offers four quite different preset *workspaces*, depending on how you want to work. For example, these workspaces determine the Ribbon components, toolbars, and other interface items that you see. AutoCAD offers both 2D and 3D environments. AutoCAD LT has only 2D environments, and the 2D environments for AutoCAD and AutoCAD LT are similar. In this section, I discuss the 2D environment. Both AutoCAD and AutoCAD LT offer two 2D workspaces: Drafting & Annotation and AutoCAD (or AutoCAD LT) Classic. The Drafting & Annotation workspace is the default workspace and displays the

Ribbon for executing commands. The AutoCAD Classic and AutoCAD LT Classic workspaces display toolbars and a menu instead.

> **NOTE**
>
> AutoCAD's 3D Modeling and 3D Basics workspaces create a 3D environment along with the 3D drawing templates `acad3D.dwt` and `acadiso3D.dwt`. (I cover templates in Chapter 2.) I cover this 3D environment in Part IV, "Drawing in Three Dimensions."

Figure 1.1 shows the default screen that appears when you first open AutoCAD or AutoCAD LT. Your screen may look somewhat different — remember that AutoCAD and AutoCAD LT can be customized in many ways — but the general features will be the same. If you see other items open on your screen, you can close all these items by clicking their Close (X) button.

> **NOTE**
>
> By default, you see a grid when you open AutoCAD. I explain how to turn off the grid in Chapter 4. The default screen color is dark gray. You can leave it that way or change the drawing area color, as I explain in Bonus Chapter 15. I use a white background for the figures in this book for clarity.

If you find yourself in a 3D environment in AutoCAD, you'll see a gray background and a perspective view. To work in 2D in AutoCAD, switch to a 2D environment, following these steps in AutoCAD:

1. From the Workspace drop-down list in the Quick Access Toolbar, choose Drafting & Annotation. This displays the Ribbon with 2D commands.

2. Choose Application Button ⇨ New. From the Select Template dialog box, choose `acad.dwt` and click Open. This places you in a 2D view.

The AutoCAD and AutoCAD LT screens consist of four important areas. These are discussed in the following sections.

Exploring the drawing area

The blank area in the middle of the screen, called the *graphics window* or *drawing area,* is where you draw. You can think of this as a sheet of drafting paper, except that this piece of paper can be any size — even the size of a huge factory or an entire county!

By default, you draw in *model space,* so called because that's where you draw your models. When you create a new drawing, by default, you are in model space, so you can just start drawing. You can lay out your drawings for plotting in *paper space,* also called a *layout.* To switch from model space to a layout, you use the Layout tab at the bottom of the drawing area. You click the Model tab to switch back to model space. (See Chapter 17 for details.)

> **NOTE**
>
> Rather than the model and layout tabs, you may see `Model` and `Layout1` buttons on the status bar. You can switch between the buttons and tabs by right-clicking either feature and choosing Display/Hide Layout and Model Tabs from the shortcut menu.

When you start to draw, you need to specify where to start drawing. One way is to use coordinates. To specify a coordinate, the universally accepted convention is to put the X coordinate first, followed by a comma, and then the Y coordinate. Examples are –3,5, 3,2, 6,–2, and –1,–1. These coordinates specify points in the drawing area. You can see the current coordinates of the cursor displayed at the lower-left corner of the AutoCAD window.

FIGURE 1.1

The AutoCAD and AutoCAD LT screens are very similar. The AutoCAD LT screen doesn't include the Express Tools tab on the Ribbon.

Navigation bar

Drawing Minimize, Maximize, and Close buttons

Ribbon   Workspace   Application Minimize, Maximize, and Close buttons

Quick Access toolbar   Title bar   Help and Support options

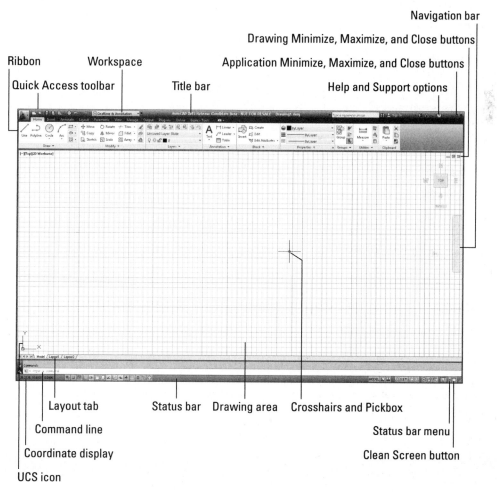

Layout tab   Status bar   Drawing area   Crosshairs and Pickbox

Command line   Status bar menu

Coordinate display   Clean Screen button

UCS icon

Chapter 4 explains how to specify coordinates. To create three-dimensional models, you need to add a Z coordinate when specifying a point. Chapter 21 discusses three-dimensional coordinates.

> **TIP**
>
> If you want the maximum amount of free space for drawing, click the Clean Screen button at the right side of the status bar to remove the Ribbon. Click the same button to get it back. You can also press Ctrl+0 to toggle between the two displays. You can double-click the active tab to cycle through three display states of the Ribbon that collapse and expand the Ribbon.

The UCS icon

Notice the symbol with two perpendicular lines and X and Y labels in the drawing area in Figure 1.1. This symbol is called the User Coordinate System (UCS) icon. The lines point to the positive directions of the X and Y axes to help you keep your bearings. (In a 3D environment, you see a Z axis as well.) You can change the look of this icon, and turn it on and off, as I explain in Chapter 8.

The crosshairs

In the drawing area of Figure 1.1, notice the intersecting lines with a small box at their intersection. The small box is called the *pickbox* because it helps you to select, or pick, objects. The lines are called *crosshairs*. They show you the location of the mouse cursor in relation to other objects in your drawing.

The ViewCube and Navigation Bar

On the right side of the drawing area, semi-faded, you see two navigational tools, the ViewCube and the Navigation Bar (or NavBar). The ViewCube is not available in AutoCAD LT. These are mostly used for 3D navigation, which I cover in Chapter 22. You can use the NavBar to zoom and pan in 2D; see Chapter 8 for more information.

Exploring the Ribbon and Quick Access Toolbar

At the top of the application window is the title bar, and directly beneath the title bar is the Ribbon. On the left side of the title bar is the Quick Access Toolbar. The Ribbon has tabs, and each tab is divided into control panels (usually called just panels), which are sections of related commands. I explain how to work with the Ribbon and the Quick Access Toolbar in Chapter 3.

> **NOTE**
>
> The AutoCAD Classic and AutoCAD LT Classic workspaces do not show the Ribbon; instead, you see toolbars, which are usually docked along the left, top, and right sides of the screen. From the Workspace drop-down list (just to the right of the Quick Access Toolbar), try switching between the Drafting & Annotation workspace and the AutoCAD or AutoCAD LT Classic workspace to see which one you prefer. In Bonus Chapter 15, I explain how to customize workspaces.

On the Home tab, in the Draw panel of the Ribbon, hover the cursor over the leftmost button. You see a tooltip that says Line, as shown in Figure 1.2. Below the tooltip, a description tells you that this button creates straight-line segments. If you continue to hover the cursor over the Line button, the tooltip expands to provide more information about the command.

You use buttons on the Ribbon to execute commands. For example, to draw a line, you click the Line button on the Draw panel of the Ribbon's Home tab. You get some practice drawing lines in the exercise that follows. (In the AutoCAD Classic or AutoCAD LT Classic workspace, you would click the Line button on the Draw toolbar to draw a line.)

If you inadvertently start a command that you don't want to use, press Esc.

FIGURE 1.2

Hovering the cursor over the Line button displays a tooltip that shows the command and a description of its function.

The Quick Access Toolbar contains a few often-used commands that are useful to have available all the time. Examples are commands to start a new drawing, open an existing drawing, and save a drawing.

ON THE WEB

Because you can customize the Ribbon and the Quick Access Toolbar to suit your needs, your screen may appear somewhat different. See Bonus Chapter 6 for information on customizing the Quick Access Toolbar, and see Bonus Chapter 10 for information on customizing the Ribbon. Both chapters are on the companion website; for more information see the Introduction and Appendix B.

TIP

You can lock the position of Ribbon panels (if they're not docked), toolbars, and windows (palettes). On the right side of the status bar, at the bottom of the screen, is a Lock icon. Click this icon to open a menu allowing you to individually lock specific window, panel, or toolbar components. You can also choose the All option and lock or unlock everything. Locking these interface components prevents you from moving them inadvertently.

Using the Application menu

When you click the Application Button, the Application menu opens, giving you access to file-related commands, as shown in Figure 1.3.

TIP

You can display the menu bar along with the Ribbon. Type menubar ↵ on the command line, and then enter 1 ↵. To hide the menu bar, enter 0 ↵. Alternatively, you can click the down arrow at the right end of the Quick Access Toolbar, and choose Show Menu Bar. Choose Hide Menu Bar to hide it.

FIGURE 1.3

The Application Button offers file-related commands, recently opened drawings, access to other open drawings, and a Search box.

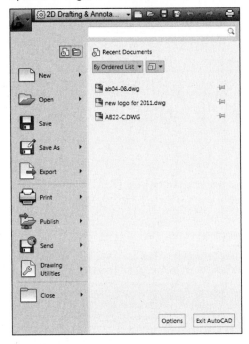

When you open the Application menu, you can type a search term in the Search text box to find a command. On the right, you see a list of drawings that you opened recently. Click the Open Documents button to show open drawings rather than recently used drawings. At the top of the list of drawings, you can click a drop-down arrow to choose to display them alphabetically *(ordered list)*, by date, or by type. To the right, you can click a drop-down arrow to display the drawings as icons, or as small, medium, or large images. However, even if you display just icons, if you hover the cursor over any drawing name, an image of the drawing appears.

The Options button, at the bottom of the Application menu, opens the Options dialog box where you can specify many settings that affect how AutoCAD works. I explain the Options dialog box in detail in Bonus Chapter 15, which you can find on the companion website.

Using the command line and dynamic input tooltip

At the bottom of the drawing area, you see a separate window showing approximately three lines of text. (You can change it to show as many lines as you like by dragging the top edge of the window up or down.) Notice the phrase, Type a command:. This is the *command line*. You can execute any command by typing it on the command line.

Even if you use a menu item or the Ribbon to execute a command, you may see a response on the command line. AutoCAD and AutoCAD LT often provide options, which you can click on the command line or type on the keyboard. Text that you type appears on the command line. For example, when you type coordinates specifying a point, they appear on the command line.

The Dynamic Input tooltip allows you to see the text that you type at the cursor. This tooltip doesn't appear until you start typing a command. You can also choose options near the tooltip. (For more information, see Chapter 3.)

To see more of the command line, press F2 to open the AutoCAD or AutoCAD LT Text Window. You can scroll back through previous commands. Press F2 again to close the window. You can also simply hide the Text window by clicking in the AutoCAD or AutoCAD LT window for easy access to the Text window later from the Windows task bar.

Exploring the status bar

At the very bottom of the screen is the *status bar* (refer to Figure 1.1). At the left are the X,Y coordinates. As you move your mouse, these coordinates change. (If they don't change, click them and move your mouse again.) The status bar also contains a number of buttons that I explain later in this book.

At the right side of the status bar is a small down arrow. Click it to open the status bar menu. This menu determines which buttons appear on the status bar. If you don't use a certain button, choose it on the menu to remove its checkmark and make it disappear. You can always go back and choose the item again to redisplay the button.

Creating a New Folder

For your work with this book, you should create a new folder so that you can save your exercise drawings where they won't get mixed up with other drawings. You should also download the drawings for the exercises and put them in two new subfolders. The following directions leave it up to you where to create these new folders.

> **CAUTION**
>
> I do not recommend creating a subfolder in the AutoCAD 2013 or AutoCAD LT 2013 folder. These folders contain the files that make up the program. If you keep your drawings here, it is too easy to make a mistake and delete necessary program files. Some people create a subfolder in the My Documents or Documents folder.

STEPS: Creating Folders for the Exercise Drawings

1. Move the cursor to the Windows task bar at the bottom of your screen and right-click the Start button.

2. Choose Explore.

3. On the left pane of Windows Explorer, click the drive where you want to create the new folder. If you don't know where to create the folder, choose the drive where AutoCAD or AutoCAD LT is installed. If you're on a network, choose the drive that represents your

computer. If you keep your work in subfolders of the My Documents or Documents folder, click that folder.

4. If you want to make a *subfolder* (a folder within a folder), choose the folder where you want to create the subfolder.

5. In Windows XP, choose File ⇨ New ⇨ Folder. In Windows Vista, click Organize ⇨ New Folder. In Windows 7, click New Folder. A new, highlighted folder, named New Folder, appears in the right pane. You may have to scroll down to see it.

6. Type **AutoCAD Bible** for the folder name and press Enter. (If you did the exercises from a previous edition of this book, such as *AutoCAD 2012 and AutoCAD LT 2012 Bible,* and you already have a folder named AutoCAD Bible, first rename the original folder to something such as ACAD2012Bible.)

7. In the left pane of Windows Explorer, click the new AutoCAD Bible folder and again create a new folder. Name it Drawings. Again, click the AutoCAD Bible folder, create a new folder, and name it Results.

8. To download the drawings for the exercises, go to www.wiley.com/go/autocad2013 bible or www.ellenfinkelstein.com/autocad2013bible, click the Drawings download link, and save the Zip file. Repeat the process for the Results drawings. (The Results download contains the final versions of the drawings in each exercise.)

9. Move the Drawings Zip file to the Drawings folder and the Results Zip file to the Results folder.

10. Unzip the files.

11. Save all drawings that you create for this book in your AutoCAD Bible folder.

CAUTION

Creating a folder for your drawings as described in the previous steps is essential before you go on to exercises in the rest of this book.

Using the Interface

If you did the Quick Start exercise, you had the experience of drawing a window, but I chose the simplest method of completing each task because I had not yet described the AutoCAD and AutoCAD LT application window. In the following exercise, you draw some simple objects, but experiment with all the features of the user interface to get a feel for how they work. (Chapter 3 explains in more detail how to use commands.) As explained in the Introduction, you type what appears in **bold**.

TIP

Don't worry if you don't understand everything you're doing. It all becomes clear as you progress through this book. If you haven't read the Introduction, now is a good time to go back and read the part that explains how to follow the exercises.

STEPS: Drawing a Line in Four Ways

1. Start AutoCAD or AutoCAD LT. This exercise assumes you are using the default Drafting & Annotation workspace in a 2D environment.

   You see a new drawing. If you are prompted for a template, choose acad.dwt (for AutoCAD) or acadlt.dwt (for AutoCAD LT).

2. From the Ribbon, choose Home tab ⇨ Draw panel ⇨ Line.

3. Move your mouse to move the crosshairs cursor around the screen. Notice the Dynamic Input tooltip that follows the cursor around, as shown in Figure 1.4. (For this figure, I turned off the grid by clicking the Grid Display button on the status bar.) If you don't see the Dynamic Input tooltip, click the Dynamic Input button on the status bar. At the same time, notice the coordinates changing on the left side of the status bar.

FIGURE 1.4

When you move the mouse, the Dynamic Input bar follows the cursor, displaying the current coordinates.

4. Anywhere on the screen, stop moving the mouse and click the left mouse button to pick a point. When you move the mouse again, the Dynamic Input bar changes to prompt you to specify the next point and to show you the angle and length of the cursor from the original point you picked, as shown in Figure 1.5.

FIGURE 1.5

After specifying the first point of a line, the Dynamic Input bar prompts you for the next point.

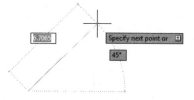

5. Pick any point to create a line segment. You see the same Dynamic Input tooltip as before, which means that you can continue to create more line segments. (Chapter 6 explains all about drawing lines.)

6. Press Enter to end the command and finish your line.

7. For your second line, type **menubar** ⏎ and then type **1** ⏎ on the command line. The menu bar appears at the top of the screen. From the menu, choose Draw⇨Line. Again, pick any point on the screen.

8. Move your mouse so you can see the length and angle tooltips. Notice the value for the length. Now type a different value and press Enter. For example, if the Length tooltip says 13.7638, type **5** ⏎.

9. Press Enter to end the command. The line's length is based on what you typed, not where the cursor was, but the line's angle is the same as it was before you typed in the length.

10. To hide the menu bar, click the down arrow at the right end of the Quick Access Toolbar and choose Hide Menu Bar near the bottom of the list of menu items.

11. For your third line, type **line** ⏎. Notice that the text appears in the Dynamic Input tooltip as you type, but not in the command line area.

12. Press Enter. You now see the command that you typed in the command line area, as well as the Dynamic Input prompt to specify the first point.

13. Click in two places to pick a start point and an endpoint.

14. This time, to end the line, right-click anywhere in the drawing area. By default, this opens a shortcut menu, but it may end the command. If so, you're done. If you see the shortcut menu, choose Enter from the shortcut menu to end the command.

15. For your fourth line, click the Workspace drop-down list on the Quick Access Toolbar at the top of your screen, and choose AutoCAD Classic or AutoCAD LT Classic. The entire interface changes: The Ribbon is gone, and in its place you see a menu bar at the top, and several toolbars. If you don't see the Draw toolbar (it's usually docked vertically on the left side of the application window), right-click any toolbar that is already displayed and choose Draw from the list of toolbars. Click the Line button on the Draw toolbar. Move the mouse so that the cursor is in the drawing area. Pick two different points and press Enter.

16. Use the Workspace drop-down list to return to the Drafting & Annotation workspace. Leave the drawing on your screen and complete the next exercise to save the drawing.

You should now have four lines on the screen. You can see how the interface offers several ways to work. You can use the method that suits you best.

Saving a Drawing

Saving a drawing on your computer is similar to saving any other file in Windows. You should get in the habit of saving your work every few minutes to avoid losing your work in case the software or your computer system crashes. Saving a drawing for the first time is different from saving it subsequently because you have to name the drawing.

NEW FEATURE
You can also save a drawing online using the Autodesk 360 service for the purpose of storage and sharing drawings with others. I cover Autodesk 360 in Bonus Chapter 5.

 To save a drawing, click Save on the Quick Access Toolbar or choose Application Button ➪ Save. If you're saving a drawing for the first time, the Save Drawing As dialog box appears, as shown in Figure 1.6.

FIGURE 1.6

The Save Drawing As dialog box

Down the left side of the dialog box are several buttons, called the *Places list*, to help you find a location to save drawings more quickly.

TIP
Conveniently, you can reorder the buttons in the Places list. Just drag any button to a new location.

Of course, you can also choose a location from the Save In drop-down list to which you want to save the file. To save a file, type a filename in the File Name text box and click Save to save the file.

AUTOCAD ONLY
The SAVEALL command of the Express Tools saves all open drawings, without closing them. Type saveall ↵ on the command line. If a drawing hasn't been saved, you are prompted for a filename. For information on installing Express Tools, see Bonus Chapter 15.

STEPS: Saving a Drawing for the First Time

 1. The four lines you created earlier in this chapter should still be on your screen. Click Save on the Quick Access Toolbar. The Save Drawing As dialog box opens.

2. Click the Save In drop-down list. Navigate to the `AutoCAD Bible` folder.

3. In the File Name text box, select the default filename that appears. Type **ab01-01** and press Enter (or click Save).

4. Keep your drawing on the screen and go to the next exercise.

AutoCAD saves your drawing under the name `ab01-01.dwg`. This numbering system will help you organize your drawings from this book and find equivalent drawings on the companion website more easily. It just means that this is the first drawing from Chapter 1 of *AutoCAD 2013 and AutoCAD LT 2013 Bible*.

Closing a Drawing and Exiting from AutoCAD and AutoCAD LT

You can close your drawing and keep AutoCAD or AutoCAD LT open. The simplest way to do this is to use the Drawing Close button at the upper-right corner of the drawing. To exit AutoCAD or AutoCAD LT, click the Close (X) box at the top-right corner of your screen. You can also exit out of AutoCAD or AutoCAD LT by typing **quit** ↵ on the command line. If you've made any changes to your drawing since last saving it, AutoCAD or AutoCAD LT asks you if you want to save your changes. Choose Yes or No as your situation requires. If you have opened more than one drawing to which you have made changes, you have a chance to save each drawing in turn.

TIP
You can double-click the Application button to close AutoCAD. This is equivalent to typing quit.

STEPS: Closing Your Drawing and Exiting AutoCAD or AutoCAD LT

1. Your drawing should still be on your screen. Choose Application Button ⇨ Close. You now see a gray screen with no drawing. (Repeat this process if you have other drawings open. Save or cancel the changes to these extra open drawings as you like.)

2. Click the Close button in the upper-right corner to exit AutoCAD or AutoCAD LT.

Summary

In this chapter, I explained how to start AutoCAD and AutoCAD LT and create a new drawing. I gave you a tour of the screen and explained how to save a drawing. This chapter provided the basis for all your work in AutoCAD and AutoCAD LT.

In this chapter, you learned the following:

- A brief history of AutoCAD and AutoCAD LT
- How to start AutoCAD and AutoCAD LT
- How to start a new drawing
- The user interface and its various sections, including the drawing area, the UCS icon, the crosshairs, the Ribbon, the Quick Access Toolbar, the command line, and the status bar
- How to start a command from the Ribbon, menu, command line, and toolbar
- How to save a drawing for the first time
- How to close a drawing and exit AutoCAD and AutoCAD LT

You may have several questions at this point, but "well begun is half done." The next chapter explains all the ways to start a new drawing as well as how to open an existing drawing.

Opening a Drawing

IN THIS CHAPTER

Using a template to start a new drawing

Customizing a template

Using the default settings to create a drawing

Opening and switching between existing drawings

Resaving a drawing with a new name

A utoCAD and AutoCAD LT offer a number of options for opening new and existing drawings. These options create a great deal of flexibility and save you time as well. You can create complex templates to avoid doing the same basic setup and drawing over and over.

Creating a New Drawing from a Template

A *template* is a special file that contains drawing settings and often objects (such as a titleblock and text). A template has a DWT filename extension. When you use a template as the basis for a new drawing, the drawing takes on all the settings and objects contained in the template. Use templates to avoid re-creating settings and redrawing objects for new drawings. AutoCAD and AutoCAD LT come with templates that you can use as is or customize. You can also create your own templates.

To create a new drawing based on a template, choose Application Button ⇨ New to open the Select Template dialog box, which lists all the available templates, as shown in Figure 2.1. Select a template to see its preview, if any. Double-click a template to create a new drawing based on that template. Because AutoCAD or AutoCAD LT opens with Drawing1.dwg, the new drawing is named Drawing2.dwg. When you save and name your drawing, the original template file is unaffected.

FIGURE 2.1

Choose a template from the Select Template dialog box.

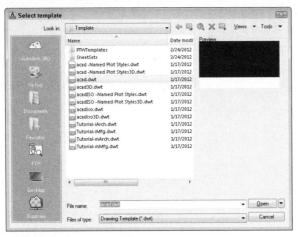

 The QNEW command is useful if you always start a new drawing based on the same template. You set a default template and then click New on the Quick Access Toolbar to start a new drawing immediately, based on that default template. To set the default template, follow these steps:

1. Choose Application Button ⇨ Options, and click the Files tab.
2. Double-click the Template Settings item.
3. Double-click the Default Template File Name for QNEW item.
4. Select the listing under the Default Template File Name for QNEW item (which says None by default).
5. Click Browse and choose the template that you want to use. Click Open.
6. Click OK to close the Options dialog box.

You can specify whether this default template uses metric or imperial measurements by setting the MEASUREINIT system variable. (System variables are discussed further in Chapter 5.) On the command line, type **measureinit** ↵. Enter **0** ↵ for imperial units or **1** ↵ for metric units.

The default template is `acad.dwt` for AutoCAD and `acadlt.dwt` for AutoCAD LT. Another default template is `acad -Named Plot Styles.dwt` or `acadlt -Named Plot Styles.dwt`, which refers to named plot styles. (See Chapter 17 for more information.)

STEPS: Opening a Drawing Based on the Default Template

1. Start AutoCAD or AutoCAD LT.
2. Choose Application Button ⇨ New.
3. From the Select Template dialog box, choose `acad.dwt` (for AutoCAD) or `acadlt.dwt` (for AutoCAD LT) from the list.
4. Click Open. You now have a blank drawing named `Drawing2.dwg`.

> **NOTE**
>
> The default workspace is Drafting & Annotation. However, you can choose another 2D workspace, AutoCAD Classic (for AutoCAD) or AutoCAD LT Classic, from the Workspace drop-down list just to the right of the Application Button or from the Workspace Switching button on the right side of the status bar. For 2D drawing in AutoCAD only, make sure that you're not in the 3D Modeling workspace. I discuss workspaces in Bonus Chapter 15.
>
> In both AutoCAD and AutoCAD LT, you may see palettes (windows) open that you don't want to use right now. You can close these by clicking their Close (X) buttons.

Working with Templates

A template contains ready-made settings to get you started drawing quickly. These settings include the size of the drawing (called *limits*), the unit type (such as *decimal* or *feet and inches*), and others. An important part of setting standards in an office where people work together on drawings is the creation of a template so that all users work with an identical setup. Templates may contain more than just settings — they often contain a complete titleblock, for example, and may include *boilerplate* (standardized) text as well.

 In Chapter 5, I explain the options available for setting up a drawing. In Bonus Chapter 3, I cover the process of setting standards for drawings.

> **CAUTION**
>
> If you're using someone else's computer, don't change the templates that come with AutoCAD or AutoCAD LT without first checking with the computer's owner. Also, if you create new templates, put them in their own folder to avoid losing them when you upgrade or reinstall AutoCAD.

Creating Your Own Templates

You may want several templates to choose from on a regular basis. For example, you may create drawings of several sizes. AutoCAD and AutoCAD LT let you create as many templates as you want. To create your own templates, either start a drawing based on a template and make the changes you want, or open an existing drawing that already has some of the settings you want and make any further changes you need. After your templates are created, you don't have to worry about most settings; they are already available for you, and you can quickly start to draw. Follow these steps:

1. Create a new drawing based on the default template or another template that has settings similar to the settings you want. You can also open an existing drawing. Make any changes you want.

2. Choose Save As from the Quick Access Toolbar.

3. In the Save Drawing As dialog box, click the Files of Type drop-down list. Choose AutoCAD Drawing Template or AutoCAD LT Drawing Template (*.dwt).

4. In the File Name text box, type a name for your template and click Save. If you are modifying an existing template, choose the template that you want to customize from the list of template files, click Save, and then click Yes at the message asking if you want to replace it.

5. In the Template Options dialog box, enter or revise the description as you want. From the Measurement drop-down list, choose English (Imperial) or Metric, depending on the type of units you plan to use. (I discuss the New Layer Notification option in Bonus Chapter 3.) Click OK.

> **TIP**
>
> Name your templates in a way that clearly differentiates them from regular drawings. You may want drawings set up for each of the standard paper sizes (A through E), with a titleblock in each. Useful names might be `tb-a.dwt`, `tb-b.dwt` (tb meaning titleblock), and so on.

Creating a Drawing with Default Settings

Occasionally, you may want to create a drawing without any settings. It is actually impossible for a drawing to have no settings at all, but you can create a drawing with the minimum possible presets. You might want to do this if you're working on someone else's computer and don't want to take the time to get rid of a large number of complex settings that aren't helpful for your work. Choose Application Button ➪ New. Instead of choosing a template, click the arrow to the right of the Open button (refer to Figure 2.1). Choose Open with No Template — Imperial or Open with No Template — Metric.

Opening an Existing Drawing

Opening a drawing in AutoCAD or AutoCAD LT is like opening a file in any Windows program. You can find existing drawings by name or by viewing a thumbnail (preview image) of the drawing. Choose Open from the Quick Access Toolbar, or choose Application Button ➪ Open. The Select File dialog box appears. Navigate to the file's location, and then choose your drawing. The Preview box enables you to look at the drawing to see if it's the one you want. (If you don't see a preview, choose Preview from the Views drop-down list in the dialog box.) Click Open.

If you have opened the drawing recently, click the Application Button, click the Recent Documents icon, and look at the Recent Documents list on the right. At the top of the file list, click the arrow button to choose By Ordered List (alphabetical — the default), By Access Date, By Size, or By Type. To the right is a small drop-down list that you can click to view icons or images of the files. When you hover the cursor over any drawing, a tooltip displays, showing you a preview of the drawing plus additional information. You can click the Pin icon next to a drawing to stick it to the list.

You can also double-click a drawing in Windows Explorer to open it. If AutoCAD or AutoCAD LT is not running, Windows loads the program and the drawing as well. If AutoCAD or AutoCAD LT is running and a drawing is active, the drawing opens as a second drawing within the program.

> **NOTE**
>
> AutoCAD WS is an online service used primarily for reviewing drawing files on the go, but you can use it to open a drawing as well. Autodesk 360 offers online storage, so you can also use it to open a drawing. For more information on both these services, see Bonus Chapter 5.

Switching Among Open Drawings

When you open more than one drawing, by default, AutoCAD and AutoCAD LT display only one button on the Windows task bar, except in Windows 7. To display a separate button for each drawing, type **taskbar** ↵ on the command line. Then type **1** ↵. If only one button shows on the task bar, switch between drawings in one of the following ways:

 • Click the Quick View Drawings button on the status bar to display previews of all the open drawings, as shown in Figure 2.2. Above the drawings, you see a second level, showing model space and the layouts (which I cover in Chapter 17) in the drawing. Click the one that you want to display. The small toolbar below the drawings lets you pin them (so they remain displayed), start a new drawing, open an existing drawing, and close Quick View.

• Go to View tab ⇨ User Interface panel ⇨ Switch Windows and choose from the drawings on the drop-down list.

 • Click the Application Button and click the Open Documents button at the top. Then choose from the files listed on the right.

FIGURE 2.2

The Quick View feature lets you see other open drawings and switch among them.

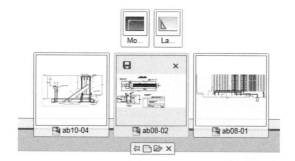

STEPS: Opening a Drawing

1. If AutoCAD or AutoCAD LT is not open, start the program.

 2. Click Open on the Quick Access Toolbar.

3. If you didn't follow the instructions in Chapter 1 for downloading and unzipping the Drawings and Results downloads from the companion website, look there for the exercise, "Creating Folders for the Exercise Drawings," and follow those instructions now. Then, in the Select File dialog box, navigate to the `Results` folder.

4. In the files list, click `abqs-01.dwg`.

5. Click Open. The drawing opens.

6. Click the Close (X) button in the upper-right corner of the drawing window to close the drawing.

Saving a Drawing under a New Name

Whether you want to use an existing drawing as a prototype or simply make a copy of a drawing, you need to save the drawing under a new name. Choose Save As from the Quick Access Toolbar or Application Button ⇨ Save As. In the Save Drawing As dialog box, type a new name in the File Name text box. Then click Save. You may also want to change the location of the new drawing by changing the folder in the Save In drop-down list box.

Summary

In this chapter, you explored the various ways of opening a drawing. You learned about:

- Starting a new drawing based on a template
- Customizing a template and creating your own templates
- Starting a new drawing with no template
- Opening an existing drawing and switching among open drawings
- Saving a drawing under a new name

In the next chapter, you read about using commands.

Using Commands

IN THIS CHAPTER

Using the Ribbon, menus, dialog boxes, toolbars, and palettes

Working with Dynamic Input and the command line

Repeating, canceling, undoing, and redoing commands

Executing a command within another command

Using the Help system

AutoCAD and AutoCAD LT have been around for a long time. As a result, the way you give the program commands — called the *user interface* — is somewhat unique. You can give the same command in several ways. In this chapter, you read about the various possibilities and start to get acquainted with all of them.

Commands are important. In a word processing program, you can simply start typing, and in a spreadsheet program, you can begin by entering data; but in most cases, nothing happens in AutoCAD or AutoCAD LT until you give it a command.

Understanding the AutoCAD and AutoCAD LT Interface

Many new commands have been added to AutoCAD and AutoCAD LT over the years. Often, older commands that were no longer necessary were kept to maintain compatibility with earlier releases. A number of these older commands, as well as certain rarely used commands, are not found in the interface. Other than this idiosyncrasy, the interface is similar to those of other Windows programs. Specifically, the Ribbon is similar to the latest version of Microsoft Office.

You use the user interface to execute commands and to specify settings and values. The user interface consists of the default Ribbon, the Quick Access Toolbar, the optional drop-down menu bar, shortcut (right-click, or contextual) menus, the optional toolbars, palettes, the dynamic input tooltip, dialog boxes, and the command line. For executing commands, all the aspects of the user interface except dialog boxes work in conjunction with the command line. Looking at the command line whenever you execute a command is important, because that command appears on the command line, and a prompt or list of options may appear as well. If you have Dynamic Input on, the tooltip also displays the prompt. (Click the Dynamic Input button on the status bar to turn it on — and off.)

Working with the Ribbon

AutoCAD 2013 and AutoCAD LT 2013 use a Ribbon, which is a horizontal, tabbed area at the top of the screen. The Ribbon contains buttons like a toolbar, but is wider. You can drag it to the left or right side of your screen to make it vertical. You can customize the Ribbon, as I explain in Bonus Chapter 10. The Ribbon is the user interface in the default workspace, Drafting & Annotation. It's also the user interface for the 3D Basics and 3D Modeling workspaces that come with AutoCAD (but not with AutoCAD LT).

The Home tab contains many of the commands that you use most often. The Ribbon is divided into control panels (panels, for short). Each panel contains a related group of commands. Other features of the Ribbon are:

- **More Commands arrows.** Many of the panels have a down arrow to the right of the panel name that you can click to expand the panel and display more buttons for commands and controls for settings that you don't use as often.
- **Dialog box launchers.** Some panels have an arrow at the right end of the panel, which opens a related dialog box or palette. This arrow is called a *dialog box launcher*.
- **Contextual tabs.** When you select certain types of objects, *contextual* tabs appear. For example, if you attach an image into a drawing and select the image, the Image tab appears.

> **NOTE**
> This book provides instructions for executing a command by using the default workspace. For information on changing the workspace, see Bonus Chapter 15. For information on customizing the user interface, see Bonus Chapter 10.

To execute a command, click the tab that you need, and click the command's button. If the button doesn't have a label, hover the cursor over the button to read its tooltip and a brief description of the button's command. If you continue to hover a little longer, the description expands, explaining the command in more detail. Some items on the Ribbon are drop-down lists from which you choose an option.

> **NOTE**
> The Ribbon and Quick Access Toolbar support *KeyTips*. KeyTips allow you to access commands and controls with a keyboard combination. To display KeyTips, press the Alt key. KeyTips are not available when you display the menu bar. The menu bar is covered in the following section.

 The Ribbon has several states that you can choose from to balance between convenience and space. The button to the right of the rightmost tab lets you toggle between the full Ribbon and three states. Choose one of the following states from the button's drop-down list, and then click the full button to return to the full Ribbon.

- **Minimize to Tabs.** Displays one row of the tab names only.
- **Minimize to Panel Titles.** Displays the tab names and the panel names for the current tab.
- **Minimize to Panel Buttons.** Displays the current tab and buttons for each of the panels.

To move the Ribbon to the left or right of your screen in a vertical configuration, right-click any blank space on the tab bar at the top of the Ribbon, and choose Undock. The Ribbon undocks and then functions like a palette, which I cover later in this chapter. You can dock it on the left or right and auto-hide it. Right-click the gray, vertical title bar for more options.

You access the Application menu by clicking the Application button at the upper-left corner of the application window. The menu contains file-related commands, such as saving, exporting, and printing (plotting).

Displaying and using menus

In the default workspace (Drafting & Annotation), the drop-down menus are hidden. You can display the menus by clicking the down arrow at the right end of the Quick Access Toolbar (at the upper-left corner of your screen) and choosing Show Menu Bar. This method lets you use the Ribbon and the menu bar together. To use a menu, choose the menu title and then the item that you want from the menu list that drops down.

Using shortcut menus

Shortcut menus appear when you right-click your mouse. The shortcut menus try to anticipate the most common tasks you might want to complete. As a result, the menu that appears when you right-click depends on the situation:

- If you have neither started a command nor selected any objects, you get the default menu when you right-click in the drawing area. Here you can cut, copy, paste, undo, pan, zoom, and so on.
- If you've selected any objects, you see the edit-mode menu, which lists the most common editing commands. Selecting one or more objects of the same or of different types affects the commands that are available.
- If you've started a command, the command-mode menu opens, letting you choose an option for that command. I explain this in more detail later in this chapter.
- Other menus include the toolbar list you get when you right-click a toolbar and the command-line history you see when you right-click the command line and choose Recent Commands.

> **TIP**
>
> In early releases, right-clicking was equivalent to pressing Enter. You can customize how right-clicking works — and that includes changing it back to the way it worked in earlier releases. Choose Application Button ⇨ Options and choose the User Preferences tab. Then click the Right-click Customization button. For more information, see Bonus Chapter 15.
>
> When you set right-click customization, you can turn on time-sensitive right-clicking. Time-sensitive right-clicking is a great feature that gives you the best of two worlds — the right mouse button can be used both as an equivalent to pressing Enter and as a way to open the shortcut menus. When you turn on time-sensitive right-clicking, a quick right-click is equivalent to pressing Enter and will repeat the last command or end any commands that require Enter to end. A longer right-click (hold your finger on the mouse button slightly longer) opens the shortcut menu. You can specify the length of time required for the longer right-click, which is 250 milliseconds by default.

Working with dialog boxes

Dialog boxes offer the user a simple way to control AutoCAD or AutoCAD LT without memorizing a lot of technical commands and option names. They guide you through a task by clearly laying out all the choices. If you're familiar with any other Windows program, you're familiar with dialog boxes. Dialog boxes provide contextual help in the form of a tooltip that provides information on an option or control. To use contextual tooltips, position the cursor over a control.

> **TIP**
> You can enter mathematical expressions for values in dialog box text boxes; start an expression with an equal sign (=). For example, in the Angle box of the Hatch and Gradient dialog box, you can enter =20+10. Press Alt+Enter to complete the process. You can also enter mathematical expressions in palette text boxes.

When you've finished using a dialog box, click OK to accept any settings you specified, or click Cancel to discard any changes. In some cases, you can click Apply to save the changes made without closing the dialog box.

Using the Quick Access Toolbar

The Quick Access Toolbar provides a quick way to execute a command with one click of the mouse. If you're not sure what a toolbar button does, hover the cursor over a button and read the tooltip. The Quick Access Toolbar contains a few often-used commands, starting with QNEW, OPEN, QSAVE, SAVEAS, PLOT, UNDO, and REDO. In Bonus Chapter 6, I explain how to customize the tools that are on this toolbar.

When you click a toolbar button, in order to complete the command, you usually need to look at the Dynamic Input tooltip or the command line to follow the prompts there. I explain the command line and Dynamic Input later in this chapter.

Managing palettes

A palette is a window that you can dock or float (like a toolbar). Palettes combine related functions in one place. AutoCAD and AutoCAD LT have several palettes that are covered throughout this book. To see palettes only when you need them, you can auto-hide them. Right-click the palette's title bar and choose Auto-hide from the shortcut menu. To dock a palette, choose Allow Docking from the same shortcut menu. You can dock and auto-hide a palette: Right-click the palette's title bar and choose Anchor Left or Anchor Right. The palette collapses to a thin vertical strip and opens only when you hover the mouse cursor over it. You can also anchor more than one palette on a side. They fit together on the right or left side and unroll to their full length when you hover the cursor over them.

Using the Tool Palettes window

 Tool palettes are another way to give AutoCAD and AutoCAD LT commands. To open the Tool Palettes window, shown in Figure 3.1, choose View tab ⇨ Palettes panel ⇨ Tool Palettes. The palettes are actually a collection of tabs that are used to organize tools with similar functionality. Because of the number of tabs, some of the tabs are bunched up at the bottom. To choose these tabs, right-click those bottom tabs and choose a tab from the list that appears. The AutoCAD LT Tool Palettes window contains fewer tabs, and some of the tabs are slightly different.

FIGURE 3.1

The Tool Palettes window, as shown in AutoCAD

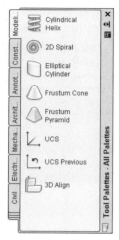

Each of the items on a tool palette is a tool. The tools on the Command Tool Samples tab contain commands that you can use. For example, you can draw a line by clicking the Line tool. The first two tools have *flyouts,* which are like toolbar flyouts. Click the small arrow and the flyout appears, containing other command buttons. Click the command button that you want in order to start that command.

 You can use tool palettes to insert objects, fill in closed areas, and add other content. For more information, see Bonus Chapter 3. I also explain how to customize tool palettes in Bonus Chapter 6. For example, you can put custom commands on a tool palette.

Using the Command Line and Dynamic Input

You can execute a command by typing it directly on the command line, directly to the right of the prompt. The command line is a place to enter commands as well as coordinates and values, as shown in Figure 3.2.

FIGURE 3.2

The command line window

The command line is actually a window that you can move like a palette. By default, it is floating along the bottom of the drawing window. The window displays the `Type a command:` prompt, where you type, and three history lines of text from the most recent input entered. You can click the arrow at the right side of the window to temporarily expand the window and see previously used commands and entered input. You can also adjust the number of history lines displayed without expanding the command line by right-clicking over the command line window and choosing Lines of Prompt History. Commands that you choose from the Ribbon, a toolbar button, a menu, or a tool palette are all echoed on the command line.

You can hide the command-line window by using the COMMANDLINEHIDE command, and display it with the COMMANDLINE command, or press Ctrl+9, which toggles the Command window on and off. Another option for the command line is to dock the Command window.

New Feature

You can customize the way the command line looks. Click the Customize button at the left end of the command line window (it looks like a wrench) and choose Options to open the Options dialog box. On the Display tab, click the Colors button and choose Command line from the Context list. Also, just to the left of the Type a Command text is a little down arrow that you can click to display recently used commands; to start a recent command, just click a command on that list.

Entering commands with Dynamic Input

You can use the Dynamic Input feature to execute commands that you type. Dynamic Input displays whatever you type in a tooltip box near the cursor. Dynamic Input also displays prompts at the cursor, so that you don't have to look down at the command line. Dynamic Input does not completely replace the command line; in some situations the command line displays necessary prompts that the Dynamic Input tooltip omits. For more information about Dynamic Input settings, see Chapter 4.

 You can turn Dynamic Input on and off by using the Dynamic Input button on the status bar. When Dynamic Input is on, a tooltip box echoes what you type, displays prompts, and then displays your responses at the cursor as you type, as shown in Figure 3.3. This input is echoed on the command line after you press Enter. When Dynamic Input is off, commands and other input that you type appear on the command line only.

FIGURE 3.3

The Dynamic Input tooltip prompts you for input and then displays your input as you type.

Understanding command names

All commands have a special one-word command name. This may or may not be the same as the wording that appears on the toolbar's tooltip or on the menu. However, you can be sure of one thing: Every command can be executed by typing its name on the command line or in the Dynamic Input tooltip. Fast typists often prefer to type the command because they find it faster than searching for a command on the Ribbon, a menu, a toolbar, or a palette. Most users use a combination of the command line and other user interface options.

Some of the commands are easy to type, such as LINE or ARC. Others are long and harder to remember, such as HATCHEDIT, DDPTYPE, or EXTERNALREFERENCES. Command names such as these can quickly drive you to use one of the user interface elements.

 If you like typing commands, you can create short versions of the command names, called *aliases*. Many are already included with AutoCAD and AutoCAD LT. Aliases are covered in Bonus Chapter 6.

You can edit what you have typed on the command line. If you type a long command or a difficult coordinate, and make a mistake, you can backspace up to the mistake and retype the last part correctly. You can also use the left and right arrow keys, the Home and End keys, and the Delete key in the same way you do in any word processing environment.

When you start to type a command, AutoCAD auto-completes it. If you pause, all commands that start with the letters you typed appear; just choose the one you want. You can change the auto-complete behavior by right-clicking in the command line window and choosing an option from the AutoComplete submenu.

> **TIP**
> You can use wildcard characters with the auto-complete feature. For example, if you type `*line`, you see a list of all commands that end with the word "line."

You can scroll through and reuse previous command-line entries. To repeat the last line you entered, press the up arrow. Press Enter to execute it. To see more of the command-line entries, press F2 on your keyboard to expand the command line window or open the Text Window when the command line window is docked. Scroll until you find the entry you want, highlight it, and then right-click and choose Paste To CommandLine (or CmdLine in the Text Window) from the shortcut menu. You now see the highlighted text on the current command line. You can copy selected text from the command-line history or the entire history to the Clipboard. You can also access a list of Recent Commands from the Text Window's shortcut menu.

> **TIP**
> Switching from the mouse to the keyboard and back is time-consuming. In general, if you're picking points by using the mouse (covered in Chapter 4), using the Ribbon and other graphic user interfaces to give commands is faster. If you're typing coordinates as you did in Chapter 1, your hands are already at the keyboard, so typing commands at the keyboard is easier.

3

Responding to commands

When you execute a command by any method, you usually need to respond to the command. AutoCAD displays a prompt that tells you what you need to do next.

The format for command prompts on the command line is as follows:

```
current instruction or [options] <current value>:
```

The current instruction explains what you need to do. For example, if you choose an editing command, the prompt usually instructs you to "Select objects." The text in the square brackets lists the various options available for the command. The angled brackets tell you the current value or default option for the command, if any.

In the Dynamic Input tooltip, you first see the following:

```
current instruction or ↓
```

If the current instruction is to specify a point, you also see the cursor's X and Y coordinates. Figure 3.4 shows a prompt for the CIRCLE command. After specifying the center of the circle, this command has a current instruction to specify the radius, an option to specify the diameter, and a current value of 1.0000, the radius of the previously drawn circle.

FIGURE 3.4

To see the options and a current value (if any) in the Dynamic Input tooltip, press the down arrow on your keyboard.

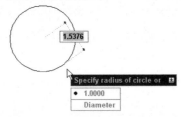

> **NOTE**
> Throughout this book, I show the prompt as it appears on the command line, because this prompt includes the options. If you are looking at the Dynamic Input tooltip, press the down arrow to display the options at the tooltip or right-click to display the shortcut menu.

When you see a prompt, the possible types of responses are as follows:

- **Specify a point.** You can pick a point by clicking with the mouse. You can also enter an X,Y coordinate or displacement — whatever you type appears both in the Dynamic Input tooltip and on the command line. Chapter 4 explains how to specify points.

- **Enter a value or text.** You type the value or the text and press Enter. If Dynamic Input is on, you see your input as you type in the tooltip but you don't see the value on the command line until you press Enter. If Dynamic Input is off, you see your input as you type on the command line.

- **Select an object.** Most editing commands require that you select one or more objects. You can click an object to select it. I explain all the other methods to select objects in Chapters 9 and 10.

- **Choose an option.** Many commands have options that you need to choose before continuing to use the command. To choose an option by using the command line, do one of the following:

NEW FEATURE

Choosing an option by clicking it on the command line is new for AutoCAD and AutoCAD LT 2013. Options have a great background so you can see where to click.

- Click the option on the command line.

- Type the one or two letters that are capitalized in the option name — usually (but not always) the first letter(s) of the option. You can type the letter(s) in lowercase. Press Enter.

- Press Enter to choose a default option or current value.

- Right-click in the drawing area and choose one of the options from the shortcut menu. This works best for options that won't need any numerical input on the command line.

To choose an option by using the Dynamic Input tooltip, press the down arrow on your keyboard to display the options. If there is a default value, you see a mark next to it. Then click one of the options.

At this point, additional options and prompts may appear; you respond in the same way that I have just described, depending on the type of information that the command needs.

In the following exercise, you practice using command options and picking points on the screen with the mouse.

STEPS: Using Command Options

1. Open a new drawing by using the `acad.dwt` or `acadlt.dwt` template. Make sure that the Drafting & Annotation workspace is chosen from the Workspace drop-down list to the right of the Application button. Close any palettes that may be open.

2. Choose Home tab ⇨ Draw panel ⇨ Polyline. (A polyline can contain both line and arc segments. I discuss polylines in Chapter 16.)

3. Look at the command line and the Dynamic Input tooltip. (If you don't see the Dynamic Input tooltip near the cursor, click the Dynamic Input button on the status bar.) You see the following prompt:

```
Specify start point:
```

You also see the current coordinate location of the cursor in the Dynamic Input tooltip. Move the mouse cursor anywhere in the middle of the screen, and click to specify the start point. This is called *picking a point*.

4. Now you see the following prompts, the first on the command line and the second in the Dynamic Input tooltip:

   ```
   Specify next point or [Arc/Halfwidth/Length/Undo/Width]:
   Specify next point or ↓
   ```

   Suppose that you want to specify the width of the polyline. Because specifying the next point is the main instruction, click the Width option on the command line. The program responds with the Specify starting width: prompt. Follow the prompts:

   ```
   Specify starting width <0.0000>: .5 ↵
   Specify ending width <0.5000>: .25 ↵
   ```

5. The prompt to specify the next point returns. Move the mouse so that your cursor is away from the first point that you picked and pick another point. You now see the same prompt repeated.

6. This time, you want to change the width. To specify the width this time, type **w** ↵. Follow the prompts:

   ```
   Specify starting width <0.2500>: ↵ to accept the default value.
   Specify ending width <0.2500>: ↵ to accept the default value again.
   ```

7. Move your mouse so that the new segment is at a different angle than the first one. Pick any point on the screen. The same prompt appears again.

8. Right-click in the drawing area to display the Dynamic Input shortcut menu. Choose Close from the menu. AutoCAD closes the polyline so that you now have a triangle, and ends the command.

   Do not save this drawing.

> **NOTE**
> You may have noticed an underscore (_) before commands. This mark allows translation to foreign languages and can be ignored.

Repeating commands

The most common way to repeat a command you have just used is to press Enter. The most recent command appears again. You can also press the Spacebar at the Type a command: prompt to repeat a command you just used. This technique works well if you want to keep one hand on the mouse and use the other hand to press the Spacebar.

If you know in advance you'll be using a command several times, you can use another technique — type **multiple** ↵. At the Enter command name to repeat: prompt, type the command name on the command line. The command automatically reappears on the command line. For example, you could type **multiple** and then **arc** if you knew you were going to draw several arcs in a row. To stop repeating the command, press Esc.

> **TIP**
> If you create a Ribbon or toolbar button that executes a customized set of actions (as I explain in Bonus Chapters 6 and 10), right-click and choose the top option of the shortcut menu to repeat the action of the custom button. You cannot press Enter to get this effect.

Using recent input

You may need to use the same input again and again. For example, you may want to draw several circles with the same radius. You can use the recent input list to choose a recently used radius instead of typing it again. You can access recent points, values (such as distances and angles), and text strings.

When you see a prompt for input, right-click and choose Recent Input from the shortcut menu. (In a few instances, no shortcut menu is available, so you can't use this feature.) You can then choose one of the recent input items from the list. You can also press the up or down arrows to cycle through the recent input in the Dynamic Input tooltip.

The Recent Input feature displays items that are appropriate for the current prompt. For example, if the prompt asks for a radius, you don't see angles or X,Y coordinates; you see only lengths.

Canceling commands

Sometimes you start a command and then realize you don't need it. In this situation, you can press the Esc key to cancel the command and then choose a different command. The `Command:` prompt reappears.

In the following exercise, you practice the techniques for repeating and canceling commands, as well as using recent input.

STEPS: Repeating and Canceling Commands

1. Start a new drawing by using the `acad.dwt` or `acadlt.dwt` template. Make sure that the Drafting & Annotation workspace is chosen from the Workspace drop-down list to the right of the Application button. Close any palettes that may be open.

2. Choose Home tab ⇨ Draw panel ⇨ Circle drop-down list ⇨ Center, Radius.

3. At the `Specify center point for circle or [3P/2P/Ttr (tan tan radius)]:` prompt, pick a center point anywhere near the center of the screen.

4. At the `Specify radius of circle or [Diameter]:` prompt, type **2** ↵. The circle appears in the drawing area.

5. Press Enter. The CIRCLE command's first prompt appears again.

6. Follow these prompts:

   ```
   Specify center point for circle or [3P/2P/Ttr (tan tan radius)]: Right-
       click and choose 2P from the shortcut menu.
   Specify first end point of circle's diameter: Pick any point on the
       screen.
   Specify second end point of circle's diameter: Press Esc.
   ```

   The prompts disappear.

7. Press the Spacebar. Looking at the Dynamic Input tooltip, you see the `Specify center point for circle or ↓:` prompt. Pick any point on the screen.

8. At the `Specify radius of circle or ↓:` prompt, press Enter to create another circle with a radius of 2.

9. Press Enter to start the CIRCLE command again. At the first prompt, right-click and choose Recent Input. Choose the top item, which is the center of the last circle you drew.

10. At the prompt to specify a radius, pick any point to create a concentric circle.

Do not save this drawing.

Undoing a command

Most Windows applications offer Undo and Redo commands. AutoCAD and AutoCAD LT are no different. AutoCAD and AutoCAD LT remember every command you execute, starting from the time you open a drawing. You can therefore undo every action and return your drawing to its condition when you opened it.

There are a few obvious exceptions. For example, if you print a drawing, you can't unprint it, and you can't unsave a drawing, either. Similarly, you can't undo commands that provide you with information, such as the coordinates of a point.

> **NOTE**
> Some commands have their own undo options. I explain these undo options when I discuss these commands throughout the book.

 Each time you click Undo on the Quick Access Toolbar, you undo one command. You can click the Undo button's drop-down list and choose an earlier command to undo that command and all later commands. If you continue back to the first command of the session, you undo all the commands and get the message:

```
Everything has been undone
```

When you start the UNDO command, which you enter on the command line, you see the following options:

```
Enter the number of operations to undo or [Auto/Control/BEgin/End/Mark/
    Back] <1>:
```

`Enter the number of operations to undo` is the default instruction. If you type a number, such as **3**, you undo your last three commands. This action is equivalent to clicking the Undo button three times. Here are the other options:

- **Auto.** Applies to a menu item that executes more than one command at a time. When Auto is On (the default), the entire menu item is undone in one step. When Auto is Off, UNDO undoes each step one at a time.

- **Control.** Offers five suboptions. All, the default, gives you the full UNDO capability. None disables the UNDO command. The One suboption enables you to undo only one step at a time, effectively turning the UNDO command into the U command. The Combine suboption groups consecutive pan and zoom operations into a single operation. The Layer suboption groups multiple operations from the Layer Properties Manager palette into a single operation.

- **Begin.** Works with the End option. This starts a group at the current point of the list of commands. Then when you use the End option, UNDO undoes all the commands in the group. The U command also undoes everything within a group.

- **End.** Marks the end of all commands in the group created by using the Begin option.

- **Mark.** Works with the Back option. It is somewhat similar to the Begin option, but you can place several marks as you work.

- **Back.** When you use this option, AutoCAD or AutoCAD LT undoes only to the most recent Mark point. The next Back option you use undoes to the Mark point before that.

As you undo commands, the command line lists the commands that are being undone. Sometimes, you see the word *Group,* which means that a group of commands is being undone. However, sometimes the word *Group* is used even for a single command. This use of the word *Group* is not significant and can be ignored.

> **TIP**
>
> You can tell AutoCAD or AutoCAD LT to combine consecutive zooms and pans when you undo commands to help you quickly get back to your previous situation. Choose Application Button ⇨ Options and click the User Preferences tab. Then check the Combine Zoom and Pan Commands check box in the Undo/Redo section. As mentioned earlier, you can also use the Combine suboption of the UNDO command's Control option.

Using the Back option when no mark has been created undoes everything you have done in a drawing session! Luckily, you get the following warning message:

```
This will undo everything. OK? <Y>
```

Type **n** ↵ if you do not want to undo everything.

Redoing a command

If you undo a command, you might realize that you want to undo the undo. This is called redoing a command. Don't confuse redoing a command with repeating a command. Redoing only applies when you have just undone a command.

 The REDO command on the Quick Access Toolbar redoes the effect of the previous UNDO command. You can redo multiple UNDO commands.

> **NOTE**
>
> The MREDO command lets you undo multiple UNDO commands at one time. You can enter it on the command line.

In the following exercise, you practice using the UNDO and REDO commands.

STEPS: Undoing and Redoing Commands

1. Start a new drawing by using `acad.dwt` or `acadlt.dwt` as the template. Make sure that the Drafting & Annotation workspace is chosen from the Workspace Switching drop-down list to the right of the Application button.

2. Choose Home tab ⇨ Draw panel ⇨ Line.

3. Follow the prompts to draw one line, and press Enter to end the command.

4. Choose Home tab ⇨ Draw panel ⇨ Arc.

5. Using the default options, pick any three points to draw an arc.

6. Choose Home tab ⇨ Draw panel ⇨ Circle.

7. Pick one point to be the center of the circle and another nearby point to specify the radius. Your drawing now contains a line, an arc, and a circle, and looks something like Figure 3.5. Of course, your objects will look different because you picked different points.

8. Click the Undo button on the Quick Access Toolbar; the circle disappears.

9. Click the Undo button on the Quick Access Toolbar; the arc disappears. Click the Undo button again; the line disappears.

10. Click the drop-down arrow to the right of the Redo button on the Quick Access Toolbar, and select Circle. All three objects reappear because they were undone by the previous UNDO commands.

Do not save this drawing. If you are continuing, keep the drawing on the screen for the next exercise.

FIGURE 3.5

Your drawing should contain a line, an arc, and a circle.

 The OOPS command restores the most recently erased object or set of objects, even if you have used other commands in the meantime. See Chapter 18 for further information.

Using one command within another command

Certain commands can be used within another command. These are called *transparent commands*. After a transparent command is completed, the original command continues its regular operation. Many transparent commands help you display the drawing differently so that you can complete the original command easily. Other transparent commands change settings. In fact, almost any command that doesn't select objects, create new objects, cause regeneration, or end the drawing session can be used transparently.

When you start transparent commands from the Ribbon or menus, they are automatically transparent. If you want to type a transparent command on the command line or in the Dynamic Input tooltip, you need to type an apostrophe (') before the command name. Experiment using transparent commands, and you'll soon find them indispensable.

Using Mice and Pucks

For the sake of simplicity, this book assumes that you're using a mouse, but some people use a digitizing tablet and a *puck* (or a stylus). A typical digitizing tablet and puck are shown in Figure 3.6. A puck often has more buttons than a mouse and also has crosshairs on a transparent area that you can use for accurately picking points from a paper drawing.

A digitizing tablet is generally configured to include an area that represents the screen you draw on as well as a customizable command area that you use for commands. This command area of the tablet functions as another menu. Usually, you would customize the tablet to suit individual needs, as explained in Bonus Chapter 10.

In the center, the puck functions like a mouse to draw, as well as to access menus and dialog box options. You can use the tablet for a process called *digitizing,* which means transferring data from paper into AutoCAD or AutoCAD LT. This transference is often done by putting a paper document directly on the tablet and using the entire tablet as a drawing area. Because the puck has crosshairs on a transparent surface, you can pick points on the drawing, which then become endpoints of lines, for example. Chapter 16 has an exercise on digitizing.

FIGURE 3.6

A digitizer and puck

3

Getting Help

AutoCAD and AutoCAD LT have so many commands with so many options that every user needs help at some time. AutoCAD and AutoCAD LT come with a very complete Help system.

 See Appendix A for help that is available on the Internet and other resources for AutoCAD and AutoCAD LT.

Getting help on a command

The easiest way to get help on a command is to start the command and press F1. The Help window appears with the content related to that command. Figure 3.7 shows the screen that opens when you type **zoom** ↵ and then press F1.

NEW FEATURE

If you are not connected to the Internet, you will be prompted to connect to the Internet. If you do not always have access to the Internet or have limited access, you can download and install the Help files locally for access when offline.

FIGURE 3.7

The Help screen for the ZOOM command

Using the main Help system

When you have a question, try the Help system. AutoCAD and AutoCAD LT come with the most complete Help documentation I have ever seen in a program. Pressing F1 (with no command active) or clicking the question mark at the right end of the title bar opens the main Help page, as shown in Figure 3.8.

To find help on a topic, enter some keywords in the Search Help text box. When you press Enter, you see a list of related topics on the left, with the first topic displayed on the right. You can scroll down the list of topics to find the one that best meets your needs. In the drop-down list to its right, choose where you want to search.

FIGURE 3.8

The main Help page in AutoCAD

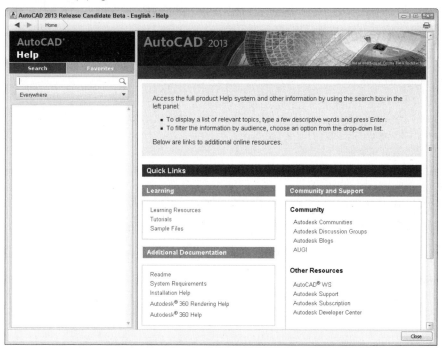

The default setting searches everywhere. Here are your other options:

- **Choose Product Help.** Displays all product topics related to the keywords entered. The search results will return documentation related to general users, developers, and administrators (IT and CAD managers).
- **Choose User.** Filters the search results to only show topics related to general features of the product.
- **Choose Developer.** Filters the search results to only show topics related to customizing or creating custom programs for the product.
- **Choose Administrator.** Filters the search results to only show topics related to installing, deploying, and authorizing the product.

You can also search the online Knowledge Base and Discussion Groups to get additional help.

Working with Help pages

When you get to the Help page of the topic you want, two features can help you find what you need:

- **Related References.** Provides links to Help on relevant commands and system variables.
- **Related Concepts.** Provides links to related Help topics.

Summary

In this chapter, you read all you need to know about how to use AutoCAD and AutoCAD LT commands. Specifically, you read about:

- Using the Ribbon
- Using menus and shortcut menus
- Using dialog boxes
- Working with toolbars
- Using tool palettes
- Understanding command names
- Using and editing the command line
- Using the Dynamic Input tooltip to enter and respond to commands
- Responding to command options and using the command line and shortcut menus
- Repeating and canceling commands
- Undoing and redoing commands
- Using transparent commands
- Using a puck and digitizing tablet to enter commands
- Getting help

In the next chapter, I explain how to specify coordinates, an essential skill before you start to draw.

Specifying Coordinates

IN THIS CHAPTER

Working with absolute, relative, and polar coordinates

Using direct distance entry, orthogonal mode, and polar tracking

Using snap settings

Toggling on and off object snaps

Finding points away from an object

Specifying points in a drawing is one of the most fundamental tasks you do in AutoCAD and AutoCAD LT. Unless you know how to specify a point, you can't draw anything real, whether a house or a gasket. Most objects you draw have a specific size, and you need to specify that information. You draw lines, arcs, and circles by specifying the coordinates of points on the screen. As with most tasks, AutoCAD and AutoCAD LT offer many ways to accomplish this.

Understanding the X,Y Coordinate System

AutoCAD and AutoCAD LT work the same way as the graphs with X and Y axes that you plotted in high school. Look at the User Coordinate System (UCS) icon shown in Figure 4.1.

 The UCS icon can take on different appearances. See Chapter 8 for details. For information on the UCS icon in 3D drawing and 3D coordinates, see Chapter 21.

The X arrow points along the X axis in the positive direction. This means that as you go in the direction of the arrow, the X coordinates increase. The Y arrow points along the Y axis in the positive direction. Using this system, every 2D point on the screen can be specified by using X and Y coordinates. This is called a *Cartesian* coordinate system. The universal convention is to place the X coordinate first, and then a comma (but no space), and then the Y coordinate. By default, the intersection of the X,Y axes is 0,0. Use negative numbers for points to the left of the X axis or below the Y axis.

FIGURE 4.1

The UCS icon shows the direction of the X and Y axes. If you're in a 3D display, you also see the Z axis.

Drawing units

When you draw in AutoCAD or AutoCAD LT, you draw in undefined units. A line from point 3,0 to point 6,0 is three units long. While you're drawing, these units can be anything — a millimeter, a centimeter, a meter, an inch, a foot, or a mile. Practically, you should know exactly what the units represent. After all, you don't want your 36-foot-wide house to end up 36 inches wide!

When you set up a drawing, you specify how units are displayed — for example, whether partial units show as decimal points or fractions. (I cover units in Chapter 5.) However, you don't actually specify what the units represent until you print or plot your drawing — covered in Chapter 17.

To ensure accuracy, you should draw full size. If you're drawing a plan for a factory that will be 120 feet long, for example, you create lines with those measurements. On the screen, you can zoom in to see small details or zoom out to see the whole factory, so that you have no reason not to use the actual line lengths. It's only when you need to print those 120-foot-long lines on a real sheet of paper that you have to specify how to plot out your drawing at a reduced scale.

Users are typically familiar only with the type of notation used in their own field of specialty, whether scientific, architectural, engineering, or whatever. However, you should be at least somewhat familiar with all the major forms of measurement notation.

> **NOTE**
>
> If you are using engineering or architectural units, AutoCAD and AutoCAD LT display parts of inches (fractions) differently than the format you must use to type them in. You must type in coordinates without any spaces because in AutoCAD a space is equivalent to pressing Enter, and that ends your input. Use a hyphen between whole and partial inches — for example, 3'2-1/2". (You can omit the " after the number because inches are assumed in engineering and architectural units if no symbol follows a number.) However, this appears on the status bar as 3'-2 1/2". This can be confusing because the hyphen is in a different place, and you see a space between the whole and partial inches.

Typing coordinates

One way to specify the location of an object is to type its coordinates by using the keyboard. You can enter several types of coordinates. Use the type of coordinates that suit your specific situation.

> **TIP**
> If you need to enter a coordinate that you've typed recently, use the Recent Input feature. Right-click and choose Recent Input from the shortcut menu. Then choose the coordinate that you want from the list that appears.

Using the Dynamic Input tooltip to enter coordinates

Dynamic Input enables you to enter text input near the cursor. In Chapter 3, I explain how to use the Dynamic Input tooltip for commands and command options. Here I explain how to use it to enter coordinates.

 The Dynamic Input button on the status bar turns Dynamic Input on and off. Dynamic Input applies to commands that you type, responses to prompts, and coordinates.

Typing coordinates in the Dynamic Input tooltip

You can type 2D coordinates in the Dynamic Input tooltip in the same way that you type them on the command line — in the format **x,y**. You can press Tab between the X and Y coordinates instead of typing a comma, but typing the comma is probably easier and therefore more accurate.

When you draw a line, after you specify the first point, you see only one tooltip box because AutoCAD assumes that you want to enter only the distance, using the current angle of the temporary line shown on the screen. However, as soon as you type a comma or press the Tab key, a second box appears so that you can enter the Y coordinate, as shown in Figure 4.2. The same situation applies when you want to move or copy an object and want to specify an X,Y displacement.

In Figure 4.2, note the lock next to the X coordinate. Before you type any part of the coordinate, both the X and Y values vary as you move the mouse. When you enter a value for the X coordinate, you fix this value, as the lock indicates. However, the Y coordinate is still unlocked until you type a value.

FIGURE 4.2

As you enter an X,Y coordinate, two boxes appear, one for each part of the coordinate.

Specifying Dynamic Input settings

You can specify how Dynamic Input works for coordinates that you type. Changing the settings gives you very different results when you type coordinates. To specify settings for the Dynamic Input feature, right-click the Dynamic Input button on the status bar and choose Settings to display the Dynamic Input tab of the Drafting Settings dialog box, as shown in Figure 4.3.

4

FIGURE 4.3

Use the Dynamic Input tab of the Drafting Settings dialog box to specify how your Dynamic Input works when you type coordinates.

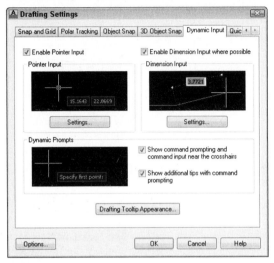

Pointer Input section

The Enable Pointer Input check box is selected by default, which means that the Dynamic Input tooltip includes an input box where you can type coordinates at the start of any command. If you uncheck this check box, you see these first coordinates only on the command line as you enter them. However, whether the check box is checked or not, as long as the Dynamic Input button is selected on the status bar, you see the input box for subsequent coordinates in a command. For example, if you are drawing a line, and the Enable Pointer Input check box is not checked, you don't see coordinates that you type for the start point in the Dynamic Input tooltip, but for the next point, you see the input box and coordinates that you type appear in that box.

Click the Settings button to open the Pointer Input Settings dialog box, as shown in Figure 4.4. Here you can make the following choices:

- **Default format for second or next points.** You can choose to default to polar or Cartesian format. The default is polar format, which shows distances. You can also choose between relative and absolute coordinates. The default is relative coordinates, which indicate a distance and direction from a previously specified point. I explain both absolute and relative formats in the next few sections of this chapter.

- **Tooltip visibility.** You can specify that you see the tooltip only when you start typing a point in response to a prompt, automatically at a prompt for a point (the default), or always.

FIGURE 4.4

The Pointer Input Settings dialog box sets important options for Dynamic Input.

> **CAUTION**
>
> The settings in this dialog box are very important for determining how all of your coordinate entries work when Dynamic Entry is turned on. If you are upgrading from an earlier release of AutoCAD, you may be used to the entry of X,Y coordinates denoting absolute, not relative, coordinates. However, with Dynamic Input turned on, the default is relative coordinates. This is a great default and will speed up your coordinate entry, but can be very confusing if you are unaware of this setting or where to change it.

Dimension Input section

The Enable Dimension Input Where Possible check box is selected by default. This section has nothing to do with dimensions! Instead, it refers to distances or lengths and sometimes angles, as opposed to points or coordinates. With this check box selected, after you indicate a first point, such as the start of a line or the center of a circle that you are drawing, you see a dimension tooltip that shows the length of the line segment or radius of the circle, as shown in Figure 4.5. You specify the length by typing in this tooltip. If you uncheck the check box, you don't see this dimension tooltip.

Click the Settings button in this section of the dialog box to open the Dimension Input Settings dialog box. Here you can change settings relating to dimension input during grip editing. I discuss grip editing in Chapter 10.

> **NOTE**
>
> If you uncheck both the Enable Pointer Input and the Enable Dimension Input Where Possible check boxes, you turn off Dynamic Input.

4

FIGURE 4.5

The so-called dimension input tooltip shows distances and angles as you draw.

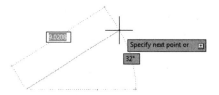

Dynamic prompts section

The Show Command Prompting and Command Input Near the Crosshairs check box enables the display of command prompts and your input in response to these prompts in the Dynamic Input tooltip. This part of Dynamic Input is supposed to take the place of the command line. However, the prompts are not an exact echo of what you see on the command line, and certain prompts do not appear in the tooltip.

Click the Drafting Tooltip Appearance button to open the Tooltip Appearance dialog box. Here you can change the color of the tooltip, change its size and transparency, and apply the settings to all drafting tooltips in AutoCAD.

Overriding Dynamic Input settings

The default Dynamic Input settings ensure that your input in the tooltip is always interpreted as polar, relative coordinates. However, you may want to override this setting for an individual coordinate. You can override this setting by using a symbol before your X coordinate as you type it. AutoCAD provides three overrides that you can use:

- **Absolute.** To override the default setting of relative coordinates and enter an absolute coordinate, type **#**. For example, you could type **#0,0** to specify the 0,0 coordinate. See the "Working with absolute Cartesian coordinates" section for more information.

- **Relative.** If you have set your Dynamic Input for absolute coordinates, you can enter @ to override the setting and type a relative coordinate. For example, you could type **@3,4**. See the "Working with relative Cartesian coordinates" and "Using polar coordinates" sections.

- **World.** Normally, coordinates that you type are interpreted in the current User Coordinate System (UCS). The default coordinate system is called the World Coordinate System (WCS). If you have created a custom coordinate system but want to enter a World Coordinate System coordinate, type * before the X coordinate. For more information, see Chapter 8 (for two-dimensional drawings) and Chapter 21 (for three-dimensional drawings).

Working with absolute Cartesian coordinates

When you type a line and enter the actual coordinates, such as a line from point 3,2 to 6,9, you are using absolute Cartesian coordinates. Absolute coordinates are measured from 0,0.

If you have Dynamic Input on with the default setting of relative units, you must enter the # symbol before entering the X portion of an absolute Cartesian coordinate when specifying the second or next point, as explained in the previous section. Here you practice entering absolute Cartesian coordinates.

STEPS: Entering Absolute Cartesian Coordinates

1. Start a new drawing by using the `acad.dwt` or `acadlt.dwt` template. Close any palettes that may be open.

2. If you have Dynamic Input on, right-click the Dynamic Input button on the status bar and choose Settings. In the Pointer Input section, click the Settings button. In the Pointer Input Settings dialog box, click the Absolute Coordinates option (unless this option is already selected). Click OK twice to return to your drawing.

3. Choose Home tab ⇨ Draw panel ⇨ Line. Follow these prompts:

   ```
   Specify first point: -10,-5 ↵
   Specify next point or [Undo]: 21,-5 ↵
   Specify next point or [Undo]: 21,49 ↵
   Specify next point or [Close/Undo]: -10,49 ↵
   Specify next point or [Close/Undo]: c ↵ (to close the rectangle)
   ```

   Most of the lines are off the screen. By default, a new drawing starts with 0,0 at the lower-left corner of your screen; therefore, negative coordinates do not show.

4. Choose View tab ⇨ Navigate 2D panel ⇨ Zoom drop-down list ⇨ Out. If you still can't see the entire rectangle, repeat the zoom out process until you can see it.

5. Start the LINE command again and follow these prompts:

   ```
   Specify first point: -8,-2 ↵
   Specify next point or [Undo]: 19,-2 ↵
   Specify next point or [Undo]: 19,21.5 ↵
   Specify next point or [Close/Undo]: -8,21.5 ↵
   Specify next point or [Close/Undo]: c ↵
   ```

4

6. Once more, start the LINE command and follow these prompts:

```
Specify first point: -8,22.5 ↵
Specify next point or [Undo]: 19,22.5 ↵
Specify next point or [Undo]: 19,46 ↵
Specify next point or [Close/Undo]: -8,46 ↵
Specify next point or [Close/Undo]: c ↵
```

7. If you changed the Dynamic Input settings in Step 1, you should change them back. Right-click the Dynamic Input button on the status bar and choose Settings. In the Pointer Input section, click the Settings button. In the Pointer Input Settings dialog box, click the Relative Coordinates option. Click OK twice to return to your drawing.

8. Save this drawing in your `AutoCAD Bible` folder as `ab04-01.dwg`.

You can now see that you've drawn a simple window, as shown in Figure 4.6.

FIGURE 4.6

A window drawn with absolute coordinates

Two questions may have occurred to you during this exercise. First, isn't there a better way of entering absolute coordinates? Typing them in is slow and prone to error. Second, how do you know the absolute coordinates for what you're drawing? Read on for the answers.

Working with relative Cartesian coordinates

In practice, you usually don't know the absolute coordinates of the points you need to specify in order to draw an object. Whether you're drawing an architectural layout, a physical object, or an electrical schematic, you don't have X,Y coordinates from which you can work. However, you often do have the measurements of what you're drawing. Usually, you start from any suitable point and work from there. In this situation, you know only the length of the lines you're drawing (if you're drawing lines). Real life doesn't have a 0,0 point. Relative coordinates were developed for these situations.

Relative coordinates specify the X and Y distance from a previous point. They are called *relative coordinates* because they have meaning relative to a point previously specified. Suppose that you need to draw a window. You can start the window from any point. From there, you have the measurements you need.

If you have Dynamic Input on — set to the default option of relative units — X,Y coordinates are automatically relative. If you have Dynamic Input off or have set Dynamic Input to absolute coordinates, as described earlier in this chapter, you specify that the coordinates are relative by using the @ symbol. For example, if you start a line by picking any point with the mouse, and you know it should be two units long, you can specify the next point as @2,0. The result is a line starting with the first point you picked and ending two units along the X axis, as shown in Figure 4.7. The line is horizontal because the Y coordinate is 0. In a relative coordinate, this means that the Y distance does not change.

FIGURE 4.7

A line whose start point could be anywhere and whose endpoint is specified with the relative point @2,0 is a horizontal line two units long.

Relative Cartesian coordinates are often used for lines drawn at 90-degree angles (that is, they are either horizontal or vertical). These are called *orthogonal lines.* However, when you create a diagonal line from point 3,3 to point @2,5, the length of the line is not immediately obvious.

When you specify a positive number, such as the 2 in @2,0, the direction is positive. If you want to draw a line in the negative direction of an axis, type a minus sign before the number.

Using polar coordinates

Another common situation is to know the distance and angle of a point from either 0,0 or a previous point. In this case, you can use *polar coordinates,* which can be either absolute or relative. Most commonly, you use relative polar coordinates.

Polar coordinates take the form distance<angle. (To type the angle symbol, use the less-than symbol on your keyboard.) If you have Dynamic Input on, set to the default options of relative coordinates, polar coordinates are automatically relative. If you have Dynamic Input off or have set Dynamic Input

to absolute coordinates, as described earlier in this chapter, you need to add the @ sign before a relative polar coordinate. If you also have the default option of polar format selected, you first see coordinates in polar format. Enter the distance, press the Tab key, and then enter the angle. You can also type the angle (<) symbol instead of using the Tab key. To switch to Cartesian format, just type a comma between the X and Y coordinates.

With Dynamic Input on, angles are measured from 0 to 180, with 0 to the right, going either clockwise or counterclockwise. Watch the dotted lines near the angle's tooltip to see exactly what the angle shown in the tooltip is measuring. You can use negative angles. With Dynamic Input off, angles are measured counterclockwise, with 0 to the right, ranging from 0 to 360.

In the following series of steps, you draw part of a portico, the decorative molding above a door or window. You'll use architectural units. In this case, only inches are used, which don't need to be specified. You can specify feet by using an apostrophe (also called a *prime*) after any number.

When typing architectural units, partial inches are indicated by fractions in the form a/b. You need to separate the fraction from the whole inches by a hyphen. This can be a little confusing because the hyphen is also used for negative numbers. For example, to draw a horizontal line of 5¼ inches in the negative direction of the X axis, you would type **-5-1/4,0**. (The 0 indicates no change in the Y axis because it is a horizontal line.)

On the Web

The drawing used in this exercise on using relative and polar coordinates, `ab04-a.dwg`, is available from the Drawings download on the companion website.

STEPS: Using Relative and Polar Coordinates

1. Open `ab04-a.dwg`, available from the Drawings download on the companion website. Close any palettes that may be open.
2. As you move your mouse around, notice that the coordinates displayed on the status bar are in architectural units (that is, in feet and inches). If the coordinates are grayed out, click them to turn them on.
3. Save the drawing in your `AutoCAD Bible` folder as `ab04-02.dwg`.

Note

The next steps involve some complex typing. If you get an error message, try typing the coordinate again. If you realize you made a mistake after ending the command, click Undo on the Quick Access Toolbar. This exercise assumes that you are using the default Dynamic Input settings of polar format and relative coordinates and that Dynamic Input is on. See the section on using the Dynamic Input tool in this chapter for details.

4. Choose Home tab ⇨ Draw panel ⇨ Line to start the LINE command. Follow these prompts:

```
Specify first point: Pick any point at the lower-left corner of your
    screen.
Specify next point or [Undo]: 0,-3/4 ↵
Specify next point or [Undo]: 75-1/4,0 ↵
Specify next point or [Close/Undo]: 0,3/4 ↵
Specify next point or [Close/Undo]: c ↵
```

5. Start the LINE command again. Follow the prompts:

    ```
    Specify first point: ↵. This starts the line at the last endpoint you
        specified.
    Specify next point or [Undo]: 4-3/4,0 ↵
    Specify next point or [Undo]: 43<40 ↵
    Specify next point or [Close/Undo]: 43<-40 ↵
    Specify next point or [Close/Undo]: -2-1/4,0 ↵
    Specify next point or [Close/Undo]: 39-7/8<140 ↵
    Specify next point or [Close/Undo]: 39-7/8<-140 ↵
    Specify next point or [Close/Undo]: ↵ to end the command.
    ```

> **NOTE**
> In this exercise, you draw a line on top of a line, which is not good drawing practice. Later in this chapter and in upcoming chapters, you learn techniques to avoid this.

6. Save your drawing. You have created a portion of a portico, which goes over a window of a house, as shown in Figure 4.8.

FIGURE 4.8

Part of a portico over a window, drawn by using relative Cartesian and polar coordinates in architectural notation.

> **TIP**
> You can type @ ↵ at the first prompt of any drawing command to indicate the most recent coordinate specified.

4

Notice that using relative coordinates, both Cartesian and polar, is much more realistic than using absolute coordinates. However, typing in coordinates is still awkward. Typing in coordinates is often the only way to get exactly what you want. Nevertheless, in many circumstances, several other techniques for specifying coordinates are easier. I discuss these techniques in the next few sections.

Using direct distance entry

One shortcut for entering coordinates is direct distance entry. You can use direct distance entry for any command that requires you to specify a distance and a direction, including both drawing and editing commands. After you specify the start point of a line, at the `Specify next point or [Undo]:` prompt, simply move the mouse in the direction you want the line to go and type in the line's length. It works best in orthogonal mode or with polar tracking (discussed in the following section), which makes specifying the exact angle easy.

Working in Orthogonal mode

Lines drawn at 0, 90, 180, and 270 degrees are orthogonal lines. When in orthogonal mode — *ortho* for short — you can only draw orthogonal lines with the mouse. Ortho Mode also affects editing. For example, with Ortho Mode on, you can move objects only vertically or horizontally. Combined with snap and grid, Ortho Mode makes drawing easier and more efficient. Ortho Mode is also great for direct distance entry.

 Click Ortho Mode on the status bar to toggle Ortho Mode on and off, or press F8. You cannot have polar tracking on at the same time that Ortho Mode is on. Polar tracking is discussed next.

> **NOTE**
> Orthogonal mode only affects points picked directly on the screen by using your mouse. Any relative or absolute coordinates that you type in the Dynamic Input tooltip or on the command line override orthogonal mode. For example, if you use a polar coordinate of 5<45 in the Dynamic Input tooltip, you'll get a line at an angle of 45 degrees, even when Ortho Mode is on.

Working with polar tracking

Polar tracking guides you, using a tooltip and vector line, when you want to draw (or edit) at an angle other than the four orthogonal angles, as shown in Figure 4.9. You can use polar tracking for orthogonal angles as well. If you have Dynamic Input on, just look for the word "Polar" to distinguish between the Dynamic Input and the polar tooltips.

Polar tracking makes it easy to use direct distance entry to specify distances for many angles. To use polar tracking, you first set the angles that you want to use.

Setting polar tracking angles

 To set the angles, right-click the Polar Tracking button on the status bar and choose Settings. The Polar Tracking tab of the Drafting Settings dialog box is displayed, as shown in Figure 4.10.

FIGURE 4.9

When polar tracking is on, a tooltip appears when you move the cursor close to one of the polar angles. Here you see a tooltip indicating an angle of 45 degrees.

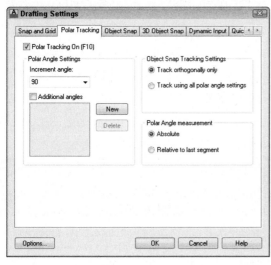

Polar tracking vector

Polar: 3'0 3/8" < 45d — Polar tracking tooltip

FIGURE 4.10

The Polar Tracking tab of the Drafting Settings dialog box

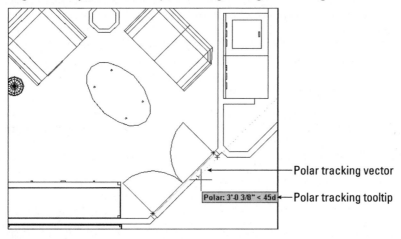

To set polar tracking, you can define two types of angles:

- **Increment angle.** To set the increment angle, click the Increment Angle drop-down arrow, where you can pick from angles that range from every 90 degrees to every 5 degrees. You can also type your own incremental angle in the text box. Polar tracking will then apply to that angle and its multiples.
- **Additional angles.** If you think that you'll need other angles, check Additional Angles, click New, and then type in an angle. You can add up to ten angles. Note that additional angles are not incremental angles — if you type 35, only 35 degrees will be marked, not 70 degrees or other multiples of 35. To delete an additional angle, select it and click Delete.

On the right side of the dialog box, you can choose how polar tracking works with object snap tracking (covered later in this chapter). You can set object snap tracking to use all the polar angle settings or limit it to orthogonal angles only. You can also set whether polar angles are measured absolutely (relative to 0 degrees) or relative to the segment drawn most recently. By default, absolute angles are used. To turn on polar tracking, check the Polar Tracking On check box in the dialog box. If you are not in the dialog box, press F10 or click the Polar Tracking button on the status bar.

To customize how polar tracking works, click Options in the Drafting Settings dialog box to open the Options dialog box with the Drafting tab on top. The following settings in the AutoTracking Settings section apply to polar tracking:

- **Display polar tracking vector** turns on and off the polar tracking vector, which is the faint dotted line that extends to the end of the screen.
- **Display AutoTrack tooltip** turns on and off the distance and angle tooltip.

Using polar tracking

To use polar tracking, you need to move the cursor slowly through the angles to allow time for the calculation and display of the vector and tooltip. Suppose that you're drawing a line. Specify the start point. To specify the second point, move the cursor in the approximate angle of the line you want to draw. When you see the polar tracking vector and tooltip, leave the mouse where it is and type the length of the line. Then press Enter to create the line with the proper length and angle. You'll find this method easier than typing polar coordinates for lines with angles specified in your polar tracking settings.

> **TIP**
> Turn on NumLock on your keyboard and use the numerical pad for typing lengths. Use the Enter key on the numerical pad as well.

You can specify a polar angle for just one command. If you're drawing a line, after specifying the first point, for example, type the angle preceded by the angle symbol (<). The next segment is then locked to that angle while you type its length. A polar angle specified in this way is called a *polar override angle* because it overrides the current polar angles in effect. Of course, a polar override is not faster than simply typing a polar coordinate, but it does let you see the angle of the line segment before you type its length.

In the following exercise, you practice using direct distance entry with Ortho Mode and polar tracking.

ON THE WEB

The drawing (`ab04-b.dwg`) used in the following exercise on using direct distance entry with Ortho Mode and polar tracking is available from the Drawings download on the companion website.

STEPS: Using Direct Distance Entry with Ortho Mode and Polar Tracking

1. Open `ab04-b.dwg`, available from the Drawings download on the companion website. Close any palettes that may be open.

2. Right-click the Polar Tracking button on the status bar, and choose 45 to set a 45° polar tracking angle.

3. Save the drawing in your `AutoCAD Bible` folder as `ab04-03.dwg`. If Ortho Mode is not on, click the Ortho Mode button on the status bar.
4. Choose Home tab ➪ Draw panel ➪ Line to start the LINE command and, at the `Specify first point:` prompt, type **2,2** ↵.
5. Move the mouse horizontally to the right and then type **.5** ↵.
6. Move the mouse up vertically (in the 90-degree direction) and then type **.5** ↵.
7. Move the mouse horizontally to the right and then type **2** ↵. Your drawing should look like Figure 4.11.

FIGURE 4.11

Drawing with direct distance entry enables you to specify coordinates by typing in a length after you move the pointer in the desired direction.

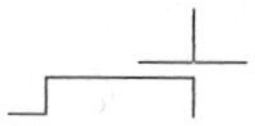

8. Move the mouse up in the 90-degree direction and then type **.5** ↵.
9. Move the mouse to the left in the 180-degree direction and then type **2** ↵.
10. Move the mouse up in the 90-degree direction and then type **.5** ↵.
11. Move the mouse to the left in the 180-degree direction and then type **.5** ↵.
12. Type **c** ↵ to close the figure. Press Enter again to end the command.

13. Click Polar Tracking on the status bar. The Ortho Mode button becomes deselected.
14. Start the LINE command again. Press Enter to start the new line from the most recent point. At the `Specify next point or [Undo]:` prompt, move the cursor diagonally up and to the left so the line is approximately in the 135-degree direction. When you see the tooltip confirming the angle, release the mouse button and type **.7071** ↵.

15. Move the cursor up until you see the polar tracking tooltip confirming a 90-degree angle. Type **.5** ↵.

16. Move the cursor diagonally in the 45-degree direction until you see the tooltip. Type **.7071** ↵. Press Enter again to end the LINE command.

17. Save your drawing. It should look like Figure 4.12.

FIGURE 4.12

The completed drawing of a bolt

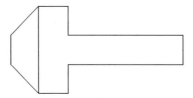

Displaying Coordinates

As you work, you can refer to the coordinate display on the status bar. This display helps you know where your cursor and objects are when you draw and is also helpful when editing, by informing you how far and in what direction you are moving or copying objects.

> **NOTE**
> You can set the Dynamic Input tooltip to show coordinates all the time, even when you're not in a command. The section on "Specifying Dynamic Input settings" gives more detail.

AutoCAD and AutoCAD LT have three coordinate display modes:

- **Dynamic absolute coordinates (absolute).** Absolute coordinates that change as you move the mouse, as shown in Figure 4.13 on the left.
- **Static absolute coordinates (off).** Absolute coordinates that change only when you specify a point, as shown in Figure 4.13 in the middle. The coordinate display is dimmed.
- **Dynamic polar coordinates (relative).** Polar coordinates that change continuously as you move the mouse, as shown in Figure 4.13 on the right. They appear after you've already specified a point and are ready to specify the next point, as when you're in the process of drawing a line.

FIGURE 4.13

Dynamic absolute coordinates, static absolute coordinates, and dynamic polar coordinates.

0.7409, 2.1450 , 0.0000	0.3485, 3.0654 , 0.0000	1.4580< 29 , 0.0000
Dynamic absolute coordinates.	Static absolute coordinates.	Dynamic polar coodinates.

To change the coordinate display, click the coordinates area on the status bar. For purposes of this chapter, I ignore the Z coordinate that follows the X and Y coordinates (in AutoCAD only). In two-dimensional drawings, the Z coordinate is always zero.

Picking Coordinates on the Screen

The easiest and quickest way to specify coordinates is to pick them directly on the screen with the mouse. Several techniques are available to help you do so accurately.

You can adjust the size of the crosshairs that cross the cursor. By default, they are 5 percent of screen size. To change the crosshair size, choose Application Button ➪ Options, and click the Display tab. In the Crosshair Size text box, type a new percentage or drag the bar to increase or decrease the percentage. Click OK.

Using Snap settings

The SNAP command is often an alternative to tedious entry of coordinates. This command restricts the cursor to an incremental distance that you choose, such as 0.5 units, whenever you are specifying a coordinate. You can set the snap spacing to anything you want. For example, if all your measurements are rounded off to the nearest 0.25 units, you can set your snap to 0.25.

NOTE

When snap is on, the cursor doesn't jump to the snap coordinate until you specify a point.

The snap technique is not very useful when you need to draw to three or more decimal places of accuracy. And when you're zoomed out in a large drawing, the snap points may be so close together that you cannot easily find the one you want. But in the right situation, snap is one of the quickest, most accurate drawing techniques available. AutoCAD and AutoCAD LT provide two types of snap settings, Grid Snap and PolarSnap.

4

Snapping to a grid

 To set the snap spacing, right-click the Snap Mode button on the status bar and choose Settings. The Drafting Settings dialog box opens, as shown in Figure 4.14. In the Snap X Spacing text box of the Snap Spacing section, type the spacing you want between snap points. Make sure that Grid Snap and Rectangular Snap are selected in the Snap Type section of the dialog box. Click OK.

FIGURE 4.14

The Snap and Grid tab of the Drafting Settings dialog box. (The AutoCAD LT dialog box is slightly different.)

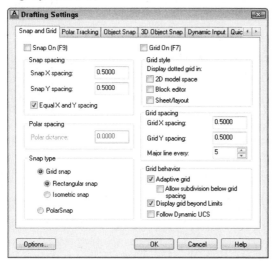

 In Chapter 8, I discuss rotating the angle of the snap and grid. Chapter 8 also discusses Isometric snap, used for isometric drawing.

Usually you want the X spacing (going across) to be the same as the Y spacing (going up and down). By default, the Equal X and Y Spacing check box is selected, so you need to specify only the X spacing; the Y spacing changes automatically to equal the X spacing. X and Y spacing will be different only if you type a different number in the Snap Y Spacing text box.

You can also turn snap on in this dialog box by clicking the Snap On check box. However, the most common way to turn snap on, after you've set the spacing, is to click the Snap Mode button on the status bar (or press F9). Click it again to turn snap off.

Snapping at polar angles

After you set polar tracking settings, discussed earlier in this chapter in the "Using polar tracking" section, you can snap to increments along the polar angles you have set. When PolarSnap is on, the polar tooltip only shows distances in increments of the snap setting. When you see the distance you want, just click. PolarSnap makes it easy to draw accurately without the need to type coordinates.

To use PolarSnap, follow these steps:

1. Right-click the Snap Mode button on the status bar and click Settings to open the Drafting Settings dialog box with the Snap and Grid tab displayed.

2. Check PolarSnap in the Snap Type section of the dialog box (see Figure 4.14).

3. Type a distance in the Polar Distance text box.

4. Click OK to close the dialog box.

5. Click Snap Mode on the status bar.

Note that PolarSnap and Grid Snap are mutually exclusive. If PolarSnap is on, the cursor will not snap to the grid. Used with polar tracking, PolarSnap is a powerful tool. Remember that you can polar track along orthogonal as well as other angles.

> **TIP**
> You can choose either PolarSnap or Grid Snap (switch between them) by right-clicking Snap Mode on the status bar. A shortcut menu lets you choose the type of snap you want, or turn both off.

Viewing with the grid

 Sometimes you may find it helpful to see a grid to help get your bearings while you draw, as shown in Figure 4.15. To toggle the grid, click Grid Display on the status bar or press F7. Notice how you can quickly judge the approximate width of a windowpane, knowing that the grid lines are half a foot apart. If you turn on snap, the grid helps you visualize the snap points. However, it is not necessary that the grid lines be set to the same spacing as the snap points.

FIGURE 4.15

A portion of a drawing with the grid turned on and set to 6 inches

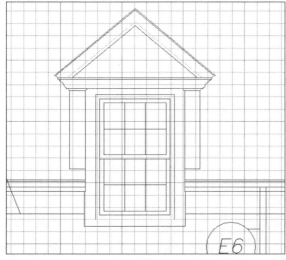

Thanks to Henry Dearborn, AIA, Fairfield, Iowa, for this drawing.

Some users find the grid annoying, but when you first start to use AutoCAD or AutoCAD LT, you may find it helpful. Even accomplished users can take advantage of the grid, especially when starting a new drawing.

To set the grid size, right-click the Grid Display button on the status bar and choose Settings to open the Drafting Settings dialog box (refer to Figure 4.14). In the Grid X Spacing text box of the Grid Spacing section, type the spacing you want between grid points. Click OK.

As with the snap feature, you usually want the X spacing (going across) to be the same as the Y spacing (going up and down). You only need to specify the X spacing; the Y spacing automatically changes to be the same, as long as the Equal X and Y Spacing check box is selected in the Drafting Settings dialog box. X and Y spacing will only be different if you type a different number in the Grid Y Spacing text box.

> **NOTE**
> You can choose to display the grid as dots instead of the default lines. In the Grid Style section of the Snap and Grid tab of the Drafting Settings dialog box, check the contexts in which you want to display dots.

You can turn on the grid in this dialog box by clicking the Grid On check box, but it's easier to click Grid Display on the status bar (or press F7). In the following exercise, you practice using PolarSnap and Grid Snap points as well as the grid.

> **ON THE WEB**
> The drawing used in the following exercise on using snap points and the grid, ab04-b.dwg, is available from the Drawings download on the companion website.

STEPS: Using Snap Points and the Grid

1. Open ab04-b.dwg, available from the Drawings download on companion website. Close any palettes that may be open.

2. Save the drawing in your AutoCAD Bible folder as ab04-04.dwg.

 3. Right-click the Snap Mode button on the status bar and choose Settings. The Drafting Settings dialog box opens with the Snap and Grid tab displayed. In the Snap Type section, make sure that Grid Snap and Rectangular Snap are selected.

4. In the Snap Spacing section, the Snap X Spacing should be 0.5.

5. In the Grid Spacing section, the Equal X and Y Spacing check box should be selected. The Grid X Spacing should be 0.5. Click OK.

6. On the status bar, click Snap Mode, Grid Display, and Ortho Mode. The grid appears. Make sure that the Object Snap and Object Snap Tracking buttons on the status bar are off.

7. Choose View tab ⇨ Navigate 2D panel ⇨ Zoom drop-down list ⇨ All.

8. Choose Home tab ⇨ Draw panel ⇨ Line to start the LINE command. At the Specify first point: prompt, click when the coordinates on the status bar show 2.0000,2.0000. (AutoCAD users can ignore the third Z coordinate, which is always 0.0000 in 2D drawings.) If you have Dynamic Input on, you'll find the coordinates in the Dynamic Input tooltip easier to read.

9. Move the mouse around and watch the coordinates. If you don't see polar coordinates (for example, 3.0000<0), right-click the coordinates and choose Relative.

10. Move the mouse to the right until the coordinates read 8.5000<0 and click. You have drawn a horizontal line with a length of 8.5 units.

11. Right-click and choose Enter to end the LINE command. The absolute coordinates reappear.

12. Right-click and choose Repeat LINE to start the LINE command again. Use the coordinate display to start the line at 1.5000,1.5000. (For the rest of this exercise, ignore the Dynamic Input tooltip.) Continue to pick points (rather than type them) and draw the following line segments, as shown in the coordinate display:

    0.5000<0
    3.0000<90
    0.5000<180
    3.0000<270

13. End the LINE command.

14. Start the LINE command and pick points, drawing the following line segments (as shown in the coordinate display) starting from 10.5000,1.50. Then end the LINE command:

    0.5000<0
    3.0000<90
    0.5000<180
    3.0000<270

15. Starting from 2.0000,4.0000 draw an 8.5-unit line at 0 degrees. End the LINE command.

16. Start the LINE command again. At the first prompt, pick 11.0000,2.0000. Right-click the Snap Mode button on the status bar and choose Settings. In the Snap Type section, choose PolarSnap. (This is equivalent to choosing the PolarSnap On feature on the Snap Mode button's shortcut menu.) In the Polar Spacing section, change the Polar Distance to 0.5. Choose the Polar Tracking tab and set the Increment Angle to 45 degrees. Click OK. Click Polar Tracking on the status bar.

17. Move the cursor in a 45-degree direction from 11.0000,2.0000 until you see the tooltip. Move along the polar tracking vector until the tooltip says 3.5000 < 45° and click. End the LINE command.

18. Right-click the Snap Mode button and choose Grid Snap On. Start the LINE command and, at the Specify first point: prompt, choose 11.0000,4.0000.

19. Right-click the Snap Mode button and choose PolarSnap On. Move the cursor in a 45-degree direction until the tooltip says 3.5000 < 45° and click. End the LINE command.

20. Save your drawing. Your drawing should look like Figure 4.16.

4

FIGURE 4.16

The completed pipe section

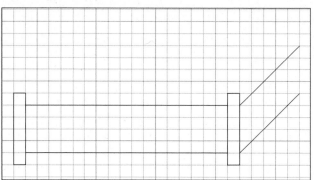

As you no doubt experienced, compared to typing in coordinates, this is a much easier way to draw. Note that drawing with Snap on works better when you're drawing small objects. However, even when drawing an office building, you spend a great deal of time working on small details that may be easier to draw with Snap on.

Using object snaps

Often you need to draw relative to an existing object. For example, you may need to start a line from the endpoint or midpoint of an existing line. *Object snaps* (OSNAPS for short) enable you to precisely specify a point by snapping to a geometrically defined coordinate on an existing object. Object Snaps provide a very precise and efficient way to draw.

Here are three ways to specify an object snap:

- Right-click, choose Snap Overrides from the shortcut menu, and then choose the object snap that you want from the menu.
- Type the object snap's abbreviation on the command line.
- Access the Object Snap shortcut menu by holding down the Shift key and right-clicking. Choose the object snap that you want from the shortcut menu.

NOTE
When you press Shift and right-click to get the Object Snap menu, the mouse pointer must be in the drawing area. If the mouse pointer is on the Ribbon or command line area, press the Esc key, or hold down the Shift key and right-click again in the drawing area.

 On multi-button mice, you can customize one of the buttons to show the Object Snap shortcut menu. I discuss customizing the mouse in Bonus Chapter 10.

When you specify an object snap, a prompt for that object snap appears on the command line. For example, if you choose a midpoint object snap, you see mid of on the command line. Unfortunately, the Dynamic Input tooltip does not show this prompt.

> **TIP**
> When you use Dynamic Input and object snaps together, the tooltip alternates between showing the Dynamic Input tooltip and the object snap tooltip, or displays them as separate tooltips. To keep all the tooltips together, set the TOOLTIPMERGE system variable to 1.

Table 4.1 lists the object snaps. Use the abbreviation to type the object snap from the keyboard.

TABLE 4.1 Object Snaps

Object Snap	Abbreviation	Uses
Endpoint	end	Lines, arcs, and so on.
Midpoint	mid	Lines, arcs, and so on.
Intersection	int	Intersection of lines, circles, arcs.
Apparent Intersection*	app	The intersection that would be created if two objects were extended until they met.
Extension	ext	Extends lines, arcs, and so on past their endpoints but in the same direction. After choosing this object snap, pause over the endpoint of a line or arc until you see a small plus sign. As you move the cursor along the extension path, a temporary extension path appears so that you can draw to or from points on the extension path.
Center	cen	Circles, arcs, ellipses.
Quadrant	qua	Nearest quadrant (0-, 90-, 180-, or 270-degree point) of a circle, arc, or ellipse.
Perpendicular	per	Arc, circles, ellipses, lines, multilines, polylines, rays, splines, or construction lines. The Deferred Perpendicular mode lets you draw a line perpendicular *from* one of these objects. Start the LINE command and choose the Perpendicular object snap. Click the object that you want to draw perpendicular from and then move the cursor away from that object. You see the Deferred Perpendicular tooltip and a temporary perpendicular line that follows your cursor along the original object. You can then complete the perpendicular line.
Parallel	par	Continues a line, polyline, and so on so that it's parallel to an existing line or other straight-line segment. After you choose this object snap, pause over the line you want to draw parallel to until you see a small parallel line symbol. As you move the cursor parallel to the object, a temporary parallel path appears to help you create the parallel segment.
Tangent	tan	Starts or continues a line from or to a point tangent with an arc, circle, or ellipse.
Node	nod	Point objects (discussed in Chapter 7) and origin point (defpoint) on dimensions (covered in Chapter 14).
Insertion	ins	Insertion point of text (see Chapter 13) or a block (see Chapter 18).
Nearest	nea	Nearest point on any object.
None	non	Turns off any object snap modes.

* Apparent Intersection also applies to 3D objects that appear to intersect because of the angle of view.

When you draw a line, you think of it as having a starting point and an ending point. After the line is drawn, however, both of these points are considered endpoints in terms of object snaps. When picking the endpoint of a line for the endpoint object snap, pick a point on the line closer to the endpoint that you want. The same applies to arcs. Although the arc prompts read Start point and End, both are considered endpoints for purposes of object snaps.

AutoSnap is a feature that helps you work with object snaps. When you move the cursor near the geometric point you have specified, such as an endpoint, you are notified in three ways:

- **Marker.** An object snap shape appears. Each object snap has a differently shaped marker.
- **AutoSnap tooltip.** A label displays the name of the object snap.
- **Magnet.** A pull gently moves the cursor toward the geometric point.

Figure 4.17 shows an endpoint marker and AutoSnap tooltip.

You can customize the AutoSnap feature to suit your needs or make it go away completely if you want. Choose Application Button ➪ Options, and click the Drafting tab. Here you can individually turn on and off the marker, the AutoSnap tooltip, and the magnet. You can also change the marker size and color. For more information, see Bonus Chapter 15.

FIGURE 4.17

AutoSnap shows you the endpoint of the line.

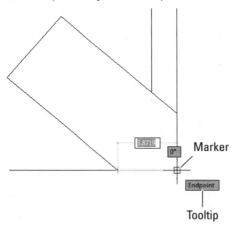

In the following exercise, you practice using object snaps.

STEPS: Using Object Snaps

1. Start a new drawing by using the `acad.dwt` or `acadlt.dwt` template. Close any palettes that may be open.

2. Save the drawing in your `AutoCAD Bible` folder as `ab04-05.dwg`.

3. Click Ortho Mode on the status bar to turn on Ortho Mode. If the Object Snap button on the status bar is on, click it to turn off running object snaps (covered in the next section).

4. Choose Home tab ⇨ Draw panel ⇨ Line to start the LINE command. Follow the prompts:

```
Specify first point: 2,7 ↵. Move the cursor downward.
Specify next point or [Undo]: 4 ↵. Move the cursor to the right.
Specify next point or [Undo]: 4 ↵. Move the cursor up.
Specify next point or [Close/Undo]: 4 ↵
Specify next point or [Close/Undo]: Press Enter to end the command.
```

Your drawing should look like Figure 4.18. The circled numbers are reference points for this exercise.

5. Choose Home tab ⇨ Draw panel ⇨ Arc drop-down list ⇨ 3-Point. Follow these prompts:

```
Specify start point of arc or [Center]: Right-click. From the shortcut
    menu, choose Snap Overrides ⇨ Endpoint.
_endp of Move the cursor to ❶ in Figure 4.18. When you see the endpoint
    marker and AutoSnap tooltip, click.
Specify second point of arc or [Center/End]: Right-click and choose
    Center.
Specify center point of arc: Press Shift and right-click. Choose Midpoint
    from the shortcut menu.
_mid of Move the cursor to ❷ and pick.
Specify end point of arc or [Angle/chord Length]: end ↵. Move the cursor
    to ❸ and pick.
```

6. Choose Home tab ⇨ Draw panel ⇨ Circle drop-down list ⇨ Center, Radius. Follow the prompts:

```
Specify center point for circle or [3P/2P/Ttr (tan tan radius)]: Choose
    Center from the Object Snap shortcut menu.
cen of Move the cursor over the arc until you see the Center marker and
    tooltip, and then click.
Specify radius of circle or [Diameter]: .75 ↵
```

4

FIGURE 4.18

These three lines are the start of a mounting bracket.

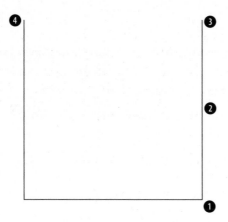

7. Start the LINE command and use any method you want to draw a line from the endpoint at ❸ to the endpoint at ❹. End the LINE command.

8. Save your drawing. It should look like Figure 4.19.

FIGURE 4.19

This is the start of a drawing of a mounting bracket (including a construction line that would later be erased). It was created by using the endpoint, midpoint, and center object snaps.

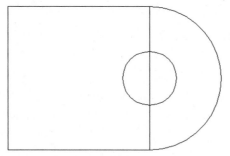

Running object snaps and Object Snap mode

The Endpoint object snap is probably the most commonly used of all the object snaps. It would be nice to have a method of using object snaps that you use often without resorting to a menu, toolbar, or keyboard entry. The solution is to set a *running object snap,* which keeps one or more object snaps on until you turn them off.

> **TIP**
>
> Many users like to work with three or four running object snaps on at once, such as Endpoint, Midpoint, Center, and Intersection. If you can't find the object snap you want because you have several object snaps near each other, press Tab to cycle through the object snaps, one by one, until you find the one that you want.

To set running object snaps, right-click the Object Snap button on the status bar and choose the object snaps that you want from the list that pops up. Because the list closes after each choice, you may want to choose Settings to open the Drafting Settings dialog box, as shown in Figure 4.20. Choose the object snaps that you want and click OK. To clear a checked object snap, click it. Click Clear All to clear all running snaps.

You use the Object Snap button on the status bar to turn on your running object snaps. If you want to turn them off temporarily, just click the Object Snap button or press F3. This capability to toggle running object snaps on and off makes it easy to work with running object snaps on almost all the time, because you can turn them off at the click of a button.

FIGURE 4.20

Use the Object Snap tab of the Drafting Settings dialog box to set running object snaps.

4

Overriding Coordinate Settings

Sometimes you're in the middle of a command and want to turn off an object snap just for a second. You're trying to pick a point and that pesky object snap marker keeps appearing just when you don't want it. Or you may want to turn Snap mode on or off for part of a command. Temporary overrides exist for this purpose. There are two kinds of temporary overrides:

- **Toggles.** You press a key or combination of keys. The setting switches on or off. You then press the same keyboard shortcut to reverse the setting. For example, if you have Ortho Mode on, you can press F8 to turn it off. To turn Ortho Mode back on, press F8 again.
- **Temporary overrides.** You press and hold a key or key combination. The setting switches on or off only while you're holding down the keyboard shortcut. The setting reverts to its original setting when you release the key or key combination. For example, if you have Ortho Mode on, you can press Shift to temporarily turn it off. As soon as you release the Shift key, Ortho Mode comes back on.

Table 4.2 lists these overrides. Note that each setting has two shortcuts, one for your left hand and one for your right hand. Use whichever one you like. You can customize the keys for these overrides. (For more information, see Bonus Chapter 10.)

TABLE 4.2   Coordinate Setting Overrides

Setting	Toggle	Temporary Override	Description
Toggle Object Snap mode	F3	Shift+A; Shift+'	Equivalent to clicking the Object Snap button on the status bar.
Turn on Object Snap mode		Shift+S; Shift+;	Use when Object Snap mode is off and you want to briefly turn it on.
Endpoint object snap		Shift+E; Shift+P	Temporarily turns on an Endpoint object snap when Object Snap mode is off.
Midpoint object snap		Shift+V; Shift+M	Temporarily turns on a Midpoint object snap when Object Snap mode is off.
Center object snap		Shift+C; Shift+,	Temporarily turns on a Center object snap when Object Snap mode is off.
Turn off Object Snap and Object Snap Tracking modes		Shift+D; Shift+L	Equivalent to deselecting both the Object Snap and the Object Snap Tracking buttons on the status bar. (I explain object tracking in the next section.)
Ortho Mode	F8	Shift	Equivalent to clicking the Ortho Mode button on the status bar.
Snap mode	F9		Equivalent to clicking the Snap Mode button on the status bar.
Polar mode	F10	Shift+X; Shift+.	Equivalent to clicking the Polar Mode button on the status bar.
Object Snap Tracking mode	F11	Shift+Q; Shift+]	Equivalent to clicking the Object Snap Tracking button on the status bar (I explain this in the next section).
Dynamic UCS mode	F6	Shift+Z, Shift+/	Equivalent to clicking the Allow/Disallow Dynamic UCS button on the status bar.
Dynamic Input	F12		Equivalent to clicking the Dynamic Input button on the status bar.

In the following exercise, you practice using running object snaps with Object Snap mode.

STEPS: Using Running Object Snaps with Object Snap Mode

1. Start a new drawing by using the `acad.dwt` or `acadlt.dwt` template. Close any palettes that may be open.

2. Save the file in your `AutoCAD Bible` folder as `ab04-06.dwg`.

 3. Right-click the Object Snap button on the status bar and choose Settings. Choose Endpoint. Uncheck all other object snaps and click OK.

4. Choose Home tab ⇨ Draw panel ⇨ Line to start the LINE command. At the prompt, enter **2,2** ↵ to start the line at coordinate 2,2.

5. Turn on Ortho Mode by clicking the Ortho Mode button on the status bar. If Object Snap mode is not on, click it on the status bar.

6. Move the mouse in the 0-degree direction and type **6** ↵.

7. Move the mouse up in the 90-degree direction, type **3** ↵, and end the LINE command.

8. Start the ARC command. At the `Specify start point of arc or [Center]:` prompt, pick the endpoint at ❶, as shown in Figure 4.21. (Look for the marker and AutoSnap tooltip.) This is the right endpoint of the horizontal line that you just drew.

FIGURE 4.21

Drawing a steam boiler with an endpoint running object snap

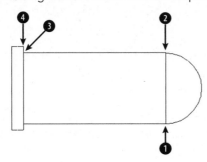

9. At the `Specify second point of arc or [Center/End]:` prompt, right-click (or press the down arrow if Dynamic Input is on) and choose End. Pick the endpoint at ❷, as shown in Figure 4.21.

10. At the `Specify center point of arc or [Angle/Direction/Radius]:` prompt, right-click (or press the down arrow if Dynamic Input is on) and choose Angle, and then type **180** ↵.

4

11. Start the LINE command and at the `Specify first point:` prompt, pick the endpoint at ❷, as shown in Figure 4.21.

12. Move the mouse to the left in the 180-degree direction, type **6** ↵, and end the LINE command.

13. Right-click the Snap Mode button on the status bar and choose Settings. Make sure that the Equal X and Y Spacing check box is selected. Click Grid Snap in the Snap Type section. Set the Snap X Spacing to 0.25. Check the Snap On check box. Click OK.

> **NOTE**
>
> If the boiler is too small, choose View tab ⇨ Navigate 2D panel ⇨ Zoom drop-down list ⇨ All.

14. Start the LINE command. At the `Specify first point:` prompt, place the cursor 0.25 units above ❸, as shown in Figure 4.21 (at 2,5.25). If you see the endpoint marker for the nearby line, press F3 to turn off the running Object Snap temporarily. Pick point 2,5.25.

15. At the `Specify next point or [Undo]:` prompt, pick point 2,1.75. (If necessary, right-click the coordinates and choose Absolute to get absolute coordinates.)

16. If Dynamic Input is not on, click the Dynamic Input button on the status bar. Follow the prompts:

```
Specify next point or [Undo]: Pick .5<180. (This means that you see a
    length tooltip of .5 and an angle tooltip of 180°.)
Specify next point or [Close/Undo]: Pick 3.5<90.
Specify next point or [Close/Undo]: (If you turned off Object Snap mode
    in Step 14, press F3 to turn it on again.) Pick the endpoint at ❹ in
    Figure 4.21.
Specify next point or [Close/Undo]: ↵
```

17. Save your drawing.

> **NOTE**
>
> Even if you have running object snaps, if you specify an object snap during a command, it overrides the running object snap. For example, having a running endpoint object snap does not mean that you can't use a midpoint object snap for any specific drawing command.

By default, if you type absolute or relative coordinates, they take precedence over any running object snaps. This lets you leave running object snaps on but override them with keyboard entry of typed coordinates whenever you want. In general, the default gives you the most control and flexibility. However, you can change this default to give running object snaps precedence. To change the default, choose Application Button ⇨ Options, click the User Preferences tab, and use the Priority for Coordinate Data Entry section of the dialog box.

Locating Points

Sometimes you need to locate a point that is not on an existing object. For example, you may need a point a certain distance and angle from an existing object. This section explains three techniques that enable you to locate points that are not on objects — object snap tracking, point filters, and the From feature.

Using object snap tracking

The purpose of object snap tracking is to let you specify a point based on the object snaps of existing objects. Temporary tracking lines are drawn from points you specify, and guide you so that you can easily specify the point that you want. Use the Object Snap Tracking button on the status bar to turn object snap tracking on and off. Object snap tracking can handle the following tasks and many more:

- You're drawing a line and have specified the start point. You want the endpoint to be exactly vertical to the endpoint of an existing line.

- You're drawing a circle inside a rectangle (which could be a hole inside a sheet-metal plate). You want the center of the circle to be exactly centered inside the rectangle, at the intersection of the midpoints of the rectangle's two sides.

- You want to start a line at the point where two existing lines would intersect if they were extended.

To start using object snap tracking, at least one object snap must be active. Turn on a running object snap, as explained in the previous sections. Then click the Object Snap Tracking button on the status bar.

With object snap tracking on, follow these steps:

1. Start a command that requires you to specify a point.

2. Place the cursor briefly over an object snap, such as the endpoint of a line, to temporarily *acquire* it. You can acquire more than one point. These acquired points are used to calculate the tracking paths. You see a small plus sign (+) over the object snap as confirmation, as shown in Figure 4.22.

FIGURE 4.22

When you pause over an object snap and then move the cursor slightly, you see a plus sign (+) at the acquired point to show that the point has been acquired and that you can now use it for object snap tracking.

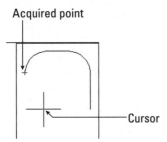

3. Move the cursor away from the object snap toward your desired point. You see the temporary alignment paths as you move the cursor over available drawing paths, as shown in Figure 4.23. If Ortho Mode is on, you see only horizontal and vertical paths. If Polar Tracking mode is on, you see polar paths based on the polar angle settings, as explained earlier in this chapter.

FIGURE 4.23

With the endpoint object snap active and Ortho Mode on, AutoCAD displays temporary alignment paths based on the acquired point.

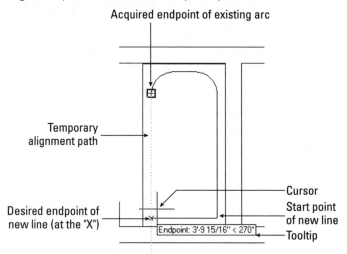

4. When you see a tooltip and a small x, click it. You can now continue or complete the command, using this point.

After you acquire a point, you can clear it in any one of three ways:

- Move the cursor back over the point's plus sign.
- Click the Object Snap Tracking button on the status bar to turn it off.
- Start any new command.

You can customize the following features of object snap tracking on the Drafting tab of the Options dialog box (choose Application Button ⇨ Options):

- Uncheck Display Polar Tracking Vector to eliminate the tracking paths.
- Uncheck Display Full-Screen Tracking Vector to display the tracking paths only from the cursor to the object snap point.
- Uncheck Display AutoTrack Tooltip to eliminate the tooltips.
- In the Alignment Point Acquisition section, choose Shift to Acquire, which will require you to hold Shift to acquire a point when the cursor is over an object snap point.

In the following exercise, you practice locating points with object snap tracking.

STEPS: Locating Points with Object Snap Tracking

1. Open ab04-c.dwg, available from the Drawings download on the companion website. Close any palettes that may be open.

2. Save the drawing as ab04-07.dwg in your AutoCAD Bible folder. This drawing is a section of a simple plan layout of an apartment. Set endpoint and midpoint running object snaps only. Make sure that Object Snap mode and Object Snap Tracking are on and that Polar Tracking and Ortho Mode are off.

3. Choose Home tab ⇨ Draw panel ⇨ Line to start the LINE command. At the Specify first point: prompt, pick the endpoint at ❶, as shown in Figure 4.24. Be sure to pick the endpoint itself, in order to acquire it.

4. At the Specify next point or [Undo]: prompt, pass the cursor over ❷. Move the cursor down a little, and you see the small plus sign showing that this endpoint has been acquired.

FIGURE 4.24

The tub, door, and sink to be completed in this plan layout.

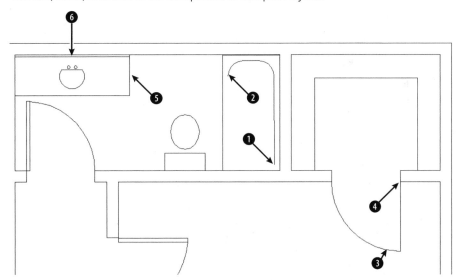

5. Move the cursor down until it is to the left of ❶ and vertical to ❷. When you see the tooltip (reading Endpoint: < 270°, Endpoint: < 180°) and the small x marking the intersection of the two points, click to end the line segment.

6. At the Specify next point or [Undo]: prompt, click at ❷ and end the LINE command.

7. Start the LINE command again. At the Specify first point: prompt, pick the endpoint of the arc at ❸, as shown in Figure 4.25. If you're not sure that you found the right endpoint, press Tab until the arc is highlighted. Make sure that you've acquired the endpoint by clicking the endpoint itself or passing the crosshairs over it.

8. At the Specify next point or [Undo]: prompt, pass the cursor over ❹ until you see the small plus sign. Move the cursor slightly to the left until you see the tooltip (reading Endpoint: < 90°, Endpoint: < 180°) and click.

9. At the Specify next point or [Undo]: prompt, pick the endpoint at ❹ and end the LINE command.

10. Choose Home tab ➪ Draw panel ➪ Circle drop-down list ➪ Center, Radius to start the CIRCLE command. At the Specify center point for circle or [3P/2P/Ttr (tan tan radius)]: prompt, pass the cursor over ❺ and then over ❻ to acquire both midpoints.

11. Move the cursor to the middle of the sink, where lines from both midpoints would intersect until you see the tooltip (reading Midpoint: < 270°, Midpoint: < 180°) and click.

12. At the Specify radius of circle or [Diameter]: prompt, type **7.5** ⏎ to complete the sink.

13. Save your drawing. It should look like Figure 4.25.

FIGURE 4.25

The completed drawing

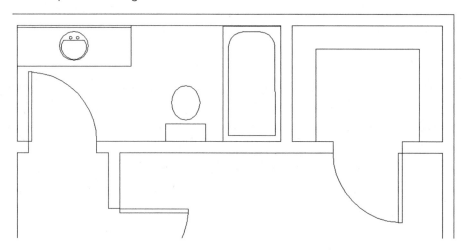

Using the temporary tracking feature

The temporary tracking feature is similar to object snap tracking, but limits you to horizontal and vertical directions. Follow these steps:

1. Start a command.

2. At a prompt to specify a point, enter **tracking** ↵ (or **tk** ↵) at the command prompt.

3. At the First tracking point: prompt, specify a point (usually using object snaps) that is horizontal or vertical to the final point that you want to specify.

4. Immediately move the cursor horizontally or vertically toward the final point that you want to specify. You see a rubber-band line.

5. At the Next point: prompt, move the cursor from the rubber-band line to specify a second point that is also vertical or horizontal to the final point.

6. Press Enter to end tracking and continue the command.

The cursor moves to the intersection of the rubber-band lines. You can now continue your command.

Finding points with point filters

Point filters enable you to specify a coordinate by using the X coordinate of one existing object snap and the Y coordinate of another. You construct an X,Y coordinate based on coordinates of existing objects. In most cases, you can use object snap tracking instead. Here's how to use point filters:

1. Start a command to draw an object.

2. To specify a coordinate, enter **.x** or **.y** ↵ on the command line. You can also find point filters on the Object Snap shortcut menu (Shift+right-click).

3. The prompt requests a point. Generally, you specify the point by using an object snap.

4. The prompt requests the other coordinate value, which you generally provide by using an object snap. (If you're working in 2D, ignore the request for a Z coordinate.)

5. Continue your command.

> **TIP**
> You don't need to use existing coordinates for both portions of the coordinate. For example, you can construct a coordinate by using the Y coordinate of an existing line and picking the X coordinate anywhere on the screen.

Finding offset points with the From feature

The From feature enables you to create a new object starting at a known distance and direction from an existing object. Here's how to use the From feature:

1. Start a command to draw an object, such as LINE.

2. Press Shift+right-click, and choose From on the shortcut menu. You can also enter **from** ↵ on the command line or in the Dynamic Input tooltip.

3. The prompt requests a base point, which you usually provide by using an object snap.

4. The prompt requests an Offset, which you provide by using relative or polar coordinates.

5. Continue the command you started (in Step 1).

NOTE

When you specify the offset for the From feature, you need to use the @ symbol to indicate relative coordinates, even if Dynamic Input is set to the default of relative coordinates. The Dynamic Input relative coordinate's setting only applies to the second coordinate that you enter.

ON THE WEB

The drawing used in the following exercise on using the From feature, ab04-06.dwg, is available from the Results download on the companion website.

STEPS: Using the From Feature

1. Open ab04-06.dwg, which you created in an earlier exercise. If you did not do the previous exercise, open the drawing, available from the Results download on the companion website. Close any palettes that may be open. Make sure Ortho Mode is on and Snap mode is off. Object Snap should be on. Set Endpoint as the running object snap.

2. Save the drawing as ab04-08.dwg in your AutoCAD Bible folder.

3. Choose Home tab ⇨ Draw panel ⇨ Line to start the LINE command.

4. From the Object Snap shortcut menu, choose From.

5. The prompt asks you for a base point. Pick the endpoint at ❶, as shown in Figure 4.26.

FIGURE 4.26

Using the From feature to complete the steam boiler

6. At the <Offset>: prompt, type **@−1,0.5** ↵.

7. You are now ready to continue the line at the Specify next point or [Undo]: prompt. Press F3 to turn off Object Snap mode. Move the cursor in the 90-degree direction and type **2** ↵.

8. Move the mouse in the 180-degree direction and type **1** ↵.

9. Move the mouse in the 270-degree direction and type **2** ↵.

10. Right-click and choose Close from the shortcut menu to close the rectangle.

11. Save your drawing. It should look like Figure 4.27.

FIGURE 4.27

The completed steam boiler

Summary

This chapter covers a great deal about specifying coordinates. You read about:

- The X,Y coordinate system
- Using Dynamic Input
- Using absolute and relative Cartesian and polar coordinates
- Direct distance entry
- Orthogonal (Ortho) mode
- Using polar tracking
- Controlling the display of coordinates on the status bar
- Grid and PolarSnap settings
- Using object snaps to specify geometric points on objects
- Temporarily overriding coordinate settings
- Using object snap tracking and point filters to locate points
- The From feature for locating points not on an object

The next chapter introduces you to the basics of setting up a drawing.

Setting Up a Drawing

O ften, the first step after you start a new drawing is to set its size and unit type. These and other setup options are discussed in this chapter. The entire process of setting up a drawing is essential for ensuring accurate results. You can save most of these settings in a template to avoid having to re-create them each time you start a new drawing.

Choosing Unit Types

One of the first tasks in setting up a drawing is to choose the unit type. Units define how objects are measured. You can save the unit type in a template.

The coordinates that you use in AutoCAD or AutoCAD LT are measured in units that can represent any real-world measurement, such as inches or millimeters. A surveyor or city planner might even use miles or kilometers as the base unit. However, different disciplines have customs that express units differently, and you should use the unit type appropriate for the type of drawing you're creating. This ensures that everyone involved understands the drawing. AutoCAD and AutoCAD LT offer five types of units, as shown in Table 5.1. The sample measurement column shows how a line 32.5 units long would be displayed in the various unit types.

TABLE 5.1 **Unit Types**

Unit Type	Sample Measurement	Description
Decimal	32.50	Number of units, partial units in decimals
Engineering	2'–8.50"	Feet and inches, partial inches in decimals
Architectural	2'–8 1/2"	Feet and inches, partial inches in fractions
Fractional	32 1/2	Number of units, partial units in fractions
Scientific	3.25E+01	Base number + exponent

Notice how the engineering and architectural units translate a line of 32.5 units into feet and inches (when using Imperial measurements). Engineering and architectural units assume a unit of 1 inch, unlike the other unit types, which can represent any measurement.

The unit type affects how coordinates are shown on the status bar and how information about objects is listed. You generally input coordinates by using the type of units you've chosen, although in some cases you can input coordinates in another unit type.

> **NOTE**
> If you're using engineering or architectural units, AutoCAD and AutoCAD LT display partial inches differently than the format you must use to type them in. You must type coordinates without any spaces, because a space is equivalent to pressing Enter, and that ends your input. Use a hyphen between whole and partial inches, for example, 3'2-1/2". (You can omit the " after the inches because inches are assumed in engineering and architectural units if no symbol follows a number.) However, this appears on the status line as 3'-2 1/2". This can be confusing because the hyphen is in a different place, and you see a space between the whole and partial inches.

Setting the drawing units

When you know the units you want to use, you set them in the Drawing Units dialog box. To set the units, choose Application Button ⇨ Drawing Utilities ⇨ Units, to open the Drawing Units dialog box, as shown in Figure 5.1. The left side of the Drawing Units dialog box enables you to choose which unit type you want to use. In the Precision drop-down list in the Length section, click the arrow and a list of precision options drops down. Click the one you want.

> **CAUTION**
> AutoCAD and AutoCAD LT round off measurements to the nearest precision value you choose. Say that you choose a precision of two decimal places, using decimal units. You want to draw a line so that it is 3.25 units long, but when you type the coordinate, by accident you press the 4 key at the end, resulting in a line 3.254 units long. This line is displayed as 3.25 units long, making it difficult for you to spot the error. Therefore, setting a higher precision than you need to show is a good idea.

Setting the angle type

As with units, your choice of angle type depends on your profession and work environment. Decimal Degrees is the default. Table 5.2 lists the types of angles.

FIGURE 5.1

The Drawing Units dialog box

TABLE 5.2 Angle Types

Angle Type Name	Sample Measurement	Description
Decimal Degrees	32.5	Degrees, partial degrees in decimals
Deg/Min/Sec	32°30'0"	Degrees, minutes, and seconds
Grads (gradians)	36.1111g	Gradians
Radians	0.5672r	Radians
Surveyor	N 57d30' E	Surveyor (directional) units

NOTE

A minute is $\frac{1}{60}$ degree and a second is $\frac{1}{60}$ minute. Gradians and radians are simply alternate ways of measuring angles. A gradian is a metric measurement equal to $\frac{1}{100}$ of a right angle. Radians measure an angle by placing a length, equal to the radius, along the circle's circumference. Radians range from 0 to $2 \times \Pi$ rather than from 0 to 360 as degrees do. A radian is approximately 57.30 degrees. Surveyor units measure angles in directions, starting with north or south and adding an angle in degrees/minutes/seconds format that shows how far the angle is from north or south and in which direction (east or west).

5

To set the angle type, choose the option you want from the Type drop-down list of the Angle section of the Drawing Units dialog box (shown in Figure 5.1).

 Changing these angle settings does not automatically change the way your dimension annotations appear. Use the Dimension Style Manager, which is discussed in Chapter 15, to change dimensions.

Setting the angle measure and direction

By convention, degrees increase in a counterclockwise direction, and you measure angles so that 0 degrees starts to the right, also called the East direction. To change the angle direction, click Clockwise in the Drawing Units dialog box. To change the direction of 0 degrees, click Direction to open the Direction Control dialog box, as shown in Figure 5.2.

FIGURE 5.2

The Direction Control dialog box

Here you can choose to have 0 degrees start in a direction other than East. You can also choose Other and type any other angle or click the Pick an Angle button to specify two points in your drawing that define the new angle. Click OK to close the Direction Control dialog box. Click OK to close the Drawing Units dialog box.

> **NOTE**
> Changing the angle direction affects what happens when you input angles and what you see in the coordinate display. It does not change the absolute coordinates, which are set according to the User Coordinate System (UCS). Chapter 8 covers using and customizing UCSs.

If you are using Dynamic Input, the angle that you see in the Dynamic Input tooltip never goes above 180°. This angle in the tooltip represents the angle to your current point and goes from 0° to 180° in both the clockwise and counterclockwise directions.

 At the bottom of the Drawing Units dialog box, you can choose units for lighting. See the discussion of lighting in Bonus Chapter 2 for more information.

STEPS: Setting Drawing Units

1. Begin a new drawing by using the `acad.dwt` or `acadlt.dwt` template. Close any palettes that may be open. If Dynamic Input isn't on, click the Dynamic Input button on the status bar. This exercise assumes that you have input of coordinates set to relative coordinates, the default setting. (For more information, see Chapter 4.)

2. Save the drawing as `ab05-01.dwg` in your `AutoCAD Bible` folder.

3. Choose Application Button ⇨ Drawing Utilities ⇨ Units, to open the Drawing Units dialog box.

4. In the Length section, choose Architectural.

5. Click the arrow to the right of the Precision drop-down list in the Length section. Choose 0'-0 1/8".

6. In the Angle section, choose Deg/Min/Sec.

7. In the Precision box, choose 0d00'.

8. In the Units to Scale Inserted Content drop-down list, set the units to Inches.

9. Click OK.

10. Choose Home tab ⇨ Draw panel ⇨ Line to start the LINE command. Follow the prompts:

    ```
    Specify first point: 2,2 ↵
    Specify next point or [Undo]: 1'<0 ↵
    Specify next point or [Undo]: 6-3/4<153 ↵
    Specify next point or [Close/Undo]: Right-click and choose Close.
    ```

11. Choose View tab ⇨ Navigate 2D panel ⇨ Zoom drop-down list ⇨ All to zoom to the entire drawing. Save your drawing. If you're continuing through the chapter, keep it open.

> **NOTE**
> You would not actually use Deg/Min/Sec for angles in an architectural drawing, but the exercise gives you the opportunity to set the angular units.

Drawing Limits

You can specify the area of your drawing, also called the *limits*. The drawing limits are the outer edges of the drawing, specified in X,Y units. You set only the width and length of the drawing. Together, these two measurements create an invisible bounding rectangle for your drawing.

Almost universally, the lower-left limit is 0,0, which is the default. Therefore, the upper-right corner really defines the drawing size. Remember that you typically draw at life size (full scale). Therefore, the size of your drawing should be equal to the size of the outer extents of what you're drawing, plus a margin for a titleblock (if you plan to add one in model space), annotation, and dimensioning. If you want to show more than one view of an object, as is common in both architectural and mechanical drawings, you need to take this into account.

To decide on the upper-right corner limits for your drawing, you need to consider what the drawing units mean for you. Generally, the smallest commonly used unit is used, often inches or millimeters. Therefore, if you're drawing a plan view of a house that is approximately 40 feet across (in the X direction) by 30 feet deep (in the Y direction), this translates to a top-right corner of 480,360.

The limits define an artificial and invisible boundary to your drawing. However, you can draw outside of the limits. The limits can affect the size of the grid, when displayed. (See Chapter 4 for more information on the grid.) The ZOOM command with the All option also uses the limits, but only if no objects are outside the limits. (See Chapter 8 for a discussion of the ZOOM command.)

To set the drawing limits, type **limits** ↵ on the command line, to start the LIMITS command. Press Enter to accept the lower-left corner default of 0,0 that appears on the command line. Then type the upper-right corner coordinate that you want and press Enter.

Understanding Scales

You need to consider the fact that your drawing will likely be plotted onto a standard paper (sheet) size. The standard orientation for drafting (and the default for most plotters) is *landscape* orientation, meaning that as you look at the drawing, the paper is wider than it is tall. Figure 5.3 shows an example. To scale a drawing onto a piece of paper in a pleasing manner requires a rectangular shape that somewhat resembles the proportions of standard paper sizes.

FIGURE 5.3

Drawings are usually oriented horizontally, as in this example.

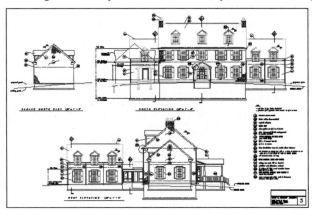

Thanks to Henry Dearborn, AIA, Fairfield, Iowa, for this drawing, which I have altered slightly.

In addition, although you specify the scale at plotting time, it helps to be aware at the outset of the scale you'll use when plotting your drawing. One important reason for establishing the scale at the beginning is to ensure that text, whether annotations or dimensions, is readable in its final plotted form. Applying a scale ensures that text remains a reasonable size even as the rest of the drawing is scaled up or down. Scale also affects linetypes that contain dots or dashes.

Some drawings are not scaled. Examples are electrical or electronic schematics, piping diagrams, and railroad schematics. These drawings are representations of electrical or electronic connections but do not resemble the actual physical object that will eventually be created from the drawing. These drawings can be any size as long as they are clear and organized.

 You can lay out various views of your drawing on an imaginary piece of paper, a *paper space layout*, to prepare it for plotting. You can annotate on the layout to avoid having to scale these components. See Chapter 17 for more information on layouts and plotting.

When determining your scale to fit a drawing on a sheet of paper, be aware that a plotter cannot print on the entire sheet. A certain amount of the margin around the edge is not available for drawing. The plotter's manual can let you know the width of this unprintable margin. On average, you can assume a half-inch margin on each side; thus you should subtract 1 inch from both the length and width sheet measurements to determine the actual drawing space. Table 5.3 shows standard U.S. sheet sizes.

TABLE 5.3   Standard Paper Sheet Sizes in the United States (in inches)

Size	Width	Height	Size	Width	Height
A	11	8½	D	34	22
B	17	11	E	44	34
C	22	17			

Table 5.4 lists standard metric sheet sizes.

TABLE 5.4   Standard Metric Paper Sheet Sizes (in millimeters)

Size	Width	Height	Size	Width	Height
A4	297	210	A1	841	594
A3	420	297	A0	1,189	841
A2	594	420			

Working with scale formats

A scale is often indicated in the format *plotted size=actual size* or *plotted size:actual size*. Because you draw at actual size, the actual size is also the drawing size. For example, a scale of ¼"=1' means that ¼ inch on the drawing, when plotted out on a sheet of paper, represents 1 foot in actual life — and in the drawing. This is a typical architectural scale. A windowpane 1 foot wide would appear ¼-inch wide on paper.

5

From the scale, you can calculate the scale *factor*. You use the factor when you set the size for text (see Chapter 13) or dimensions (see Chapter 15). The left side of the scale equation must equal 1, and the two numbers must be in the same measurement (for example, both in inches). This requires some simple math. For 1/4"=1', you would calculate as follows:

1/4"=1'

1"=4'   Both sides of the equation multiplied by 4

1"=48"   4' converted to 48"

Therefore, the scale factor is 48. This means that the paper plot is $\frac{1}{48}$ of real size.

In mechanical drawing, you might draw a metal joint that is actually 4 inches long. To fit it on an 8½-x-11-inch sheet of paper, you could use a 2"=1" scale, which means that 2" on the paper drawing equals 1" in actual life and the drawing. Calculate the scale factor:

2"=1"

1"=1/2"

The scale factor is 1/2. Thsmeans that the paper plot is twice the real size.

Most professions use certain standard scales. Therefore, you do not usually have a choice to pick any scale you want, such as 1":27'. Instead, the conventions of your profession, client, or office dictate a choice of only a few scales. Some typical architectural scale factors are:

- 192: 1/16" = 1'
- 96: 1/8" = 1'
- 48: 1/4" = 1'
- 24: 1/2" = 1'
- 12: 1" = 1'

Civil engineering scales are somewhat different and range to larger sizes — a bridge is bigger than a house. Some typical scale factors are 120 (1" =10') and 240 (1" =20').

Metric scales can be used for any purpose. Example scale factors are 10000 (1mm = 10 meters), 5000 (1mm = 5 meters), 1000 (1mm = 1 meter), or 100 (1cm = 1 meter).

Using annotative scales

You can assign an *annotative property* to certain objects so that they automatically resize to the proper scale when you lay out the drawing for plotting. The following types of objects can be annotative:

- Text (see Chapter 13)
- Dimensions and leaders (see Chapters 14 and 15)
- Hatches (see Chapter 16)

- Blocks (see Chapter 18)
- Attributes (see Chapter 19)

You would use annotative scaling when you need to display your drawing at more than one scale. For example, you might display the entire drawing at one scale and a detail at another scale. (See Chapters 13, 14, 15, 16, 17, and 18 for more information on annotative styles and objects.)

Using annotative objects avoids the necessity to manually figure out how large these objects need to be; when you scale them, they will be the proper size. For example, if your drawing scale will be 1:48, and you want your text to be 1/4" high, then you would need to multiply the desired height of the text (1/4") by the scale factor to get a text height of 12. However, by setting the annotative scale for the text to 1/4" = 1'-0", you can simply set the height of the text to 1/4" and not worry about the calculations.

The procedure for creating annotative objects differs somewhat for each type of object, but the overall process is the same:

1. If necessary, create an annotative style and make it current. Annotative text, dimensions, and multileaders require an annotative style.

2. Decide on the scales that you will use for each object. For example, you might have two text objects each at a different scale, or one text object that you need to display at two different scales.

 3. If you want each text object to have a different scale, turn off the ANNOAUTOSCALE system variable. This system variable, when on, automatically adds scales to annotative objects as you add annotative scales; the result is that each object has more than one scale. To turn ANNOAUTOSCALE off, click the icon on the right side of the status bar to the right of the Annotation Scale pop-up list. When on, there's a yellow lightning bolt; when off, the lightning bolt is gray.

4. Set the annotation scale for the first object. To do so, click the Annotation Scale button at the right side of the status bar to display the scale list and choose the scale you want. For example, choose 1/4" = 1'-0" if you plan to display the text at the 1/4" = 1'-0" scale.

5. Create the object.

6. When you're ready to plot, you can set the desired annotative scale, and plot. You can also create viewports and set their scale. See Chapter 17 for details and an exercise using annotative objects.

If you want one object to have more than one scale, you can add an annotative scale to it. Follow these steps:

1. Select the object and right-click in the drawing area.

2. Choose Annotative Object Scale⇨Add/Delete Scales to open the Annotation Object Scale dialog box, as shown in Figure 5.4.

5

FIGURE 5.4

The Annotation Object Scale dialog box enables you to add an annotation scale to an annotation object.

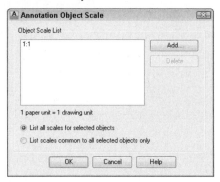

3. Click Add to display the Add Scales to Object dialog box, where you can choose one or more scales.

4. Click OK twice to close both dialog boxes.

You can also open the dialog box by displaying the Properties or Quick Properties palette, clicking the Annotative Scale item, and clicking the Ellipsis button that appears.

 For each scale that you assign to an object, AutoCAD or AutoCAD LT automatically creates a representation of that object in an appropriate size. Therefore, you may have a text object shown at three sizes. At any time, you can view any single scale for an annotative object, or view all its scales. If you don't see all scales of an annotative object, click the Annotation Visibility button on the right side of the status bar. This button controls the ANNOALLVISIBLE system variable. By default, it is on, displaying all scales. When you turn it off, you see only the text for the current annotative scale. To immediately plot, you would turn off this system variable so that you plot only the text for the current annotative scale.

Customizing the scale list

You generally choose a scale during the process of laying out a drawing. AutoCAD and AutoCAD LT have a list of scales from which you can choose. You can find this list in several places (which I discuss throughout the book):

- On the Annotation Scale list on the status bar, as mentioned earlier
- In the Add Scales to Object dialog box, also mentioned earlier
- In the VP Scale list of the status bar, when you select a viewport (see Chapter 17)

- In the Plot Scale section of the Page Setup and Plot dialog boxes (see Chapter 17)
- In the Standard Scale item of the Properties and Quick Properties palettes when a viewport is selected (see Chapter 17)
- In the Sheet Set Manager, when placing a view on a layout (see Bonus Chapter 3)

You might use unusual scales in your office or want a list that includes only the scales that you use. You can customize the scale list for this purpose. To customize the scale list, choose Annotate tab ⇨ Annotation Scaling panel ⇨ Scale List. The Edit Drawing Scales dialog box opens, as shown in Figure 5.5.

FIGURE 5.5

Use the Edit Drawing Scales dialog box to create your own custom scales.

To add a new scale, click Add. In the Add Scale dialog box, name the scale. The name is what will show on the list. Then define the scale by completing the Paper Units and Drawing Units text boxes. For example, to add a 1:12 scale, you would name the scale 1:12, set the Paper Units to 1 and the Drawing Units to 12.

To delete scales that you don't use, select the scale and click Delete. You can also edit existing scales (select the scale and click Edit), move them up or down in the order of the list, and reset the list (click Reset) to its original status. Click OK when you're done.

> **NOTE**
> AutoCAD 2013 stores a default scale list in the Windows registry. You can customize this list by going to Application Button ⇨ Options, choosing the User Preferences tab, and clicking Default Scale List. This list will appear in all drawings. However, you can still use the Edit Drawing Scales dialog box (see Figure 5.5) to edit the scale list within any drawing file, so this list can vary with the drawing. To reset a scale list in a drawing to match the scale list in the Windows registry, click the Reset button in the Edit Drawing Scales dialog box.

5

Deciding on a scale and sheet size

As soon as you know the size of your drawing and the scale appropriate for your situation, you need to consider the sheet size of the paper on which you want to plot. Again, you often find that certain factors limit your choices. Your plotter or printer may be limited to certain sheet sizes. The conventions used in your discipline or working environment also affect your decision. You may be working on a series of drawings that are all to be plotted on the same size sheet of paper.

As an example, the architectural drawing in Figure 5.3 is 175 feet wide by 120 feet high. The two most typical scales for a drawing of a house are $\frac{1}{4}$"=1' and $\frac{1}{8}$"=1'. On a small plotter, you might have a choice of sheet sizes A, B, or C. The following steps show the calculations you need to do in order to decide on a scale, obtain the scale factor, and determine the appropriate sheet size.

In this exercise, you practice determining the scale and sheet size. You need only a sheet of paper and a pencil. Use Figure 5.3 as a reference.

STEPS: Determining the Scale and Sheet Size

1. To calculate the plotted size of the drawing at 1/4"=1', you can start with the width, which is 175'. Take one-quarter of 175 to get the width of the drawing in inches, which is 43$\frac{3}{4}$".

2. Take one quarter of the height, 120', to get the height of the drawing in inches, which is 30".

3. A C-size sheet (see Table 5.3) is 22"×17", which is too small for a 43$\frac{3}{4}$"×30" drawing.

4. Recalculate the drawing at 1/8"=1'. Take one-eighth of 175 to get 21$\frac{7}{8}$. Take one-eighth of 120 to get 15".

5. The actual drawing space (minus the margins the printer requires) on a C-size sheet is about 21"×16". The height of the drawing at this scale is adequate, but the width is $\frac{7}{8}$" too long. Therefore, the best option is to simply make the drawing $\frac{7}{8}$" narrower because the drawing has some extra room. This lets you fit the drawing on a C-size sheet.

6. To calculate the scale factor of a 1/8"=1' scale, multiply 1' by 8 to get 8' and convert it to inches, which is 96 (8×12).

Rearranging the views, dimensions, and text on a drawing to fit a standard scale factor and sheet size is a typical task. There is no actual setup step for setting the drawing scale, but you use it when you insert text or dimensions and when you plot the drawing.

Creating a Titleblock

A *titleblock* is a rectangle that includes spaces for the drawing title, company name, drafter name, and so on. It generally comes with a border that bounds your drawing. Many drawings require titleblocks. You can insert an existing titleblock in two ways:

- When creating a new drawing, choose Application Button ⇨ New to open the Select Template dialog box. Choose one of the templates that include a titleblock, either one that comes with

AutoCAD or a custom template that you created. For example, `Tutorial-iArch.dwt` includes a titleblock and border that fit on a D-size sheet. The titleblock and border appear on a layout tab. (Chapter 17 covers layouts.)

- After you open a drawing, you can insert a drawing of a titleblock into it. Choose Home tab ⇨ Block panel ⇨ Insert. (Chapter 18 covers blocks.) In the Insert dialog box, type the name of the drawing or block, or click Browse to find it. To insert the file or block at 0,0 with no scaling or rotation, uncheck all the Specify On-Screen check boxes. Check Explode if you expect to edit text included as part of the titleblock. Click OK.

To find the location of the templates, choose Application Button ⇨ Options, and click the Files tab. Double-click Template Settings and then double-click Drawing Template File Location. You see the path to the location displayed. (The path is very long!) This folder may be hidden in Windows Explorer. For instructions on displaying hidden folders, go to Windows Help and type **hidden folders** in the search box.

 As explained in Chapter 2, you can create your own titleblock, make a template from it, and then start a drawing based on that template.

Specifying Common Setup Options

A few other items are generally set up in advance and are included in a template. Other chapters of this book cover the following:

- **Layers** (covered in Chapter 11) enable you to organize your drawing into meaningful groups. In an architectural drawing, for example, you might create layers for walls, doors, and electrical fixtures.
- **Text styles** (covered in Chapter 13) enable you to format the font and other text characteristics.
- **Table styles** (covered in Chapter 13) format tables.
- **Multileader styles** (covered in Chapter 14) create styles for multileaders.
- **Dimension styles** (covered in Chapter 15) format the dimensions that measure your objects.

If you know that you'll frequently use snap, grid, and ortho modes (covered in Chapter 4) in certain drawings, and you know the suitable settings for snap and grid, you can set these and save them in a template because these settings are saved with the drawing. In other cases, you might want to leave them off and turn them on only when you need them.

Many settings, such as running object snaps, the type of snap (grid or polar), and the polar distance, are saved in the Windows registry, not in your drawing. As a result, when you open AutoCAD or AutoCAD LT, they're automatically set to the same setting that you had when you last closed the program, regardless of the setting in the drawing. Therefore, you cannot save these settings in a template.

5

System Variables

When you change AutoCAD or AutoCAD LT settings, such as the unit type, angle type, drawing limits, blip marks, snap mode (on or off), grid mode, or ortho mode, you are actually changing *system variables*. These are settings that are stored in each drawing or in the Windows registry (which stores settings that apply to all drawings). Usually, you don't need to pay any direct attention to them, but they're the nuts and bolts behind the dialog boxes that you use to change the settings. When you start customizing AutoCAD, you need to learn about them because programming code and script files (macros) cannot access dialog boxes. Also, a few system variables are accessible only by typing them on the command line. Some system variables store information about a drawing or its environment, such as the drawing name and path. These are *read-only*, meaning that you cannot change them. They are often used in AutoLISP programs (AutoCAD only).

Information about each system variable, where it is stored, its default value, and whether it is read-only is in the Help system. At the command line, enter the system variable you want to know more about and press F1. In the Options dialog box (Application Button ➪ Options), system variables that are stored in a drawing have a drawing file icon next to them. You can type system variables on the command line, just like regular commands. The Express Tools (AutoCAD only) contain an editor (choose Express Tools tab ➪ Tools panel ➪ System Variables [the SYSVDLG command]) that enables you to view and edit system variable values in a dialog box; the command also provides helpful supporting information.

On the Web

The drawing used in the following exercise on setting drawing aids and creating a template, `ab05-01.dwg`, is available from the Results download on the companion website.

STEPS: Setting Drawing Aids and Creating a Template

1. If you did the exercise on setting drawing units, use that drawing; otherwise, open `ab05-01.dwg`, available from the Results download on the companion website.

2. Save the drawing as `ab05-02.dwg` in your `AutoCAD Bible` folder.

3. Right-click the Snap Mode button on the status bar, and choose Settings.

4. On the Snap and Grid tab, the snap spacing is set to ½". In the Grid Spacing section, change the X and Y spacing to 1". Make sure that the Snap Type is set to Grid Snap and Rectangular Snap. Click OK.

5. Click Snap Mode and Grid Display on the status bar to turn them on. Make sure that Object Snap Mode is turned off.

6. Choose Application Button ➪ Drawing Utilities ➪ Units. Change the Angle Type back to Decimal Degrees (if necessary). Click OK.

7. Using the coordinate display as your guide, start the LINE command and draw line segments from 2.5, 1.5 to .5<270 to 11<0 to .5<90. End the LINE command.

8. Restart the LINE command. Again use the coordinate display to draw line segments from 2,2 to .5<270 to 12<0 to .5<90. End the LINE command.

9. Save your drawing. It should look like Figure 5.6. Notice how the grid and snap settings facilitate the drawing process.

   The architectural units create a different drawing experience than decimal units would. Setting up a drawing creates a drawing environment suited to your work needs.

FIGURE 5.6

The final architectural drawing

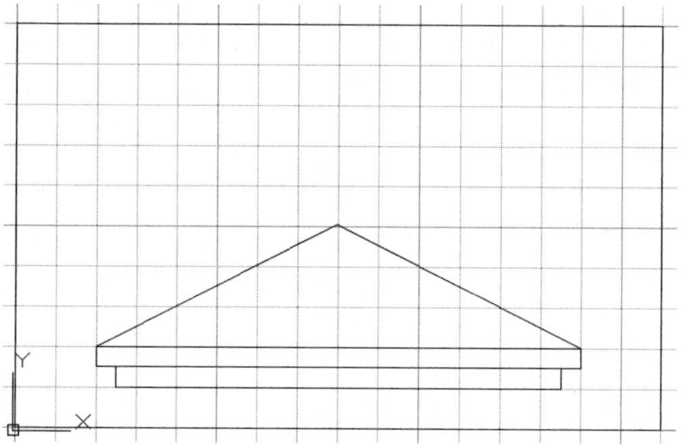

10. To change the limits, type **limits** ↵ on the command line. Press Enter to keep the lower-left corner coordinate of 0,0. At the next prompt, type **16,10** ↵ to specify the upper-right corner limits.

11. Choose Application Button ⇨ Save As. In the Save Drawing As dialog box, click the Files of Type drop-down list and choose AutoCAD Drawing Template (*.dwt) or AutoCAD LT Drawing Template (*.dwt). Notice that you're automatically in the Template folder.

12. In the File Name text box, change the name to archroof.dwt. Click Save.

13. In the Template Options dialog box, type **Arch units, 16,10 limits, snap & grid** and click OK. The Measurement drop-down list should be set to English.

14. Choose Application Button ⇨ New. Choose the archroof template and click Open. A new drawing is created based on the template.

15. Move the cursor around and look at the coordinate display to confirm that the grid is set to 1", although the snap is set to ½".

    Do not save this new drawing.

Summary

This chapter explained setting up a drawing so that it behaves the way you want it to. You read about:

- Setting the unit type
- Setting the angle type, measurement, and direction
- Drawing limits
- Using scales and calculating a scale factor
- Setting drawing aids and creating a template that includes the settings that you want

This chapter ends Part I, "AutoCAD and AutoCAD LT Basics." Now that you know the basics, you can go on to Part II, "Drawing in Two Dimensions." The next chapter covers drawing simple lines, polygons, rectangles, and infinite construction lines.

Part II

Drawing in Two Dimensions

IN THIS PART

Drawing Simple Lines

IN THIS CHAPTER

Working with the LINE command

Using the RECTANG command

Using the POLYGON command

Building construction lines

Drawing rays

L ines are the most commonly drawn object in 2D AutoCAD drawings — you'll use the LINE command a lot! Straight edges just happen to be very common in the real world. Related commands for drawing rectangles, polygons, and construction lines are also important, so you should have all these commands in your arsenal. This chapter explains how to draw all these types of objects.

Using the LINE Command

The LINE command draws straight line segments. Part I includes several exercises in which you draw lines. However, the LINE command has several options, and you can still learn a few tricks of the trade by focusing on the LINE command itself.

 To draw a line, choose Home tab ⇨ Draw panel ⇨ Line. At the Specify first point: prompt, specify any point. Continue to specify points until you're finished. Press Enter to end the command. You can also right-click and choose Enter from the shortcut menu. The LINE command assumes that you will use it over and over. For this reason, the command continues to prompt you until you press Enter.

If you continue to draw line segments, the subsequent prompts are different. Here's how to use them:

- The command displays the Specify next point or [Undo]: prompt for the next two segments. Right-click (or press the down-arrow key if you have Dynamic Input turned on) and choose Undo (or type u ↵) to undo only the last line segment that you created — without exiting the LINE command.

- After creating at least two line segments, the command displays the Specify next point or [Close/Undo]: prompt. Right-click (or press the down-arrow key if you have Dynamic Input on) and choose Close (or type c ↵) to automatically draw a line from the endpoint of the last segment to the original start point, thereby creating a closed figure. You can continue to use the Undo option as well.

If you previously drew a line, press Enter at the `Specify first point:` prompt to start the line at the endpoint of the last line. If you most recently drew an arc, press Enter to start the line at the endpoint of the arc and draw it tangent to the arc.

STEPS: Using the LINE Command

1. Start a new drawing by using the `acad.dwt` or `acadlt.dwt` template.

> **NOTE**
>
> This exercise assumes that you have Dynamic Input on (click the Dynamic Input button on the status bar to turn it on, if necessary) and that you are using the default settings of polar format and relative coordinates. Make sure that the Drafting & Annotation workspace is chosen from the Workspace drop-down list on the Quick Access Toolbar. Close any palettes that may be open.

2. Save the drawing in your `AutoCAD Bible` folder as `ab06-01.dwg`.

3. Choose Home tab ⇨ Draw panel ⇨ Line to start the LINE command. At the `Specify first point:` prompt, choose any point in the center of your drawing.

4. Click the Ortho Mode button on the status bar.

5. Move the cursor to the right in the 0-degree direction and type **.4667** ↵.

6. Type **.7341<129** ↵. (Instead of typing the < symbol, you can press the Tab button to move to the Dynamic Input angle tooltip.)

7. Move the cursor to the right in the 0-degree direction and type **.4668** ↵.

8. Assume that this was a mistake. Type **u** ↵.

9. The `Specify next point or [Close/Undo]:` prompt reappears. With the cursor still in the 0-degree direction, type **.4667** ↵.

10. Type **c** ↵ to close the figure. This ends the LINE command.

11. Start the LINE command again.

12. At the `Specify first point:` prompt, press Enter. The line starts at the previous endpoint.

13. Type **.8071<270** ↵ and press Enter to end the LINE command.

14. Save your drawing. It should look like Figure 6.1.

FIGURE 6.1

The completed gate valve symbol

Other aspects of lines are covered elsewhere in this book. Chapter 11 explains how to draw dashed and dotted lines. Chapter 16 explains how to create *polylines*, which combine line segments and arcs into one object. Chapter 16 also covers *multilines* and *dlines* — sets of parallel lines that you draw all at once. Chapter 21 discusses how to draw 3D lines and polylines.

Drawing Rectangles

The RECTANG command draws rectangles. Rectangles are used in all disciplines. The RECTANG command has a number of options that specify how the rectangle appears and how you define the rectangle's dimensions.

 To draw a rectangle, choose Home tab ⇨ Draw panel ⇨ Rectangle/Polygon drop-down menu ⇨ Rectangle. The first prompt is as follows:

```
Specify first corner point or [Chamfer/Elevation/Fillet/Thickness/
    Width]:
```

Select one of the options. If you don't want to use any of the options, just specify one corner of the rectangle, using any method of specifying a coordinate.

The RECTANG command creates a *polyline*, meaning that all four sides of the rectangle are one object, rather than four separate line objects. Chapter 16 covers polylines. You can chamfer and fillet the corners as you create the rectangle. (Chapter 10 covers chamfering and filleting.) You can also specify a width for the rectangle's line (see Chapter 16), or create a 3D box by using the elevation and thickness options (see Chapter 21).

If you use one of the options, the first prompt returns so that you can specify the first corner point or use another option. After you specify the first point, you see the Specify other corner point or [Area/Dimensions/Rotation]: prompt.

To immediately create the rectangle, specify the corner diagonally opposite the first corner that you specified. You can use any method of specifying coordinates. For example, if you know that the rectangle should be 6 inches wide and 3 inches high, you can specify the second point as 6,3. (If Dynamic Input is turned off or set to absolute coordinates, add the @ symbol before the X,Y coordinates.) You can also use one of the options below:

- **Area.** If you know the area of the rectangle, and only its length or width, then use this option. First you enter the area. Then you specify either the length or the width, and AutoCAD calculates the side that you didn't specify, based on the area you entered.

- **Dimensions.** If you know the length and width of the rectangle, then use this option (although it may be simpler to specify the opposite corner, as I described earlier). You are prompted for the length and width. You then need to move the mouse to specify if you want the second corner to be above and to the right, or in any other direction from the first corner. When you see the rectangle you want, click it.

- **Rotation.** If you want to rotate the rectangle as you create it, then simply enter a rotation angle and pick the opposite corner. Alternatively, instead of entering a rotation angle, you can pick two points to specify a rotation angle and then pick the opposite corner. This last option is great if you want to align the rectangle with an existing object.

Drawing Polygons

The POLYGON command enables you to draw multisided, closed figures with equal side lengths. You can draw polygons that have from 3 to 1,024 sides. To draw a polygon, choose Home tab ⇨ Draw panel ⇨ Rectangle/Polygon drop-down menu ⇨ Polygon. Like the RECTANG command, the POLYGON command creates a polyline, meaning that the entire polygon is one object, rather than a series of line segments.

First specify the number of sides. Then choose one of three methods of defining the polygon, as described in Table 6.1.

TABLE 6.1 POLYGON Command Options

Option	Description
Edge	Right-click and choose the Edge option. Specify the two endpoints of any edge of the polygon to complete the polygon.
Inscribed in circle	After specifying the center, right-click and choose Inscribed in Circle. Then specify the radius from the center to a vertex (point). This defines the polygon with reference to an imaginary circle whose circumference touches all the vertices of the polygon.
Circumscribed about circle	After specifying the center, right-click and choose Circumscribed about Circle. Then specify the radius from the center to the midpoint of a side. This defines the polygon with reference to an imaginary circle whose circumference touches all the midpoints of the polygon's sides.

If you type a number for the radius, then the bottom edge of the polygon is horizontal. However, if you pick a point for the radius with your mouse, you can specify the orientation of the polygon. As you rotate the mouse cursor around the center, you see the polygon rotate. Click when you like what you see.

 When you type a number for the radius, the bottom edge aligns with the snap rotation angle, which is usually 0. Chapter 8 explains how to change this angle.

In the exercise that follows, I indicate inches with a double prime (") and feet with a single prime ('). You may find this notation clearer when a measurement has both feet and inches, but you do not actually need to type the double prime for inches. When you have a measurement that is only in inches, it saves time to leave out the double prime.

ON THE WEB

The drawing used in this exercise on drawing rectangles and polygons, `ab06-a.dwg`, is available from the Drawings download on the companion website.

STEPS: Drawing Rectangles and Polygons

1. Open `ab06-a.dwg`, available from the Drawings download on the companion website.

2. Save the drawing in your `AutoCAD Bible` folder as `ab06-02.dwg`. Verify that snap and grid are on, set at 1". Object Snap should be off.

3. Choose Home tab ⇨ Draw panel ⇨ Rectangle/Polygon drop-down menu ⇨ Rectangle.

4. At the `Specify first corner point or [Chamfer/Elevation/Fillet/Thickness/Width]:` prompt, move the cursor to 0'-1",0'-1" and click. At the `Specify other corner point or [Area/Dimensions/Rotation]:` prompt, type **2'1",1'9"** ↵.

5. Start the RECTANG command again. At the `Specify first corner point or [Chamfer/Elevation/Fillet/Thickness/Width]:` prompt, Shift+right-click and choose the From object snap. Pick the bottom-left corner of the rectangle. At the `<Offset>:` prompt, type **@2,2** ↵ to start the second rectangle 2 inches up and 2 inches to the right of the first rectangle.

6. At the `Specify other corner point or [Area/Dimensions/Rotation]:` prompt, type **1'9",1'3"** ↵.

7. Right-click and choose Repeat RECTANG. At the prompt, find 0'8",1'7" (on a snap point) and click. At the `Specify other corner point or [Area/Dimensions/Rotation]:` prompt, type **11,2** ↵. (You don't need to type the double-prime for inches.)

8. Again, start the RECTANG command. At the prompt, find 1'1",1'8" and click. At the `Specify other corner point or [Area/Dimensions/Rotation]:` prompt, type **1,-5** ↵.

9. Choose Home tab ⇨ Draw panel ⇨ Rectangle/Polygon drop-down menu ⇨ Polygon. At the `Enter number of sides <4>:` prompt, type **5** ↵. At the `Specify center of polygon or [Edge]:` prompt, type **0'10,1'8** ↵ to indicate the center.

10. At the `Enter an option [Inscribed in circle/Circumscribed about circle] <I>:` prompt, press Enter to accept the default. This means that you indicate the radius from the center to the vertices. (If your prompt shows <C> as the default, type **i** ↵.)

11. At the `Specify radius of circle:` prompt, type **1/2** ↵. AutoCAD or AutoCAD LT draws the pentagon.

12. Repeat Steps 9 through 11, using a center of 1'5",1'8".

13. Start the POLYGON command again. At the `Enter number of sides <5>:` prompt, type **3** ↵.

14. At the `Specify center of polygon or [Edge]:` prompt, right-click and choose the Edge option.

15. At the `Specify first endpoint of edge:` prompt, choose the top-left corner of the faucet rectangle (1'1",1'8"), which is on a snap point.

16. At the `Specify second endpoint of edge:` prompt, choose the top-right corner of the faucet rectangle to complete the triangle.

17. Turn off the grid to get a better look at the drawing. You have completed the sink, which should look like Figure 6.2. Save your drawing.

FIGURE 6.2

The completed sink, drawn with rectangles and polygons

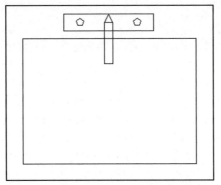

*Thanks to Bill Wynn of New Windsor, Maryland, for this drawing, which he created
in his AutoCAD class as part of a plan drawing of an entire house.*

Creating Construction Lines

Sometimes you want to create a line that is used solely for the purpose of reference. A construction line is a temporary or reference line used to help you draw or to show a relationship between objects. For example, you might want to do the following:

- Draw two lines from the midpoints of two perpendicular lines so that you can use their intersection as the center for a circle.
- Draw a line from one object to another to visually indicate the relationship between the two objects.
- Show the relationship between equivalent parts of a model shown in front and right-side views.
- Draw a line through the center of an object shown in cross-section so that you can show dimensions from the centerline to the edge of the object.

You could use regular lines for these purposes. However, construction lines (also known as xlines) are unique in that they extend infinitely in both directions. This makes them especially useful for seeing the relationships among various objects in your drawing.

Of course, construction lines are not actually infinite. However, they extend to the edge of the drawing area on your screen, and if you zoom out to see more of your drawing, they expand so that they always extend to the edge of the screen. The object snap tracking feature (covered in Chapter 4) sometimes eliminates the need for construction lines; nevertheless, sometimes you can work more easily having a line visible for several commands and then erasing it.

If you zoom to show the extents of your drawing, AutoCAD or AutoCAD LT ignores the xlines and shows you just the extents of the regular objects in your drawing. Chapter 8 covers the ZOOM command.

The XLINE command offers several ways to create construction lines. Start the command by choosing Home tab ⇨ Draw panel (expanded) ⇨ Construction Line. You see the following prompt:

```
Specify a point or [Hor/Ver/Ang/Bisect/Offset]:
```

Table 6.2 lists the possible options. AutoCAD or AutoCAD LT continues to prompt you for more points so that you can continue to draw construction lines — much like the LINE command. Press Enter to end the command.

TABLE 6.2   XLINE Command Options

Option	Description
Specify a point	This option enables you to define the construction line with two points. At the first prompt, specify a point. At the `Specify through point:` prompt, specify another point. The first point becomes the base point for subsequent construction lines that you can draw by specifying other through points.
Hor	To draw a construction line parallel to the X axis, type **h** ↵ to specify the Horizontal option. The command responds with the `Specify through point:` prompt. Specify one point. This is useful for drawing a series of horizontal construction lines.
Ver	To draw a construction line parallel to the Y axis, type **v** ↵ to specify the Vertical option. The command responds with the `Specify through point:` prompt. Specify one point.
Ang	Type **a** ↵ (for Angle). The command responds with the `Enter angle of xline (0) or [Reference]:` prompt. If you enter an angle, the command asks for a through point. You can also type **r** ↵ and select a line as a reference, and then provide an angle and a through point. AutoCAD or AutoCAD LT then calculates the angle of the construction line from the angle of the reference line. This is useful for drawing a series of construction lines at a specified angle.
Bisect	To draw a construction line that bisects an angle (divides the angle in half), type **b** ↵. The command responds with the `Specify angle vertex point:` prompt. Choose any point that you want the construction line to pass through. Then at the `Specify angle start point:` prompt, choose a point that defines the base of the angle. At the `Specify angle end point:` prompt, choose a point that defines the end of the angle.
Offset	To create a construction line parallel to a line, type **o** ↵. You can specify the offset distance by typing in the number or using the Through option to pick a point through which the construction line should pass. Either way, the next step is to select a line. If you specified an offset distance, the command displays the `Specify side to offset:` prompt. Respond by picking a point on the side of the selected line on which you want the construction line to appear.

Creating Rays

Rays are similar to construction lines, except they start at a specific point and extend to infinity in one direction only. If you need a line to extend in only one direction, using a ray may be less confusing.

> **NOTE**
> You can use most object snaps with construction lines and rays. (You can't use an endpoint for construction lines or a midpoint for rays.) You can edit construction lines and rays like any other object.

 To draw a ray, choose Home tab ⇨ Draw panel (expanded) ⇨ Ray. At the `Specify start point:` prompt, specify the start point for the ray. At the `Specify through point:` prompt, specify another point. AutoCAD or AutoCAD LT continues to ask for through points. Press Enter to end the command.

> **ON THE WEB**
> The drawing used in this exercise on drawing construction lines and rays, `ab06-b.dwg`, is available from the Drawings download on the companion website.

STEPS: Drawing Construction Lines and Rays

1. Open `ab06-b.dwg` available from the Drawings download on the companion website.

2. Save the drawing as `ab06-03.dwg` in your `AutoCAD Bible` folder.

 3. Choose Home tab ⇨ Draw panel (expanded) ⇨ Construction Line.

4. At the `Specify a point or [Hor/Ver/Ang/Bisect/Offset]:` prompt, choose point ❶, as shown in Figure 6.3.

5. At the `Specify through point:` prompt, choose point ❷, as shown in Figure 6.3.

FIGURE 6.3

A pipe with cross-section

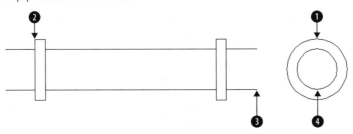

6. Press Enter to end the command. Notice that the drawing has been set up so that the construction line is drawn in green and with a noncontinuous linetype. This is to distinguish it from the main drawing. (See Chapter 11 for details on how to set up a drawing in this way.)

7. Choose Home tab ⇨ Draw panel (expanded) ⇨ Ray.

8. At the `Specify start point:` prompt, choose point ❸, as shown in Figure 6.3.

9. At the `Specify through point:` prompt, choose point ❹, as shown in Figure 6.3. Press Enter to end the command.

10. Save your drawing.

Summary

This chapter covered the ins and outs of lines. You read about:

- Using the LINE command
- Drawing rectangles
- Drawing polygons
- Creating construction lines, including xlines that extend infinitely in both directions and rays that extend infinitely in one direction

The next chapter explains how to draw curves and point objects. Curves include circles, arcs, ellipses, and donuts.

6

Drawing Curves and Points

A utoCAD and AutoCAD LT offer a number of ways to create curved objects. You can draw circles, arcs, ellipses, and donuts (also spelled as doughnuts). In this chapter, I also cover point objects, which are neither curves nor lines but don't deserve their own chapter.

 Several complex objects — such as polylines, splines, regions, and boundaries — involve curves. These objects are covered in Chapter 16.

Drawing Circles

Circles are common objects in drawings. In mechanical drawings, they often represent holes or wheels. In architectural drawings, they may be used for doorknobs, trash baskets, or trees. In electrical and piping schematics, they are used for various kinds of symbols.

Understanding the circle options

 The CIRCLE command provides six ways to draw a circle. To draw a circle, choose Home tab ⇨ Draw panel ⇨ Circle, and follow the prompts. You can just click the Circle button and follow the options on the command line, or access the options by clicking the button's drop-down menu. Table 7.1 describes how to use these options. You can access the options directly by clicking the down arrow below to the Circle button on the Ribbon.

TABLE 7.1   Six Ways to Draw a Circle

Option	Description
Center, Radius	This option is the default. Specify the center and then the radius. You can type the radius as a distance, or pick a point where you want the circumference to be.
Center, Diameter	Specify the center. Choose the `Diameter` option and type the length of the diameter, or pick a point to specify the diameter.
2P (2 Points)	Choose the `2p` option. Specify one point on the circumference, and then an opposite point on the circumference. These two points define the diameter of the circle.
3P (3 Points)	Choose the `3p` option. Specify three points on the circumference.
Tan, tan, radius (Tangent, Tangent, Radius)	Choose the `Ttr` option. The CIRCLE command prompts `Specify point on object for first tangent of circle:` and provides an aperture to let you pick a point. Then the command prompts `Specify point on object for second tangent of circle:` and you pick a second point. These points can be any points on the object(s) to which you want your circle to be tangent. Finally, type a radius.
Tan, tan, tan (Tangent, Tangent, Tangent)	This option is available only from the Circle's drop-down menu on the Ribbon. You are prompted for three points, and AutoCAD automatically applies the Tangent object snap to each point.

TIP

You can also create a circle tangent to other objects by using the two-point (2P) method or three-point (3P) method, picking those points with the Tangent object snap.

Creating circles

Drawing circles is fairly straightforward. Often, you can use object snaps to define part of the circle. In the following exercise, you practice using the most common methods of creating a circle.

ON THE WEB

The drawing used in the following exercise on drawing circles, `ab07-a.dwg`, is available from the Drawings download on the companion website.

STEPS: Drawing Circles

1. Open `ab07-a.dwg`, available from the Drawings download on the companion website.

2. Save the file as `ab07-01.dwg` in your `AutoCAD Bible` folder. This is a drawing of an air compressor from which all the circles have been removed. Make sure that Object Snap is turned on. Set a running object snap of Endpoint only. You should be in the default Drafting & Annotation workspace (if necessary, choose it from the Workspace drop-down list on the Quick Access Toolbar).

 3. Choose Home tab ⇨ Draw panel ⇨ Circle drop-down menu ⇨ 2-Point. At the `Specify first end point of circle's diameter:` prompt, pick the endpoint at ❶, as shown in Figure 7.1. At the `Specify second end point of circle's diameter:` prompt, pick the endpoint at ❷.

FIGURE 7.1

The air compressor without its circles

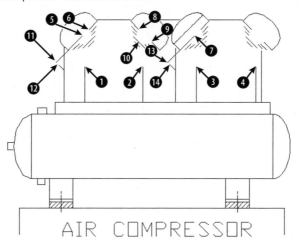

4. Repeat the CIRCLE command by right-clicking and choosing Repeat CIRCLE. Right-click and choose 2P from the shortcut menu. Pick the endpoints at ❸ and ❹, as shown in Figure 7.1.

5. Repeat the CIRCLE command by pressing Enter. At the `Specify center point for circle or [3P/2P/Ttr (tan tan radius)]:` prompt, pick the endpoint at ❺. At the `Specify radius of circle or [Diameter]:` prompt, pick the endpoint at ❻.

6. Repeat the CIRCLE command. At the `Specify center point for circle or [3P/2P/Ttr (tan tan radius)]:` prompt, pick the endpoint at ❼. At the `Specify radius of circle or [Diameter]:` prompt, right-click and choose Diameter; and then type **.25** ↵.

7. Repeat the CIRCLE command by right-clicking and choosing Repeat CIRCLE. At the `Specify center point for circle or [3P/2P/Ttr (tan tan radius)]:` prompt, right-click and choose 3P. At the `Specify first point on circle:` prompt, pick the endpoint at ❽, as shown in Figure 7.1. At the `Specify second point on circle:` prompt, pick the endpoint at ❾. At the `Specify third point on circle:` prompt, choose the Midpoint object snap and pick the midpoint at ❿.

8. For the last circle on the right, choose any method that you want to use to draw a circle. The circle should be the same size and placement as the second circle from the left.

9. Repeat the CIRCLE command. At the `Specify center point for circle or [3P/2P/Ttr (tan tan radius)]:` prompt, choose the Center object snap and pick ❼. At the `Specify radius of circle or [Diameter]:` prompt, type **.05** ↵.

10. Repeat Step 9 to create a circle inside the circle whose center is at ❺ and whose radius is 0.05.

11. Repeat the CIRCLE command. At the `Specify center point for circle or [3P/2P/Ttr (tan tan radius)]:` prompt, pick the endpoint at ⓫. At the `Specify radius of circle or [Diameter]:` prompt, pick the endpoint at ⓬.

12. Repeat Step 11, choosing the endpoint at ⓭ for the center of the circle and the endpoint at ⓮ for its radius, as shown in Figure 7.1.

13. Save your drawing. It should look like Figure 7.2.

FIGURE 7.2

The completed air compressor

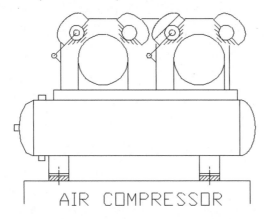

Thanks to the U.S. Army Corps of Engineers at Vicksburg, Mississippi, for this drawing.

 It may have occurred to you that this task would have been easier if you could simply have copied one circle to another location instead of creating each circle from scratch. I cover copying in Chapter 9.

Drawing Arcs

An arc is a portion of a circle. Therefore, to define an arc, you have to define not only a circle — for example, by specifying a center and a radius — but also the start and endpoints of the arc. The ARC command offers several methods for defining an arc. The method you pick depends on the information that you have about the arc that you want to draw.

 You can close an arc to create a circle by using the JOIN command. You can also use the BREAK command to create an arc from a circle. For more information, see Chapter 10.

Understanding arc options

After you understand the parts of an arc, you can choose the options that suit your needs. Figure 7.3 shows the parts of an arc that you can use to draw an arc.

FIGURE 7.3

The parts of an arc

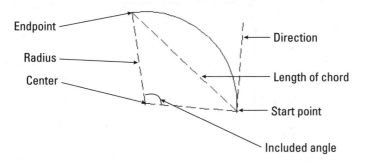

Figure 7.4 shows the flow of the arc options. When you start the ARC command, you have two options, Start Point and Center. Depending on how you start, more options become available.

You can also press Enter at the first arc prompt to draw another arc starting from the endpoint of the most recently drawn arc, line, polyline, or other object. The new arc continues in the same direction as the end of the first object. The only other prompt is the endpoint.

FIGURE 7.4

The ARC command options

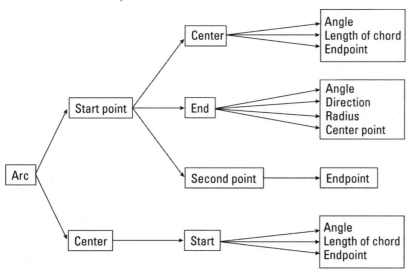

Creating arcs

 To draw an arc, choose Home tab ➪ Draw panel ➪ Arc, and follow the prompts. You can just click the Arc button and follow the options on the command line, or access the options by clicking the button's drop-down menu. Object snaps are often helpful when drawing arcs.

When drawing an arc by using the Start, End, and Radius options, the three specifications actually define two possible arcs, one minor and one major. The ARC command draws the minor arc by default, in the counterclockwise direction. (A minor arc is less than half a circle.) If you enter a negative number for the radius, the command draws the major arc. The options requiring an angle also define two possible arcs, one drawn counterclockwise and one drawn clockwise. AutoCAD and AutoCAD LT draw the counterclockwise arc by default. If you type a negative number for the angle, the arc is drawn clockwise.

> **ON THE WEB**
> The drawing used in the following exercise on drawing arcs, `ab07-b.dwg`, is available from the Drawings download on the companion website.

STEPS: Drawing Arcs

1. Open `ab07-b.dwg`, available from the Drawings download on the companion website.

2. Save the file as `ab07-02.dwg` in your `AutoCAD Bible` folder. Ortho mode is on, and units are set to Fractional. Right-click the Object Snap button on the status bar and set running object snaps for Intersection, Center, and Endpoint. Make sure that Object Snap is on. You should be in the default Drafting & Annotation workspace (if necessary, choose it from the Workspace drop-down list on the Quick Access Toolbar or the Workspace Switching button on the status bar). In this exercise, you draw part of the sealing plate shown in Figure 7.5 from scratch; therefore, the drawing is blank.

3. Choose Home tab ➪ Draw panel ➪ Line to start the LINE command. Start at a coordinate of 2,3 and use Direct Distance Entry to create a 7-unit horizontal line to the right. End the LINE command. (See Chapter 4 for a full explanation of how to use Direct Distance Entry.)

4. Draw another line starting at 5-1/2,1-5/8 and draw it 2-3/4 units long in the 90-degree direction. End the line. These two lines are centerlines and would ordinarily appear in a different color and linetype than the object you're drawing. (You can read about colors and linetypes in Chapter 11.)

5. Choose Home tab ➪ Draw panel ➪ Circle drop-down menu ➪ Center, Radius to draw a circle with its center at the intersection of the two lines (use the Intersection object snap) and a radius of 11/16.

6. Use the Center object snap to draw another circle with the same center as the first circle and a radius of 1.

7. Draw a third circle, using the From object snap (Shift+right-click to open the Object Snap menu, and then choose From). For the base point, use the Center object snap and pick either of the first two circles that you drew. The offset is @-1-15/16,0 (this means 1-15/16 units to the left of the center of the first two circles). Its radius is ³/₈.

8. Draw a fourth circle. Use the From object snap again. For the base point, use the Center object snap and pick either of the first two circles. The offset is @1-15/16,0. The radius is ³/₈.

FIGURE 7.5

The dimensioned sealing plate for a valve

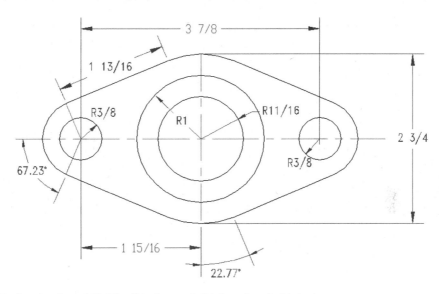

Thanks to Jerry Bottenfield of Clow Valve Company in Oskaloosa, Iowa, for this drawing.

9. Choose Home tab ⇨ Draw panel ⇨ Arc drop-down menu ⇨ 3-Point. Follow the prompts:

   ```
   Specify start point of arc or [Center]: Choose the From object snap.
   Base point: Use the Center object snap to pick the center of the leftmost
        circle.
   <Offset>: @-5/8,0 ↵
   Specify second point of arc or [Center/End]: Right-click and choose
        Center. Use the Center object snap to pick the center of the leftmost
        circle.
   Specify endpoint of arc or [Angle/chord Length]: Right-click and choose
        Angle. Drag the cursor above the circle.
   Specify included angle: 67.23 ↵
   ```

10. Start the LINE command. At the `Specify first point:` prompt, press Enter to continue the line in the same direction as the end of the arc. At the `Length of line:` prompt, type **1-13/16** ↵. End the LINE command.

11. Start the ARC command again. Follow the prompts:

   ```
   Specify start point of arc or [Center]: Use the Endpoint object snap to
        pick the end of the line that you just drew.
   Specify second point of arc or [Center/End]: Right-click and choose
        Center. Use the Center object snap and pick any point on one of the
        large central circles.
   Specify end point of arc or [Angle/chord Length]: Use Endpoint object
        snap to pick the lower end of the vertical construction line.
   ```

12. Repeat the ARC command. Follow the prompts:

Specify start point of arc or [Center]: *Right-click and choose Center. Use the Center object snap and pick any point on one of the large central circles.*
Specify start point of arc: *Use the Endpoint object snap to pick the endpoint of the arc that you just completed.*
Specify end point of arc or [Angle/chord Length]: *Right-click and choose Angle. Drag the cursor above the circle.*
Specify included angle: **22.77** ⏎

13. Start the LINE command. At the `Specify first point:` prompt, press Enter to continue the line in the same direction as the end of the arc. At the `Length of line:` prompt, type **1-13/16** ⏎. End the LINE command.

14. Start the ARC command. Follow the prompts:

Specify start point of arc or [Center]: *Use the Endpoint object snap to pick the endpoint of the line that you just drew.*
Specify second point of arc or [Center/End]: *Right-click and choose End.*
Specify end point of arc: Choose the From object snap.
_from Base point: *Use the Center object snap to pick the center of the rightmost circle.*
<Offset>: **@5/8,0** ⏎
Specify center point of arc or [Angle/Direction/Radius]: **r** ⏎
Specify radius of arc: **5/8** ⏎

15. Save your drawing. Your drawing should look like Figure 7.6. You can complete this drawing in Chapter 10 by creating a mirror image.

FIGURE 7.6

The partially completed sealing plate is created by using lines, circles, and arcs.

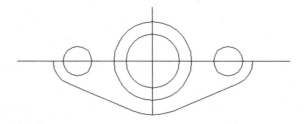

Creating Ellipses and Elliptical Arcs

You can create ellipses (ovals) as well as elliptical arcs, which are partial ellipses. Like a circle, an ellipse has a center. The difference, of course, is that an ellipse has a longer radius along its major axis and a shorter radius along its minor axis.

Understanding ellipse options

You can draw an ellipse by defining the center first. Another option is to define the axis endpoints first. If you want to draw an elliptical arc, you must specify the start and end angles.

The default option is to specify endpoints 1 and 2 of the first axis. Then you specify the second distance of the axis, which is the distance from the first axis line to the circumference along the second axis.

Instead of specifying a second axis distance, you can choose the Rotation option. The Rotation option defines the minor axis by specifying an angle from 0 degrees to 90 degrees, which is the ratio of the major axis to the minor axis. (Actually, the command only accepts up to 89.4 degrees.) When the angle is 0, you get a circle. As the angle increases, the ellipse gets flatter and flatter until you reach 89.4 degrees. A 45-degree angle results in a minor axis whose length is the square root of the major-axis length.

Instead of specifying endpoints, you can use the Center option to specify the center of the ellipse. Then specify the endpoint of the first axis, which can be either the major or the minor axis. Finally, specify the other axis distance, which is the radius from the center to the circumference along the second axis. Again, instead of specifying the second axis distance, you can define the ellipse by using the Rotation option.

Understanding elliptical arc options

To draw an elliptical arc, use the Arc option of the ELLIPSE command. The first prompts are the same as for an ellipse. Then the command continues with the `Specify start angle or [Parameter]:` prompt, offering the following options:

- **Start angle.** This option is the default. Specify the start angle, which the command redefines to start along the major axis. The command responds with the `Specify end angle or [Parameter/Included angle]:` prompt.
- **End angle.** Specify the end angle to complete the ellipse arc.
- **Included angle.** After specifying the start angle, you can complete the arc by specifying the included angle from the start point to the endpoint, going counterclockwise.
- **Parameter.** Choose this option to define the arc portion by the ellipse's area rather than by its included angle (which defines the arc portion by its circumference). The command responds with the `Specify start parameter or [Angle]:` and `Specify end parameter or [Angle/Included angle]:` prompts. By typing in angles, you define the percent of the full ellipse's area that you want to include. (For example, starting at 15 degrees and ending at 105 degrees includes 90 degrees and therefore draws one quarter of an ellipse.) The options in brackets let you return to regular angle specification.

Drawing ellipses and elliptical arcs

To draw an ellipse, choose Home tab ⇨ Draw panel ⇨ Ellipse, and follow the prompts. You can just click the Ellipse button and follow the options on the command line, or access the options by clicking the button's drop-down menu. In addition to the information that the command explicitly requests in the prompts, you need to know the angle of the first axis that you define. Not all ellipses are horizontal or vertical. You control the orientation when you stipulate the second point of the first axis. The second axis is automatically perpendicular to the first axis.

To draw an elliptical arc, choose Elliptical Arc from the Ellipse button's drop-down menu or use the Arc option of the ELLIPSE command. When you draw an elliptical arc, the command introduces a helpful but sometimes confusing feature: While you're defining the arc angles, the command redefines 0 degrees along the major axis. This helps you to define the included angle in an orientation that relates to the ellipse, rather than the usual orientation where 0 degrees is to the right.

In this exercise, you practice drawing ellipses and elliptical arcs.

ON THE WEB

The drawing used in the following exercise on drawing ellipses and elliptical arcs, `ab07-c.dwg`, is available from the Drawings download on the companion website.

STEPS: Drawing Ellipses and Elliptical Arcs

1. Open `ab07-c.dwg`, available from the Drawings download on the companion website.

2. Save the file as `ab07-03.dwg` in your `AutoCAD Bible` folder. The drawing shows an empty conference room. Snap is on, and set to 6". Ortho mode and Object Snap should be on, with a running object snap set for Endpoint only. You should be in the default Drafting & Annotation workspace (if necessary, choose it from the Workspace drop-down list on the Quick Access Toolbar or the Workspace Switching button on the status bar).

3. Choose Home tab ⇨ Draw panel ⇨ Ellipse drop-down menu ⇨ Center. At the `Specify center of ellipse:` prompt, choose 8',10', which is a snap point. At the `Specify endpoint of axis:` prompt, move the cursor to the right until the coordinates read 3'<0 and click. (If necessary, right-click the coordinates on the status bar and choose Relative, or look at the Dynamic Input tooltips.) At the `Specify distance to other axis or [Rotation]:` prompt, move the cursor up until the coordinates read 6'6"<90 and click. This completes the conference table.

4. Repeat the ELLIPSE command. Follow the prompts:

   `Specify axis endpoint of ellipse or [Arc/Center]:` *Right-click and choose Arc (or choose Home tab⇨ Draw panel⇨ Ellipse drop-down list⇨Elliptical Arc).*
   `Specify axis endpoint of elliptical arc or [Center]:` *Right-click and choose Center.*
   `Specify center of elliptical arc:` *Pick 8',3', a snap point.*
   `Specify endpoint of axis:` *Move the cursor to the right until the coordinates read 1'<0 and pick. (You can also look at the Dynamic Input tooltips.)*
   `Specify distance to other axis or [Rotation]:` *Move the cursor up until the coordinates read 6"<90 and pick.*
   `Specify start angle or [Parameter]:` **162** ↵
   `Specify end angle or [Parameter/Included angle]:` **18** ↵

5. Turn off Ortho mode. Start the LINE command. At the `Specify first point:` prompt, use the Endpoint running object snap and pick the right side of the elliptical arc. At the `Specify next point or [Undo]:` prompt, right-click the coordinates and choose Absolute (if necessary), and press and hold Shift+A to temporarily override Object Snap mode while you pick the snap point 8'6",3'. End the LINE command.

6. Start the LINE command. At the `Specify first point:` prompt, use the Endpoint object snap to pick the left side of the ellipse arc. At the `Specify next point or [Undo]:` prompt, press and hold Shift+A while you pick the snap point 7'6",3'. End the LINE command.

7. Start the ELLIPSE command. Follow the prompts:

    `Specify axis endpoint of ellipse or [Arc/Center]:` *Right-click and choose Arc.*
    `Specify axis endpoint of elliptical arc or [Center]:` *Use the Endpoint object snap to pick the free endpoint of the line on the right.*
    `Specify other endpoint of axis:` *Use the Endpoint object snap to pick the free endpoint of the line on the left.*
    `Specify distance to other axis or [Rotation]:` **3<90** ↵ (If you don't have Dynamic Input on and set to the default of relative coordinates, then type @ before the distance.)
    `Specify start angle or [Parameter]:` *Use the Endpoint object snap to pick the free endpoint of the line on the right.*
    `Specify end angle or [Parameter/Included angle]:` *Use Endpoint object snap to pick the free endpoint of the line on the left.*

8. Choose Home tab ⇨ Draw panel ⇨ Ellipse drop-down menu ⇨ Axis, End. At the `Specify axis endpoint of ellipse or [Arc/Center]:` prompt, pick point 2',18', a snap point. At the `Specify other endpoint of axis:` prompt, pick point 2',16', also a snap point. (The coordinates on the status bar display this point in absolute coordinate mode. The Dynamic Input tooltips show 2' and 90°.) At the `Specify distance to other axis or [Rotation]:` prompt, move the cursor to the right until the coordinates read 6<0. (Right-click the coordinates and choose Relative, if necessary.) This is also a snap point. Click the mouse button to complete the small side table.

9. Save your drawing. It should look like Figure 7.7.

FIGURE 7.7

The conference room with a conference table, a chair, and a side table.

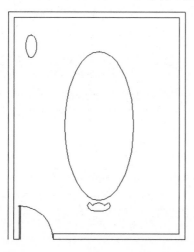

Making Donuts

A donut is a wide polyline that looks like two concentric circles, with the area between the circles filled in. You define a diameter for the inner and outer circles. Donuts are often used in electrical drawings to create symbols. If the inner circle's radius is zero, you create a filled-in circle.

The setting of the FILL command determines whether the donut is filled. Type **fill** ↵ and type **on** ↵ or **off** ↵. FILL is on by default. Turning FILL off displays a radial pattern of lines, rather than a solid fill. Type **regen** ↵ to update existing donuts to the new FILL setting.

Understanding DONUT options

The DONUT command has the following prompts:

- `Specify inside diameter of donut <0.5000>`. Type the diameter of the inside circle or pick two points to specify the inside diameter. The number in brackets is the last inside diameter that you defined, or 0.5 if you haven't previously used the DONUT command in this drawing session.

- `Specify outside diameter of donut <1.0000>`. Type the diameter of the outside circle or pick two points to specify the outside diameter. The outside diameter must be larger than the inside diameter. The number in brackets is the last outside diameter that you defined, or 1.0 if you haven't previously used the DONUT command in this drawing session.

- `Specify second point`. If you define the inside or outside diameter by picking a point, the command asks for a second point. Use this technique if you're using object snaps to define the diameters.

- `Specify center of donut or <exit>`. Specify the center of the donut. Pressing Enter ends the command.

Drawing donuts

To draw a donut, choose Home tab ⇨ Draw panel (expanded) ⇨ Donut. Then specify the inner and outer diameters and the center. The DONUT command continues to prompt for centers so that you can place additional donuts. Press Enter to end the command. You draw some donuts in the next exercise.

> **NOTE**
> You can use the hatch feature to fill in any object with a solid fill, with a great deal more flexibility in the shape of your objects. (Chapter 16 discusses hatching.) As a result, the DONUT command is not as essential as it once was.

Placing Points

A point simply marks a coordinate. Points are generally used for reference. It is sometimes helpful to mark a point that you will use later as a guide to place an object or to help you return an object to its original position. When it's no longer needed, you may erase the point. This is a typical construction method. In some cases, the From object snap or object snap tracking can be used rather than a point.

The DIVIDE and MEASURE commands place point objects along an object. Chapter 12 covers these commands.

Changing the point style

Because points can be hard to see, and because various disciplines have different conventions for drawing point objects, AutoCAD and AutoCAD LT provide 20 types of point styles that you can use in your drawing. Before you draw a point, you should set the point style. You can save this setting in your template.

Choose Home tab ⇨ Utilities panel (expanded) ⇨ Point Style (the DDPTYPE command) to open the Point Style dialog box, as shown in Figure 7.8. To set the point style, click the option showing the style that you want. Then set the point size, which has the following options.

FIGURE 7.8

The Point Style dialog box

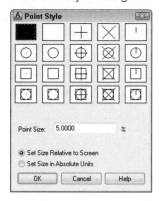

- **Set Size Relative to Screen.** Use this option if you want the point to always appear the same size, no matter how much you zoom in and out — for example, when you're using the point as a reference. The size is set as a percentage of the screen. This option is the default, with the size set to 5 percent of the screen.
- **Set Size in Absolute Units.** Use this option if you want the point to have a real size, just like any other object. The size is set in units. Use this option when you want the point to stay the same size relative to other objects in your drawing.

When you are done, click OK to close the dialog box.

Creating points

After you determine the point style, you're ready to create points. Choose Home tab ⇨ Draw panel (expanded) ⇨ Multiple Points. At the Specify a point: prompt, specify the point that you want, either by picking a point on the screen or by typing coordinates. (You can specify a Z coordinate to create a point in 3D space. For more information, see Chapter 21.) You can use object snaps to specify the point. When you choose the POINT command from the Draw panel, the command automatically repeats the prompt so that you can continue to specify points. To end the command, press Esc. When you type **point** ↵ on the command line, the command ends after you specify one point.

STEPS: Drawing Donuts and Points

1. Open ab07-d.dwg, available from the Drawings download on the companion website.

2. Save the file as ab07-04.dwg in your AutoCAD Bible folder. The drawing contains a rectangle and connecting wires for an electrical switch. Make sure that Object Snap is on. Set running object snaps for Endpoint, Center, Node, and Quadrant. This exercise assumes that you have Dynamic Input on, with the default setting of relative coordinates.

3. Choose Home Tab ⇨ Utilities panel (expanded) ⇨ Point Style. The Point Style dialog box opens. Choose the third point type, which is the plus sign. Set Size Relative to Screen should be selected. The Point Size should be 5.0000. Click OK.

4. Choose Home tab ⇨ Draw panel (expanded) ⇨ Multiple Points. Follow the prompts:

   ```
   Specify a point: Use the From object snap. (Shift+right-click to open the
       Object Snap shortcut menu.)
   Base point: Use the Endpoint object snap to pick the top-left corner of
       the rectangle.
   <Offset>: @.08,-.09 ↵
   Specify a point: Press Esc to complete the command.
   ```

5. Choose Home tab ⇨ Draw panel (expanded) ⇨ Donut. Follow these prompts:

   ```
   Specify inside diameter of donut <0.5000>: .04 ↵
   Specify outside diameter of donut <1.0000>: .06 ↵
   Specify center of donut or <exit>: Use the Node object snap to pick the
       point that you drew.
   Specify center of donut or <exit>: @.19,0 ↵
   Specify center of donut or <exit>: ↵
   ```

6. Start the POINT command again. Follow the prompts:

   ```
   Specify a point: Press Shift+right-click and choose Mid Between 2 Points
       from the shortcut menu.
   First point of mid: Use the Center object snap to pick the center of the
       right-hand donut. (You may have to press Tab until you get the Center
       object snap, and not a Quadrant object snap.)
   ```

> Second point of mid: *Press Shift+right-click and choose Perpendicular from the shortcut menu. Press and hold Shift to temporarily turn on Ortho mode and pick the lower horizontal line of the rectangle. Release the Shift key.*
>
> Specify a point: *Press Esc.*

7. Choose Home tab ⇨ Draw panel ⇨ Line to start the LINE command. Follow the prompts:

> Specify first point: *Use the Quadrant object snap to pick the right (0 degrees) quadrant of the left donut. If you don't see the Quadrant tooltip or AutoSnap marker, press Tab until it appears.*
>
> Specify next point or [Undo]: *Use the Node object snap to pick the point that you just drew. End the LINE command.*

8. Save your drawing. It should look like Figure 7.9.

FIGURE 7.9

In the completed electrical switch, the points show as plus signs.

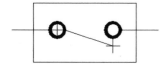

Summary

In this chapter, you learned how to draw curved objects and points in AutoCAD and AutoCAD LT. You discovered:

- All the ways to draw circles
- How to define and draw an arc
- How to define an ellipse and an elliptical arc
- How to draw a donut
- How to set the point style and draw points

In the next chapter, you learn how to display your drawing for the greatest ease and comfort.

Viewing Your Drawing

Often you may need to zoom in to see a particular part of a drawing more closely or move the display in a certain direction to reveal an area that is hidden. You may also want to save a view so that you can return to it at some other time. In this chapter, you will read about controlling the display of your drawing to meet all your drawing needs and increase your productivity. This chapter covers viewing a 2D drawing.

> **NOTE**
> This entire chapter assumes that you're using the Drafting & Annotation workspace and (for AutoCAD) the 2D Wireframe visual style. To check, choose Drafting & Annotation workspace from the Workspace drop-down list on the Quick Access Toolbar or the Workspace Switching button on the status bar. To set the visual style to 2D Wireframe, click the Visual Style Controls at the upper-left corner of the drawing area (it's the third of three bracketed settings), and then choose the 2D Wireframe option. Visual styles are mostly used for 3D drawings. I cover viewing 3D drawings in Chapter 22.

Regenerating and Redrawing the Display

AutoCAD and AutoCAD LT are *vector programs,* which means that they store information about objects in your drawing in terms of coordinates and equations. To display your drawing on your computer screen, the programs convert the vector information to pixels. Occasionally, you may need to re-display the objects on your screen. One way is to recalculate the entire drawing, in a process called *regenerating* (the REGEN command). Another way is to quickly access a virtual screen from your computer's memory; this is called *redrawing* (the REDRAW command). Keep in mind that redrawing is quicker than regenerating.

When should you use the REDRAW and REGEN commands?

- Use the REDRAW command to remove blips or to quickly refresh the screen. To redraw the screen, type **redraw** ↵ at the command line.
- Use the REGEN command whenever you want to recalculate and redisplay the entire drawing. In common usage, the word *regen* refers to the REGEN command as well as *regenerate* or *regeneration*. To regenerate the entire drawing, type **regen** ↵ at the command line.

Panning

Often you cannot see the entire drawing on your screen. You therefore need a way to see the parts of your drawing that are not currently visible. To *pan* means to move the display without changing the magnification. The word *pan* refers to the expression of panning a camera across a scene or view. You pan to view a different part of your drawing.

The PAN command moves the display in the direction and distance that you indicate without changing the magnification. *Real-time* panning moves the drawing as you move the cursor.

 To pan the drawing, click and hold down the middle button or wheel on your mouse. Alternatively, click the Pan button on the Navigation bar, which appears on the right side of the drawing area (by default). The cursor changes to a hand. With the cursor anywhere in your drawing, click and drag in the direction that you want the objects to go. You can pan transparently, while you're in the middle of another command.

> **NOTE**
> The Navigation bar is a floating toolbar that sits on the right side of the drawing window (by default) and contains tools for panning, zooming, and 3D navigation (3D Orbit), as well as the SteeringWheels and the Show Motion feature. The Navigation bar is transparent until you hover the mouse cursor over it. You can turn the Navigation bar on and off with the NAVBAR command, or click the Viewport Controls (the first of three bracketed settings at the upper-left corner of the drawing area), and then choose Navigation Bar.

> **TIP**
> You can pan past the edge of the screen (actually the viewport). This means that when the cursor reaches the edge of the screen, you can continue moving your mouse in the same direction to continue the pan.

If you use the Pan button on the Navigation bar, then to leave Pan mode, press Esc or Enter, or start any command by using the Ribbon, a menu, or a toolbar. You can also right-click to open the shortcut menu and choose Exit or one of the other view options. If you pan by using the mouse wheel (or middle button), you don't need to press Esc or Enter to leave Pan mode.

Using the ZOOM Command

The ZOOM command enables you to zoom in and out of your drawing, like the zoom lens of a camera. When you zoom in, everything is magnified so that you can see it more easily, but you see less of the entire drawing. When you zoom out, objects look smaller, but you can see more of the drawing. The ZOOM command has several options that make it easy to see just what you need at an appropriate size.

You can zoom by rotating the mouse wheel forward to zoom in and backward to zoom out. There is no Zoom cursor, and you don't need to press Esc or Enter to leave Zoom mode. Alternatively, you can click the Zoom button's down arrow on the Navigation bar and then choose Zoom Realtime from the drop-down menu. The cursor changes to a magnifying glass with a plus sign on one side and a minus sign on the other side. To zoom in, click and drag up in the direction of the plus sign. To zoom out, click and drag down in the direction of the minus sign. Press Esc or Enter to leave Zoom mode.

> **TIP**
> You can zoom past the edge of the screen (actually the viewport). As you move the mouse up or down to zoom, when you reach the edge of the viewport, continue to move the mouse in the same direction to continue the zoom in or out. To control how much you zoom for each incremental movement of the wheel, change the ZOOMFACTOR system variable.

Understanding ZOOM options

The ZOOM command has many options that let you fine-tune the process. Start the command by choosing one of the options on the Zoom drop-down menu of the Navigation bar, or go to View tab⇨Navigate 2D panel and choose one of the options on the Zoom drop-down menu there. Table 8.1 outlines the Zoom options.

TABLE 8.1 Zoom Options

Button	Option	Description
	Extents	Zooms to the outer extents of the drawing. You can also double-click the wheel of your mouse.
	Window	Lets you define a rectangular window as the boundaries of the new display. When you use Zoom Window, the command displays everything in the window that you specify but reshapes the display to fit your screen. As a result, you may see objects that were outside the specified window. You don't need to specify this option separately, because the command initially prompts you to specify the first corner of a window. When you do so, you're prompted for the opposite corner.
	Previous	Redisplays the most recent display of your drawing.
	Realtime	Displays the Zoom cursor and lets you drag up to zoom in and down to zoom out. Press Esc or Enter to exit Realtime Zoom mode.
	All	Zooms the display to the greater of the drawing extents or the drawing limits.
	Dynamic	Enables you to zoom and pan in one operation. This option is covered in the following section.

continued

TABLE 8.1 *(continued)*

Button	Option	Description
	Scale	Lets you enter a number to scale the display relative to the drawing limits (a kind of absolute scaling). Enter a number followed by **x** to scale the display relative to the current view (relative scaling). Enter a number followed by **xp** to scale the display relative to paper space units (discussed in Chapter 17). A number less than 1 (such as 0.5) reduces the size of the objects on the screen (by half when you use 0.5). A number greater than 1 (such as 2) increases the size of the objects on the screen (to twice the size when you use 2).
	Center	Lets you specify a new center for the display, and then a new magnification/height. The current magnification/height is shown in brackets for your reference. Type a smaller number to increase the magnification, making the objects larger. Type a larger value to decrease the magnification, making the objects smaller.
	Object	Lets you zoom in to selected objects.
	In	Uses the Scale option with a value of 2x. See the Scale option. It's only available from the Ribbon drop-down list.
	Out	Uses the Scale option with a value of 0.5x. See the Scale option. It's only available from the Ribbon drop-down list.

When you use one of the Zoom options, you see the objects in your drawing become larger or smaller in a smooth transition. To turn off this feature, use the VTOPTIONS command. In the View Transitions dialog box that opens, uncheck the Enable Animation for Pan & Zoom check box.

> **NOTE**
> When you undo consecutive ZOOM or PAN commands, they count as one operation. Because people often use several ZOOM or PAN operations together, combining them helps you to get back to your previous state more quickly. To disable this feature, choose Application Button ⇨ Options. On the User Preferences tab, uncheck the Combine Zoom and Pan Commands check box in the Undo/Redo section.

> **TIP**
> After you zoom and pan, you may want to go back to previous views of your drawing. On the View tab, in the Navigate 2D panel, the Back button lets you easily do so. After you use the Back button, the Forward button lets you reverse the Back operation. It's similar to using the Back and Forward buttons in your web browser.

Using ZOOM Dynamic

The Dynamic option of ZOOM enables you to pan and zoom in one operation. When you start ZOOM Dynamic, you see the virtual screen area of the drawing in a blue, dashed rectangle; this view box represents the drawing extents or limits, whichever is greater. Your current view is bounded in a green, dashed rectangle. Your cursor changes, based on the two modes of ZOOM Dynamic. Each time you click the left mouse button, you switch modes. Here's how the two modes work:

- **Pan mode.** The view box contains an X and can move freely around any displayed area of the drawing.
- **Zoom mode.** The view box contains an arrow. The left side of the box is fixed at the point where you changed to Zoom mode. As you move the cursor, the box expands or shrinks, letting you zoom to any magnification.

When the view box displays the view that you want, click the right mouse button and choose Enter (or press Enter). The command pans and zooms to show that view. Figure 8.1 shows the screen during a ZOOM Dynamic operation.

FIGURE 8.1

Using ZOOM Dynamic

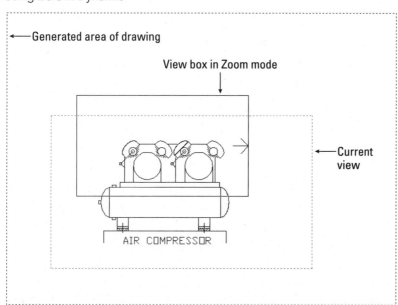

ON THE WEB

The drawing used in the following exercise on panning and zooming, ab08-a.dwg, is available from the Drawings download on the companion website.

STEPS: Panning and Zooming

1. Open ab08-a.dwg from the Drawings download on the companion website. This is a drawing of a warehouse, as shown in Figure 8.2.

2. To read the text in the lower-right corner, choose Zoom Window from the Zoom drop-down menu on the Navigation bar.

3. At the Specify corner of window, enter a scale factor (nX or nXP), or [All/Center/Dynamic/Extents/Previous/Scale/Window/Object] <real time>: prompt, pick ❶, as shown in Figure 8.2. At the Specify opposite corner: prompt, pick ❷. AutoCAD or AutoCAD LT zooms in to display the window that you specified.

FIGURE 8.2

A drawing of a large warehouse, with shelving and conveyor belts

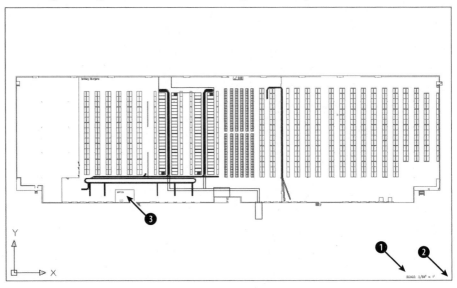

Thanks to Bryan Kelly of ATI Corporation, Fairfield, Iowa, for this drawing.

 4. Choose View tab ⇨ Navigate 2D panel ⇨ Zoom drop-down menu ⇨ All.

 5. Choose View tab ⇨ Navigate 2D panel ⇨ Back. You return to the previous display.

 6. If you have a mouse with a wheel or middle button, double-click it. Otherwise, choose Zoom Extents from the Zoom drop-down menu on the Navigation bar. The drawing fills the screen. In this drawing, the drawing extents are similar to the drawing limits, so that you see little difference between using Zoom All and Zoom Extents.

 7. Choose Navigation bar ⇨ Zoom drop-down menu ⇨ Zoom Center. At the Specify center point: prompt, pick ❸, as shown in Figure 8.2. At the Enter magnification or height <5315.176>: prompt, type **500** ↵. You zoom in on the office.

 8. Choose Zoom Realtime from the same Zoom drop-down menu. Place the cursor at the top of the drawing, then click and drag to the bottom of the screen. The display zooms out about 200 percent.

9. Choose Zoom Scale from the Navigation bar's Zoom drop-down menu. Type **2x** ↵. The display zooms in, doubling the scale of the view and returning you approximately to the previous view of the office.

10. Press and hold your mouse's wheel and move the mouse to the left, horizontally, until the office is on the left side of the screen. Or, choose Pan from the Navigation bar, drag to the left with the mouse's pick button, and then press Enter to exit Pan Realtime mode.

11. Choose Zoom Dynamic from the Navigation bar's Zoom drop-down menu. You now see the entire drawing. The current view is shown with a green dashed line. The cursor is a box with an X in it. You are now in Pan mode. To zoom in on the right side of the warehouse, move the Pan box to the lower-right corner of the warehouse and click with the pick (left) button.

12. You are now in Zoom mode. The Zoom box contains an arrow. Move the mouse to the left to shrink the Zoom box. Notice that the Zoom box is fixed at its left side. When the Zoom box is about half of its original size, left-click again.

13. You are back in Pan mode again. Move the Pan box to the bottom-right corner of the warehouse. Right-click and choose Enter to zoom in on this new view. Your display should look approximately like Figure 8.3.

FIGURE 8.3

The new view of the drawing after using Zoom Dynamic

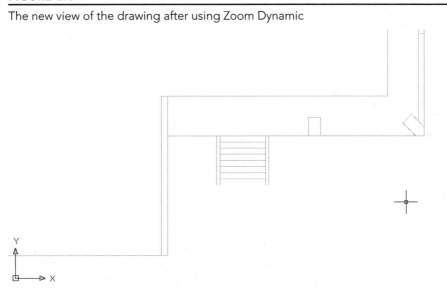

14. Choose Extents from the Navigation bar's Zoom drop-down menu. Do not save your drawing. If you're continuing to the next exercise, leave the drawing open.

Using the SteeringWheels

The SteeringWheel is a navigation device that allows you to zoom and pan from a single interface. It also lets you rewind through previous displays. This wheel is an all-in-one navigation tool for both 2D and 3D use and comes in several configurations. For more information on 3D navigation, see Chapter 22. In AutoCAD LT, the wheel offers only 2D navigation tools. Figure 8.4 shows the default SteeringWheel configuration in AutoCAD.

FIGURE 8.4

The SteeringWheel is a quick navigation device that hovers at the cursor.

To display the SteeringWheel, click the SteeringWheels button on the Navigation bar or from the Viewport Controls drop-down list at the upper-left corner of the drawing area. This starts the NAVSWHEEL command. The SteeringWheel appears at the cursor (and follows the cursor as you move it) and is divided into sections (called *wedges*), each of which offers a different navigational aid. To use the default wheel configuration, do one of the following:

- **Pan.** Place the cursor over the Pan wedge, click and hold the pick button, and drag in the direction you want to pan. When you click, you immediately see the Pan cursor.
- **Zoom.** Place the cursor over the Zoom wedge, and then click and hold the pick button. Drag up or to the right to zoom in. Drag down or to the left to zoom out. When you click, you immediately see the Zoom cursor.
- **Rewind.** Click and hold the Rewind wedge. You see a series of thumbnails showing previous views. Drag over the thumbnails and release the mouse when you see the view that you want to restore. Click the Rewind wedge to restore the previous view.
- **Orbit.** Click and hold the Orbit wedge to view your drawing in various 3D views. I discuss Orbit in Chapter 22 (AutoCAD only).
- **Center.** Click a pivot point for 3D navigation. I discuss this feature more in Chapter 22 (AutoCAD only).
- **Walk.** Lets you walk through a 3D drawing. I discuss walking through a drawing in Chapter 22 (AutoCAD only).
- **Look.** Swivels the 3D view. I discuss this further in Chapter 22 (AutoCAD only).
- **Up/Down.** Moves the view along the Y axis, like going up or down in an elevator. I discuss this further in Chapter 22 (AutoCAD only).

To exit, press Esc or Enter or click the wheel's X button. To configure the wheel, right-click and choose SteeringWheel Settings. In the SteeringWheels Settings dialog box, you can configure both 2D and 3D features. For example, you can change the wheel's size and opacity, and display a mini wheel, which is a smaller version of the SteeringWheel. You can also quickly choose one of the configurations from the shortcut menu. The SteeringWheels Settings dialog box and option are in AutoCAD only.

Creating Named Views

After you've done a lot of panning and zooming in a drawing, you may find that you return to the same part of your drawing again and again, especially if the drawing undergoes a lot of changes. In a large drawing, it can take some time to display the part of the drawing that you want. You can speed up the process by saving views.

A view can show any part of your drawing at any magnification. After you have the display that you want, you give the view a name and then save it. AutoCAD or AutoCAD LT then lets you retrieve that view at any time, without zooming or panning.

Saving a view

First display the view that you want to save on the screen. Then choose View tab ⇨ Views panel ⇨ View Manager to start the VIEW command and open the View Manager, as shown in Figure 8.5.

FIGURE 8.5

The View Manager dialog box

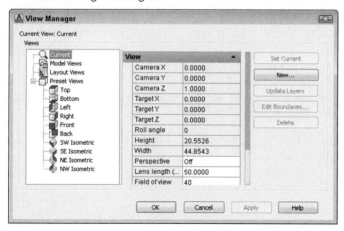

The Views pane lists the following types of views:

- **Current.** The current display.
- **Model views.** All named views, including cameras, in model space. *Model space* is where you draw. I cover the concept of model space in Chapter 17. Cameras are a way to define 3D views (they are not available in AutoCAD LT); I explain cameras in Chapter 22.
- **Layout views.** All named views created in a layout (paper space). A layout is a mechanism for laying out your drawing in preparation for plotting. I explain layouts in Chapter 17.
- **Preset views.** Preset views that come with AutoCAD and AutoCAD LT. These are the same views that you see by choosing View tab ⇨ Views panel ⇨ Views drop-down list or the View Controls in the upper-left corner of a viewport (AutoCAD only).

When you choose a view in the Views panel, you see its properties in the central panel of the View Manager dialog box. The available properties depend on the type of view. You can use the properties panel to change most of a view's properties; however, some are for information only and are not editable. Some of the properties only apply to 3D views, and some are not available in AutoCAD LT. Table 8.2 lists the properties that may appear in the View Manager.

TABLE 8.2   View Properties

Property	Description
Name	Named model and layout views, and cameras.
Category	The category that you specify when you create a new named view. A category is optional and applies only to model and layout views. If you specify a category, it appears on the Sheet Views tab of the Sheet Set Manager (covered in Bonus Chapter 3).
Viewport Association	Specifies whether the view is associated with a viewport on a sheet in a sheet set. This applies only to layout views.
UCS	The name of the User Coordinate System (UCS) saved with the view. When you create a named view, you can save a UCS with that view. I cover UCSs later in this chapter.
Layer snapshot	Specifies whether the current layer states are saved with the view. You can save this *layer snapshot* with a model or layout view. I cover layer states in Chapter 11.
Location	Specifies the layout tab name when you define a named view on a layout tab. See Chapter 17 for a discussion of layout tabs.
Annotation Scale	Stores the annotation scale that was current when you defined the model view. See Chapter 17 for more on annotation scales.
Visual style	Specifies a visual style for the view. This applies only to model views. I explain visual styles in Chapter 22; they apply mostly to 3D drawings. For 2D drawings, the visual style is 2D Wireframe.
Background	Specifies a background for the model view. Backgrounds apply only to 3D model views (AutoCAD LT does not offer backgrounds). Choose Solid, Gradient, or Image to open the Background dialog box or Sun & Sky to open the Adjust Sun & Sky Background dialog box. I cover backgrounds more in Chapter 22.
Live section	Specifies a live section object applied to the model view. See Chapter 24 for more on live sections.
View type	Displays the type of *shot*, used for animation and playbacks. I discuss creating animated presentations (the ShowMotion feature) later in this chapter.
Transition type	Displays the type of transition between views, when shown as an animated presentation (the ShowMotion feature).
Transition duration	Displays the length of the transition between shots.
Playback duration	Displays the length of the display of the shot, when played back as an animated presentation.
Camera X	Displays the X coordinate of the view's camera. This is for information only and does not apply to layout views.

Property	Description
Camera Y	Displays the Y coordinate of the view's camera. This is for information only and does not apply to layout views.
Camera Z	Displays the Z coordinate of the view's camera. This is for information only and does not apply to layout views.
Target X	Displays the X coordinate of the view's target. This is for information only and does not apply to layout views.
Target Y	Displays the Y coordinate of the view's target. This is for information only and does not apply to layout views.
Target Z	Displays the Z coordinate of the view's target. This is for information only and does not apply to layout views.
Roll angle	Displays the angle that the view is tilted around the line of site. This is for information only and does not apply to layout views.
Height	Displays the height of the view. This is for information only and does not apply to camera views.
Width	Displays the width of the view. This is for information only and does not apply to camera views.
Perspective	Specifies whether a view is a perspective view. This applies to model views and is read-only in AutoCAD LT. I discuss perspective views in Chapter 22.
Lens length (mm)	Specifies the lens length in millimeters. This applies to perspective views only. The LENSLENGTH system variable controls the default value for this setting. Changing this value also changes the Field of View setting, which is another way of expressing this setting.
Field of view	Specifies the field of view of a perspective view. Changing this value also changes the Lens Length setting. This does not apply to layout views.
Front plane	Specifies the offset for the front clipping plane if you enabled front clipping. Clipping applies to 3D views only.
Back plane	Specifies the offset for the back clipping plane if you enabled back clipping.
Clipping	Turns clipping on or off.

To create a new named view, click New to open the New View / Shot Properties (or New View in AutoCAD LT) dialog box, as shown in Figure 8.6. Type a name for your view in the View Name text box. To specify a view, you use the View Properties tab in AutoCAD.

View names can be up to 255 characters and can include spaces. As explained in Table 8.2, you can save a category, a layer snapshot, a User Coordinate System, a live section, and a visual style with a view. Select the Current Display option to use the current display as the view. Otherwise, click the Define View Window button, and specify a window around the view that you want. Press Enter to return to the New View / Shot Properties (New View in AutoCAD LT) dialog box.

Click OK to return to the View Manager dialog box, where you see your new view listed. Click New again to define another new view or click OK to return to your drawing.

8

FIGURE 8.6

The New View / Shot Properties dialog box, with the View Properties tab active.

> **TIP**
>
> In a very large drawing, you might create views as soon as you create the titleblock — for example, one for each quadrant of the drawing and another for the titleblock lettering. This helps you move quickly from one section of the drawing to another. As you determine the need for more specific views, you can add them.

Displaying a view

The easiest way to display a view is to select a view from the View Controls in the upper-left corner of a viewport; or you can choose View tab ⇨ Views panel, and click the Views drop-down list, where you can find the named views that you created. Alternatively, choose View tab ⇨ Views panel ⇨ View Manager, choose your view, click Set Current, and click OK.

Managing named views

You can use the View Manager to manage named views. You can also find these features by right-clicking inside the View Manager.

- To delete a view, choose the view that you want to delete and click the Delete button or press the Delete key on your keyboard.

- To rename a view, select it, type a new name in the Properties pane (next to the Name property), and press Enter.

- To change the layer states that you saved with the view, change the states of any layers before opening the dialog box. Then open the View Manager dialog box, choose a named view, and click Update Layers. The view now uses the current layer settings. (I explain layers in Chapter 11.)

- To edit the boundaries of a view, choose the Edit Boundaries button. You are now back in your drawing and the current view boundaries are shown in black or white (depending on the color of your background). At the prompts, specify the two opposite corners that you want to serve as boundaries for the view and press Enter.

Creating animated presentations from named views

You can create a presentation that displays one named view after another to show the drawing to a client or colleague. In essence, you create a slide show from named views in your drawing. Each view can have a transition, as well as timing for the transition and the display of the view itself. Together, these properties are called a shot. *ShowMotion,* a looping feature, lets you create an ongoing display of views. This feature is not available in AutoCAD LT. You define the shot on the Shot Properties tab of the New View / Shot Properties dialog box, as shown in Figure 8.7.

To configure the shot, first choose one of the view types:

- **Cinematic.** Allows you to choose a movement for the view. Most of the options are appropriate for 3D drawings only. The options are Zoom In, Zoom Out, Track Left, Track Right, Crank Up, Crank Down, Look, and Orbit. Each movement has its own settings. Try them out and click the Preview button to see what they look like.

- **Still.** Displays a still view. You can specify the duration of the view.

- **Recorded Walk.** Lets you record a walk-through of a 3D model. I discuss this feature in Chapter 22.

Next, choose a transition from the Transition Type drop-down list. Then enter a duration for the transition in the Transition Duration text box. Finally, change the options under the Motion section as desired based on the transition type selected. Click OK when you're done.

FIGURE 8.7

Use the Shot Properties tab of the New View / Shot Properties dialog box to create and configure a presentation of your drawing.

> **TIP**
>
> The Fade from Black into This Shot option looks best with a black background. The Fade from White into This Shot option looks best with a white background. See Bonus Chapter 15 for instructions on changing the background color of the drawing area.

To play the show or use other related features, click ShowMotion on the Navigation bar to start the NAVSMOTION command. At first, you see one window, displaying the drawing, along with some navigation tools. However, if you move the cursor over that window, thumbnails of all the views appear, as shown in Figure 8.8.

FIGURE 8.8

The ShowMotion feature creates a slide show from named views.

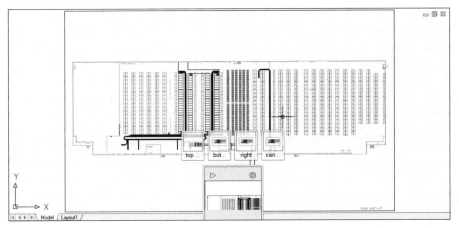

Use the navigation tools to do the following:

- Click any view to display that view.
- Click the Pin button to pin the ShowMotion box, so that it doesn't disappear when you click elsewhere in the drawing area.
- Click the Play All button to play the slide show. Click in the drawing area to hide the ShowMotion window (if it isn't pinned) so that it doesn't obscure the show.
- Click the Stop button to stop the slide show.
- Click the Turn On Looping button to repeat the playback over and over.
- Click the New Shot button to open the New View / Shot Properties dialog box, with the Shot Properties tab on top so that you can create a new view and define its shot properties.

To edit the properties of a shot, right-click the thumbnail of an individual shot and choose Properties, or use the EDITSHOT command and enter the name of the shot. The View / Shot Properties dialog box opens, where you can change the settings of the shot.

ON THE WEB

The drawing used in the following exercise on working with views, ab08-a.dwg, is available from the Drawings download on the companion website.

STEPS: Working with Views

1. Open ab08-a.dwg, available from the Drawings download on the companion website if it is not already open from the previous exercise.

2. Save the file as ab08-01.dwg in your AutoCAD Bible folder.

3. Choose View tab ➪ Views panel ➪ View Manager to open the View Manager.

4. Click New to open the New View / Shot Properties (New View in AutoCAD LT) dialog box, with the View Properties tab on top if you are using AutoCAD.

5. In the View Name text box, type **top left**.

6. Click the Define View Window button to return to your drawing temporarily.

7. At the Specify first corner: prompt, pick the top-left corner of the drawing. At the Specify opposite corner: prompt, pick somewhere around the center of the warehouse. Press Enter to return to the New View / Shot Properties (New View in AutoCAD LT) dialog box.

8. If you are using AutoCAD LT, go to the next step. Click the Shot Properties tab. Check that the View Type is set to Still. Change the Transition Duration to **0.5** seconds. In the Motion section, change the Duration to **1** second.

9. Click OK.

10. Click New again. Type **bottom left** in the text box of the New View / Shot Properties (or New View in AutoCAD LT) dialog box.

11. Click the Define View Window button. At the Specify first corner: prompt, pick the bottom-left corner of the drawing. At the Specify Opposite corner: prompt, again pick around the center of the warehouse. Press Enter.

12. If you are using AutoCAD LT, go to the next step. Click the Shot Properties tab. Again, change the Transition Duration to **0.5** seconds. In the Motion section, change the Duration to **1** second, as you did previously.

13. Click OK. The View Manager dialog box should list both of your views. Click OK to close the View Manager.

14. Choose View tab ➪ Views panel ➪ View Manager. If necessary, expand the Model Views item, and choose bottom left. Click Set Current, and then click OK. AutoCAD or AutoCAD LT displays the view.

 15. If you are using AutoCAD LT, go to the next step. Click ShowMotion on the Navigation bar. Click the Play button. The ShowMotion feature displays the two views, one after the other, using the transition and timing that you specified.

16. Save your drawing. The views that you created are now part of the drawing database.

Using named views to manage a drawing

Using named views provides three additional advantages:

- You can use named views when you open a drawing so that one of its views is immediately displayed.

- You can open only the part of a drawing contained in a view (AutoCAD only).

- You can turn a named view into a floating viewport for plotting purposes.

I explain these techniques in the next three sections.

A drawing with a view

After you've saved views, you can use them to open a drawing so that a view is immediately displayed. Click Open on the Quick Access Toolbar. In the Select File dialog box, choose the file that you want to open and check the Select Initial View check box. Then click Open. In the Select Initial View dialog box, choose the view that you want to display, and click OK.

Partially opening a drawing

You may have a very large drawing that is slow and cumbersome to work with when it is completely loaded. For example, if you have a surveyor's drawing of an entire county, but you need to work only with one plat, you can open a named view containing only that plat. This feature is not available in AutoCAD LT.

To partially open a drawing from within AutoCAD, follow these steps:

1. Click Open on the Quick Access Toolbar to open the Select File dialog box.

2. Choose a drawing and then click the Open button's drop-down menu. Choose Partial Open to open the Partial Open dialog box, as shown in Figure 8.9.

FIGURE 8.9

Use the Partial Open dialog box to open only the part of a drawing contained in a named view.

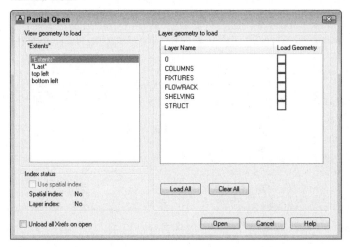

3. Choose a view from the list of named views.

4. Check the check box of one or more layers. To include all the layers, click Load All. If you don't include at least one layer, no objects are loaded. (Chapter 11 covers layers.) Click Open.

After you've partially opened a drawing, you can load more of the drawing. Enter **partialload** ↵ on the command line. This command is functional only if the current drawing has been partially opened. AutoCAD opens the Partial Load dialog box. You can change the view. To display the entire drawing (from whatever is loaded), choose the default view, *Extents*. Check the layers that you want to include or click Load All. Click OK to load the newly specified view and layers.

Using named views with sheet sets

You can combine layouts from more than one drawing into a sheet set. Sheet sets are a powerful way to organize many layouts. I cover them in detail in Bonus Chapter 3. However, at this point you should know that named views have a value beyond helping you display an area of your drawing. They can become your final layout for plotting.

Suppose that you're drawing a mechanical model with a top view, a side view, and a section view. In the final plot, you want to display these three views on one sheet of paper. Without sheet sets, you would create three floating viewports and individually pan and zoom to get the three views. (For more information on floating viewports, see the "Floating viewports" sidebar in this chapter, as well as Chapter 17.) Using the sheet-set feature as you work, you can create named views of the three parts of the drawing. Then you can use those same views to create the floating viewports for plotting.

Working with Tiled Viewports

Tiled viewports enable you to divide up the screen into rectangular bounding boxes. You can then show different views of your drawing in each viewport — at one time. The purpose of tiled viewports is to help you draw. For example:

- You can see the whole drawing in one viewport and a zoomed-in portion of that drawing in another viewport.
- You can see widely separated views of a large drawing at one time.

 There are two types of viewports — *tiled* and *floating.* For more information on floating viewports, see the "Floating viewports" sidebar in this chapter. For a detailed discussion, turn to Chapter 17.

Actually, you're already using a tiled viewport because the regular single view of your drawing on the Model tab that you've been working with represents the default of a one-tile viewport. Tiled viewports have the following characteristics:

- No matter how many viewports you have, they always collectively take up the entire screen. They are not separate entities but a way of dividing the screen.
- Only one viewport can be active at a time. The active viewport has a bold border and the Navigation bar is displayed (when enabled).
- The crosshairs appear only in the active viewport.
- The UCS (User Coordinate System) icon (if set to On) appears in each viewport.
- The viewport controls and ViewCube are displayed in each viewport (when these features are enabled).
- Any change that you make to your drawing in one viewport automatically appears in every other viewport (or in viewports that show the part of the drawing where you made the change).
- You can create up to 64 viewports — but you'll never want to create that many!
- You can begin a command in one viewport and finish it in another. For example, you can start a line in one viewport, switch to a second viewport, and end the line there.
- You can save and restore viewport configurations.

Figure 8.10 shows a drawing divided into three tiled viewports. Each viewport shows a different view of the same drawing.

FIGURE 8.10

A drawing showing three tiled viewports with a different view in each viewport

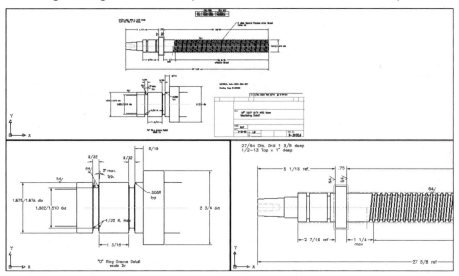

Thanks to Jerry Bottenfield of Clow Valve Company, Oskaloosa, Iowa, for this drawing.

Configuring tiled viewports

Creating tiled viewports involves deciding how you want to divide the screen. A set of tiled viewports is called a *configuration*. A few simple configurations come with AutoCAD and AutoCAD LT, but you can create your own by further dividing up any of the viewports. You can also join two adjacent viewports. Finally, you can always return to the default of one viewport.

Creating tiled viewports

 To add viewports, choose View tab ⇨ Model Viewports panel ⇨ Named. The Viewports dialog box opens; click the New Viewports tab, shown in Figure 8.11. You choose the configuration that you want on the New Viewports tab. You see a preview of the configuration on the right.

If you have named views in your drawing, you can specify a view for each viewport to display. Click a viewport in the Preview pane and choose a named view from the Change View To drop-down list at the bottom of the dialog box. You can also choose a visual style from the Visual Style drop-down list if you are using AutoCAD. If your drawing is in 3D, you can choose 3D from the Setup drop-down list, and AutoCAD creates standard orthogonal views in the viewports. When you've specified your viewport configuration, click OK to return to your drawing.

The Viewports dialog box is usually the best place to start creating viewports. However, if the standard configurations do not meet your needs, you can use one of them as a starting point and then use the other options.

Notice the Apply To drop-down list at the bottom-left corner of the Viewports dialog box in Figure 8.11. By default, the tiled viewport configurations apply to the entire display, meaning that they replace your current configuration. You can also choose to apply the configuration to the viewport that is currently displayed in the drawing area. The active viewport has a bold border and crosshairs. To make a viewport active, click anywhere inside that viewport. Then choose View tab ⇨ Model Viewports panel ⇨ Named, click the New Viewports tab, choose Current Viewport from the Apply To drop-down list, and then choose the configuration that you want for that viewport.

FIGURE 8.11

The Viewports dialog box makes it easy to choose a configuration.

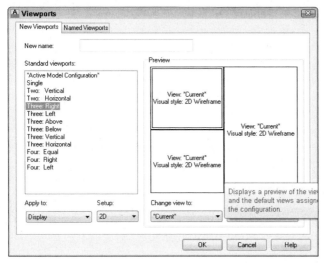

Let's say that you have four equal viewports, and the top-left viewport is active. If you choose the Four: Equal configuration from the Viewports dialog box while the top-left viewport is active and apply it to the current viewport, the top-left viewport is divided into four viewports. Now you have seven viewports in the drawing.

Removing tiled viewports

One way to remove a tiled viewport is to join it to another viewport. To join one viewport to another, choose View tab ⇨ Model Viewports panel ⇨ Join. At the `Select dominant viewport <current viewport>:` prompt, click the viewport that you want to retain or press Enter if you want to retain the current viewport. At the `Select viewport to join:` prompt, click the adjacent viewport that you want to join into the dominant viewport. When the two viewports merge, you lose the display in the second viewport. Together, the adjacent viewports must form a rectangle.

To remove all tiled viewports, return to the single viewport configuration. Choose View tab ⇨ Model Viewports panel (expanded) ⇨ Viewport Configuration drop-down menu ⇨ Single. The display in the current viewport remains.

Using tiled viewports

After you've created the viewport configuration that you want, the first step is to create the views that you need in each viewport. Just click in a viewport, and zoom and pan until you have the view that you want.

One of the great advantages of viewports is that you can draw from one viewport to another. In a large drawing, you may need to draw a line from one end of the drawing to another, but when you display the entire drawing, you can't see the detail well enough to specify where to start and end the line. To draw from one viewport to another, just click the viewport where you want to start. Start a command, specifying any necessary coordinates. To continue the command in a second viewport, click to activate that viewport. Continue the command, specifying coordinates as necessary.

You can also use viewports to edit your drawing. All commands except those that change the display — such as zooming, panning, and creating views — can be started in one viewport and continued in another.

Saving and restoring viewport configurations

You can save a tiled viewport configuration. Then you can restore it when needed. Viewport configuration names can be up to 255 characters and can include spaces.

After you create a viewport configuration that you like, choose View tab ⇨ Model Viewports panel ⇨ Named if you aren't already in the Viewports dialog box. Click the New Viewports tab and type a name in the New Name text box. Click OK.

After returning to one viewport or using a different configuration, you can restore a named viewport configuration. Choose View tab ⇨ Model Viewports panel ⇨ Named to open the Viewports dialog box with the Named Viewports tab on top. Choose the viewport that you want to restore from the list, and click OK.

Floating Viewports

AutoCAD and AutoCAD LT have two types of viewports: *tiled viewports*, which are discussed here, and *floating viewports*, which I cover in Chapter 17. These two types of viewports have many similarities, but they have different purposes. Whereas the purpose of tiled viewports is to help you draw and edit your drawing, you use floating viewports to lay out your drawing for plotting.

Floating viewports create layouts, which enable you to treat your screen like a sheet of paper. You create floating viewports and perhaps a titleblock on this electronic sheet of paper. You can create one or more layouts. Each floating viewport can show a different view of your drawing — just like tiled viewports. But floating viewports then let you plot all those views on one sheet of paper. You can't do that with tiled viewports, which are just devices to let you temporarily display your drawing in a way that helps you draw and edit. However, you can also draw and edit by using floating viewports.

Tiled viewports are covered here because they are appropriate for learning how to draw and edit your drawing. Floating viewports are covered in Chapter 17 because you use them to lay out your drawing for plotting.

STEPS: Creating, Naming, and Restoring Tiled Viewport Configurations

1. Open `ab08-b.dwg`, available from the Drawings download on the companion website.

2. Save the file as `ab08-02.dwg` in your `AutoCAD Bible` folder.

 3. Choose View tab ⇨ Model Viewports panel ⇨ Named to open the Viewports dialog box.

4. Click the New Viewports tab. In the listing at the left of the dialog box, choose Three: Above. Click OK. You see three tiled viewports.

5. Click the bottom-right viewport. Choose View tab ⇨ Navigate 2D panel ⇨ Zoom drop-down menu ⇨ Window and choose a window around the left portion of the threaded model (the upper part of the drawing).

6. Click the bottom-left viewport. Again choose Window from the Zoom drop-down menu and choose a window around the bottom-left portion of the drawing (not including the title-block).

7. Click the top viewport. Choose View tab ⇨ Navigate 2D panel ⇨ Zoom drop-down menu ⇨ Extents. Figure 8.12 shows the results.

8. Choose View tab ⇨ Model Viewports panel ⇨ Named. Click the New Viewports tab. In the New Name text box, type **3 view O Ring** and click OK.

FIGURE 8.12

The three tiled viewports now display three different views.

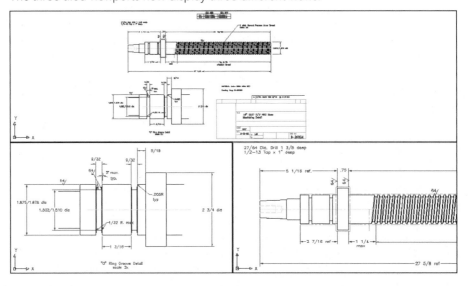

9. With the top viewport still active, choose View tab ⇨ Model Viewports panel ⇨ Viewport Configurations drop-down menu ⇨ Single to display the view shown in the last active viewport.

10. Choose View tab ⇨ Model Viewports panel ⇨ Named.

11. Choose 3 view O Ring and click OK to restore the viewport configuration, including the views in each viewport.

12. Save your drawing.

Using Snap Rotation

Not all 2D drawings are vertical and horizontal. In some drawings, significant portions of your objects need to be at nonorthogonal angles. One example is an auxiliary view to show the "true size" of an inclined surface. Sometimes it helps to rotate the crosshairs to match the major angles of the drawing.

Consider Figure 8.13. A great deal of this drawing is at an angle. You could handle this in five ways:

FIGURE 8.13

In 2D drawings such as this, you should consider various options, such as rotating the snap or creating a new UCS.

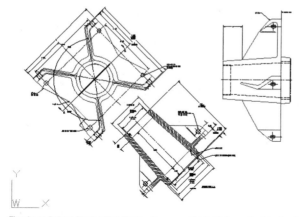

Thanks to Robert Mack of The Dexter Company, Fairfield, Iowa, for this drawing.

- Draw as normal, specifying the necessary angles.
- Rotate the snap, which also rotates the grid and crosshairs.
- Use the ViewCube to rotate the drawing.
- Create a new User Coordinate System (UCS). (Creating a new UCS is covered later in this chapter.)
- Draw the entire model vertically and rotate it afterward.

If you need to draw several objects at a certain angle, such as 45 degrees, you can rotate the snap to that angle. The crosshairs rotate to follow suit. This technique works best when the decimal point accuracy required lets you draw by using snap points. You can also use this technique to guide the cursor at an appropriate angle for direct distance entry, although polar tracking is another way to accomplish the same task.

To change the snap rotation angle, you use the SNAPANG system variable. Enter **snapang** ↵ on the command line. At the `Enter new value for SNAPANG <0>:` prompt, enter an angle. Note that you can also set an X base and a Y base. This simply ensures that the grid goes through a point of your choice, which is very important if you're using Snap mode to draw. Setting X and Y bases does not change the coordinates, which are tied to the UCS. (The UCS is discussed in the next section.) To set the base, use the SNAPBASE system variable on the command line and specify a coordinate for the base. You can use an object snap.

 You can use the ID command to get the coordinates of a point. Then use these coordinates as the X and Y bases. Chapter 12 covers the ID command.

TIP
You can use the ViewCube to rotate the drawing, along with the UCS icon and the grid. I cover the ViewCube in Chapter 22, because it's most often used in 3D drawings. When you place the cursor outside the edge of the ViewCube, you see a circle that you can drag clockwise or counterclockwise to rotate the drawing.

Understanding User Coordinate Systems

You can create a new User Coordinate System (UCS) rather than rotate the snap angle. The results are similar, except that when you create a UCS, you also affect the X,Y coordinates. The UCS is much more flexible when you start drawing in three dimensions.

By default, a drawing is set up by using a *World Coordinate System*. This sets the origin of the X,Y points at 0,0 and the angles using the familiar East (right-facing) equals 0 degrees system. Figure 8.14 shows the UCS icon in its default display in a 2D environment. The X axis is red and the Y axis is green.

FIGURE 8.14

The UCS icon in its default display

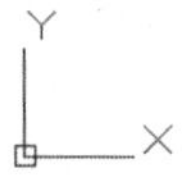

You can easily create your own UCS and even save it for future use in the drawing. To define a UCS in a 2D drawing, you indicate the angle of the X and Y axes and an origin point. The origin point then becomes the new 0,0 coordinate. You have several options for specifying the UCS. If you don't see the UCS, see "Controlling the UCS icon" later in this section.

Understanding UCS options

Understanding the UCS options will help you create a new UCS more easily, based on the information that you have available. The easiest way to create a new UCS is to select and drag the icon.

To change the UCS by dragging the icon, click the icon so that selection handles appear at the origin and the ends of the X and Y axes. (In 3D drawings, you'll also see a handle on the Z axis.) You can do any of the following:

- To move the origin, click the intersection of the axes (the square handle), move the cursor to the desired location, and then click.
- To rotate the X and Y axes, click one of the axis handles (the circular handles), move the cursor until the axes are at the desired angle, and then click.
- To return the UCS to the World Coordinate System, click it, position the cursor over the origin and choose World from the menu that appears.

In a 3D drawing, if you choose Move and Align from the menu that appears when you click the icon, the UCS automatically aligns itself to an origin or object that you specify.

Another way to create a UCS is to choose View tab ⇨ Coordinates panel and click one of the options, as listed in Table 8.3. You can also right-click on the UCS icon. The Coordinates panel is only displayed in the 3D Modeling and 3D Basics workspaces (AutoCAD only) by default. If the Coordinates panel is not displayed, display the Coordinates panel by clicking the View tab and then right-clicking over the tab. Choose Show Panels ⇨ Coordinates.

TABLE 8.3 UCS Options

Button	Option	Meaning
	World	Specifies the default UCS, with the X axis horizontal, the Y axis vertical, and the origin at the initial 0,0 location.
	Origin	Specifies a new 0,0 point of your choice, relative to the current origin.
	View	Aligns the X and Y axes with the current view. Used in 3D drawing. This option arbitrarily sets the origin.
	X	Keeps the current origin and rotates the Y and Z axes around the current X axis. You specify the angle. This is used in 3D drawing.
	Y	Keeps the current origin and rotates the X and Z axes around the current Y axis. You specify the angle. This is used in 3D drawing.
	Z	Keeps the current origin and rotates the X and Y axes around the current Z axis. You specify the angle. This option can be used in 2D drawing.
	Object	Enables you to align the UCS with an object. In general, this option uses the most obvious object snap as the origin and aligns the X axis with the object. For example, when you choose a line, the endpoint nearest your pick point becomes the origin and the X axis aligns with the angle of the line. When you choose a circle, the X axis points toward the point that you pick on the circumference.
	Z-Axis Vector	Specifies which way the Z axis points. This option is not used in 2D drawing.
	Face	Aligns the UCS with the face of a 3D solid.
	3 Point	Enables you to specify three points. The first point is the origin, the second point indicates the positive direction of the X axis, and the third point indicates the positive direction of the Y axis.

159

Saving and restoring a custom UCS

After you create a UCS, you can save it so that you can easily switch back and forth between the World Coordinate System and your UCS. To save a UCS, follow these steps:

1. Specify the UCS as described in the previous section.

2. Right-click the UCS icon and choose Named UCS⇨Save.

3. Type a name for the UCS and press Enter. The name can be up to 255 characters and can include spaces.

To restore a saved UCS, again right-click the UCS icon, choose Named UCS, and then click the UCS that you want to use. To delete a saved UCS, choose View tab⇨Coordinates panel⇨UCS, Named UCS to open the UCS dialog box. With the Named UCSs tab current, select the UCS and press the Delete key. When you're done, click OK to close the dialog box.

Controlling the UCS icon

When you start a new drawing, the UCS icon is at the bottom left of your drawing at 0,0. By default, the icon remains at 0,0 even if you pan around the drawing. The icon may, therefore, end up in the middle of your drawing. If 0,0 is off the screen, then the icon reverts to the bottom-left corner.

You can turn off the UCS icon completely. If you aren't working with customized UCSs, you often have no reason to see the UCS in a 2D drawing. If you want the UCS icon on, you can also display it only at the bottom left of your drawing. This keeps the icon out of the way so that it does not obstruct your drawing.

If you create a new UCS, keeping the UCS icon at the 0,0 point (the origin) of your new UCS helps you to get your bearings. A plus sign appears in the icon to indicate the origin. However, if the origin is out of the current display or so close to the edge that the icon won't fit, the UCS icon appears at the lower-left corner of your drawing anyway.

To control the UCS icon, first display the Coordinates panel on the View tab, if it is hidden. To do so, right-click the View tab itself, choose Show Panels, and then click Coordinates. Then choose View tab⇨Coordinates panel, and click the dialog box launcher arrow to the right of the panel name to open the UCS dialog box. On the Settings tab, you can control the UCS icon with the following items:

- **On.** Toggles the display of the UCS icon on and off. You can also turn the display on and off by choosing View tab⇨Coordinates panel⇨Display UCS Icon drop-down menu.
- **Display at UCS Origin Point.** Toggles the placement of the UCS icon at the origin on and off.
- **Apply to All Active Viewports.** Applies the preceding two settings to all viewports, rather than to just the current viewport.
- **Allow Selecting UCS icon.** Lets you manipulate the UCS icon to change the UCS.

You can customize the look of the UCS icon. To do this, choose View tab⇨Coordinates panel⇨UCS Icon, Properties to open the UCS Icon dialog box, as shown in Figure 8.15. As you make changes, you can see the result in the preview box. Alternatively, you can right-click the UCS icon and choose UCS Icon Settings⇨Properties.

FIGURE 8.15

Use the UCS Icon dialog box to customize the look of the UCS icon.

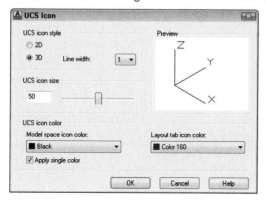

Choose between 2D and 3D styles. The 3D style shows the Z axis (AutoCAD only), but you won't see it when you're looking at your model from the top (called *Plan view*). You can choose a line width from 1 to 3, 1 being the default.

You can change the size of the icon. Just drag the slider up and down to get the result you like. Finally, you can change the color of the icon, both in model space and in paper space layouts. (I cover paper space layouts in Chapter 17.) Click OK to close the dialog box.

ON THE WEB

The drawing used in the following exercise on drawing with a custom UCS, `ab08-c.dwg`, is available from the Drawings download on the companion website.

STEPS: Drawing with a Custom UCS

1. Open `ab08-c.dwg`, available from the Drawings download on the companion website. This exercise assumes that you have Dynamic Input on, with the default relative coordinates setting.

2. Save the file as `ab08-03.dwg` in your `AutoCAD Bible` folder. Ortho Mode and Object Snap should be on. Set a running object snap for Endpoints only.

 3. Right-click the UCS icon and choose Rotate Axis ⇨ Z. Because no objects exist in the drawing, you cannot easily use the 3 Point or Object options that might otherwise be useful.

4. At the `Specify rotation angle about Z axis <90>:` prompt, type **45** ↵. The UCS icon and crosshairs are displayed at a 45-degree angle.

5. Choose Home tab ⇨ Draw panel ⇨ Line. At the prompt, pick a point in the middle of your screen. At the `Specify next point or [Undo]:` prompt, type **@1.25<90** ↵. End the LINE command.

6. Choose Home tab ⇨ Draw panel ⇨ Rectangle/Polygon drop-down menu ⇨ Rectangle. Choose the From object snap. At the `Base point:` prompt, use the Endpoint object snap to pick the endpoint of the line that you just drew. At the `<Offset>:` prompt, type **@.875,0** ↵. At the

Specify other corner point or [Area/Dimensions/Rotation]: prompt, type
@-5.5,1.5 ↵. The command creates the rectangle at the proper angle.

7. Start the LINE command again. Follow the prompts:

Specify first point: *Choose the From object snap.*
Base point: *Use the Endpoint object snap to pick point* ❶ *in Figure 8.16.*
<Offset>: *Type* **@-.875,0** ↵
Specify next point or [Undo]: *Move the cursor in the 90° direction (it*
looks like the 135° direction because of the rotated UCS). **.625** ↵
Specify next point or [Undo]: *Move the cursor in the 180° direction.*
3.75 ↵
Specify next point or [Close/Undo]: *Move the cursor in the 270°*
direction. **.625** ↵
Specify next point or [Close/Undo]: ↵

8. Start the LINE command again. Turn on Object Snap Tracking on the status bar and follow
the prompts:

Specify first point: *Pass the cursor over* ❷ *and then over* ❸ *in Figure*
8.16 to acquire these points. Move the cursor to ❹ *at the*
intersection of the two temporary tracking lines and click.
Specify next point or [Undo]: *Move the cursor in the 270° direction*
relative to the UCS. **1.25** ↵.
Specify next point or [Undo]: ↵

FIGURE 8.16

Using a customized UCS to start to draw a detail for a drill

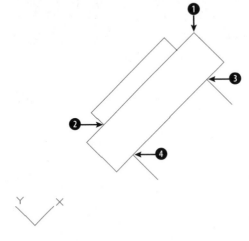

9. Because you would normally continue working on this drawing, you should save the UCS.
Right-click the UCS icon and choose Named UCS ⇨ Save. Type **Rotated 45** and press Enter.

10. Right-click the UCS icon and choose World. The UCS icon and crosshairs return to their familiar angle.

11. To return to the Rotated 45 UCS, again right-click the UCS icon and choose Named UCS⇨Rotated 45.

12. Save your drawing.

> **TIP**
>
> After creating a new, rotated UCS such as the one in the previous exercise, type plan (to start the PLAN command) and use the Current UCS option to remove the rotation. Now you aren't working at an angle in your UCS. To return to the World UCS, type plan again and choose the World option to return to your drawing's previous state.

Creating Isometric Drawings

An *isometric* drawing is a 2D drawing made to look like a 3D drawing. By drawing parallelograms instead of squares, the drawing gives the impression of being in three dimensions. However, most people use true 3D tools these days. For more information, see Part IV of this book.

Understanding isometric planes

The ISOPLANE (short for isometric plane) command rotates the crosshairs to the special angles required for isometric drawing. You then toggle the ISOPLANE setting from left to right to top, to draw on each of the three "planes." As you do so, the angles of the crosshairs, snap, and grid change to the appropriate angles. As you toggle among the planes, you see the crosshairs take on various configurations of these angles. Figure 8.17 shows the standard isometric cube. You can see three sides — left, right, and top. In the figure, the crosshairs are set to the right isometric plane.

FIGURE 8.17

The isometric cube

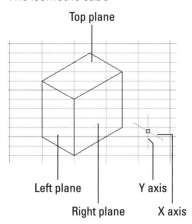

Top plane

Left plane

Right plane

Y axis

X axis

Drawing in Isometric mode

To start Isometric mode, right-click the Snap button on the status bar and choose Settings to open the Drafting Settings dialog box. On the Snap and Grid tab, in the Snap Type section, choose Grid Snap (if it is not already selected), and then Isometric Snap to enter Isometric mode. Click OK. After you're in Isometric mode, press F5 to toggle from plane to plane.

Drawing lines in Isometric mode is fairly straightforward if the lines are parallel to one of the isometric plane angles. Circles and arcs in Isometric mode must be drawn as ellipses and elliptical arcs. When you're in Isometric mode, the ELLIPSE command has an Isocircle option.

> **TIP**
>
> Use snap points and object snaps as often as possible in an isometric drawing. Also, you can enlarge crosshairs to better visualize the isometric planes. (Choose Application Button ⇨ Options and click the Display tab. Then set the Crosshair Size value to 100.) The grid is also a helpful aid. Polar coordinate display is very helpful while drawing isometrically. The coordinates are easier to understand than the unusual absolute snap point coordinates created by ISOPLANE.

Summary

In this chapter, you read how to control the display of your drawing. You learned about:

- The PAN and ZOOM commands, including real-time pan and zoom and ZOOM options
- Using the SteeringWheels
- Saving several views of your drawing so that you can retrieve them quickly
- Creating animated presentations of your drawing
- Creating tiled viewports, as well as naming and displaying useful viewport configurations
- Rotating the snap and grid
- Creating a User Coordinate System, saving a UCS, and then restoring it
- Setting the snap style to isometric to create isometric drawings

In the next chapter, you discover how to start editing your drawings.

Editing Your Drawing with Basic Tools

IN THIS CHAPTER

Making changes to a drawing

Working with the selection set of objects

N o drawing project is ever completed without changes. You make changes in a drawing for many reasons. Some editing processes are simply part of the drawing process, such as copying an object rather than drawing it a second time from scratch. Other types of editing involve making changes to many objects at once, such as moving an entire section of a drawing to make room for additional objects. You often also need to erase, move, rotate, and resize objects.

Editing a Drawing

In order to edit an object, you need to select it. AutoCAD and AutoCAD LT offer numerous techniques for selecting objects. In this chapter, I cover basic editing commands as well as most of the ways to select objects. The rest of the 2D editing commands, as well as additional selection and editing methods — grips, the Properties palette, selection filters, and groups — are covered in the next chapter.

Most of the editing commands are on the Home tab in the Modify panel. In most cases, you can do either one of the following:

- Start the command first and then select the objects to which the command applies.
- Select the objects first and then start the command.

The question of which comes first, the command or the object, is covered later in this chapter.

> **NOTE**
>
> Although you can use the editing tools that I describe in this chapter in a 3D environment, this chapter assumes that you are working in a 2D environment. (AutoCAD LT doesn't offer a 3D environment.) To make sure that you're in a 2D environment, set the workspace to AutoCAD Classic or Drafting & Annotation (choose it from the Workspace drop-down list on the Quick Access Toolbar or Workspace Switching button on the status bar) and set the visual style to 2D Wireframe (use the 2D Wireframe option of the `vscurrent` command or the Visual Style Controls in the upper-left corner of a viewport). If you still see the Z axis on the UCS icon, choose View tab ⇨ Views panel ⇨ 3D Navigation drop-down list ⇨ Top or click the View Controls in the upper-left corner of a viewport and choose Top. Another method is to set the workspace to Drafting & Annotation, and then start a new drawing based on the default `acad.dwt` or `acadlt.dwt` template.

Understanding object-selection basics

When you start to edit drawings, it is important to first learn how to select objects. The simplest selection technique is to place the *pickbox* — the box at the intersection of the crosshairs — over the object and click with the pick button on the mouse. This is known as *picking* an object.

When you pass the cursor over an object before choosing any editing command, the object becomes thicker and dashed. This *rollover highlighting* helps you to know which object you will select when you click. This feature is helpful in a busy drawing with many objects close together or overlapping. I explain how to fine-tune the effect at the end of this chapter. You also see a rollover tooltip that displays some basic properties of the object.

If you start an editing command before selecting an object, the command responds with the `Select objects:` prompt. When you then pick an object to select it, AutoCAD or AutoCAD LT highlights it, usually by making the object dashed, as shown on the left side of Figure 9.1.

The command continues to provide `Select objects:` prompts so that you can select other objects. Continue to select objects until you have selected all the objects that you want to edit. Then press Enter to end the `Select objects:` prompt.

When you select an object before choosing an editing command, the lines of the selected object become dashed and you also see one or more small boxes, called *grips,* as shown on the right side of Figure 9.1 for a line. Chapter 10 covers grips. In the next few exercises, you use this picking technique to select objects. Other selection methods are covered later in this chapter.

FIGURE 9.1

On the left, the selected line is dashed. On the right, the selected line also displays grips.

Erasing objects

 The ERASE command is very simple — it has no options. To erase an object, select the object and choose Home tab ⇨ Modify panel ⇨ Erase, or press Delete on the keyboard. Alternatively, choose Erase and then select the object.

 The PURGE command erases two kinds of undesirable objects that sometimes mistakenly exist in a drawing — zero-length lines and empty text objects. I cover the PURGE command more in Chapter 11.

 The OVERKILL command deletes duplicate objects, including duplicate or overlapping lines, arcs, and polylines. It also combines partially overlapping or contiguous objects. To delete duplicate objects, follow these steps:

1. Choose Home tab ⇨ Modify panel (expanded) ⇨ Delete Duplicate Objects.

2. At the `Select objects:` prompt, select all objects that might contain duplicates (which usually aren't visible). You can also type **all** ↵ to select all objects in your drawing. (For more information on selecting objects, see the "Selecting Objects" section later in this chapter.)

3. Press Enter to end the selection process. The Delete Duplicate Objects dialog box opens.

4. Choose the options you want and click OK. (You can choose to ignore certain properties. By default, these properties are not ignored, so OVERKILL will not delete overlapping lines, for example, if they are on different layers. I explain most of these properties, including layers, in Chapter 11.)

You see a message on the command line stating the number of duplicate objects that were deleted.

ON THE WEB
The drawing used in the following exercise on picking and erasing objects, `ab09-a.dwg`, is available from the Drawings download on the companion website.

STEPS: Picking and Erasing Objects

1. Open `ab09-a.dwg`, available from the Drawings download on the companion website.

2. Save the file as `ab09-01.dwg` in your `AutoCAD Bible` folder. The drawing shown in Figure 9.2 is a schematic of a gas extraction well.

3. To erase the line at point ❶ of Figure 9.2, move the mouse until the pickbox at the intersection of the crosshairs is anywhere over the line. The line thickens and is dashed. Click the line. Now the line is dashed and displays grips.

 4. Choose Home tab ⇨ Modify panel ⇨ Erase. The line is erased.

5. Right-click and choose Repeat ERASE.

6. At the `Select objects:` prompt, pick the line at point ❷, as shown in Figure 9.2.

7. The command responds with `1 found` and repeats the `Select objects:` prompt. Right-click to end the `Select objects:` prompt. The line is erased.

8. Save your drawing.

9

FIGURE 9.2

The gas extraction well schematic

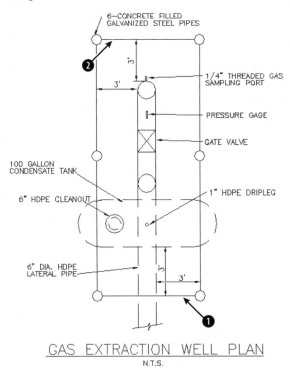

Thanks to the Army Corps of Engineers for this drawing.

 The OOPS command restores the most recently erased object and is covered in Chapter 18.

Moving objects

Use the MOVE command to move objects in your drawing. You need to specify the distance and direction that you want the object to move.

 To move an object, select it and choose Home tab ⇨ Modify panel ⇨ Move. Alternatively, choose Move and then select the object. When you start the MOVE command and then select an object, the command responds with the following prompt:

```
Specify base point or [Displacement] <Displacement>:
```

You now have two ways of specifying how to move the object or objects:

- **Displacement method.** At the prompt, state the entire displacement as an X,Y coordinate such as 2,3 or a polar coordinate such as 2<60. The command responds with the `Specify second point or <use first point as displacement>:` prompt. Because you've already specified all the necessary information, press Enter. AutoCAD or AutoCAD LT uses the first point you indicated as the displacement (the default) and moves the object. (Because the word *displacement* already implies the relative distance from the object, you do not use @, even if you have Dynamic Input on and set to Absolute coordinates.)

> **TIP**
>
> The MOVE command remembers the most recent displacement throughout a session. To move an object the same displacement as you just moved another object, press Enter at the `Specify base point or [Displacement]` `<Displacement>:` prompt. At the `Specify displacement <2.0000, 3.0000, 0.0000>:` prompt, you see in angled brackets the last displacement that you previously typed. Press Enter to move the object using this displacement.

- **Base point/second point method.** At the `Specify base point or [Displacement]` `<Displacement>:` prompt, pick a base point. This can be anywhere in your drawing but is usually on or near the object that you want to move. When you specify a base point, choose an object snap on the object or a nearby, related object for exact results. At the `Specify second point or <use first point as displacement>:` prompt, specify the distance and angle of movement either by picking a second point on the screen or by typing a relative coordinate. (If you have Dynamic Input on, set to the default of relative coordinates, you don't need to add the @ symbol before the coordinates.)

The displacement method requires less input and is simpler when you know the exact displacement so that you can type it in. The only disadvantage is that as soon as you type in the displacement, you sometimes see a confusing temporary drag line and copy of your object or objects. Ignore this display and press Enter. Your object or objects move as you specified. The base point/second point method works best when you want to move an object relative to another object on the screen.

You can use PolarSnap with the base point/second point method to move an object. Turn on PolarSnap and, if necessary, use the Drafting Settings dialog box to set the increment. If the polar distance is 0, you can set it to a new value. AutoCAD and AutoCAD LT use the Snap X spacing value that you specified in the Drafting Settings dialog box. At the first prompt, pick a point such as an object snap on the object. At the second prompt, drag the object in the desired direction. Use the tooltip to guide you and then click.

You can use drag-and-drop to move objects if you aren't too particular about where they end up. Here's how it works:

1. Pick an object.
2. Continue to pick as many objects as you want to move. They all show grips.
3. Pick any of the objects, but not on a grip. Keep the mouse button pressed until the cursor changes to an arrow with a small rectangle.
4. Drag the object(s) to any other location in your drawing.

For a little more control over the placement of your objects, you can use the Windows Clipboard. Pick the object(s) that you want to move. Right-click and choose Cut from the shortcut menu. Right-click a second time and choose Paste. At the prompt for an insertion point, you can pick with an object snap

9

or by typing coordinates. However, you can't control the base point (which is 0,0) as you can with the MOVE command, because it's always the lower-left corner of the object or of a bounding box around the object.

TIP

You can press and hold Ctrl as you use one of the arrow keys to nudge an object, that is, move it slightly in any of the four orthogonal directions.

ON THE WEB

The following exercise on moving objects has both Imperial and metric versions. The drawings used in the exercise, `ab09-b.dwg` and `ab09-b-metric.dwg`, are available from the Drawings download on the companion website.

STEPS: Moving Objects

1. Open `ab09-b.dwg` or `ab09-b-metric.dwg`, available from the Drawings download on the companion website.

2. Save the file as `ab09-02.dwg` or `ab09-02-metric.dwg` in your `AutoCAD Bible` folder. This drawing shows the plan of a bathroom. Each object is a *block,* a set of objects that you can select as one object. (Chapter 18 covers blocks.) Make sure that Object Snap mode is turned on. Set a running object snap for Intersection only.

3. Pick anywhere on the tub to select it. Notice the rollover highlighting before you click, and the grip and dashed lines that appear after you click. Choose Home tab ⇨ Modify panel ⇨ Move. Follow the prompts:

   ```
   Specify base point or [Displacement] <Displacement>: Move the cursor to
       the Intersection at ❶ in Figure 9.3 and click.
   Specify second point of displacement or <use first point as
       displacement>: Move the cursor to the Intersection at ❷ in Figure
       9.3 and click.
   ```

   The tub moves to the bottom-right corner of the bathroom.

4. Choose Move again. Follow the prompts:

   ```
   Select objects: Pick the sink.
   Select objects: ↵
   Specify base point or [Displacement] <Displacement>: 4'<0 (1200<0) ↵
   Specify second point of displacement or <use first point as
       displacement>: ↵
   ```

   The sink moves 4 feet (1200mm) to the right.

5. Click Snap Mode on the status bar to turn it on. Now, right-click Snap Mode. Choose PolarSnap On (unless it is already on, in which case it is unavailable). Click Polar Tracking on the status bar.

FIGURE 9.3

The bathroom plan

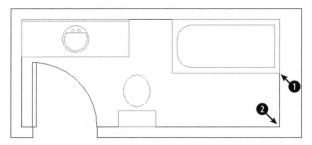

Thanks to Bill Wynn of New Windsor, Maryland, for this drawing.

6. Pick the toilet and choose Move again. At the `Specify base point or [Displacement]`
    `<Displacement>:` prompt, pick the intersection at the bottom-left corner of the toilet
    tank. At the `Specify second point or <use first point as displacement>:`
    prompt, move the toilet to the left until you see `0'-6"<180°` (150<180°) on the tooltip,
    and click. The toilet moves 6 inches (150mm) to the left. (If you can't get the right tooltip,
    check your polar angle settings.)

7. Save your drawing.

Copying objects

Copying is very similar to moving. In fact, the only difference is that AutoCAD or AutoCAD LT does not
remove the object from its original spot, so you end up with two objects rather than one.

To copy an object, select it and choose Home tab ⇨ Modify panel ⇨ Copy. Alternatively, choose Copy
and then select the object. When you start the COPY command and have selected an object, the command responds with the following prompt:

```
Specify base point or [Displacement/mOde] <Displacement>:
```

> **TIP**
>
> The COPY command lets you create a linear, non-associative array, using the Array option. It's an easy way to create a row
> of objects. I cover arrays in Chapter 10.

You now have two ways of specifying where to copy the object or objects:

*   **Displacement method.** At the `Specify base point or [Displacement/mOde]`
    `<Displacement>:` prompt, state the entire displacement as an X,Y coordinate such as 2,3 or
    a polar coordinate such as 2<60. The command responds with the `Specify second point`
    `or [Array] <use first point as displacement>:` prompt. Because you've already
    specified all the necessary information, press Enter. The command uses the first point that
    you indicated as the displacement (the default), copies the object, and ends the command.
    (Because the word *displacement* already implies the relative distance from the object, you do
    not use @, even if you have Dynamic Input on and set to Absolute coordinates.)

9

> **TIP**
>
> The COPY command remembers the most recent displacement throughout a session. To copy an object the same displacement as you just copied any object, press Enter at the `Specify base point or [Displacement/mOde]` `<Displacement>:` prompt. At the `Specify displacement <2.0000, 3.0000, 0.0000>:` prompt, you see in angled brackets the last displacement that you previously typed. Press Enter to copy the object using this displacement.

● **Base point/second point method.** At the `Specify base point or [Displacement/ mOde] <Displacement>:` prompt, pick a base point. This can be anywhere in your drawing. At the `Specify second point or [Array] <use first point as displacement>:` prompt, specify the distance and angle of movement either by picking a second point on the screen or by typing in a relative coordinate. (If you have Dynamic Input on and set to the default of relative coordinates, you don't need to add the @ symbol before the coordinates.)

If you use the base point/second point method, the COPY command continues to prompt you for additional copies. However, scripts and other routines use the earlier functioning, in which the command ends after creating one copy. After you make one copy, you see the `Specify second point or [Array/Exit/Undo] <Exit>:` prompt. Press Enter to use the Exit option and end the command.

> **NOTE**
>
> The COPYMODE system variable lets you specify if you want the COPY command to repeat or not. By default, as I just described, COPY repeats. Set the system variable's value to 1 to end the COPY command after one copy. You can also change how the COPY command works as you use it, with the Mode option. Choose either the Single or Multiple (the default) suboption.

If you've created more than one copy, the Undo option enables you to undo the last copy that you created. You can then continue to make more copies or end the command.

You can use PolarSnap to copy objects in the same way that you use it to move objects. For details, see the previous section. You can also use drag-and-drop to copy objects. Follow the steps in the previous section on moving objects, but press and hold the Ctrl key as you drag the object. Notice the plus sign in the cursor's rectangle. As also described in the previous section, you can use the Clipboard to copy and paste objects from one location in a drawing to another.

> **TIP**
>
> The Add Selected feature (ADDSELECTED command) lets you create a new object that has the same properties as an existing object. For example, you can create a new line that has the same color as an existing line. To use the Add Selected feature, select an existing object that has the properties you want, right-click in the drawing area, and choose Add Selected. Follow the prompts to create a new object.

> **ON THE WEB**
>
> The drawing used in the following exercise on copying objects, `ab09-c.dwg`, is available from the Drawings download on the companion website.

STEPS: Copying Objects

1. Open ab09-c.dwg, available from the Drawings download on the companion website.

2. Save the file as ab09-03.dwg in your AutoCAD Bible folder. This drawing shows part of an electrical schematic. Make sure that Object Snap is turned on. Set a running object snap for Endpoint only.

3. Use ZOOM Window to zoom into the area of the drawing marked ❶, as shown in Figure 9.4. This shows a 24-volt transformer.

FIGURE 9.4

The electrical schematic

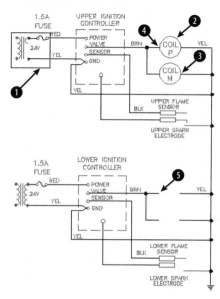

Thanks to Robert Mack of the Dexter Company, Fairfield, Iowa, for this drawing.

4. Note that three of the arcs that make up the right side of the transformer are missing. Pick the arc at ❶, as shown in Figure 9.5. Choose Home tab ➪ Modify panel ➪ Copy. Follow the prompts:

```
Specify base point or [Displacement/mOde] <Displacement>: Pick the
    endpoint at the top of the arc at ❷ (see Figure 9.5).
Specify second point or [Array] <use first point as displacement>: Pick
    the endpoint at the bottom of the first arc at ❸.
Specify second point or [Array/Exit/Undo] <Exit>: Pick the endpoint at
    the bottom of the second arc at ❹.
Specify second point or [Array/Exit/Undo] <Exit>: Pick the endpoint at
    the bottom of the third arc at ❺.
Specify second point or [Array/Exit/Undo] <Exit>: ⏎
```

FIGURE 9.5

Close-up of the transformer

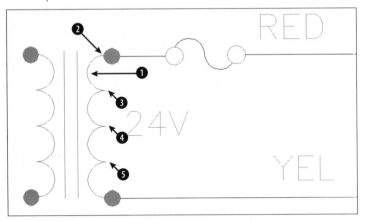

5. Use ZOOM Previous to return to your previous view.

6. Pick the circle at ❷, as shown in Figure 9.4 (which shows the entire schematic section). Note the grips. You also want to select the text inside the circles, but it's hard to see because of the grips. Press Esc to remove the grips.

7. Choose Copy again. Now select the circle at ❷, shown in Figure 9.4, again. This time no grips obscure the text. Separately pick both lines of text inside the circle.

8. Continuing to select objects to copy, select the circle at ❸, as shown in Figure 9.4. Also select the two lines of text inside the circle. Right-click to end the Select objects: prompt.

9. At the Specify base point or [Displacement/mOde] <Displacement>: prompt, pick the endpoint at ❹, as shown in Figure 9.4. At the Specify second point or [Array] <use first point as displacement>: prompt, pick the endpoint at ❺, as shown in Figure 9.4. Press Enter to end the COPY command. This action copies the two circles with the text.

10. Save your drawing.

Copying and moving objects from one drawing to another

If you use other Windows programs, you often cut, copy, and paste objects. In AutoCAD and AutoCAD LT, these commands are called CUTCLIP, COPYCLIP, and PASTECLIP. (The CLIP refers to the Windows Clipboard.) Although the MOVE and COPY commands provide more accuracy within one drawing, you can use the Clipboard to move and copy objects from one drawing to another.

You can copy objects from one drawing to another by using the drag-and-drop technique. The easiest way is to open both drawings and then choose View tab⇨ User Interface panel⇨ Tile Vertically. Select the object(s) that you want to copy, point to one of them, and drag them to the second drawing. However, you don't have much control over the exact placement of the new objects. From drawing to drawing, AutoCAD or AutoCAD LT copies the objects instead of moving them.

For more control over the placement of your objects, use the Windows Clipboard. A special feature, Copy with Base Point, gives you control over the placement of your objects. Follow these steps:

1. Pick the object(s) that you want to copy.
2. Right-click and choose Clipboard⇨Copy with Base Point from the shortcut menu.
3. At the `Specify base point:` prompt, specify a base point. An object snap is a good idea here. This action copies the object(s) to the Clipboard, including the base point.
4. Switch to the second drawing.
5. Right-click in the drawing area and choose Clipboard⇨Paste. At the prompt for an insertion point, specify the insertion point by picking, using an object snap, or typing coordinates. This action pastes the object.

To copy the object(s) to the same coordinates as the original drawing, in Step 5 choose Clipboard⇨Paste to Original Coordinates from the shortcut menu. AutoCAD or AutoCAD LT pastes the object(s) in the second drawing, matching the coordinates. Depending on your drawing, you may need to ZOOM and PAN to see the copy.

You cannot specify a base point for moving (cutting) an object, but you can specify the insertion point when you paste it. The lower-left extent of the selected object(s) is the base point.

 You can drag objects from a drawing into another application, such as a word-processing document. For more information on working with AutoCAD or AutoCAD LT and other applications, see Bonus Chapter 4.

Rotating objects

If your design changes or you drew at an incorrect angle, you may need to rotate one or more objects. You can easily rotate an object or objects around a base point that you specify. The base point is usually an object snap point on the object. To indicate the rotation, specify an angle of rotation. As explained in Chapter 4, by default, zero degrees is to the right, and degrees increase counterclockwise. (To change the default, choose Application Button⇨Drawing Utilities⇨Units.) By specifying a negative angle, you can rotate objects clockwise.

 To rotate an object, choose Home tab⇨Modify panel⇨Rotate. Alternatively, select an object and then choose Rotate. At the `Specify base point:` prompt, indicate the point around which you want to rotate. At the `Specify rotation angle or [Copy/Reference]:` prompt, type an angle at the command line.

> **TIP**
>
> Use the Copy option to create a copy of the original object. After you use this option, the same prompt returns so that you can specify a rotation angle. You end up with two objects, one at the original rotation angle and one at the new rotation angle.

The most recent rotation angle that you specify becomes the default for other rotations during the same session. For example, if you rotate an object 330°, the next time you rotate an object, the prompt appears as `Specify rotation angle or [Copy/Reference] <330>:.` Press Enter to rotate the object using the default rotation.

The purpose of the Reference option is to let you specify an absolute rotation angle for an object. For example, let's say you want to rotate a line, whose angle you don't know, to 45°. At the `Specify the reference angle <0>:` prompt, you type in an angle or specify an angle by picking two points. These can be object snap points on the object that specify the object's current angle; in the example, you would use the endpoints of the line. At the `Specify the new angle or [Points] <0>:` prompt, type or pick a new angle or specify two points to determine the new angle. You can also pick an object snap on another object in the drawing to indicate this new angle. In the example, you would enter **45** to rotate the line to 45°. You can use the Reference option to align the object with the X or Y axis or with another object in your drawing.

ON THE WEB

The drawing used in the following exercise on rotating objects, `ab07-03.dwg`, is available from the Results download on the companion website.

STEPS: Rotating Objects

1. Open `ab07-03.dwg`, available from the Results download on the companion website. If you did the exercise on ellipses in Chapter 7, you can open this drawing from your `AutoCAD Bible` folder.

2. Save the file as `ab09-04.dwg` in your `AutoCAD Bible` folder. This drawing shows a conference room, as shown in Figure 9.6.

3. Set Center, Quadrant, and Perpendicular running object snaps. Object Snap mode should be on. Polar Tracking should be off.

4. Pick the small elliptical table at the top-left corner of the conference room. Choose Home tab ⇨ Modify panel ⇨ Rotate.

FIGURE 9.6

The conference room

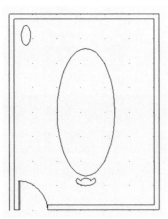

5. At the `Specify base point:` prompt, pick the top quadrant of the ellipse. At the `Specify rotation angle or [Copy/Reference]:` prompt, type **90** ↵. This action rotates the small table 90 degrees around the base point.

6. Click Snap Mode on the status bar to turn off snap.

7. To make a copy of the chair and rotate it at the same time, start the ROTATE command. At the `Select objects:` prompt, pick the arc that makes the back of the chair at the bottom of the drawing. The command responds `1 found`. Continue to pick the two lines that make the armrests and the arc that makes the front of the chair, making sure, each time, that you see the response `1 found`, for a total of 4. Press Enter to end the `Select objects:` prompt.

8. To copy and rotate the selected chair, follow the prompts:

   ```
   Specify base point: Use the Center object snap to select the center of
       the large table.
   Specify rotation angle or [Copy/Reference] <90>: Right-click and choose
       Copy.
   Specify rotation angle or [Copy/Reference] <90>: 180 ↵
   ```

9. Start the COPY command and select the four objects in the new chair. Press Enter to end object selection. Follow the prompts:

   ```
   Specify base point or [Displacement/mOde] <Displacement>: Use the Center
       object snap to select the center of the arc that makes up the back of
       the chair.
   Specify second point or [Array] <use first point as displacement>: Pick a
       point about a third of the way around the right side of the
       conference table.
   Specify second point or [Array/Exit/Undo] <Exit>: Pick a point about
       halfway around the right side of the conference table.
   Specify second point or [Array/Exit/Undo] <Exit>: Pick a point about two-
       thirds of the way around the right side of the conference table.
   Specify second point or [Array/Exit/Undo] <Exit>: ↵
   ```

10. Start the ROTATE command and select the four objects in the first of the three chairs (the top one) that you just created. Right-click to end object selection. At the `Specify base point:` prompt, pick the Center object snap of either arc of the chair. At the `Specify rotation angle or [Copy/Reference]:` prompt, move the cursor around, watch the image of the chair rotate, and click when the chair faces the angle of the table.

11. Repeat Step 10 for the second chair.

12. Start the ROTATE command and select the four objects in the last chair that you created by using the COPY command. Follow the prompts:

    ```
    Specify base point: Choose the Center object snap of either of the chair
        arcs.
    Specify rotation angle or [Copy/Reference]: Right-click and choose
        Reference from the shortcut menu.
    Specify the reference angle <0>: Use the Quadrant object snap to pick the
        back arc of the chair.
    Specify second point: Use the Quadrant object snap to pick the front arc
        of the chair.
    Specify the new angle or [Points] <0>: Use the Perpendicular object snap
        to choose the conference table next to the chair.
    ```

13. Save your drawing.

9

Scaling objects

Scaling, or resizing, objects is another common editing task in AutoCAD or AutoCAD LT. As with rotating objects, you specify a base point, usually an object snap on the object. The base point is the one point on the object that does not move or change as you scale the object. The most common way to resize an object is to specify a scale factor. The current object has a scale factor of 1. Therefore, to increase the size of the object, type in a number greater than 1. For example, a scale factor of 2 doubles the size of the object. To decrease the size of the object, type in a number less than 1. A scale factor of 0.25 creates an object one quarter of its previous size. The most recent scale factor that you specify becomes the default for other scaling operations during the same session.

Use the Copy option to create a copy of the original object. After you use this option, the same prompt returns so that you can specify a scale factor. You end up with two objects, one at the original scale and one at the new scale.

As with the ROTATE command, you can scale by using the Reference option to specify an absolute length. You specify the reference length, usually the current length of the object, by typing it in or using object snaps on the object. At the `Specify new length or [Points] <0'-1">:` prompt, you can type a new length or pick two points. You can use the Points option to match the size of another existing object.

To scale an object, choose Home tab ➪ Modify panel ➪ Scale, and select the object. Alternatively, you can select the object and choose Scale.

ON THE WEB

The drawing used in the following exercise on scaling objects, `ab09-d.dwg`, is available from the Drawings download on the companion website.

STEPS: Scaling Objects

1. Open `ab09-d.dwg`, available from the Drawings download on the companion website.

2. Save the file as `ab09-05.dwg` in your `AutoCAD Bible` folder. This drawing, shown in Figure 9.7, shows part of a valve that is manufactured in several sizes. In this exercise, you scale both views to represent a different-sized valve piece. Ensure that Object Snap is on. Set running object snaps for Quadrant and Endpoint.

3. Choose Home tab ➪ Modify panel ➪ Scale. At the `Select objects:` prompt, pick both circles in the top view (they're actually arcs because they're broken at the bottom) and the two short lines at the bottom of the circles. Press Enter to end object selection. Follow the prompts:

   ```
   Specify base point: Use the Quadrant object snap to pick the left
       quadrant of the inner circle.
   Specify scale factor or [Copy/Reference]: Right-click and choose
       Reference.
   Specify reference length <1.000>: Use the Quadrant object snap to pick
       the left quadrant of the inner circle again.
   Specify second point: Use the Quadrant object snap to pick the right
       quadrant of the inner circle.
   Specify new length or [Points] <1.000>: 1 ↵
   ```

   Because the distance between the two quadrants that you chose is 2.5 units, the SCALE command scales the objects to 40 percent (1 divided by 2.5).

FIGURE 9.7

The valve piece in two views

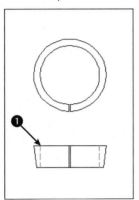

Thanks to Jerry Bottenfield of Clow Valve Company, Oskaloosa, Iowa, for this drawing.

4. Right-click and choose Repeat SCALE. Select all eight lines in the bottom view, including the green dashed lines. Be sure that you see 1 found each time. If necessary, use ZOOM Window to zoom in. Right-click to end object selection after you finish selecting the lines. Follow the prompts:

   Specify base point: *Use the Endpoint object snap at point* **❶** *in Figure 9.8.*
   Specify scale factor or [Copy/Reference]: **.4** ↵

5. Save your drawing. It should look like Figure 9.8.

FIGURE 9.8

The valve piece has now been scaled down.

9

Using the CHANGE command

The CHANGE command changes the endpoint of a line and the radius of a circle. Note that you can also use grips, and the Properties or Quick Properties palettes (these are covered in the next chapter) to change line endpoints and circle radii (among other object properties).

> **NOTE**
>
> You can use the CHANGE command to change text (which I cover in Chapter 13), the text and text properties of block attributes (not yet contained in a block), as well as the location and rotation of blocks (Chapter 18), but other newer commands do those jobs better. The Properties option of this command can change many object properties, but it's generally easier to use the Properties or Quick Properties palettes. However, these features of the CHANGE command can be useful when writing scripts or AutoLISP code, covered in the Bonus Chapters on the companion website.

To change an object, select it and type **change** ⏎ on the command line. Alternatively, you can type **change** ⏎ on the command line and select the object.

> **CAUTION**
>
> The CHANGE command works differently, depending on whether you select lines or circles. For this reason, it can give unexpected results if you choose lines and circles at the same time.

Changing lines

If you select one line, the CHANGE command changes the endpoint closest to where you picked the line. The command prompts you for a change point. When you pick the point, the command brings the endpoint of the line to that change point, as shown in Figure 9.9. You can use an object snap to specify the change point. If Ortho Mode is on, the line becomes orthogonal, bringing the endpoint of the line as close as possible to the change point that you specify, as shown in Figure 9.9.

FIGURE 9.9

Using the CHANGE command on one line

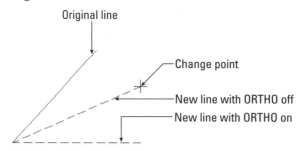

If you select more than one line, CHANGE works differently: It moves the nearest endpoints of all the lines to the change point so that all the lines meet at one point, as shown in Figure 9.10.

FIGURE 9.10

Using the CHANGE command on several lines. The original lines are shown as continuous. The new lines, after using the CHANGE command, are dashed.

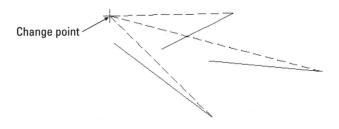

Change point

Changing circles

Changing the radius of a circle has the same result as scaling it. When you select a circle, the command prompts you for a change point. AutoCAD or AutoCAD LT resizes the circle so that it passes through the new point. You can also press Enter. You then get a prompt to enter a new radius.

If you select more than one circle, the command moves from circle to circle, letting you specify a new radius for each, one at a time. You can tell which circle is current because of its drag image, which lets you drag the size of the circle.

Selecting Objects

If you've been following through this chapter's exercises, you've probably thought it tedious to pick several objects one at a time. Imagine trying to individually pick every object in a drawing just to move all the objects one-half unit to the left! Of course, there is a better way. In fact, AutoCAD and AutoCAD LT offer many ways of selecting objects. Selected objects are called the *selection set* of objects.

Selecting objects after choosing a command

When you choose an editing command, you see the Select objects: prompt. This prompt has 18 options (16 if you are using AutoCAD LT) — all you could ever want for selecting objects — but these options are not shown on the command line or in the Dynamic Input prompt. To specify an option, type the option abbreviation. Because the Select objects: prompt repeats until you press Enter, you can combine options to select objects for any command. In the following list of options, the capitalized letters of the option are the abbreviation that you type (uppercase or lowercase letters work when you type) at the Select objects: prompt.

- **Window.** The Window option lets you pick two diagonal corners that define a window. All objects entirely within the window are selected. Figure 9.11 shows the process of picking the window on the left and the result on the right — to indicate that the selected objects are highlighted, they display dashed rather than continuous lines. As you move your mouse to specify the second diagonal corner, a blue transparent rectangle appears to help you preview which objects will be selected.

FIGURE 9.11

Selecting objects with a window. The window selects only objects that lie entirely within the window.

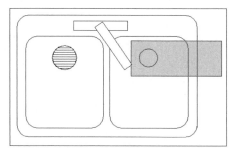 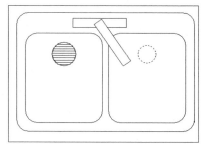

- **Last.** The Last option selects the last object created that is on a visible layer within the current view. (See Chapter 11 for more about layers.) Often you create an object and then want to move or copy it. In this situation, the Last option is an easy way to select the object that you just created.

- **Crossing.** Crossing enables you to pick two diagonal corners that define a window. All objects entirely or partly within the window are selected. As you move your mouse to specify the second diagonal corner, a green transparent rectangle appears to help you preview which objects will be selected. Figure 9.12 shows the process of picking the window on the left and the result on the right — the selected objects are highlighted.

- **BOX.** The BOX option is a combination of the Window and Crossing options. If you pick the two window corners from left to right, the selection functions as if you used the Window option. If you pick the two points from right to left, the selection functions as if you used the Crossing option. By default, you can select objects this way without specifying the BOX option. See the description of implied windowing later in this chapter.

- **ALL.** The ALL option selects all objects on thawed and unlocked layers in the drawing. (I discuss layers in Chapter 11.) Use the ALL option when you want to select everything, including objects that you can't currently see on the screen.

FIGURE 9.12

Selecting objects with a crossing window. The crossing window selects any objects that lie within or partly within the window.

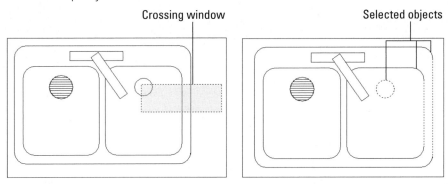

- **Fence.** The Fence option enables you to specify a series of temporary lines to select any object crossing the lines. Figure 9.13 shows the process of defining a selection fence on the left and the result on the right — the selected objects are highlighted.

FIGURE 9.13

Using a fence to select objects

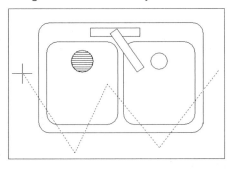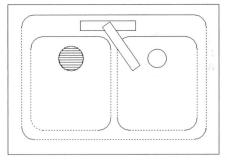

- **WPolygon.** The Window Polygon option (WPolygon) is like the Window option, except that you create a polygon rather than a rectangular window. This option selects all objects that lie entirely within the polygon.
- **CPolygon.** The Crossing Polygon option (CPolygon) is like the Crossing option, except that you create a polygon rather than a rectangular window. This option selects all objects that lie entirely or partly within the window.
- **Group.** The Group option selects a named group of objects. (Chapter 10 covers groups.) If you need to work regularly with a certain set of objects, you can place them in a group and then easily select them with one click.

- **Remove.** The Remove option enables you to deselect objects. After you use this option, all objects that you select are deselected and are therefore removed from the selection set. Use the Add option to once again select objects.

> **TIP**
>
> An alternative to using Remove to deselect objects is to press Shift and deselect objects by picking or implied windowing. Implied windowing is discussed later in this chapter.

- **Add.** The Add option sets the selection mode to add objects to the selection set. Use the Add option after using the Remove option to start selecting objects again.
- **Multiple.** The Multiple option turns off highlighting as you select objects. However, you cannot preview which objects are in the selection set.
- **Previous.** The Previous option automatically selects all objects that you selected for the previous command. Objects selected and edited by using grips are not remembered for this option. (The next chapter covers grips.)
- **Undo.** The Undo option deselects the object(s) selected at the last `Select objects:` prompt. (If you removed objects from the selection set at the last `Select objects:` prompt, Undo reselects them.)
- **AUto.** The AUto option combines picking with the BOX option. By default, you can select objects this way without specifying this option. See the description of implied windowing later in this chapter.
- **SIngle.** When you specify this option, you get another `Select objects:` prompt. You select objects by using any option, and then AutoCAD immediately ends the selection process. You don't have to press Enter.
- **SUbobject.** The SUbobject option is used only for 3D solids and allows you to select vertices, edges, and faces. For more information, see Chapter 24. (AutoCAD only)
- **Object.** This option ends the selection of subobjects so that you can select other objects. (AutoCAD only)

Cycling through objects

If you have many objects close together in a drawing, it can be hard to select the object or point that you want. You could always zoom in, but another trick is to use *selection cycling.*

When you hover the crosshairs over two or more overlapping objects, an icon with two overlapping rectangles appears near the crosshairs. When you click on a point where objects overlap, the Selection dialog box appears, listing the objects, so that you can easily select the one you want. Hover over an object's listing in the dialog box to see the corresponding object highlight in the drawing. To select an object, click its item in the dialog box. Continue selecting other objects or use an editing command to work with the selected object.

 Click the Selection Cycling button on the status bar to turn on or off the display of the Selection dialog box. Right-click the Selection Cycling button and choose Settings to control the display of the Selection dialog box.

> **TIP**
> At the `Select objects:` prompt, place the cursor over the area where more than one object overlaps. Then hold down the Shift key and press the Spacebar. One object is highlighted. If it is not the one you want, with the Shift key still down, press the Spacebar again to cycle through the objects. When the object that you want is highlighted, pick the object. You can continue to select other objects or end object selection by pressing Enter.

Selecting objects before choosing a command

If you select objects before choosing a command, your options are more limited than if you choose a command first. Nevertheless, you have enough flexibility for most situations. The reason for the limitation is that the `Command:` prompt is active, and anything that you might type at the keyboard to indicate a selection option could be confused with a command. You can pick the object to highlight it, use implied windowing, or use the SELECT command on the command line to select objects in advance.

> **TIP**
> To select all objects, choose Home tab ⇨ Utilities panel ⇨ Select All, or press Ctrl+A. Choosing Select All or pressing Ctrl+A cancels the current command, so you need to use these options before you start a command.

The purpose of the SELECT command is simply to select objects. This command then saves these objects for use with the Previous selection option. Choose an editing command and type **p** ↵ at the `Select objects:` prompt to select the objects that you selected with the SELECT command.

> **TIP**
> The SELECTSIMILAR command allows you to select objects in a drawing that are similar to a selected object or objects. Select one or more objects, then right-click and choose Select Similar from the shortcut menu. The objects remain selected when you then choose an editing command, so you can immediately apply that command to the selected objects. Use the Settings option to control which object properties AutoCAD uses to compare the selected objects with others that are in the drawing. I cover object properties in Chapter 11.

Implied windowing

Implied windowing is equivalent to the Auto selection option discussed earlier in this chapter. By default, implied windowing is always active. As a result, implied windowing is useful for selecting objects before or after choosing a command. By carefully choosing which way you create a selection window, you determine how you select objects:

- **From left to right.** If the first window corner is to the left of the second one, you create a regular selection window. The window selects all objects entirely within the window.

- **From right to left.** If the first window corner is to the right of the second one, you create a crossing window. The crossing window selects all objects that lie entirely or partially within the window.

9

STEPS: Selecting Objects

1. Open ab09-e.dwg, available from the Drawings download on the companion website, as shown in Figure 9.14.

2. Save the file as ab09-06.dwg in your AutoCAD Bible folder. Make sure that Object Snap mode is on. Set running object snaps for Endpoint and Perpendicular.

3. Draw a line from ❶ to ❷, as shown in Figure 9.14. You will use this later to illustrate the Last selection option.

FIGURE 9.14

A kitchen floor plan

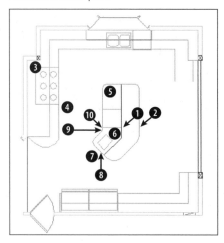

4. Type **select** ⏎.

5. To select the six-burner stovetop, pick a point near ❸, being careful that the pickbox at the intersection of the crosshairs doesn't touch any object. Transparently zoom in and back out, if necessary. Then move the mouse to ❹, again making sure not to pick on any object, and pick again. The objects that you have chosen appear dashed to indicate that they have been selected.

6. To select the last object that was created — the line drawn in Step 1 — type **l** ↵. It now appears dashed.

7. Turn off Object Snap mode. To select the interior lines on the kitchen's island by using a fence, type **f** ↵. Then pick points ❺, ❻, and ❼. Press Enter to end the fence.

8. Type **r** ↵ at the Select objects: prompt (the prompt changes to Remove objects:) and pick the line at ❽ to remove the external island line picked in Step 7. At this point, all the selected items should be dashed, as shown in Figure 9.15.

FIGURE 9.15

Kitchen floor plan with all selected items shown with dashed lines

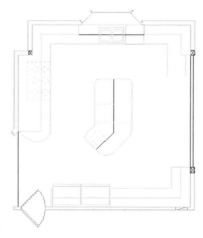

9. Press Enter to complete the command.

10. Turn on Object Snap mode. Start the MOVE command. At the Specify base point or [Displacement] <Displacement>: prompt, pick the endpoint at ❾, as shown in Figure 9.14. At the Specify second point or <use first point as displacement>: prompt, pick the endpoint at ❿. All the objects move.

11. Save your drawing.

Customizing the selection process

You can customize the way that you select objects. To do so, choose Application Button⇨Options to open the Options dialog box and click the Selection tab, as shown in Figure 9.16. The next few sections describe the settings on the left side of this tab.

FIGURE 9.16

The Selection tab of the Options dialog box

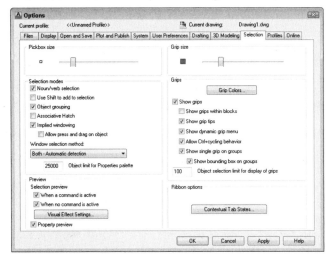

Pickbox Size

The pickbox is the box that you see at the intersection of the crosshairs when selecting (or picking) objects. The Pickbox Size area lets you set the size of the pickbox.

> **NOTE**
>
> If Noun/verb Selection is off and grips are disabled, no pickbox appears at the intersection of the crosshairs until you start an editing command and the command line displays the `Select objects:` prompt. However, if either Noun/verb Selection or grips are on, the pickbox is always at the crosshairs, letting you select objects at any time.

Noun/verb selection

As you already know, the editing process consists of two parts: using a command, such as COPY or MOVE, and selecting objects. In AutoCAD/AutoCAD LT lingo, *noun* means an object in your drawing. *Verb* refers to a command because a command acts on an object. This option lets you decide whether you want to be able to select objects before starting a command.

In Windows programs, you typically select objects before starting a command. For example, if you're using Microsoft Word and want to erase a sentence, you select the sentence first, and then press Del.

By default, Noun/verb selection is active. With this option enabled, you can select objects first, without giving up the ability to choose commands first. This gives you maximum flexibility. Most commands let you choose an object first, but a few don't because they require a specific order for selecting objects. For those commands, the selected object is ignored and you just follow the prompts.

The advantage of selecting objects first is that, when you switch between Windows programs, you don't have to change habitual ways of selecting objects. The disadvantage of selecting objects first is that some AutoCAD and AutoCAD LT commands don't let you select objects first, which can be confusing. Also, when you select objects first, grips appear — sometimes obscuring the objects that you need to select.

Use Shift to Add to Selection

The Use Shift to Add to Selection option is not checked by default. In AutoCAD and AutoCAD LT, you often select more than one object at a time for editing. As a result, when you select a second object, the first object stays selected. If you check the Use Shift to Add to Selection option, then after selecting one object, you must hold down Shift to select any additional objects.

Object grouping

Groups are sets of objects that you name. Creating groups of objects is discussed in the next chapter. If object grouping is on (the default) when you select one object in a group, all the objects in the group are automatically selected.

Associative Hatch

The Associative Hatch option selects boundary objects when you select a hatch within the boundary. This option is off by default. Checking this option is equivalent to setting the PICKSTYLE system variable to 2. Chapter 16 covers hatches.

Implied windowing

Implied windowing means that if you pick any point not on an object, AutoCAD or AutoCAD LT assumes that you want to create a selection window. By default, this option is on. This is controlled by the PICKAUTO system variable; the default value is 1. You can then pick the opposite corner to select objects. If you pick the corners from left to right, you get a standard selection window. If you pick the corners from right to left, you get a crossing window.

This option applies only when you start a command and see the Select objects: prompt. If you turn this option off, you can still enter the Window or Crossing selection options manually (by typing **c** ↵ or **w** ↵). When selecting objects before starting the command, implied windowing is always on.

Allow Press and Drag on Object

One of the ways to select objects is to create a window that includes a number of objects. If the Allow Press and Drag on Object option is checked, you need to pick at one corner of the window and, without releasing the pick button, drag the cursor to the diagonally opposite corner. This type of action is typical of Windows programs. By default, this option is off, which means that to create a window, you pick at one corner of the window, release the mouse button, and pick again at the diagonally opposite corner. This setting does not affect the ZOOM Window operation, which always requires two separate picks, one for each corner. Implied windowing must be enabled first before you can select this option.

9

When you set the PICKAUTO system variable to 2, you can click on an object, but drag the cursor to create a window for selection. In other words, if after clicking on an object, you move the cursor without releasing the mouse button, you can use a window to select objects instead of selecting just the object under the cursor.

Selection Preview

The Selection Preview option applies to rollover highlighting and the transparent selection rectangle. You can specify whether you want these effects to appear only if a command is active or even when no command is active (when you are selecting objects before choosing a command).

Click the Visual Effect Settings button to open the Visual Effect Settings dialog box, where you can specify the following settings:

- **Rollover highlighting.** In the Selection Preview Effect section, you can control the highlighting of faces (of 3D objects) and lines. Highlighting makes lines thicker, dashed, or both. The default is to show both. Click the Advanced Options button to exclude certain types of objects from the rollover highlighting effect.

- **Selection effect.** In the Area Selection Effect section, you can turn the effect off, change the colors for the window (as well as crossing rectangles and polygons), and change the opacity percentage.

 The Ribbon Options section of the Selection tab lets you customize when certain Ribbon tabs appear, based on the type of object selected or the active command. I cover this topic in Bonus Chapter 10.

Summary

All drawings need to be edited, either as part of the drawing process or to make corrections. In this chapter, you read about:

- Erasing objects
- Moving objects
- Copying objects
- Rotating objects
- Scaling objects
- Using the CHANGE command on lines and circles
- The many ways of selecting objects
- Customizing the object-selection features

The next chapter covers the more advanced editing commands and options.

Editing Your Drawing with Advanced Tools

IN THIS CHAPTER

Using advanced copying and moving commands: MIRROR, ARRAY, OFFSET, and ALIGN

Using advanced resizing commands: TRIM, EXTEND, STRETCH, and LENGTHEN

Using construction commands: BREAK, JOIN, CHAMFER, and FILLET

Building a revision cloud

Using a wipeout to hide objects

Editing an object's properties

Editing objects with grips

Editing objects with the Quick Properties palette

This chapter completes the discussion, started in the preceding chapter, of geometric editing commands — covering the more complex commands you can use to refine the details of your drawing. These commands enable you to copy, move, resize, break, and cover objects, as well as construct corners. I also discuss grips, which make it easy to move, copy, mirror, rotate, scale, and stretch objects, and I explain how to use the Quick Properties palette and the Properties palette to edit objects. In the Chapter 10 Addendum, I discuss three ways to control the selection of objects — groups, filters, and the Quick Select feature as well as how to constrain objects using parameters.

> **NOTE**
> Although you can use the editing tools that I describe in this chapter in a 3D environment, this chapter assumes that you are working in a 2D environment, using the default Drafting & Annotation workspace. (AutoCAD LT doesn't offer a 3D environment.) To make sure that you're in a 2D environment, set the workspace to Drafting & Annotation (from the Workspace Switching list on the Quick Access toolbar or the status bar) and set the visual style to 2D Wireframe (type vscurrent and choose the 2D Wireframe option). If you still see the Z axis on the UCS icon, choose View tab ⇨ Views panel ⇨ Views drop-down list ⇨ Top. Another method is to set the workspace to Drafting & Annotation, and then start a new drawing based on the default `acad.dwt` or `acadlt.dwt` template.

Copying and Moving Objects

Three commands enable you to copy objects in very specific ways. MIRROR creates a mirror image. ARRAY copies objects in a rectangular or circular pattern. OFFSET creates parallel objects. Although these commands make copies of objects, they produce a result that would be difficult or impossible to produce simply by using the COPY command. The ALIGN and 3DALIGN commands move objects by aligning them with other objects in the drawing.

Mirroring objects

Many drawings have symmetrical elements. Often, especially in mechanical drawings, you can create one half or one quarter of a model and complete it simply by mirroring what you have drawn.

 To mirror, select an object or objects and then choose Home tab ⇨ Modify panel ⇨ Mirror. Alternatively, start the MIRROR command first and then select an object or objects.

The command prompts you for the first and second points of the mirror line. This is an imaginary line across which the command creates the mirrored object. The length of the line is irrelevant — only its start point and direction are important.

> **TIP**
> Most mirror lines are orthogonal. Therefore, after you specify the first mirror point, you can turn on Ortho Mode and move the mouse in the direction of the second point. You can then quickly pick the second point. Polar tracking can also easily guide you to specify an orthogonal mirror line.

The command then asks if you want to erase the source objects. The source objects are the objects you have selected to mirror. If you want to keep them, type **n** ↵ or press Enter. You keep the source objects when you're building a symmetrical model and want the mirror image to be added to the original object(s). Type **y** ↵ when you want to edit an object (change its orientation) so that only the mirror image is retained in the drawing.

> **ON THE WEB**
> The drawing that you need for the following exercise on mirroring objects, ab07-02.dwg, is available from the Results download on the companion website

STEPS: Mirroring Objects

1. Open ab07-02.dwg, available from the Results download on the companion website. If you completed the exercise on arcs in Chapter 7, you can open this drawing from your AutoCAD Bible folder.

2. Save the file as ab10-01.dwg in your AutoCAD Bible folder. Make sure Object Snap mode is on. Set a running object snap for Intersection only.

3. Choose Home tab ⇨ Modify panel ⇨ Erase. At the Select objects: prompt, pick the line and two arcs to the bottom right of the two centerlines, and then press Enter. The resulting model should look like Figure 10.1.

4. Choose Home tab ⇨ Modify panel ⇨ Mirror. At the `Select objects:` prompt, pick the remaining exterior line and two arcs, and press Enter.

5. At the `Specify first point of mirror line:` prompt, pick intersection ❶, as shown in Figure 10.1. At the `Specify second point of mirror line:` prompt, pick intersection ❷.

6. The command prompts `Erase source objects? [Yes/No] <N>:` Press Enter to accept the default, No.

FIGURE 10.1

A partially completed mounting plate

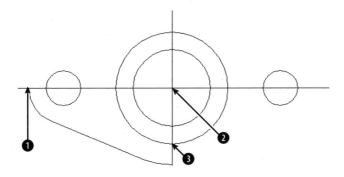

7. Start the MIRROR command again. At the `Select objects:` prompt, type **p** ↵ to pick the original lines. Then pick the new exterior line and two arcs, and press Enter.

8. At the `Specify first point of mirror line:` prompt, pick intersection ❷. At the `Specify second point of mirror line:` prompt, pick intersection ❸. Press Enter again at the `Erase source objects? [Yes/No] <N>:` prompt.

9. The command completes the mounting plate. Save your drawing. It should look like Figure 10.2.

FIGURE 10.2

The completed mounting plate

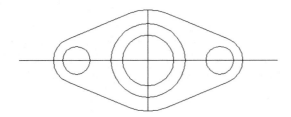

10

Using the ARRAY command

The ARRAY command creates a rectangular, polar (circular), or path-guided pattern by copying the object(s) you select as many times as you specify. The ARRAY command is a powerful drawing tool. It can quickly create large numbers of objects, thus saving a huge amount of time and effort.

Creating a rectangular array

A rectangular array creates a grid of rows and columns of one or more objects. Figure 10.3 shows an existing rectangular array on the right and the process of creating a rectangular array on the left. To create a rectangular array, follow these steps:

FIGURE 10.3

After selecting objects for a rectangular array, you see a 4 x 3 array.

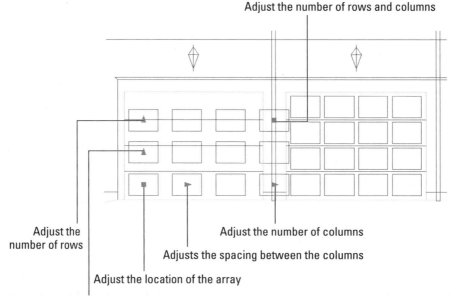

Adjust the number of rows and columns

Adjust the
number of rows

Adjust the number of columns

Adjusts the spacing between the columns

Adjust the location of the array

Adjust the spacing between the rows

Thanks to Henry Dearborn, AIA, Fairfield, Iowa, for this drawing.

NEW FEATURE

When you start to create a polar array and select the object and the array's center, AutoCAD automatically displays an initial rectangular array of four columns and three rows.

1. Choose Home tab ⇨ Modify panel ⇨ Array drop-down menu ⇨ Rectangular Array to start the ARRAYRECT command.

> **NOTE**
>
> You can also type array ↵ on the command line, and then choose one of the options to specify a rectangular, path, or polar array.

2. At the `Select objects:` prompt, select the object(s) you want to array and press Enter to end selection. You can choose the objects before starting the command if you want.

3. You immediately see a 4-column x 3-row array. At the `Select grip to edit array or [ASsociative/Base point/COUnt/Spacing/COLumns/Rows/Levels/eXit] <eXit>:` prompt, you can use one of three ways to specify the number of, and the distance between, the rows and columns:

   - **Multi-functional grips.** Use the grips, labeled in Figure 10.3, to adjust the number of rows and columns and the spacing.

   - **Options.** Use the Count option to specify the number of rows and columns or use the Rows or Columns options. You can also use the Angle option to rotate the array.

   - **Array Creation tab.** You can specify the number of rows and columns and the spacing in the panels of the Array Creation tab that appears when you are creating an array.

4. Press Enter to complete the array and exit the command or use one of the following options:

   - **Associative.** By default, arrays are associative. Use this option to toggle on and off the associativity of the array.

   - **Base point.** You can specify a base point as the basis for the rest of the array. Usually, you would accept the default point on the object you are arraying, but you can choose any other point.

   - **Levels.** This option lets you specify the number of, and spacing for, levels (for a 3D array).

To edit an array, select the array. The Array tab appears and you see the same multi-functional grips on the array, as shown in Figure 10.4.

FIGURE 10.4

When you select an array, you can edit it using grips or the Array Creation tab.

You can edit the properties of a rectangular array in the following ways:

- **Move.** Hover the cursor over the base point's square grip. This is usually on the object you selected to array. You see a menu with two options — Move and Level Count. Choose the Move option, and then specify the new location for that base point.

- **Change the row and column count.** Hover the cursor over the square grip diagonally opposite the base point grip and choose the Row and Column Count option. Then drag the cursor away from the base point to add rows and/or columns, just as you would while creating the

10

array. The arrow grips furthest from the base point grip allow you to individually adjust the number of rows and columns in the drawing. Alternatively, use the top text box of the Columns and Rows panels on the Array Creation tab.

- **Change the spacing between rows or columns.** Click the arrow grip near the base point grip — one controls rows and the other controls columns. Then type the distance. Alternatively, use the middle row of text boxes in the Columns or Rows panel on the Array Creation tab.

- **Change the total width and height of the array.** Hover the cursor over the square grip diagonally opposite the base point grip and choose the Total Row and Column Spacing option. Then drag to expand the entire width and/or height of the array. When you hover the cursor over arrow grips furthest from the base point grip, you can choose the Total Column Spacing and Total Row Spacing options to adjust the overall spacing for columns or rows on screen. Alternatively, use the bottom row of text boxes of the Columns or Rows panels on the Array Creation tab.

Use the Levels panel for a 3D array. For more information, see Chapter 24. The Base Point button lets you choose a new location for the base point, but doesn't move the array itself.

You can also edit the objects in the array using the Options panel of the Array Creation tab. To edit an object in the array and apply the change to all objects in the array, follow these steps:

1. Select a rectangular array.
2. Go to Array Creation tab ⇨ Options panel ⇨ Edit Source.
3. At the `Select item in array:` prompt, select any of the array items.
4. You see a dialog box explaining that you can edit source objects in an Array Editing state and that you should enter **ARRAYCLOSE** to exit that state. Click OK.
5. All items except the item you selected are now dashed. Click the item you selected and edit it using grips or editing commands. The changes appear on all the array items.
6. Enter **arrayclose** ↵ and click Yes to save your changes. Alternatively, from the Edit Array panel, choose Save Changes.

To replace one item in an array with an existing object elsewhere in the drawing, but leave the rest of the objects in the array unchanged, follow these steps:

1. Select a rectangular array.
2. Go to Array Creation tab ⇨ Options panel ⇨ Replace Item.
3. At the `Select replacement objects:` prompt, select the new object(s) and end selection.
4. At the `Select base point of replacement objects or [Key Point] <centroid>:` prompt, select a base point, usually on the replacement object, press Enter to use the centroid, or use the Key Point option.

> **NOTE**
>
> The key point is a constraint on the source object that you specify as a base point. When you edit the source object, the base point of the array stays on the key point that you specified.

5. At the `Select an item in the array to replace or [Source objects]:` prompt, select the object in the array that you want to replace. You can select multiple objects. Press Enter to end object selection.

6. Press Enter to exit the ARRAYEDIT command.

> **CAUTION**
>
> When you use the Edit Source button, you execute the ARRAYEDIT command, which persists until you use the ARRAYCLOSE command — type it on the command line — and choose to save or discard the changes you made. Alternatively, you can choose one of the options (Save Changes or Discard Changes) from the Edit Array panel. If you forget to use the ARRAYCLOSE command in one of these ways, every object that you draw will become an array!

Arraying objects around a center point (polar array)

A polar array creates copies of one or more objects arrayed in a circle around a center point. An example of a polar array is shown in Figure 10.5.

FIGURE 10.5

The pulley was drawn with one spoke, as shown on the left. A polar array created the additional spokes.

Adjust the angle between the items

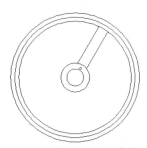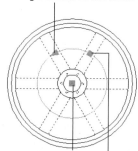

Adjusts the location of the array

Stretches the radius; also specifies
the row and level counts

Thanks to Robert Mack of the Dexter Company, Fairfield, Iowa, for this drawing.

> **NEW FEATURE**
>
> When you start to create a polar array and select the object and the array's center, AutoCAD automatically displays an initial polar array of six objects.

10

To create a polar array, follow these steps:

1. Choose Home tab ⇨ Modify panel ⇨ Array drop-down menu ⇨ Polar Array to start the ARRAYPOLAR command. At the prompt, select the object or objects that you want to array. You can choose the objects first if you want.

2. At the `Specify center point of array or [Base point/Axis of rotation]:` prompt, specify the center of the array around which to array the selected objects. You immediately see a polar array with six copies of the object you selected.

3. At the prompt, you can choose one of three ways to configure the polar array:

   - **Multi-functional grips.** Use the grips, labeled in Figure 10.3, to adjust the number of rows (around the center) and levels, stretch the radius, move the array, and change the angle between the objects.

   - **Options.** Use the command options to set the base point for the array, as well as specify the number of rows, number of items, angle between the items, and the number of levels. You can also rotate the items in the array.

   - **Array Creation tab.** You can specify all the parameters in the panels of the Array Creation tab that appears when you are creating an array.

4. Press Enter to accept the array and exit the command or use one of the options to make further changes.

You can use the Base Point option to specify which point on the last object selected AutoCAD or AutoCAD LT uses to array the objects. The command makes a calculation of the distance from the center point of the array to a base point on the last object selected. Otherwise, the command uses a default point based on the type of object selected. If you are arraying more than one object, you may not obtain the result you want without specifying the base point. Even for one object, you may want to change the base point that is used. Editing a polar array is similar to editing a rectangular array, described just previously.

TIP
The COPY command has an Array option that lets you create a linear array. You can specify a second point to set a distance between objects or use the Fit option to fit the copied objects between the first and last copies of the object. I cover the COPY command in Chapter 9.

ON THE WEB
The drawing that you need for the following exercise on arraying objects, ab10-a.dwg, is available from the Drawings download on the companion website.

STEPS: Arraying Objects

1. Open ab10-a.dwg, available from the companion website.

2. Save the file as ab10-02.dwg in your AutoCAD Bible folder. It looks like Figure 10.6. Object Snap mode should be on. Set Center and Intersection running object snaps.

FIGURE 10.6

A partially completed mounting bracket

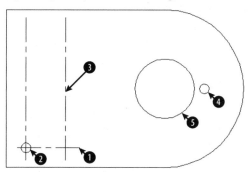

3. Choose Home tab ⇨ Modify panel ⇨ Array drop-down menu ⇨ Rectangular Array.

4. At the `Select objects:` prompt, pick the horizontal centerline **1**, shown in Figure 10.6, and then press Enter.

5. At the `Select grip to edit array or [Associative/Base point/COUnt/Spacing/COLumns/Rows/Levels/eXit] <eXit>:` prompt, on the Array Creation tab, in the Rows text box of the Rows panel, type **4** ⏎. In the Columns text box of the Columns panel, type **1**.

6. Note that the Between text box in the Rows panel has a value of 1, which is what you want. (Otherwise, you would type a different value there.) You should see a total of four horizontal lines, as shown in Figure 10.7.

7. Press Enter to accept the array.

8. To add the holes to the pattern, repeat the ARRAYRECT command.

9. At the `Select objects:` prompt, pick circle **2**, shown in Figure 10.6, and then press Enter. You see a 4 x 3 array.

10. Click the arrow grip at the lower-right corner of the array, drag to the left until you see two columns, and click.

11. Click the arrow grip at the upper-left corner of the array, drag upward until you see four rows, and click.

12. On the command line, click the Spacing option, and then click the Unit Cell option. At the `Specify first corner point of unit cell:` prompt, pick the lower-left intersection of the lines (the center of the circle at **2**). At the `Specify opposite corner:` prompt, pick the intersection of the right vertical centerline and the second horizontal centerline near **3**, as shown in Figure 10.6.

13. Press Enter to accept the array.

14. To create a six-hole bolt circle, pick hole **4**, as shown in Figure 10.6.

15. Choose Home tab ⇨ Modify panel ⇨ Array drop-down menu ⇨ Polar Array.

16. At the `Specify center point of array or [Base point/Axis of rotation]:` prompt, pick the center of the large circle at **5**, as shown in Figure 10.6.

10

17. Because AutoCAD's default is to create a six-item polar array, you don't have to do anything more! Just press Enter to accept the array.

18. Save your drawing. It should look like Figure 10.7.

FIGURE 10.7

The completed mounting bracket

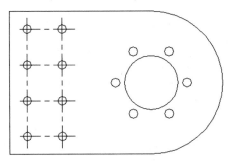

Arraying objects along a path

You can array one or more objects along a line, polyline, 3D polyline, arc, circle, ellipse, spline, or helix. Figure 10.8 shows a bush arrayed along a spline path, representing a walkway.

FIGURE 10.8

You can array an object along a path.

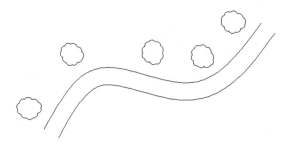

To array an object along a path, follow these steps:

1. Choose Home tab ⇨ Modify panel ⇨ Array drop-down menu ⇨ Path Array.

2. At the `Select objects:` prompt, select the object(s) you want to array and press Enter to end selection. You can choose the objects before starting the command if you want.

3. At the `Select path curve:` prompt, select the object you want to use as the path.

4. At the `Select grip to edit array or [ASsociative/Method/Base point/Tangent direction/Items/Rows/Levels/Align items/Z direction/eXit] <eXit>:` prompt, you can choose one of three ways to specify the array:

   - **Multi-functional grips.** Use the square grip to adjust the number of rows (offset from the path) and levels or move the array. Use the arrow grip to change the distance between the items.

   - **Options.** Use the command's options to set the base point for the array, as well as to specify the number of rows, number of items, and number of levels. You can also align the items in the array or change the Z direction of the levels. The Tangent Direction option lets you specify the orientation of the first arrayed item relative to the path.

   - **Array Creation tab.** You can specify all the parameters in the panels of the Array Creation tab that appears when you are creating an array.

5. Press Enter to accept the array.

NEW FEATURE

The Method option lets you choose between Measure (keeps the distance between objects if you modify the path) and Divide (keeps the number of objects if you modify the path).

 In Chapter 12, I cover the DIVIDE and MEASURE commands, which similarly place a block along a distance, either dividing the spacing evenly or specifying the distance between the blocks.

To edit a path array, use the same procedure described earlier for editing rectangular arrays. The Array tab contains options to align items and change the Z direction.

Offsetting objects

The OFFSET command creates lines or curves parallel to one existing object. The beauty of this command is apparent when you start to create complex objects, such as polylines, which are covered in Chapter 16. Polygons and rectangles are *polylines,* which means that all the line segments are one object. For example, using OFFSET, you can create concentric polygons in one step. Figure 10.9 shows two concentric polygons. The outside polygon was created with the POLYGON command, and the inside polygon was created by using OFFSET.

FIGURE 10.9

Use the OFFSET command to create concentric polygons.

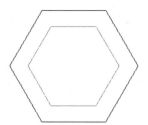

10

To offset an object, choose Home tab ➪ Modify panel ➪ Offset.

The command responds with the following list of settings and prompt:

```
Current settings: Erase source=No Layer=Source OFFSETGAPTYPE=0
Specify offset distance or [Through/Erase/Layer] <Through>:
```

The settings show how the OFFSET command's options will function. Set the Erase option to Yes to erase the selected object and leave only the offset. Use the Layer option to specify if you want the new object to be on the same layer as the source object or on the current layer.

The OFFSET command offers two ways to specify the offset:

- If you type an offset distance, the command responds with the `Select object to offset or [Exit/Undo] <Exit>:` prompt. You can select one object. Then the `Specify point on side to offset or [Exit/Multiple/Undo] <Exit>:` prompt appears. Pick a point to indicate on which side of the object you want to create the offset copy. The command creates the offset and continues to show the `Select object to offset or [Exit/Undo] <Exit>:` prompt so that you can offset other objects by using the same offset distance. Press Enter to exit the command.

- If you want to indicate a *through point* (a point that the offset passes through, such as an object snap on another object), type **t** ↵ or right-click and choose Through from the shortcut menu. The command displays the `Select object to offset or [Exit/Undo] <Exit>:` prompt. Pick one object. At the `Specify through point or [Exit/Multiple/Undo] <Exit>:` prompt, pick a point through which you want the offset to go to create the offset.

Use the Undo option if you don't like the result of the offset. After you offset an object, the prompt repeats so that you can offset additional objects. Press Enter to end the command.

STEPS: Using the OFFSET Command

1. Open ab10-b.dwg, available from the companion website.

2. Save the file as ab10-03.dwg in your AutoCAD Bible folder. It looks like Figure 10.10. Set a running object snap for Center, and turn on Object Snap mode.

FIGURE 10.10

A tension arm for a commercial dryer

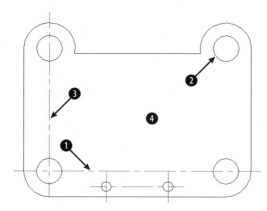

Thanks to Robert Mack of the Dexter Company, Fairfield, IA for this drawing.

3. Choose Home tab ⇨ Modify panel ⇨ Offset. Follow the prompts:

```
Specify offset distance or [Through/Erase/Layer] <Through>: ↵ or specify
    the Through option if it does not appear as the default.
Select object to offset or [Exit/Undo] <Exit>: Pick ❶ in Figure 10.10.
Specify through point or [Exit/Multiple/Undo] <Exit>: Pick the center
    of ❷.
    Select object to offset or [Exit/Undo] <Exit>: ↵
```

This action copies the centerline through the upper circles.

4. Repeat the OFFSET command. At the Specify offset distance or [Through/Erase/Layer] <Through>: prompt, type **4-19/64** ↵. Pick the centerline ❸ at the Select object to offset or [Exit/Undo] <Exit>: prompt, and then click near ❹ at the Specify point on side to offset or [Exit/Multiple/Undo] <Exit>: prompt. Press Enter to end the command. The vertical centerline appears 4-19/64 units to the right of the original.

5. Save your drawing. It should look like Figure 10.11.

10

FIGURE 10.11

The completed tension arm

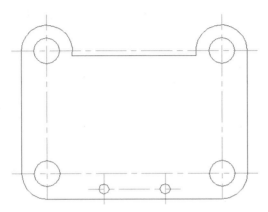

Aligning objects

The ALIGN and 3DALIGN commands let you move and rotate an object or objects in one procedure. They are useful in both 2D and 3D environments. By specifying where selected points on an object move, you can align the object with other objects in your drawing, as shown in Figure 10.12. You can align in two ways:

- **ALIGN command.** This command prompts you by point. You specify the first source point (on the object you're aligning), and then the first destination point (where that source point will end up). Then you specify the second set of source and destination points. For 3D, you go on to a third set. Finally, you can scale the selected object to match the destination points.

- **3DALIGN command.** This command prompts you by object. You specify two or three points on the source object, and then the points at the destination location. As you specify destination points, you see the object move and align in real time. You cannot scale the object. See Chapter 24 for an exercise that uses the 3DALIGN command in 3D editing.

AUTOCAD ONLY

AutoCAD LT doesn't include the 3DALIGN command.

Aligning requires several steps. Even so, it can save you time when you need to move and rotate at the same time, especially if you don't know the rotation angle that you need.

FIGURE 10.12

Aligning a door with a wall

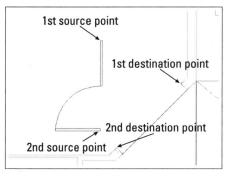
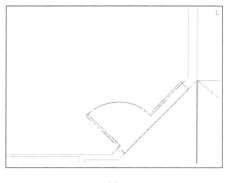

Before   After

Using the ALIGN command

If you prefer to think, "This point will go here and that point will go there," use the ALIGN command. You can also scale the object that you're aligning. Choose Home tab ⇨ Modify panel (expanded) ⇨ Align and select an object or objects. You can also select the object or objects first. In AutoCAD LT, type **align** at the command line to align objects. Then follow these steps:

1. The prompt asks for the first source point. Specify a point, usually an object snap on the object that you want to move.

2. The prompt asks for the first destination point. Specify the point where you want the first source point to end up.

3. The prompt asks for the second source point. If you press Enter, AutoCAD simply moves the selected objects. To continue to align, specify another point, usually another object snap on the object that you want to move.

4. The prompt asks for the second destination point. Specify the point where you want the second source point to end up.

5. The prompt asks for the third source point. You use this for 3D alignment, to specify how you want to rotate the object in the third dimension. For 2D alignment, press Enter to continue the command.

6. The prompt displays the `Scale objects based on alignment points? [Yes/No] <N>:` prompt. If the distances between the source and destination points are not the same, type **y** if you want to scale the original object so that the source and destination points match exactly.

10

Using the 3DALIGN command

If you like to think, "These are the points on the source object that I want to align and then these are the destination points that I want to align them to," and if you don't need to scale your object, use the 3DALIGN command. To align an object by using the 3DALIGN command, enter **3dalign** ↵ on the command line, and select an object or objects. You can also select the object or objects first. (In the 3D Modeling workspace in AutoCAD, you can choose Home tab ⇨ Modify panel ⇨ 3D Align.)

Then follow these steps:

1. The message, Specify source plane and orientation, explains that you now need to specify the source points, which define the plane and orientation of the source object. The first prompt asks for the base point. Specify a point, usually an object snap on the object that you want to move. This point will match the first destination point. You can use the Copy option to make a copy of the object rather than move it. If you use the Continue option here, you only move the object.

2. The prompt asks for the second point. Specify another point on the source object. This point will match the second destination point. Use the Continue option to start specifying destination points.

3. The prompt asks for the third point. In 3D models, you need the third point to specify the plane.

4. The message, Specify destination plane and orientation, explains that you now need to specify the destination points for the base points you just specified. The prompt asks for the first destination point. Specify the point where you want the first base point to end up. As soon as you do this, the object moves to match the first base and destination points so that you can see how the object will look.

5. The prompt asks for the second destination point. The second base point will match this point. If you press Enter at this point, the command aligns the object with the X axis of the current UCS.

6. The prompt asks for the third destination point. You use this for 3D alignment, to specify how you want to rotate the object in the third dimension. For 2D alignment, you can place the cursor on either side of the aligning line you specified, to mirror the object in either direction. When you see the direction that you want, press Enter to end the command and align the object.

ON THE WEB

The drawing used in the following exercise on aligning objects in two dimensions, ab10-c.dwg, is in the Drawings download on the companion website.

STEPS: Aligning Objects in Two Dimensions

1. Open ab10-c.dwg, available from the companion website.

2. Save the file as ab10-04.dwg in your AutoCAD Bible folder. It looks like Figure 10.13. Set a running object snap for Endpoint.

FIGURE 10.13

A base assembly for a commercial washing machine

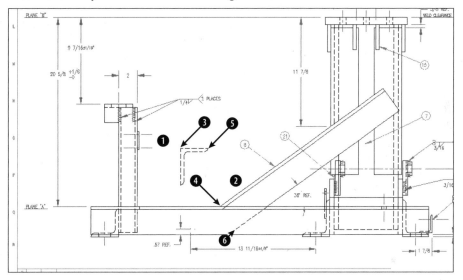

Thanks to Robert Mack of the Dexter Company, Fairfield, Iowa, for this drawing.

3. Choose Home tab ⇨ Modify panel (expanded) ⇨ Align or type **align** ↵, and follow the prompts:

```
Select objects: Select the horizontal angle by using a window, picking
    near ❶ and then ❷. Press Enter to end object selection. This angle
    needs to be aligned with the long, diagonal support angle.
Specify first source point: Pick the endpoint at ❸ in Figure 10.13.
Specify first destination point: Pick the endpoint at ❹.
Specify second source point: Pick the endpoint at ❺.
Specify second destination point: Pick the endpoint at ❻.
Specify third source point or <continue>: ↵
Scale objects based on alignment points? [Yes/No] <N>: ↵ to accept the
    default No answer.
```

4. Save your drawing. It should look like Figure 10.14.

10

FIGURE 10.14

The washing machine base

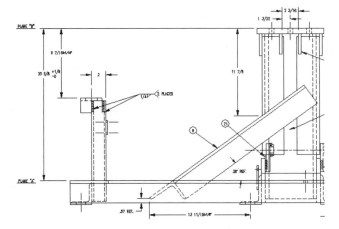

Resizing commands

Four editing commands resize objects in specific ways. The TRIM and EXTEND commands change the endpoint of an object to meet another object. LENGTHEN lets you lengthen or shorten a line, polyline, arc, or elliptical arc. STRETCH is used to stretch (longer or shorter) a group of objects, letting you change their direction at the same time.

Trimming objects

As you edit a drawing, you may find that lines or arcs that once perfectly met other objects now hang over. To trim an object, you must first specify the *cutting edge,* which defines the point at which to cut the object you want to trim. You define the cutting edge by selecting an object. You can select several cutting edges and several objects to trim at one time, as shown in Figure 10.15. When you select an object to trim, you must pick the object on the side that you want trimmed (not on the side that you want to remain). A common use for the TRIM command is to create intersections of walls in architectural floor plans.

> **TIP**
> While using the TRIM command, you can switch to extending objects by pressing the Shift key as you select objects to trim.

FIGURE 10.15

Trimming two objects by using two cutting edges

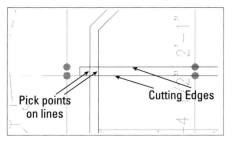
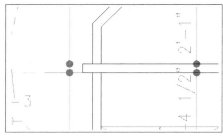

Before trimming   After trimming

The object you want to trim does not have to actually intersect the cutting edge. You can trim an object to a cutting edge that would intersect the object if extended. This is called *trimming to an implied intersection,* an example of which is shown in Figure 10.16.

FIGURE 10.16

Trimming two arcs to an implied intersection

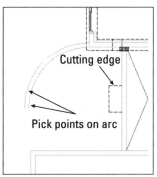
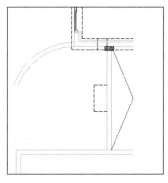

Before trimming   After trimming

You can trim arcs, circles, ellipses, elliptical arcs, hatches, lines, polylines, xlines, rays, and splines. You can use 2D helixes, polylines, arcs, circles, ellipses, elliptical arcs, lines, rays, regions, splines, text, or xlines as cutting edges. An object can be used as both a cutting edge and an object to be trimmed in the same trimming process. You can also trim to objects within blocks. (Chapter 18 covers blocks.)

10

To trim an object, choose Home tab⇨Modify panel⇨Trim/Extend drop-down menu⇨Trim. The command displays the `Current settings: Projection=UCS, Edge=None Select cutting edges . . . Select objects or <select all>:` prompt. The prompt lets you know the values of the two system variables that affect trimming. The Projection setting is used only for 3D models and can trim based on either the current UCS or the current view. The Edge setting is used for implied intersections. When Edge is set to Extend, the command trims to the implied intersection of the cutting edge and the object to be trimmed. At this prompt, pick the object(s) that you want to use as a cutting edge or press Enter to select all objects as edges. Press Enter to end object selection.

You can trim to an actual or an *implied* intersection (an intersection that would exist if objects were extended):

- If you want to trim to an actual intersection, at the `Select object to trim or shift-select to extend or [Fence/Crossing/Project/Edge/eRase/Undo]:` prompt, select the objects that you want to trim. You can use the Fence option to draw lines that crisscross the objects that you want to trim. Use the Crossing option to select the objects with a crossing window. Be sure to pick each object between the cutting edge and the end you want to trim off. Press Enter to end object selection. This action trims the object(s).

- If you want to trim to an implied intersection, at the `Select object to trim or shift-select to extend or [Fence/Crossing/Project/Edge/eRase/Undo]:` prompt, type **e** ↵. The Extend option responds with the `Enter an implied edge extension mode [Extend/No extend] <No extend>:` prompt. Type **e** ↵. Then select the objects that you want to trim at the `Select object to trim or shift-select to extend or [Fence/Crossing/Project/Edge/eRase/Undo]:` prompt. Be sure to pick each object at or near the end that you want to trim. Press Enter to end object selection and trim the object(s).

Use the Undo option if the results of the trim are not what you want. You can then continue to select objects to trim. The eRase option lets you erase an object instead of trimming it, without leaving the TRIM command.

ON THE WEB

The drawing used in the following exercise on trimming objects, `ab10-d.dwg`, is in the `Drawings` download on the companion website.

STEPS: Trimming Objects

1. Open `ab10-d.dwg`, available from the companion website.

2. Save the file as `ab10-05.dwg` in your `AutoCAD Bible` folder. It looks like Figure 10.17.

 3. Choose Home tab⇨Modify panel⇨Trim/Extend drop-down menu⇨Trim. At the `Select objects or <select all>:` prompt, pick lines at ❶ and ❷, shown in Figure 10.17, and then press Enter.

4. At the Select object to trim or shift-select to extend or [Fence/Crossing/
   Project/Edge/eRase/Undo]: prompt, again pick lines at ❶ and ❷, as shown in Figure
   10.17. Be sure to pick them outside the intersection, as shown. Press Enter to end the command.

   The command trims the lines. Each line is used as the cutting edge for the other line.

FIGURE 10.17

A schematic of an air compressor

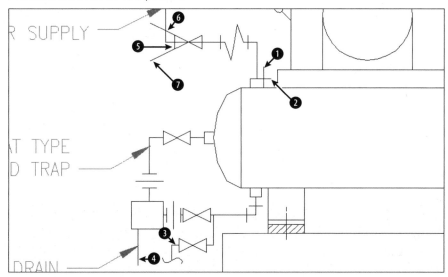

5. Again start the TRIM command. At the Select objects or <select all>: prompt, pick
   the line at ❸, shown in Figure 10.17, and press Enter.

6. At the Select object to trim or shift-select to extend or [Fence/Crossing/
   Project/Edge/eRase/Undo]: prompt, right-click and choose Edge. Then right-click and
   choose Extend at the Enter an implied edge extension mode [Extend/No extend]
   <Extend>: prompt.

7. Pick the line at ❹, shown in Figure 10.17, to trim the line. Press Enter to end the command.

8. Start the TRIM command again. At the Select objects or <select all>: prompt, pick
   ❺ and press Enter. At the Select object to trim or shift-select to extend or
   [Fence/Crossing/Project/Edge/eRase/Undo]: prompt, pick the lines at ❻ and ❼.
   Press Enter to end the command.

9. Save your drawing. It should look like Figure 10.18.

10

FIGURE 10.18

The completed clamp in two views

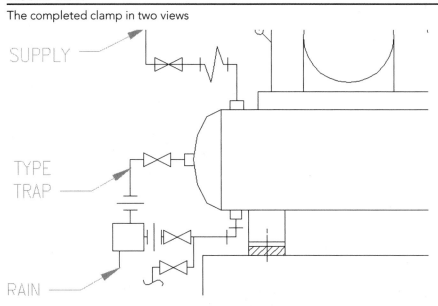

Extending objects

The EXTEND command has similar prompts to the TRIM command, but instead of trimming objects to a cutting edge, it extends them to a *boundary edge* (see Figure 10.19). As with TRIM, when you select an object to extend, you must pick the object on the side that you want extended (not on the side that you want left as is).

FIGURE 10.19

Extending two lines by using an arc as the boundary edge

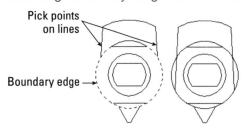

The object you want to extend does not have to actually intersect the boundary edge after its extension. You can extend an object to a boundary edge that would intersect the extended object if it were longer. This is called extending to an implied intersection, an example of which is shown in Figure 10.20.

FIGURE 10.20

Extending a line to an implied intersection

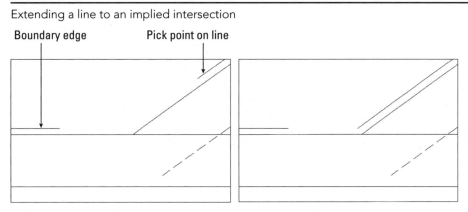

You can extend arcs, elliptical arcs, lines, open polylines, and rays. You can use 2D helixes, polylines, arcs, circles, ellipses, elliptical arcs, lines, rays, regions, splines, text, or xlines as boundary edges. An object can be used as both a boundary edge and an object to be extended in the same extending process.

TIP
While using the EXTEND command, you can switch to trimming objects by pressing the Shift key as you select objects to trim.

 To extend an object, choose Home tab ⇨ Modify panel ⇨ Trim/Extend drop-down menu ⇨ Extend. The command displays the Current settings: Projection=UCS, Edge=Extend Select boundary edges ... Select objects or <select all>: prompt. The prompt lets you know the values of the two settings that affect how the object is extended. Projection is used only for 3D models and can extend based on either the current UCS or the current view. Edge is used for implied intersections. When Edge is set to Extend, the command extends to the implied intersection of the boundary edge and the object to be extended. At this prompt, pick the object(s) that you want to use as the boundary edge(s) or press Enter to select all objects. Press Enter to end object selection. You can extend an actual or implied intersection:

- If the extension will result in an actual intersection, at the Select object to extend or shift-select to trim or [Fence/Crossing/Project/Edge/Undo]: prompt, select objects to extend. You can use the Fence option to draw lines that crisscross the objects you want to extend. Use the Crossing option to select the objects with a crossing window. Be sure to pick each object at the end that you want to extend. Press Enter to end object selection and extend the object(s).

- If you want to extend to an implied intersection, at the prompt, right-click and choose Edge. The option responds with the `Enter an implied edge extension mode [Extend/No extend] <Extend>:` prompt. Right-click and choose Extend. Then select the objects that you want to extend at the `Select object to extend or shift-select to trim or [Fence/Crossing/Project/Edge/Undo]:` prompt. Be sure to pick each object at the end that you want to extend. Press Enter to end object selection and extend the object(s).

Use the Undo option if the results of the extension are not what you want. You can then continue to select objects to extend. You can use the Fence object selection method to select objects to extend the side of the object that the fence line crosses.

STEPS: Extending Objects

1. Open ab10-e.dwg, available from the companion website.

2. Save the file as ab10-06.dwg in your AutoCAD Bible folder. It looks like Figure 10.21.

3. Choose Home tab ⇨ Modify panel ⇨ Trim/Extend drop-down menu ⇨ Extend. At the Select objects or <select all>: prompt, pick the line at ❶, shown in Figure 10.21, and then press Enter.

FIGURE 10.21

An electrical schematic

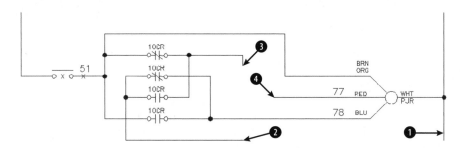

4. At the Select object to extend or shift-select to trim or [Fence/Crossing/ Project/Edge/Undo]: prompt, pick the line at ❷, as shown in Figure 10.21. Press Enter to finish selecting objects. The command extends the line.

5. Repeat the EXTEND command. At the `Select objects or <select all>:` prompt, pick the lines at ❸ and ❹, shown in Figure 10.21, and then press Enter.

6. At the `Select object to extend or shift-select to trim or [Fence/Crossing/Project/Edge/Undo]:` prompt, right-click and choose Edge. Right-click and choose Extend at the `Enter an implied edge extension mode [Extend/No extend] <No extend>:` prompt.

7. Pick lines ❸ and ❹, shown in Figure 10.21, again at the points shown. The lines extend to meet. Press Enter to end the command.

8. Save your drawing. It should look like Figure 10.22.

FIGURE 10.22

The completed electrical schematic

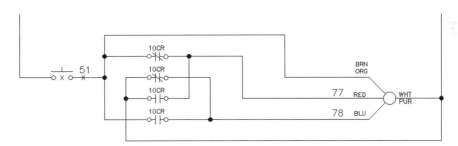

Lengthening and shortening objects

The LENGTHEN command both lengthens and shortens. It works on open objects, such as lines, arcs, and polylines, and also increases or decreases the included angle of arcs. AutoCAD and AutoCAD LT offer several ways of defining the new length or included angle. Use LENGTHEN if you want to lengthen or shorten an object when there is no available intersecting edge or boundary to use with TRIM or EXTEND.

In the LENGTHEN command, the length of an arc is measured along its circumference. Don't confuse this with the Length of Chord option of the ARC command, which refers to the length of a line stretched from one endpoint of the arc to the other endpoint.

To lengthen (or shorten) an object, choose Home tab ⇨ Modify panel (expanded) ⇨ Lengthen. You cannot select objects before the LENGTHEN command. The command responds with the `Select an object or [DElta/Percent/Total/DYnamic]:` prompt. Choose one of the following options:

- **Select object.** This is the default. However, its purpose is to display the current measurements of the object. This can help you to decide how to define the final length or angle of the object. The current length is displayed at the command line, and the previous prompt is repeated.

10

- **DElta.** Right-click and choose DElta. *Delta* means the change, or difference, between the current and new length or included angle. The option responds with the `Enter delta length or [Angle] <0.0000>.` prompt. If you want to change an included angle, right-click and choose Angle. Then type the change in the included angle. Otherwise, simply type the change in the length of the object. A positive number increases the length or included angle. A negative number decreases the length or included angle.

- **Percent.** Right-click and choose Percent. At the `Enter percentage length <100.0000>:` prompt, type in what percent of the original object you want the final object to be. Amounts over 100 lengthen the object. Amounts under 100 shorten the object. You cannot change an included angle by using this option.

- **Total.** Right-click and choose Total. At the `Specify total length or [Angle] <1.0000>:` prompt, you can either choose the Angle suboption, as described for the DElta option, or use the default total-length option. Either way, you enter the total angle or length you want.

- **DYnamic.** Right-click and choose DYnamic. This option lets you drag the endpoint of the object closest to where you picked it. You can use an object snap to specify the new endpoint.

After you've used an option to specify the length you want, you see the `Select an object to change or [Undo]:` prompt. Here you select the object you want to change. Be sure to pick the endpoint of the object for which you want to make the change.

The same prompt continues so that you can pick other objects by using the same length specifications. Choose Undo to undo the last change. Press Enter to end the command.

TIP

You can lengthen a line with grips and dynamic input. (I cover grips later in this chapter.) Select a line, hover over one of the endpoint grips, and choose Lengthen. (The default is to stretch the line, which can also lengthen the line. The difference is that the Lengthen feature gives you both incremental and total options.) By default, the amount you enter will be the incremental length — that is, the change in the length — but you can press the Tab key to switch to specifying the total length. You can tell which option is functioning by seeing which dynamic input tooltip is active.

ON THE WEB

The drawing that you need for the following exercise on lengthening and shortening objects, `ab10-f.dwg`, is available from the `Drawings` download on the companion website.

STEPS: Lengthening and Shortening Objects

1. Open `ab10-f.dwg`, available from the companion website.

2. Save the file as ab10-07.dwg in your AutoCAD Bible folder. It is a capacitor symbol from an electrical schematic, as shown in Figure 10.23.

FIGURE 10.23

A poorly drawn capacitor symbol

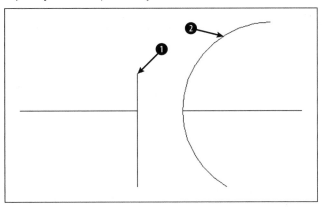

3. Select the line at ❶. Hover over the top endpoint grip and choose Lengthen from the menu that appears. You should see two dynamic input text boxes. The one that's active should be the top one; if not, press the Tab key. Move the cursor upward, above the current endpoint of the line. Type **.07** ↵ and press Esc.

This action lengthens the line by .07 unit.

4. Choose Home tab ➪ Modify panel (expanded) ➪ Lengthen, and follow the prompts:

```
Select an object or [DElta/Percent/Total/DYnamic]: Pick the arc at ❷ in
    Figure 10.23.
Current length: 0.407, included angle: 150
Select an object or [DElta/Percent/Total/DYnamic]: Right-click and choose
    Total.
Specify total length or [Angle] <1.000)>: Right-click and choose Angle.
Specify total angle <57>: 120 ↵
Select an object to change or [Undo]: Pick the arc at ❷ in Figure 10.23.
Select an object to change or [Undo]: ↵
```

This action shortens the arc.

5. Save your drawing. It should look like Figure 10.24.

10

FIGURE 10.24

The completed capacitor symbol

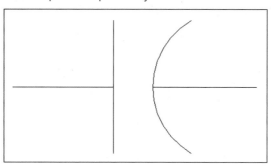

Stretching objects

The STRETCH command is generally used to stretch groups of objects. For example, you can use this command to enlarge a room in a floor plan. You can also shrink objects. You can change not only the length of the objects but the angle as well. You use a crossing window to choose the objects to be stretched. All objects that cross the boundaries of the crossing window are stretched. All objects that lie entirely within the crossing window are merely moved. Successful stretching involves precise placement of the crossing window. Figure 10.25 shows the process of stretching a garage. Note that the walls that cross the boundaries of the crossing window are stretched. However, the dormer that is entirely within the crossing window is just moved. This maintains the integrity of the model.

You cannot stretch circles, text, or blocks. You can stretch arcs, although the results may not be what you expect.

The real power of the STRETCH command is in stretching a number of objects at once. However, you can also stretch one line. The results are similar to using the CHANGE command to change the endpoint of a line or to editing with grips (discussed later in this chapter).

 To stretch objects, choose Home tab ⇨ Modify panel ⇨ Stretch. The command responds with the `Select objects to stretch by crossing-window or crossing-polygon . . .` instruction and then the `Select objects:` prompt. Create the crossing window and select the objects that you want to stretch. (You can also use a crossing polygon — type **cp** at the `Select objects:` prompt.) After completing the crossing window, check to see which objects are highlighted. This helps you avoid unwanted results. You can use the object selection Remove option (type **r** ⏎ at the Command prompt) to remove objects by picking the objects that you don't want to stretch or move. Then use the Add option (type **a** ⏎) to continue selecting objects if necessary.

FIGURE 10.25

Stretching a garage

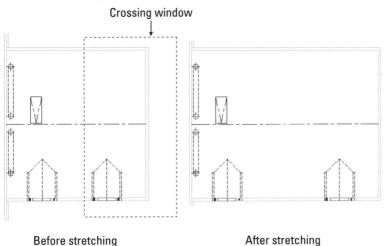

Before stretching   After stretching

The STRETCH command remembers the most recent displacement throughout a session. To stretch an object by the same displacement that you most recently used, press Enter at the `Specify base point or [Displacement] <Displacement>:` prompt. At the `Specify displacement <0.0000, 0.0000, 0.0000>:` prompt, you see in angled brackets the last displacement that you used. Press Enter to stretch the object using this displacement.

> **TIP**
> You can use multiple crossing windows to select the objects that you want to stretch. You can also pick to select objects, although these objects are simply moved.

When you've finished selecting objects, you see the `Specify base point or [Displacement] <Displacement>:` prompt. This step is just like moving objects, and you can respond in two ways:

- Pick a base point. At the `Specify second point or <use first point as displacement>:` prompt, pick a second point. Object snap and PolarSnap are helpful for picking these points.

- Type a displacement without using the @ sign. For example, to lengthen the objects by 6 feet in the 0-degree direction, type **6'<0** ↵. Then press Enter at the `Specify second point or <use first point as displacement>:` prompt.

> **TIP**
> Usually, you want to stretch at an orthogonal angle. If you're going to stretch by picking, turn Ortho mode on. Object snaps, polar tracking, and Snap mode are other helpful drawing aids for stretching.

10

When specifying a displacement by typing at the keyboard, you can use both positive and negative distances. For example, 6'<180 is the same as –6'<0. Both would stretch the objects 6 feet to the left.

STEPS: Stretching Objects

1. Open `ab10-g.dwg`, available from the companion website.

2. Save the file as `ab10-08.dwg` in your `AutoCAD Bible` folder. This drawing is the plan view of a garage, as shown in Figure 10.26. Turn on polar tracking by clicking Polar Tracking on the status bar. Click Snap Mode on the status bar and then right-click the Snap Mode button to make sure that PolarSnap is on (the PolarSnap item will be unavailable if it is already on); otherwise, choose PolarSnap On. Turn on Object Snap mode and set a running object snap to Endpoint.

 3. Choose Home tab ⇨ Modify panel ⇨ Stretch. At the `Select objects:` prompt, pick ❶, as shown in Figure 10.26. At the `Specify opposite corner:` prompt, pick ❷. The prompt notifies you that it found 32 objects. Press Enter to end object selection.

FIGURE 10.26

A plan view of a garage

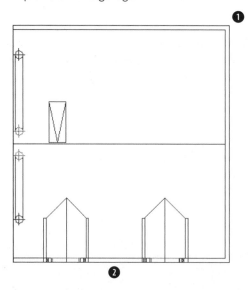

4. At the `Specify base point or [Displacement] <Displacement>:` prompt, pick the endpoint at the bottom-right corner of the garage. At the `Specify second point or <use first point as displacement>:` prompt, move the cursor to the right until you see the polar tracking tooltip. Click when the tooltip says 6'-0"<0. (If you can't find it, type **6',0** ↵. If you're not using Dynamic Input or have Dynamic Input set to absolute coordinates, add the @ symbol first.) This action stretches the garage by 6 feet.

5. Save your drawing. It should look like Figure 10.27.

FIGURE 10.27

The longer garage

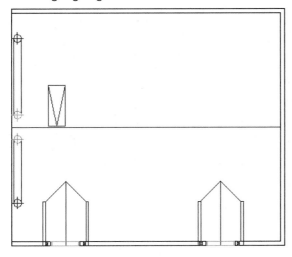

Using Construction Commands

Four additional commands are commonly used in the process of constructing models. The BREAK command removes sections of objects at points that you specify. The JOIN command joins co-linear lines, polylines, arcs, elliptical arcs, or splines, and can close arcs and elliptical arcs into circles and ellipses. CHAMFER creates corners, and FILLET creates rounded corners.

Breaking objects

Drawing a long line and then breaking it into two or more shorter lines is often much easier than drawing two separate lines. A common use for BREAK is to break a wall at a door or a window in an architectural floor plan. You specify two points on the object, and the command erases whatever is between those two points. Typically, you use object snaps to specify the points. Sometimes, you can use TRIM to break an object, but if you have no convenient cutting edge, you may find BREAK more efficient.

10

You can break lines, polylines, splines, xlines, rays, helixes, circles, arcs, elliptical arcs, and ellipses. To break a line, choose Home tab ⇨ Modify panel (expanded) ⇨ Break. You cannot select the object first. The command responds with the `Select object:` prompt. (Notice that you can only select one object to break.) At this prompt, you have two choices:

- Select the object at one of the break points that you want to create. You then see the `Specify second break point or [First point]:` prompt. Because you have already specified the first point, you can now specify the second point. The command breaks the object between the two points.

- Select the object by using any method of object selection. You then see the `Specify second break point or [First point]:` prompt. Right-click and choose First point. At the `Specify first break point:` prompt, pick the first break point. At the `Specify second break point:` prompt, pick the second break point. The command breaks the object between the two points.

> **TIP**
>
> Sometimes you may want to break an object into two pieces at a point, without erasing any part of the object. Choose Home tab ⇨ Modify panel (expanded) ⇨ Break at Point to help you easily break an object at a point. After selecting the object, pick where you want to break the object at the `Specify first break point:` prompt. The two new objects look the same as before on the screen — until you select one of the objects. AutoCAD and AutoCAD LT use @ to signify the last point entered; thus, the first and second break points are the same.

You can use BREAK to shorten an object. Pick one point on the object where you want the new endpoint to be. Pick the other point past its current endpoint to cut off the object at the point you picked on the object.

Joining objects

The opposite of breaking objects is joining them. The JOIN command lets you join lines, polylines, arcs, elliptical arcs, and splines. The objects must be along the same linear, circular, or elliptical path. The objects can overlap, have a gap between them, or touch end to end.

 To join objects, choose Home tab ⇨ Modify panel (expanded) ⇨ Join. At the `Select source object or multiple objects to join at once:` prompt, select the objects that you want to join (or select one object first, then additional objects). Press Enter to end selection. AutoCAD joins the objects.

A nice touch is the ability to close arcs (to circles) and elliptical arcs (to ellipses), but you can't select multiple arcs or elliptical arcs at one time. If your first object is either type of arc, you see the `Select arcs to join to source or [cLose]:` prompt. Use the cLose option to close the arc.

> **TIP**
>
> You can reverse the direction of lines, polylines, splines (see Chapter 16), and helixes (see Chapter 21) with the REVERSE command. The direction of these objects influences how noncontinuous linetype patterns (covered in Chapter 11) flow, such as from left to right, or from right to left. Choose Home tab ⇨ Modify panel (expanded) ⇨ Reverse.

STEPS: Breaking and Joining Objects

1. Open `ab10-h.dwg`, available from the companion website.

2. Save the file as `ab10-09.dwg` in your `AutoCAD Bible` folder. This is a site plan, as shown in Figure 10.28. Turn on Object Snap mode and set running object snaps for Endpoint and Intersection.

3. Choose Home tab ⇨ Modify panel (expanded) ⇨ Break. At the `Select object:` prompt, pick the line at ❶ in Figure 10.28. At the `Specify second break point or [First point]:` prompt, pick ❷. This action shortens the line.

4. Repeat the BREAK command. At the `Select object:` prompt, pick the circle (it's a maple tree) anywhere along its circumference. At the `Specify second break point or [First point]:` prompt, right-click and choose First point. At the `Specify first break point:` prompt, pick the intersection at ❸. At the `Specify second break point:` prompt, pick the intersection at ❹ to break the circle.

5. Let's say that you decide this is a mistake. Choose Home tab ⇨ Modify panel (expanded) ⇨ Join. At the `Select source object or multiple objects to join at once:` prompt, select the circle (tree) that you just broke into an arc and press Enter to end selection. At the `Select arcs to join to source or [cLose]:` prompt, right-click and choose cLose. The arc becomes a full circle again.

6. To break the line at ❺, click the Object Snap Tracking button on the status bar. Start the BREAK command again. Follow the prompts:

    `Select object:` *Pick the line at* ❺.
    `Specify second break point or [First point]:` *Right-click and choose First point.*
    `Specify first break point:` *Move the cursor to* ❻ *to acquire it as a tracking point. Then move the cursor to the right onto the line you are breaking. When you see the Endpoint: Intersection tooltip, click. (You have no visual confirmation yet that you picked the right point.)*
    `Specify second break point:` *Move the cursor to* ❼ *to acquire it as a tracking point. Then move the cursor onto the line you are breaking.* At the Endpoint: **4'-2 3/4"<0.0000** *tooltip, click.*

10

FIGURE 10.28

A site plan

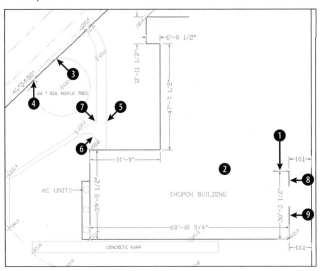

7. Start the JOIN command. At the `Select source object or multiple objects to join at once:` prompt, select the line at ❽. At the `Select objects to join:` prompt, select the line at ❾. Press Enter to end the selection and join the lines into one.

8. Save your drawing. It should look like Figure 10.29.

FIGURE 10.29

The edited site plan

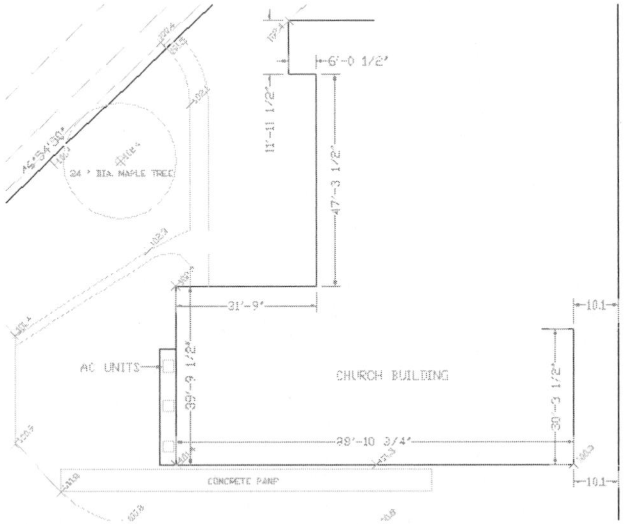

Creating chamfered corners

The CHAMFER command creates corners from two nonparallel lines. You can also chamfer xlines, rays, and polylines. You can simply extend the lines to meet at an intersection (a square corner), or create a beveled edge. If you create a beveled edge, you define the edge by either two distances or one distance and an angle relative to the first line that you're chamfering. Figure 10.30 shows the elements of a chamfered corner.

FIGURE 10.30

A chamfered corner

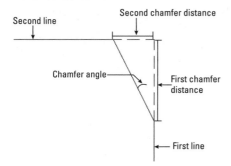

Chamfering is a two-step process. First you define how you want to chamfer the corner, specifying either two distances from the corner or a distance and an angle. Then you select the two lines that you want to chamfer.

To chamfer, choose Home tab ⇨ Modify panel ⇨ Chamfer/Fillet drop-down menu ⇨ Chamfer. You cannot select objects before the CHAMFER command. The command responds with the (TRIM mode) Current chamfer Dist1 = 0.0000, Dist2 = 0.0000 Select first line or [Undo/ Polyline/Distance/Angle/Trim/mEthod/Multiple]: prompt. The command starts by listing the current settings. (The CHAMFER command remembers the last-used chamfer data.) You can define two distances from a corner or one distance and an angle:

- To define two distances from the corner, right-click and choose Distance. At the Specify first chamfer distance <0.0000>: prompt, type the first chamfer distance or press Enter to accept the default (which is the last distance that you defined). At the Specify second chamfer distance <0.0000>: prompt, type the second distance. The default for this is always the first chamfer distance because equal chamfer distances are so common.

- To define a distance (from the corner) and an angle, right-click and choose Angle. At the Specify chamfer length on the first line <1.0000>: prompt, enter a distance. This is the same as the first chamfer distance. At the Specify chamfer angle from the first line <0.0000>: prompt, type the angle between the first line and the chamfer line.

Now that you have specified the settings that you want, you're ready to chamfer. Your distances or distance and angle are displayed as you just specified them. The command repeats the `Select first line or [Undo/Polyline/Distance/Angle/Trim/mEthod/Multiple]:` prompt. Select the first line. If you aren't creating a chamfer with equal distances, the order in which you select the lines is important. The command trims the first line selected by the first distance, and the second line selected based on either the second distance or the angle. At the `Select second line or shift-select to apply corner or [Distance/Angle/Method]:` prompt, select the second line to chamfer the lines.

After selecting the first line, you can hover the cursor over the second line to see a preview of what the chamfer will look like. While previewing the results of the chamfer, use the Distance, Angle, and Method options to adjust the final results of the chamfer before selecting the second line.

If the lines already intersect, the command trims them to create a corner. The pick points on intersecting lines should be on the part of the lines that you want to keep, not on the part of the lines that you want to trim off.

> **TIP**
>
> To quickly create a square corner if you have non-zero settings, press Shift as you select the second line. Of course, you can still set each distance to zero.

 Choose the Polyline option to chamfer an entire polyline at once. Chapter 16 covers polylines, and Chapter 24 discusses chamfering 3D models.

By default, CHAMFER trims the original lines that it chamfers. If you want to keep the full original lines when you add the chamfer line, choose the Trim option and choose No Trim. Use the Multiple option to continue the prompts and chamfer several corners in one command. The Undo option lets you undo your last chamfer and try again.

> **ON THE WEB**
>
> The drawing used in the following exercise on chamfering lines, `ab10-i.dwg`, is in the `Drawings` download on the companion website.

STEPS: Chamfering Lines

1. Open `ab10-i.dwg`, available from the companion website.

2. Save the file as `ab10-10.dwg` in your `AutoCAD Bible` folder. This drawing is a very small section of a "porcupine" mixer, as shown in Figure 10.31.

 3. Choose Home tab ⇨ Modify panel ⇨ Chamfer/Fillet drop-down menu ⇨ Chamfer. CHAMFER states the current mode and distances. At the `Select first line or [Undo/Polyline/ Distance/Angle/Trim/mEthod/Multiple]:` prompt, pick ❶, as shown in Figure 10.31. At the `Select second line or shift-select to apply corner or [Distance/ Angle/Method]:` prompt, pick ❷. (If the current distances are not zero, press Shift as you pick ❷.) The command chamfers the two lines to make a corner. (If this doesn't work, you may have the Trim option set to No Trim. Change the setting to Trim and try again.)

FIGURE 10.31

A mechanical drawing showing a small section of a "porcupine" mixer

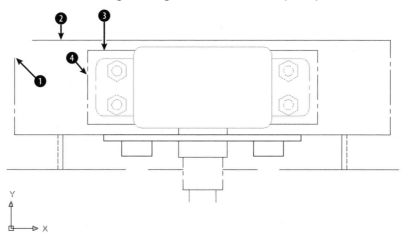

4. Repeat the CHAMFER command. Follow the prompts:

   ```
   Select first line or [Undo/Polyline/Distance/Angle/Trim/mEthod/Multiple]:
       Right-click and choose Angle.
   Specify chamfer length on the first line <1>: 9/16 ↵
   Specify chamfer angle from the first line <0>: 45 ↵
   ```

5. At the Select first line or [Undo/Polyline/Distance/Angle/Trim/mEthod/
   Multiple]: prompt, pick ❸, as shown in Figure 10.31. At the Select second line or
   shift-select to apply corner or [Distance/Angle/Method]: prompt, pick ❹.
   The command chamfers the two lines, as shown in Figure 10.32.

6. Save your drawing.

Creating rounded corners

The FILLET command creates rounded corners, replacing part of two lines with an arc. Fillets are often
used in mechanical drawings. In certain cases, you can use FILLET instead of the ARC command to create arcs. As with CHAMFER, you can fillet lines, xlines, rays, and polylines — they can even be parallel. You can also fillet circles, arcs, elliptical arcs, and ellipses.

 You can insert a spline between two selected lines or curves using the BLEND command, I cover splines and
the BLEND command in Chapter 16.

The FILLET command defines the fillet arc by its radius. (I cover arcs in Chapter 7.)

10

FIGURE 10.32

The edited drawing after using the CHAMFER command

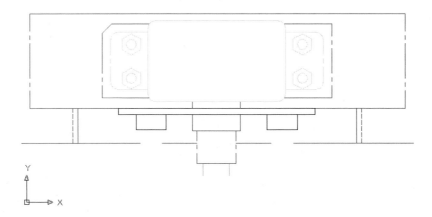

Like chamfering, filleting is a two-step process. First you define the radius of the fillet arc. Then you select the two lines that you want to fillet. You cannot select objects before the FILLET command.

To fillet, follow these steps:

1. Choose Home tab ⇨ Modify panel ⇨ Chamfer/Fillet drop-down menu ⇨ Fillet. The command responds with the `Current settings: Mode = TRIM, Radius = 0.0000 Select first object or [Undo/Polyline/Radius/Trim/Multiple]:` prompt.

2. Right-click and choose Radius.

3. At the `Specify fillet radius <0.0000>:` prompt, type the radius you want. The default is either 0.0000 or the last radius that you specified.

4. The command repeats the `Select first object or [Undo/Polyline/Radius/Trim/Multiple]:` prompt. Select the first object that you want to fillet.

5. At the `Select second object or shift-select to apply corner or [Radius]:` prompt, select the second object that you want to fillet. This action creates the fillet.

If you hover the cursor over the second object before selecting it, you see a preview of the fillet. While previewing the results of the fillet, use the Radius options to adjust the final results of the fillet before selecting the second line.

By default, FILLET trims the original lines that it fillets, but the FILLET command recalls the last setting you used. If you want to keep the full original lines when you create a fillet, right-click and choose the Trim option, and then choose No Trim.

 Choose the Polyline option to fillet an entire polyline at once. Chapter 16 covers polylines, and Chapter 24 discusses filleting 3D models.

Filleting with a zero radius gives the same results as chamfering with distances set to zero. (See the previous section on chamfering.) If your existing settings are non-zero, you can press Shift as you select the second object to create a square corner.

The order in which you select the two objects to be filleted is not important. However, *where* you pick the objects is quite important. If two objects intersect, the command keeps the objects on the same side of the intersection as your pick point and fillets them. Those parts of the objects on the far side of the intersection are erased.

When you fillet arcs and lines, if more than one fillet is possible, FILLET connects the endpoints closest to your pick points. Filleting circles and lines can produce unexpected results. Sometimes you need to experiment to find the proper pick points.

TIP

Use the Multiple option to continue the prompts and fillet several corners in one command.

ON THE WEB

The drawing used in the following exercise on filleting objects, ab10-i.dwg, is in the Drawings download on the companion website.

STEPS: Filleting Objects

1. Open ab10-i.dwg, available from the companion website.
2. Save the file as ab10-11.dwg in your AutoCAD Bible folder. This is the same drawing used in the previous exercise. It is shown in Figure 10.33.

FIGURE 10.33

A mechanical drawing showing a small section of a "porcupine" mixer

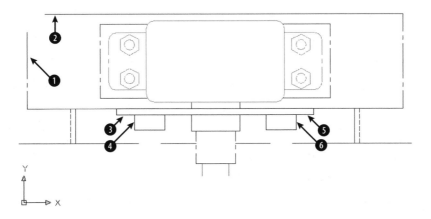

3. Choose Home tab ➪ Modify panel ➪ Chamfer/Fillet drop-down menu ➪ Fillet. At the `Select first object or [Undo/Polyline/Radius/Trim/Multiple]:` prompt, right-click and choose Radius. At the `Specify fillet radius <1/2>:` prompt, type **5/8** ↵.

4. At the `Select first object or [Undo/Polyline/Radius/Trim/Multiple]:` prompt, pick the line at ❶, as shown in Figure 10.33. At the `Select second object or shift-select to apply corner or [Radius]:` prompt, pick the line at ❷ to fillet the two lines.

5. Repeat the FILLET command. At the `Select first object or [Undo/Polyline/ Radius/Trim/ Multiple]:` prompt, right-click and choose Radius. At the `Enter fillet radius <5/8>:` prompt, type **1/4** ↵.

6. At the `Select first object or [Undo/Polyline/Radius/Trim/Multiple]:` prompt, right-click and choose Multiple. Pick the line at ❸, as shown in Figure 10.33. At the `Select second object or shift-select to apply corner or [Radius]:` prompt, pick the line at ❹ to fillet the two lines. The prompts continue. This time pick at ❺ and ❻.

7. If you want, you can connect the two loose lines that the fillets created and create some more fillets in the drawing.

8. Save your drawing. It should look like Figure 10.34.

FIGURE 10.34

The filleted drawing

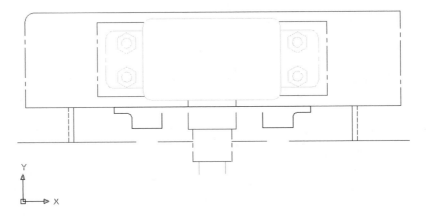

Creating a Revision Cloud

You may need to mark areas of your drawings that contain revisions in order to draw attention to these revisions. A common method is to draw a *revision cloud* around the revised objects. Figure 10.35 shows a drawing with a revision cloud, which is a series of arcs that indicate that an area of the drawing has been revised.

FIGURE 10.35

The revision cloud shows where the drawing has been modified.

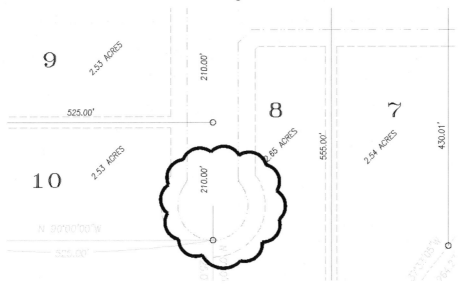

To create a revision cloud, follow these steps:

1. Choose Home tab ⇨ Draw panel (expanded) ⇨ Revision Cloud.
2. At the `Specify start point or [Arc length/Object/Style] <Object>:` prompt, you can choose from three options:
   - To change the length of the arc, right-click and choose Arc Length. Then specify a new arc length. For a variable, hand-drawn look, you can specify a minimum arc length and a maximum arc length that is up to three times the length of the minimum.
   - To change a closed object into a revision cloud, right-click and choose Object. Then pick a circle, ellipse, closed polyline, or closed spline. You can choose to reverse the direction of the revision cloud. The object is converted to a revision cloud, and the command ends.

10

- To choose from two available cloud styles, right-click and choose Style. At the next prompt, choose either the Normal or Calligraphy option. A calligraphy revision cloud has a variable line width so that it looks as if you drew it with a calligraphy pen.

3. Click where you want the revision cloud to start. You also see an instruction, `Guide cross-hairs along cloud path . . .`, which means that you don't have to pick to create the arcs. You just have to move the crosshairs along the path of the desired cloud.

4. Move the crosshairs counterclockwise to create a circular or elliptical shape. When you approach the start point, the command ends automatically. (You can end the cloud at any time by pressing Enter.)

> **NOTE**
> If you want, you can pick each arc endpoint to control the size of the arcs. However, if you move the crosshairs farther than the arc length, an arc is created automatically. REVCLOUD multiplies the arc length by the Overall Scale factor (see Chapter 15) to adjust for different scale factors.

Hiding Objects with a Wipeout

A *wipeout* covers existing objects in order to clear space for some annotation or to indicate that the covered objects will be changed and should therefore be ignored. A wipeout is a polygonal area with a background that matches the background of the drawing area. The WIPEOUT command creates a polygon of the same color as the background of your drawing area.

To create a wipeout, follow these steps:

1. Choose Home tab ⇨ Draw panel (expanded) ⇨ Wipeout.
2. At the `Specify first point or [Frames/Polyline] <Polyline>:` prompt, specify the first point of a shape that will cover existing objects. To use a polyline as the shape, right-click and choose Polyline. (The polyline can't contain any arcs when you use it for this purpose.) Then select the polyline and choose whether or not to erase the polyline.
3. At the `Specify next point or [Undo]:` prompt, if you specified a point, specify the next point.
4. At the `Specify next point or [Close/Undo]:` prompt, specify another point or use the Close option to close the wipeout shape. You can also press Enter to end the command and use the shape that you specified.

By default, the wipeout has a frame around it, using the current layer's color. You can hide the frames of all wipeouts by starting the WIPEOUT command, choosing the Frames option, and choosing Off.

> **NEW FEATURE**
> The Frames option has a new suboption, `Display but not plot`, which lets you display frames while editing a drawing, but plot without the frames. You can also control wipeout frames using the WIPEOUTFRAME system variable. The FRAME system variable does the same thing, but also applies to images, underlays, and xrefs.

ON THE WEB

In AutoCAD (but not AutoCAD LT), you can control objects by specifying parameters that constrain their relationships with other objects or their measurements. For example, you can constrain one line to be always perpendicular to another line, or you can constrain the diameter of a circle to a specific value. Using parameters adds intelligence to your drawing and helps to ensure accuracy of the entire drawing when you modify objects. Parameters can also save a huge amount of time that you would otherwise need to spend editing objects, because when you change one object, other objects automatically adjust to comply with their constraints. I cover this advanced topic fully in the Chapter 10 Addendum on the companion website.

Double-Clicking to Edit Objects

You can double-click objects to edit them. What happens after you double-click depends on the type of object. In most cases, double-clicking an object just opens the Quick Properties palette where you can change the object's properties. For more information about using the Quick Properties palette, see the section, "Editing with the Quick Properties Palette," later in this chapter.

When you double-click certain types of objects in a drawing, you see a dialog box that is specific to these objects, or a related editing command starts:

- **Attribute definition.** Opens the Edit Attribute Definition dialog box (the DDEDIT command). See Chapter 19 for more information.
- **Attribute within a block.** Opens the Enhanced Attribute Editor dialog box (the EATTEDIT command). See Chapter 19 for more information.
- **Block.** Opens the Edit Block Definition dialog box. You can choose the block from a list and click OK to enter the Block Editor. See Chapter 18 for more information.
- **Image.** Opens the IMAGEADJUST command. See Bonus Chapter 4 for more information.
- **Livesection.** Starts the LIVESECTION command. See Chapter 24 for more information.
- **Mline.** Opens the Multilines Edit Tools dialog box (the MLEDIT command). Mlines are not available in AutoCAD LT, which has a similar feature, called Dlines. See the Chapter 16 Addendum for more information.
- **Mtext or leader text.** Opens the In-Place Text Editor (the MTEDIT command). See Chapter 13 for more information.
- **Polyline.** Starts the PEDIT command.
- **Spline.** Starts the SPLINEDIT command.
- **Text (TEXT commands).** Opens the In-Place Text Editor (the DDEDIT command). See Chapter 13 for more information.
- **Xref.** Opens the Reference Edit dialog box (the REFEDIT command). See Chapter 20 for more information.

 You can customize what happens when you double-click an object. For example, you could choose to display the Quick Properties palette rather than the Reference Edit dialog box when you double-click an xref. See Bonus Chapter 10 for details.

10

The DBLCLKEDIT system variable specifies whether double-clicking activates the default editing command or dialog box. To turn off double-clicking to edit objects, choose Application Button ➪ Options and click the User Preferences tab. In the Windows Standard Behavior section of the dialog box, uncheck the Double Click Editing check box.

Editing with Grips

Grips offer a way to edit objects without choosing commands. By using grips, you can quickly stretch, move, rotate, scale, copy, and mirror objects.

When you select an object without first choosing a command, the object appears highlighted with *grips* — small boxes at preset object snap points. (If you don't see grips, they may be turned off. See the "Customizing grips" section later in this chapter to find out how to turn them back on.) You can continue to select more objects in this way.

If you click to activate a grip, you can use the grip to manipulate the object. When the grip is activated, it turns red (by default). An activated grip is also called a *hot grip,* as shown in Figure 10.36. In some cases, you activate more than one grip at a time. To activate more than one grip, hold down Shift and then click the grips. If you activate a grip in error, click it again to deactivate it. Grips are so called because you can "hold on to" the object by dragging the grips with the mouse.

After you activate a grip, right-click with the mouse to open the Grip shortcut menu, which lists all the grip options. You can also press the Spacebar or Enter to cycle through five possible commands on the command line.

FIGURE 10.36

When moving a line, grips appear at preset object snaps. You use the hot grip to manipulate an object.

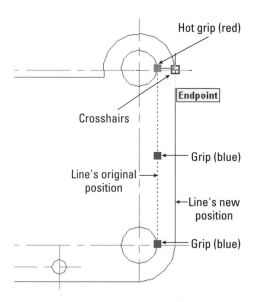

As long as you're familiar with the STRETCH, MOVE, COPY, ROTATE, SCALE, and MIRROR commands, you can easily learn how to accomplish the same edits by using grips because the prompts are similar. After you complete the edit, the object remains highlighted and the grips remain so that you can further edit the object. If you want to edit another object, press Esc once to remove the grips. Then select another object or objects or choose another command.

> **NOTE**
>
> If you use Dynamic Input, you can customize how many and which tooltips appear when you grip edit. Right-click the Dynamic Input button on the status bar and choose Settings to open the Drafting Settings dialog box with the Dynamic Input tab on top (I explain this dialog box in Chapter 4). Click the Settings button in the Dimension Input section to open the Dimension Input Settings dialog box. The settings here apply to grip editing. By default, the Show 2 Dimension Input Fields at a Time option is selected. Although this setting usually works well, you can go down to one input field or specify additional fields. When you select multiple grips to edit an object, no Dynamic Input field appears.

Stretching with grips

Stretching with grips involves understanding how the grip points relate to the object. For example, you cannot stretch a line from its midpoint — if you think about it, there's no way to define in which direction to stretch the line. Also, you cannot stretch a circle, you can only scale it. Aside from these types of limitations, anything goes.

Stretching one line

You can stretch one line. The result is similar to using the CHANGE command to change a line's endpoint. To stretch a line, select it, and click the grip at the endpoint that you want to stretch. You see the `Specify stretch point or [Base point/Copy/Undo/eXit]:` prompt on the command line.

STRETCH is the first grip-editing command on the command line. Simply specify the new endpoint for the line, using any method of specifying a coordinate, to stretch the line. The other options work as follows:

- Base point lets you define a base point — other than the activated grip — and a second point. Right-click to open the Grip shortcut menu and choose Base Point. The option displays the `Specify base point:` prompt. Define a base point. Again you see the original `Specify stretch point or [Base point/Copy/Undo/eXit]:` prompt. Define the second stretch point to stretch the line.

- Copy puts you in Multiple mode. Right-click to open the Grip shortcut menu and choose Copy. Again you see the original `Specify stretch point or [Base point/Copy/Undo/eXit]:` prompt. Specify a new point to keep the original line, and create a new line stretched to the new point. You can continue to create new stretched lines.

- Undo undoes the last edit. Right-click to open the Grip shortcut menu and choose Undo.

- eXit returns you to the Command prompt. Right-click to open the Grip shortcut menu and choose Exit. Esc also returns you to the Command prompt.

Stretching multiple lines

Stretching more than one line at a time is similar to the most common use of the STRETCH command. However, it can also be somewhat confusing.

10

When you stretch multiple lines, you should activate endpoint grips to stretch lines, and activate midpoint grips to move lines. Picking all those grips accurately can be difficult and time-consuming. For this reason, stretching multiple lines works best with simple models.

To stretch multiple lines, follow these steps:

1. Choose the objects that you want to stretch. The objects are highlighted and display grips. You can use any method of choosing objects — you are not limited to crossing windows.

2. Hold down Shift and pick each grip that you want to stretch. If there are internal objects that you want to move with the stretch, select their grips, too; these include the midpoints of the lines and arcs, and the centers of the circles.

3. Release Shift and pick a grip to use as a base point. You see the `Specify stretch point or [Base point/Copy/Undo/eXit]:` prompt.

4. Specify a new stretch point. You can also use any of the other options.

At the end of this section on grips, you have the opportunity to try them out in an exercise.

Moving with grips

It's easy to move objects with grips. First, choose all the objects that you want to move. Then click any grip to activate it. This becomes the base point. Right-click to open the Grip shortcut menu and choose Move or press the Spacebar once. At the `Specify move point or [Base point/Copy/Undo/eXit]:` prompt, use any method to specify the second point. The selected objects move. The other options work similarly to the Stretch grip options, explained previously.

Rotating with grips

Rotating with grips is very similar to using the ROTATE command. First, choose all the objects that you want to rotate. Then click any grip to activate it. This becomes the base point. Right-click to open the Grip shortcut menu and choose Rotate. At the `Specify rotation angle or [Base point/Copy/Undo/Reference/eXit]:` prompt, type in a rotation angle or pick a point to rotate the objects. The other options work similarly to the Stretch grip options, explained previously, except for the Reference option, which works like the Reference option for the ROTATE command. (See Chapter 9.)

Scaling with grips

Scaling with grips is very similar to using the SCALE command. First, choose all the objects that you want to scale. Then click any grip to activate it. This becomes the base point. Right-click to open the Grip shortcut menu and choose Scale. At the `Specify scale factor or [Base point/Copy/Undo/Reference/eXit]:` prompt, type a scale factor to scale the objects. The other options work similarly to the Stretch grip options, explained previously, except for the Reference option, which works like the Reference option for the SCALE command. (See Chapter 9.)

Mirroring with grips

Mirroring with grips is similar to using the MIRROR command. First, choose all the objects that you want to mirror. Then click any grip to activate it. This becomes the first point of the mirror line.

Right-click to open the Grip shortcut menu. Choose Mirror. At the `Specify second point or [Base point/Copy/Undo/eXit]:` prompt, specify the second point of the mirror line to mirror the objects. The other options work similarly to the Stretch grip options.

CAUTION
By default, AutoCAD and AutoCAD LT erase the original objects. To keep the original objects, you must use the Copy option. This feature is the opposite of the MIRROR command, where the default is to keep the original objects.

ON THE WEB
The drawing that you need for the following exercise on editing with grips, `ab10-k.dwg`, is available from the `Drawings` download on the companion website.

STEPS: Editing with Grips

1. Open `ab10-k.dwg`, available from the companion website.

2. Save the file as `ab10-13.dwg` in your `AutoCAD Bible` folder. This is a small section of a drive block, seen from above, as shown in Figure 10.37. Make sure that Ortho mode and Object Snap mode are on.

3. Use a selection window to select the entire model. Now hold down Shift and place a selection window around the small circles and rectangle at the center of the model to deselect them.

4. Pick the grip at ❶, shown in Figure 10.37, to activate it. You see the `Specify stretch point or [Base point/Copy/Undo/eXit]:` prompt.

5. Right-click and choose Mirror from the shortcut menu. You see the `Specify second point or [Base point/Copy/Undo/eXit]:` prompt.

6. Right-click and choose Copy so that the original objects that you mirror are not deleted.

7. At the `Specify second point or [Base point/Copy/Undo/eXit]:` prompt, move the cursor to the right. You can see the mirror image of the model. Pick any point to the right (in the 0-degree direction) of the activated grip.

FIGURE 10.37

This small section of a drive block, seen from above, can be edited with grips.

10

8. Right-click and choose Exit to return to the command line. Press Esc to deselect all of the objects.

9. Zoom out a little so that you can see the entire model. Use a large selection window to select all the objects, including the small rectangle and circles in the middle. Everything should be highlighted and display grips.

10. Pick the grip at ❷, shown in Figure 10.37, to activate it. Right-click and choose Rotate from the shortcut menu. At the `Specify rotation angle or [Base point/Copy/Undo/Reference/eXit]:` prompt, type **90** ↵. This action rotates the model.

11. Pick the bottom-right grip to activate it. Right-click and choose Scale from the shortcut menu. At the `Specify scale factor or [Base point/Copy/Undo/Reference/eXit]:` prompt, type **.5** ↵. This action scales the model.

12. Pick the grip at the midpoint of the bottom line. Press the Spacebar once to activate the Move option. At the `Specify move point or [Base point/Copy/Undo/eXit]:` prompt, type **0,–3** ↵. The model should look like Figure 10.38.

FIGURE 10.38

The drive block section, after several grip edits, looks a little like a cookie jar.

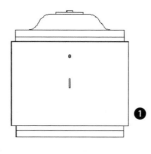

13. Press Esc to remove all grips. Define a crossing window by picking first at ❶, and then at ❷ (see Figure 10.38).

14. Hold down Shift and pick all the grips along the bottom three lines. Release Shift and pick the grip at the middle of the bottom line. At the `Specify stretch point or [Base point/Copy/Undo/eXit]:` prompt, type **0,1** ↵ to shrink the model.

    If the stretch does not come out right (it might be hard to see and activate all the grips), choose Undo from the Standard toolbar to undo the stretch and try again.

15. Save your drawing.

Customizing grips

You can turn grips on and off and customize their size and color. Choose Application Button ➪ Options and click the Selection tab. Use the right side of the dialog box, as shown in Figure 10.39.

FIGURE 10.39

Use the right side of the Option dialog box's Selection tab to customize grips.

By default, grips are enabled. Also by default, grips are turned off for blocks. (Chapter 18 covers blocks.) When grips are off for blocks, you see only one grip when you select a block; this is its insertion point. When grips for blocks are on, you see all the grips you would normally see for objects.

In the Grips section, you can choose the colors that you want for grips. Click the Grip Colors button to open the Grip Colors dialog box. There you can separate set colors for unselected and selected grips, the color that appears when you hover your cursor over a grip, and the color of the grip's contour (outline).

The Grip Size section lets you drag the slider bar to set the size of the grips. Click OK after you have made the desired changes.

Editing with the Quick Properties Palette and the Properties Palette

The Quick Properties palette and Properties palette are windows that show the properties of a selected object and allow you to change those properties by entering or choosing new values. The Quick Properties palette is small and is useful for simple, quick changes; it is also highly customizable. The Properties palette offers more options for each object.

Using the Quick Properties palette

By default, when you select an object, the Quick Properties palette appears, displaying some basic properties of the object, such as its layer, color, and linetype. Other properties that appear depend on the type of object. For example, you see the length of a line, as shown in Figure 10.40. To change an object's properties, enter or choose a new value in the Quick Properties palette. If you select more than one object, you see properties that apply to all the selected objects.

10

TIP

The QUICKPROPERTIES command lets you select objects for display in the Quick Properties palette. You can then see their properties. Type quickproperties ⏎ on the command line.

FIGURE 10.40

The Quick Properties palette shows you an object's properties in a small space and allows you to change those properties.

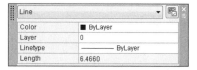

NEW FEATURE

When you use the Quick Properties palette to edit an object's properties and you hover your mouse over a property choice, you see a preview of the result on the object. For example, if you hover over a layer with a different color, you see the object displayed in that layer's color.

You can configure the Quick Properties palette in several ways:

- **Customize.** Click the Customize button at the upper-right corner of the palette to open the Customize User Interface (CUI) editor, where you can define which objects open the palette and which properties appear. For more information, see Bonus Chapter 10.

- **Settings.** Click the Options button beneath the palette's Close button at the upper-right corner, and choose Settings to open the Quick Properties tab of the Drafting Settings dialog box, where you can control the functioning of the panel in one location. You can also set the default height of the palette to display more or fewer properties.

- **Location Mode.** Click the Options button beneath the palette's Close button at the upper-right corner, and choose Location Mode ➪ Cursor or Static. By default, the palette displays at the cursor. Choose Static to display the palette in the drawing area, wherever you drag it. These options control the QPLOCATION system variable.

- **Auto-Collapse.** By default, the palette is small and you usually need to expand it to see all the properties. You can uncheck this option to display the palette big enough to show all the properties.

TIP

Click the Quick Properties button on the status bar to turn the Quick Properties palette on and off.

The rollover tooltip is a smaller version of the Quick Properties palette that appears when you hover your cursor over an object, without selecting it. You can't change properties in the rollover tooltip; they're just for your information. You can customize which properties appear, and synchronize the tooltip, with the Quick Properties palette; see Bonus Chapter 10 for more information.

Using the Properties palette

The Properties palette displays an extended list of the properties of selected objects. You can also use the Properties palette to change the properties of objects.

 To open the Properties palette, click View tab ⇨ Palettes panel ⇨ Properties, or press Ctrl+1. The Properties palette, shown in Figure 10.41, opens on your screen.

FIGURE 10.41

Use the Properties palette to edit objects and their properties.

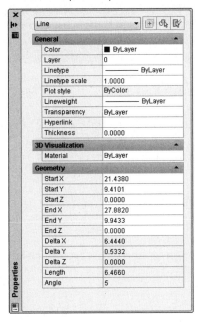

The auto-hide feature of the Properties palette makes it easy to work with the palette open all the time. Whenever the cursor moves off the palette, it collapses to just display the title bar. To auto-hide the palette, right-click the title bar and choose Auto-hide. You can also dock it; choose Anchor Left or Anchor Right from the title bar's shortcut menu. The Allow Docking item should also be checked; if it isn't, choose it from the same shortcut menu.

> **TIP**
> The Properties palette has its own undo function. Right-click the palette (but not on the item that you changed) in the Properties palette and choose Undo. Multiple levels of undo are available. For more information about palettes, see Bonus Chapter 3.

10

You can use the Properties palette to directly edit objects and to edit other object properties as well:

- You can change the layer, color, linetype, linetype scale, lineweight, and transparency of objects (see Chapter 11).
- You can edit text and text properties (see Chapter 13).
- You can edit plot styles (see Chapter 17).
- You can edit blocks (see Chapter 18).
- You can edit hyperlinks (see Bonus Chapter 5).

NEW FEATURE

When you use the Properties or Quick Properties palettes to edit an object's properties and you hover your mouse over a property choice, you see a preview of the result on the object. For example, if you hover over a layer with a different color, you see the object displayed in that layer's color.

To change values in the Properties palette, do one of the following:

- Click a value, select the text, type a new value, and press Enter.
- Click a value, click the down arrow to the right of the value, and choose from the drop-down list.

 - Click a value, click the Pick a Point button, and specify a new point by picking on the screen.

The information that you see in the Properties palette depends on the object selected. If you select more than one object, the palette shows properties that are common to those objects.

Working with object selection in the Properties palette

The Properties palette has three buttons in its upper-right corner: the Toggle Value of PICKADD Sysvar button, the Select Objects button, and the Quick Select button. These buttons all relate to selecting objects.

The Toggle Value of PICKADD Sysvar button turns PICKADD on and off. PICKADD changes how you select more than one object. When it's on (set to 1), which is the default, you can continue to select objects and they're added to the selection set. When it's off (set to 0), you need to press Shift to add objects to the selection set; otherwise, selecting an object deselects previously selected objects. Here's how to change the PICKADD variable:

 - When you see the 1, PICKADD is off. Click the button to turn PICKADD on.

 - When you see the plus, PICKADD is on. Click the button to turn PICKADD off.

 The Select Objects button enables you to select objects for editing in the Properties palette. After you select the objects you want, you can change their properties. If you're going to pick objects or use implied windowing, the Select Objects button offers no advantage. You can just select the objects and apply changes in the Properties palette. However, if you want to use a fence or polygon method of selection, the Select Objects button is helpful. Follow these steps:

1. Click the Select Objects button.

2. On the command line, type the selection method that you want (such as **f** for fence) as you would if a command were active or you had started the SELECT command.

3. Select the objects that you want.

4. Press Enter to end object selection.

5. Use the Properties palette to make the desired changes. (You can also start an editing command to use with the selected objects.)

 The Quick Select button opens the Quick Select dialog box, which is covered in Chapter 10 Addendum. Click the Properties palette's close box to close the window. I cover the Properties palette further in the next chapter and in later chapters as appropriate.

> **ON THE WEB**
>
> Sometimes you need a more powerful way to select objects. For example, you may want to select all the lines in your drawing to change their color, check the arc radii of all your fillets, or find short line segments that should be erased. Two powerful features, Quick Select and the FILTER command, let you create filters to select objects. These topics are covered fully in the Chapter 10 Addendum on the companion website.
>
> Another feature, groups, lets you create groups of objects that you can select together. I also cover this topic in the Chapter 10 Addendum on the companion website.

Summary

This chapter covered all the more advanced editing commands. You read about:

- Mirroring objects
- Creating rectangular, polar, and path arrays
- Creating an offset of an object
- Aligning objects
- Trimming and extending objects
- Stretching objects
- Lengthening (and shortening) objects
- Breaking and joining objects
- Creating chamfered corners and fillets for square, beveled, and rounded corners
- Drawing revision clouds and using wipeouts
- Using grips to stretch, move, mirror, rotate, and scale objects
- Double-clicking objects to edit them
- Using the Quick Properties panel and the Properties palette to see the properties of objects and edit them

In the next chapter, I cover layers, colors, linetypes, and lineweights.

10

Organizing Drawings with Layers and Object Properties

IN THIS CHAPTER

Working with layers in your drawing

Changing object color, linetype, lineweight, and transparency

Changing linetype spacing

Specifying which properties you want to match

U ntil you learn about layers, you draw everything in black or white. Drawing everything in one color is not a very good way to draw — besides, it's boring! If everything is the same color, it's hard to distinguish the various elements of a drawing. If you've followed the exercises throughout this book, you've opened some drawings from the companion website that used various colors and linetypes (such as dashed lines). For example, in some of the architectural drawings, you may have noticed that the walls are a different color than the fixtures in the kitchen. When you create text and dimensions, covered in Chapters 13, 14, and 15, you almost always use a color that stands out from the main model that you're drawing. You can also create objects with varying line widths, called *lineweights*. Finally, you can set the transparency of objects. This use of color, linetype, lineweight, and transparency helps to organize your drawings, making them easier to understand.

Most often, you assign color, linetype, lineweight, and transparency to a layer. A layer is simply an organizational tool that lets you organize the display of objects in your drawing. Every object must be on a layer, and every layer must have a color, a linetype, a lineweight, and a transparency value. You define layers to meet your drawing needs. Layers, colors, linetypes, lineweights, and transparency are called *object properties*. You can easily change any object's properties. This chapter explains how to create and change these object properties to organize your drawing.

Working with Layers

Layers offer powerful features that enable you to distinguish all the various elements of your drawing. In an architectural drawing, for example, you'll commonly create layers for walls, doors, windows, plumbing, electrical fixtures, structural elements, notes (text), dimensions, and so on. Mechanical drawings might use center, hidden, hatch, object, and titleblock layers. Each discipline has its own conventions, and where you work you might have specific conventions that you must follow.

Creating layers is an important part of setting up a drawing, in addition to the setup features covered in Chapter 5. You should create and save layers in your templates so that they're available to you when you start to draw. Layers give you many ways to organize your drawing. For example, you can:

- Assign different colors, linetypes, lineweights, and transparency to layers.
- Assign the various colors to different pens in a pen plotter, resulting in a paper drawing with varying colors or line widths.
- Control the visibility of layers. Making a layer invisible lets you focus on just the objects that you need to draw or edit.
- Control which objects are plotted.
- Lock a layer so that objects on that layer cannot be edited.

 You can also assign a plot style to a layer. A *plot style* is a group of settings that affects how your drawing is plotted. Chapter 17 covers plot styles.

Understanding layers

Besides having a color, linetype, lineweight, and transparency value, every layer must have a name. All drawings come with a default layer, called layer 0 (zero). Its color is black/white (depending on the background color of the drawing area), its linetype is Continuous, its lineweight is Default (0.010 inch or 0.25 mm), and its transparency is 0 (opaque). Most of the exercises in this book up to this point have used layer 0. To create a new layer, you must give it a name, a color, a linetype, a lineweight, and a transparency value. You can then start drawing on that layer.

Layers have four *states*:

- **On/Off.** On layers (the default) are visible. Off layers are invisible and are regenerated with the drawing. Off layers are not plotted.

- **Thawed/Frozen.** Thawed layers (the default) are visible. Frozen layers are invisible and are *not* regenerated with the drawing. However, when you thaw a frozen layer, the drawing regenerates. If you have floating viewports on a layout (covered in Chapter 17), you can also freeze a layer just in the current viewport, or only for new viewports that you create. You can also create a layer that is frozen in all viewports. Frozen layers are not plotted.
- **Unlocked/Locked.** Unlocked layers (the default) are visible and editable. Locked layers are visible but cannot be edited.
- **Plottable/Not Plottable.** Plottable layers are plotted. Not plottable layers are not plotted. This setting affects only layers that are on or thawed, because off and frozen layers are not plotted anyway.

Creating new layers

 To create a new layer, choose Home tab ⇨ Layers panel ⇨ Layer Properties. The Layer Properties Manager palette opens, as shown in Figure 11.1. This palette lists all current layers and their properties. You can also create new layers and modify existing ones. The left panel allows you to filter the list of layers. For more information on layer filtering, see the section, "Filtering the layer list," later in this chapter.

> **NOTE**
>
> The Layer Properties Manager is a palette that you can auto-hide and dock. Changes that you make to layer properties and states in the palette apply immediately in your drawing.

FIGURE 11.1

The Layer Properties Manager is the place to manage all your layers.

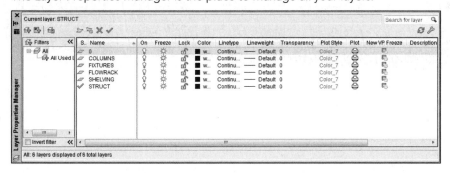

Table 11.1 explains the columns in the palette. For a description of the icons in most of the columns, see Table 11.2, later in this chapter.

TABLE 11.1 Columns in the Layer Properties Manager

Column Name	Description
Status	The status of each layer. A darker layer icon is used, and a lighter icon is unused. The current layer shows a checkmark.
Name	The name of the layer. To change the layer, click once to display a border and click again to type a new name.
On	The current on/off state of a layer. Click to turn the layer on or off.
Freeze	The current freeze/thaw state of a layer. Click to freeze or thaw a layer.
Lock	The current locked/unlocked state of a layer. Click to lock or unlock a layer.
Color	The current color of the layer. Click to change the color.
Linetype	The current linetype of the layer. Click to change the linetype.
Lineweight	The current lineweight of the layer. Click to choose a new lineweight.
Transparency	The current transparency (from 0 to 90) of the layer. Click to choose or enter a new value.
Plot Style	The current plot style of the layer. Click to select a new plot style. (Chapter 17 covers plot styles.)
Plot	The current plottable/not plottable state of the layer. Click to make the layer plottable or not plottable.
New VP Freeze	The current freeze/thaw state of the layer in new floating viewports that you create. Click to freeze or thaw the layer in new viewports. This column is displayed only if you have floating viewports and a layout tab is active. (Chapter 17 covers floating viewports.)
Description	A place to enter a description of a layer.

 When you open the Layer Properties Manager with a layout active, five additional columns appear that let you override layer properties for specific viewports. I explain this feature in more detail in Chapter 17.

To adjust the display in the Layer Properties Manager, you can do the following:

- Display or hide the Filters pane by clicking the double-arrow icon at the top of that pane.
- Change the width of any column in the Layer Properties Manager by placing the cursor over the line dividing two column headings and dragging.
- Double-click the line dividing two columns to minimize/maximize the width of the column to the left.
- Click any column head to sort the layers by that column. Click again to sort in the opposite order.
- Right-click any heading and display a shortcut menu where you can choose which columns you want to see.
- Drag any column to any location to specify the order of the columns.
- Right-click any heading and choose Freeze or Unfreeze Column (depending on the current status). Freezing a column forces it to the left of a gray, vertical line and holds it visible, even if you scroll to the right.
- Resize the entire dialog box by dragging on any side.

Naming the layer

Click the New Layer button in the Layer Properties Manager. A new layer appears, named `Layer1`. The name is highlighted so that you can immediately type in a new name for the layer. Press Enter after you type the name.

Next to the New Layer button is the New Layer VP Frozen in All Viewports button for creating a layer that is frozen in all viewports. I discuss freezing layers in viewports in Chapter 17.

11

> **TIP**
>
> If you want a new layer to have the same color and/or linetype as an existing layer, choose that existing layer and click New Layer. The new layer inherits the properties and states of the selected layer. You can then make any changes that you want.

Layer names can be up to 255 characters long and may include spaces. Layer names retain the uppercase/lowercase characters that you type. Layer names may not include the following symbols: < > / \ " ; ? * | , = `.

Assigning a color

To change the default color, move the cursor to the color box in the same row as the new layer. Click to open the Select Color dialog box, shown in Figure 11.2, with the Index Color tab displayed.

FIGURE 11.2

The Select Color dialog box

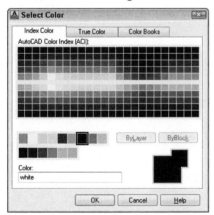

Click the color that you want. At the bottom of the dialog box, the color's name or number appears along with a sample of the color. Click OK to close the dialog box and return to the Layer Properties Manager.

Note that the Index Color tab offers you a choice of standard colors, gray shades, and a fuller palette of colors. The standard colors are the original colors that AutoCAD (and then AutoCAD LT) offered, and they're the ones often used, even today. These colors have both a name and a number, whereas other colors have only a number (an *index*). The standard colors are red (1), yellow (2), green (3), cyan (4), blue (5), magenta (6), and white (7). For more color choices, click the True Color tab, as shown in Figure 11.3.

> **NOTE**
>
> You can choose any color you want for the background color of a drawing, but commonly it is a black, white, or off-white screen. The default screen is almost black and the default color for 7 is black, but the color is called white. When you work on a black screen, objects using the color of 7 appear white (or else they would be invisible), and vice versa. To change the screen color, choose Application Button ⇨ Options and click the Display tab. Then click the Colors button under the Window Elements section. For a 2D drawing, choose 2D Model Space from the Context list box and choose Uniform Background (Background in AutoCAD LT) from the Interface Element list box. Then use the Color drop-down list to specify a color.

FIGURE 11.3

The True Color tab of the Select Color dialog box offers a more precise way to define color.

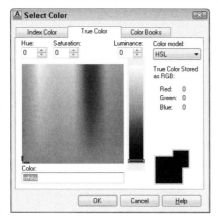

To define a color, first choose the color model from the Color Model drop-down list. Choose a color model based on familiarity or existing specifications. You have two choices:

- **HSL (Hue, Saturation, Luminance).** Hue is the actual wavelength of light that defines the color. Saturation is the purity or intensity of the color. Luminance is the brightness of the color.

- **RGB (Red, Green, Blue).** Defines a color according to the intensity of red, green, and blue in the color.

If you choose the HSL color model, specify the color as follows:

1. Specify the hue by dragging the crosshairs horizontally across the colors, or type a value from 0° to 360° in the Hue text box.

2. Specify the saturation by dragging the crosshairs vertically over the colors, or type a value from 0% to 100% in the Saturation text box.

3. Specify the luminance by dragging the bar on the color slider, or type a value from 0% to 100% in the Luminance text box.

If you choose the RGB color model, specify the red color by dragging the color bar, or type a value from 1 to 255 in the Red text box. Do the same for the green and blue color values.

You can also choose a color by using the Color Books tab. The Color Books tab displays colors in *color books*. Color books are files that define colors. AutoCAD includes several Pantone color books. Pantone is a commonly used system of matching colors that is often used for printing on paper and fabric.

To use a color from a color book, follow these steps:

1. On the Color Books tab of the Select Color dialog box, choose a color book from the Color Book drop-down list.

2. Drag the color slider or use the up and down arrows to choose a "page" of the color book. On the left, you see the colors for that page. A page can hold up to ten colors.

3. Choose one of the colors on the left side of the dialog box.

4. Click OK.

Choosing a linetype

The default linetype is a continuous line, but you can use many other linetypes. These linetypes are repeating patterns of dashes and/or dots and spaces, although they can also include text and shapes. Linetypes are covered more fully later in this chapter.

To change the default linetype, move the cursor to the Linetype column in the new layer's row. Click to open the Select Linetype dialog box, as shown in Figure 11.4.

FIGURE 11.4

The Select Linetype dialog box

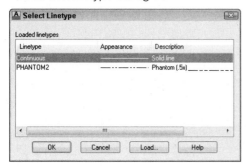

If the linetype that you want appears on the list, click the linetype and choose OK to close the dialog box. If the linetype does not appear, you need to load the linetype. Click Load to open the Load or Reload Linetypes dialog box, as shown in Figure 11.5.

Linetypes are stored in text (ASCII) files with the filename extension LIN. The standard linetypes are in `acad.lin` in AutoCAD and in `acadlt.lin` in AutoCAD LT. You can create your own linetypes and store them in these files. You can also store them in another file that you create with the extension `.lin`. Click File at the top of the dialog box if you want to load a linetype from a file that you created. Choose the linetype file that you want to load and click Open.

FIGURE 11.5

The Load or Reload Linetypes dialog box

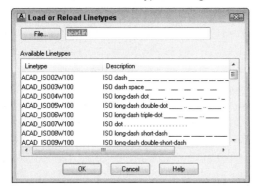

 See Bonus Chapter 8 for a full discussion on creating custom linetypes.

Choose the linetype to load and click OK. You return to the Select Linetype dialog box. The loaded linetype now appears on the list. Choose it and click OK. You're now back in the Layer Properties Manager dialog box and the layer now uses that linetype.

Assigning a lineweight

 A lineweight assigns a width to a line. When you give a layer a lineweight, every object on that layer has the same lineweight, unless you assign that specific object a different lineweight. A lineweight can help to distinguish various elements of your drawing, both on-screen and on paper. For example, you could use a thicker lineweight to indicate planned construction changes, for dimension lines, or to represent the true width of an object. The Show/Hide Lineweight button on the status bar toggles the display of lineweights on and off. By default, lineweight display is off.

To set a lineweight for a layer, click the Lineweight column of that layer to open the Lineweight dialog box, as shown in Figure 11.6. Choose a lineweight and click OK.

FIGURE 11.6

When you click the Lineweight column of the Layer Properties Manager, the Lineweight dialog box opens so that you can choose a lineweight.

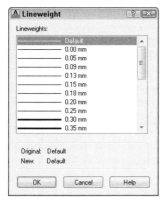

Lineweights have the following features:

- The default lineweight value for layers and objects is called DEFAULT, which has a value of 0.010 inch or 0.25 mm.
- On the Model tab, where you draw, lineweights are displayed in relation to pixels, the unit of measurement for computer screens. A lineweight of 0 is displayed with a width of 1 pixel. Wider lineweights are calculated proportionally to the actual width of the lineweight. The lineweight display on the Model tab does not change as you zoom in or out.
- On Layout tabs (covered in Chapter 17), lineweights are displayed in real-world units as they will be plotted. Lineweights act like other objects in your drawing and look bigger or smaller as you zoom in and out.
- By default, lineweights are measured in millimeters. You can format lineweights by choosing Home tab ⇨ Properties panel ⇨ Lineweight drop-down list ⇨ Lineweight Settings. The Lineweight Settings dialog box opens, as shown in Figure 11.7. The Lineweights section lists available lineweights. Choose a default lineweight from the Default drop-down list. The Adjust Display Scale slider determines how lineweights are displayed on the Model tab. Adjust this setting if you use several closely related lineweights but can't distinguish them on your screen. The Display Lineweight check box turns the display of lineweights on and off, which is the same as clicking the Show/Hide Lineweight button on the status bar.

If you don't want to use lineweights, you can just ignore them and display every object by using the default lineweight.

FIGURE 11.7

The Lineweight Settings dialog box lets you format how lineweights are measured and displayed.

Assigning a transparency value

A transparent object lets you see other objects behind it. Actually, you can make objects only partially transparent, because a completely transparent object would be invisible. You can set transparency from 0 (completely opaque) to 90.

 When you specify transparency for a layer, every object on that layer has the same transparency. In most cases, you'll use transparency for solid hatch fills, which are covered in Chapter 16. Generally, you won't notice transparency for the outlines that define most objects, such as lines, circles, and rectangles, unless you use a very thick lineweight.

To set a transparency value for a layer, click the Transparency column of that layer to open the Layer Transparency dialog box. Then either choose a default value from the drop-down list or enter a new value. You can specify a value from 0 to 90. Click OK. If you want objects to be opaque, you can ignore the transparency value. After you've set your new layer's color, linetype, lineweight, and transparency in the Layer Properties Manager, you're ready to use the layer.

> **NOTE**
> Many people have CAD standards that restrict which layers should be in a drawing. You can specify that you want to receive a notification whenever a new layer is added to a drawing. Then you can decide if the layer meets your CAD standards. For more information, see Bonus Chapter 3, where I cover CAD standards.

> **ON THE WEB**
> The drawing used in the following exercise on creating layers, ab11-a.dwg, is available from the Drawings download on the companion website.

STEPS: Creating a New Layer

1. Open ab11-a.dwg, available from the Drawings download on the companion website.
2. Save the file as ab11-01.dwg in your AutoCAD Bible folder.

3. Choose Home tab ⇨ Layers panel ⇨ Layer Properties to open the Layer Properties Manager.

4. Click the New Layer button. A new layer named `Layer1` appears, highlighted. Type **Walls** ↵ as the name for the new layer.

5. Click the color square in the Color column to open the Select Color dialog box. Choose the blue square from the Standard Colors and click OK.

6. Choose the New Layer button again to create another new layer. Type **Hidden** ↵.

7. Click the color square in the Color column to open the Select Color dialog box.

8. In the Select Color dialog box, click the True Color tab. From the Color Model drop-down list, choose RGB. In the Color text box, type **141,218,189.** (In some instances, you may have to re-choose RGB from the Color Model drop-down list to make the Color text box active.) Press Tab. You should see a teal (blue-green) color. Click OK.

9. In the main layer listing, click Continuous in the same row as the Hidden layer to open the Select Linetype dialog box. Click Load to open the Load or Reload Linetypes dialog box. Scroll down until you see the HIDDEN linetype. Choose it and click OK. In the Select Linetype dialog box, choose HIDDEN and click OK.

10. Click the Description column for the Hidden layer. (If you can't see this column, which is usually the rightmost column, drag the edge of the palette that is opposite the title bar to widen the palette. Click again so that a text cursor appears. Type **teal, hidden lines** ↵.

11. Select the Walls layer by clicking its name. Choose the New Layer button again to create another new layer with the same properties as the Walls layer. Type **Fill** ↵.

12. Click the color square in the Color column to open the Select Color dialog box. Choose the green square from the Standard Colors and click OK.

13. Click in the Transparency column of the Fill layer's row to open the Layer Transparency dialog box. Choose 40 from the drop-down list. Click OK.

14. Close or auto-hide the palette.

15. Choose Home tab ⇨ Layers panel and click the Layer drop-down list to see a list of the three layers that you just created. Click again to close the drop-down list.

16. Save your drawing.

Using layers

To use a layer that you have just created, click the Set Current icon in the Layer Properties Manager or double-click the layer's name. Objects that you create now are drawn on that layer and display with the layer's color, linetype, and lineweight. (The lineweight shows only if the Show/Hide Lineweight button on the status bar is on.)

After you have the layers you need, you need to switch from layer to layer as you draw. To do so, choose Home tab ⇨ Layers panel ⇨ Layer drop-down list, as shown in Figure 11.8.

FIGURE 11.8

The Layer drop-down list

The Layer drop-down list has three display modes:

- If no object is selected, it displays the current layer.
- If one or more objects are selected, it displays the layer of the selected object(s).
- When objects on varying layers are selected, the Layer drop-down list goes blank, indicating that more than one layer is included in the selection.

To check the current layer, make sure that no object is selected. If necessary, press Esc to deselect any objects.

To open the Layer drop-down list, click its down arrow. You see a list of all of your layers, including their states and colors. When you pass the mouse over the items, a tooltip tells you what they mean. The Layer drop-down list has three functions:

- It switches the current layer so that you can draw on a new layer.
- It changes the certain states of any specific layer on the list.
- It changes the layer of a selected object.

Switching the current layer

To switch the current layer, make sure that no object is currently selected, click the Layer drop-down list arrow, and click the name of the layer that you want to be current. Be careful to click only the name — otherwise, you may change the layer's state. After you click a new layer name, the drop-down list automatically closes.

 Choose Home tab ⇨ Layers panel ⇨ Previous to undo changes that you made to layer settings. It's like an UNDO command for the Layer Properties Manager.

Changing a layer's state

After you create a layer, you can manage that layer — and all the objects on that layer — by changing its states. You can change some layer states through the Layer drop-down list; others must be changed in the Layer Properties Manager. Each layer state has different properties and uses:

- **On/Off.** Turn layers off when seeing objects on those layers interferes with the drawing process. For example, if you want to edit only objects on your Object layer, but objects on other layers are nearby, you can turn off the other layers and easily select the objects on the Object layer with a window. Then turn the other layers back on. The on/off state is available on the Layer drop-down list.

- **Thaw/Freeze.** You can freeze layers for reasons similar to those that lead you to turn off layers. In general, freeze layers when you want to work without those layers for a longer period of time. The thawed/frozen state is available on the Layer drop-down list.

- **Thaw/Freeze in Current Viewport.** You may want to freeze or thaw layers in some floating viewports but not in others. (I cover floating viewports in Chapter 17.) For example, if you want to display dimensions in one viewport but not in others, freeze your dimensions layer in all the viewports except one. You can change this state on the Layer drop-down list if you're working on a layout. You can also click the Current Viewport Freeze icon in the Layer Properties Manager.

- **Thaw/Freeze in New Viewports.** You can also freeze or thaw layers in future viewports that you create. For example, after you display dimensions or text in one viewport, you may want to make sure that they won't appear in any new viewports that you create. This state is available in the New Viewport Freeze column of the Layer Properties Manager.

> **TIP**
>
> Three commands help you hide and display objects, although not by layer: The ISOLATEOBJECTS command hides all objects except those that you select. After selecting objects, right-click in the drawing area and choose Isolate ⇨ Isolate Objects. The HIDEOBJECTS command hides selected objects. Select the objects, right-click in the drawing area, and choose Isolate ⇨ Hide Objects. The UNISOLATEOBJECTS command undoes either of the previous commands, displaying objects that those commands hid. Right-click in the drawing area and choose Isolate ⇨ End Object Isolation.

> **NOTE**
>
> When you make several layer property changes in a row and then undo them, AutoCAD and AutoCAD LT count these changes as one change. Therefore, Undo brings you back to the state before the first change. You can change this behavior by choosing Application Button ⇨ Options, clicking the User Preferences tab, and unchecking the Combine Layer Property Change check box in the Undo/Redo section.

- **Unlock/Lock.** Lock a layer when you want to ensure that objects on that layer are not changed. You can still use objects on locked layers for reference (for example, you can use their object snaps). Click the Lock/Unlock icon on the Layer drop-down list.

> **NOTE**
>
> When you select an object on a locked layer, it doesn't display grips, because you can't edit it.

- **Plot/No Plot.** Make a layer not plottable when you want to create reference text or revision marks on your drawing but don't want to plot them. You may also have a drawing that contains both actual and planned structures; this feature enables you to plot showing only the actual structures. Being able to change a layer's plottable state makes it possible for you to create variations on your drawing, perhaps for different users, such as electricians, plumbers, and roofers. The plot/no plot state is available in the Plot column of the Layer Properties Manager.

> **TIP**
>
> Both the off and frozen states make layers invisible. The purpose of the frozen/thawed layer states is to reduce regeneration time — this is the main difference between On/Off and Thawed/Frozen layer visibility options. However, today's computers are faster, and recent releases of the software have reduced the need for regeneration. Because thawing a layer causes a regeneration, whereas turning a layer back on only causes a redraw, you actually save a regeneration by using On/Off rather than Thawed/Frozen.

Click any of the state icons to toggle a layer's state. For example, if you want to freeze a layer, click its sun icon; it switches to a snowflake icon. Table 11.2 shows the icons for each state.

TABLE 11.2   Layer State Icons

State	Icon	State	Icon
On		Off	
Thawed (in all viewports)		Frozen (in all viewports)	
Thawed (in new viewports)		Frozen (in new viewports)	
Unlocked		Locked	
Plottable		Not plottable	

When you change a layer's state from the Ribbon, the drop-down list stays open so that you can change the state of more than one layer at a time. Click the top of the list to close it.

> **CAUTION**
>
> Be careful when editing a drawing with layers that are frozen or off — it's easy to forget about them. For example, you could move a whole section of your drawing and inadvertently leave the frozen objects in that section behind.

Saving layer states

Often you work with sets of layer states. For example, you may lock certain layers during part of the editing process to avoid changing objects on those layers. You may also set some layers as not plottable just before final plotting, but want them plotted for a draft plot. You may also want to temporarily change the properties of certain layers — color, linetype, lineweight, transparency, and plot style — and then change them back.

You could spend a lot of time adjusting all these layer states and properties. Instead, you can save and restore sets of layer states — the properties and states of all the layers in a drawing. You can save layer states to automate the process of restoring layer states and properties by saving the set of all layer states and properties. After you save this set, you can restore it at any time. The term *layer states* includes the set of all layer states as well as their properties (such as color and linetype).

You can also export layer state settings to a file. You can then use the layer-state settings in another drawing with the same or similar layers.

To save a layer state, follow these steps:

1. Set all the layer states and properties the way you want them. Usually, you've already done this and should save the state before making changes that you plan to reverse later on.

2. Choose Home tab ⇨ Layers panel ⇨ Layer State drop-down list ⇨ Manage Layer States to open the Layer States Manager dialog box, as shown in Figure 11.9. Alternatively, you can click the Layer States Manager icon in the Layer Properties Manager.

FIGURE 11.9

The Layer States Manager dialog box

3. Click New and type a name for your layer state in the New Layer State Name text box of the New Layer State to Save dialog box. If you want, type a description. Click OK.

4. Back in the Layer States Manager, choose the layer states and properties that you want to save in the Layer Properties to Restore section. (If you don't see this section, click the More Restore Options right-arrow button at the lower-right corner of the dialog box.)

> **CAUTION**
>
> States and properties that you do not save are not affected later when you restore the layer state. For example, if you save only the on/off state and then change both a layer's on/off state and its color, when you restore the layer state, only the on/off state is returned to its original setting; the layer retains its new color.

5. If you want your drawing to look exactly as it did when you saved the layer state (in terms of layers), check the Turn Off Layers Not Found in Layer State check box. Any new layers that you create after saving the layer state are then turned off when you restore your layer state.

6. Click Close.

The Layer States Manager enables you to manage layer states in the following ways:

- **Restore.** Click the Restore button to restore a saved layer state.
- **Delete.** Click the Delete button to delete a layer state.
- **Import.** Click Import to import a layer state that has been previously exported as an `.las` file. Importing a layer state gives you access to layer states that others have saved. Click Import to open the Import Layer State dialog box.

> **NOTE**
>
> You can also import a layer state from a DWG (drawing), DWT (template), or DWS (standards) file. (Standards files are covered in Bonus Chapter 3.) In the Import Layer State dialog box, choose the type of file you want from the Files of Type drop-down list. Also, the Layer States Manager includes layer states from xrefs. (See Chapter 20 for information about xrefs.)

- **Export.** Click Export to export the settings of a layer state in an LAS file. Exporting a layer state gives others access to your layer-state settings.

To rename a layer state, click its name, type a new name, and press Enter. After you finish using the Layer States Manager, click Close to close the dialog box.

Changing an existing object's layer

Sometimes you need to change the layer of an object or objects that you've already drawn. You can do this easily by selecting one or more objects and clicking the layer name that you want for the object in the Layer drop-down list of the Layers panel on the Home tab. The list automatically closes.

> **NOTE**
>
> If you turn off Noun/Verb selection, as I explain in Chapter 9, you cannot select an object and change its layer from the Layer drop-down list. Instead, you can change the layer in the Properties palette.

You can also change an object's layer in the Quick Properties palette or the Properties palette. You can open the Quick Properties palette by selecting an object, and then right-clicking in the drawing area and choosing Quick Properties. You can also enable Quick Properties on the status bar to open the Quick Properties palette automatically when you select an object. To use the Properties palette, choose View tab ⇨ Palettes panel ⇨ Properties or press Ctrl+1. Use the Properties palette if you want to change more than one property of an object at one time.

> **CAUTION**
>
> It's easy to inadvertently change an object's layer. Make sure that objects are not selected (press Esc) if you're about to use the Layer drop-down list just to change the current layer.

Making an object's layer current

 If you're adding an object, you usually want to draw on the same layer as an existing object. You could select the object to see what layer it's on, press Esc to deselect the object, and then choose that layer from the Layer drop-down list to make it current. However, this process is easier with the Make Object's Layer Current button. Choose Home tab ⇨ Layers panel ⇨ Make Object's Layer Current, select an object, and click the button. That object's layer is now current.

Using special layer tools

A set of layer tools that were once in the Express Tools collection are very helpful for working with layers. Table 11.3 lists the Layer tools and what they do.

TABLE 11.3 **Layer Tools**

Layer Tool Name	Menu	Description
LAYWALK	Home tab ⇨ Layers panel (expanded) ⇨ Layer Walk	A full-featured command that helps you to see which objects are on which layers. Using the dialog box and the shortcut menu, you can list the number of objects on each layer, count the total number of layers, save layer states, and purge unused layers.
LAYMCH	Home tab ⇨ Layers panel ⇨ Match	Changes the layer of selected objects to match that of another selected object.
LAYCUR	Home tab ⇨ Layers panel (expanded) ⇨ Change to Current Layer	Changes the selected object's layer to the current layer.
COPYTOLAYER	Home tab ⇨ Layers panel (expanded) ⇨ Copy Objects to New Layer	Copies objects while changing the copy to the layer that you specify.
LAYISO	Home tab ⇨ Layers panel ⇨ Isolate	Turns off all layers except the layer of an object that you select, to isolate a specific layer. You can lock and fade layers. (I explain this command further after this table.)

continued

TABLE 11.3   *(continued)*

Layer Tool Name	Menu	Description
LAYUNISO	Home tab ⇨ Layers panel ⇨ Unisolate	Restores the state of layers that existed before you used LAYISO. (I explain this command further after this table.)
LAYVPI	Home tab ⇨ Layers panel (expanded) ⇨ VP Freeze in All Viewports except Current	Freezes all layers except the layer of an object that you select in all viewports except the current one, isolating the selected layer in the current viewport. (See Chapter 17 for information on viewports.)
LAYOFF	Home tab ⇨ Layers panel ⇨ Off	Turns the layer of the selected object(s) off.
LAYON	Home tab ⇨ Layers panel (expanded) ⇨ Turn All Layers On	Turns all layers on.
LAYFRZ	Home tab ⇨ Layers panel ⇨ Freeze	Freezes the layer of the selected object(s).
LAYTHW	Home tab ⇨ Layers panel (expanded) ⇨ Thaw All Layers	Thaws all layers.
LAYLCK	Home tab ⇨ Layers panel (expanded) ⇨ Lock	Locks the layer of the selected object(s).
LAYULK	Home tab ⇨ Layers panel (expanded) ⇨ Unlock	Unlocks all layers.
LAYMRG	Home tab ⇨ Layers panel (expanded) ⇨ Merge	Changes the layer of all objects on the first layer selected to the second layer selected. The first layer is purged.
LAYDEL	Home tab ⇨ Layers panel (expanded) ⇨ Delete	Deletes objects from the specified layer and purges that layer.

The LAYISO command can lock layers (other than the one you're isolating) and fade those layers instead of turning them off. The default is to lock layers and fade them by 50 percent. You can change the default by using the Settings option. For example, you can choose to turn off the layers or change the fade percentage. Use the LAYUNISO command to unisolate layers. Choose Home tab ⇨ Layers panel (expanded). Then drag the Locked Layer Fading slider to the left or right to decrease or increase fading. You can also specify Layer Isolate controls in the Layer Settings dialog box, which I discuss in the next section of this chapter.

ON THE WEB

The drawing used in the following exercise on working with layers, `ab11-b.dwg`, is available from the Drawings download on the companion website.

STEPS: Working with Layers

1. Open `ab11-b.dwg`, available from the Drawings download on the companion website.

2. Save the file as `ab11-02.dwg` in your `AutoCAD Bible` folder. This drawing is shown in Figure 11.10. The current layer is 0. Make sure that Object Snap is on. Set running object snaps for Endpoint and Quadrant. Turn Infer Constraints off.

FIGURE 11.10

This gas extraction well plan drawing needs to be completed.

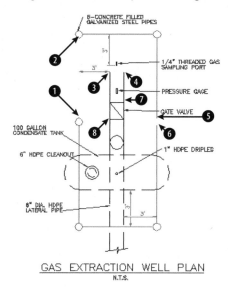

Thanks to the Army Corps of Engineers for this drawing.

3. From Home tab ⇨ Layers panel, click the Layer drop-down list and click PIPES to change the current layer to Pipes.

4. Start the LINE command. Draw a line from ❶ to ❷, shown in Figure 11.10, using the Quadrant running object snap.

5. Click the Layer drop-down list and click OBJECT to change the current layer to Object.

 6. Click the Layer drop-down list and click the On/Off icon of the Dim layer. Click again at the top of the list to close it.

7. Start the CIRCLE command. Right-click and choose 2p to use the two-point option. Draw a circle from the endpoint of ❸ to ❹, shown in Figure 11.10, using the Endpoint running object snap.

8. Without changing the layer, start the CIRCLE command and again use the 2p option. Draw a circle between the endpoints at ❺ and ❻.

9. The last circle was drawn on the wrong layer. To change its layer, select the circle. Then click the Layer drop-down list and choose PIPES. Press Esc to remove the grips and see the result.

The circle is now on the Pipes layer. Notice that the current layer is still Object in the Layer display.

10. Pick any red object (the Pipes layer). Choose Home tab ⇨ Layers panel ⇨ Make Object's Layer Current. The Pipes layer is now the current layer. Draw a line from the right quadrant of the circle at ❶ to the left quadrant of the circle at ❺ and ❻, as shown in Figure 11.10.

11. You want to draw a line on the Object layer. This is the previous layer that you used. Choose Home tab ⇨ Layers panel ⇨ Previous. The Object layer is now the current layer.

12. Draw a line from the endpoint at ❼ to the endpoint at ❽.

13. Pick any text to see what layer it is on. The Layer drop-down list changes to show the Text layer. Press Esc to clear the current selection. Choose Home tab ⇨ Layers panel ⇨ Match and choose the text gas extraction well plan at the bottom of the drawing. Then select one of the blue text objects in the drawing. The text gas extraction well plan is now on the Text layer.

14. Save your drawing. It should look like Figure 11.11.

FIGURE 11.11

The completed drawing

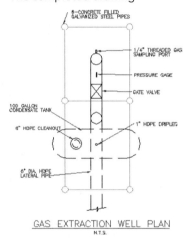

Modifying layers

Sometimes you need to change the layers that you display in the Layer Properties Manager to facilitate working with only certain layers. You may also need to change the properties of a layer, such as its color or linetype. Changing a layer's properties is a powerful tool because every object on that layer is automatically regenerated with the new properties. Other layer housekeeping tasks are renaming and deleting layers. You use the Layer Properties Manager for these functions.

Managing columns in the Layer Properties Manager

If you have many layers in a drawing, sorting can help you find the layers on which you need to work. You can sort the layer listing in a drawing by any column, by clicking once on the column title. Click again to see the list in reverse order. Long layer names display a tooltip with the entire layer name.

> **NOTE**
>
> If sorting by layer name does not appear to be working, increase the value for the MAXSORT system variable, which determines the maximum number of symbols that AutoCAD or AutoCAD LT sorts. Type maxsort ↵ on the command line and enter a larger number. Press Enter.

You can change the order of the columns by dragging them. For example, you may want to place the Color column next to the Name column. You can also choose which columns appear in the Layer Properties Manager. Right-click any column name and uncheck any column that you don't want to see. This choice remains until you change it. If you want to see a column again, right-click a column name again and check that column. As mentioned earlier in this chapter, you can freeze certain columns so that they always appear to the left, even if you scroll to the right. Right-click a column name and choose Freeze Column.

Filtering the layer list

Some complex drawings may have dozens of layers, and you may have a hard time finding the layer that you want in the Layer Properties Manager. You can filter the layer list so that you only see the layers that you want. This makes it easy to change a group of layers at once. The Filter Tree panel on the left side of the Layer Properties Manager contains one filter, All Used Layers, as well as the default that displays all layers. To display only used layers, click the All Used Layers filter in the Filter Tree panel.

> **NOTE**
>
> If you don't see the Filter Tree panel, right-click in the Layer Properties Manager and choose Show Filter Tree or click the double arrow on the left side of the palette.

You can create your own filters. There are two types of filters:

- **Properties filter.** Defines a filter by the properties of the layer. For example, you can create a filter that displays only green layers or layers that start with the letter *A*.
- **Group filter.** Defines a filter by selecting layers that go into a filter. A group filter offers complete flexibility to filter layers. For example, you might want to create a group filter that contains all your text, annotation, and dimension layers.

 To create a properties filter, click the New Property Filter button to open the Layer Filter Properties dialog box, as shown in Figure 11.12. Notice that the Filter Definition pane at the top has the same columns as the Layer Properties Manager.

FIGURE 11.12

The Layer Filter Properties dialog box

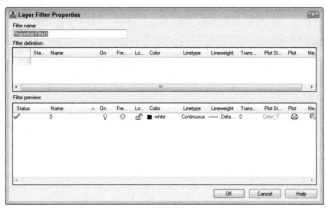

Name the filter in the Filter Name text box. To choose a property, you use the Filter Definition pane. Click in the first row of that property's column. Then do one of the following:

- If a drop-down arrow appears, click the arrow and choose one of the options from the drop-down list. (To remove a property, choose the blank line at the top of the drop-down list.)
- If an ellipsis button appears, click the button and choose a property from the dialog box that opens. For example, you can choose a layer color from the Select Color dialog box. (To remove a property, select the text, press Delete, and click anywhere outside the column.)
- To specify a filter for a named property, such as the name or linetype of a layer, you can use wildcards. The two most common wildcard characters are * (asterisk), which replaces any number of characters, and ?, which replaces any single character. For example, you could set the layer name filter to h* and the color to magenta. The resulting filter would include only magenta layers whose names start with the letter *H*.

As you work, the Filter Preview pane shows the results of your filter. When you're done, click OK. The Layer Properties Manager now shows only the layers that match your filter specifications.

 To create a group filter, open the Layer Properties Manager and click the New Group Filter button. Enter a name for the filter in place of the default name that appears. In the Filter Tree panel, choose a filter that displays the layers you need, such as All. Then simply drag the layers that you want onto the group filter's name.

TIP

To add layers by selecting objects that are on the layers you want, right-click the filter and choose Select Layers ⇨ Add. You return to your drawing where you can select objects. Press Enter to end object selection.

 To display all layers except the ones specified by any filter, click Invert Filter. If you want to filter the Layer drop-down list on the Layers panel or Layer toolbar in the same way, click the Settings button. In the Layer Settings dialog box that opens, check Apply Layer Filter to Layer Toolbar. This dialog box also lets you specify settings for the Layer Isolate feature (locking and fading). (I discuss the New Layer Notification section in Bonus Chapter 3.) Click OK.

> **TIP**
>
> When you work with a large number of layers, think carefully about how you name them. Naming layers in groups is common. For example, if you have several text layers, you could name them Text Title, Text Notes, and Text Schedule. A systematic layer-naming scheme makes it easy to filter the layers that you need, which in turn makes it easy to make changes to groups of layers.

Changing a layer's color, linetype, lineweight, and transparency

You can modify the color of a layer. To do so, open the Layer Properties Manager, and choose the color swatch of the layer that you want to modify. The Select Color dialog box opens. Choose a color and click OK. For more information about choosing colors, see the section, "Assigning a color," earlier in this chapter.

To change a layer's linetype, click the layer's linetype in the Layer Properties Manager. There you can either choose a loaded linetype or load a linetype if necessary. Click OK.

To change a layer's lineweight, click the layer's lineweight. Choose a new lineweight from the Lineweight dialog box and click OK.

To change a layer's transparency, click the layer's transparency value. Choose or enter a new value in the Layer Transparency dialog box. Click OK.

> **TIP**
>
> You can modify more than one layer at a time. In the Layer Properties Manager, right-click and choose Select All to choose all the layers. Choose Clear All to deselect all the layers. You can choose a range of layers by clicking the first layer in the range, holding Shift, and clicking the last layer in the range. Finally, you can choose individual layers by pressing Ctrl for each additional layer. Changes that you make to color, linetype, lineweight, or transparency affect all the selected layers.

 When you're ready to lay out a drawing for plotting, you generally work on a layout and create floating viewports. You can change the properties of a layer in a viewport. For example, you might want a layer to appear in a different color when you display it in a small detail view from the color that you want in a larger context. It's also common to freeze layers in a viewport. For more information, see Chapter 17 where I cover overriding layer properties for layouts and viewports.

Renaming layers

Thinking out your layer-naming scheme in advance is best. Many disciplines and organizations have layer-naming standards. However, sometimes you simply need to rename a layer.

To rename a layer, open the Layer Properties Manager. Click the name of the layer, and then click a second time. A border appears, and the name is highlighted. Type the new name and press Enter. Alternatively, you can right-click the layer name and choose Rename Layer from the shortcut menu or just press F2.

Deleting layers

 To delete a layer, open the Layer Properties Manager. Click the name of the layer and click the Delete Layer button.

 Layer and linetype definitions add to the size of your drawing because they're kept in the drawing's database. Therefore, eliminating layers and linetypes that you aren't using is worthwhile. You can delete them, but sometimes it's hard to know which layers contain no objects. The PURGE command lets you delete many types of unused definitions, including layers and linetypes. I cover the PURGE command in Bonus Chapter 3.

STEPS: Modifying Layers

1. Open `ab11-c.dwg`, available from the Drawings download on the companion website.

2. Save the file as `ab11-03.dwg` in your `AutoCAD Bible` folder.

 3. Choose Home tab ⇨ Layers panel ⇨ Layer Properties.

 4. Click the New Property Filter button. In the Filter Name text box, type **M layers**. In the Name column, type **m*** to list all layers starting with the letter *M*. Click OK. The layer list now shows only those layers.

5. In the Layer Properties Manager, click the top layer. Hold Shift and click the next-to-last layer. All the layers except for Mydims are selected. Click anywhere in the Linetype column to open the Select Linetype dialog box and choose Dashed. Click OK. Notice that all the selected layers now have a dashed linetype. You can now see that the layers that you selected have the dashed linetype.

6. In the Layer Properties Manager, choose Mydims. Click it a second time so that the name of the layer is highlighted. Type **Titles** ↵ to change the name of the layer. Close or collapse the Layer Properties Manager.

11

7. Start the ERASE command and pick anywhere on the titleblock (it is all one object) and the three labels FRONT, TOP, and RIGHT SIDE. Press Enter to end the command.

8. Again display the Layer Properties Manager. In the Filter Tree panel, click All to display all the layers.

9. Click the Settings. In the Layer Settings dialog box, check the Indicate Layers in Use check box at the bottom of the dialog box. Click the OK button.

10. Scroll down the list of layers and choose Titles. Click Refresh. You can see that its Status icon is off, indicating that the layer contains no objects. Click the Delete Layer button.

11. Save your drawing.

Manipulating Object Color, Linetype, Lineweight, and Transparency

The properties of layers — color, linetype, lineweight, and transparency — can also apply directly to objects. You can assign a color, linetype, and lineweight to an object. You can also set a current color, linetype, and lineweight so that all the future objects that you draw have those properties, regardless of the properties assigned to their layer. In most cases, you should avoid assigning properties directly to objects because you lose the organizational value of layers. When you create a layer, and assign it a color, linetype, lineweight, and transparency, those properties of the object are *ByLayer*. This means that the object picks up those properties from the properties of its layer.

You can also assign plot styles to objects. See Chapter 17 for more information. When you create a block with objects whose properties are ByBlock and you insert the block, it takes on the current color (or the color of the current layer). (For more information about blocks and layers, see Chapter 18.)

Because it's so helpful to organize object properties by layer, you can use the SETBYLAYER command to return objects' properties to ByLayer. Choose Home tab ⇨ Modify panel (expanded) ⇨ Set to ByLayer. At the `Select objects or [Settings]:` prompt, select objects. At the `Change ByBlock to ByLayer? [Yes/No] <Yes>:` prompt, choose Yes if you want to change the properties of objects in blocks to ByLayer. At the `Include blocks? [Yes/No] <Yes>:` prompt, choose Yes if you want to include blocks that are in the selection set. (Chapter 18 covers blocks.) All objects that you selected become ByLayer and therefore pick up the properties of their layer (unless you chose objects that were set to ByBlock and chose No at the first prompt).

If you choose the Settings option at the first prompt, the SetByLayer Settings dialog box opens, where you can choose which properties you want to set to ByLayer. For example, if you had an object whose color was set to green and whose linetype was set to Dashed, you could uncheck the Linetype check box to change the color to ByLayer, but leave the linetype set to Dashed.

Changing an object's color

You can control an object's color by using the Color drop-down list, which you can find by choosing Home tab ⇨ Properties panel. You can also change an object's color by using the Quick Properties palette that opens when you select an object, or in the Properties palette. For more information about choosing colors, see the section, "Assigning a color," earlier in this chapter. As with the Layer drop-down list, the Color drop-down list shows the color of any selected object. When you create a layer, assign it a color, and draw with that layer, the color is displayed as ByLayer.

The ByBlock color creates objects by using color 7 (white or black, depending on the screen color), but if the objects are placed in a block, the block takes on the current color when inserted. (For information about blocks, see Chapter 18.)

The best practice for organizing a drawing is to assign colors by layer. It can be confusing if related elements, such as centerlines in a mechanical drawing, appear in different colors. Also, if you see another line with the same color and linetype as most centerlines, you may assume that it's a center-line in the wrong place. It is standard practice to organize colors by layer.

Colors have a special significance because when you plot, you can assign colors to pens — although you can also use plot styles (see Chapter 17). If you use a color-based system, color is the basis that you use for plotting with various width pens or colors. You may want to temporarily change the color of an object to emphasize it in a plot or for some other reason. However, you should generally refrain from directly changing the color of objects.

If you need to change the color of an object, here are two ways to do it:

- To change just an object's color, select the object. Click the Color drop-down list by choosing Home tab ⇨ Properties panel, or the Quick Properties palette, and then choose the color that you want.
- If you want to change other properties at the same time, select the object and open the Properties palette (press Ctrl+1). There you can change all the properties of the object. To change the color, choose Color and click the drop-down arrow that appears. Choose the color that you want.

You can always change an object's color back to ByLayer, using the same technique, or by using the SETBYLAYER command, described in the preceding section.

Changing the current color

When you change the current color, all future objects are drawn using that color, regardless of their layer. In general, you should do this only when you have a special need for two objects to be on one layer but have different colors. An example might be text in a titleblock. You might want the text to have the same layer so that you can freeze it and thaw it (or turn it on and off) easily without having to remember that the text and titleblock are on two separate layers. If you also want part of the text to have a different color, change the current color before typing in that part of the text. Remember to change the current color back to ByLayer before drawing anything else.

To change the current color, make sure that no object is selected. Then click the Color drop-down list on the Properties panel on the Home tab. You can also open the Properties palette and choose the color that you want. To use a color not on the list, choose Select Color to open the Select Color dialog box. (See the section "Assigning a color" earlier in this chapter for more information on assigning colors.) To change the current color back to ByLayer, use the same techniques and choose ByLayer or use the SETBYLAYER command. You have an opportunity to do an exercise on changing colors after the "Changing the current lineweight" section.

Altering an object's linetype

Linetypes work according to the same principles as colors. You can change the linetype of an existing object or objects. You can control an object's linetype by using the Linetype drop-down list in the Properties panel of the Home tab, or in the Quick Properties palette. The Linetype drop-down list shows the linetype of any selected object. When you create a layer, assign it a linetype, and draw with that layer, the linetype is displayed as ByLayer.

The ByLayer linetype simply means that the linetype of the object is taken from the linetype of the object's layer.

The best way to organize a drawing is to assign linetypes by layer. It can be confusing if similar elements, such as plat borders in a surveyor's drawing, appear in different linetypes. Also, if you see another line with the same color and linetype as most plat borders, you may assume that it's a plat border in the wrong place.

If you need to change the linetype of an object, you have two options:

- To change an object's linetype, select the object. Click the Linetype drop-down list in the Properties panel of the Home tab, or in the Quick Properties palette, and then choose the linetype that you want.
- Select the object and open the Properties palette. Click the Linetype item, and then click the drop-down arrow that appears. Choose from one of the linetypes.

You can always change an object's linetype back to ByLayer, using the same methods or with the SETBYLAYER command, discussed earlier in this chapter.

As discussed in the "Assigning a linetype" section earlier in this chapter, you need to load a linetype before you can use it for the first time. To load a linetype, choose Home tab ⇨ Properties panel ⇨ Linetype drop-down list. Choose Other to open the Linetype Manager. Choose Load to open the Load or Reload Linetypes dialog box, choose the linetype file (if not the default), and choose the linetype that you want to load. Click OK. Choose the linetype again in the Linetype Manager and click OK to return to your drawing.

To filter the list of linetypes, choose from the Linetype Filters drop-down list box in the Linetype Manager.

Altering the current linetype

You can also change the current linetype. When you change the current linetype, all future objects that you draw have that linetype and are not drawn according to their layer's assigned linetype. In general, you should do this only when you have a special need for two objects to be on one layer but have different linetypes. An example might be a table containing notes in one corner of a drawing. You might want the lines that make up the table to have the same layer so that you can freeze it and thaw it (or turn it on and off) easily without having to remember that the table is on two separate layers. If you also want some of the lines to have a different linetype, change the current linetype before adding those lines. Remember to change the current linetype back to ByLayer before drawing anything else.

To change the current linetype, click the Linetype drop-down list and choose the linetype that you want, first making sure that no objects are currently selected. You can also use the Properties palette. To change the current linetype back to ByLayer, choose ByLayer for the linetype or use the SETBYLAYER command, discussed earlier in this chapter.

Changing an object's lineweight

Lineweights let you represent objects with varying line widths. The widths can represent the width of a pen in a pen plotter that will be used to plot that object. Lineweights can also be used as an organizational tool, to distinguish certain types of objects just as colors and linetypes do. Finally, you can use lineweights to represent the actual properties of objects, such as the width of wires in an electrical schematic.

Lineweights work according to the same principles as colors and linetypes. You can control an object's lineweight by using the Lineweight drop-down list in the Properties panel of the Home tab. The Lineweight drop-down list shows the lineweight of any selected object. When you create a layer, assign it a lineweight, and draw with that layer, the lineweight is displayed as ByLayer.

As with colors and linetypes, the best way to organize a drawing is to assign lineweights by layer. If you need to change the lineweight of an object, do one of the following:

- Select the object. Click the Lineweight drop-down list in the Properties panel of the Home tab and choose the lineweight that you want.
- Select the object and open the Properties palette. To change an object's lineweight, click Lineweight, and then click the drop-down arrow that appears. Choose from one of the lineweights.

Changing the current lineweight

You can also change the current lineweight. When you change the current lineweight, all future objects that you draw have that lineweight and are not drawn according to their layer's assigned lineweight.

To change the current lineweight, click the Lineweight drop-down list and choose the lineweight that you want, first making sure that no objects are currently selected. You can also use the Properties palette. To change the current lineweight back to ByLayer, choose ByLayer as the lineweight or use the SETBYLAYER command, discussed earlier in this chapter.

Altering an object's transparency

Transparency lets you see multiple layers of objects. Most often, you would use transparency for filling closed areas, such as the inside of a circle or rectangle. (You create fills using the HATCH command; I cover hatches in Chapter 16.) You may want to allow an image or text to show through an object that is on top.

Transparency works according to the same principles as colors and linetypes. You can control an object's transparency by using the Transparency slider in the Properties panel of the Home tab. The Transparency slider shows the transparency value of any selected object. When you create a layer, assign it a transparency value, and draw with that layer, the transparency is displayed as ByLayer.

As with colors and linetypes, the best way to organize a drawing is to assign transparency by layer. However, you may want to make an object transparent temporarily so that you can see objects behind it. If you need to change the transparency of an object, do one of the following:

- Select the object. Click the Transparency slider in the Properties panel of the Home tab, and drag it to the transparency value that you want.
- Select the object and open the Properties palette. Click Transparency, and then type the transparency value (from 0 to 90) that you want.

Altering the current transparency

You can also change the current transparency. When you change the current transparency, all future objects that you draw have that transparency and are not drawn according to their layer's assigned transparency.

To change the current transparency, click the Transparency slider and drag it to display the value that you want, first making sure that no objects are currently selected. You can also use the Properties palette. To change the current transparency back to ByLayer, choose ByLayer as the transparency or use the SETBYLAYER command, discussed earlier in this chapter.

On the Web
The drawing used in the following exercise on changing colors, linetypes, and lineweights, `ab11-d.dwg`, is available from the Drawings download on the companion website.

STEPS: Changing Colors, Linetypes, Lineweights, and Transparency

1. Open `ab11-d.dwg`, available from the Drawings download on the companion website.
2. Save the file as `ab11-04.dwg` in your `AutoCAD Bible` folder. This is an elevation view of a lavatory cabinet, as shown in Figure 11.13. Turn Selection Cycling on (if it isn't already on) by clicking the Selection Cycling button on the status bar.

FIGURE 11.13

A lavatory cabinet

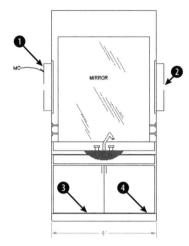

Thanks to the Army Corps of Engineers for this drawing.

3. Pick one of the reflection lines in the mirror. Notice that the color is red but the layer's color, as shown in the Layer drop-down list, is Magenta. Select all the reflection lines. Choose Home tab ⇨ Properties panel, click the Color drop-down list, and choose ByLayer from the top of the list. Press Esc to remove the grips.

4. Select the green dimension at the bottom of the cabinet. (The dimension is all one object.) To make it more visible, click the Color drop-down list and choose Red. Press Esc to see the result.

5. Pick the lines at ❶ and ❷, as shown in Figure 11.13. On the Home tab in the Properties panel, click the Linetype drop-down list and choose the Hidden linetype. Press Esc so that the hidden lines are no longer selected.

6. Select the dashed arc that represents the bottom curvature of the sink. In the Selection dialog box that opens, click Arc. In the Properties panel, click the Lineweight drop-down list and choose 0.30 mm. Press Esc. Click the Show/Hide Lineweight button on the status bar to turn on the display of lineweights and see the result.

7. Select the sink's fill. Click the Home tab. In the Properties panel, expand the panel and drag the Transparency slider to about 50. Press Esc to deselect the fill. The arc at the edge of the sink is now much more visible.

8. In the Properties panel, click the Color drop-down list box and choose Cyan to make it the current color.

9. Start the RECTANG command. Draw a rectangle inside the left cabinet. The exact size and placement are not important. Use the COPY command to copy the rectangle to the right cabinet. To copy, use an intersection object snap at point ❸ as the base point and ❹ as the second point of displacement. The rectangles are drawn in cyan.

10. Save your drawing. It should look like Figure 11.14.

FIGURE 11.14

The finished cabinet

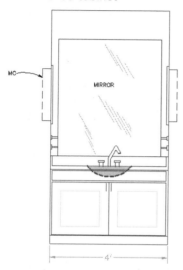

Working with Linetype Scales

A noncontinuous linetype is a repeating pattern of dots, dashes, and spaces. Linetypes can also include repeating text or shapes. You may find that the linetype patterns in your drawing are too long or short for clarity. The linetype scale may even be so big or so small that the line looks continuous. How often the pattern is repeated is affected by three factors:

- The linetype definition
- The global linetype scale
- The individual object's linetype scale

Changing linetype spacing by using a different linetype

One choice is to change the linetype. A number of linetypes come in short, medium, and long variations, such as Dashedx2, Dashed, and Dashed2, as shown in Figure 11.15.

FIGURE 11.15

A number of the standard linetypes come in three variations, such as Dashedx2, Dashed, and Dashed2.

AutoCAD's `acad.lin` and AutoCAD LT's `acadlt.lin` contain a number of ISO linetypes that meet the specifications of the International Standards Organization. Your organization or field of specialty may require the use of these linetypes. The ISO linetype pattern definitions are much longer than the other linetype definitions. You may need to make adjustments to the linetype scale as a result.

Changing linetype spacing by changing the global linetype scale

Another choice is to change the global linetype scale, which affects all noncontinuous linetypes in your drawing. AutoCAD and AutoCAD LT multiply the linetype definition by the global linetype scale to calculate the length of each repetition of the linetype:

- Linetype scales larger than 1 result in longer sections — and fewer repetitions of the linetype definition per unit.
- Linetype scales smaller than 1 result in shorter sections — and more repetitions of the linetype definition per unit.

 You can also change the scale of a linetype that appears in a viewport on a layout. For more information, see Chapter 17.

When you change the linetype scale, the drawing regenerates to change all the linetypes. Figure 11.16 shows three versions of a drawing with linetypes at linetype scales of 0.5, 1, and 2. As you can see, a scale of 2 is too large and a scale of 0.5 is too small. A scale of 1 is just right. (Goldilocks would have been happy with it.)

FIGURE 11.16

Three versions of a drawing, using linetype scales of 0.5, 1, and 2

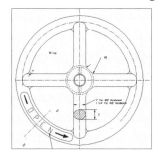 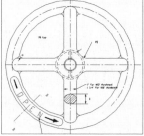 

For purposes of drawing, you simply want to make sure that you can distinguish the linetype both when you can see the entire drawing on the screen and when you zoom in close. The main reason to scale linetypes is for plotting. A linetype scale that works for a drawing of a house on-screen may appear continuous when you plot it at a scale factor of 1 = 96.

If you want the linetype to appear exactly according to its definition, use the scale factor for the linetype scale. Chapter 5 covers scale factors. If the scale factor doesn't give you the results that you want, try a linetype scale of one quarter to one half of the scale factor — in the 1 = 96 example, you might use a linetype scale of 24 or 48.

To change the linetype scale, choose Home tab⇨Properties panel⇨Linetype drop-down list⇨Other (the LINETYPE command) to open the Linetype Manager, as shown in Figure 11.17. Click Show Details if the lower portion of the dialog box is not displayed.

FIGURE 11.17

The Linetype Manager dialog box

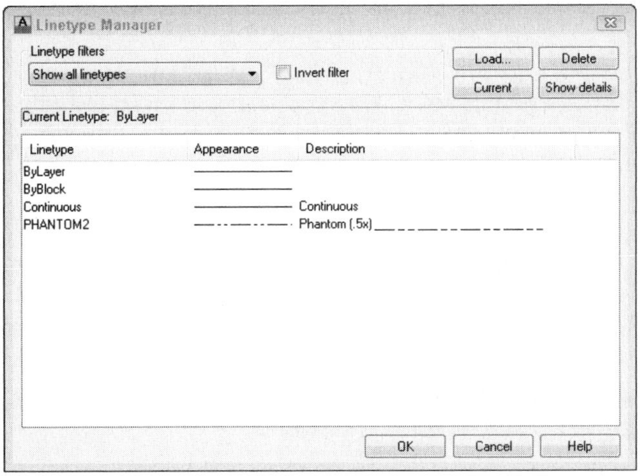

In the Global Scale Factor text box, type the scale factor that you want. Click OK. The drawing regenerates, changing the scale of every noncontinuous linetype in the drawing.

TIP

The global linetype scale is held in the LTSCALE system variable. You can change the linetype scale by typing ltscale ⏎ at the command line and typing a scale.

Altering linetype spacing by changing the object linetype scale

On occasion, you may want the linetype spacing to be different for one object — or a small group of objects — only. Perhaps the object is too small to show the linetype pattern or you want to set it off visually. The *current object linetype scale* works like setting a current color or linetype — all objects drawn after you set the object linetype scale are drawn with the new linetype scale. In most cases, you want to make sure that you change the current object linetype scale back to its default of 1 after using it for that one object or group of objects.

Changing the current object linetype scale

To change the linetype scale, choose Home tab ⇨ Properties panel ⇨ Linetype drop-down list ⇨ Other to open the Linetype Manager. Click Show Details if the lower portion of the dialog box is not displayed. In the Current Object Scale text box, type the scale factor that you want. Click OK. Now all objects that you draw use the current object linetype scale. When you're done drawing objects at that linetype scale, remember to change the linetype scale back to 1.

The current object linetype scale is held in the CELTSCALE system variable. You can also change the current object linetype scale by typing **celtscale** at the command line and typing in a scale.

If you have also set the global linetype scale to a value other than 1, AutoCAD and AutoCAD LT multiply the two linetype scales to calculate the final result. For example, if you have a global linetype scale of 12 and a current object linetype scale of 0.5, objects you draw will have a resulting linetype scale of 6.

Changing an existing object's linetype scale

You will often draw an object without setting a special object linetype scale and then decide that you want to change its linetype scale. To change an object's linetype scale, select the object and open the Properties palette. Click Linetype Scale and then type the new linetype scale. This linetype scale affects only the selected object. It does not affect the global linetype scale.

 You can import layers and linetypes (as well as other types of drawing content and definitions) from other drawings, using the Content Explorer. I cover this feature in Chapter 12.

ON THE WEB
The drawing used in the following exercise on changing linetype scales, `ab11-e.dwg`, is available from the Drawings download on the companion website.

STEPS: Changing Linetype Scales

1. Open `ab11-e.dwg`, available from the Drawings download on the companion website.

2. Save the file as `ab11-05.dwg` in your `AutoCAD Bible` folder. This drawing is of a bushing, as shown in Figure 11.18. Notice that the linetype doesn't show clearly on the short line at ❶ and in the small circle at ❷.

FIGURE 11.18

This drawing of a bushing has two noncontinuous linetypes.

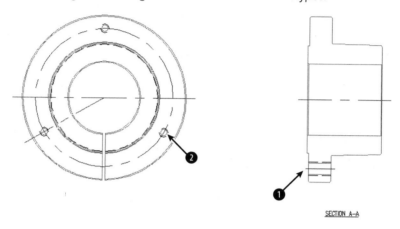

SECTION A–A

Thanks to Robert Mack of the Dexter Company, Fairfield, Iowa, for this drawing.

3. Choose Home tab ⇨ Properties panel ⇨ Linetype drop-down list ⇨ Other. Click Show Details to open the Details section of the Linetype Manager, if necessary. Change the Global scale factor to 0.5. Click OK. The drawing regenerates. Note that the circles are better, but the short line at ❶ still looks like a continuous line.

4. Choose the line at ❶. Choose View tab ⇨ Palettes panel ⇨ Properties (or press Ctrl+1) to open the Properties palette (if it isn't already open). Click Linetype Scale and change it to 0.5. Press Enter. Press Esc to remove the grips and see the result. Notice the difference in the line, which now has a linetype scale of 0.5 (global) times 0.5 (object) = 0.25.

5. Save your drawing. It should look like Figure 11.19.

FIGURE 11.19

FIGURE 11.19

The drawing's noncontinuous lines are now more appropriate.

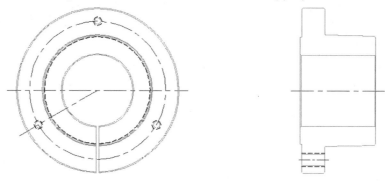

SECTION A–A

ON THE WEB

Rtltscal gives you real-time control over linetype scales. This is a VBA application. Look in `\Software\Chapter11\rtltscal.dvb`.

AutoCAD enables you to *translate* layers. For example, you can specify that all objects on layer `dashed` be changed to the layer `hidden`. Use this feature to maintain layer standards that you have set up. Bonus Chapter 3 fully covers layer translating. This feature is not available in AutoCAD LT.

Matching Properties

You may be familiar with the Format Painter button available in many Windows applications. AutoCAD and AutoCAD LT offer something similar that enables you to specify which properties you want to match. AutoCAD calls this process *matching properties*.

An object can have so many properties that this can be a useful tool. To match properties, you need two objects, a source object and a destination object (or objects). Follow these steps to match properties:

 1. Choose Home tab ⇨ Clipboard panel ⇨ Match Properties. You see a Format Painter cursor with a pickbox. On the command line, you see the `Select source object:` prompt.

2. Choose the object whose properties you want to match (the source object).

TIP

You can choose the source object first and then start the command.

---

3. Then you see the `Select destination object(s) or [Settings]:` prompt. If you want to match all the object's properties, select the object(s) that you want to receive the matching properties, that is, the destination object(s).

4. If you want to match only some of the object's properties, right-click and choose Settings to open the Property Settings dialog box, as shown in Figure 11.20. Uncheck all the properties that you don't want to match and click OK. The previous prompt returns. Select the object(s) that you want to receive the matching properties, that is, the destination objects(s).

FIGURE 11.20

The Property Settings dialog box

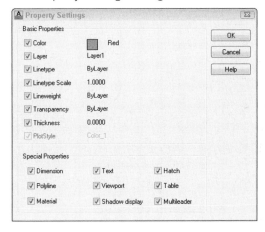

5. Press Enter to end object selection and match the properties.

Summary

In this chapter, you read all about layers, colors, linetypes, and lineweights. You learned about:

- Using layers to help you organize your drawings by assigning the same properties to related objects
- Creating a layer by giving it a name, color, linetype, lineweight, and transparency in the Layer Properties Manager
- Changing the layer of existing objects
- Setting layer states — On/Off, Thawed/Frozen, Unlocked/Locked, and Plottable/Not Plottable
- Changing the properties of existing layers
- Saving sets of layer states and properties and later restoring them
- Filtering the layer listing

- Purging unused layers and linetypes
- Altering the color, linetype, lineweight, and transparency of any object
- Globally changing the linetype scale, changing the current linetype scale, and changing the object linetype scale of existing objects
- Utilizing the Match Properties feature to copy properties from one object to one or more destination objects

The next chapter explains how to get detailed information from your drawing.

Obtaining Information from Your Drawing

IN THIS CHAPTER

Obtaining drawing-wide information

Obtaining information about objects

Measuring and segmenting objects

Your drawing is intelligent in many ways. For example, several commands can give you the details of each object. In addition, you can view listings that provide information about your drawing as a whole. You can also list system variables, which I've mentioned previously in this book, along with their current settings.

You can perform calculations on objects that may assist you in certain drawing tasks. For example, you can divide an object into any number of segments by placing point objects along the object, or you can place point objects at a specified distance along the object. You can use AutoCAD's calculator, which not only does regular numerical calculations but also works with coordinates and geometric points on objects. This chapter shows you how to discover the hidden data in your drawing.

Getting Drawing-Level Information

Some information applies to the drawing as a whole or even to your computer system as a whole, rather than to individual objects. This information can be important when there is a problem or when you simply need to find the status of system variables.

Listing the status of your drawing

The STATUS command is available only in AutoCAD and provides a standard list of information that can be very helpful. The most common use for STATUS is to troubleshoot problems. You can send the listing to a colleague in another office who needs to work on the same drawing. Your colleague can then work more easily by using the same settings that you have used. Enter **status** ↵ on the command line. Figure 12.1 shows a sample status listing.

FIGURE 12.1

A sample listing from the STATUS command

```
Model space uses    X:     0'-0"   Y: -4'-11 1/2" **Over
                    X:     6'-0"   Y:     0'-0"
Display shows       X: -2'-6 3/4"  Y: -4'-6 1/2"
                    X: 10'-0 3/4"  Y: 0'-9 1/4"
Insertion base is   X:     0'-0"   Y:     0'-0"   Z:
0'-0"
Snap resolution is  X:     0'-6"   Y:     0'-6"
Grid spacing is     X:     1'-0"   Y:     1'-0"
Current space:      Model space
Current layout:     Model
Current layer:      "0"
Current color:      BYLAYER -- 7 (white)
Current linetype:   BYLAYER -- "CONTINUOUS"
Current material:   BYLAYER -- "Global"
Current lineweight: BYLAYER
Current elevation:      0'-0" thickness:      0'-0"
Fill on  Grid off  Ortho off  Qtext off  Snap off  Tablet off
Object snap modes:    Center, Endpoint, Intersection, Midpoint,
Extension
```

The command lists the number of objects in your drawing, followed by the limits and extents of the drawing, and the extents of the current display on your screen. Other items are the snap and grid spacing as well as the current layer, color, linetype, and lineweight.

Obviously, much of this information is available without using the STATUS command. The easiest items to find are the current layer, color, linetype, and lineweight, which are visible in the Layers and Properties panels on the Home tab of the Ribbon. However, you would have to use a number of commands to obtain other information such as the snap and grid spacing and the drawing limits. STATUS puts it all together in one listing.

Listing system variables

The SETVAR command provides a listing of all the system variables and their settings. It may be quicker to view system-variable settings by using the SETVAR command than by typing each individual system variable on the command line. For more information about how AutoCAD and AutoCAD LT store settings in system variables, see Chapter 5.

Too many system variables exist to show the entire listing here, but a few can convey the wealth of information that is available, as shown in Figure 12.2.

Although some system variables allow a variety of values, many are either on or off. In general, a setting of 1 means on and 0 means off.

You can set most system variables in a dialog box. For example, in Chapter 11, I covered setting the LTSCALE system variable in the Linetype Manager. However, some system variables are available only by typing them on the command line.

You can use SETVAR to set system variables that are not read-only, as well as to list them. To list the system variables, enter **setvar** ↵ on the command line. At the Enter variable name or [?]: prompt, type **?** ↵. At the Enter variable(s) to list <*>: prompt, press Enter to list all the system variables, or type the name of a variable. (You can use the * and ? wildcards in the name.) The command either lists all the system variables or just the variable you typed.

FIGURE 12.2

A partial SETVAR listing

```
only)
ACTPATH          ""
ACTRECORDERSTATE 0                              (read
only)
ACTRECPATH       "C:\Users\Ellen\appdata\roaming\autodesk
\autocad 2013 release..."
ACTUI            6
AFLAGS           16
ANGBASE          0
ANGDIR           0
ANNOALLVISIBLE   1
ANNOAUTOSCALE    -4
ANNOTATIVEDWG    0
APBOX            0
APERTURE         10
AREA             0'-0"                          (read
only)
ATTDIA           0
ATTIPE           0
```

> **NOTE**
>
> Read-only system variables are for information only and cannot be changed. An example is LOGINNAME (AutoCAD only), which shows the name of the current user who is registered on the system. Other system variables can be changed.

If you type a variable, the command prompts you for a new value so that you can change it. For example, if you type **celtscale** ↵, you see the Enter new value for CELTSCALE <1.0000>: prompt. You can then change the system variable by typing in a new value. You can also press Enter to accept the current setting.

Tracking drawing time

You can track the time you spend working on a drawing. This feature is most often used for billing time to clients, or when your boss wants to see how much you're accomplishing.

 Chapter 17 covers the PLOTSTAMP command, which can optionally make a log file of plotting activity. Bonus Chapter 3 explains how to keep a log file of your overall drawing activity.

To use the TIME command, enter **time** ↵ on the command line.

The following explains the listing that you see when using the TIME command:

- **Current time.** The current date and time. The time is displayed to the nearest millisecond.
- **Created.** The date and time when the drawing was created.
- **Last updated.** The date and time of the last save of the drawing.
- **Total editing time.** Accumulates the time spent in the drawing from session to session, not including plotting time or time that you worked on the drawing and quit without saving your changes.

- **Elapsed timer.** Also accumulates time spent in the drawing, although you can turn this feature on and off and reset it.

- **Next automatic save in.** Shows when your drawing will automatically be saved. Choose Application Button ⇨ Options and click the Open and Save tab to set how often you want to automatically save your drawing.

You can think of total editing time as your car's odometer, and elapsed time as a timer that is similar to a trip meter that some cars have to enable you to time a specific trip.

At the end of the listing, you see the `Enter option [Display/ON/OFF/Reset]:` prompt. The Display option re-displays the listing with updated times. ON and OFF turn the elapsed time on and off. The Reset option resets the elapsed time to zero.

AUTOCAD ONLY

The Express Tools contain a tool called EDITTIME (enter edittime ↵ on the command line) that tracks active editing time.

Using Object-Level Information

Several commands and features exist solely to provide information about the objects in your drawing.

Listing objects

The LIST command displays information about selected objects. The information displayed depends on the object. For example, the LIST command gives you the radius of a circle and the length of a line.

 To list an object, choose Home tab ⇨ Properties panel ⇨ List, or type **list** ↵ on the command line. Figure 12.3 shows a typical listing for a line.

FIGURE 12.3

A typical listing for a horizontal line

```
Command: list
Select objects: 1 found
Select objects:
                LINE        Layer: "0"
                            Space: Model space
                    Handle = 646
            from point, X=     0'-0"  Y=     0'-0"  Z=     0'-0"
              to point, X=     6'-0"  Y=     0'-0"  Z=     0'-0"
        Length =     6'-0",  Angle in XY Plane =       0
                    Delta X =     6'-0", Delta Y =      0'-0", Delta
Z =     0'-0"
```

Table 12.1 explains the information that you see when you list an object.

TABLE 12.1   LIST Command Information

Data	Comments
Layer	Lists the object's layer. If any of the properties, such as the color, linetype, lineweight, or transparency, are not ByLayer or ByBlock, then AutoCAD lists these as well.
Space	Tells you whether the object is in model space or paper space. (Chapter 17 covers paper space.)
Handle	Every object in your drawing has a handle. Your drawing's internal database uses handles to keep track of objects.
From point	Because the example in Figure 12.3 lists a line, it shows the start point.
To point	The endpoint of the line.
Length	The line's length.
Angle in XY Plane	The line's angle. This line is horizontal, and so its angle is zero.
Delta X	The change in the X coordinate from the start point to the endpoint.
Delta Y	The change in the Y coordinate from the start point to the endpoint.
Delta Z	The change in the Z coordinate from the start point to the endpoint.

The Layer drop-down list in the Layers panel and drop-down lists in the Properties panel make it easy to tell an object's layer, color, linetype, lineweight, and transparency. Later in this chapter, I explain how you can use the Properties and Quick Properties palettes to see most of the same information, and more; you can also use them to change the information.

Finding coordinates

 You can find the coordinate of any point. Choose Home tab ⇨ Utilities panel (expanded) ⇨ ID Point. The ID command prompts you for a point. You can use any means of specifying a point, although object snaps or snap mode are useful. Here is a typical listing:

```
X = 61' -5 1/8"  Y = 32'  -4 5/8"  Z = 0'  -0"
```

CAUTION

If you're working in 3D, be aware that if you check the Replace Z Value with Current Elevation check box on the Drafting tab of the Options dialog box, you may get inaccurate results when you pick points for the ID and DIST commands. For more information on this option, see Chapter 21, where I discuss 3D coordinates.

Measuring objects

The MEASUREGEOM command measures distance, radius, angle, area, and volume. You can use this information to check dimensions (covered in Chapter 14) or to make calculations that you need for drawing. To start the MEASUREGEOM command, choose Home tab ⇨ Utilities panel ⇨ MEASUREGEOM drop-down menu. Then choose the option that you want. Note that the last-used option displays on top and you have to click the drop-down menu to access the other options.

Here's how to use the options:

- **Distance.** Specify two points. The result shows you the distance, angle in the XY plane, angle from the XY plane (for 3D models), and the delta (change) of X, Y, and Z coordinates.

- **Radius.** Select an arc or circle. The result shows you the radius and diameter.

- **Angle.** Select an arc, circle, or line, or press Enter to specify the vertex of the angle. If you select an arc, the result immediately shows you its included angle. If you select a circle, do so by specifying the first point of the desired angle, and then specify the second angle endpoint. If you select a line, then select a second line.

- **Area.** Specify the first corner point and then subsequent points, in a roundabout manner (not diagonally opposing corners) and press Enter to get the total. Or, use the Object suboption to select an object. You can also use the Add Area suboption to keep a running total, and the Subtract Area suboptions to remove areas, until you get just the combination of areas that you want. The Arc suboption lets you find the area of an arc, assuming that the two endpoints are joined by a line. In addition to the area, the Area option returns the perimeter for closed areas, the length for open areas, and the circumference for circles. You can't calculate the area of an arc.

- **Volume.** Specify the first corner point and then subsequent points, in a roundabout manner (not diagonally opposing corners), all on the XY plane, and press Enter to get the total. Then enter a height. Or, use the Object suboption to select an object. (You can select a 2D object and specify a height.) You can also use the Add Volume suboption to keep a running total, and the Subtract Volume suboptions to remove volumes, until you get just the combination of volumes that you want.

You can use any means of specifying the necessary points, but remember that object snaps or snap mode are useful for accuracy. After using an option, type **x** ↵ to end the command, or choose another option.

You can also use the BOUNDARY command to create one polyline or region from a complex area. (Chapter 16 covers boundaries and polylines.) You can then use the MEASUREGEOM's Area option and its Object suboption instead of picking points.

STEPS: Measuring Geometry

1. Open `ab12-a.dwg` or `ab12-a-metric.dwg`, available from the Drawings download on the companion website.

2. On the Navigation bar, click the Zoom button's drop-down menu and choose Zoom Window. Define a window to zoom in on the parcels of land labeled D and E, as shown in Figure 12.4. Object Snap should be on with a running object snap for Endpoint.

FIGURE 12.4

The MEASUREGEOM command can calculate properties of the objects that make up the land parcels.

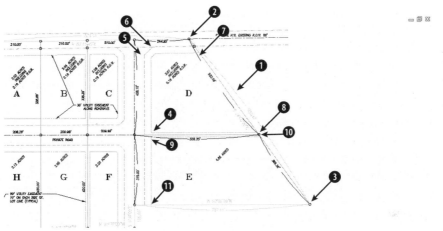

Thanks to Bill Maidment of Caltech, Inc., Fairfield, Iowa, for this drawing.

3. Choose Home tab ⇨ Properties panel (expanded) ⇨ List. At the `Select objects:` prompt, pick ❶, shown in Figure 12.5. Press Enter to end object selection. Note the surveyor's units.

4. Choose Home tab ⇨ Utilities panel ⇨ MEASUREGEOM drop-down menu ⇨ Distance. At the `Specify first point:` prompt, choose the endpoint at ❷, shown in Figure 12.5, using the Endpoint running object snap. At the `Specify second point:` prompt, choose the endpoint at ❸. Type **x** ↵ to end the command. Here's the result:

Imperial drawing:

```
Distance = 922.42, Angle in XY Plane = S 36d0'0" E, Angle from XY
    Plane = E
Delta X = 542.18, Delta Y = -746.25, Delta Z = 0.00
```

Metric drawing:

```
Distance = 281.153, Angle in XY Plane = 144d0'0.00»,  Angle from XY
    Plane = 90d0'0.00»
Delta X = 165.258, Delta Y = -227.458,  Delta Z = 0.000]
```

5. Choose Home tab ⇨ Utilities panel (expanded) ⇨ ID Point. At the `Specify point:` prompt, pick the endpoint at ❹. Here is the result:

Imperial drawing:

```
X = 6065.67 Y = 3775.58 Z = 0.00
```

Metric drawing:

```
X = 1002.341 Y = 394.567 Z = 0.000
```

6. Choose Home tab ⇨ Utilities panel ⇨ MEASUREGEOM drop-down menu ⇨ Area. At the `Specify first corner point or [Object/Add area/Subtract area/eXit] <Object>:` prompt, right-click and choose Add Area to start Add mode. At the `Specify first corner point or [Object/Subtract area/eXit]:` prompt, pick ❹, by using the Endpoint running object snap. At the `(ADD mode) Specify next point or [Arc/Length/Undo]:` prompt, continue to pick ❺, ❻, ❼, and ❽. Press Enter. The command line lists the area and perimeter. (Your figures may be different if you picked different points.)

Imperial drawing:

```
Area = 123575.16, Perimeter = 1480.17
Total area = 123575.16
```

Metric drawing:

```
Area = 11480.508, Perimeter = 451.156
Total area = 11480.508
```

7. At the `Specify first corner point or [Object/Subtract area/eXit]:` prompt, pick ❾. At the `(ADD mode) Specify next point or [Arc/Length/Undo]:` prompt, pick ❿, ❸, and ⓫. Press Enter to complete the point selection. The command line reports the area and perimeter of the second area and adds the two areas together to give you the total area. Type **x** ↵ twice to end the command.

Imperial drawing:

```
Area = 183399.88, Perimeter = 1884.62
Total area = 306975.04
```

Metric drawing:

```
Area = 17038.407, Perimeter = 574.433
Total area = 28518.914
```

8. Do not save the drawing. Keep it open if you're continuing to the next exercise.

NOTE

The MASSPROP command is mostly used for 3D drawings, but it can also be used on *regions*, which are 2D solid surfaces, such as a shape cut from sheet metal. This command provides area and perimeter but also other engineering calculations, such as centroids, moments of inertia, the product of inertia, and so on. Chapter 24 covers this command further.

Getting information from the Properties palette

You can also obtain information about an object by selecting it and opening the Properties palette. Choose Home tab ⇨ Properties panel and click the dialog box launcher on the panel's title, or press

Ctrl+1. In Chapter 11, I discuss using this Properties palette to change layer, color, linetype, and line-weight properties. As you can see in Figure 12.5, the palette also lists the line's start and endpoints; delta (change) in X, Y, and Z; length; and angle — much like the LIST command. However, you can change the start and endpoints directly in the palette.

FIGURE 12.5

The Properties palette lists information about a selected object.

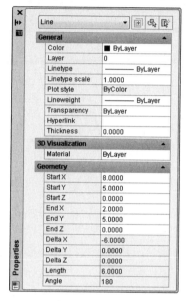

Getting information from the Quick Properties palette

The Quick Properties palette appears by default whenever you double-click an object or select an object when Quick Properties is enabled on the status bar. The palette contains a smaller set of properties about an object than the Properties palette. Like the Properties palette, you can change the properties. Figure 12.6 shows the Quick Properties palette for a line.

FIGURE 12.6

The Quick Properties palette pops up when you select or double-click an object and displays editable properties for that object.

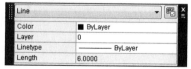

Click the Quick Properties button on the status bar to turn off the display of this palette when you select an object; however, the Quick Properties palette still appears when you double-click an object. You can customize what properties appear on the Quick Properties palette. For more information, see Bonus Chapter 6.

TIP
The QUICKPROPERTIES command (you can just type qp ↵) prompts you to select objects to view their properties in the Quick Properties palette. It works even if the Quick Properties button on the status bar is off. The panel disappears when you deselect the objects.

Accessing Drawing Components

When you create a drawing, you not only create objects, but you also create a complex structure to support those objects. You create named blocks, layers, layouts, text styles, dimension styles, multileader styles, table styles, and linetypes to help define those objects. And you spend a lot of time creating them! All these named drawing components can be reused and organized for greater efficiency, using the Content Explorer or the DesignCenter.

Using the Content Explorer

You can use the Content Explorer to easily drag named drawing components from one drawing to another. You can access this drawing content from drawings on your hard drive, on a network drive, or over the Internet. You never need to re-create them.

You can do the following with the Content Explorer:

- Search for, insert, and open drawings.
- Search for and insert named drawing components, including blocks, xrefs, layers, text styles, table styles, multileader styles, dimension styles, linetypes, and layouts. You can also access custom objects that are created by third-party applications.
- Search text in single-line text, multi-line text, attributes, leaders, multilines, and dimensions.
- Save searches.
- Access content on the Autodesk Seek website, which contains a catalog of product drawings that you can use in your drawing.

You can search locally and on networks. When you search on a network, other computers need to have Autodesk Content Service installed.

 To open the Content Explorer, choose Plug-Ins tab ⇨ Content panel ⇨ Explore. The Content Explorer palette opens, as shown in Figure 12.7. The Content Explorer indexes content in folders that you specify; these are called *watched folders*.

FIGURE 12.7

The Content Explorer palette displays watched folders.

Watched folders

Add Current Configuration to Saved Searches

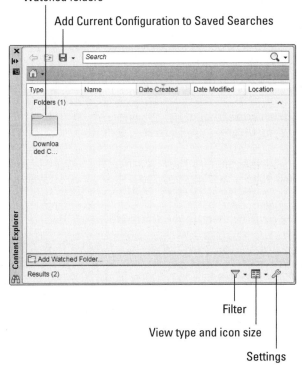

Filter

View type and icon size

Settings

To add a watched folder, click Configure Settings near the bottom of the palette. In the Configure Settings dialog box, click Add Watched Folder on the right. Then in the Select Watched Folder dialog box, navigate to a folder, select it, and click OK. In the Edit Watched Folder dialog box that opens, you can specify whether the folder is private or public (shared). You can also specify a network path. Click OK and then click Close to return to the Content Explorer palette. AutoCAD starts indexing the content in these folders, which can take a while. When the process is complete, you can search for components. Use the navigational tools at the upper-left corner of the palette to go back a step, go to the Home page (the list of watched folders), and so on.

NEW FEATURE

You can now index any type of file that you can attach to your drawing, such as PDF files and raster images.

TIP

To add multiple watched folders at once, open Windows Explorer, and then select and drag multiple folders into the main (root) level of the Content Explorer palette.

Double-click a folder to display its contents and double-click a drawing to display its components. To add a component, drag it onto the drawing area. You can also do the following:

- **Insert a drawing as a block.** Drag it onto the drawing area, or for more precision, right-click and choose Insert to start the INSERT command.
- **Open a drawing.** Right-click the drawing and choose Open.
- **Insert a drawing as an xref.** Right-click the drawing and choose Attach.
- **Open the parent drawing of a block.** Right-click a block and choose Open Drawing.

At the lower-right corner are three icons:

- **Toggle Filter.** Click the drop-down arrow to filter which components you see.
- **Toggle Icon Size.** Click the drop-down arrow to change the icon size and switch between icon and detail view.
- **Configure Settings.** Click to open the Configure Settings dialog box, where you can see more information about your watched folders, and statistics about their indexing. You can also add network content.

You can search for components by typing a search term in the Search box.

> **TIP**
> When you find a component by searching, go to the file to see if it has any other components that you may also want, right-click, and choose the Go to Folder. There you can double-click that file to see its other components.

Finding components with the DesignCenter

 Like the Content Explorer, the DesignCenter is a feature that allows you to find drawing components. It has been around for quite some time. To open it, choose View tab ⇨ Palettes panel ⇨ DesignCenter or press Ctrl+2. The DesignCenter is shown in Figure 12.8.

The Folders tab displays a tree view of any location — your hard drive, network, or the Internet — that you can access. Click the plus sign next to a drive or folder to display its contents. A selected drawing displays its named components in the content area on the right side of the palette. (Use the Views drop-down list to choose the type of display that you want.) You can also click the plus sign next to a drawing to display these components in the tree view. Then click a component type, such as blocks, to see a list of the blocks in the drawing, as shown in Figure 12.8. Click Preview on the DesignCenter toolbar to see a preview in the preview pane of blocks, drawings, and raster images. Click Description to display a description, if one is saved. To narrow your search, you can click two other tabs in the DesignCenter:

- **The Open Drawings tab** displays currently open drawings.
- **The History tab** displays the most recently opened drawings.

FIGURE 12.8

The DesignCenter with the Folders tab displayed

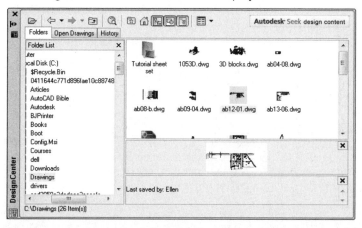

TIP

If you have old blocks that don't have preview icons, use the BLOCKICON command and press Enter at the first prompt to automatically create preview icons of all the blocks in a drawing.

The DesignCenter includes a Search feature to help you find components when you don't know the name of their drawing or that drawing's location.

 Choose Search from the DesignCenter toolbar to open the Search dialog box. (You can also right-click in the Content area and choose Search.) Here's how to use the Search dialog box:

- **Click the Look For drop-down list to choose what you're looking for.** You can look for blocks, dimension styles, drawings, drawings and blocks, hatch pattern files, hatch patterns, layers, layouts, linetypes, multileader styles, table styles, text styles, and xrefs.

- **Click the In drop-down list to specify the drive that you want to search.** By default, the Search subfolders check box is checked so that the search looks in all folders and subfolders within the drive.

- **Use the tabbed area to specify the name of the components that you want.** The tab's name and content change, depending on what you chose in the Look For drop-down list. For example, if you chose Layers, the tab is called Layers and asks you for the name of the layer. If you're looking for drawings, you have three tabs to work with:

  - The **Drawings** tab enables you to look for a drawing by filename (the default), title, subject, author, or keywords. Choose one of these options in the In the Field(s) drop-down list. Then type the text that you want to look for in the Search for the Word(s) text box. You can use the wildcards * (to substitute for any number of characters) and ? (to substitute for any one character). Specifying a drawing's title, subject, and keywords is discussed later in this chapter.

- The **Date Modified** tab enables you to search by the last date that the file was saved or modified. You can specify a range of dates, or look in the last *x* days or months.

- The **Advanced** tab enables you to search for text in drawing descriptions, block names, attribute tags, and attribute values. You can also search here by drawing size.

- When you've created your specifications, click Search Now.

 See Chapter 18 for information on creating block descriptions when you create a block. The main reason for creating a block description is to display it in the DesignCenter and use it in a search on the Advanced tab, as just described. For more information on searching for drawings, see Bonus Chapter 3.

The `Favorites` folder contains shortcuts to actual files. The files remain in their original locations. You'll find an `Autodesk` subfolder within the `Favorites` folder where you can store shortcuts to drawings and other files that you use often. You can then easily open the `Favorites` folder and find these files. `Favorites` is one possible place to keep drawings that contain block libraries. To add a shortcut to `Favorites`, right-click the drawing (or other file) in the DesignCenter and choose Add to Favorites.

 To access the drawings in `Favorites`, click Favorites on the DesignCenter toolbar. You can also right-click the Content pane and choose Favorites. The `Favorites` folder appears in the Content pane. To move, copy, or delete shortcuts from `Favorites`, right-click the Content pane and choose Organize Favorites.

As soon as you have the item that you need in the Content pane, you can insert it into your drawing. If you used the Search window to locate a file, then you can also insert the item directly from the results that you find. Here's how to insert drawing components into your drawing:

- **Inserting drawings.** To insert an entire drawing into your drawing, choose the drawing's folder in the navigation pane so that the drawing appears in the content area. Drag the drawing's icon onto the drawing area. The command line prompts you for an insertion point, scale, and rotation angle, using the -INSERT command (the command-line version of the INSERT command). If you right-click the drawing, you can choose to insert the drawing as a block, or attach it as an xref.

- **Opening drawings.** To open a drawing, display the drawing in the Content pane, right-click it, and choose Open in Application Window.

- **Inserting blocks.** If you drag the block's icon onto the drawing area, the drawing uses *Autoscaling*, which compares the current drawing's units with those of the block, and scales the block appropriately, using the value set in the Drawing Units dialog box (which I explain in Chapter 5; choose Application Button ⇨ Drawing Utilities ⇨ Units). The block takes on the default scale and rotation. If you double-click the block's icon or right-click it and choose Insert Block, the Insert dialog box opens, where you can specify the insertion point, scale, and rotation. Right-click and choose Insert and Redefine Block to update an existing block definition and insert a reference of the block into the drawing.

- **Inserting raster images.** You can insert raster (bitmap) images directly into your drawing. To attach a raster image, drag its icon onto the drawing area. The command line prompts you for an insertion point, scale, and rotation angle. You can also double-click or right-click an image and choose Attach Image to display the Attach Image dialog box.

See Bonus Chapter 4 for more information on raster images, including determining which type of files you can import, attaching images, clipping images, and controlling how they're displayed.

> **TIP**
>
> Knowing the appropriate scale of an image before inserting it is often difficult. When you move the cursor at the `Specify scale factor or [Unit] <1>:` prompt, you can see a bounding box that will help you visualize the resulting size of the image.

- **Attaching an xref.** To attach or overlay an xref, double-click or right-click its icon and choose Attach as Xref to open the Attach External Reference dialog box. Choose either Attachment or Overlay in the Reference Type section. Specify an insertion point, scale, and rotation (or choose to specify them on-screen), and click OK. If you drag the xref onto the drawing area, you see prompts on the command line that are similar to those of the INSERT command.

- **Inserting layers and styles.** To insert a layer, layout, linetype, text style, table style, multileader styles, or dimension style into a drawing, drag its icon onto the drawing area. Of course, these items don't appear in your drawing area, but they're added to the drawing's database.

You can drag multiple items at one time. To select a contiguous group, click the first item, press and hold Shift, and click the last item. To select multiple individual items, click the first item, press and hold Ctrl, and click any other item that you want to insert. You can also double-click an item to insert it.

> **CAUTION**
>
> The insertion process does not check for duplicate layer names. If you try to insert a layer with the same name as a layer in your current drawing, you see a message: `Layer(s) added. Duplicate definitions will be ignored.` You should check for duplicate layer names before trying to insert layers from the DesignCenter.

If you make changes in the structure of a folder while the DesignCenter is open — for example, by deleting a drawing by using Windows Explorer — right-click the navigation or Content pane and choose Refresh. The DesignCenter re-reads the data and refreshes the list.

Purging unused components

 Unused components, such as layers, blocks, and linetypes, can make your drawing larger than necessary. You can use the PURGE command to remove them from your drawing's database. To purge components, choose Application Button ⇨ Drawing Utilities ⇨ Purge. The Purge dialog box opens, as shown in Figure 12.9.

FIGURE 12.9

The Purge dialog box

> **NOTE**
>
> The Incremental Save Percentage option may prevent a purge during a drawing session from removing all unreferenced layers or linetypes from the drawing. To avoid this, you can either set incremental save to zero, or save the drawing and reopen it and then immediately use the PURGE command. To set this option, choose Application Button ⇨ Options and then click the Open and Save tab in the Options dialog box.

At the top of the Purge dialog box, you can choose to view objects that you can purge or objects that you cannot purge. Why would you want to view objects that you cannot purge? Sometimes it's hard to figure out why you can't purge a certain object, and the dialog box has a handy feature that lets you select an object and view possible reasons why it cannot be purged.

To start purging, choose View Items You Can Purge. A plus sign (+) next to each type of object indicates that it contains purgeable objects. Click the plus sign to display the specific items.

To purge an individual item, select it and click Purge. Check the Confirm Each Item to Be Purged option if you want to see a dialog box asking you to confirm each purge. Click Purge All to purge all possible items. Check the Purge Nested Items option to purge items within other named objects. Usually, these are layers, linetypes, and so on inside blocks.

12

> **TIP**
>
> You can select more than one item at a time to purge. To select an additional item, press and hold Ctrl as you click. To select a contiguous group of items, click the first item in the group, press and hold Shift, and then select the last item in the group.

After you're done purging, click Close to close the Purge dialog box.

Dividing and Spacing Objects

The DIVIDE command divides an object into equally spaced sections. The MEASURE command divides an object into sections of a specified length. These commands are useful in many fields. For example, you may need to space bolt holes evenly around the edge of a bushing, or place fence studs along the edge of a plot every 5 feet.

 You can create a path array and specify a distance between the objects you are arraying (similar to the MEASURE command) or use the ARRAY command's Divide option to space the objects evenly. I cover the ARRAY command in Chapter 10.

Dividing objects

The DIVIDE command divides an object into equal sections. DIVIDE does not break the object — it simply places point objects along the selected object. You can use the Node object snap if you want to draw from those points.

 To divide an object, choose Home tab ⇨ Draw panel (expanded) ⇨ Divide. Select the object that you want to divide. The command responds with the `Enter the number of segments or [Block]:` prompt. Enter the number of segments that you want to create. AutoCAD places the point objects and ends the command.

> **NOTE**
>
> Remember that you can set the point display by choosing Home tab ⇨ Utilities panel (expanded) ⇨ Point Style. An easy-to-see point style is especially useful for the DIVIDE command. Specify the point style *before* using the command.

For example, to create eight segments, you need to place seven point objects. If you have in your mind the number of point objects that you want, simply add one when specifying the number of segments.

You can use the Block option to place a block of your choice along the object rather than a point object. The block must already exist in your drawing. (Chapter 18 covers blocks and how to insert them.) If you choose the Block option (right-click and choose Block), the option responds with the `Enter name of block to insert:` prompt. Type the name of the block. The prompt asks, `Align block with object? [Yes/No] <Y>`. Answer Y or N, depending on whether you want to align the block with the angle of the object.

Figure 12.10 shows an electrical schematic. Here you want to divide a line so that you can evenly space wires entering the ignition module. Four wires need to come in so that the line is divided into five segments by an easy-to-see point object.

FIGURE 12.10

Dividing a line into five segments by using point objects

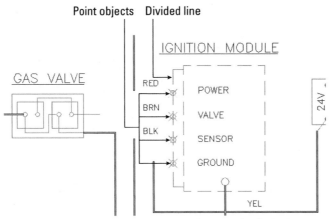

Thanks to Robert Mack of the Dexter Company, Fairfield, Iowa, for this drawing.

You can practice using the DIVIDE command after the next section.

Measuring objects

The MEASURE command is similar to the DIVIDE command, except that you specify the distance between point objects rather than the total number of segments. The command starts measuring from the endpoint closest to where you pick the object. MEASURE does not break the object — it simply places point objects along the object. You can use the Node object snap if you want to draw from those points.

 To measure an object, choose Home tab Draw panel (expanded) ⇨ Measure. Select the object that you want to measure. The command responds with the `Specify length of segment or [Block]:` prompt. Type the segment length where you want to place the point objects and end the command.

Remember that you can set the point display by choosing Home tab ⇨ Utilities panel (expanded) ⇨ Point Style. An easy-to-see point style is especially useful for the MEASURE command. Specify the point style *before* using the command.

As with the DIVIDE command, you can place a block along the object by using the Block option, as long as the block exists in your drawing. The option prompts you for the name of the block and lets you choose whether you want to align the block with the object. The prompt asks for the segment length, and you type in the lengths between the points, as described earlier.

STEPS: Using the DIVIDE and MEASURE Commands

1. Open `ab12-a.dwg`, available from the Drawings download on the companion website, if it isn't already open from the previous exercise.

2. If you didn't do the previous exercise, on the Navigation bar, click the Zoom button's drop-down menu and choose Zoom Window. Specify a window to zoom in to the parcels labeled D and E, as shown in Figure 12.11.

3. Choose Home tab ⇨ Utilities panel (expanded) ⇨ Point Style and choose the fourth style in the first row. Choose Set Size Relative to Screen and set the size to 5% (the default). Click OK.

4. Choose Home tab ⇨ Draw panel (expanded) ⇨ Divide. At the `Select object to divide:` prompt, choose ❶, shown in Figure 12.11. At the `Enter the number of segments or [Block]:` prompt, type **3** ↵. The command places two points along the line, dividing it into three segments. (If you want, draw lines from the points perpendicular to the opposite side of the parcel to divide it into three parcels.)

5. Choose Home tab ⇨ Draw panel (expanded) ⇨ Measure. At the `Select object to measure:` prompt, choose ❷, shown in Figure 12.11. At the `Specify length of segment or [Block]:` prompt, type **120** ↵. The command places two points along the line.

6. Do not save your drawing.

FIGURE 12.11

The site plan zoomed in to parcels D and E

ON THE WEB

AutoCAD's calculator is a flexible tool, with many advanced features. Use it when you need to do calculations to get a distance or coordinate. I cover the calculator in the Chapter 12 Addendum, available on the companion website.

Summary

A great deal of information is available to you in each drawing. In this chapter you read about:

- Getting a general status listing
- Listing system variable settings
- Tracking drawing time
- Getting information about individual objects by using the LIST and ID commands
- Measuring objects, and calculating area and perimeters
- Using the Properties palette to display all an object's properties
- Finding, accessing, and purging drawing components
- Dividing and measuring objects by placing point objects along them

In the next chapter, I explain how to create and edit text.

Creating Text

IN THIS CHAPTER

Creating and editing single-line text

Creating text styles

Working with multiline (paragraph) text, including annotative text

Working with tables

Linking to data and extracting object data

Managing text to improve performance

Using the FIND command

Checking spelling

Every drawing includes text that labels or explains the objects in the drawing; this text is often called *annotation*. In each release, the capabilities of the text feature have improved so that you can now easily format and edit text to provide a professional appearance to your drawing. A wide range of font, alignment, and spacing options is available. You can also import text from a word processor. This chapter tells you all that you need to know about creating text in AutoCAD and AutoCAD LT.

Creating Single-Line Text

A great deal of text in a drawing consists of short labels or comments. Use single-line text when you want each line of text to be a separate object or when you're creating a small amount of text. Single-line text has fewer options than the multiline text that I explain later in this chapter, but it's easy to create and accurately place in a drawing.

 It is very easy to create a single line of text by using the defaults, such as font and height. Choose Annotate tab ⇨ Text panel ⇨ Text drop-down menu ⇨ Single Line. This starts the TEXT command.

Follow the prompts:

```
Current text style: "Standard" Text height: 0.2000 Annotative: No
Specify start point of text or [Justify/Style]: Pick a start point for the
    text.
Specify height <0.2000>: Type a height and press Enter, or just press
    Enter to accept the default.
Specify rotation angle of text <0>: Type a rotation angle and press Enter,
    or just press Enter to accept the default.
```

> *You see a cursor at the insertion point. Type one line of text. Press*
> *Enter. You can continue to type more lines of text.*
> *Press Enter at a blank line to end the command. You can also click*
> *another location on the screen to start a new text object.*

> **NOTE**
>
> You cannot use the Return (usually the right) button of the mouse or the Spacebar to end the command. You can type -text on the command line to use the original TEXT behavior, which ends the command after one line of text. There is also a command called DTEXT, which functions just like the TEXT command in recent releases of AutoCAD, but in earlier releases functioned differently. The 'D' in DTEXT stands for dynamic text, which allowed you to see the text in the drawing as you typed it. When working with script files, menus, or AutoLISP files; you must use the TEXT command (rather than the DTEXT command) for script files, menus, or AutoLISP routines. (See the Bonus Chapters on this book's companion website for more information.)

The next section covers the Justify option. The Style option and the Annotative property are discussed later in this chapter.

One advantage of TEXT is that each line of text is a separate object, making it easy to move or copy individual lines of text. Unfortunately, you cannot control the spacing between the lines.

TEXT remembers the location of the previous line of text even if you've used other commands in the meantime. To continue text below the last line of text that you have created, press Enter at the `Specify start point of text or [Justify/Style]:` prompt.

Justifying single-line text

When you pick a start point for text, the relationship between the start point and the actual letters is determined by the justification. The start point is also called the *insertion point*. When you want to refer to text by using object snaps, you use the Insertion object snap. If you select text without first choosing a command, grips appear at the insertion point as well as at the bottom-left corner.

By default, text is left-justified; therefore, there is no left justification option. To change the text's justification, right-click and choose Justify at the `Specify start point of text or [Justify/ Style]:` prompt. The command responds with this bewildering prompt:

```
Enter an option [Align/Fit/Center/Middle/Right/TL/TC/TR/ML/MC/MR/BL/
    BC/BR]:
```

Align and Fit offer two ways to fit text into a specified space. Both respond with the same two prompts:

```
Specify first endpoint of text baseline:
Specify second endpoint of text baseline:
```

Specify the beginning and the end of the text line. Align then prompts you for the text and squeezes or stretches the text to fit within the text line. The height of the text changes accordingly, to maintain the proportions of the font.

Fit adds the `Specify height <0.2000>:` prompt. Type the height that you want and then type the text. Fit also squeezes or stretches the text to fit within the text line, but maintains the text height that you specified, distorting the font letters to fit the space. Figure 13.1 shows an example of normal, aligned, and fitted single-line text.

FIGURE 13.1

Normal (left-justified), aligned, and fitted text

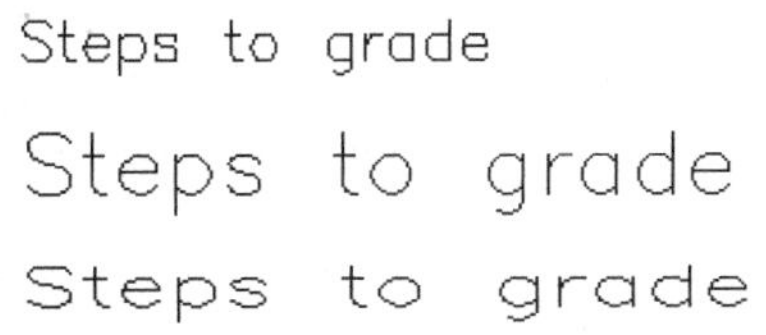

Steps to grade

Steps to grade

Steps to grade

Here is an explanation of the other justification options:

- **Center.** Text is centered around the insertion point. The insertion point is on the baseline.
- **Right.** Text is right-justified from the insertion point. The insertion point is on the baseline.
- **Middle.** Text is centered both vertically and horizontally. The vertical center point is measured from the bottom of the lowest to the top of the tallest possible letter.
- **TL, TC, TR (top-left, top-center, top-right).** The insertion point is at the top of the highest possible letter, and the text is left-, center-, or right-justified, respectively.
- **ML, MC, MR (middle-left, middle-center, middle-right).** Text is centered vertically. The vertical center point is measured from the bottom of the lowest to the top of the tallest possible letter. Text is left-, center-, or right-justified, respectively.
- **BL, BC, BR (bottom-left, bottom-center, bottom-right).** The insertion point is below the lowest descending letter. Text is left-, center-, or right-justified, respectively.

TIP

If you know the option abbreviation of the justification that you want, you can use it at the `Specify start point of text or [Justify/Style]:` prompt.

Setting the height

Setting the height of text is fairly straightforward. The default is 0.2 units. The main point to consider is the scale factor. If you're drawing a house and plan to plot it at 1" = 8' (1 = 96), you need to figure out how big to make the text so that you can still read it when it is scaled down.

For example, if you want the text to be 0.2 units high and your scale factor is 96, your text needs to be 19.2 inches high (0.2 × 96). On the other hand, if you're drawing a very small object, such as a computer chip, and your scale is 0.10, then your text needs to be 0.02 inches high.

AutoCAD and AutoCAD LT calculate text height in units. Most word processors calculate text height in points. A point is $1/72$ of an inch (0.3527mm). Therefore, 12-point text, a standard for most business letters, is about 0.17 inches (4.3mm) high. The default of 0.2 units, if you're using inches as your unit, is just over 14 points.

You can create *annotative* single-line text, using an annotative text style. This feature automatically scales text according to your scale. For more information, see the section "Understanding Text Styles" later in this chapter. To make existing single-line text annotative, select the text and change the

Annotative property in the Properties palette from No to Yes. For more information about changing the scale of text, see the section "Editing single-line text" later in this chapter.

Setting the rotation angle

The final prompt in TEXT is the rotation angle. This angle applies to the entire line of text, not to individual characters. (You can specify slanted text, called *obliqued text*, using the STYLE command covered later in this chapter.) Figure 13.2 shows text rotated to 315 degrees.

FIGURE 13.2

Text rotated to 315 degrees

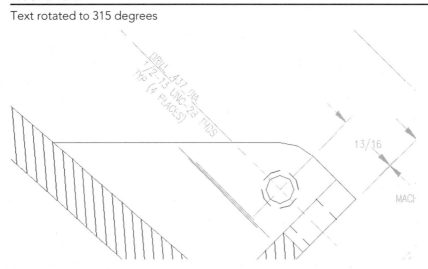

Adding special characters and formatting

To create special characters and formats for single-line text, you have to use codes. These codes are shown in Table 13.1.

TABLE 13.1   Special Character Codes for Text Fonts

Code	Results
%%o	Toggles the overscore mode on/off
%%u	Toggles the underscore mode on/off
%%d	Draws a degree symbol (°)
%%p	Draws a plus/minus tolerance symbol (±)
%%c	Draws a circle-diameter dimensioning symbol (Ø)

Figure 13.3 displays text using some of these codes, along with the entries that created them.

FIGURE 13.3

Using special characters and formatting with text fonts

<u>35.3</u> not 35.8	%%u35.3%%u not 35.8
⌀1.5	%%c1.5
±.002	%%p.002

On the Web

The drawing used in the following exercise on creating text with TEXT, `ab13-a.dwg`, is available from the Drawings download on the companion website.

STEPS: Creating Text with TEXT

1. Open `ab13-a.dwg`, available from the Drawings download on the companion website.
2. Save the file as `ab13-01.dwg` in your `AutoCAD Bible` folder. This is a master-bathroom plan drawing, as shown in Figure 13.4. Make sure that Object Snap is on. Set running object snaps for Endpoint, Midpoint, and Intersection.

13

FIGURE 13.4

The master bathroom

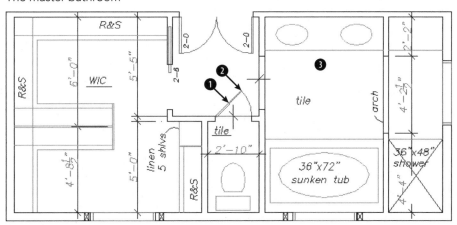

3. Choose Annotate tab ⇨ Text panel ⇨ Text drop-down menu ⇨ Single Line. Follow the prompts:

```
Current text style: "ROMANS" Text height: 0'-4 1/2" Annotative: No
Specify start point of text or [Justify/Style]: Right-click and choose
   Justify.
```

```
Enter an option [Align/Fit/Center/Middle/Right/TL/TC/TR/ML/MC/MR/BL/BC/
    BR]: Right-click and choose BC.
Specify bottom-center point of text: Use the Midpoint running object snap
    to pick ❶ in Figure 13.4.
Specify rotation angle of text <0>: Pick the endpoint at ❷.
Enter text: 2-0 ↵
Enter text: ↵
```

4. Start the TEXT command again. Follow the prompts:

```
Specify start point of text or [Justify/Style]: Right-click and choose
    Justify.
Enter an option [Align/Fit/Center/Middle/Right/TL/TC/TR/ML/MC/MR/BL/BC/
    BR]: Right-click and choose Middle.
Specify middle point of text: Pick ❸ in Figure 13.4. (This point doesn't
    have to be exact.)
Specify rotation angle of text <45>: 0 ↵
Enter text: %%UMASTER BATH ↵
Enter text: ↵
```

Save your drawing. It should look like Figure 13.5.

FIGURE 13.5

The master-bathroom plan drawing with added single-line text

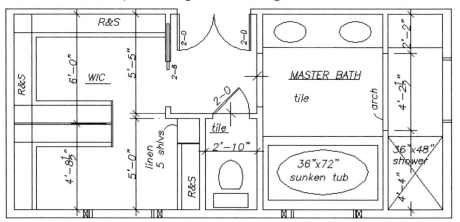

Editing single-line text

As with any drawing object, the need often arises to edit your text. The most common way to edit single-line text is to use the DDEDIT command. Double-click the text to start the command. Remember that each line of text created with TEXT is a separate object.

The text appears in a border with your text highlighted in an edit box. You can start typing to completely replace the text or click where you want to change part of the text and use standard Windows techniques to edit the text. Press Enter or click anywhere outside the border. DDEDIT prompts you to select another annotation object. Press Enter to end the command.

You can also change text by using the Quick Properties palette. Select any text and click in the Contents item of the Quick Properties palette to edit the text. To use the Properties palette, select any text object and open the Properties palette (press Ctrl+1). Here you can edit the text content as well as every other conceivable property, including layer, linetype, lineweight, color, insertion point, justification, rotation angle, and others that I cover in the section on text styles.

Scaling text

If you want to scale text and use the SCALE command, the text may move, depending on the base point you use. Instead, you can use the SCALETEXT command to change the scale of selected text without moving the text insertion point. This command works with either one text object or several at once. All the text objects stay in their original location.

To use SCALETEXT, follow these steps:

1. Choose Annotate tab ⇨ Text panel (expanded) ⇨ Scale.

2. Select the text objects that you want to scale.

3. At the `Enter a base point option for scaling [Existing/Left/Center/Middle/Right/TL/TC/TR/ML/MC/MR/BL/BC/BR] <Existing>:` prompt, press Enter to use the existing insertion point of the selected text, or choose a new base point. (Your last choice for this prompt becomes the new default, so if you used another option, type **e** ↵.) These options are the same as the Justify options described earlier in this chapter.

4. At the `Specify new model height or [Paper height/Match object/Scale factor] <3/32>:` prompt, right-click and choose Scale Factor to specify a scale factor, just as you would for the SCALE command (see Chapter 9). You can also type a new height or use the Match Object option to match the height of the selected text objects to another existing text object. The prompt asks you to select an object with the desired height. For annotative text only, you can specify a paper height, which means the height you want the text to appear when plotted.

5. If you have chosen the Scale Factor option, then type the factor that you want at the `Specify scale factor or [Reference] <2>:` prompt.

6. If you want to specify the scale factor with reference to existing text or a value, use the Reference option. At the `Specify reference length <1>:` prompt, type a length or specify two points that measure the reference length. At the `Specify new length:` prompt, type a value or pick two points to indicate the new length.

13

If you want to scale text to automatically fit a drawing scale, you can use annotative text, which I cover in the next section.

Justifying text

The JUSTIFYTEXT command lets you change the justification of selected text objects without moving the text. To use JUSTIFYTEXT, choose Annotate tab ⇨ Text panel (expanded) ⇨ Justify. Then select the text objects that you want to modify. At the `Enter a justification option [Left/Align/Fit/Center/Middle/Right/TL/TC/TR/ML/MC/MR/BL/BC/BR] <Left>:` prompt, right-click and choose the justification that you want.

ON THE WEB

The drawing used in the following exercise on editing text, `ab13-b.dwg`, is available from the Drawings download on the companion website.

STEPS: Editing Text

1. Open `ab13-b.dwg`, available from the Drawings download on the companion website.

2. Save the file as `ab13-02.dwg` in your `AutoCAD Bible` folder. This is an air and vacuum release valve, as shown in Figure 13.6.

3. Double-click the text `1/2" PIPING`. A highlighted border appears around the text. Select only the text 1/2 and type **3/8**. Press Enter or click anywhere outside the text border. The DDEDIT prompt continues to prompt you to select another annotation object. Press Enter to end the command.

4. Display the Properties palette (press Ctrl+1). Click Quick Select in the Properties palette. In the Quick Select dialog box, choose Text from the Object Type drop-down list. In the Operator drop-down list, choose Select All. Click OK to select all the text objects in the drawing.

FIGURE 13.6

An air and vacuum release valve

Thanks to the Army Corps of Engineers for this drawing.

5. In the Properties palette, choose Layer. From the Layer drop-down list, choose TEXT. Choose Color. From the Color drop-down list, choose ByLayer. All text is now on the TEXT layer using the ByLayer color. Press Esc to remove the grips and see the result.

6. Select the text at the bottom of the drawing that reads N.T.S. From the grips you can tell that it has a middle-left justification. Choose Annotate tab ⇨ Text panel (expanded) ⇨ Justify, or type **justifytext** ↵ on the command line. At the prompt, type **bc** ↵.

   The command ends. You can select the text again to see that the insertion point grip is now at the bottom center of the text.

7. Choose Annotate tab ⇨ Text panel (expanded) ⇨ Scale, or type **scaletext** ↵ on the command line. Follow the prompts:

   ```
   Select objects: Select the two lines of text at the bottom of the
       drawing.
   Select objects: ↵
   Enter a base point option for scaling
   [Existing/Left/Center/Middle/Right/TL/TC/TR/ML/MC/MR/BL/BC/BR] <BC>: Type
       e ↵ to use the existing base point.
   Specify new model height or [Paper height/Match object/Scale factor]
       <1/8">: Right-click and choose Scale factor.
   Specify scale factor or [Reference] <2">: Type 1.5 ↵
   ```

8. You can click the Properties palette's Close button to close it. Save your drawing.

Understanding Text Styles

You may not always want to use the default font. You can create text styles that give you full creative control over the font, font style (bold, italic, or both), character width, obliquing angle, and text height. You can even design backward, upside-down, and vertical text. (Vertical text is like the text that you occasionally see on the spine of a book. It goes down rather than to the right.)

Each text style

- Has a name and several properties
- Is saved with the drawing
- Can be made current when you want to use it
- Can be renamed and deleted

Creating text styles is part of the typical drawing setup procedure. You should include text styles in your drawing templates. AutoCAD and AutoCAD LT come with two types of fonts: the original .shx fonts, which are created by using *shape* files; and TrueType fonts, which are used by most Windows applications.

 See Bonus Chapter 9 for instructions on creating shape files and your own fonts.

Creating a new text style

To create a new text style, choose Home tab ⇨ Annotation panel (expanded) ⇨ Text Style or Annotate tab ⇨ Text panel and click the panel's dialog box launch arrow. This starts the STYLE command and opens the Text Style dialog box, as shown in Figure 13.7.

FIGURE 13.7

The Text Style dialog box

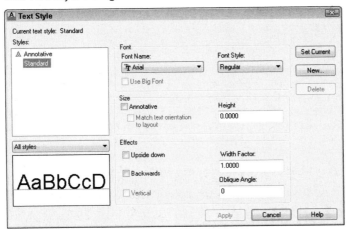

Choose New to open the New Text Style dialog box. Type the name of your new text style and click OK. Text style names can be up to 255 characters and can include spaces. You return to the Text Style dialog box where you can define the new text style.

At the top left of the Text Style dialog box is a list of currently defined styles in the drawing. At the lower-left corner is a preview of the style that is selected in the Styles list.

Font

In the Font section of the Text Style dialog box, you specify the font name and font style. Click the Font Name drop-down list arrow to see the list of fonts. Fonts with the double-T icon are TrueType fonts. The other fonts are defined in a shape file that has the SHP filename extension. They are compiled into a file with the SHX filename extension for faster access. For more information on working with fonts, see Bonus Chapter 9.

Click a font to choose it and see a preview in the Preview pane at the lower-left corner of the dialog box. If the font that you've chosen supports different styles, such as bold or italic, you can choose one of them in the Font Style drop-down list. None of the AutoCAD or AutoCAD LT fonts supports font styles, but many of the TrueType fonts do.

> **NOTE**
>
> AutoCAD supports fonts with many characters (called *big fonts*), such as Japanese and Chinese. To use these fonts, check the Use Big Font check box. The Font Style drop-down list changes to become the Big Font drop-down list, where you can choose from a list of big fonts.

Size

The Size section of the dialog box lets you specify the height of the text. There are two types of height:

- **Height in the drawing.** If you are going to use the text style in the main drawing area (model space, where you draw and edit), use the Height text box to enter the height of the text. Remember to take into account the scale factor, if necessary.

- **Height in a viewport.** If you are going to use the text style for text that you will display in a scaled viewport on a layout, check the Annotative check box. Then use the Paper Text Height text box to enter the height of the text. You don't need to adjust for the scale factor when you enter a height, because annotative objects facilitate that process for you. I cover layouts and using annotative objects in Chapter 17.

> **AUTOCAD ONLY**
>
> If you check the Annotative check box, you can also check the Match Text Orientation to Layout check box. If you rotate the viewport by using the MVSETUP command, with the Align ⟳ Rotate view options, the text remains horizontal and does not rotate.

13

In both types of height, you can leave the height at zero if you want to be able to vary the text height within that one style. If the height is zero, the TEXT command prompts you for a height when you use these commands to place text.

> **CAUTION**
>
> If you create a text style using a height other than zero and then use that text style when you define a dimension style, the text style height overrides the text height that you specify in the dimension style. See Chapter 15 for more information on dimension styles.

Effects

In the Effects section, you specify the orientation, width factor, and oblique angle of the text style. The default width factor of characters is set to 1. You can specify a smaller number to compress text and a larger number to expand it, as shown in Figure 13.8.

FIGURE 13.8

Text using different width factors

Width = 1.5   Bearing   Housing
Width = .8   Bearing Housing

The term *oblique angle* refers to the angle of the individual letters. It is generally used to create an effect, such as italic text. You don't need to use an oblique angle if you're using a TrueType font that supports italic text.

The angle definition used to define oblique text is different from the angle definition used for other objects. Up and down text, which is normal text, has a zero oblique angle. A positive angle slants the text to the right; this is typical for italic text. A negative angle slants the text to the left. Figure 13.9 shows text with a positive and negative oblique angle.

FIGURE 13.9

Text using different oblique angles

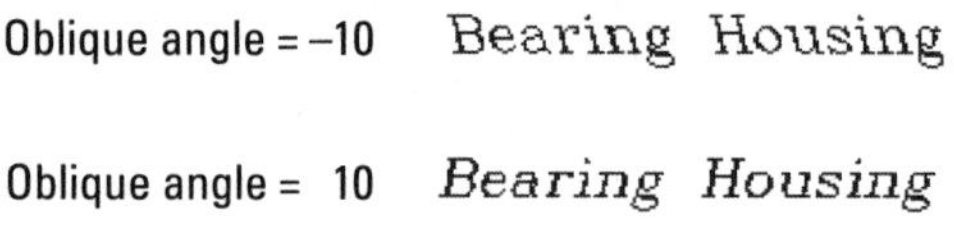

Oblique angle = –10   Bearing Housing

Oblique angle = 10   *Bearing Housing*

You can create text that is backward (like a mirror image) or upside down. Some fonts also let you create vertical text. Figure 13.10 shows an example of each kind of text. Check the appropriate check box to create the effect that you want.

FIGURE 13.10

Upside-down, backward, and vertical text

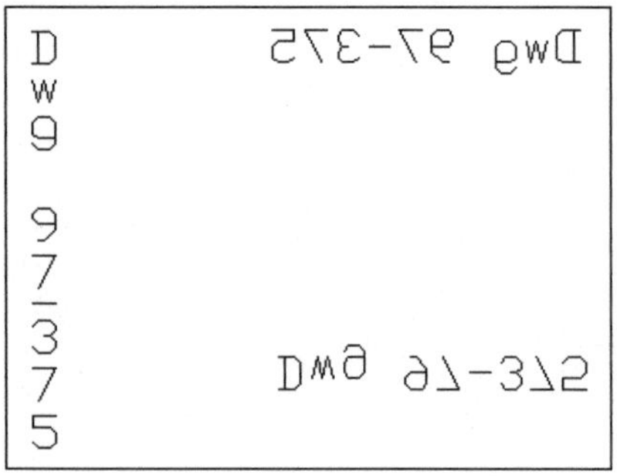

After you finish defining your text style, click Apply to make it current. Click Close to return to your drawing.

Renaming and deleting text styles

You can rename and delete text styles easily. To rename a text style, start the STYLE command to open the Text Style dialog box. Select the text style, click the text style's name again, enter a new name, and press Enter.

To delete a text style, choose it from the Styles list box of the Text Style dialog box and click Delete. A message box asks you to confirm the deletion. Click OK to delete the text style. You cannot delete a text style that is being used.

ON THE WEB
The drawing used in the following exercise on creating text styles, ab13-b.dwg, is available from the Drawings download on the companion website.

STEPS: Creating Text Styles

1. Open ab13-b.dwg, available from the Drawings download on the companion website.

2. Save the file as ab13-03.dwg in your AutoCAD Bible folder.

3. Choose Home tab ⇨ Annotation panel (expanded) ⇨ Text Style to open the Text Style dialog box. Click New. In the New Text Style dialog box, type **Notes** and click OK.

4. From the Font Name drop-down list, choose romans.shx. In the Height text box, enter a height of **1/16"**. In the Width Factor text box, enter a width factor of **.95**. In the Oblique Angle text box, type **10**. Click Apply to make the new style current. Click Close.

5. Start the TEXT command. At the Specify start point of text or [Justify/Style]: prompt, pick a start point at the lower-left corner of the drawing. At the Specify rotation angle of text <0>: prompt, press Enter. At the prompt, type **Note: Not drawn to scale.** ↵. Press Enter again to end the command.

6. Save your drawing. It should look like Figure 13.11. If you're going on to the next exercise, keep this drawing open.

FIGURE 13.11

The addition of text using a new text style

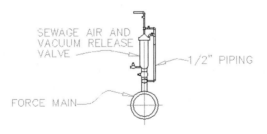

Modifying a text style

To change a style, choose Home tab ⇨ Annotation panel (expanded) ⇨ Text Style. From the Styles list box in the Text Style dialog box, choose the text style that you want to change. Make changes in the same way that you did when creating the style. Choose Apply and then Close. The drawing regenerates, and the text that uses the style that you changed is modified accordingly. This is a powerful way to control the look of text in your drawing.

NOTE
Unfortunately, only changes to the font and text style affect current text. Other changes, such as width factor, oblique angle, orientation, and height, are ignored. However, new text takes on these other changes.

Making a style current or changing a text object's style

You can choose the current style when you use one of the text commands. If you use TEXT, the command displays the `Specify start point of text or [Justify/Style]:` prompt. Right-click and choose Style. (The prompt also displays the current style, height, and annotative setting.) If you know the name of the style that you want to use, type it and press Enter. The `Specify start point of text or [Justify/Style]:` prompt repeats. You can choose the Justify option or pick a start point to continue the command.

If you use MTEXT, the In-Place Text Editor opens, as explained in the next section. Choose the text style that you want from the Style drop-down list.

An easy way to make a style current or to change the text style of existing text is to choose Home tab ⇨ Annotation panel (expanded) ⇨ Text Style drop-down list or Annotate tab ⇨ Text panel ⇨ Text Style drop-down list. To make a style current, choose the style from the Text Style drop-down list with no text selected. To change the text style of existing text, select the text and choose a new style from the list. You can also change the style of selected text in the Quick Properties palette or the Properties palette.

Importing a text style

You can use the Content Explorer to import features from other drawings. (For more information, see Chapter 12.) To import a text style from a drawing in an indexed folder in the Content Explorer, follow these steps:

1. Choose Plug-ins tab ⇨ Explore.
2. In the left pane, navigate to the drawing that has the text style that you want.
3. Double-click the drawing icon.
4. Scroll down to the `Text Styles` section.
5. Drag the text style that you want onto the drawing area.

ON THE WEB
The drawing used in the following exercise on modifying text styles, `ab13-03.dwg`, is available from the Results download on the companion website.

STEPS: Modifying Text Styles

1. If you have `ab13-03.dwg` open from the previous exercise, continue to use it for this exercise. Otherwise, open `ab13-03.dwg`, available from the Results download on the companion website.

2. Save the file as `ab13-04.dwg` in your `AutoCAD Bible` folder.

3. The note at the bottom-left corner of the drawing uses the Notes text style. Choose Home tab ⇨ Annotation panel (expanded) ⇨ Text Style. In the Text Style dialog box, make sure that the Notes style name is selected, and then choose `italic.shx` from the Font Name drop-down list. Choose Apply and then Close.

4. The drawing regenerates, and the font of the text changes.

5. Save your drawing.

Creating Multiline Text

Single-line text is awkward when you want to type lengthy text. The main disadvantage is that single-line text does not wrap text to the next line to keep a neat right margin. Multiline text solves this problem and also offers more formatting options compared to single-line text. The entire paragraph of multiline text is one object. Don't confuse multiline text, which is also called *paragraph text,* with *multilines* (which I cover in Chapter 16).

Using the In-Place Text Editor

To create paragraph text, choose Home tab ⇨ Annotation panel ⇨ Text drop-down list ⇨ Multiline Text. This starts the MTEXT command. The prompt tells you the current style, text height, and whether or not the style is annotative. For example:

```
Current text style: "ROMANS" Text height: 4 1/2" Annotative: No
```

The command continues with the `Specify first corner:` prompt. Specify one corner of a bounding box to indicate where to place the text. At the `Specify opposite corner or [Height/ Justify/Line spacing/Rotation/Style/Width/Columns]:` prompt, specify the diagonally opposite corner of the bounding box. The Text Editor tab appears on the Ribbon. You can choose one of the other prompt options to specify the text properties before you type the text. Some of these options are also available in the In-Place Text Editor, which opens after you specify the bounding box. Figure 13.12 shows the Text Editor tab and the In-Place Text Editor.

> **NOTE**
> You can use the MTEXTTOOLBAR system variable to display the Text Formatting toolbar. Change its value to 1 to display both the Text Formatting toolbar and Ribbon tab.

> **TIP**
>
> When you specify the corners of the Mtext bounding box, you see sample text at the cursor to give you an idea of the actual current height of the text. You can change the sample text with the MTJIGSTRING system variable.

FIGURE 13.12

The Text Editor tab and the In-Place Text Editor

Type your text in the bounding box. The In-Place Text Editor wraps the text to the next line when the text meets the right side of the bounding box that you specified. Although you've created a bounding box with four sides, only the *paragraph width* (that is, the left and right margins) limits the text. If you type too much text for the bounding box, the bounding box expands vertically. To format selected or new text, use the buttons on the panels of the Text Editor tab of the Ribbon. In the Style panel, you can do the following:

- **Style.** Choose any text style by clicking the Text Style button and choosing from the thumbnail images.

- **Annotative.** Click to turn the annotative feature on or off.

- **Text Height.** Choose a height from the drop-down list or type a new height in the Text Height box.

In the Formatting panel, you can do the following:

- **Bold.** If Bold style is supported for the font, select text and click the Bold button.
- **Italic.** If Italic style is supported for the font, select text and click the Italic button.
- **Font.** Choose any font from the Font drop-down list.
- **Underline.** Select text and click the Underline button.
- **Overline.** To overscore selected text, click the Overline button.
- **Color.** Choose ByLayer or any color from the Color drop-down list. To choose from additional colors, choose Select Color to open the Select Color dialog box. (See Chapter 11 for details on using this dialog box.)
- **Strikethrough.** Click to add a strikethrough line to selected text.
- **Case.** Choose from the drop-down list to make selected text all uppercase or lowercase.
- **Background Mask.** Opens the Background Mask dialog box. This feature creates a background around your text that covers other objects so that you can easily read the text. Check the Use

Background Mask check box. Specify a border offset factor to create a margin around the text. A margin setting of 1 does not create any margin. Then check the Use Drawing Background Color check box to use the color of your drawing screen, or choose another color from the drop-down list. Click OK.

- **Oblique Angle (in the expanded Formatting panel).** Enter a number that represents an angle from upright to specify the angle for the selected characters. For example, you can use the oblique angle to create italicized text. A negative value angles text to the left.

- **Tracking (in the expanded Formatting panel).** Enter a number in the text box to specify the spacing between letters of selected text. The number works like a scale factor.

- **Width Factor (in the expanded Formatting panel).** Enter a number in the text box to specify the width of selected letters. The number works like a scale factor.

- **Stack (in the expanded Formatting panel).** Toggles stacking and unstacking fractions. (This option only appears if you select appropriate characters.) Use this option to stack characters if they are not numerals or immediately before or after the three AutoStack symbols (slash, pound sign, and carat). Select the text, and choose Stack. You can use the same process to unstack text that you previously stacked. If you select stacked fractions, you can also right-click and choose Stack Properties to configure the fraction in the Stack Properties dialog box. See the sidebar, "Creating stacked fractions automatically," for more details on creating fractions.

TIP

To create an exponent (or superscript), type a number and then a carat, as in 2^. Select the number and the carat, and then choose Stack. To create a subscript, type a carat, and then the number, as in ^2, and then stack it.

In the Paragraph panel, you can control formatting that applies to an entire paragraph, as follows:

- **Justification.** Choose a justification from the Justification drop-down list. The justifications are discussed in the "Justifying single-line text" section earlier in this chapter.

- **Bullets and Numbering.** Displays a submenu that lets you manage bullets and numbering:
  - **Off.** Removes bullets and numbering from the selected text.
  - **Numbered.** Creates a numbered list.
  - **Lettered.** Lets you create lettered lists. You can choose uppercase or lowercase letters.
  - **Bulleted.** Creates a bulleted list.
  - **Start.** Restarts numbering (or lettering) from the beginning.
  - **Continue.** Continues numbering (or lettering) from the last list.
  - **Allow Auto-list.** Automatically starts a numbered list if you type **1.**, a lettered list if you type **A.**, or a bulleted list if you type a dash (-) or an asterisk (*).
  - **Use Tab Delimiter Only.** Creates a list only if you use a tab after some text, and not when you use a space. On by default.
  - **Allow Bullets and Lists.** Turns on the feature that automatically numbers (or letters) items that are in a list. For example, if you delete an item, the rest of the items are automatically adjusted.

13

- **Line Spacing.** Set line spacing in multiples of single-line spacing. You can choose More to open the Paragraph dialog box, discussed later in this list.
- **Default.** Sets the default alignment, usually left-justified.
- **Left.** Left-justifies text and sets the insertion point to the left of the text.
- **Center.** Centers text and sets the insertion point to the center of the text.
- **Right.** Right-justifies text and sets the insertion point to the right of the text.
- **Justify.** Aligns both the left and right margins on the text.
- **Distribute.** Spreads out the text to meet the left and right margins.
- **Paragraph.** Click the dialog box launcher arrow at the right side of the panel's title bar to open the Paragraph dialog box, shown in Figure 13.13, where you can specify the following settings:

FIGURE 13.13

The Paragraph dialog box offers one place where you can specify many settings relating to paragraphs.

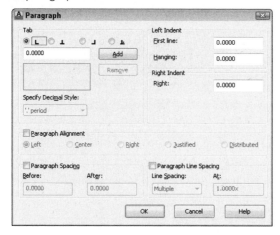

- **Tabs.** You can choose left, center, right, and decimal tabs, as well as their position. Click Add to add the tab. A decimal tab centers text around a decimal point. (If you choose a decimal tab, you can choose a decimal style from the Specify Decimal Style drop-down list — period, comma, or space.)
- **Paragraph Alignment.** Check the Paragraph Alignment check box and choose Left, Center, Right, Justified, or Distributed. These buttons are also on the Paragraph panel.
- **Paragraph Spacing.** Sets spacing between paragraphs. You can set spacing both before and after, but if you set both, the two values are added.

- **Left Indent.** Sets the left margin for the first line of a paragraph and the rest of the paragraph. Use this indentation for creating bulleted and numbered lists. To indent an entire paragraph, use both first-line and paragraph indentation. You can also use the two left triangle indent markers on the Text Editor ruler.

- **Right Indent.** Sets the right margin for the paragraph. You can also use the right triangle indent marker on the Text Editor ruler.

- **Paragraph Line Spacing.** You can set the spacing of lines of text within a paragraph. For example, from the Line Spacing drop-down list, you can choose Multiple to Single or Double-space lines. Choose Exactly to specify the distance between lines in units — great for inserting text into titleblocks. Choose At Least to set a minimum spacing — this is good for situations when you have text or symbols of varying heights and want to leave room for the larger items. For simple formatting, you can use the Line Spacing button in the Paragraph panel.

- **Combine Paragraphs** (on the expanded Paragraph panel). Combines separate paragraphs into one. Select the paragraphs that you want to combine before applying the command.

> **TIP**
> To set indentation and tabs on the In-Place Text Editor's ruler, drag the first-line indent marker (the top triangle at the left of the ruler) or the paragraph indent marker (the bottom triangle) to the left or right. To set a tab, click on the ruler where you want the tab. To delete a tab, drag a tab marker off the ruler. Note that the bullets and numbering feature makes these settings less important than previously.

The Insert panel enables you to do the following:

- **Columns.** Create multiple-column text. You have the following options:
  - **No Columns.** Creates one column of text.
  - **Dynamic Columns.** The default option, which creates columns based on the amount of text. Text automatically flows from one column to the next. The vertical height of the bounding box does not change as you add text; if you enter more text than can fit in the box, another column automatically starts, with no limit. You can set column height to automatic or manual (the default), using the submenu.
  - **Static Columns.** Creates a set number of columns of a specified height and width. Text automatically flows from one column to the next, but you can specify the number of columns.
  - **Insert Column Break.** Forces a column break. Place the cursor at the desired location and press Alt+Enter.
  - **Column Settings.** Opens the Column Settings dialog box. Here you can specify the type of columns, their width, height, and gutter (the spacing between columns).

13

> **TIP**
> You can grip-edit column text. Use one of the lower grips to change the vertical height. Use the right-facing arrow to change the column width.

- **Symbol.** Insert the degree, plus/minus, or diameter symbol, a non-breaking space, and a number of other symbols. You can also choose Other to open the Windows Character Map to select any of the available symbols. Click a symbol, and then click Select. Click Copy and then click the Close button to close the Windows Character Map. In the In-Place Text Editor, press Ctrl+V to paste the symbol.
- **Field.** Insert a field into the text. For more information, see the section "Inserting Fields" later in this chapter.

In the Spell Check panel, you can do the following:

- **Spelling Check.** Find misspelled words in the selected Mtext object. Be sure to place the cursor at the beginning of the text. Misspelled words are underlined with a dashed red line. You can then right-click to choose from suggested words. At the end of this chapter, I explain how to check the spelling of an entire drawing.
- **Edit Dictionaries.** You can edit the dictionaries that AutoCAD and AutoCAD LT use to check spelling. I discuss this process at the end of this chapter.
- **Check Spelling Settings.** Click the dialog box launcher arrow at the right side of the panel's title bar to open the Check Spelling Settings dialog box, where you can specify which types of words to exclude from spell checking.

In the Tools panel, you have the option to do the following:

- **Find and Replace.** Open the Find and Replace dialog box so that you can find or replace specified text. If you want the search to match the case of the specified text, choose Match Case. If you want to restrict the search to whole words that match the specified text, choose Find Whole Words Only. If you only want to find text, ignore the Replace text box. To both find and replace text, enter text in both boxes. Make sure that the cursor is at the beginning of the text if you want to search the entire Mtext object. At the end of this chapter, I explain how to find and replace text in an entire drawing.

> **TIP**
> You can check the Use Wildcards check box and use wildcards, such as * (any number of characters) and ? (any single character) to search for text. You can check the Match Diacritics check box to match words with diacritical marks. Finally, you can check the Match Half/Full Width Forms check box to refine searching for text in East Asian languages.

- **Import Text** (on the expanded Tools panel). Opens the Select File dialog box, which lets you choose a text (TXT) or Rich Text Format (RTF) file to import. (Rich Text Format preserves formatting from application to application, while text-only documents do not retain formatting.) Find the file, choose it, and click Open to place the text in the In-Place Text Editor. The maximum file size is 256K. I cover other techniques for importing text later in this chapter.
- **AutoCAPS** (on the expanded Tools panel). Automatically changes newly typed and imported text to uppercase, even if the Caps Lock key is not on. (And it's a cute pun on AutoCAD.)

On the Options panel, you can find the following:

- **Character Set** (on the More drop-down list). Lets you choose the language that you want to work with, so that you have the characters that you need for that language.
- **Remove Formatting** (on the More drop-down list). Removes character formatting, such as bold and italic, paragraph formatting (such as indenting), or all formatting.

- **Editor Settings** (on the More drop-down list). Opens a submenu that lets you toggle the display of the Text Formatting toolbar and control if the editor uses WYSIWYG (what you see is what you get). You can also create a temporary opaque background for the In-Place Text Editor that may help you to edit text more easily if the text overlaps other objects. This background disappears when you close the editor. Finally, you can choose the color of the highlight when you select text.
- **Ruler.** Turn the ruler on and off.
- **Undo.** Undo the last Mtext edit.
- **Redo.** Redo the last undo operation.

In the Close panel, click Close Text Editor to close the editor. You can also close the editor by clicking anywhere outside the editor or by pressing Ctrl+Enter.

Right-click in the editor to display the shortcut menu. The shortcut menu contains many of the options that are on the Ribbon. Here I discuss the options that are not available on the Ribbon.

- **Select All.** Selects all the text in the current Mtext object.
- **Cut.** Places selected text in the Windows Clipboard and removes it from the editor.
- **Copy.** Places selected text in the Windows Clipboard without removing it from the editor.
- **Paste.** Places text from the Windows Clipboard.
- **Paste Special.** Opens a submenu where you can paste without character formatting, paragraph formatting, or any formatting at all.

The TEXTTOFRONT command moves all text in your drawing to the front (top) of the drawing order. For the background mask to work, your text needs to be on top, so that you can use this command when you are creating text with background masks. The display order of objects is controlled by the DRAWORDER command, which I discuss in Bonus Chapter 4.

You can snap to the corners of the Mtext bounding box by using the node object snap. (See Chapter 4 for an explanation of object snaps.) To turn this feature off, change the OSNAPNODELEGACY system variable to 1.

Creating Stacked Fractions Automatically

You can create automatic stacked fractions and tolerances as you type by using a system similar to those described earlier for creating special characters with TEXT. You can also type unstacked fractions (as in 1/2); select the fraction text and choose Stack from the expanded Formatting panel. To create stacked fractions as you type, open the In-Place Text Editor and follow these steps:

1. Type the numerator, which is the character that you want on top.

2. Type the character that defines the fraction format that you want (see the example):

   - Type a slash (/) to create a fraction separated by a horizontal line.

   - Type a pound symbol (#) to create a fraction separated by a diagonal line.

   - Type a caret (^) to create a tolerance stack, which is like a fraction separated by a horizontal line, except that there is no horizontal line.

continued

continued

3. Type the denominator.

4. Type a space (or other nonnumeric character). The AutoStack Properties dialog box opens.

5. Choose the option you want to create the stacked fraction:

   ■ Uncheck Enable AutoStacking to disable the automatic stacked fraction feature.

   ■ Uncheck Remove Leading Blank if you want to retain a space between whole numbers and fractions.

   ■ Choose whether you want the slash to result in a fraction with a horizontal line or a fraction with a slash. This choice does not affect how the pound sign and carat work. If you want the slash to result in a fraction with a slash (which would seem to make more sense), then you do not have an automatic way to create a fraction with a horizontal line.

   ■ Check Don't Show This Dialog Again; Always Use These Settings to stop the dialog box from opening when you create automatic stacked fractions.

   ■ Click OK to create the stacked fraction, or Cancel to leave the numbers as you typed them.

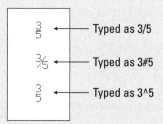

AutoStack works only with numerals immediately before and after the slash, pound sign, and carat. You can also set the properties of individual stacked fractions. Select and right-click the fraction in the In-Place Text Editor and choose Stack Properties from the shortcut menu. In the Stack Properties dialog box, you can change the following properties:

■ **Text.** Edit the upper and lower text.

■ **Style.** Change the fraction style. (Refer to the example under Step 2 for the three possible styles.)

■ **Position.** Position the fraction so that the top, center, or bottom is aligned with other text.

■ **Text Size.** Change the size of the numbers that make up the fraction. Fraction numbers are usually smaller than regular numbers.

Specifying and changing line spacing

You can specify the spacing between lines in multiline text before you open the Multiline Text Editor. (You can also use the Paragraph dialog box when you're in the editor, as described previously.) Line spacing is useful for fitting text into a schedule or table in your drawing. Of course, you can also use the table feature, which I discuss in the "Creating Tables" section later in this chapter. To set line spacing to an exact unit distance, follow these steps:

1. Start the MTEXT command.

2. At the `Specify first corner:` prompt, pick the first corner of your Mtext box.

3. At the `Specify opposite corner or [Height/Justify/Line spacing/Rotation/ Style/Width/Columns]:` prompt, choose the Line Spacing option.

4. At the `Enter line spacing type [At least/Exactly] <At least>:` prompt, choose Exactly.

5. At the `Enter line spacing factor or distance <1x>:` prompt, type a number, such as **1x** for specifying a one-unit space between lines of text. (If you type **1x**, you get single-line spacing, which varies according to the size of the text.)

6. Continue with the command.

This setting persists for future Mtext objects. To change existing line spacing, select (do not double-click) the multiline text object. Open the Properties palette and set one or more of the following:

- **Line space factor.** Specifies line spacing as a multiple of lines. Single-line spacing is 1.0000, and double-line spacing is 2.0000.

- **Line space distance.** Specifies line spacing in units. Use this measurement (along with a line space style of Exactly) to fit text into an existing table or schedule.

- **Line space style.** Choose At Least (the default) to adjust line spacing based on the height of the largest character in the line of text. Choose Exactly to specify line spacing that is the same, regardless of differences in character height.

Specifying width and rotation

To change the width of an Mtext object, you can use its right triangular grip. Select the Mtext object and drag the grip to the desired location. You can use the Properties palette to change the width and height. You can specify the exact width when creating the Mtext object by using the Width option after you specify the first corner of the Mtext bounding box. Otherwise, you generally specify the width by picking the two corners of the Mtext bounding box.

> **TIP**
> When the In-Place Text Editor is open, you can change the width of the Mtext object by dragging on the right edge of the ruler.

To rotate an existing Mtext object, use the Properties palette's Rotation item, or use the top-left square grip, as follows:

1. Select the Mtext object.

2. Click the grip to make it "hot."

3. Right-click and choose Rotate.

4. At the `Specify rotation angle or [Base point/Copy/Undo/Reference/eXit]:` prompt, pick a new location for the grip or type a rotation angle.

You can also specify the rotation while creating the Mtext object. Use the Rotation option that appears on the command line after you specify the first corner.

Creating text for different scales

You may plan to display certain sections of your drawing at more than one scale. For example, you may want to show the entire model at a 1:4 scale, but a detail of the model at a 1:1 scale. If you have some text next to the model and want that text to appear at both scales, you have a problem — how do you get the text to appear the same size in both places? Without addressing this problem, your text will be either too big or too small at one of the scales. Another situation may be that you want one text object to appear at one scale, but another to appear at a different scale.

You create displays of various scales by using floating viewports on a layout. I cover viewports and layouts in Chapter 17. However, if you know the scales you want to use, you can plan for this situation while you're in the drawing and editing stage by using *annotative* text.

Annotative objects create representations at various scales that you can automatically display at those scales when you lay out your drawing for plotting. The following objects can be annotative: text, dimensions, geometric tolerances, multileaders, blocks, and attributes. Text styles, dimension styles, and multileader styles can also be annotative; if you create an object using an annotative style, then the object is annotative. See the chapters that cover each of these objects for more information on their annotative property.

Previously, to create text that appeared in viewports of different scales, you needed to create a separate layer for each scale. You could then put the text on different layers and turn off the layers that you didn't want in each viewport. You might also have created separate text styles for each text object. This was a complicated and time-demanding task. Annotative text can eliminate the need for separate layers and text styles when you need to display text at more than one scale.

To create annotative text, follow these steps:

1. Create an annotative text style and make it current. To create an annotative text style, see the "Understanding Text Styles" section earlier in this chapter. AutoCAD also comes with a text style named `Annotative` that you can use.

2. Decide on the scales that you will use for each text object. For example, you might have two text objects each at a different scale, or one text object that you need to display at two different scales.

 3. If you want each text object to have a different scale, turn off the ANNOAUTOSCALE system variable. When this system variable is on, it automatically adds scales to annotative objects as you add annotative scales; the result is that each object has more than one scale. To turn ANNOAUTOSCALE off, click the icon on the right side of the status bar to the right of the Annotation Scale list. The tooltip reads "Automatically Add Scales to Annotative Objects When the Annotation Scale Changes." When on, there's a yellow lightning bolt; when off, the lightning bolt is gray.

4. Set the annotation scale for the first text object. To do so, click the Annotation Scale button at the right side of the status bar to display the scale list and choose the scale you want. For example, choose 1:4 if you plan to display the text in a viewport at the 1:4 scale. (The first time you add an annotative object to a drawing, a dialog box may open automatically, asking you for the scale.)

In Chapter 5, I explain scales in general and how to edit the scale list.

5. Start the TEXT or MTEXT command and enter the text.

6. Repeat Steps 4 and 5 for each separate scale and text item.

7. When you're ready to plot, you can set the desired annotative scale, and plot. You can also create viewports and set their scale. See Chapter 17 for details and an exercise using annotative objects.

If you want one text object to have more than one scale, you can add an annotative scale to it. Follow these steps:

1. Select the text.

2. Choose Annotate tab ⇨ Annotation Scaling panel ⇨ Add/Delete Scales to open the Annotation Object Scale dialog box, as shown in Figure 13.14. You can also display the Properties palette, click the Annotative Scale item, and click the Ellipsis button that appears.

3. Click Add to display the Add Scales to Object dialog box, where you can choose one or more scales.

4. Click OK twice to close both dialog boxes.

FIGURE 13.14

You can add or delete scales for annotative objects in the Annotation Object Scale dialog box.

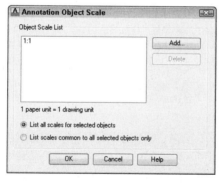

 At any time, you can view the text for any single scale, or view the text for all scales. (This applies to all types of annotative objects, not just text.) Remember that you may have one or more scales for any one text item. If you don't see all the scales of an annotative object, click the Annotation Visibility button on the right side of the status bar. This button controls the ANNOALLVISIBLE system variable. By default, it is on, displaying all scales. When you turn it off, you see only the text for the current annotative scale. To immediately plot, you would turn off this system variable so that you plot only the text for the current annotative scale.

If you want to change a text object that is not annotative to one that is annotative, you can use the Properties palette. Follow these steps:

1. Select the text.

2. Display the Properties palette.

3. In the Properties palette, select the Annotative property and choose Yes from the drop-down list. The Annotative Scale property is displayed in the Properties palette when the Annotative property is set to Yes.

4. Select the Annotative Scale property and click the Ellipsis button that is displayed to open the Annotation Object Scale dialog box, shown in Figure 13.14.

5. Click Add to display the Add Scales to Object dialog box, where you can choose one or more scales.

6. Click OK twice to close both dialog boxes.

Editing paragraph text

To edit paragraph text, double-click the text to start the In-Place Text Editor.

Make your changes in the editor. The techniques are similar to those in any word processor. You can:

- Select text and press the Delete key to delete the text, or type to replace the selected text.
- Click to move the insertion point to where you want to insert text and start typing. (To type over text, press Insert to enter overtype mode.)
- Use the Ribbon, Text Formatting toolbar, or shortcut menu (right-click) to change formatting.

To change characters, you must first highlight the characters. This lets you make height or font changes to individual words or even letters. When changing properties that affect the entire paragraph, such as justification, you do not first highlight the characters.

If you right-click in the In-Place Text Editor with the cursor on a field, you have options to edit the field, update it, or convert it to regular text. For more information about fields, see the section "Inserting Fields" later in this chapter.

ON THE WEB

Mmt combines two Mtext objects into one Mtext paragraph. Look in `\Software\Chapter13\Mmt` on the companion website. Txtexprt exports text to a text file. It's in `\Software\Chapter13\txtexprt`. These features work with AutoCAD only.

Importing text

As mentioned earlier, you can import text by using the In-Place Text Editor. You can also import text in three other ways:

- You can use drag-and-drop to insert text from a .txt file into a drawing. Open Windows Explorer and locate the file. Position the Explorer window so that you can see the filename and your drawing at the same time. Click the file and drag it to your drawing. The new text becomes multiline text in the drawing.

- You can copy text from another file to the Windows Clipboard. Open the other file, select the text, and copy the text to the Windows Clipboard. Return to your drawing by clicking the AutoCAD or AutoCAD LT button on the Windows task bar. Choose Home tab ⇨ Clipboard panel ⇨ Paste drop-down menu ⇨ Paste (or press Ctrl+V). If you double-click this text, the original application opens.

- If you have the In-Place Text Editor open, you can paste the text directly into the editor. Right-click in the editor and choose Paste (or press Ctrl+V). You can then format the text.

 For more information on importing text, see Bonus Chapter 4.

ON THE WEB

The files used in the following exercise on creating multiline text, `ab13-c.dwg` and `ab13-c.txt`, are available from the Drawings download on the companion website.

STEPS: Creating Multiline Text

1. Open `ab13-c.dwg`, available from the Drawings download on the companion website.

2. Save the file as `ab13-05.dwg` in your `AutoCAD Bible` folder. This is a plat drawing, as shown in Figure 13.15.

FIGURE 13.15

The plat drawing

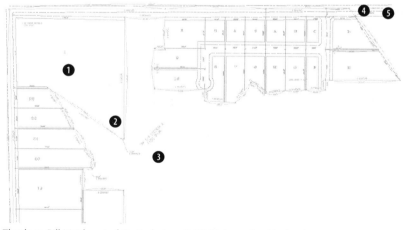

Thanks to Bill Maidment of Cantech, Inc., Fairfield, Iowa, for this drawing.

3. Choose Home tab ➪ Annotation panel ➪ Text drop-down menu ➪ Multiline Text. At the prompts, pick points ❶ and ❷, shown in Figure 13.15. The Text Editor tab is displayed. In the Text Height box in the Style panel, type a height of **12.5** and press Enter. In the main editing box, type the following:

   Containing 108.33 acres including 5.97 acres existing R.O.W. and 4.56 acres proposed R.O.W.

4. Highlight the text 108.33 and click Underline in the Formatting panel. In the Paragraph panel, choose Justification ➪ Middle Left. Click outside the text editor to place the text.

5. Open Windows Explorer (right-click Start and choose Explorer or Open Windows Explorer). Find ab13-c.txt on the companion website. Move the Windows Explorer window so that you can see both ab13-c.txt and your drawing screen. Drag ab13-c.txt from the Windows Explorer window to ❸, shown in Figure 13.15, and release the mouse button. If necessary, pick a grip and click at the proper location.

6. Select the text and open the Properties palette (press Ctrl+1). Next to the Defined Width item, type **500** ↵. Next to the Defined Height item, type **12.5** ↵.

7. Zoom in on the new text. This text was originally single-line text in an older drawing. You can see why you wouldn't want to retype it!

8. Choose View tab ➪ Navigate 2D panel ➪ Back to return to your original view. Repeat this process, this time choosing the Window option to zoom in to the area bounded by ❹ and ❺. Set the current layer to 0, which is a gray color.

9. Above the text about the proposed R.O.W. (right of way) is a yellow centerline. You want to place text on that line. Choose Home tab ➪ Annotation panel ➪ Text drop-down menu ➪ Multiline Text.

10. At the prompt, pick ❹ and ❺, centering the bounding box around the yellow centerline. In the Text Height box of the Style panel, change the text to 12.5. The text style should be ROMANS. Type the following text:

    64TH AVE N.W. EXISTING R.O.W. 66' – CURRENT

11. Press the Spacebar to add a space after CURRENT. From the Insert panel, choose Symbol ➪ Center Line to add the centerline symbol to the end of the text.

12. To add a background mask so that the yellow centerline doesn't make the text hard to read, choose Background Mask from the Formatting panel. In the Background Mask dialog box, select the Use Background Mask check box. Choose Red as the background color and click OK. Click anywhere outside the In-Place Text Editor to place the text. You can see that it uses the centerline symbol and has a red background that hides the yellow centerline behind the text.

13. Start the MTEXT command. At the prompts, define a border somewhere in the middle of the drawing. The width should be equal to about three of the plats that you see at the top. Type **Plat Acreage** ↵.

14. Type **1.**, press Tab, and type **22.93** ↵. Be sure to insert a tab after the period. AutoCAD or AutoCAD LT automatically creates a numbered list when you use this format. You should now see the number two with a period after it (2.).

15. Finish the rest of the numbered list as follows:

    2. 2.85 ↵
    3. 1.51 ↵
    4. 1.38

16. Click anywhere outside the In-Place Text Editor area to end the MTEXT command.

17. Zoom to the Previous display to return to your original view. Save your drawing.

Creating Tables

Tables, which are often called schedules, are very common in drawings. You can save your formatting in table styles for consistency among drawings. You should save table styles in your templates.

Inserting a table

 To insert a table, choose Home tab ⇨ Annotation panel ⇨ Table, to start the TABLE command. The Insert Table dialog box opens, as shown in Figure 13.16.

FIGURE 13.16

Use the Insert Table dialog box to create a table in your drawing.

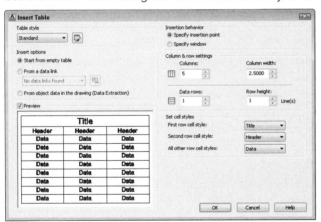

On the left side of the Insert Table dialog box, you see a preview of how the table will look. By default, you see either the Standard table style or the last table style that you used. Choose the table style that you want from the Table Style name drop-down list. In the next section, I explain how to define a table style.

In the Insert Options section, you can choose from three options for getting data into the table:

- **Start from empty table.** Use this option when you want to manually enter the data.
- **From a data link.** This option creates a table from Microsoft Excel spreadsheet data or a comma-delimited (CSV) file. When you choose this option, most of the rest of the Insert Table dialog box is unavailable.
- **From object data in the drawing (Data Extraction).** This option creates a table from properties of existing objects in the drawing (AutoCAD only).

If you choose to start from an empty table, you can choose from one of the following options in the Insertion Behavior section of the dialog box:

- **Specify insertion point.** You place the table in your drawing by specifying an insertion point (the default). You use the Column & Row Settings section to specify the number of columns and their width, as well as the number of rows and their height (in terms of lines of text).
- **Specify window.** You pick a point at the upper-left and then lower-right corner of the table. You use the Column & Row Settings section to specify the number of columns and the line height of the rows. As you move the mouse to the right, the columns widen, and as you move the mouse downward, additional rows are added. Click when you see the size that you want.

In the Set Cell Styles section, you specify which cell styles go where. See the next section for an explanation of cell styles. By default, the First Row Cell Style uses the Title cell style, the Second Row Cell Style uses the Header cell style, and All Other Row Cell Styles use the Data cell style. If you create your own cell styles, you can choose them from the drop-down lists here.

If the table style shown is what you want, click OK. Then specify an insertion point or window to place the table.

 You can also add a table to a tool palette and insert a table from the tool palette. For more information on tool palettes, see Bonus Chapter 3.

Specifying a table style

 You have a great deal of control over how your table looks. You can make it plain or fancy. To design your table, you create a table style by choosing Home tab ⇨ Annotation panel (expanded) ⇨ Table Style to open the Table Style dialog box, as shown in Figure 13.17. Alternatively, you can click the Launch the Table Style Dialog button in the Table Style section of the Insert Table dialog box or choose Annotate tab ⇨ Tables panel and then click the panel's dialog box launcher arrow.

FIGURE 13.17

The Table Style dialog box gives you the tools to create tables with style.

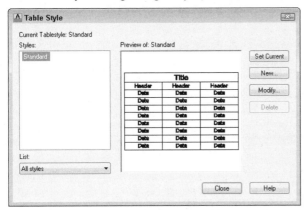

On the left side of the Table Style dialog box is a list of styles. From the List drop-down list at the bottom, you can choose to display all styles or only styles that are in use in your drawing. To make a table style current, choose the style that you want and click Set Current.

TIP

An easier way to make a table style current is to choose the table style from the Table Style drop-down list in the Annotation panel (expanded) of the Home tab or the Tables panel on the Annotate tab. Choose your table style before you start to create a table. You can also import table styles from the Content Explorer. (For more information on the Content Explorer, see Chapter 12.)

To create a new style, click the New button. In the Create New Table Style dialog box, enter a name in the New Style Name text box. From the Start With drop-down list, choose an existing table style as a basis for your new style. The new table style inherits the properties of this existing style so that you have to specify only the differences that you want. Then click Continue to open the New Table Style dialog box, as shown in Figure 13.18.

NOTE

You can select an existing table in the drawing as a starting point. In the Starting Table section, click the button to select a table in your drawing.

As you define your new table style, the preview panel shows you the results. You use the Cell Styles drop-down list to format data in the cells of the table, column headers, and the table's main title. Each category is one of the preexisting *cell styles* — data, header, and title — but you can create your own.

FIGURE 13.18

The New Table Style dialog box is the place to define a new table style.

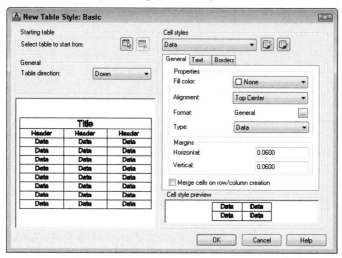

You use the three tabs to define general, text, and border formatting for each cell style. In this way, you format the entire table. The three cell styles are very similar, but have slightly different defaults. For example, the Title cell style has centered text and a larger height than the headers and data cells.

 To create a cell style as you work, first click the Create a New Cell Style button in the Cell Styles section of the dialog box. In the Create New Cell Style dialog box, enter a name and choose an existing cell style to start from. Click Continue. You return to the New Table Style dialog box, where you can now specify formatting.

 At any time, you can manage cell styles by clicking the Manage Cell Styles Dialog button. In the Manage Cell Styles dialog box, you can rename and delete existing cell styles.

General properties

The General tab lets you define the following properties:

- **Fill color.** Click the Fill Color drop-down list to choose a color, or choose Select Color to open the Select Color dialog box. The default is None, which shows the background color of your drawing area.

- **Alignment.** Use the Alignment drop-down list to specify the text alignment within each cell. For example, you might want to use Middle Center for the title and column headings, and Middle Left for the data cells.

- **Format.** Click the Ellipsis button to open the Table Cell Format dialog box, where you can specify the data format. The default is general, which is good for text, but you can also format data for angles, currency, dates, decimal numbers, percentages, points, text, and whole numbers. Click the Additional Format button to open the Additional Format dialog box, where you can add a prefix or suffix, specify the number separator, and format zero suppression. The Additional Format button is not available for all data types.

- **Type.** Choose Data or Label. Use a label cell for a header or title. If you break a table into sections, then you can repeat label cells for each section. It's common to repeat headers when breaking a table.

- **Margins.** The cell margins are the space between the text and the cell borders. The horizontal margins affect the left and right sides of the text, while the vertical margins affect the top and bottom of the text. Enter a value in the Horizontal and Vertical text boxes.

Check the Merge Cells on Row/Column Creation check box for titles that you want to span across an entire table.

Text properties

The Text tab lets you specify properties for cells. You can choose a text style from the Text Style drop-down list or click the Ellipsis button to open the Text Style dialog box. (See the "Understanding Text Styles" section earlier in this chapter.)

You can also specify the text height (if the text style has a height of 0), a text color, and a text angle. The default text color is ByBlock, which means that the text color is the same as the actual table — which is a block. (I explain blocks and the ByBlock attribute in Chapter 18.) You can also choose ByLayer, which gives the text the properties of the current layer.

Border properties

Use the Borders tab to specify the properties of the lines around the cells. Choose one of the border buttons to specify which borders you want to see. For example, for the data cells, if you choose Outside Borders, the data area of the table will not have any grid lines between the data cells, only around the outside of the cells.

> **CAUTION**
> If you inadvertently create a table style with only outside borders, you may not notice the absence of borders in your drawing, where grid lines show between the cells so that you can more easily fill in the table. Choose Preview on the Plot panel of the Output tab on the Ribbon to see the final result more accurately.

Choose a border lineweight from the Lineweight drop-down list. For example, you may want a slightly thicker lineweight for the title cell. If you don't want to use continuous lines, then choose a linetype from the Linetype drop-down list. Then choose a color from the Color drop-down list. If you leave the ByBlock defaults, the lineweight, linetype, and color will match the layer of the table. Check Double Line to show two lines instead of one along the edge of the border for a cell. You control the spacing between the double lines with the value in the Spacing box.

Completing the table style

Repeat the process of specifying general, text, and border properties for each of the three cell styles or your own styles. You access the styles from the Cell Styles drop-down list.

13

If you're creating your own cell styles, you specify which cell style goes where when you insert the table. (See Figure 13.17 earlier in this chapter.) Remember that you choose a cell style for the first row (usually the title), second row (usually the headers), and for all other rows (usually the data cells). Therefore, you would usually create three cell styles, one for each of these categories.

When you're done, click OK to return to the Table Style dialog box. Click Close. If you opened the Table Style dialog box from the Insert Table dialog box, then you're back in the Insert Table dialog box. If you opened the Table Style dialog box separately, open the Insert Table dialog box as described earlier in this chapter and choose the table style you want from the Table Style drop-down list. Either way, specify any other settings you want and insert the table.

Adding data to a table

You can add data to a table from three sources:

- You can enter data by typing it.
- You can link to external data — a Microsoft Office Excel worksheet or comma-delimited (CVS) file.
- You can extract data from existing objects in the drawing (AutoCAD only).

You choose which method you want to use in the Insert Options section of the Insert Table dialog box. I discuss the first two methods in the next two sections.

AutoCAD Only
AutoCAD LT includes the ability to create a table from external data, but not from object data.

Entering data into a table

After you've placed a table, you can then enter data into the table. The cursor is automatically placed in the first cell, and you can just start typing. Press Tab to move to the next cell or press an arrow key to move to an adjacent cell. Continue in this way until you have completed the table. Figure 13.19 shows an example of a table.

FIGURE 13.19

A nicely styled schedule of parts

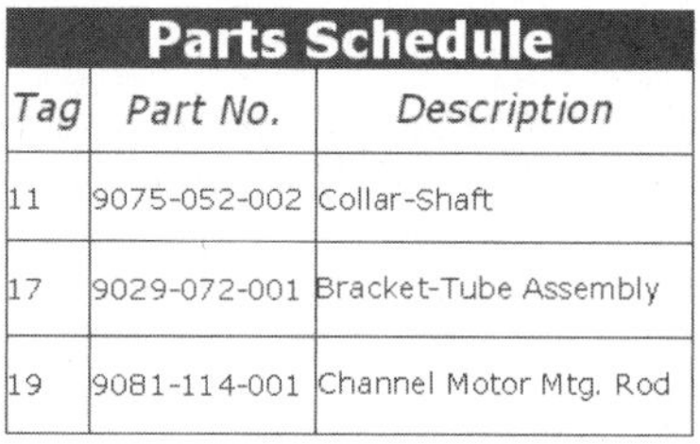

Parts Schedule		
Tag	Part No.	Description
11	9075-052-002	Collar-Shaft
17	9029-072-001	Bracket-Tube Assembly
19	9081-114-001	Channel Motor Mtg. Rod

You can insert a field into any cell in a table. Select a blank cell, right-click, and choose Insert ⇨ Field. For more about fields, see the "Inserting Fields" section, later in this chapter. You can also insert blocks into a table. (I explain blocks in Chapter 18.) To do so, select a blank cell, right-click, and choose Insert ⇨ Block.

You can create tables that function like a spreadsheet. To enter a formula into a cell, follow these steps:

1. Select the cell.

2. Right-click and choose Insert ⇨ Formula.

3. Choose one of the suboptions.

   - **Sum.** Adds rows or columns. At the `Select first corner of table cell range:` prompt, pick inside the first cell. At the `Select second corner of table cell range:` prompt, pick inside the last cell. You see the formula listed in the cell, for example, =Sum(C3:C5).

   - **Average.** Averages rows or columns. At the `Select first corner of table cell range:` prompt, pick inside the first cell. At the `Select second corner of table cell range:` prompt, pick inside the last cell. You see the formula listed in the cell, for example, =Average(C3:C5).

   - **Count.** Counts the number of cells in a row or column. At the `Select first corner of table cell range:` prompt, pick inside the first cell. At the `Select second corner of table cell range:` prompt, pick inside the last cell. You see the formula listed in the cell, for example, =Count(C3:C5).

   - **Cell.** Displays the value of another cell. At the `Select table cell:` prompt, select the cell that you want to display. You see the formula listed in the cell, for example, =C3.

   - **Equation.** Lets you write your own equation. You just see an equal sign (=) in the cell. Enter the equation, for example =A3+B4.

You also see row headings (1, 2, 3, and so on) and column headings (A, B, C, and so on), so that you can easily determine any cell's address.

4. Press Enter to place the value of the formula.

Linking to external data

You can create a table that links to external data that was created in Microsoft Excel or that is in comma-delimited (CSV) format. The link maintains its connection, so that if you change the spreadsheet, the table in your drawing also changes. You also have the option to change the external data from within AutoCAD.

 In Bonus Chapter 1 on the companion website, I cover the external database connectivity feature. While this feature also allows you to connect to Microsoft Access databases and other types of databases, it's more complicated to use.

To create a linked table, you first need a Microsoft Excel or CSV file. Make sure that you know the file's name and location. Then choose Home tab ⇨ Annotation panel ⇨ Table. From the Insert Options section of the Insert Table dialog box, choose From a Data Link. For the rest of the dialog box, see the section "Creating Tables" earlier in this chapter.

 To connect to a link you've already created, choose it from the drop-down list. To create a new link to a spreadsheet, click the Launch the Data Link Manager Dialog button to open the Select a Data Link dialog box. Choose Create a New Excel Data Link. In the Enter Data Link Name dialog box, enter a meaningful name and click OK.

The New Excel Data Link dialog box opens. Click the Ellipsis button at the right to choose a Microsoft Excel file. When you click Open, you return to the New Excel Data Link dialog box. Select the Preview check box to list your data link.

In the Link Options section, you can choose which sheet you want to use, and you can link to a named range (you can name ranges of cells in Microsoft Excel) or you can specify a range, such as A1:H20. Click OK to return to the Select a Data Link dialog box, where your data link is now listed and highlighted. Click OK to return to the Insert Table dialog box. You should see your table in the Preview box.

Click OK one more time and specify an insertion point to insert the table into your drawing. You may have to resize the table to avoid unwanted word wrapping in the cells. (See the upcoming section, "Modifying a table," for instructions.) Figure 13.20 shows the result.

FIGURE 13.20

You can create a table that links to Excel data.

Code	Style	Exterior	Interior	Rough Opening
A	Casement	Ultrex	Wood	2 5"x3'11" 5/8"
B	Casement	Ultrex	Wood	2 5"x4'11" 5/8"
C	Casement	Ultrex	Wood	2 5"x4'11" 5/8"
D	Awning	Ultrex	Wood	2 5"x1'-11 5/8"
E	Transom	Wood	Wood	N/A

When you create a linked table, it's locked to prevent changes; this makes sense, because the content should come from the Microsoft Excel spreadsheet. However, you can unlock it and make changes; you can save these changes back to the spreadsheet to keep the two data sources the same. To unlock data (both content and formatting), select one or more cells, right-click, and choose Locking ⇨ Unlocked. After changing the data, select the table (the whole table must be selected) and right-click. Choose Write Data Links to External Source.

Extracting data from drawing objects

You can create a table that contains information about the objects in your drawing. For example, you might want to display the number of window blocks and their location. If a circle represents trees and bushes in a landscaping plan, you could list the number of circles and their layer; perhaps you have a tree and a bush layer. You can extract data from all objects, not just blocks. For information about extracting data from blocks using attributes, see Chapter 19. You cannot extract data from drawing objects in AutoCAD LT.

To create a table from object data, choose Home tab ⇨ Annotation panel ⇨ Table. In the Insert Table dialog box (see Figure 13.16 earlier in this chapter), choose From Object Data in the Drawing (Data Extraction) in the Insert Options section and click OK. Page 1 of the Data Extraction Wizard opens, as shown in Figure 13.21.

Choose to create a new extraction or edit an existing one. If you want to create a new extraction, you can use one of two types of files as a template to use settings you've specified previously:

- **DXE.** When you create a data extraction table, AutoCAD creates a DXE file that contains settings for the extraction.
- **BLK.** When you extract attribute information from blocks, you can save a BLK file, which is a template that defines the settings for the extraction.

13

FIGURE 13.21

The Data Extraction Wizard guides you through the process of creating a table from object data.

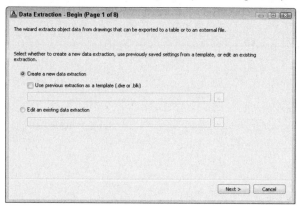

The following explains how to create a new data extraction without a template. Choose Create a New Data Extraction and click Next. The Save Data Extraction As dialog box opens, so you can save a DXE file; this is the file that you can use in the future as a template. Choose a name and location and click Save.

On the Define Data Source (Page 2 of 8) page of the wizard, you define which objects you want to include and where they come from. You can use a Sheet Set, which is a collection of drawings (covered in Bonus Chapter 3) or choose any drawings that you want. The Drawing Files and Folders box lists the drawings and their locations. If you want to use objects from other drawings, click Add Drawings. To add all the drawings in a folder, click Add Folder.

If you choose multiple drawings, you create a table from all the objects in those drawings. If you want to select specific objects, you can do so only in the current drawing. In that case, choose the Select Objects in the Current Drawing option. The following assumes that you are selecting objects in the current drawing.

Click the Settings button to open the Data Extraction - Additional Settings dialog box, shown in Figure 13.22, where you define which types of objects you want to include. These settings are particularly important if you are extracting data from entire drawings (rather than selecting objects) and you have blocks or xrefs in those drawings. (I cover blocks in Chapter 18 and xrefs in Chapter 20.) Choose whether you want to extract data from blocks and xrefs and whether to include xrefs in the block count. You can also choose whether to include objects only in model space or all objects in the drawing, meaning also objects in layouts. (See Chapter 17 for coverage of layouts.)

 You're now ready to select objects. Click the Select Objects in the Current Drawing button. You return to your drawing, where you select objects. End selection to return to the wizard. Click Next.

FIGURE 13.22

You can specify what kinds of objects you want to include in your data extraction.

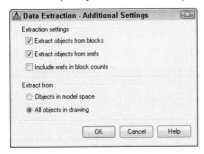

The Select Objects page shows the objects you've selected. You can choose to display only blocks or only non-blocks, instead of the default, which is to display all object types. If you're interested in blocks, you can choose to include only blocks with attributes. Finally, you can choose to display objects that are currently in use because some blocks may be defined but not inserted into the drawing. (See Chapter 19 for information about attributes.) Then click Next.

On the Select Properties page, you specify which properties of the objects you want to include. The properties come in 10 categories:

- **3D Visualization.** Includes materials assigned to objects. (See Chapter 25.)
- **Attribute.** Includes blocks and dynamic blocks with attributes. (See Chapter 19.)
- **Drawing.** File-related information including the author, date created, dated accessed, location, name, size, total editing time, and so on.
- **Dynamic blocks.** Properties of dynamic blocks. (See Chapter 18.)
- **General.** Includes color, layer, linetype, linetype scale, plot style, thickness, and hyperlink.
- **Geometry.** Depending on the type of object, can include area; center; circumference; diameter; length; radius; start angle; total angle; delta (change) in X, Y, and Z; start of X, Y, and Z coordinates; and so on.
- **Misc.** Includes closed (or open).
- **Pattern.** Includes hatch pattern properties, which I cover in Chapter 16.
- **Table.** Includes table properties.
- **Text.** Includes single or multiline text properties.

For each category, you can choose which property you want to include by checking the check boxes. As you can see, your choices depend on why you're extracting the data. In some cases, you may want drawing information for archiving purposes; in other cases, you may be interested only in geometry data. When you're done, click Next.

13

On the Refine Data page, you can reorder and sort columns, filter the results, combine identical rows, specify if you want a count or a name column, add formulas, and include external data. Click on a column and right-click for numerous options, including the ability to rename and hide columns. Click on any column to sort by that column, and click again to reverse the sorting order. Right-click and choose Filter Options to open the Filter dialog box, which is similar to the Quick Select feature (described in Chapter 10), but has fewer options.

> **TIP**
>
> When extracting data, you can add formulas such as totals to a column. Right-click the column and choose Insert Totals Footer. You can choose Sum, Max, Min, or Average. You can also create a new column from data in other columns. Right-click any column and choose Insert Formula Column. Use the Insert Formula Column dialog box to specify the formula. Click OK.

Click the Full Preview button to see what the table will look like in a new window; then click the window's Close button to return to the wizard and click Next.

On the Choose Output page, you can choose to create a table and insert it into a drawing, output the data to an external file (XLS, CSV, MDB, or TXT), or both. If you choose to create an external file, click the Ellipsis button to browse to a location and give the file a name. Then click Next.

If you chose to create a table, you now choose a table style or manually set up the table. Then click Next. The Finish page explains that you need to specify an insertion point for the table and that the external file you requested (if any) will be created when you click the Finish button. Click the Finish button and you're done.

Modifying a table

You may need to change the data in a table, or you may want to change the way the table looks. Either way, you can modify a table easily. However, you need to know some of the techniques involved, because tables in AutoCAD and AutoCAD LT are a little different from tables in your word processor.

Changing the text

Changing the text of a table is like changing any multiline text. Double-click the text inside a table, being careful not to double-click the grid lines. The In-Place Text Editor opens. You can use any of the techniques for editing text that I discuss in the "Editing paragraph text" section earlier in this chapter. You can change the properties of the text so that they don't match the table style. For example, you can change the height or font of the text.

Changing table properties

You can also change properties of the table itself. Open the Properties palette (press Ctrl+1) and select the table. Here, you can modify any conceivable table property, including its layer, its color, the number of rows or columns, or any of its style properties. If you want to revert to old-fashioned lines, you can explode the table. Of course, you can no longer edit the table as a table anymore; you just have lines and text.

To select the entire table, click any gridline of the table. You see grips at the corners of the table and at several other cell junctions. To understand editing tables with grips, imagine that the left side of the table is the stable side, while the right side of the table is the flexible side. The top-left grip is the base point for the entire table. You can do the following edits with grips:

- **Upper-left grip.** Moves the entire table. You can right-click after selecting the grip to rotate, scale, or make a copy of the table.
- **Upper-right grip.** Stretches the table horizontally. As you change the width of the table, the columns also stretch proportionally.
- **Lower-left grip.** Stretches the table vertically. As you change the height of the table, the rows also stretch proportionally.
- **Lower-right grip.** Stretches the table both vertically and horizontally. The columns and rows adjust proportionally.
- **Top-of-column grip.** Adjusts the width of the column to the left or right of the grip. The entire table adjusts accordingly. If you press Ctrl while moving a column grip, the adjacent columns adjust, but the width of the table remains unchanged.
- **Bottom-center grip.** Adjusts the table break height. Drag the grip up or down to adjust the height at which the table breaks into additional tables. See "Breaking a table into sections" for more information.

If you select the table and right-click, then you can use the shortcut menu to make additional changes to the table. For example, you can size columns or rows equally or remove property overrides. If you make a change to a cell, such as the cell's alignment or color, you can use the Remove All Property Overrides item on the shortcut menu to change the cell's properties back to match the rest of the table.

Changing cell properties

To select a cell, click inside that cell. You can also click a column or row header, or drag across several cells to select them. The Table Cell tab appears on the Ribbon. (If you're using the AutoCAD Classic workspace, you'll see a Table toolbar.)

In the Rows panel, the following items are available:

- **Insert Above.** Inserts a row above the selected cell or row.
- **Insert Below.** Inserts a row below the selected cell or row.
- **Delete Row(s).** Deletes the selected row or the row of the selected cell.

In the Columns panel, the following items are available:

- **Insert Left.** Inserts a column to the left of the selected cell or row.
- **Insert Right.** Inserts a column to the right of the selected cell or row.
- **Delete Column(s).** Deletes the selected column or the column of the selected cell.

In the Merge panel, you have the following options:

- **Merge Cells.** Merges selected cells. You need to select multiple cells. (See techniques for doing so after this list.) The suboptions let you merge by row or by column. By merging cells, you can create complex table structures.
- **Unmerge Cells.** Unmerges selected cells that you previously merged.

In the Cell Styles panels, the following options are available:

- **Match Cell.** Matches cell properties. At the `Select destination cell:` prompt on the command line, pick another cell that you want to have the same properties. The prompt repeats until you press Enter.
- **Cell Alignment.** Changes the alignment of the text in the cell, using the standard text-alignment options available for multiline text.
- **Cell Styles.** Enables you to choose a cell style for the selected cell from the drop-down list. You can also choose to create a new cell style or manage existing cell styles.
- **Background Fill.** Sets a background color for the selected cell.
- **Edit Borders.** Opens the Cell Border Properties dialog box, where you can specify border properties for that individual cell.

The Cell Format panel has two options:

- **Locking.** Locks or unlocks the format and/or the data of the selection. Text from external links or data extraction is locked by default.
- **Data Format.** Allows you to choose a format from a drop-down list. Choose Custom Table Cell Format to open the Table Cell Format dialog box, where you can change the data type and format.

The Insert panel has the following options:

- **Block.** Opens the Insert a Block in a Table Cell dialog box, where you can select the block that you want to insert, specify the block's alignment in the cell, and set its scale and rotation angle. If you select the AutoFit check box, the block is automatically scaled to fit the table cell.
- **Field.** Lets you insert or edit a field. I discuss fields in the next section of this chapter.
- **Formula.** Lets you insert a formula, as explained in the "Entering data into a table" section earlier in this chapter.
- **Manage Cell Contents.** Applies when you have more than one block in a cell. The Manage Cell Content dialog box opens, where you can change the order of the blocks and change the way they're laid out.

In the Data panel, the following options are available:

- **Link Cell.** Enables you to link the selected cell to a Microsoft Excel file. For more information, see the section "Linking to external data" earlier in this chapter.
- **Download from Source.** Updates links, if available, from an external spreadsheet, in case that spreadsheet has changed.

You can access some additional options by right-clicking with a cell or cells selected:

- **Remove All Property Overrides.** Removes any formatting that you applied to the selected cell.
- **Edit Text.** Opens the In-Place Text Editor so that you can edit text.
- **Delete All Contents.** Deletes any text or block in the current cell.
- **Columns ⇨ Size Columns Equally.** Makes two or more columns that you select equally wide.
- **Rows ⇨ Size Rows Equally.** Makes all your rows an equal height.
- **Properties.** Opens the Properties palette so that you can change the cell's properties.
- **Quick Properties.** Opens the Quick Properties palette so that you can change the cell's properties.

When you edit a table, column and row headers appear so that you can easily refer to cells in your formulas. You can change the background color of these headers to make the text clearer. Select a table, right-click, and choose Table Indicator Color. You can then choose a color in the Select Color dialog box.

You can select multiple cells and apply changes to those cells. To select multiple cells, use one of the following techniques:

- Click a row or column header to select an entire row or column.
- Click inside one cell and drag over the other cells that you want to select. Release the mouse button at the last cell.
- Click inside one cell, hold down Shift, and click inside the last cell that you want to select.

13

> **TIP**
>
> To enter the same text in multiple cells, select the cells. Then open the Properties palette and enter the text in the Contents item. The text appears in all the selected cells.

You can export a table to comma-delimited (`.csv`) format. You can then open the table data with a database or spreadsheet program. To export a table, follow these steps:

1. Select the table.
2. Right-click and choose Export.
3. In the Export Data dialog box, choose a name and location for the file.
4. Click Save.

Breaking a table into sections

Sometimes you need to fit a table into a tight space; to do so, you might want to break up the table into two or more sections.

Breaking a table is easy, but you can also access a number of settings to fine-tune how it works. To break a table, click it once to select it. Then drag the cyan down arrow, located at the bottom of the table, upward to the point where you want the table to break (see Figure 13.23), and click.

FIGURE 13.23

You can break a table by dragging upward on the Table Breaking arrow.

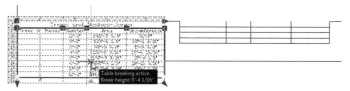

To adjust breaking settings, open the Properties palette. In the Table Breaks section, you can set the direction of subsequent sections, repeat top labels, and repeat bottom labels. You can also manually set the position of sections, individually set the height of subsequent sections (otherwise, they're the same size as the first section), and set the spacing between the sections. In this example, I chose to repeat top labels; you can see the result in Figure 13.24.

TIP

To disable table breaks, change the Enabled property of a table in the Properties palette to No.

FIGURE 13.24

After breaking, the table appears in two sections with top labels on each section.

Trees and Bushes-Jones			
Trees or Bushes	Diameter	Area	Circumference
1	10'-0"	942'-5 3/4"	31'-5"
1	8'-0"	603'-2 1/4"	25'-1 9/16"
1	2'-0"	37'-8 3/8"	6'-3 3/8"
1	4'-0"	150'-9 9/16"	12'-6 13/16"
1	5'-0"	235'-7 7/16"	15'-8 1/2"

Trees and Bushes-Jones			
Trees or Bushes	Diameter	Area	Circumference
1	6'-0"	339'-3 1/2"	18'-10 3/16"
1	15'-0"	2120'-6 7/8"	47'-1 1/2"
1	20'-0"	3769'-10 15/16"	62'-10"
8			

ON THE WEB

The drawing used in the following exercise on creating tables, `ab13-c.dwg`, is available from the Drawings download on the companion website.

STEPS: Creating Tables

1. Open `ab13-c.dwg`, available from the Drawings download on the companion website. This is the same drawing used in the previous exercise.

2. Save the file as `ab13-06.dwg` in your `AutoCAD Bible` folder.

 3. Choose Home tab ⇨ Annotation panel ⇨ Table. You'll create a table showing some of the plat numbers and their acreage.

4. In the Insert Table dialog box, click the Launch the Table Style Dialog button to the right of the Table Style Name drop-down list.

5. In the Table Style dialog box, click New. In the Create New Table Style dialog box, enter **Acreage Schedule** in the New Style Name text box. The Start With text box should read `Standard`. Click Continue. The New Table Style dialog box opens.

6. Make sure that the Data cell style appears in the Cell Styles drop-down list. To the right, click the Create a New Cell Style button, so that you can save the formatting that you will specify. In the Create New Cell Style dialog box, enter **Plat Data** and click Continue.

7. On the General tab, you want to set the numbers in the table to be right-aligned, so choose Middle Right from the Alignment drop-down list. In the Cell Margins section, change both the Horizontal and Vertical text box values to **5**.

8. Click the Text tab. From the Text Style drop-down list, choose ROMANS. In the Text Height text box, enter **12.5**.

9. To format the column headers, choose Header from the Cell Style drop-down list. Again, click the Create a New Cell Style button, name the cell style **Plat Header**, and click Continue. On the General tab, leave the alignment as Middle Center, but change the cell margins to **5**. On the Text tab, again set the Text Style to ROMANS and the Text Height to **12.5**.

10. Choose Title from the Cell Style drop-down list. Create a new cell style named **Plat Title**. Make the following changes:

    - **General tab.** Change the cell margins to **5**. From the Fill Color drop-down list, choose Blue.

    - **Text tab.** Choose ROMANT (for a different look). Change the Text Height to **13.5** to make the title text bigger than the rest of the table text. Click the Text Color drop-down list and choose Select Color. From the Select Color dialog box, choose the light gray color (254) on the Index Color tab. Click OK to return to the New Table Style dialog box.

    - **Borders tab.** From the Color drop-down list, choose Blue to match the fill. Click the All Borders button.

11. Click OK to return to the Table Style dialog box. Then click Close to return to the Insert Table dialog box.

12. In the Insertion Behavior section of the dialog box, make sure that the insertion behavior is set to `Specify insertion point`. In the Columns & Row Settings section, set the number of columns to 2 and the column width to 100. Set the number of data rows to 5. The row height should be 1 (which means one row high).

13. In the Set Cell Styles section, set the First Row Cell Style to Plat Title, set Second Row Cell Style to Plat Header, and set All Other Row Cell Styles to Plat Data. Then click OK.

14. In your drawing, pick an insertion point anywhere in the lower-right area of the drawing. The In-Place Text Editor opens. Because you need to zoom in first, click anywhere outside the editor and do a Zoom Window around the table. Then double-click the table to open the In-Place Text Editor again, with the cursor in the title cell.

13

> **TIP**
> To zoom in without exiting the In-Place Text Editor, you can use the wheel of your mouse (if you have one). I explain how to zoom with the mouse wheel in Chapter 8.

15. Complete the data for the four plats, shown in Figure 13.25, pressing Tab to go from cell to cell.

16. Type **Total** in the last row. Then choose Text Editor tab ⇨ Paragraph panel ⇨ Justification drop-down list ⇨ Middle Left.

17. Click anywhere outside the In-Place Text Editor and then click the lower-right cell to select it. Right-click the cell and choose Insert ⇨ Formula ⇨ Sum from the shortcut menu.

18. At the `Select first corner of table cell range:` prompt, click anywhere inside cell B3. At the `Select second corner of table cell range:` prompt, click anywhere inside cell B6. Press Enter. Your table should look like Figure 13.25.

19. Save your drawing.

FIGURE 13.25

The plat acreage table

Plat	Acreage
1	22.93
2	2.85
3	1.51
4	1.38
Total	28.67

Inserting Fields

Most drawings contain information about the drawing, such as the last date it was revised, the person who saved the drawing, or the sheet number in a sheet set. Draft plots often contain additional information, such as the time and drawing name. You may also want to insert information about drawing objects, such as the area or circumference of a circle. Fields store information and allow you to insert it into a drawing. You can also place fields in block attributes, which I discuss in Chapter 19. When your drawing changes, you can update the fields to keep them current. You can insert fields anywhere that you might normally use text. As you start using fields, you'll think of many uses for them. You can format the text of a field in the same way that you format any multiline text.

Creating fields

To create a new field as a multiline text object, you can use two methods:

- Choose Insert tab ⇨ Data panel ⇨ Field (the FIELD command).
- Open the In-Place Text Editor or any other text box where you can enter text, right-click in the editor or text box, and choose Insert Field from the shortcut menu.

Whichever method you use, the Field dialog box opens, as shown in Figure 13.26.

The Field dialog box offers a huge variety of fields. To give you an idea of the possibilities, here are the available categories of fields:

- **Date & Time.** Offers various formats for inserting dates and times.
- **Document.** Relates to data that you complete in the Properties dialog box. (Choose Application Button ⇨ Drawing Utilities ⇨ Drawing Properties.) I cover the Properties dialog box in Bonus Chapter 3.
- **Linked.** Creates a field from a hyperlink.
- **Objects.** Offers properties relating to block attributes, formulas in tables, named objects (such as named views, layers, blocks, and so on), and objects (any drawing object that you select).
- **Other.** Displays values of AutoLISP variables (AutoCAD only), diesel expressions, and system variables.
- **Plot.** Displays plot-related information such as scale, sheet size, and orientation.
- **SheetSet.** Displays values relating to sheet sets. (I cover sheet sets in Bonus Chapter 3.)

FIGURE 13.26

Use the Field dialog box to choose, format, and insert a field into your drawing.

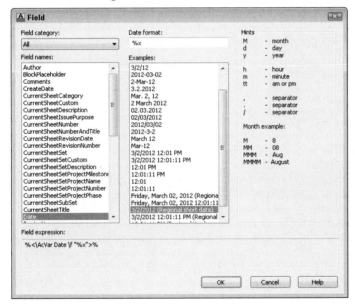

Note that there are two date-related fields. The `CreateDate` field creates a date based on the current date. This field does not change if you open the drawing on a future date. For example, you can use this field to show the last time a drawing was updated. The `Date` field always shows the current date.

To insert a field, follow these steps:

1. Choose a field category from the Field Category drop-down list. You can use the All category to display all the fields. The other categories help you to filter the fields.

2. From the Field Names list, choose the field that you want to use.

3. Depending on the field that you choose, you can usually select a format or example for the field. For example, you can choose a date format (such as m/d/yyyy) or a text format (such as title case).

4. Click OK.

   - If you opened the Field dialog box by choosing Insert tab ⇨ Data panel ⇨ Field, the FIELD command starts, and you see the `Specify start point or [Height/Justify]:` prompt. Pick a start point or use one of the options.

   - If you started the MTEXT command first, the value of the field appears in the In-Place Text Editor. Click outside the editor to place the text, and close the editor.

By default, fields appear in your drawing with a gray background. This background doesn't plot. If you want, you can remove the background by choosing Application Button ⇨ Options, and clicking the User Preferences tab. In the Fields section, uncheck the Display Background of Fields check box. Click OK to close the Options dialog box. Figure 13.27 shows an example of a titleblock that uses fields.

FIGURE 13.27

Filling in a titleblock is easier when you use fields.

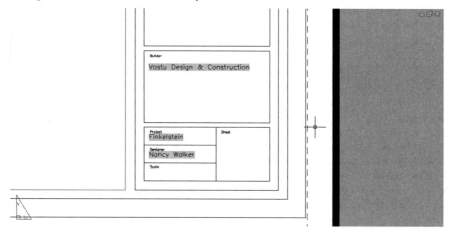

Editing and updating fields

To edit a field, double-click the field's text to open the In-Place Text Editor. Select the text, right-click, and choose Edit Field. The Field dialog box opens. You edit a field in the same way that you define the field originally. When you're done, click OK. The field is reevaluated immediately. Close the In-Place Text Editor to place the edited field.

By default, a field is evaluated and updated, if necessary, whenever you open, save, plot, eTransmit, or regenerate a drawing. (See Bonus Chapter 5 for information on eTransmitting a drawing.) You can change when AutoCAD updates a field by choosing Application Button⇨Options, and clicking the User Preferences tab. In the Fields section, click Field Update Settings. Check or uncheck the items that you want, and then click Apply & Close. Click OK to close the Options dialog box.

You can manually update a field if you want. For example, you may have an object field that displays the radius of a circle. If you resize the circle, you probably want to update the field.

To update a field, double-click the field to open the In-Place Text Editor. Select the text, right-click, and choose Update Field. Close the In-Place Text Editor to return to your drawing. Another method is to select the field and choose Insert tab⇨Data panel⇨Update Fields (the UPDATEFIELD command). You can press Ctrl+A to select all the objects in your drawing.

You can convert a field to text. Open the In-Place Text Editor. Select the text in the field, right-click, and choose Convert Field to Text.

What happens to fields when you save a 2005 or later drawing to an earlier release of AutoCAD? The fields display as their last value in the older drawing but are not updated.

ON THE WEB

The drawing used in the following exercise on using fields, `ab13-d.dwg`, is available from the Drawings download on the companion website.

13

STEPS: Using Fields

1. Open `ab13-d.dwg`, available from the Drawings download on the companion website. Save the file as `ab13-07.dwg` in your `AutoCAD Bible` folder. This drawing is zoomed in on the titleblock.

2. To set some of the drawing properties, choose Application Button⇨Drawing Utilities⇨Drawing Properties. On the Summary tab, type the following in the Title field: **6" thru 12" 2727 EPV Valves**.

3. On the Custom tab, click Add. Enter the following two fields and values, and click OK after each:

   ```
   Drafter    Enter your initials
   Dwg No     SK-1972
   ```

4. Click OK to return to your drawing.

5. Choose Home tab⇨Annotation panel⇨Text drop-down menu⇨Multiline Text. Pick two boundary points within the Title box of the titleblock. The In-Place Text Editor opens. Right-click and choose Insert Field to open the Field dialog box.

6. From the Field Category drop-down list, choose Document. From the Field Names list, choose Title. From the Format list, choose Title Case. Click OK. Click anywhere outside the In-Place Text Editor to place the field.

7. Again start the MTEXT command. Pick two boundary points within the Dwg No box of the titleblock. In the In-Place Text Editor, right-click and choose Insert Field to open the Field dialog box.

8. From the Field Names list, choose Dwg No. Click OK. Click anywhere outside the In-Place Text Editor to place the field.

9. Choose Insert tab ⇨ Data panel ⇨ Field. From the Field Category drop-down list, choose Date & Time. From the Field Names list, choose CreateDate. From the Format list, choose M/d/yy (fourth from the top). Click OK.

10. Pick a point within the Date box of the titleblock.

11. If necessary, move the text so that it fits better in the titleblock. Save your drawing. The titleblock should look like Figure 13.28.

FIGURE 13.28

The titleblock after adding some fields

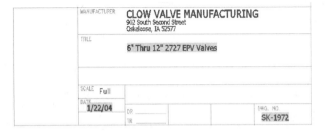

Managing Text

Text is a complex object type that increases your drawing size and adds redraw and regeneration time. TrueType fonts can have an impact on how long it takes to open and save a file. The techniques described in this section help you to manage text and improve performance while editing your drawing.

Using Quicktext

The QTEXT command replaces all text with rectangles that approximate the placement of the original text. All text objects, including dimensions, attributes, and tolerances, are affected. To use QTEXT, type **qtext** ⏎ on the command line. Type **on** ⏎ to display the rectangles; type **off** ⏎ to return to regular text. Then type **regen** ⏎ at the command line. Quicktext takes effect only after a regeneration; it does not apply to OLE objects that you have pasted into a drawing from the Windows Clipboard (see Bonus Chapter 4).

Using AutoCAD and AutoCAD LT fonts

AutoCAD and AutoCAD LT fonts are simpler than TrueType fonts, and offer a range of complexity. The simplest font is `txt.shx`. You can easily define a text style by using an AutoCAD or AutoCAD LT font and then change the font to something nicer just before plotting. Be aware that the text may take up more or less space than before.

When your drawing cannot find the specified font, it uses an alternate font. This may happen if you receive a drawing from someone else that uses a custom or third-party font that you don't have. You can specify the alternate font by choosing Application Menu ⇨ Options, and clicking the plus sign next to Text Editor, Dictionary, and Font File Names on the Files tab. Choose Alternate Font File to specify the alternate font, which is `simplex.shx` by default.

You can further control the fonts used in your drawing by customizing the Font Mapping File, `acad.fmp` (or `acadlt.fmp`). The format is `current_font; font_to_substitute`. (You need to use the actual filenames of the fonts.) To substitute a simpler font for the Arial Black font, you can add the following line:

```
Ariblk.ttf;simplex.shx
```

To find the Windows TrueType fonts, look in the `Fonts` subfolder of your `Windows` folder.

> **NOTE**
> To find `acad.fmp` (or `acadlt.fmp`), choose Application Button ⇨ Options, and click the File tab. Double-click Text Editor, Dictionary, and Font File Names. Double-click Font Mapping File. Click the path list to view the location of `acad.fmp` (or `acadlt.fmp`). AutoCAD and AutoCAD LT only read the font-mapping file when you open a new drawing, so any changes that you make are effective only after you start a new drawing.

Turning off text layers

Turning off (or freezing) text layers can reduce regeneration time dramatically; this is a good reason to give text its own layer. Don't forget to turn off dimension text, as well. Dimensions (see Chapter 14) are usually placed on a separate layer.

Using MIRRTEXT

When you mirror sections of your drawing that include text, you usually don't want any backward text (unless you're Alice going through the looking glass). The MIRRTEXT system variable controls whether text is mirrored or retains its normal orientation. The default value for MIRRTEXT is off, so mirrored text is not backward. The text is copied to the mirrored location, but reads from left to right (if that's the direction of the language that you're using).

If you do want to mirror the text, type **mirrtext** ↵. At the `Enter new value for MIRRTEXT <0>:` prompt, type **1** ↵ to turn MIRRTEXT on. This system variable is saved with the drawing, so you may still need to change it when you open older drawings.

> **AUTOCAD ONLY**
> Express Tools has a number of text routines that you may find very helpful. Table 13.2 lists these tools.

TABLE 13.2 **Express Tools for Text**

Command	Ribbon Location	Description
RTEXT	Express Tools tab ⇨ Text panel (expanded) ⇨ Remote Text	Displays text from an outside file. You can specify the text style, height, and rotation. Use RTEDIT on the command line to edit remote text.
TEXTFIT	Express Tools tab ⇨ Text panel ⇨ Modify Text drop-down menu ⇨ Fit	Stretches or shrinks Text objects (but not Mtext) to fit between two points.
TEXTMASK	Express Tools tab ⇨ Text panel (expanded) ⇨ Text Mask	Creates a wipeout, 3D face, or 2D solid object behind the text, with a little extra space around the text. You can use this to make text on top of a hatch more legible.
TEXTUNMASK	Express Tools tab ⇨ Text panel (expanded) ⇨ Text Unmask	Removes a text mask.
TXTEXP	Express Tools tab ⇨ Text panel ⇨ Modify Text drop-down menu ⇨ Explode	Transforms Text or Mtext into geometrical shapes.
TXT2MTXT	Express Tools tab ⇨ Text panel ⇨ Convert to Mtext	Converts Text objects to Mtext objects.
ARCTEXT	Express Tools tab ⇨ Text panel ⇨ Arc Aligned	Aligns text along an arc.
TORIENT	Express Tools tab ⇨ Text panel ⇨ Modify Text drop-down menu ⇨ Rotate	Rotates multiple text, Mtext, and attribute definitions to a specified angle without moving them, or aligns them so that they're horizontal or right-side up for easy reading.
TCIRCLE	Express Tools tab ⇨ Text panel ⇨ Enclose in Object	Encloses selected Text or Mtext inside a circle, a *slot* (a rectangle, but with arcs at each end), or a rectangle.
TCOUNT	Express Tools tab ⇨ Text panel ⇨ Auto Number	Numbers lines of text by adding a prefix or suffix, or by overwriting the text.
TCASE	Express Tools tab ⇨ Text panel ⇨ Modify Text drop-down menu ⇨ Change Case	Offers the following ways to change the case of text: uppercase, lowercase, sentence case, title case, and toggle case.

Finding Text in Your Drawing

 In a large, complex drawing with a lot of text, you may have difficulty finding specific text that you need to edit. The FIND command lets you find and replace text anywhere in your drawing — not only single-line text and multiline text but also text in tables, block attributes, dimensions, hyperlink descriptions, and hyperlinks. To use the FIND command, choose Annotate tab ⇨ Text panel ⇨ Find Text, enter the text you want to find in the Ribbon's text box, and click the Find Text button. The Find and Replace dialog box opens, as shown in Figure 13.29.

Here's how to use the Find and Replace dialog box:

1. If the text you want to find isn't in the Find What text box, enter it now. Use the drop-down list to choose recently used text strings.

2. If you want to replace the text that you find with new text, type it in the Replace With text box. This box also includes a drop-down list of recently used text strings.

3. If you want to limit or expand the scope of your search, use the Find Where drop-down list. If you selected objects before starting the FIND command, this drop-down list displays Selected Objects. You can choose Entire Drawing from this list. You can also click the Select Objects button to return to your drawing and select objects. The FIND command then limits its search to selected objects. Choose Current Space/Layout to look for the text string only on the Model or layout tab that is current.

FIGURE 13.29

The Find and Replace dialog box finds text anywhere in your drawing.

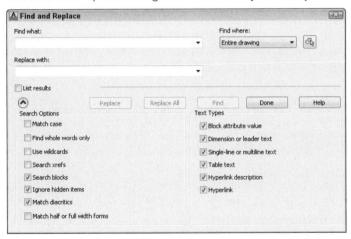

4. Click the More Options down arrow to expand the dialog box and specify the type of text that FIND will search in the Text Types list. By default, it searches all types of text, including attributes (Chapter 19), dimensions (Chapter 14), tables, and hyperlinks (Bonus Chapter 5). The command can find text in fields, as well.

5. In the Search Options list, you can also choose the Match Case and Find Whole Words Only options. You can also choose to use wildcards, search xrefs and blocks, ignore hidden items, match diacritics (such as accent marks), and match half/full width forms (for East Asian languages).

> **NOTE**
> Hidden items are text on frozen or off layers, text in block attributes using invisible mode, and text in dynamic block visibility states.

6. Click Find or Find Next to find the next instance of the text string. The drawing zooms in to the text and moves the dialog box so that it doesn't cover up the text.

7. Click Replace to replace the text string with the replacement text. Click Replace All to replace all instances of the text string with the replacement text.

8. Check the List Results check box to list the results that have been found.

9. After you're finished, click Done to close the dialog box.

Checking Your Spelling

If you take pride in the accuracy of your drawings, you might as well make sure that the text is spelled correctly. You can use the SPELL command to check your spelling. The spelling checker acts just like the one in your word processor.

If you want, you can select some objects first. Choose Annotate tab ⇨ Text panel ⇨ Check Spelling to open the Check Spelling dialog box, as shown in Figure 13.30.

FIGURE 13.30

The Check Spelling dialog box

From the Where to Check drop-down list, choose Entire Drawing, Current Space/Layout, or Selected Objects. (I cover layouts in Chapter 17.) Click the Settings button to open the Check Spelling Settings dialog box, where you can choose if you want to include dimension text (see Chapter 14), block attributes (see Chapter 19), or external references (see Chapter 20). You can also ignore capitalized words (proper names), words that include numbers, uppercase words, words with mixed cases, such as EllenFinkelstein.com, and words containing punctuation. Click OK when you're done.

In the Check Spelling dialog box, click Start. When the first misspelled word appears in the Not in Dictionary text box, you have the following options:

- **Add to Dictionary.** Choose Add to Dictionary to add the word to the dictionary. The word will not appear again as misspelled.
- **Ignore.** Choose Ignore to ignore the current instance of this word only.
- **Ignore All.** Choose Ignore All to ignore all instances of this word.
- **Change.** Select the suggested word that you want, and choose Change to change the current instance of the word to the suggested word that you selected.
- **Change All.** Select the suggested word that you want, and choose Change All to change all instances of the word to the suggested word that you selected.

Notice that the drawing zooms in and highlights each word. The command automatically moves from word to word until you see the message `Spelling Check Complete`. Click OK and click Close to close the Check Spelling dialog box.

When you edit text, the Text Editor tab appears, which contains a Spell Check panel. Click the dialog box launcher arrow at the right end of the panel's title bar to open the Check Spelling Settings dialog box, where you can specify which type of text you want to include in spell checks and set options for ignoring certain types of text, such as capitalized words. You can change the main and custom spelling dictionaries. To change the main dictionary, choose one from the Main Dictionary drop-down list; these are dictionaries in different languages. Choose Dictionaries from the Check Spelling dialog box to open the Dictionaries dialog box, as shown in Figure 13.31.

The custom dictionary is the dictionary that you add to when you click Add in the Dictionaries dialog box. It is a simple text file that includes words that you have added during spelling checks, as well as a list of drawing-related words that come with the file. You can add words to the custom dictionary by typing them in the Content text box and clicking Add.

TIP

Another way to edit the custom dictionary is to open the file directly with a text editor. The custom dictionary is called `sample.cus`. To find `sample.cus`, choose Application Button⇨ Options, and click the File tab. Double-click Text Editor, Dictionary, and Font File Names. Then double-click Custom Dictionary File. Click the path list to view the location of `sample.cus`.

FIGURE 13.31

The Dictionaries dialog box

You can use a different custom dictionary. For example, it can be useful to use the same dictionary in your drawing as you use in your word processor. Here's how to use the Microsoft Word dictionary:

1. Find Word's custom dictionary. If necessary, choose Start ⇨ Find (or Search) and use the Windows Find dialog box to find the file or click Start and type the file name in the Search text box. Search for `custom.dic`. You can open this file with Notepad and edit it directly.

2. As explained in the previous Tip, find the location of `sample.cus`. Use Windows Explorer to copy `custom.dic` to that folder. You can hold down Ctrl as you drag it from one folder to another or use the right mouse button to click the file, choose Copy, and then paste it in its new location.

3. Click `custom.dic` to highlight it. Click it again and change its filename extension to `.cus`. Press Enter. Windows asks you whether you are sure you want to do this. Click Yes.

4. Click Dictionaries in the Check Spelling dialog box to open the Dictionaries dialog box. From the Current Custom Dictionary drop-down list, choose Manage Custom Dictionaries, and click Add. Find the file, and click Open.

5. Click Close three times to return to your drawing.

Summary

In this chapter, you learned how to create, edit, and manage text. You read about:

- Using TEXT to create single-line text
- Editing single-line text
- Creating text styles to control the formatting of your text, including creating annotative text styles

- Utilizing MTEXT for creating and editing paragraph text, including using the In-Place Text Editor
- Importing text
- Creating tables to clearly display data, including linking to external data and extracting object data
- Using fields to automate the insertion of text
- Managing text for the fastest display
- Finding and replacing text
- Checking spelling in your drawing and editing the spelling dictionaries

In the next chapter, you read about how to create dimensions.

13

Drawing Dimensions

Dimensions are an important part of most drawings. Dimensions indicate the measurement of the models that you've created and are used in the manufacturing process. The dimensions in AutoCAD and AutoCAD LT offer a great deal of flexibility. In this chapter, I cover the process of drawing dimensions. In the next chapter, I explain how to customize the format of your dimensions by using dimension styles. (Even though you should create a dimension style before you dimension, you need to understand dimensions before you can create a style; therefore, I cover dimensions first.)

Working with Dimensions

You usually add dimensions after you complete all or most of a drawing. When you dimension a drawing all at once, you can create a unified, organized look for your dimensions. Before you can dimension a drawing, you need to understand the elements of a dimension and how to prepare for dimensioning.

 In Chapter 17, I explain how to dimension a drawing on a paper space layout and also how to work with *annotative* dimensions that automatically scale according to the scale of the drawing. In Chapter 15, I explain how to create a dimension style, including one that is annotative.

Understanding the elements of a dimension

A dimension is a complex object, containing many parts. Figure 14.1 shows a typical linear dimension using the default dimension style. Mechanical drawings use dimensions that look like this.

FIGURE 14.1

The parts of a dimension

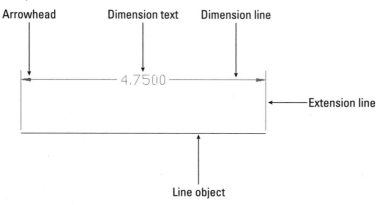

The parts of a dimension are

- **Extension lines.** These extend from the dimensioned object to the dimension line and arrowheads. A small gap usually separates the dimensioned object and the start of the extension lines. Extension lines visually clarify the extents of the object being dimensioned.

> **NOTE**
> Relative to dimensions, the word *extension* (or *extend*) is used in two other ways besides referring to extension lines. First, the extension line itself usually extends from the object being dimensioned past the dimension line. You can specify the amount of this extension. Second, in architectural dimensions, the dimension line extends past the extension lines. You can specify this extension as well.

- **Dimension text.** This tells you the actual measurement of the dimensioned object. You can format this text in decimals, fractions, scientific units, and so on.
- **Dimension line.** This extends between the extension lines.
- **Arrowheads.** These mark the intersection of the dimension line and the extension lines. They can take several forms, such as tick marks, open arrows, or dots.

Dimensions have two important characteristics:

- **Dimensions are blocks.** Blocks are groups of objects that you can manipulate as one object. As a result, if you pick a dimension, all parts of the dimension are selected. Blocks are covered in Chapter 18.

- **Dimensions are associative.** This means that an association connects the dimension and the object it dimensions. If you change the size of the object, the dimension automatically adjusts appropriately.

You can format all parts of a dimension individually. You generally format a dimension by creating a *dimension style,* which is a named set of formats for dimensions — just as a text style is a named set of formats for text. (Dimension styles are the topic of the next chapter.)

 You can constrain the dimensions of objects using dimensional constraints, which I cover in Chapter 10.

Preparing to dimension

Dimensioning requires some preparation to get the result that you want. Before starting to create dimensions, you should prepare as follows:

1. Create a layer for your dimensions. It's important that dimensions be easily distinguishable from the rest of your drawing. The color is usually a contrast to that of your models. For example, if your models are black (and you're working on a white screen), you might want your dimensions to be green, magenta, or cyan.

> **TIP**
>
> If you often turn layers on and off (or freeze and thaw them), you may want to create a separate dimension layer for each layer of drawing data. For example, if you dimension an electrical layer that you turn off regularly, you can have a special `Dim-elec` dimension layer that you can turn off with the electrical layer.

> **NOTE**
>
> If you're dimensioning an existing drawing that was created in a pre-2002 version of AutoCAD or AutoCAD LT, turn on associative dimensioning with the DIMASSOC system variable. Type dimassoc ↵ on the command line and type 2 ↵ at the prompt. (You can also choose Application Button ⬠ Options, click the User Preferences tab, and check the check box in the Associative Dimensioning section of the dialog box. Then click OK.)

2. Create a text style for your dimensions. If you want your dimensions to be annotative, make sure that the text style is annotative. For more information on text styles, see Chapter 13.

> **TIP**
>
> Set the height of the text style to zero. You can then set the text height when you create the dimension style. If you do specify a fixed height in your text style, that height overrides any height that you specify in the dimension style.

3. Right-click the Object Snap button on the status bar and set all the running object snaps that you need. Endpoint and Intersection are a necessity. Add Center and Quadrant if you need to dimension arcs and circles. Click the Object Snap button on the status bar to turn it on.

4. Create a dimension style. If you want your dimensions to be annotative, make sure that the dimension style is annotative. The next chapter covers dimension styles. Annotative dimensions are valuable when you will be displaying your model at more than one scale, in separate viewports.

14

5. Save your dimension layer, dimension text style, and dimension style in your drawing templates.

6. If you want your dimensions to be annotative, change to the desired annotation scale, using the Annotation Scale list on the status bar. (You can add or delete annotation scales later if you need to.)

The Home tab's Annotation panel offers most of the dimensioning commands. You can find the complete set on the Annotate tab in the Dimensions panel.

Drawing Linear Dimensions

Just as the most common objects are lines, the most common dimensions are linear dimensions. Use linear dimensions for lines, or a straight segment of a polyline. You can also use a linear dimension for arcs and circles — you get the linear length of the arc (not its perimeter length) and the diameter of the circle.

Specifying the dimensioned object

To dimension a line, choose Home tab ⇨ Annotation panel ⇨ Dimension drop-down menu ⇨ Linear or Annotate tab ⇨ Dimensions panel ⇨ Dimension drop-down menu ⇨ Linear. The DIMLINEAR command responds with the `Specify first extension line origin or <select object>:` prompt. You can now proceed as follows:

- If you're dimensioning more than one object, such as the distance from the endpoint of one line to the endpoint of another line, pick the first extension line origin. At the `Specify second extension line origin:` prompt, pick the second extension line origin. The two points on the objects that you pick define the length of the dimension.

- If you're dimensioning one object, press Enter at the `Specify first extension line origin or <select object>:` prompt. The `Select object to dimension:` prompt appears. Pick the object.

> **CAUTION**
> Always use the Select Object option if possible, for the most reliable results. Proper association of dimensions with their objects depends on the points that you specify. If you can't select an object and the point you need to specify is an intersection, don't click on the intersection. Instead, click on the object that you want to measure near the intersection and let the object snap specify the intersection for you. If you're not using the Select Object option, always use an object snap for accuracy.

At the `Specify dimension line location or [Mtext/Text/Angle/Horizontal/Vertical/Rotated]:` prompt, pick a point for the location of the dimension line. As you move the mouse, you can see the results on your screen, as shown in Figure 14.2. If you want an exact location, you can type in a relative coordinate, such as **@0,.5** to specify that the dimension line should be 0.5 units from the object. Snap mode may also work well for you, depending on the drawing environment.

FIGURE 14.2

Picking a dimension line location for a linear dimension

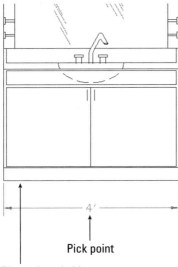

Pick point

Dimensioned object

Object snap tracking makes it a snap to pick points for dimensioning. For example, if you're dimensioning a house, your first extension line origin may be the outside corner of the house, but the second extension line origin may be an inner wall. At the `Specify first extension line origin or <select object>:` prompt, move the cursor over the inner wall endpoint to acquire it. Move the cursor back to the line you're dimensioning and click when you see the tooltip showing the snap point you chose. The dimension goes just where you need it.

ON THE WEB

The drawing used in the following exercise on drawing linear dimensions, `ab14-a.dwg`, is available from the Drawings download on the companion website.

14

STEPS: Drawing Linear Dimensions

1. Open `ab14-a.dwg`, available from the Drawings download on the companion website.

2. Save the file as `ab14-01.dwg` in your `AutoCAD Bible` folder. This is a plan of a bedroom, as shown in Figure 14.3. Ortho mode and Object Snap should be on. Set a running object snap for Endpoint only. Object Snap Tracking should be off. The current layer should be set to `Dim`.

FIGURE 14.3

A bedroom plan

3. Choose Home tab ⇨ Annotation panel ⇨ Dimension drop-down menu ⇨ Linear. Because you are dimensioning the vertical length of the room, you really want the dimension to be attached to the bottom and top horizontal lines, so that if you move those lines to make the room longer or shorter, the dimension changes. At the `Specify first extension line origin or <select object>:` prompt, pick ❶, shown in Figure 14.3, close enough to the corner to get the endpoint object snap marker. At the `Specify second extension line origin:` prompt, pick ❷ in the same way. At the `Specify dimension line location or [Mtext/Text/Angle/Horizontal/Vertical/Rotated]:` prompt, move the cursor to the right until you have sufficient space for the dimension text and click.

4. Repeat the DIMLINEAR command. At the `Specify first extension line origin or <select object>:` prompt, press Enter. At the `Select object to dimension:` prompt, pick ❸ (the window), shown in Figure 14.3. At the `Specify dimension line location or [Mtext/Text/Angle/Horizontal/Vertical/Rotated]:` prompt, move the cursor down until you have sufficient space for the dimension text and click.

5. Save your drawing. It should look like Figure 14.4.

Using dimension options

You can also use one of the options offered at the command prompt to further control the final dimension. Dimension options control the text and the angle of the dimension.

FIGURE 14.4

The bedroom with two linear dimensions

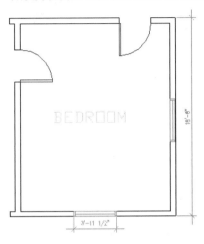

MText

The Mtext option lets you replace the calculated dimension text or add a prefix or suffix to it. When you right-click and choose Mtext at the `Specify dimension line location or [Mtext/Text/ Angle/Horizontal/Vertical/Rotated]:` prompt, the In-Place Text Editor opens. The Text Editor tab appears on the Ribbon and the dimension text is highlighted in your drawing. For more information on using the In-Place Text Editor, see Chapter 13. (If you are using the AutoCAD Classic or AutoCAD LT Classic workspace, you'll see the Text Formatting toolbar.)

The best use of the Mtext option is to add some text before or after the measurement, such as **TYP** (typical, used when one dimension applies to several objects) or **subject to final approval**. To add text before the measurement, simply start typing. To add text after the measurement, press the End or right arrow key and then type. To replace the existing text, click the text to select it and enter the replacement text. Then click outside of the In-Place Text Editor to close it.

> **NOTE**
> Typing your own dimension text is most commonly used where a dimension represents several sizes and refers to a size chart elsewhere in the drawing. For example, the text "Dim A" might be used for this purpose. If you replace the existing text, you can obtain the original text again by editing the dimension (double-click the dimension) and clearing the Text Override item in the Properties palette.

If the measurement text itself does not appear the way you want it, you should change the annotation specifications in the dimension style. You can also specify a prefix or suffix (such as *mm*) for all dimensions, as I explain in the next chapter. When you delete the text and type your own dimension text, you lose the ability of the dimension's measurement to automatically adjust to any change in the object's size.

Text

The Text option also lets you change dimension text but does not open the In-Place Text Editor. Instead, you can quickly retype the entire dimension text as you want it on the command line.

Angle

The angle of the text (horizontal, vertical, or aligned) is specified in your dimension style. However, you can use this option to change the angle of the dimension text for a particular circumstance. Right-click and choose Angle to get the `Specify angle of dimension text:` prompt. Type in an angle or pick two points to align the text with an existing object.

Horizontal/Vertical

The DIMLINEAR command assumes that you want a horizontal dimension if you select a horizontal object or two definition points running horizontally — ditto for a vertical dimension. Also, if you want to draw a vertical dimension of an object at an angle, you can specify this by simply moving the mouse cursor horizontally when specifying the dimension line location, as shown in Figure 14.5. The vertical dimension measures the change in the Y coordinates of the line, not the length of the line. If for some reason you need to force either a horizontal or vertical dimension, you can use the vertical or horizontal options.

FIGURE 14.5

By dragging the mouse cursor to the right after specifying the two endpoints, you can create a vertical dimension for this angled line.

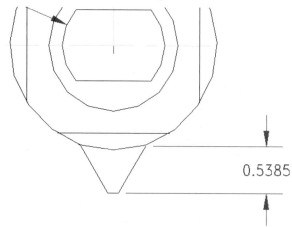

Rotated

Use a rotated linear dimension when the length that you want to dimension is not parallel to the extension line origins. Just as the vertical dimension in Figure 14.5 does not measure the length of the line to which its extension lines extend, a rotated linear dimension does not measure a specific object, but the distance of an imaginary line parallel to the dimension line. Rotated dimensions are not very common, but when you need them, they're the only way to get the dimension measurement that you need.

To use a rotated dimension, start a linear dimension, pick the two extension line origins, and choose the Rotated option. At the `Specify angle of dimension line <0>:` prompt, type the angle (or pick two points) to draw the dimension.

Figure 14.6 shows a hexagonal steppingstone with a rotated linear angle. The extension lines of the dimension extend to a line at 104.5 degrees, but in this case you want to measure a length at an angle of 135 degrees. Note that the dimension really measures an imaginary line parallel to the dimension line, shown in the figure as a dashed line, rather than the side of the hexagon.

FIGURE 14.6

Drawing a rotated linear dimension for a hexagonal steppingstone

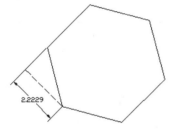

2.2229

Creating jogged dimension lines

A jog line is a zigzag used to indicate that the displayed measurement doesn't match the length of an object. For example, you might shorten an object to display it within a certain area, but manually override the dimension text to show the proper length. In this case, the jog line indicates that the visual length of the line is not to scale (NTS).

 First you create a linear or aligned dimension. (You may have modified the measurement text, as explained previously in this chapter in the discussion of the Mtext option.) Then you add the jog line, using the DIMJOGLINE command. Choose Annotate tab ⇨ Dimensions panel ⇨ Dimension, Dimjogline. At the `Select dimension to add jog or [Remove]:` prompt, select a dimension. At the `Specify jog location (or press ENTER):` prompt, press Enter to place the jog line midway between the dimension text and the first extension line, as shown in Figure 14.7. Alternatively, you can pick a location for the jog line.

You can move the jog line by stretching its grip. Select the dimension, select the jog line's grip, and move it to another location.

FIGURE 14.7

You can add a jog line to a dimension to indicate that the displayed measurement is different from the length of the dimensioned object.

Drawing Aligned Dimensions

When you want to dimension a linear object that is not orthogonal, use an aligned dimension. The dimension lines of an aligned dimension are always parallel to the object, unlike rotated dimensions. An aligned dimension measures the actual length of the object, not a vertical or horizontal distance that you dimension with a linear dimension. Therefore, your choice of linear, linear rotated, or aligned dimension depends on the distance that you want to measure. Figure 14.8 shows several aligned dimensions.

FIGURE 14.8

Three aligned dimensions

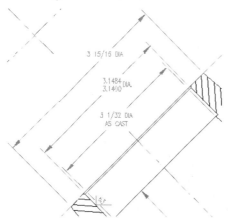

Specifying the dimensioned object

To create an aligned dimension, choose Home tab ⇨ Annotation panel ⇨ Dimension drop-down menu ⇨ Aligned or Annotate tab ⇨ Dimensions panel ⇨ Dimension drop-down menu ⇨ Aligned. This starts the DIMALIGNED command. The command responds with the `Specify first extension line origin or <select object>:` prompt. As with linear dimensions, you can now either pick two extension line origins or press Enter to select an object.

You then see the `Specify dimension line location or [Mtext/Text/Angle]:` prompt. Pick a point for the location of the dimension line. If you want an exact location, you can type in a relative coordinate, such as @2<45.

Using the options

After you've chosen what you want to dimension, you have three options: Mtext, Text, and Angle. The previous section discusses these options in detail.

STEPS: Drawing Aligned Dimensions

1. Open `ab14-b.dwg`, available from the Drawings download on the companion website.

2. Save the file as `ab14-02.dwg` in your `AutoCAD Bible` folder. This is part of a floor plan of a house, as shown in Figure 14.9. Object Snap should be on. Set running object snaps to Endpoint and Intersection.

FIGURE 14.9

A section of a floor plan of a house

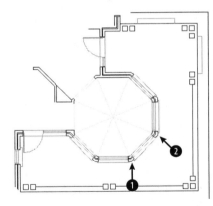

3. Choose Home tab ⇨ Annotation panel ⇨ Dimension drop-down menu ⇨ Aligned. Follow the prompts:

```
Specify first extension line origin or <select object>: Choose ❶ in
    Figure 14.9.
Specify second extension line origin: Choose ❷ in Figure 14.9.
Specify dimension line location or
```

```
[Mtext/Text/Angle]: Right-click and choose Mtext. In the In-Place Text
    Editor, press the End key on the keyboard and type a space, then type
    Typ. Click outside of the In-Place Text Editor.
Specify dimension line location or
[Mtext/Text/Angle]: Pick a location for the dimension line.
```

4. Save your drawing. It should look like Figure 14.10.

FIGURE 14.10

The house plan with an aligned dimension

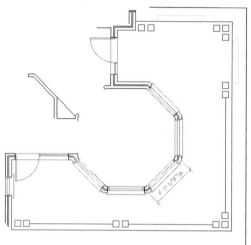

Creating Baseline and Continued Dimensions

Often, you want to create a whole series of attached, connected dimensions. You can accomplish this in two ways:

- *Baseline* dimensions are a series of dimensions that all start from one point. The first extension line is the same for all the dimensions. The second dimension includes the first dimension plus an additional distance, and so on.

- *Continued* dimensions are a series of dimensions that are all attached. The second dimension starts where the first dimension ends, and so on. Each dimension measures a different object or distance.

Figure 14.11 shows both baseline and continued linear dimensions. You can also create baseline and continued angular and ordinate dimensions. Quick Dimension, covered later in this chapter, can quickly create baseline and continued linear dimensions. Here I cover the traditional method.

FIGURE 14.11

A floor plan of a house using both baseline and continued dimensions

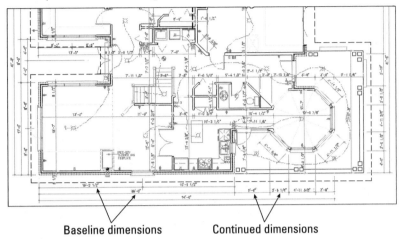

Baseline dimensions   Continued dimensions

Drawing baseline dimensions

To draw a baseline dimension, first create one linear, angular, or ordinate dimension in the regular way. (Angular and ordinate dimensions are covered later in this chapter.) Then choose Annotate tab ⇨ Dimensions panel ⇨ Continue/Baseline drop-down menu ⇨ Baseline. The command responds with the `Specify a second extension line origin or [Undo/Select] <Select>:` prompt.

If the previous dimension was a linear, angular, or ordinate dimension, the command uses the second extension line as the base for the new baseline dimension. Specify a new second extension line origin, and the command creates the baseline dimension with the same first extension origin as the original dimension and the new second extension origin that you just specified.

If you don't want to work with the previous dimension in the drawing, press Enter. The command responds with the `Select base dimension:` prompt. Be careful to pick the dimension closer to the side you want to use as the baseline. The command then prompts you to specify a second extension line origin.

The command continues to prompt you for second extension line origins so that you can quickly create a chain of baseline dimensions. At each prompt, you can right-click and choose Undo to undo the previous dimension. You can also press Enter at any time and select a different dimension from which to work. Press Esc to end the command (or press Enter twice).

Drawing continued dimensions

Continued dimensions work similarly to baseline dimensions. To continue a dimension, first create one linear, angular, or ordinate dimension in the regular way. Then choose Annotate tab ⇨ Dimensions panel ⇨ Continue/Baseline drop-down menu ⇨ Continue. The command responds with the `Specify a second extension line origin or [Undo/ Select] <Select>:` prompt.

14

If the previous dimension was a linear, angular, or ordinate dimension, the command uses the second extension line as the beginning of the new continued dimension. Specify a new second extension line origin to create the continued dimension.

If you don't want to continue from the previous dimension in the drawing, press Enter. The command responds with the `Select continued dimension:` prompt. Be careful to pick the dimension closer to the side from which you want to continue. You then get a prompt to specify a second extension line origin.

The command continues to prompt you for second extension line origins so that you can quickly create a chain of continued dimensions. At each prompt, you can right-click and choose Undo to undo the previous dimension. You can also press Enter at any time and select a different dimension from which to work. Press Esc to end the command (or press Enter twice).

On the Web

This exercise has both Imperial and metric versions. The drawings used in the following exercise on drawing baseline and continued dimensions — `ab14-b.dwg` (the Imperial drawing) and `ab14-b-metric.dwg` (the metric drawing) — are available from the Drawings download on the companion website.

STEPS: Drawing Baseline and Continued Dimensions

1. Open `ab14-b.dwg` or `ab14-b-metric.dwg`, available from the Drawings download on the companion website.

2. Save the file as `ab14-03.dwg` or `ab14-03-metric.dwg` in your `AutoCAD Bible` folder. This is the same drawing used in the previous two exercises, as shown in Figure 14.12. Object Snap should be on with running object snaps for Endpoint and Intersection.

3. Turn on Ortho mode and Object Snap Tracking on the status bar.

4. Choose Annotate tab ⇨ Dimensions panel ⇨ Dimension drop-down menu ⇨ Linear. Follow the prompts:

   ```
   Specify first extension line origin or <select object>: Pick the endpoint
       at ❶ in Figure 14.12.
   Specify second extension line origin: Pass the cursor over ❸ to acquire
       it for object snap tracking. Move the cursor to the right so that
       it's vertically under ❶, and click when you see the [Ortho: <270°,
       Extension: <0° tooltip.
   Specify dimension line location or [Mtext/Text/Angle/Horizontal/Vertical/
       Rotated]: Pick a dimension line location to the right of the model.
   ```

5. Choose Annotate tab ⇨ Dimensions panel ⇨ Continue/Baseline drop-down menu ⇨ Continue.

   At the `Specify a second extension line origin or [Undo/Select] <Select>:` prompt, move the cursor over the endpoint or intersection at ❹ to acquire it for object snap tracking. Move the cursor to the right, vertically below ❶, and click when you see the tooltip.

This action places the continued dimension. Notice that the dimension may use a leader to place the text if there is not enough room between the extension lines. (If the leader is placed to the left, select it and pick the grip on the text. Pick a point to the right of the model and click to move the leader to the right.)

FIGURE 14.12

A house plan with an octagonal ceiling

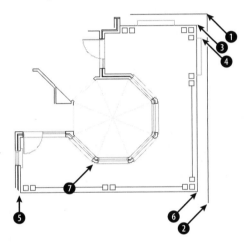

6. The command repeats the `Specify a second extension line origin or [Undo/Select] <Select>:` prompt. Pick the endpoint at **2**, shown in Figure 14.12, to place the dimension. Press Enter twice to end the command.

7. Start the DIMLINEAR command. Follow the prompts:

    `Specify first extension line origin or <select object>:` *Choose the endpoint at* **5** *in Figure 14.12.*

    Follow these prompts:

    `Specify second extension line origin:` *Move the cursor over* **7** *to acquire it. Move the cursor down so that it's horizontal to* **5**. *When you see the Ortho: <0°, Extension: <270° tooltip, click.*
    `Specify dimension line location or [Mtext/Text/Angle/Horizontal/Vertical/Rotated]:` *Pick a dimension line location fairly close to the line you dimensioned, leaving just enough room for the dimension text.*

8. Choose Annotate tab ⇨ Dimensions panel ⇨ Continue/Baseline drop-down menu ⇨ Baseline. At the `Specify a second extension line origin or [Undo/Select] <Select>:` prompt, pick the endpoint or intersection at **6**, shown in Figure 14.12. Press Enter twice to end the command.

9. Save your drawing. It should look like Figure 14.13.

FIGURE 14.13

The floor plan with baseline and continued dimensions

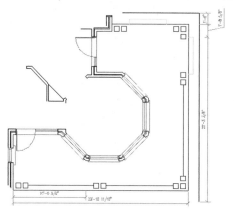

Dimensioning Arcs and Circles

When you dimension an arc or a circle, you measure its radius or diameter. It's also common to mark arc and circle centers to clarify what you're measuring. Arc and circle dimensions are most commonly used in mechanical drawings.

Marking arc and circle centers

Circle and arc centers are often marked in mechanical drawings because the center is an important aspect of a circle or arc but is not obvious without a mark. You set the size and type of mark when you create a dimension style, as explained in the next chapter. You can use a center mark (a small cross) or centerlines, as shown in Figure 14.14.

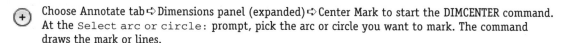

Choose Annotate tab ⇨ Dimensions panel (expanded) ⇨ Center Mark to start the DIMCENTER command. At the Select arc or circle: prompt, pick the arc or circle you want to mark. The command draws the mark or lines.

Dimensioning arc lengths

To dimension the length of an arc, choose Home tab ⇨ Annotation panel ⇨ Dimension drop-down menu ⇨ Arc Length or Annotate tab ⇨ Dimensions panel ⇨ Dimension drop-down menu ⇨ Arc Length. This starts the DIMARC command. You can dimension the length of an arc or an arc segment in a polyline. At the Select arc or polyline arc segment: prompt, select an arc. At the Specify arc length dimension location, or [Mtext/Text/Angle/Partial/Leader]: prompt, pick where you want the dimension line (which is an arc) to appear. The command automatically adds an arc symbol before the measurement. You can specify the arc symbol above the measurement or choose to display no symbol — you set this in your dimension style. Figure 14.15 shows an example of an arc length dimension.

You can also choose the Mtext, Text, or Angle option, as described in the section "Drawing Linear Dimensions." The Partial option lets you dimension part of an arc. At the prompts, you specify where you want to start and end the dimension. The Leader option inserts an arrow pointing to the arc.

FIGURE 14.14

Circles — one with a center mark and the other with centerlines

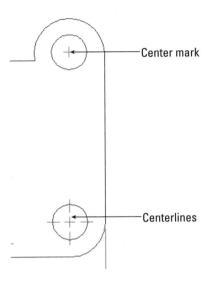

Center mark

Centerlines

Creating radial dimensions

To dimension the radius of a circle or arc, choose Home tab ⇨ Annotation panel ⇨ Dimension drop-down menu ⇨ Radius or Annotate tab ⇨ Dimensions panel ⇨ Dimension drop-down menu ⇨ Radius. The command responds with the `Select arc or circle:` prompt. Select an arc or circle. At the `Specify dimension line location or [Mtext/Text/Angle]:` prompt, pick where you want the dimension line to appear. The command automatically adds an R before the measurement to indicate the radius, as shown in Figure 14.15.

You can also choose the Mtext, Text, or Angle option, as described in the "Drawing Linear Dimensions" section earlier in this chapter.

FIGURE 14.15

The circle's radius dimension uses a leader (a line and arrow pointing to the object) because the circle is too small to place the dimension inside it. The arc displays an arc length dimension.

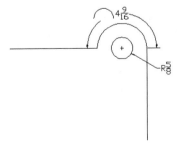

14

A radius dimension usually passes through the center of the arc or circle. If you are dimensioning a large arc or circle, you may find that you can't see the center at the same time as you see the circumference without zooming out too far. In this instance, you can use the jogged radial dimension, which lets you specify an arbitrary center for the arc or circle. Choose Home tab➪Annotation panel➪ Dimension drop-down menu➪Jogged or Annotate tab➪Dimensions panel➪Dimension drop-down menu➪Jogged.

You can create an extension arc (similar to an extension line) for a radius dimension that extends beyond the end of an arc. This allows you to place the dimension anywhere in the circle of which the arc is a part. When you specify the location of the dimension, just move the cursor past the arc's endpoint and continue around to the desired point.

Creating diameter dimensions

To dimension the diameter of an arc or circle, choose Home tab➪Annotation panel➪Dimension drop-down menu➪Diameter or Annotate tab➪Dimensions panel➪Dimension drop-down menu➪Diameter. The command responds with the `Select arc or circle:` prompt. Select an arc or circle. At the `Specify dimension line location or [Mtext/Text/Angle]:` prompt, pick where you want the dimension line to appear. The command automatically adds the diameter symbol before the measurement to indicate the dimension. You can create an extension arc (similar to an extension line) for a diameter dimension that extends beyond the end of an arc, in the same way I described just previously for a radius dimension.

You can also choose the Mtext, Text, or Angle option, as described in the section "Drawing Linear Dimensions."

Dimensioning Angles

You have several options for dimensioning angles. You may want to dimension the angular relationship between two lines, but the lines may intersect at their midpoints or may not intersect at all. Therefore, you need to specify the vertex of the angle you want to dimension. Figure 14.16 shows an angular dimension with the points used to define it.

To create an angular dimension, choose Home tab➪Annotation panel➪Dimension drop-down menu➪ Angular or Annotate tab➪Dimensions panel➪Dimension drop-down menu➪Angular. This starts the DIMANGULAR command. The command displays the `Select arc, circle, line, or <specify vertex>:` prompt, and responds differently, depending on what you select:

- If you press Enter, the command asks for the angle vertex, the first angle endpoint, and the second angle endpoint. These three points define the angle.
- If you select an arc, the command dimensions the entire arc, using the arc's center as the angle vertex.

- If you select a circle, the command uses the pick point as the first angle endpoint and the circle's center as the angle vertex. You then see the `Specify second angle endpoint:` prompt. Pick a point on the circle.
- If you select a line, the command asks for a second line. The command measures the angle between the two lines. If the lines don't intersect, the command uses their implied intersection as the angle vertex.

FIGURE 14.16

An angular dimension

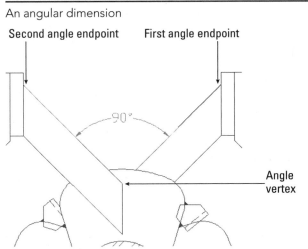

Thanks to Mary Redfern of the Bethlehem Corporation, Easton, Pennsylvania, for this drawing.

After you define the angle, the command responds with the `Specify dimension arc line location or [Mtext/Text/Angle/Quadrant]:` prompt. Pick a point for the dimension arc line — which is the same thing as a dimension line, except that the command uses an arc for angular dimensions.

The Quadrant option lets you lock the location of the dimension line to a specified quadrant of the circle in which the angle lies. For example, you can fix the dimension line outside two lines forming an angle while placing the text within those two lines. After choosing the Quadrant option, at the `Specify quadrant:` prompt, click where you want the dimension line to appear. You can then specify any location for the text of the dimension line. You can also choose the Mtext, Text, or Angle option, as covered in the section "Drawing Linear Dimensions."

14

379

Dimensioning Minor, Major, and Supplemental Angles

When two lines meet at an angle, they create two angles, the *minor angle* and the *major angle*. The angle that is less than 180 degrees is the minor angle. The major angle is always more than 180 degrees. You can also measure the *supplemental angle*, which is the difference between 180 degrees and the minor angle. These angles are shown here.

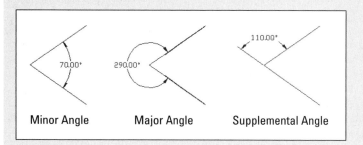

Minor Angle   Major Angle   Supplemental Angle

Here's how you create each type of dimension. Start the DIMANGULAR command. The command responds with the Select arc, circle, line, or <specify vertex>: prompt.

To dimension the minor angle, select both lines. Then at the Specify dimension arc line location or [Mtext/Text/Angle/Quadrant]: prompt, place the dimension arc line inside the angle. (You can also press Enter, specify the angle vertex and the two lines, and place the dimension arc line inside the angle.)

To dimension the major angle, press Enter. Do not select the lines. At the prompts, specify the angle vertex and the two lines. At the Specify dimension arc line location or [Mtext/Text/Angle/Quadrant]: prompt, place the dimension arc line outside the angle.

To dimension the supplemental angle, select both lines. At the Specify dimension arc line location or [Mtext/Text/Angle/Quadrant]: prompt, place the dimension arc line outside the angle.

As you can see, how you specify the angle and where you place the dimension arc line determine which angle you measure.

In the following exercise, you practice drawing radial, diameter, and angular dimensions.

ON THE WEB

The drawing used in the following exercise on drawing radial, diameter, and angular dimensions, ab14-c.dwg, is available from the Drawings download on the companion website.

STEPS: Drawing Radial, Diameter, and Angular Dimensions

1. Open ab14-c.dwg, available from the Drawings download on the companion website.
2. Save the file as ab14-04.dwg in your AutoCAD Bible folder. This is a view of a bearing housing for an industrial washing machine, as shown in Figure 14.17. Object Snap mode should be on. Set running object snaps to Endpoint, Intersection, and Center.

3. Choose Annotate tab⇨Dimensions panel (expanded)⇨Center Mark. At the Select arc or circle: prompt, pick one of the four small circles at the corners of the model. Repeat the command for the other three circles.

4. Choose Annotate tab⇨Dimensions panel⇨Dimension drop-down menu⇨Diameter. At the Select arc or circle: prompt, choose the outer of the two circles at ❶, shown in Figure 14.17. At the Specify dimension line location or [Mtext/Text/Angle]: prompt, pick a location for the dimension line.

FIGURE 14.17

A bearing housing for an industrial washing machine

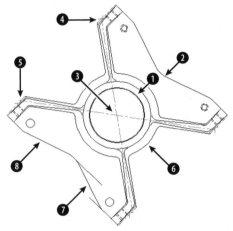

Thanks to Robert Mack of the Dexter Company, Fairfield, Iowa, for this drawing.

5. Choose Annotate tab⇨Dimensions panel⇨Dimension drop-down menu⇨Radius. At the Select arc or circle: prompt, choose ❷, shown in Figure 14.17. At the Specify dimension line location or [Mtext/Text/Angle]: prompt, pick a location for the dimension line to the left of the arc. To move the text outside the figure, select it, hover the cursor over the grip on the dimension text and then choose Move Text Only from the menu. Specify a location to the right of the arc.

6. Choose Annotate tab⇨Dimensions panel⇨Dimension drop-down menu⇨Angular. Follow the prompts:

Select arc, circle, line, or <specify vertex>: ↵
Specify angle vertex: *Pick* ❸ *in Figure 14.17.*
Specify first angle endpoint: *Pick the endpoint at* ❹. *(Press Tab if necessary until you see the endpoint tooltip.)*
Specify second angle endpoint: *Pick the endpoint at* ❺.
Specify dimension arc line location or [Mtext/Text/Angle/Quadrant]: *Choose a location for the dimension line.*

14

7. Repeat the DIMANGULAR command. At the `Select arc, circle, line, or <specify vertex>:` prompt, pick the arc at ⑥. At the `Specify dimension arc line location or [Mtext/Text/Angle/Quadrant]:` prompt, pick a location for the dimension line.

8. Choose Annotate tab ⇨ Dimensions panel ⇨ Dimension drop-down menu ⇨ Arc Length. At the `Select arc or polyline arc segment:` prompt, again pick the arc at ⑥. At the `Specify arc length dimension location, or [Mtext/Text/Angle/Partial]:` prompt, pick a location for the dimension line farther out than the previous dimension that you drew.

9. Start the DIMANGULAR command. At the `Select arc, circle, line, or <specify vertex>:` prompt, pick ⑦, shown in Figure 14.17. At the `Select second line:` prompt, pick ⑧. At the `Specify dimension arc line location [Mtext/Text/Angle/Quadrant]:` prompt, pick a location for the dimension line to the left of the model.

10. Save your drawing. It should look like Figure 14.18.

FIGURE 14.18

The bearing housing with center marks, radial and diameter dimensions, arc length, and angular dimensions

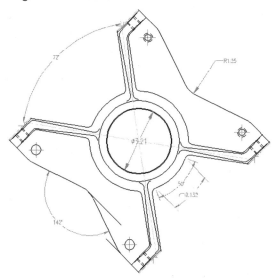

Creating Ordinate Dimensions

Ordinate dimensions are used in mechanical drawing. They dimension an object by labeling X or Y coordinates based on a 0,0 coordinate placed somewhere on the model. Figure 14.19 shows a drawing with some ordinate dimensions.

To place the 0,0 coordinate on the model, choose View tab ➪ Coordinates panel ➪ Origin. (If the Coordinates panel is not displayed, right-click over the View tab and choose Show Panels ➪ Coordinates.) At the prompt, pick a point on the model, using object snaps for an exact measurement. If you want to check the UCS, choose View tab ➪ Coordinates panel ➪ UCS Icon drop-down menu ➪ Show UCS Icon. As long as there is room, the UCS icon moves to the new 0,0 coordinate.

FIGURE 14.19

Ordinate dimensions in a mechanical drawing of a tension arm for a commercial dryer

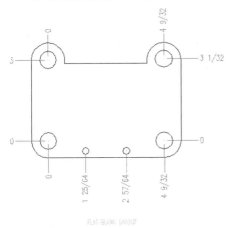

To create an ordinate dimension, choose Home tab ➪ Annotation panel ➪ Dimension drop-down menu ➪ Ordinate or Annotate tab ➪ Dimensions panel ➪ Dimension drop-down menu ➪ Ordinate. This starts the DIMORDINATE command. At the `Specify feature location:` prompt, pick the part of the model that you want to dimension. Running object snaps with Object Snap turned on makes this an easy task.

At the `Specify leader endpoint or [Xdatum/Ydatum/Mtext/Text/Angle]:` prompt, pick the endpoint for the leader. The location where you pick the leader endpoint determines which coordinate to dimension — the X coordinate (Xdatum) or Y coordinate (Ydatum). Pick the leader endpoint perpendicular from the coordinate's axis that you want to measure. To measure an X coordinate, move up or down from the feature you selected. To measure a Y coordinate, move left or right to pick the leader endpoint.

Usually you work with Ortho mode on to create straight lines. If you need to create bent lines to avoid previously drawn dimensions, turn Ortho mode off. If you pick a leader endpoint at a nonorthogonal angle from the feature, you may need to force the measurement of the coordinate that you want by using either the Xdatum or Ydatum option. Use the Mtext option to open the In-Place Text Editor and edit the dimension text. Use the Text option to change all the text on the command line.

To perfectly line up the dimensions, when specifying the leader endpoint, use object tracking to track the endpoint of the previous leader. You can also turn on SNAP.

14

STEPS: Drawing Ordinate Dimensions

1. Open ab14-d.dwg, available from the Drawings download on the companion website.

2. Save the file as ab14-05.dwg in your AutoCAD Bible folder. This drawing shows a simple sheet-metal template, as shown in Figure 14.20. Snap should be on and a snap distance of 0.25 units set. Right-click the Snap Mode button on the status bar and make sure that Grid Snap is on.

FIGURE 14.20

A sheet-metal template

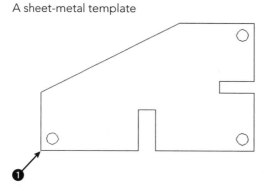

3. Choose View tab ⇨ Coordinates panel ⇨ Origin or right-click over the UCS icon and choose Origin. At the Specify new origin point <0,0,0>: prompt, pick ❶, shown in Figure 14.20.

4. Choose Home tab ⇨ Annotation panel ⇨ Dimension drop-down menu ⇨ Ordinate. At the Specify feature location: prompt, choose ❶, shown in Figure 14.20. At the Specify leader endpoint or [Xdatum/Ydatum/Mtext/Text/Angle]: prompt, pick a point 0.5 units to the left of ❶, as shown in Figure 14.21. (Because Snap is on, this is easy. If necessary, click the coordinates at the lower-left corner of the screen until you get polar coordinates to display in the lower-left area of the drawing screen.)

5. Repeat the DIMORDINATE command. At the Specify feature location: prompt, choose ❶, shown in Figure 14.20. At the Specify leader endpoint or [Xdatum/Ydatum/Mtext/Text/Angle]: prompt, pick a point 0.5 units below ❶.

6. Continue to dimension the drawing, using Figure 14.21 as a guide. (You can type **multiple** ↵ **dimordinate** ↵ to automatically repeat the command. Press Esc when you no longer need the command.)

7. Save your drawing.

FIGURE 14.21

The dimensioned template

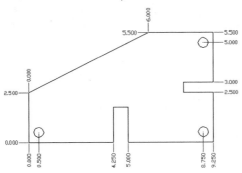

Drawing Leaders

Leaders are lines pointing to objects. At the end of a leader, you place any text that you want. Use leaders to label objects or provide explanatory text. Leaders do not calculate dimension text, but if you use an object snap to place the arrow point, they follow along if you move the object. Figure 14.22 shows two leaders.

Multileaders are leaders that support multiple lines. You format a multileader by configuring multileader styles. Multileader styles can be annotative, which allows them to scale automatically to the current annotative/viewport scale.

Creating a multileader

 To create a multileader by using the default style and settings, choose Home tab ⇨ Annotation panel ⇨ Multileader drop-down menu ⇨ Leader or Annotate tab ⇨ Leaders panel ⇨ Multileader. This starts the MLEADER command. (Earlier QLEADER and LEADER commands still exist, but they offer fewer options.) At the `Specify leader arrowhead location or [leader Landing first/Content first/ Options] <Options>:` prompt, specify where you want the tip of the arrow (the *head* of the leader) to go. If you want a precise point, you may want to use an object snap. At the `Specify leader landing location:` prompt, specify where you want the end of the line to go. This line will be next to the text or block.

The In-Place Text Editor opens, where you can enter the text for the leader. (See Chapter 13 for a discussion of the text editor.) You can use the editor to format the text at this time. For example, you can choose an existing text style, a font, or a font size. Close the editor to place the leader. The command adds a short horizontal *landing line* that connects a diagonal arrow to the text.

14

FIGURE 14.22

Use leaders to point to objects and add explanatory text.

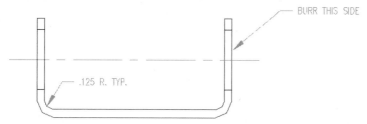

When you start the MLEADER command, you have the following options at the first prompt:

- **leader Landing first.** Lets you first specify the point where the line meets the text. If you choose this option, AutoCAD continues to prompt you for the leader landing first.
- **Content first.** Lets you specify a location for the text label, and then enter the text.
- **Options.** Displays the following suboptions:
    - **Leader type.** Offers you options relating to the leader. You can use the Type suboption to choose a straight line (the default), a spline, or no line at all. Choose the Landing suboption to choose whether or not you want a landing, and if so, its length.
    - **leader lAnding.** Lets you choose whether you want a landing (Yes) or not (No).
    - **Content type.** Lets you choose whether you want the leader to end with Mtext (the default), a block, or nothing. If you choose the Block suboption, you enter the name of the block. (Blocks are covered in Chapter 18.)
    - **Maxpoints.** Lets you specify the maximum number of points of the line. A three-point line will have three vertices.
    - **First angle.** Lets you enter an angle to constrain the first angle after the arrowhead segment. For example, you could constrain the angle to 90°.
    - **Second angle.** If you specified more than two points, you can constrain a second angle.
    - **eXit options.** Exits the Options prompts and returns you to the main prompts for the MLEADER command.

Editing multileaders

To add or remove a leader, you use the MLEADEREDIT command. Go to Home tab ➪ Annotation panel ➪ Multileader drop-down menu ➪ Add Leader or Annotate tab ➪ Leaders panel, choose Add Leader to add a leader, select the multileader, and specify the endpoint of the new arrowhead(s). Choose Remove Leader to remove a leader on a multileader that has more than one; select the multileader, specify which leader line to remove, and press Enter to end the command.

> **TIP**
>
> You can press the Ctrl key and pick a segment of a multileader to select just that segment. You can then change the properties of that segment in the Properties palette (Ctrl+1).

Creating a multileader style

Although you have a lot of settings available when you create a multileader, you can best define its look by using a multileader style. Because you save a style, you can easily use it again and again.

 To create a multileader style, choose Home tab ⇨ Annotation panel (expanded) ⇨ Multileader Style, or Annotate tab ⇨ Leaders panel and click the dialog box launcher arrow on the panel title, to open the Multileader Style Manager, as shown in Figure 14.23.

FIGURE 14.23

The Multileader Style Manager

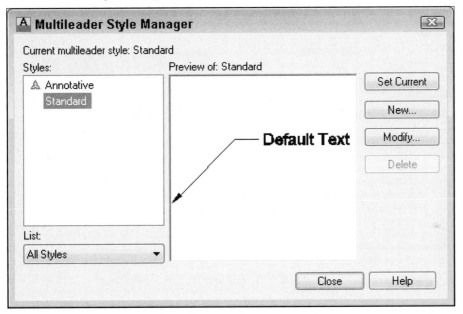

To create a new style, click the New button to open the Create New Multileader Style dialog box. Here you name your style and choose an existing style as a basis for the style. You can also specify that the style should be annotative by checking the Annotative check box. Note that if you want the multileaders to be annotative, then any blocks and text styles that they use need to be annotative, as well.

 Annotative objects scale automatically to the current annotative/viewport scale when you plot them. For more information, see Chapter 17. For information about annotative text styles, see Chapter 13. I cover blocks in Chapter 18.

When you've named your style, click Continue to open the Modify Multileader Style dialog box, shown in Figure 14.24 with the Leader Format tab displayed. If you choose an existing multileader style from the Multileader Style Manager and click Modify, you get to this same dialog box.

FIGURE 14.24

Define a multileader style in the Modify Multileader Style dialog box

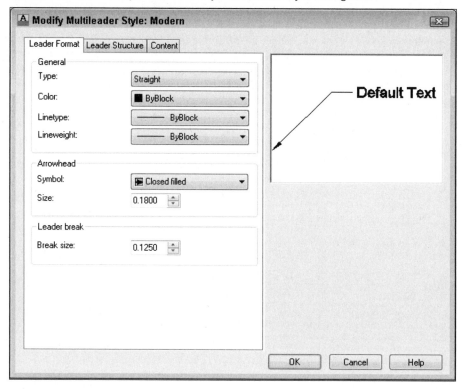

On the Leader Format tab, you can format the line and the arrow as follows:

- **Type.** Choose Straight, Spline (curved), or None from the drop-down list.
- **Color.** Choose a color from the drop-down list. These are the same colors that you can choose for any object. For more information, see Chapter 11. The default is ByBlock, which means that the leader takes on the color of the current layer (or the current color).
- **Linetype.** Choose a linetype from the drop-down list. Choose Other to open the Select Linetype dialog box, where you can choose a loaded linetype, or load another linetype. (I explain linetypes in Chapter 11.)
- **Lineweight.** Choose a lineweight from the drop-down list. (Chapter 11 discusses lineweights.)
- **Symbol.** In the Arrowhead section, you can choose the type of arrow you want to use from the drop-down list.
- **Size.** Enter an arrowhead size, or use the up and down arrows to change the current size.
- **Break size.** Enter a value for a break to use with the DIMBREAK command. (I explain the DIMBREAK command later in this chapter.)

On the Leader Structure tab, shown in Figure 14.25, you specify some more detailed information about the leader's line:

- **Maximum Leader Points.** By default, a leader line has two points. You can allow for more vertices by adding points.

- **First Segment Angle.** You can constrain the angle of the first segment, which is horizontal by default. Choose from 15° increments up to 90°.

- **Second Segment Angle.** You can constrain the angle of the second segment, which is horizontal by default. Choose from 15° increments up to 90°.

- **Automatically Include Landing.** In the Landing Settings section, you can decide whether you want a horizontal landing (the short line next to the text). Uncheck the check box if you don't want one.

- **Set Landing Distance.** To specify the length of the landing line, check this check box and enter a value in units.

- **Annotative.** In the Scale section, check this check box to make the multileaders annotative, as explained earlier in this section. If the multileaders are not annotative, you can automatically scale them to the scale of the viewport or specify a scale for all multileaders.

FIGURE 14.25

The Leader Structure tab of the Modify Multileader Style dialog box lets you specify detailed information about the leader line.

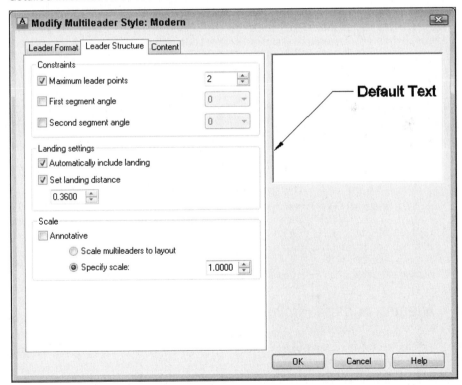

The Content tab offers settings related to text and the label part of the leader. First, you specify the Multileader Type, which can be Mtext, a block, or nothing at the end of a leader.

If you choose Mtext (multiline text), you specify default text content (if any), the text style, text angle, and text color. You specify the text height (which is the paper height if the style is annotative). You can force the text to be left-justified in all situations. Check the Frame Text check box to put a box around the text. Finally, you specify how the landing line attaches to the text and the gap between the landing line and the text.

> **TIP**
>
> You can control the spacing between the text and its frame, using the Landing Gap value in the Leader Connection section of the Content tab. The Content tab also has a check box, Extend Leader to Text, which extends the leader beyond the text bounding box, so that it reaches the text itself.

> **NOTE**
>
> You can click the Ellipsis button next to the Text Style item to open the Text Style dialog box, where you can create a new text style or modify an existing one. You can specify a vertical attachment (from the top or bottom of the leader text) as well as a horizontal attachment (from the side of the leader text).

If you choose a block, you either specify one of several standard blocks or your own block (User Block). The standard blocks are detail callout, slot, circle, box, hexagon, and triangle. The blocks contain attributes (discussed in Chapter 19) that allow you to add a number (or a letter) inside each shape. For example, you might label various parts of the drawing A, B, and C. Usually, you would then have some annotation elsewhere to provide further information about these objects. You also choose how the landing line attaches to the block and the block's color.

> **TIP**
>
> You can scale the block. Enter a scale in the Scale text box. You see the result immediately in the preview pane.

Throughout this process, the preview window displays a representation of how the multileader will look. Note, however, that several features depend on how you insert the leader. For example, you don't see any difference in the preview when you constrain the leader line's angles. When you're done, click OK and then Close to return to your drawing.

Your multileader style is now current, and you can use it to draw multileaders. To change a current style, choose it from the Multileader Style drop-down list in the Leaders panel of the Annotate tab. You can also find it by choosing Home tab ➪ Annotation panel (expanded) ➪ Multileader Style. To change the style of an existing multileader, select it and choose the desired style.

Aligning and combining leaders

Two commands allow you to align multileaders and combine them. You align leaders to make them look more orderly, using the MLEADERALIGN command. There are several options that you can use, depending on the desired result.

To start the command, choose Home tab ⇨ Annotation panel ⇨ Multileader drop-down menu ⇨ Align or Annotate tab ⇨ Leaders panel ⇨ Align. At the `Select multileaders:` prompt, select the multileaders that you want to align.

At the `Select multileader to align to or [Options]:` prompt, you specify the multileader that you want to act as a basis for the others. The command then aligns the other multileaders with this one. At the `Specify direction:` prompt, you can specify a direction for the alignment. This default use of the command does not align the multileader lines or the arrows, just the end of the landing line nearest the Mtext or block. In most cases, you'll probably want to use a vertical alignment; in this case, the ends of the landing lines align, all in a row. However, you can use any direction. As you move the cursor, you see a preview of the results. When you like what you see, click.

> **TIP**
>
> When you select multileaders for the MLEADERALIGN command, you can include other objects, and the command filters them out. This makes it easy to use a window to select a number of multileaders that are interspersed among other objects.

Instead of selecting the multileader to align to, you can select the Options option and choose one of the following suboptions:

- **Distribute.** Lets you specify the two points between which the landing lines of all the selected multileaders fit, evenly spaced. For example, you can evenly space four multileaders between two points in this way. After you use this option, the command continues to default to this mode so that you can distribute other sets of multileaders. Use Options to switch to another mode.

- **Make leader segments parallel.** Makes the leader lines parallel, without changing their endpoints. Select the multileader that you want to align the others to. After you use this option, the command continues to default to this mode. Use Options to switch to another mode.

- **Specify spacing.** You specify a spacing, in units, between each of the multileaders. Then you specify which multileader to align the others to and the direction; all of them line up (according to the ends of their landing lines), spaced according to the spacing you specified. After you use this option, the command continues to default to this mode. Use Options to switch to another mode.

- **Use current spacing.** Uses the current spacing between the ends of the landing lines. This is the default mode; as described previously, you specify which multileader to align the others to and the direction.

The MLEADERCOLLECT command works only with multileaders that use blocks as their content. The purpose of this command is to group separate leaders into one leader with all the blocks connected. For example, if you are using multileaders to point out objects that need additional annotation, multiple comments might apply to one object. You would then need a multileader that ended with more than one letter or number. Figure 14.26 shows three individual multileaders before and after being collected, using a vertical arrangement.

14

FIGURE 14.26

You can collect several multileaders that end in blocks into one multileader.

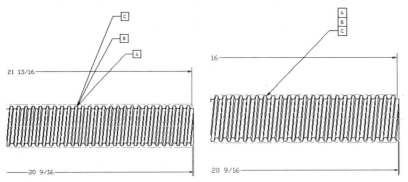

To collect a multileader, remember that you need a style that uses blocks rather than Mtext. To collect them, choose Home tab ⇨ Annotation panel ⇨ Multileader drop-down menu ⇨ Collect or Annotate tab ⇨ Leaders panel ⇨ Collect. At the `Select multileaders:` prompt, select the multileaders in the order you want them to appear. This is important, because the command groups them according to how you select them.

However, the command also uses the last multileader you choose for its final location (assuming they point to different locations). For example, if you first choose a block labeled 1 and then choose a block labeled 2, the final multileader will point to the location of label 2. If necessary, you can easily move the multileader by using its grips.

At the `Select multileaders:` prompt, choose the multileaders, taking into account the final order and location you want, as I just described. At the `Specify collected multileader location or [Vertical/Horizontal/Wrap] <Horizontal>:` prompt, specify where the blocks will now appear. You can see a preview as you move the cursor. You can also choose one of the following options:

- **Vertical.** Places the blocks in a vertical line.
- **Horizontal.** Places the blocks in a horizontal line.
- **Wrap.** Lets you specify either a width or a number of blocks. After that, the blocks wrap to the next line.

After you choose an option, the previous prompt repeats. Specify a location for the collected multileader.

AutoCAD Only

The Express Tools include the QLDETACHSET command, which detaches a leader's annotation from the leader line, to create two separate objects. Choose Express Tools tab ⇨ Dimension panel ⇨ Annotation Attachment drop-down list ⇨ Detach Leaders from Annotation. QLATTACH attaches leaders and MText objects. Choose Express Tools tab ⇨ Dimension panel ⇨ Annotation Attachment drop-down list ⇨ Attach Leader to Annotation. These tools work with leaders that you create with the QLEADER command; they don't apply to the new multileaders.

STEPS: Drawing Multileaders

1. Open `ab14-e.dwg`, available from the Drawings download on the companion website.

2. Save the file as `ab14-06.dwg` in your `AutoCAD Bible` folder. This is a drawing of a set of pulleys, as shown in Figure 14.27. Object Snap mode should be turned off. Click the Show/Hide Lineweight button on the status bar to turn it on (if necessary).

3. Choose Annotate tab ⇨ Leaders panel and click the dialog box launcher arrow on the right side of the panel title, to open the Multileader Style Manager. Click New, enter **Bold** in the New Style Name text box, make sure that the Annotative check box is checked, and click Continue. You'll create a multileader style that stands out by its color and width.

4. On the Leader Format tab, choose Green from the Color drop-down list. Choose 0.40 mm from the Lineweight drop-down list.

5. On the Leader Structure tab, check the Set Landing Distance check box (if necessary) and change the value to **1/2**.

6. On the Content tab, change the Text Style to `DIMTXT`. Check the Frame Text check box. Click OK to return to the Multileader Style Manager. The Bold style should be selected. Click Close to return to your drawing. You should see the Bold style displayed in the Multileader Style drop-down list of the Multileaders panel on the Annotate tab.

FIGURE 14.27

A set of pulleys

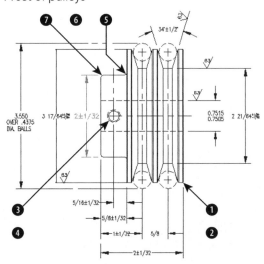

7. Choose Annotate tab ⇨ Leaders panel ⇨ Multileader. The Select Annotation Scale dialog box may open to remind you to set the annotation scale. Leave the default of 1:1 and click OK.

    Follow the prompts:

    ```
    Specify leader arrowhead location or [leader Landing first/Content first/
        Options] <Options>: Pick ❶ in Figure 14.27 (near but not on the
        drawing object).
    Specify leader landing location: Pick ❷.
    The In-Place Text Editor opens. Enter BREAK EDGES ↵. Enter TYP (8)
        PLACES. Click anywhere outside the editor.
    ```

8. Repeat the MULTILEADER command. Pick points ❸ and then ❹, shown in Figure 14.27. This time, type **DRILL 'F' HOLE**. Again, click anywhere outside the editor to place the multileader.

9. Repeat the MULTILEADER command. Pick points ❺ and ❻. The text should be **1/16 R**. If the AutoStack Properties dialog box appears after you type the fraction, uncheck the Enable AutoStacking check box and click OK. Click outside the editor to place the multileader.

10. To add a leader to the last multileader, choose Annotate tab ⇨ Leaders panel ⇨ Add Leader. Select the last leader that you drew. Specify ❼ and then press Enter.

11. Save your drawing. It should look like Figure 14.28.

FIGURE 14.28

The pulleys with three multileaders

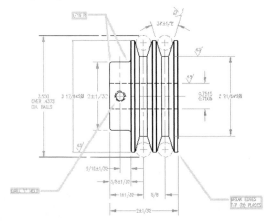

Using Quick Dimension

Quick Dimension enables you to dimension several objects at one time. You can use Quick Dimension for baseline, continued, and ordinate dimensions. You can also dimension multiple circles and arcs. Later in this chapter, I explain how you can use Quick Dimension to edit dimensions as well. Although

Quick Dimension may seem like the answer to all your dimension-related prayers, you can't use it in every case. However, it works well in "mass-production" situations. Dimensions created with the QDIM command are fully associative, so that any changes that you make to objects automatically update their associated dimensions.

Here's how it works, in three easy steps:

1. Choose Annotate tab ⇨ Dimensions panel ⇨ Quick Dimension.

2. At the `Select geometry to dimension:` prompt, select all the objects that you want to dimension. You can't use object snaps; you need to select objects. If you select an object in error, type **r** ↵ and then pick the object again to remove it. Then type **a** ↵ to start adding objects again.

3. At the `Specify dimension line position, or [Continuous/Staggered/ Baseline/Ordinate/Radius/Diameter/datumPoint/Edit/seTtings] <Continuous>:` prompt, right-click and choose the type of dimension that you want to create. Figure 14.29 shows a set of continuous dimensions. The Datum Point option sets a new base point for baseline and ordinate dimensions. You can press Enter to use the type of dimension that you just used previously because that shows as the default. The command immediately creates the dimensions for you.

FIGURE 14.29

A set of continuous dimensions created with Quick Dimension

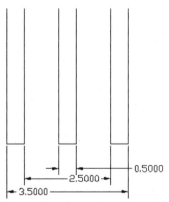

ON THE WEB
The drawing used in the following exercise on using Quick Dimension to create dimensions, `ab14-f.dwg`, is available from the Drawings download on the companion website.

14

STEPS: Using Quick Dimension to Create Dimensions

1. Open ab14-f.dwg, available from the Drawings download on the companion website.

2. Save the file as ab14-07.dwg in your AutoCAD Bible folder. This is the same drawing that you used in the previous exercise, except that some of the dimensions have been removed (see Figure 14.30). Object Snap mode should be turned off.

FIGURE 14.30

You can use Quick Dimension to dimension the circles and create continuous dimensions.

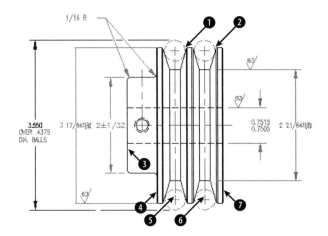

3. Choose Annotate tab ⇨ Dimensions panel ⇨ Quick Dimension. Follow the prompts:

```
Select geometry to dimension: Pick the circle at ❶ in Figure 14.30.
Select geometry to dimension: Pick the circle at ❷.
Select geometry to dimension: ↵
Specify dimension line position, or
[Continuous/Staggered/Baseline/Ordinate/Radius/Diameter/datum Point/Edit/
    seTtings]
<Staggered>: Right-click and choose Radius.
Specify dimension line position, or
[Continuous/Staggered/Baseline/Ordinate/Radius/Diameter/datum Point/Edit/
    seTtings]
<Radius>: Pick a point on the left circle at about 80 degrees from the
    right quadrant.
```

Quick Dimension places the radius dimensions.

4. Repeat the QDIM command. Follow the prompts:

```
Select geometry to dimension: Pick the line at ❸ in Figure 14.30.
Select geometry to dimension: Pick the line at ❹.
Select geometry to dimension: Pick the vertical centerline at ❺.
Select geometry to dimension: Pick the vertical centerline at ❻.
Select geometry to dimension: Pick the line at ❼.
Select geometry to dimension: ↵
Specify dimension line position, or
[Continuous/Staggered/Baseline/Ordinate/Radius/Diameter/datumPoint/Edit/
    seTtings]
<Staggered>: Right-click and choose Baseline.
Specify dimension line position, or
[Continuous/Staggered/Baseline/Ordinate/Radius/Diameter/datumPoint/Edit/
    seTtings]
<Baseline>: Pick a point below the model.
```

Quick Dimension places the baseline dimensions.

5. Save your drawing. It should look approximately like Figure 14.31.

FIGURE 14.31

The model with added radius and baseline dimensions

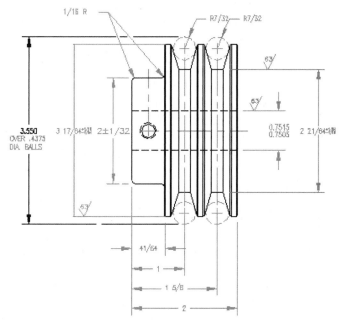

Creating Inspection Dimensions

Inspection dimensions specify how often you want the manufacturer of a part to check its measurements, and sometimes to what tolerance. For example, you may want 50 percent of the parts to be checked and require that they be accurate to within $1/16$ of an inch. Inspection dimensions allow you to add a label and inspection percentage to an existing dimension. Figure 14.32 shows an inspection dimension, using a rounded frame. You create inspection dimensions by selecting an existing dimension.

FIGURE 14.32

An inspection dimension adds a label and an inspection percentage to a dimension for the purpose of quality control.

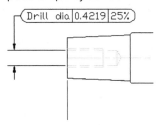

 To create an inspection dimension, first select an existing dimension. Then choose Annotate tab ⇨ Dimensions panel ⇨ Inspect to start the DIMINSPECT command and open the Inspection Dimension dialog box, as shown in Figure 14.33.

FIGURE 14.33

Use the Inspection Dimension dialog box to format inspection dimensions.

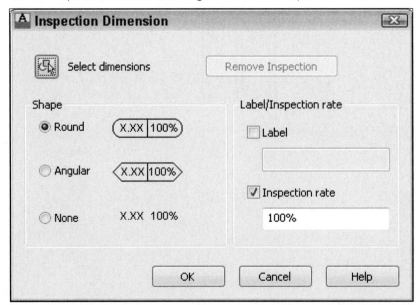

If you haven't already selected a dimension, you can click the Select Dimensions button and do so at this point. In the Shape section, choose the Round, Angular, or None option. In the Label/Inspection Rate section, check the Label check box if you want to add a text label. Then enter the text of the label. The Inspection Rate check box is checked by default. Enter an inspection rate and click OK. To change the values of an inspection dimension, select it and use the Misc section of the Properties palette.

Creating Geometric Tolerances

You can use the TOLERANCE command to create geometric tolerances. (For another way to specify tolerances, see Chapter 15.) This command creates feature control frames, which define tolerances. This method of denoting tolerances conforms to international standards such as ISO (International Standards Organization), ANSI (American National Standards Institute), or JIS (Japanese Industrial Standards). Figure 14.34 shows a drawing that uses tolerance feature-control frames.

FIGURE 14.34

An example of tolerance feature-control frames

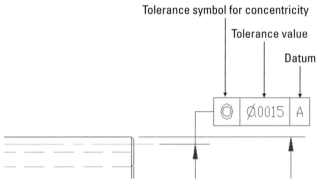

Thanks to Jerry Butterfield of Clow Value Company, Oskaloosa, Iowa, for this drawing.

Starting the tolerance frame

Creating a tolerance frame is a step-by-step process that depends on what information you want to include. To start the frame, choose Annotate tab ⇨ Dimensions panel (expanded) ⇨ Tolerance, which starts the TOLERANCE command and opens the Geometric Tolerance dialog box, as shown in Figure 14.35.

Use this dialog box to build the frame. The frame enables you to create two rows of two tolerances and three datum references (for up to three dimensions), as well as a projected tolerance zone value and a symbol and datum identifier. You'll rarely, if ever, use all the features in the frame.

FIGURE 14.35

The Geometric Tolerance dialog box

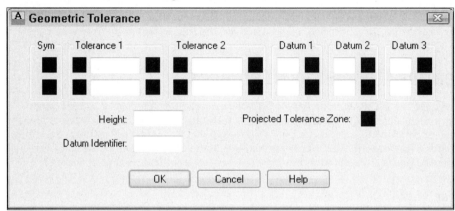

Follow these steps to build the frame:

1. Click the first Sym box to open the Symbol dialog box, as shown in Figure 14.36.

   FIGURE 14.36

   Use the Symbol dialog box to choose the symbol for the type of geometry for which you want to specify tolerance.

   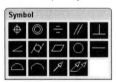

2. Choose the symbol for the geometric characteristic that you are tolerancing. (Table 14.1 explains these symbols.) If you don't need a symbol, click the blank box. The Symbol dialog box disappears.

3. To insert a diameter symbol before the first tolerance, click the black Dia box to the left of the text box in the Tolerance 1 section.

4. Type the tolerance value in the Value box.

5. If you want to specify a material condition, click the black MC box to the right of the text box. The Material Condition dialog box opens, as shown in Figure 14.37. Choose the symbol that you want. The dialog box disappears.

6. If desired, complete a second tolerance.

7. If desired, type a datum in the Datum box of the Datum 1 section, usually A.

8. If desired, add a material condition, using the same method described in Step 5.

FIGURE 14.37

The Material Condition dialog box

9. If desired, type in datum references in the Datum 2 and Datum 3 sections, usually B and C with material conditions.

10. If you need to specify a projected tolerance zone for a perpendicular part, type a value in the Height box. Then click the Projected Tolerance Zone box to insert the Projected Tolerance Zone symbol.

11. Finally, if you want to specify a datum identifier, type the identifier letter in the Datum Identifier box.

12. Click OK to return to your drawing.

If you choose a material condition symbol and then change your mind, click the MC box again and choose the blank square to delete your symbol.

TABLE 14.1 **Tolerance Symbols**

Symbol	Name	Symbol	Name
◎	Position	▱	Flatness
◎	Concentricity	○	Circularity
=	Symmetry	▬	Straightness
//	Parallelism	⌒	Surface profile
⊥	Perpendicularity	⌒	Line profile
∠	Angularity	↗	Circular runout
⌭	Cylindricity	↗↗	Total runout

Inserting the tolerance frame

After you complete the frame, you're returned to your drawing with the `Enter tolerance location:` prompt on the command line. Specify any point to insert the frame.

Editing a tolerance frame

To edit a geometric tolerance, select it and open the Properties palette. To change the text, click the Text Override item and then click the Ellipsis button at the right. The Geometric Tolerance dialog box opens, and you can make any changes that you need. Click OK to return to your drawing.

STEPS: Creating Geometric Tolerances

1. Open `ab14-g.dwg`, available from the Drawings download on the companion website.

2. Save the file as `ab14-08.dwg` in your `AutoCAD Bible` folder. This drawing of a gear operator is shown in Figure 14.38. The Dim layer is current.

FIGURE 14.38

A mechanical drawing using geometric tolerances

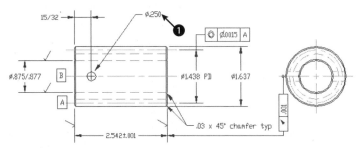

3. Choose Annotate tab ⇨ Dimensions panel (expanded) ⇨ Tolerance. In the Geometric Tolerance dialog box, click the top-left box, labeled Sym.

4. The Symbol dialog box opens. Choose the top-left symbol (for position).

5. In the Tolerance 1 section of the Geometric Tolerance dialog box, click the next black box, which is the Dia box, to insert the diameter symbol. In the Value box, type **.004**. Click the next black box, which is the MC box. In the Material Condition dialog box, choose the first image tile (for Maximum material condition).

6. In the Datum 1 section, type **B** in the Datum box. Click OK.

7. At the `Enter tolerance location:` prompt, pick ❶, shown in Figure 14.38, to place the geometric tolerance.

8. Save your drawing. It should look like Figure 14.39.

FIGURE 14.39

The drawing with the added geometric tolerance frame

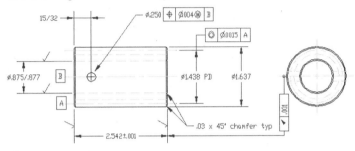

Editing Dimensions

Dimensions have many properties — text size, arrowhead size, text placement, and so on. You change most of these properties by changing the dimension style — either globally changing all dimensions using that style, or overriding a dimension style setting for a particular dimension. The next chapter covers dimension styles, but here I cover several other ways to edit dimensions.

Editing associativity

The DIMASSOC system variable specifies whether dimensions are associative. Here are the settings:

- **0** creates exploded dimensions. Each part of the dimension is a separate object, and there is no association between the dimension and the object that it dimensions.

- **1** creates nonassociative dimensions. The dimension is all one object but is not updated if the object that it dimensions is changed.

- **2** creates associative dimensions. The dimension is all one object and is updated if the object that it dimensions is changed.

> **CAUTION**
>
> By default, new drawings created in AutoCAD 2013 and AutoCAD LT 2013 are associative. However, drawings created in releases prior to 2002 or if you use an old drawing template are not associative. If you open pre-2002 release drawings and save them as 2013 drawings, you should change the DIMASSOC system variable's value to 2.

14

DIMREASSOCIATE

Use the DIMREASSOCIATE command to associate dimensions with their objects. You need to use this command when you open drawings that were dimensioned without the DIMASSOC system variable being set to 2 (typically, drawings created in releases prior to AutoCAD 2002.) You might also need to use this command when dimensions become disassociated from their objects, perhaps through some editing process, or to reassociate dimensions after you've disassociated them for some reason.

The Disassociated option of the DIMREASSOCIATE command allows you to select all dimensions that are not associated with an object snap point on an object.

To use DIMREASSOCIATE, follow these steps:

1. Choose Annotate tab ⇨ Dimensions panel (expanded) ⇨ Reassociate.

2. At the `Select objects or [Disassociated]:` prompt, select the dimensions that you want to associate. Press Enter to end object selection. Use the Disassociated option if you want to select all dimensions in the drawing that are currently not associated an object.

    You see a prompt that varies according to the type of dimension you've selected. For example, for linear dimensions, you see the `Specify first extension line origin or [Select object] <next>:` prompt. At the same time, you see a marker in the form of an X that corresponds to the prompt, as shown in Figure 14.40. The marker indicates an *association point* (a point that connects an object and all or part of its dimension). If the X has a box around it, the dimension is already associated with the point marked by the X.

> **NOTE**
>
> If you use the wheel of a mouse to pan or zoom, the X disappears. Press Esc and start the command again or type 'redraw ↵.

FIGURE 14.40

When you associate a dimension with an object, an association point appears on the object.

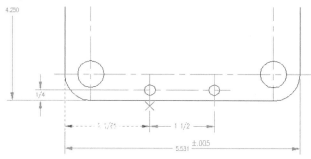

3. Use an object snap to specify the location of the X (whether the same location as shown or a different location) or use the Select Object option to select an object (right-click and choose Select Object). To skip to the next prompt without associating the dimension to the marked point, press Enter.

4. Continue to respond to the prompts in turn. The command prompts you through all the dimensions you selected.

> **CAUTION**
> When specifying object snaps, be careful that you choose the point you want. For example, if you use an endpoint object snap where two lines meet, you cannot be sure of which line's endpoint you've chosen. When you move or stretch the line that you expect to be associated with the dimension, you may find that the dimension doesn't budge. That's because it's actually associated with a different line. Selecting the object itself is often a better solution, because the dimension is associated with the object.

DIMDISASSOCIATE

Occasionally, you may want to edit a dimension in such a way that you need to remove its associativity. Perhaps you need to squeeze it into a tight corner. For these times, use the DIMDISASSOCIATE command by typing it on the command line. At the prompt, select the dimensions that you want to disassociate from their objects.

> **NOTE**
> You cannot disassociate dimensions that are on locked layers. Unlock the layer first and then disassociate the dimension.

DIMREGEN

The DIMREGEN command updates the locations of all associative dimensions. This command, which you type on the command line, is needed only if:

- You pan or zoom with a wheel mouse in a paper space layout while model space is active.
- You open a drawing containing dimensioned objects that have been edited with a previous release of AutoCAD or AutoCAD LT.
- You open a drawing containing external references that are dimensioned in the current drawing, and dimensioned objects in the external reference have been changed.

Using the DIMEDIT command

The DIMEDIT command offers four ways to edit dimensions. The advantage of this command is that you can change more than one dimension at a time. Type **dimedit** ⏎ on the command line. The command responds with the `Enter type of dimension editing [Home/New/Rotate/Oblique] <Home>:` prompt. Right-click to choose one of the options:

- **Home.** Moves dimension text to its default position as defined by the dimension style.
- **New.** Lets you type new text to replace the existing text. The In-Place Text Editor opens, showing zeros to represent the dimension text. You can use this option to add a suffix, such as TYP (typical), to several dimensions.

14

- **Rotate.** Rotates the dimension text. This works like the rotation angle for text.
- **Oblique.** Angles the extension lines of the dimension. Use this when you have several dimensions close together that interfere with each other. Specify the final angle of the extension lines, *not* the rotation from the current angle.

> **NOTE**
> The Annotate tab ⇨ Dimensions panel (expanded) ⇨ Oblique item executes the DIMEDIT command with the Oblique option.

As soon as you choose an option, DIMEDIT prompts you to select objects. You can select as many dimensions as you want. You have the opportunity to use the DIMEDIT command in an exercise after the next section.

Using the DIMTEDIT command

The DIMTEDIT command repositions dimension text. To start the command, choose Annotate tab ⇨ Dimensions panel (expanded) and choose one of the options described in the following list. Although its name gives the impression that you can edit the text content, you can only change its position. Also, you can edit only one dimension at a time. The command responds with the `Select dimension:` prompt. Select a dimension.

At the `Specify new location for dimension text or [Left/Right/Center/Home/Angle]:` prompt, you can use the cursor to pick a text location. You can also right-click and choose one of the options:

- **Left Justify.** Left-justifies the text of linear, radial, or diameter dimensions.
- **Center Justify.** Centers the text of linear, radial, or diameter dimensions.
- **Right Justify.** Right-justifies the text of linear, radial, or diameter dimensions.
- **Restore Default Text Position (Home).** Returns dimension text to its default position and angle.
- *Text* **Angle.** Rotates dimension text. This option is equivalent to the Rotate option of the DIMEDIT command.

> **ON THE WEB**
> The drawing used in the following exercise on using DIMEDIT and DIMTEDIT to edit dimensions, `ab14-h.dwg`, is available from the Drawings download on the companion website.

STEPS: Using DIMEDIT and DIMTEDIT to Edit Dimensions

1. Open `ab14-h.dwg`, available from the Drawings download on the companion website.
2. Save the file as `ab14-09.dwg` in your `AutoCAD Bible` folder. This is a civil engineering drawing whose dimensions need some editing (see Figure 14.41).
3. The dimension at ❶ in Figure 14.41 is not in the proper units because the text was entered explicitly as 14.41 units. To correct this error, enter **dimedit** ↵ on the command line. At the `Enter type of dimension editing [Home/New/Rotate/Oblique] <Home>:` prompt,

right-click and choose New. The In-Place Text Editor opens, showing zeros. Because you want the original text, click outside of the In-Place Text Editor. At the `Select objects:` prompt, pick ❶. Press Enter to end object selection. (You could correct several dimensions this way.) This action corrects the dimension, automatically creating the text in the current units.

4. The dimension text at ❷ in Figure 14.41 is too close to the dimension line of the vertical dimension that crosses it. Choose Annotate tab ⇨ Dimensions panel (expanded) ⇨ Right Justify. At the `Select dimension:` prompt, pick ❷. This action moves the text to the right.

5. Save your drawing.

FIGURE 14.41

A dimensioned civil engineering drawing

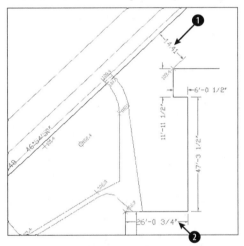

Flipping dimension arrows

Sometimes you might want to place an arrow outside the extension line, but facing inward. For example, you might do this in a tight space. Figure 14.42 shows a dimension with a flipped arrow.

FIGURE 14.42

You can flip an arrow so that it displays outside the extension line, pointing inward.

To flip an arrow, select a dimension when no command is active. Pass the cursor over the grip closest to the arrow you want to flip. From the menu that appears, choose Flip Arrow. Repeat the process to unflip the arrow. When you are done flipping arrows, press Esc to clear the grips from the dimensions.

Editing dimension text

You can edit dimension text as you would any other multiline text object. Enter **ddedit** ↵ on the command line. At the `Select an annotation object or [Undo]:` prompt, choose the dimension. The In-Place Text Editor opens. Using the In-Place Text Editor for dimension text has already been covered in this chapter under the Mtext option of the dimensioning commands.

Using the Properties palette to edit dimensions

You can edit dimensions by using the Properties palette just as you can edit the properties of any other object. Select any dimension and open the Properties palette. You see the properties of the dimensions that you can edit. You can also edit dimensions in the Quick Properties palette; however, fewer properties are available.

Many of these settings make more sense after you learn about dimension styles, which are covered in the next chapter. For example, the listings for Primary Units, Alternate Units, Fit, Lines & Arrows, Text, and so on duplicate the tabs in the New Dimension Style and Modify Dimension Style dialog boxes. You can change the color, layer, lineweight, and linetype. To override the automatic dimension text, enter the text in the Text Override field of the Text section of the Properties palette or the Quick Properties palette.

> **TIP**
> You can create a background mask like the one that you can create for multiline text. (For more information, see Chapter 13.) If dimension text covers other objects, select the dimension and open the Properties palette (Ctrl+1). Choose a color from the Fill Color drop-down list in the Text section. For the background mask to work, the dimension needs to be on top of any other objects that it overlaps. To bring a dimension to the top, use the TEXTTOFRONT command.

> **NOTE**
> You can convert a dimension to a dimensional constraint. For the complete discussion of constraints, see Chapter 10. Enter dimconstraint ↵ on the command line and select the dimension to convert.

Changing annotative scales

Dimension and multileader styles can be annotative, meaning that they can automatically change scale based on the scale of a viewport on a layout. (I discuss viewports and layouts in Chapter 17.) I've mentioned in this chapter how to make a dimension and multileader style annotative.

You can change the annotative scales of any dimension or multileader that uses an annotative style by using the OBJECTSCALE command. Follow these steps:

1. Select the dimension or multileader. (You can select more than one.)
2. Open the Properties palette. In the Misc section, click the Annotative Scale item to display the Ellipsis button.
3. Click the Ellipsis button to open the Annotation Object Scale dialog box.
   - To add an annotation scale, click the Add button. Choose a scale from the Add Scales to Object dialog box and click OK.
   - To delete an annotation scale, select it and click the Delete button.
4. Click OK.

> **TIP**
> You can also select one or more annotative objects, right-click in the drawing area, and choose Annotative Object Scale.

Spacing dimensions equally apart

Sometimes, after you've created a number of linear or angular dimensions, you realize that they would look neater if they were equally spaced. Rather than re-create or move them, you can use the DIMSPACE command to space existing dimensions. You can let the command determine the spacing automatically, or you can specify a spacing.

In order for this command to work, the dimensions must meet the following conditions:

- They must be linear or angular dimensions.
- They must be in a group of the same kind of dimension. For example, you might have all linear dimensions. If one is rotated, they must all be rotated; if one is aligned, they must all be aligned.
- The dimensions must be parallel (for linear) or concentric (for angular).
- The dimensions must share an extension line.

To space dimensions, choose Annotate tab ⇨ Dimensions panel ⇨ Adjust Space. At the `Select base dimension:` prompt, select a dimension close to which you want to place the other dimensions. At the `Select dimensions to space:` prompt, select the rest of the dimensions that you want to space.

At the `Enter value or [Auto] <Auto>:` prompt, enter a spacing or use the Auto option to let the command figure out the spacing itself. You can use a value of 0 to align the dimensions along the same horizontal or vertical line.

Breaking dimensions

It's not good form for dimensions to cross other dimensions or objects. Many disciplines break a dimension or extension line where it crosses an object with a small space. This gives the appearance that the object is in front of the dimension. You can break dimensions or multileaders by using the DIMBREAK command.

The great feature of DIMBREAK is that if you move the object to another location where it still crosses the dimension, the break moves accordingly.

 To break a dimension or multileader, choose Annotate tab ➪ Dimensions panel ➪ Break. At the `Select dimension to add/remove break or [Multiple]:` prompt, select the dimension you want to break. At the `Select object to break dimension or [Auto/Manual/Remove] <Auto>:` prompt, select the object that crosses the dimension. The `Select object to break dimension:` prompt repeats so that you can select another object that crosses the dimension, if any. Otherwise, press Enter to end the command.

You can use the Manual option to specify two points on the dimension line or extension line. In this way, you can set the size of the break yourself. However, if you use the Manual option, the break does not update if you move the crossing object.

Use the Multiple option at the first prompt to create breaks in more than one dimension at a time. You then select the dimensions. At the `Select object to break dimensions or [Auto/Remove] <Auto>:` prompt, choose the Auto option so that you can break all the dimensions.

If you want to remove an existing break, use the Remove option.

You can set a break size when you create a dimension or multileader style. For dimensions, use the Break Size text box on the Symbols and Arrows tab of the Modify Dimension Style dialog box. For Multileaders, use the Break Size text box on the Leader Format tab of the Modify Multileader Style dialog box.

Using Quick Dimension to edit dimensions

You can also use Quick Dimension to edit dimensions, whether created with QDIM or some other dimensioning command. When you select the geometry and dimensions you want to edit, you see an X at each eligible edit point, as shown in Figure 14.43.

Here's what you can do with QDIM:

- You can join two dimensions by removing the edit points between them.
- You can split a dimension into two dimensions by adding edit points within the existing dimension.
- You can move the dimension line.
- You can change the type of dimension.

FIGURE 14.43

When you edit with QDIM, you see an X at eligible edit points.

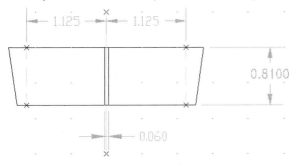

> **CAUTION**
>
> Editing with QDIM works best when the geometry is simple. Unless you can select only the geometry and dimensions that you want to work with, you'll end up changing dimensions that you don't want to edit.

To edit dimensions with QDIM, follow these steps:

1. Choose Annotate tab ⇨ Dimensions panel ⇨ Quick Dimension.

2. At the `Select geometry to dimension:` prompt, select the geometry and the dimensions that you want to edit.

3. At the `Specify dimension line position, or [Continuous/Staggered/ Baseline/Ordinate/Radius/Diameter/datumPoint/Edit/seTtings] <Continuous>:` prompt, right-click and choose Edit. You see a cross at each eligible edit point.

4. At the `Indicate dimension point to remove, or [Add/eXit] <eXit>:` prompt, you can:

   - Select the points of the dimensions you want to remove. If you see two possible edit points in line with each other that could be creating the dimension you want to remove, select both of them.

   - Right-click and choose Add. Use object snaps to add one or more points.

   - Right-click and choose Exit to continue with the command.

5. At the `Specify dimension line position, or [Continuous/Staggered/ Baseline/Ordinate/Radius/Diameter/datumPoint/Edit/seTtings] <Continuous>:` prompt, right-click and choose an option if you want to change the type of dimension.

6. The prompt repeats. Pick a location for the new set of dimensions.

7. Press Enter to end the command and update the dimensions.

14

Using grips to edit dimensions

Grips are ideal for moving dimension lines and text. The grips at the dimension line endpoints and the text insertion point are quite useful for making adjustments in dimensions. (I discuss grip editing in Chapter 10.)

To move a dimension line closer or farther from the dimensioned object, pick the dimension to display the grips. Pick one of the grips at the endpoints of the dimension line to highlight it. The `Specify stretch point or [Base point/Copy/Undo/eXit]:` prompt appears. Drag the dimension line to the desired location. Press Esc to remove the grips.

To move dimension text, pick the dimension to display the grips. Pick the grip on the dimension text to highlight it. Drag the dimension text to its desired location.

You can also grip-edit multileaders in the same way. These also have two triangular grips that you can use to change the length of the landing line.

Grips for dimensions and multileaders are multi-functional. When you select a dimension or multileader and pass the cursor over a grip, a list of editing options appears. For example, if you pass the cursor over a grip on a dimension line of a linear dimension, you see Stretch, Continue Dimension, Baseline Dimension, and Flip Arrow options.

Editing objects and dimensions together

Because dimensions are associative, when you edit objects, the dimensions automatically adjust to the new object measurements. Stretching the object with the STRETCH command or grips is usually the best way to accomplish this. The object and the dimension adjust at the same time.

ON THE WEB

The drawing in the following exercise on using DDEDIT, QDIM, grips, and STRETCH to edit dimensions, `ab14-i.dwg`, is available from the Drawings download on the companion website.

STEPS: Using DDEDIT, QDIM, Grips, and STRETCH to Edit Dimensions

1. Open `ab14-i.dwg`, available from the Drawings download on the companion website.

2. Save the file as `ab14-10.dwg` in your `AutoCAD Bible` folder. This is a cross-section of a valve part, as shown in Figure 14.44.

3. To replace the dimension marked Ht., type **ddedit** ↵ on the command line. At the `Select an annotation object or [Undo]:` prompt, choose the dimension at ❶, shown in Figure 14.44. The In-Place Text Editor opens with the text displayed. Select the current text and type **<>**. Click outside the editor. The command automatically creates the original measured dimension. Press Enter to end the command.

4. Select the two dimensions marked ❷, shown in Figure 14.44. Also select the cyan centerline and the two green hidden lines. Choose Annotate tab ⇨ Dimensions panel ⇨ Quick Dimension. At the first prompt, right-click and choose Edit. At the `Indicate dimension point to remove, or [Add/eXit] <eXit>:` prompt, choose the dimension point (each point is marked with an X) on the cyan centerline. Right-click and choose eXit. At the `Specify dimension line position, or [Continuous/Staggered/Baseline/Ordinate/Radius/Diameter/datumPoint/Edit/seTtings] <Continuous>:` prompt, place the dimension line where it was previously. (You can use the outside arrows as a guide.)

FIGURE 14.44

A dimensioned cross-section of a valve part

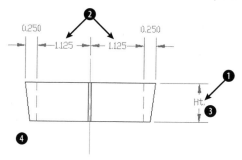
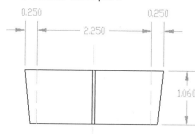

5. Pick the dimension at ❶. Pass the cursor over the grip on the text. Choose Move with Dim Line and drag slightly to the left to place the dimension and its text closer to the object that you are dimensioning.

6. Choose Home tab ⇨ Modify panel ⇨ Stretch. Follow the prompts:

```
Select objects: Pick at ❸.
Specify opposite corner: Pick at ❹.
9 found
Select objects: ↵
Specify base point or [Displacement] <Displacement>: 0,-.25 ↵
Specify second point or <use first point as displacement>: ↵
```

The valve part stretches, and the dimension that measures its height changes accordingly.

7. Save your drawing. It should look like Figure 14.45.

FIGURE 14.45

The edited valve part

Summary

The dimension features in AutoCAD and AutoCAD LT enable you to dimension almost anything. In this chapter, you read about:

- Creating linear, radial, dimension, angular, and ordinate dimensions
- Formatting and creating multileaders
- Dimensioning with the Quick Dimension feature
- Creating inspection dimensions
- Creating tolerances
- Editing dimensions

In the next chapter, I continue the subject of dimensions by explaining how to gain total control with dimension styles.

Creating Dimension Styles

IN THIS CHAPTER

Introducing dimension styles

Classifying a new dimension style

Altering dimension styles

In Chapter 14, you drew many dimensions using the default dimension style. However, you can create your own dimension styles to control the way dimensions appear. Once you're familiar with dimensions, you can learn how to customize them to suit your needs.

Understanding Dimension Styles

You should create your dimension styles before dimensioning. Some drawings have several dimension styles, although a drawing can look confusing if it has too many dimension styles. In general, you create a dimension style, save it in your template drawings, and (you hope) rarely have to deal with it again, except to override a setting for a unique situation.

The various disciplines each have their own standards and customs regarding dimensions. Dimension styles are flexible enough to accommodate any type of dimensioning practice.

 To create a dimension style, choose Annotate tab ⇨ Dimensions panel, and click the dialog box launcher arrow at the right end of the panel title bar to open the Dimension Style Manager, as shown in Figure 15.1. The current dimension style is shown as Standard, which is the default dimension style.

The Dimension Style Manager is the master control room for managing dimensions. Here you create new dimension styles and modify existing ones.

The preset Standard dimension style is most appropriate for mechanical drafting. Whichever type of drafting you do, you'll probably need to make some changes to the default dimension style or create a new dimension style. A preview of the current dimension style is shown at the right side of the dialog box.

To create a new style, click New to open the Create New Dimension Style dialog box, as shown in Figure 15.2. Type a new name in the New Style Name text box. In the Start With drop-down list, choose which existing dimension style you want to use as a basis for the new dimension style. If you have more than one to choose from, choose the style that most resembles the new style you want to create.

FIGURE 15.1

The Dimension Style Manager

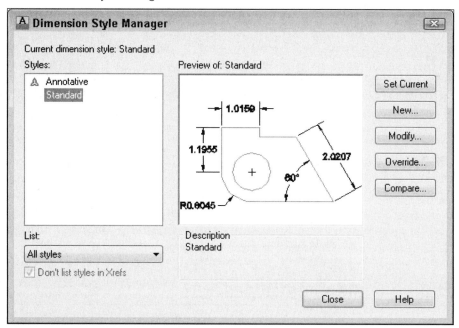

FIGURE 15.2

The Create New Dimension Style dialog box

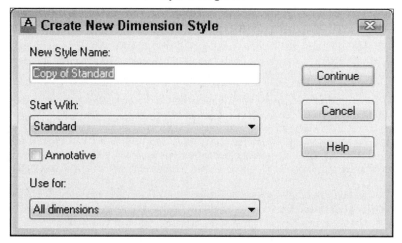

If you want dimensions that use this dimension style to be annotative, check the Annotative check box. Annotative dimensions are valuable when you will be displaying your model at more than one scale, in separate viewports.

> **NOTE**
> *Annotative* objects automatically scale according to the scale of model space or a viewport on a layout. You use a layout to lay out a drawing for plotting, and viewports display various views of the drawing. Each viewport can have a different scale, and annotative objects automatically adjust in size accordingly. I discuss annotative objects more in Chapter 17.

The Use For drop-down list lets you decide whether you want to use the dimension style for all dimensions or only for a specific type of dimension; you can choose from Linear, Angular, Radius, Diameter, Ordinate, or Leaders and Tolerances. Usually, you create a dimension style for all dimension types. Later in this chapter, I explain how to create variants of dimension styles for specific types of dimensions. When you're done, click Continue.

You can also use the Dimension Style Manager to rename an existing dimension style. Click its name to select it. Click it a second time to see an edit box. Type the new name and press Enter.

Defining a New Dimension Style

Dimension styles have many components, and so the process of defining a dimension style is complex. Your task is organized for you by the tabs of the dialog box.

When you click Continue in the Create New Dimension Style dialog box, the New Dimension Style dialog box opens, as shown in Figure 15.3.

Managing dimension lines

An important part of defining a dimension style is specifying how the dimension lines and extension lines look, which you do on the Lines tab of the New Dimension Style dialog box. In Chapter 14, I illustrate the parts of a dimension. Refer to Figure 14.1, if necessary.

Dimension lines

To set the color of the dimension line so that it differs from that of the rest of the dimension, click the Color drop-down list and choose a color. Choose Select Color to open the Select Color dialog box if you want to use a nonstandard color. Remember, a dimension is a block — that is, it is one object. The default color is ByBlock so that dimensions take on the color of the current layer or color setting. In general, you should have a separate layer for dimensions so that the entire dimension is the color set for that layer. Use this setting only if you want the dimension lines to be a different color from your dimension layer color. The arrowheads do not have a separate color setting and always follow the dimension-line setting.

 See Chapter 11 for a discussion of how to use the Select Color dialog box. See Chapter 18 for coverage of blocks.

15

FIGURE 15.3

The New Dimension Style dialog box with the Lines tab displayed

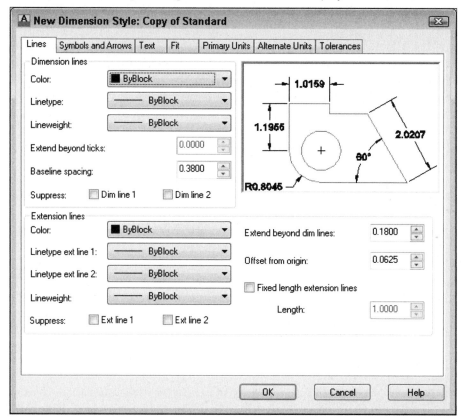

To specify a linetype for a dimension, choose one from the Linetype drop-down list. If the linetype that you want isn't on the list, then you need to load it. To do this, choose Other to open the Select Linetype dialog box. (For more information on loading linetypes, see Chapter 11.) The default lineweight is ByBlock, which means that it takes on the lineweight of the current layer. To set a lineweight for the dimension line, click the Lineweight drop-down list and choose a lineweight. In general, you want your objects to stand out, so dimensions should have a lineweight the same as, or narrower than, the objects that you're dimensioning.

The Extend Beyond Ticks text box determines how far the dimension lines extend past the extension lines. When you have arrowheads at the ends of the dimension lines, the Extension option is unavailable. However, if you choose Architectural Tick, Oblique, Dot Small, Integral, or None in the Arrowheads section of the dialog box, the Extend Beyond Ticks option becomes available. This type of extension is typical for architectural drafting. Figure 15.4 shows a dimension with an architectural tick and a 0.1-unit extension.

The Baseline spacing text box determines the distance between successive dimension lines when you create baseline dimensions with the DIMBASELINE command. This specification creates evenly spaced dimension lines. (In Chapter 14, I discuss the DIMSPACE command, which lets you evenly space any linear or angular dimensions.)

FIGURE 15.4

A typical architectural dimension showing the text above one dimension line, an architectural tick, and the dimension line extending slightly beyond the extension lines

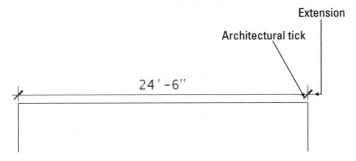

In some dimension styles, the dimension text splits the dimension line into two parts, as shown in Figure 15.5. This creates two dimension lines. You can suppress — that is, turn off — the first or second dimension line (or both dimension lines) by checking the appropriate box (or boxes). The first line is nearest where you specified the first extension-line origin. (If you selected an object instead of specifying two extension-line origins, you may not be able to predict which dimension line is the first and which is the second. Experiment.) You would usually suppress dimension lines when they interfere with other dimensions or with objects in your drawing. (The DIMBREAK command, which I cover in Chapter 14, breaks dimensions where they cross objects. You may be able to break a dimension instead of suppressing one of the dimension lines.)

FIGURE 15.5

A typical mechanical dimension with text splitting two dimension lines

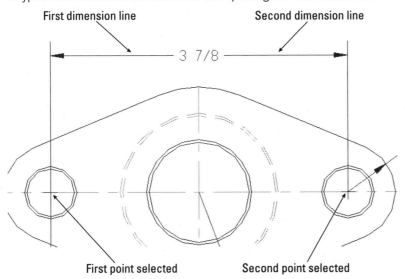

Extension lines

As with dimension lines, you can pick a color for the extension lines that differs from that of the rest of the dimension. Click the Color drop-down list and choose a color. Choose Select Color to open the Select Color dialog box if you want a nonstandard color. The default color is ByBlock so that extensions take on the color of the current layer or color setting.

You can choose a separate linetype for each extension line. Choose the linetype that you want from the drop-down lists. If the linetype that you want isn't listed, click Other to open the Select Linetype dialog box, where you can load the linetype that you need. You can also choose a lineweight from the Lineweight drop-down list.

Extension lines typically extend slightly past the dimension line, as you can see in some of the figures in this chapter. Use the Extend Beyond Dim Lines text box to specify this extension distance.

Extension lines don't usually touch the object that they dimension to make it easier to distinguish the dimension from the object. Use the Offset from Origin text box to define the distance from the specified points on the object to the extension lines.

Extension lines usually vary in length throughout a drawing, depending on the shape of the objects that you're dimensioning. However, sometimes you may want the extension lines to all be the same length, even if they don't reach near their objects. This method avoids dimension lines crossing each other when you're dimensioning a complex shape.

To specify fixed-length extension lines, check the Fixed Length Extension Lines check box and specify the length in the Length text box.

You can suppress the first or second extension line (or both lines) so that either or both are not visible. To do this, check the appropriate box (or boxes). Figure 15.6 shows a dimension with the first extension line suppressed.

FIGURE 15.6

A dimension with the first extension line suppressed

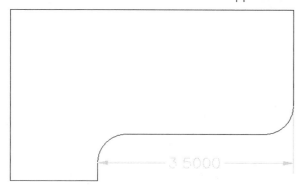

Defining symbols and arrows

The Symbols and Arrows tab organizes your settings related to arrowheads and certain dimension-related symbols, as shown in Figure 15.7. For example, you can define center marks and arc length symbols on this tab.

FIGURE 15.7

The Symbols and Arrows tab lets you define arrowheads and fine-tune dimension symbols.

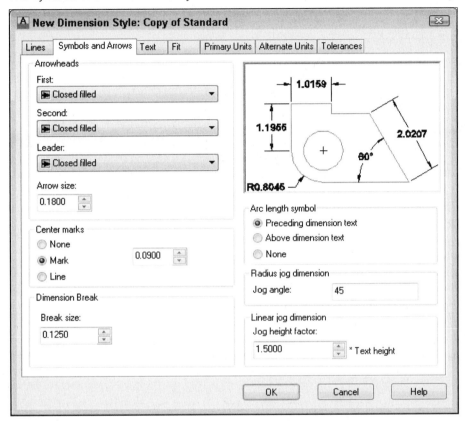

Defining arrowheads

The Arrowheads section controls the arrowheads at the ends of dimension lines. You don't actually have to use arrowheads, as you saw in Figure 15.4. You can also set the first and second arrowheads individually. However, if you change the first arrowhead, the second one follows suit, assuming that you want both ends of the dimension to look the same. To specify two different arrowheads, choose an arrowhead in the first drop-down list and then in the second drop-down list.

You can create and use your own arrowhead:

1. In any drawing, create the arrowhead that you want with a unit size of 1.

2. Make a block out of it. For an arrow-shaped block, pick the point of the arrow for the insertion point and create it pointing to the right. You may have to experiment with the right insertion point. Save the block. (See Chapter 18 for instructions on creating blocks. You can't use annotative blocks as arrowheads.)

3. In the first and second drop-down lists, choose User Arrow. The Select Custom Arrow Block dialog box opens, displaying the blocks available in the drawing.

4. Choose the block that you want from the drop-down list.

15

5. Click OK.

Figure 15.8 shows a dimension with a user arrow.

FIGURE 15.8

A dimension with a user arrow

Set the size of the arrowhead in the Arrow Size text box. As explained later in this chapter in the discussion of scale, you should use the final size that you want to see when the drawing is plotted on paper.

Defining symbols

The Center Marks section of the Symbols and Arrows tab in the New Dimension Style dialog box specifies how you want to mark the centers of arcs and circles when you choose Annotate tab ⇨ Dimensions panel (expanded) ⇨ Center Mark (the DIMCENTER command). In the Center Marks section, choose Mark to create a small cross, Line to create a cross plus four lines that cross, or None. Figure 15.9 shows a circle with centerlines and an arc with a center mark.

Specify the size of the center mark or centerline in the text box to the right of the Center Marks section. For center marks, the size is the distance from the intersection of the two lines to their endpoints. If you use centerlines, the size also determines the distance from the circle quadrants to the end of the centerlines.

FIGURE 15.9

A circle with a centerline and an arc with a center mark

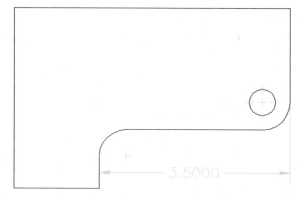

In the Dimension Break section, specify the break size. A dimension break is a gap in the dimension where it crosses an object. I discuss dimension breaks (the DIMBREAK command) in Chapter 14.

The Arc Length Symbol section is for specifying the location of the symbol used when you dimension arc lengths. By default, the symbol goes before the dimension value, but you can choose to put it on top or omit it completely. For more information on arc length dimensions, see Chapter 14.

The Radius Jog Dimension section lets you specify the angle used when you create a jogged dimension for circles or arcs with large radii. A jogged dimension is a small dimension that doesn't reach to the center of the circle or arc. For more information on jogged dimensions, see Chapter 14.

In the Linear Jog Dimension section, specify a jog height factor for linear jogs. A jog is a zigzag symbol that indicates that the object is not drawn to scale, usually due to space limitations. For more information, see Chapter 14. You specify the size in relation to the text height for the dimension. The default is 1.5 times the text height. I discuss dimension text height in the next section.

Because the Standard dimension style is closest to mechanical drafting standards, in the following exercise you start to create an architectural dimension style, using the Standard style as a base. This requires you to make a maximum number of changes, thereby letting you become as familiar as possible with the dimension style settings. Here you practice controlling dimension lines and arrows.

ON THE WEB
The drawing used in the following exercise on controlling dimension lines and arrows, `ab15-a.dwg`, is available from the Drawings download on the companion website.

STEPS: Controlling Dimension Lines and Arrows

1. Open `ab15-a.dwg`, available from the Drawings download on the companion website.

2. Save the file as `ab15-01.dwg` in your `AutoCAD Bible` folder. This drawing is an elevation of a garage, as shown in Figure 15.10. Ortho Mode and Object Snap should be on. Set running object snaps for Endpoint and Intersection. The Dim layer is current.

3. To see what the Standard dimension style looks like, choose Annotate tab ⇨ Dimensions panel ⇨ Dimension drop-down menu ⇨ Linear. At the `Specify first extension line origin or <select object>:` prompt, pick ❶, shown in Figure 15.10. At the `Specify second extension line origin:` prompt, pick ❷. At the `Specify dimension line location or [Mtext/Text/Angle/Horizontal/Vertical/Rotated]:` prompt, pick a location for the dimension line below the line that you dimensioned. The arrows and text are so small that you can't even see them.

4. Choose View tab ⇨ Navigate 2D panel ⇨ Zoom drop-down menu ⇨ Zoom Window and specify a window near ❶ and the left end of the dimension. Press Enter to repeat the ZOOM command, and then enter **p** ↵ to perform a Zoom Previous. Zoom in on the center of the dimension to see the text. Do a Zoom Previous again. As you can see, this dimension needs some modification.

5. Choose Annotate tab ⇨ Dimensions panel, and click the dialog box launcher arrow on the right side of the panel title bar. The current dimension style should be Standard. Click New. In the New Style Name text box, type **Arch 48** and click Continue.

15

6. Click the Symbols and Arrows tab if it isn't on top. In the Arrowheads section, choose Oblique from the first drop-down list. The size should be 3/16".

7. Click the Lines tab. In the Dimension Lines section, type **3/32** in the Extend Beyond Ticks text box. (Because of the units precision setting — which you set with the UNITS command — this value is rounded off to 1/8" in the display, although the value is still 3/32.) Click OK to return to the Dimension Style Manager.

8. In the Dimension Style Manager, notice that the arrows have been changed to ticks in the preview. Click Close.

9. Select the dimension that you created in Step 3. Choose Annotate tab ➪ Dimensions panel ➪ Dimension Style drop-down list, and choose Arch 48. Press Esc. The dimension now has the geometry settings that you just made. To check it out, do a Zoom Window to the left end of the dimension. You can see that the oblique mark has replaced the arrow. Do a Zoom Previous.

10. Save your drawing. Keep this drawing open if you're continuing on to the next exercise.

FIGURE 15.10

The garage elevation

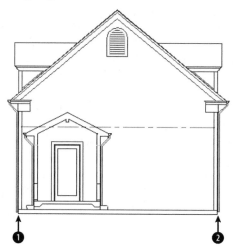

GARAGE SOUTH ELEV 1/4" = 1'-0"

Managing dimension text

You can format the text of the dimension for readability and to match other text in your drawing. In the New Dimension Style dialog box, the Text tab, shown in Figure 15.11, controls text appearance, placement, and alignment.

Text appearance

You have full control over dimension text appearance, as you do over any other text in your drawing. To specify a text style for your dimension text, choose a text style from the Text style drop-down list. You may want to create a special text style, such as Dim Text, for dimension text, to give you the flexibility to alter dimension text without changing other text in your drawing. Create the dimension text style before creating your dimension style. If you want the dimension to be annotative, its text style should also be annotative.

 See Chapter 13 for a discussion of text styles.

Choose a color from the Text Color drop-down list. You can pick a color for the dimension text that differs from that of the rest of the dimension. The default color is ByBlock so that dimensions take on the color of the current layer or color setting. Use this setting only if you want the dimension text to be a different color from your dimension layer color. To choose a nonstandard color, choose Select Color from the drop-down list to open the Select Color dialog box.

FIGURE 15.11

The Text tab of the New Dimension Style dialog box

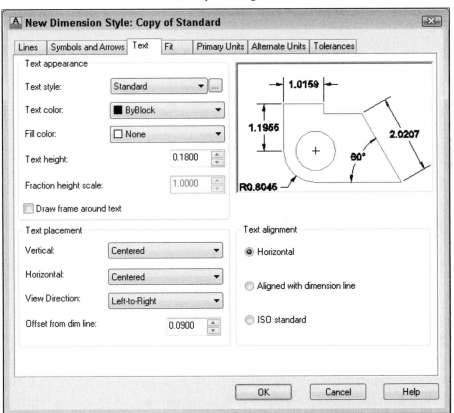

You can create a block of color around the dimension text so that if other objects are behind the dimension, you can still read the dimension text clearly. To add a color, choose one from the Fill Color drop-down list.

Choose the height for your dimension text. When you set the text style height to zero, you can set the height in the New Dimension Style dialog box. Otherwise, the text style height takes over. It's much easier to make all your dimension style adjustments in one place than to make changes in the text style as well.

If your unit type uses fractions, use the fraction height scale to set a ratio of fraction text to whole text. This option is available only if your units specify the use of fractions. You may want the fractions to be smaller than whole numbers. A scale of 0.5 makes the fractions half the size of whole numbers; the resulting overall fraction is slightly higher than the whole numbers of the dimension text.

Some dimension styles require a border around the dimension text. If you want to include a rectangular border, check the Draw Frame Around Text check box.

Text placement

The Vertical drop-down list affects how text is justified relative to the dimension line. As you make changes, be sure to look at the preview to see whether the results are what you want. You have the following options:

- **Centered.** Centers the text in the dimension line, breaking the dimension line into two. This is typical for mechanical drafting. You can see an example in Figure 15.5.
- **Above.** Places text above the dimension line. This is typical for architectural drafting. You can see an example in Figure 15.4.
- **Outside.** Places the text on the side of the dimension line that is farthest from the object that you're dimensioning.
- **JIS.** Places text in conformation to the Japanese Industrial Standards rules, which vary the placement according to the angle of the dimension line.
- **Below.** Places text below the dimension line.

The Horizontal drop-down list affects the placement of dimension text between the extension lines. Here again, you have a handy visual confirmation of your choice. You have the following choices:

- **Centered.** This is the default. It centers text between the two extension lines.
- **At Ext Line 1.** Places the text next to the first extension line. The first extension line is always the first point that you specified at the `Specify first extension line origin or <select object>:` prompt. The picture and the words Horizontal Justification can be especially confusing for vertical dimensions. If you aren't consistent in how you pick your dimensions, you can get some strange results.
- **At Ext Line 2.** Places the text next to the second extension line. The comments for the previous option apply to this option as well.
- **Over Ext Line 1.** Places the text over the first extension line. The comments for the At Ext Line 1 option apply to this option as well.
- **Over Ext Line 2.** Places the text over the second extension line. The comments for the At Ext Line 1 option apply to this option as well.

The View Direction drop-down list affects the direction of the text. You have two choices:

- **Left-to-Right.** Displays the text starting on the left reading to the right.
- **Right-to-Left.** Displays the text starting on the right reading to the left.

Use the Offset from Dim Line text box to set the gap between the dimension text and the dimension line. This sets the DIMGAP system variable. If the dimension line is broken, the gap is the space between each side of the dimension text and the two dimension lines. If the dimension line is unbroken and the text is above the line, the gap is the space between the bottom of the text and the dimension line. The gap also controls the space between the box created for Basic tolerance dimensions and the text inside them. Basic tolerances are discussed in the "Formatting tolerances" section later in this chapter.

> **TIP**
> When trying to fit dimension text, lines, and arrows into a narrow space, AutoCAD and AutoCAD LT also use the gap (the DIMGAP value) to calculate the minimum space required on either side of the dimension text. Therefore, reducing the gap can help fit more of the dimension elements between the extension lines.

Text alignment

Different disciplines have different standards for aligning dimension text. The Text Alignment section of the Text tab affects how the text is aligned relative to the dimension line, as follows:

- **Horizontal.** Keeps text between the extension lines horizontal, regardless of the angle of the dimension line (typical of mechanical drawings).
- **Aligned with Dimension Line.** Keeps text at the same angle as the dimension line (typical of architectural drawings).
- **ISO Standard.** Uses the ISO standard, which aligns text with the dimension line when text is inside the extension lines, but aligns text horizontally when text is outside the extension lines (because of a tight fit).

> **ON THE WEB**
> The drawing used in the following exercise on defining dimension text, ab15-01.dwg, is available from the Results download on the companion website.

STEPS: Defining Dimension Text

1. If ab15-01.dwg is open from the previous exercise, use it for this exercise as well. Otherwise, open ab15-01.dwg, available from the Results download on the companion website.

2. Save the file as ab15-02.dwg in your AutoCAD Bible folder.

3. Choose Annotate tab ⇨ Dimensions panel, and click the dialog box launcher arrow on the right side of the panel title bar. The Arch 48 dimension style should be current. Choose Modify to continue working on the Arch 48 dimension style. Click the Text tab.

4. In the Text Appearance section, choose ROMANS as the text style.

5. In the Text Placement section, choose Above from the Vertical drop-down list.

15

6. In the Text Alignment section, choose Aligned with Dimension Line. Although mechanical dimensions usually require horizontal text, architectural dimensions require that the text be aligned with the dimension line.

7. Click OK and then click Close to update the dimension to include the changes. The text is still too tiny to see clearly.

8. Save your drawing. Keep this drawing open if you're continuing on to the next exercise.

Fitting dimensions into tight spaces

When there is not enough room to place the arrowheads, dimension line, and text between the extension lines, some elements of the dimension need to go outside the extension lines. The Fit tab, shown in Figure 15.12, lets you specify how you want to handle this situation.

FIGURE 15.12

The Fit tab of the New Dimension Style dialog box

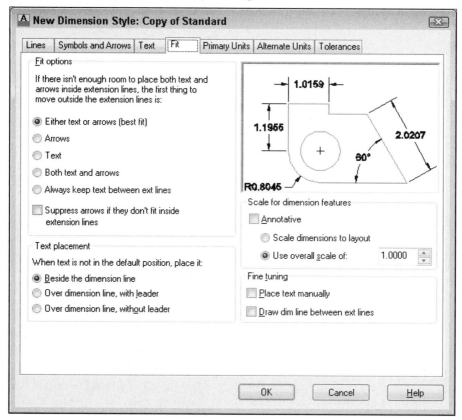

Fit Options

The Fit Options section determines which elements are moved outside the extension lines — text, arrows, or both — when they can't fit inside the extension lines. These are among the hardest of the dimension styles options to understand, yet they can greatly affect how your dimensions appear.

> **CAUTION**
>
> The Fit options specify what goes *outside* the extension lines. For example, choose the Arrows option to place the arrows outside the extension lines if there is not enough room for them. Be careful, or you'll get a result that is the opposite of what you intended.

Here are your choices:

- **Either Text or Arrows (Best Fit).** Puts whatever fits inside the extension lines. The arrowheads might fit inside and the text might not, or the other way around. If there isn't enough room for either text or arrows, then they both go outside the extension lines. Figure 15.13 shows a dimension using this option.

FIGURE 15.13

A narrow dimension using the Either Text or Arrows (Best Fit) option

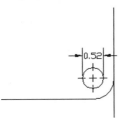

- **Arrows.** If there is not enough room for both the text and the arrows between the extension lines, the arrows go outside and the text goes between the arrows. Figure 15.14 shows a dimension using this option. The results of this option happen to look the same as Figure 15.13, but a different setting produced them.

FIGURE 15.14

A narrow dimension using the Arrows option

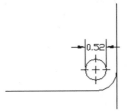

15

- **Text.** If there isn't enough room for the text and the arrows between the extension lines, the text goes outside and the arrows go between them. Figure 15.15 shows a dimension using this option.

FIGURE 15.15

A narrow dimension using the Text option

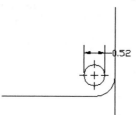

- **Both Text and Arrows.** Keeps the text and arrows together — between the extension lines if there is enough room, and outside the extension lines if there is not. Figure 15.16 shows a dimension using this option.

FIGURE 15.16

A narrow dimension using the Both Text and Arrows option

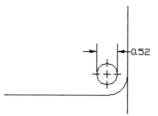

- **Always Keep Text between Ext Lines.** As it says, this option always keeps the text between the extension lines, even if they don't fit. Figure 15.17 shows a dimension using this option.

FIGURE 15.17

A narrow dimension using the Always Keep Text between Ext Lines option

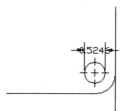

- **Suppress Arrows If They Don't Fit Inside the Extension Lines.** Use this check box to suppress the display of arrows completely if they don't fit inside the extension lines (instead of putting them outside). This option is used together with one of the previous options. Figure 15.18 shows a dimension using this option with the Either Text or Arrows (Best Fit) option.

FIGURE 15.18

A narrow dimension using the Suppress Arrows If They Don't Fit Inside the Extension Lines option along with the Either Text or Arrows (Best Fit) option

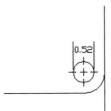

Text Placement

The Text Placement section determines where you want the dimension text when it isn't in its default position, due to a tight fit. Your options are:

- **Beside the Dimension Line.** Places the dimension text next to the dimension line, but outside the extension lines. Figure 15.19 shows a dimension using this option, as well as the same dimension edited to move the text off the model. You can move the text anywhere to the left or the right of the dimension line, but not above or below it. Editing dimensions is covered later in this chapter.

FIGURE 15.19

Dimension text is placed beside the dimension line when it doesn't fit inside the extension lines. You can move the text from side to side. On the right, the text has been moved to the right slightly so that it doesn't cross the model.

- **Over Dimension Line, with Leader.** Places the dimension text over the dimension line and between the extension lines with a leader from the dimension line to the text. You can move the text anywhere to suit your needs and dimensioning conventions, as shown in Figure 15.20.

FIGURE 15.20

Dimension text is placed over the dimension line with a leader. On the right, the text has been moved to the right of the model.

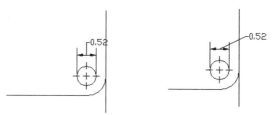

- **Over Dimension Line, without Leader.** Places the dimension text over the dimension line and between the extension lines with no leader, as shown in Figure 15.21. You can move the text anywhere.

FIGURE 15.21

Dimension text is placed over the dimension line without a leader.

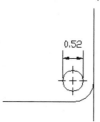

Scale for Dimension Features

The Scale for Dimension Features section lets you specify the scale factor. The reason you need to specify a scale factor is because you may have to scale the drawing when you plot it. The scale factor adjusts the size of dimension text (unless a nonzero text style height controls the text), arrowheads, spacing, and so on. It has no effect on the content of dimension text — that is, it does not affect actual measurements. So many size options are possible in a dimension style that you could spend all day trying to multiply each size option by the scale. Then if you have to change the scale of the drawing, you would need to recalculate all the size specifications. Setting the Overall Scale factor tells AutoCAD or AutoCAD LT to automatically multiply every size specification by the scale factor.

To scale dimensions according to the scale of the layout, check the Scale Dimensions to Layout option. You would use this feature if you plan to use more than one viewport, each with a different scale factor. If not, you can choose an overall scale, which would be the scale factor that you plan to use; check the Use Overall Scale Of option and enter a scale.

The annotative feature, which is available for text, hatches, blocks, dimensions, and multileaders, replaces the previous dimension scaling. Therefore, when you check the Annotative check box, the two options become unavailable.

Scale factors are discussed in detail in Chapter 5. See Chapter 17 for a discussion of scaling dimensions in a paper space layout (including the use of annotative dimensions) and placing dimensions on a layout.

In the Fine Tuning section, if you check the Place Text Manually option, the horizontal text placement settings are ignored, and the point that you pick at the `Specify dimension line location or [Mtext/Text/Angle/Horizontal/Vertical/Rotated]:` prompt is used. Before you click, as you move the cursor along the dimension line, you can see the text following the cursor.

Check the Draw Dim Line Between Ext Lines option to force a dimension line between the extension lines, even when there isn't room for text or arrows, as shown in Figure 15.22.

FIGURE 15.22

A dimension with a forced dimension line

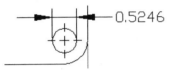

ON THE WEB

The drawing used in the following exercise on setting dimension fit, `ab15-02.dwg`, is available from the Results download on the companion website.

STEPS: Setting Dimension Fit

1. If `ab15-02.dwg` is open from the previous exercise, use it for this exercise as well. Otherwise, open `ab15-02.dwg`, available from the Results download on the companion website.

2. Save the file as `ab15-03.dwg` in your `AutoCAD Bible` folder.

3. Choose Annotate tab ⇨ Dimensions panel, and click the dialog box launcher arrow on the right side of the panel title bar. Make sure that the Arch 48 dimension style is current. Choose Modify to continue working on the Arch 48 dimension style.

4. On the Fit tab, in the Text Placement section, choose Over Dimension Line, with Leader.

5. In the Fine Tuning section, check Draw Dim Line Between Ext Lines. Architectural dimensions customarily place a line between the extension lines, even if the text cannot fit.

6. Because the drawing's scale is ¼"=1', or 1:48, type **48** in the Use Overall Scale Of text box.

15

7. Click OK. Click Close to return to your drawing.

8. Save your drawing. You can finally see the dimension! It should look like Figure 15.23. Keep this drawing open if you're continuing on to the next exercise.

FIGURE 15.23

As a result of changing the overall scale, the dimension is now legible.

GARAGE SOUTH ELEV 1/4" = 1'-0"

Defining primary units

The primary units define the type of units used to display the dimension in your drawing. You need to set primary units separately from the units for the drawing, which affect coordinate display but not dimensions.

Click the Primary Units tab, shown in Figure 15.24, to set the format and precision for linear and angular dimensions. You should already be familiar with setting units, which I discuss in Chapter 5. You must set your units for dimensions separately.

Linear Dimensions

To get the look and accuracy that you want, you should specify the format and precision of your linear dimensions. The New Dimensions Style dialog box provides settings for linear dimensions. You have the following options:

- Choose a format from the Unit Format drop-down list. You have the same choices as in the Drawing Units dialog box: Scientific, Decimal, Engineering, Architectural, and Fractional, as well as an additional option, Windows Desktop.

FIGURE 15.24

The Primary Units tab of the New Dimension Style dialog box

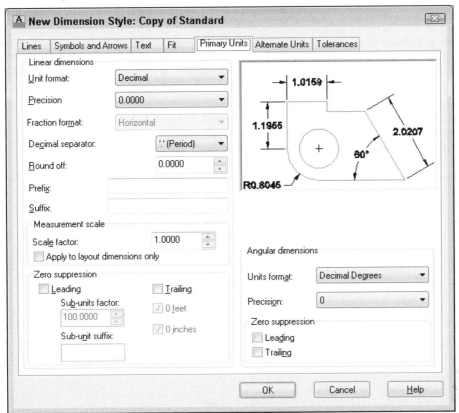

- Choose a precision (the number of decimal points or the fraction denominator) from the Precision drop-down list.
- Choose a fraction format from the Fraction Format drop-down list. This option is available only if the unit format that you chose uses fractions. Horizontal places a horizontal line between stacked numerators and denominators. Diagonal uses a diagonal slash between the stacked numerator and denominator. Not Stacked uses a diagonal line between the numerator and denominator, which are not stacked. You can see the effect of each choice in the preview box.

15

- Choose a decimal separator. This option is available only if the format that you chose uses decimals. You can choose from a period, a comma, or a space.
- Use the Round Off text box to round off linear dimension distances. For example, you can round to the nearest 0.1 unit or ½ inch.
- Use the Prefix and Suffix boxes to add a prefix or suffix that you want to place before or after every dimension. For example, you might want to add a suffix of mm after every dimension if you're measuring in millimeters and giving the drawing to a client who usually sees dimensions in inches.

You can use the Scale Factor text box to set a scaling factor for linear dimensions, including radial and diameter dimensions, and ordinal dimensions. This factor changes the actual measurement text. For example, if you draw a line 2.5 units long and you specify a linear scale of 0.5, the object is dimensioned as 1.25 units. You could set this scale to 25.4 to use metric measurements on a drawing that you have created with U.S. measurements. This can occur if you're sending the same drawing to certain clients in the United States and other clients elsewhere in the world. You can also use this scale in conjunction with alternate units, as explained in the next section.

Check the Apply to Layout Dimensions Only option to apply the linear scaling factor only to layout (paper space) dimensions.

In the Zero Suppression section, choose whether you want to suppress leading and trailing zeros. If you suppress leading zeros, a number such as 0.375 appears as .375. If you suppress trailing zeros, a number such as 3.7500 appears as 3.75.

If you suppress leading zeros, you can choose to display a measurement of less than one unit in a *subunit*, which is an alternative, smaller unit. You can use subunits with decimal units only. For example, if your units represent feet, instead of displaying a dimension value as `0.25 feet`, you may want to display the measurement as `3"`.

To do so, first check the Leading check box, to suppress leading zeros. Then specify the Sub-Units Factor value to set the number of subunits per unit. In the previous example, you would set the Sub-Units Factor to 12, because there are 12 inches in a foot. (If your units represent meters, you could set the Sub-Units Factor to 100 to show units of less than one in centimeters.)

Use the Sub-Units Suffix text box to specify a suffix for the dimension text. In the example you would set this value to `"`, to represent inches. AutoCAD multiples the actual value (.25) by the subunit factor (12), adds the suffix, and displays the results (3"). (If your units represent meters and you want to show centimeters for subunits, set the suffix to cm.)

For architectural units, you can choose to suppress 0 feet and 0 inches. If you suppress 0 feet, a number such as 0'-8" becomes 8". If you suppress 0 inches, a number such as 6'-0" becomes 6'.

Angular Dimensions

To get the look and accuracy that you need for angular dimensions, you should also set their format and precision. The Angular Dimensions section of the Primary Units tab lets you format angular measurements. You have the following options:

- Choose from Decimal Degrees, Degrees Minutes Seconds, Gradians, and Radians.
- Choose a precision from the Precision drop-down list.

In the Zero Suppression section, choose whether you want to suppress leading and trailing zeros for angular dimensions. For example, an angle of 37.0° would appear as 37° with the trailing zero suppressed.

Defining alternate units

If you want, you can show an alternate set of units in your dimensions. The most common use of this feature is to show millimeters and inches together. Alternate units appear in square brackets. To show alternate units, click the Alternate Units tab of the New Dimension Style dialog box, as shown in Figure 15.25. Check the Display Alternate Units check box.

As you can see, this dialog box is very similar to the Primary Units tab, discussed in the previous section. Notice the default scale of 25.40 in the Multiplier for Alt Units text box. There are 25.4 millimeters to an inch. If your primary units are millimeters, you can set the linear scale to 0.03937, which is the number of inches to a millimeter. Of course, if your units are not inches but meters, miles, or something else, you need to make the appropriate calculations. Figure 15.26 shows two dimensions with alternate units.

FIGURE 15.25

The Alternate Units tab of the Modify Dimension Style dialog box

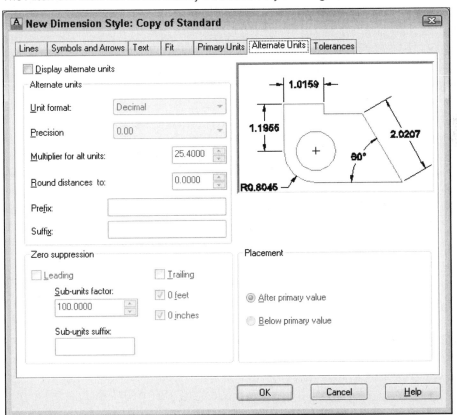

FIGURE 15.26

Dimensions showing both U.S. and metric measurements

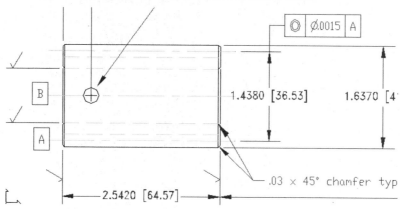

Thanks to Jerry Bottenfield of Clow Valve Company, Oskaloosa, Iowa, for this drawing.

In the Placement section, choose one of the options to place alternate units after or below the primary units.

ON THE WEB

The drawing used in the following exercise on defining primary units, ab15-03.dwg, is available from the Results download on the companion website.

STEPS: Defining Primary Units

1. If ab15-03.dwg is open from the previous exercise, use it for this exercise as well. Otherwise, open ab15-03.dwg, available from the Results download on the companion website. Ortho Mode and Object Snap should be on. Set running object snaps for Endpoint and Intersection. The Dim layer is current.

2. Save the file as ab15-04.dwg in your AutoCAD Bible folder.

3. Choose Annotate tab ⇨ Dimensions panel, and click the dialog box launcher arrow on the right side of the panel title bar. The Arch 48 dimension style should be current. Choose Modify to continue working on this dimension style. Click the Primary Units tab.

4. In the Unit Format drop-down list, choose Architectural.

5. In the Precision drop-down list, change the precision to 0'-0 1/8".

6. In the Fraction format drop-down list, choose Diagonal.

7. In the Zero Suppression section, uncheck the 0 Inches check box because architectural dimensions sometimes show 0 inches.

8. Click the Text tab. In the Fraction Height Scale text box, type **.75**.

9. Click OK. In the Dimension Style Manager, click Close to return to your drawing. The dimension is automatically updated and now looks appropriate for an architectural drawing.

10. To see how the stacked fractions appear, create a linear dimension from ❶ to ❷, as shown in Figure 15.27. If necessary, zoom in to see the dimension text clearly.

FIGURE 15.27

The dimension style is now complete.

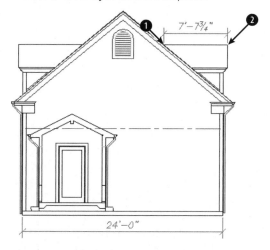

11. Return to the previous view if you zoomed in. Save your drawing. It should look like Figure 15.27.

Formatting tolerances

Tolerances are used in mechanical drafting to specify how much deviation is allowed from the exact measurement when the model is manufactured. Format the tolerance notation on the Tolerances tab of the New Dimension Style dialog box. The Tolerances tab is shown in Figure 15.28.

The Tolerances tab formats regular dimensions. You can also create special Tolerance control frames, which have the same purpose, but are separate object types. I cover them in Chapter 14.

15

FIGURE 15.28

The Tolerances tab of the New Dimension Style dialog box

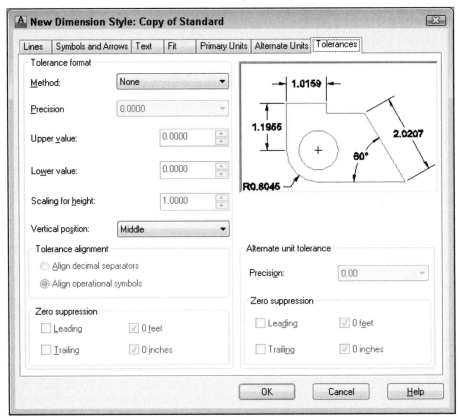

Use the Tolerance Format section to specify how you want the tolerances to be displayed. You can choose one of four tolerance methods from the Method drop-down list, as shown in Figure 15.29:

- **Symmetrical** tolerances have the same upper and lower amounts and are shown with a plus/minus sign. The Upper Value text box is active so that you can type in the tolerance amount.
- **Deviation** tolerances can have different upper and lower amounts and are therefore shown after separate plus and minus signs. When you choose a deviation tolerance, the Upper Value and Lower Value text boxes become active.
- **Limits** dimensions include the upper and lower tolerances in the measurement. Use the Upper Value and Lower Value text boxes to type in the upper and lower tolerance amounts.
- **Basic** dimensions place the dimension in a box.

FIGURE 15.29

Four types of tolerances

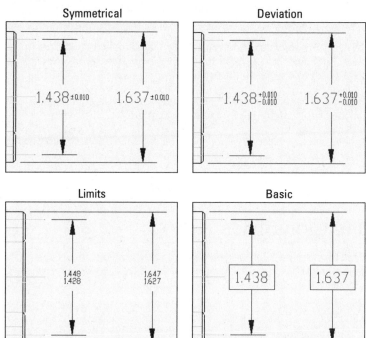

In the Precision drop-down list, choose a precision value. Use the Upper Value text box to set the tolerance value for symmetrical tolerances. For deviation and limits tolerances, use both the Upper Value and Lower Value text boxes.

The Scaling for Height text box lets you scale the height of the tolerance relative to the dimension text height. Using smaller text for the tolerances is common. A value of 1 creates tolerance text that is equal to the dimension text height. A setting of 0.5 creates tolerance text that is half the size of regular dimension text.

Use the Vertical Position drop-down list to determine how the tolerances are aligned with the main dimension text. This setting has the greatest effect on Deviation tolerances that display two lines of text for the one dimension text line. You have the following choices:

- **Bottom.** Aligns the tolerance text with the bottom of the dimension text.
- **Middle.** Aligns the tolerance text with the middle of the dimension text.
- **Top.** Aligns the tolerance text with the top of the dimension text.

15

> **NOTE**
> The Vertical position setting also applies to stacked fractions, determining how the fractions are justified with the whole-number dimensions.

If you choose a Limits or Deviation tolerance, you can specify the alignment of stacked upper and lower tolerance values. You can align the values by the decimal separators (such as a decimal point) or by the operational symbols (such as the plus-minus symbol).

Use the Zero Suppression section to suppress leading or trailing zeros, or feet and inches. See the preceding explanation of the Primary Units tab for more information.

If you've turned on alternate units, you can separately set the precision and zero suppression for alternate unit tolerances in the Precision text box.

Click OK, and then click Close to return to your drawing. You're ready to start dimensioning!

Changing Dimension Styles

You may need to edit dimension styles. Whether you want to use a different dimension style for a certain object or change the properties of a dimension style, you have the flexibility you need. You can change dimensions in the following ways:

- Choose a new dimension style.
- Create a variant of a dimension style for a certain type of dimension.
- Modify the characteristics of the dimension style in use.
- Override the dimension style with different dimension options for one dimension that you want to be an exception.

Chapter 14 covers some dimension editing techniques. This section explains how to make changes related to dimension styles.

Choosing a new current dimension style

To start using another dimension style, click the Dimension Style drop-down list in the Dimensions panel of the Annotate tab or the expanded Annotation panel of the Home tab, and choose the dimension style that you want to use.

Existing dimensions remain unchanged, but any new dimensions that you add from this point forward will use the new current dimension style.

Creating a variant of a dimension style

Create a variant of a dimension style for a specific type of dimension, such as a leader or angular dimension. You might have an architectural dimension style with ticks (rather than arrows) at the end of the dimension lines, but you might want angular dimensions to have open arrows. Here are the steps to do this:

1. Choose Annotate tab ⇨ Dimensions panel, and click the dialog box launcher arrow on the right side of the panel title bar.

2. Click New.

3. From the Use For drop-down list, choose the type of dimension that you want to use with the new variant.

4. Click Continue.

5. Make the changes that you want, using the techniques described earlier in this chapter.

6. Click OK to return to the Dimension Style Manager. Here you see the variant listed under its base (parent) dimension style.

7. Click Close.

Dimensions of the type that you specified now take on the characteristics of the variant. For example, angular dimensions would have an open arrow.

Modifying a dimension to use a new dimension style

You can change the dimension style used by an existing dimension. Select the dimension and then choose a new dimension style from the Dimension Style drop-down list in the Dimensions panel of the Annotate tab or the expanded Annotation panel of the Home tab.

Another method of changing a dimension's style is to open the Properties palette (press Ctrl+1) and select one or more dimensions. In the Properties palette, click the Dim Style item in the Misc section and choose a new dimension style from the drop-down list. You can also change the dimension style of a selected dimension in the Quick Properties palette.

TIP

Select any dimension to open the Quick Properties palette, where you can change some of the properties of that dimension.

Modifying dimension styles

You can easily change a dimension style. The advantage of changing a dimension style is that all dimensions using that style are automatically updated. To change a style:

1. Choose Annotate tab ⇨ Dimensions panel, and click the dialog box launcher arrow on the right side of the panel title bar.

2. Choose the dimension style that you want to change from the list of styles.

3. Choose Modify.

4. AutoCAD opens the Modify Dimension Style dialog box, which is exactly the same as the New Dimension Style dialog box. Use the settings on all the tabs and make the changes that you want. Click OK to close these dialog boxes and return to the Dimension Styles Manager.

5. Click Close.

All dimensions automatically change to reflect the changed dimension style.

15

> **TIP**
> You can create a new dimension style from an existing dimension on the fly by using the Properties palette. Select a dimension and open the Properties palette. Click the arrow next to the type of change that you want to make, and make the change. After you're done, right-click in the drawing area and choose Dimension Style ⇨ Save as New Style. The New Dimension Style dialog box opens so that you can give the dimension style a name. Click OK.

Overriding a dimension style

Sometimes you want to make an exception to a style for one dimension — for example, when suppressing an extension line in a tight space. It isn't often worthwhile to create a new dimension style for such a situation. To override a dimension style, simply change the properties of the dimension by using the Properties palette.

You can also create an override to the current dimension style. The override is like a subset of the dimension style. After you create the override, all new dimensions that you create using the dimension style include the override changes. To revert back to the original dimension style, you must delete the override. You also have the option to incorporate the override into the dimension style or save it as a new style.

To create a dimension style override, follow these steps:

1. Choose Annotate tab ⇨ Dimensions panel, and click the dialog box launcher arrow on the right side of the panel title bar.

2. Choose the dimension style for which you want to create an override (if it isn't already selected).

3. In the Dimension Style Manager, click Override.

4. The Override Current Style dialog box opens, which is just like the New (or Modify) Dimension Style dialog box. Make the changes that you want by using any of the tabs. Click OK.

5. In the Dimension Style Manager, you see the style override listed beneath the dimension style that you selected. Click Close.

New dimensions that you create using the dimension style that you selected now include the override properties.

> **TIP**
> To quickly override a dimension's style, select the dimension. Then right-click and choose one of two options. Precision lets you quickly choose from 0 to 6 decimal places. The Dimension Style option creates a new style from the selected dimension. If you place the cursor over a grip on the dimension line or text, you can choose additional options to move the dimension text or flip the dimension line arrow outside the extension line.

To stop using the override, open the Dimension Style Manager, right-click the style override to open the shortcut menu, and do one of the following:

- Choose Delete to delete the override.

- Choose Save to Current Style to incorporate the override properties into the current dimension style.

- Choose Rename to create a new dimension style from the override. You see a selection box around the name. Type a new dimension style name and press Enter. This action removes the override and replaces it with the new dimension style.

Removing the override using this method doesn't change dimensions that you've already created with the override. To remove a style override on an existing dimension, select a dimension containing an override, right-click, and choose Remove Style Overrides.

Updating dimensions

The Dimensions panel of the Annotate tab includes an Update button. This command updates selected dimensions so that they use the current dimension style, including any overrides that you may have just made. Use this command when you realize that you want to include some existing dimensions in the overrides that you've made.

Comparing dimension styles

You can compare a dimension style with the current dimension style. To do this, follow these steps:

1. Choose Annotate tab ⇨ Dimensions panel, click the dialog box launcher arrow on the right side of the panel title bar, and choose Compare. The Compare Dimension Styles dialog box opens, as shown in Figure 15.30.

FIGURE 15.30

The Compare Dimension Styles dialog box enables you to compare the properties of two dimension styles.

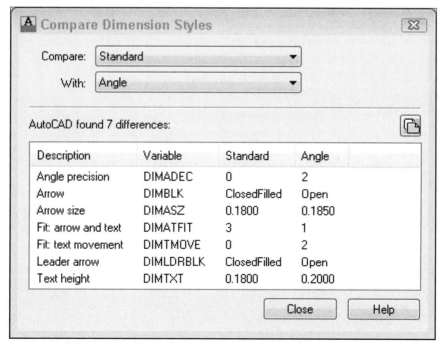

445

2. In the Compare and With drop-down lists, choose the two dimension styles that you want to compare. The resulting list shows the differences by system variable.

3. Click Close twice to return to your drawing.

TIP

Click the Copy button at the right side of the Compare Dimension Styles dialog box to copy the comparison to the Clipboard. You can then paste it into another document, for example, an e-mail message to a client.

 You can use the Content Explorer to import dimension styles from other drawings. I cover the Content Explorer in Chapter 12.

AutoCAD Only

The Express Tools offer two commands, DIMIM and DIMEX, which enable you to save (export) and retrieve (import) dimension styles. Type these commands on the command line. For information on installing Express Tools, see Bonus Chapter 15.

On the Web

The drawing used in the following exercise on changing dimension styles, ab15-b.dwg, is available from the Drawings download on the companion website.

STEPS: Changing Dimension Styles

1. Open ab15-b.dwg, available from the Drawings download on the companion website.

2. Save the file as ab15-05.dwg in your AutoCAD Bible folder. This is a tension arm for a commercial dryer, as shown in Figure 15.31. Ortho Mode and Object Snap should be on. Set running object snaps for Endpoint, Intersection, and Center. The Dim layer is current.

3. The current dimension style is CIR. Choose Annotate tab ⇨ Dimensions panel ⇨ Dimension Style to open the drop-down list, and choose LIN.

4. Choose Annotate tab ⇨ Dimensions panel ⇨ Dimension drop-down menu ⇨ Linear to start the DIMLINEAR command. At the `Specify first extension line origin or <select object>:` prompt, choose the endpoint at ❶, shown in Figure 15.31. (If necessary, press Tab until you see the endpoint tooltip.) At the `Specify second extension line origin:` prompt, choose the intersection at ❷. At the `Specify dimension line location or [Mtext/Text/Angle/Horizontal/Vertical/Rotated]:` prompt, choose an appropriate location above the bottom-most dimension.

5. Choose Annotate tab ⇨ Dimensions panel, and click the dialog box launcher arrow on the right side of the panel title bar. Choose Override and click the Tolerances tab. Change the Tolerance Method to None. Click the Lines tab. In the Extension Lines section, check the Suppress: Ext Line 1 option to suppress the first extension line. Click OK. In the Dimension Style Manager, click Close.

6. Start the DIMLINEAR command again. At the `Specify first extension line origin or <select object>:` prompt, choose the intersection at ❷, shown in Figure 15.31. At the `Specify second extension line origin:` prompt, choose the intersection at ❸. At the `Specify dimension line location or [Mtext/Text/Angle/Horizontal/`

Vertical/Rotated]: prompt, pick the endpoint object snap at the right side of the previous dimension's dimension line in order to align the two dimensions.

7. The first dimension (the one you created in Step 4) needs to be updated to remove the tolerance. Choose Annotate tab ⇨ Dimensions panel ⇨ Update. At the `Select objects:` prompt, choose the first dimension. Right-click to end object selection and update the dimension.

8. To list the overrides, choose Annotate tab ⇨ Dimensions panel, and click the dialog box launcher arrow on the right side of the panel title bar. Click Compare. In the Compare Dimension Styles dialog box, `<style overrides>` should be displayed in the Compare drop-down list, and LIN should be displayed in the With drop-down list. You see a list of the overrides, which are the only differences between the two. Click Close.

9. To remove the overrides (no tolerance and the first extension line suppressed), right-click `<style overrides>` in the Dimension Style Manager and choose Delete. You get the message, `Are you sure you want to delete "<style overrides>"?` Click Yes. Click Close to return to the drawing.

10. Start the DIMLINEAR command again. At the `Specify first extension line origin or <select object>:` prompt, choose the intersection at ❹, shown in Figure 15.31. At the `Specify second extension line origin:` prompt, choose the intersection at ❺. At the `Specify dimension line location or [Mtext/Text/Angle/Horizontal/Vertical/Rotated]:` prompt, pick an appropriate location to the right of the model.

11. To compare the CIR and LIN dimension styles, open the Dimension Style Manager again. Choose Compare. LIN should appear in the Compare drop-down list. Choose CIR from the With drop-down list. The result is a list of the differences. Click Close twice to return to your drawing.

12. Save your drawing. It should look like Figure 15.32.

FIGURE 15.31

The tension arm needs some additional dimensions.

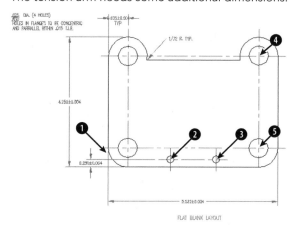

FIGURE 15.32

The dimensions have been added.

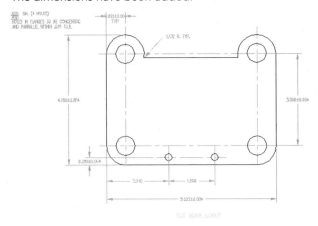

Summary

In this chapter, you gained a thorough understanding of how to use dimension styles to organize your dimensions. You read how to:

- Define a dimension's lines and arrows
- Define dimension text style and placement
- Create an annotative dimension style
- Fit dimensions into small spaces
- Define the primary and alternate measuring units
- Format tolerances
- Create a variant of a dimension style for specific types of dimensions
- Change dimension style used by a dimension
- Modify a dimension style and update all dimensions that use that style
- Override a dimension style for temporary changes
- Update existing dimensions
- Compare dimension styles
- Copy dimension styles from other drawings, using the Content Explorer

In the next chapter, you learn how to draw complex objects.

Drawing Complex Objects

IN THIS CHAPTER

Drawing and editing polylines

Creating and editing splines

Creating regions and boundaries

Using hatches to fill closed areas

Working with the SKETCH command

AutoCAD and AutoCAD LT offer a number of complex objects that can help you create accurate, professional drawings. Polylines are single objects that can combine line segments and arcs. Splines are mathematically controlled curves that are based on points that you specify. Regions and boundaries create complex shapes from existing objects. Hatches create various types of fills inside closed objects. Sketching is a way to create freehand drawings. In this chapter, I introduce you to these complex objects and explain how to use them. An addendum to this chapter, on the companion website, covers multilines, dlines, and digitizing paper drawings.

Creating and Editing Polylines

Polylines are single objects that combine line segments and arcs. In certain situations, being able to edit an entire set of lines and arcs as one object is useful. Polylines can have a width, which can vary from the start point to the endpoint of each segment. Polylines ensure that all the vertices of a series of lines and arcs actually touch. They're also useful as a basis for 3D drawing. In short, polylines are a neat, clean way to draw.

The RECTANG and POLYGON commands create polylines. Figure 16.1 shows a few examples of polylines.

FIGURE 16.1

Four examples of polylines

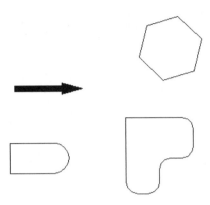

Using the PLINE command

To draw a polyline, choose Home tab ⇨ Draw panel ⇨ Polyline. This starts the PLINE command. The command responds with the `Specify start point:` prompt. Specify the start point. The main PLINE prompt is `Specify next point or [Arc/Close/Halfwidth/Length/Undo/Width]:`, which offers the following options:

- **Arc.** Draws arcs. This option opens up a set of arc suboptions, which are explained after this list.
- **Close.** Closes a polyline by drawing a line from the endpoint of the last line segment to the start point of the polyline. This option appears only after you've picked a second point.
- **Halfwidth.** Defines half of the width of the polyline — the distance from the center of the polyline to its edge. The option asks you for the starting halfwidth and the ending halfwidth, enabling you to create polylines that are tapered.
- **Length.** Specifies the length of the next line segment. The option draws the line segment in the same direction as the last line segment or tangent to the last arc.
- **Undo.** Undoes the last line segment.
- **Width.** Defines the width of the polyline. The option asks you for the starting width and the ending width.
- **Specify next point.** Enables you to create a line segment. This is the default option.

Like the LINE command, PLINE continues to prompt you for more points, repeating the entire prompt each time. When you're done, press Enter to end the command.

Generating Linetypes on Polylines

When you create a polyline with a noncontinuous linetype, you may find that the linetype doesn't appear properly along the polyline. One reason is that the segments of the polyline may be too short to fit the entire linetype definition — in this case the polyline appears continuous. You can choose to generate the linetype continuously along the polyline instead of starting the linetype definition anew at each vertex. This results in a more normal-looking linetype along the polyline. To do this, you need to turn on the PLINEGEN system variable. To turn on PLINEGEN, type **plinegen** ↵ and then **1** ↵.

As explained in the section "Editing polylines with the PEDIT command" later in the chapter, you can also modify the display of linetypes for existing polylines.

If you choose Arc, you see the `Specify endpoint of arc or [Angle/CEnter/CLose/` `Direction/Halfwidth/Line/Radius/Second pt/ Undo/Width]:` prompt. Most of the options are similar to the ARC command options. For details, see Chapter 7. The arc options are as follows:

- **Angle.** Specifies the included angle.
- **CEnter.** Specifies the arc's center.
- **CLose.** Closes the polyline by drawing an arc from the endpoint of the last arc to the start point of the polyline.
- **Direction.** Specifies the direction of the arc from the start point.
- **Halfwidth.** Defines half of the width of the polyline — the distance from the center of the polyline to its edge. The option asks you for the starting halfwidth and the ending halfwidth.
- **Line.** Returns you to the main polyline prompt so that you can draw line segments.
- **Radius.** Specifies the arc's radius.
- **Second pt.** Specifies the second point of the arc.
- **Undo.** Undoes the last arc.
- **Width.** Defines the width of the polyline. The option asks you for the starting width and the ending width.
- **Specify endpoint of arc.** Specifies the endpoint of the arc. This is the default. This option creates an arc tangent to the previous arc (continuing in the same direction).

PLINE continues to display the arc submenu until you use the Line suboption or end the command by pressing Enter.

On the Web

The drawing that you need for the following exercise on drawing polylines, ab16-a´.dwg, is available from the Drawings download on the companion website.

STEPS: Drawing Polylines

1. Open ab16-a.dwg, available from the companion website.
2. Save the file as ab16-01.dwg in your AutoCAD Bible folder. It shows a small section of a drive block, as shown in Figure 16.2. In this exercise, you complete part of the drawing.

Ortho Mode and Object Snap should be on. Set running object snaps to Endpoint, Midpoint, and Intersection. Layer 3 is current. This exercise assumes that you have Dynamic Input (the Dynamic Input button on the status bar) on, set to the default of relative coordinates.

FIGURE 16.2

A small section of a drive block

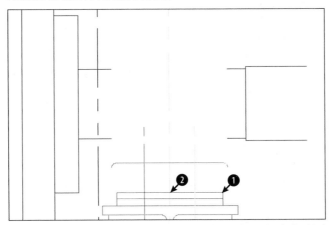

Thanks to Mary Redfern of the Bethlehem Corporation, Easton, Pennsylvania, for this drawing.

 3. Choose Home tab ⇨ Draw panel ⇨ Polyline. Follow the prompts:

    ```
    Specify start point: Press Shift+right-click and choose the From object
         snap.
    Base point: Choose ❶ in Figure 16.2.
    <Offset>: @-1/2,0 ↵
    Specify next point or [Arc/Halfwidth/Length/Undo/Width]: Move the cursor
         in the 90-degree di rection and type 3/32 ↵.
    ```

 4. Type **a** ↵ to continue with an arc. At the `Specify endpoint of arc or [Angle/CEnter/ CLose/Direction/Halfwidth/Line/Radius/Second pt/Undo/Width]:` prompt, type **3/16,3/16** ↵.

 5. Type **l** ↵ to continue with a linear segment. At the `Specify next point or [Arc/Close/ Halfwidth/Length/Undo/Width]:` prompt, move the cursor in the 0-degree direction and type **11/32** ↵.

 6. Type **a** ↵ to continue with an arc. At the prompt, type **3/16,3/16** ↵.

 7. Type **l** ↵ to continue with a linear segment. At the prompt, move the cursor in the 90-degree direction and type **6-3/32** ↵.

 8. Type **a** ↵ to continue with an arc. At the prompt, type **-5/16,5/16** ↵.

9. To create the last arc, type **r** ↵. Follow the prompts:

```
Specify radius of arc: 5-5/8 ↵
Specify endpoint of arc or [Angle]: Choose the From object snap.
Base point: Choose point ❷ in Figure 16.2.
<Offset>: @0,7-1/4 ↵
```

10. Press Enter to exit the PLINE command.

11. Save your drawing. It should look like Figure 16.3.

FIGURE 16.3

The completed polyline

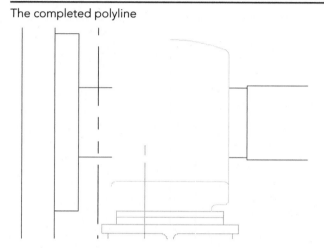

Editing polylines with the PEDIT command

 Because polylines can be quite complex, there is a special command, PEDIT, to edit them. To edit a polyline, choose Home tab ⇨ Modify panel (expanded) ⇨ Edit Polyline. The command responds with the `Select polyline or [Multiple]:` prompt. When you select a polyline, you see the `Enter an option [Close/Join/Width/Edit vertex/Fit/Spline/Decurve/Ltype gen/Reverse/ Undo]:` prompt. The options are:

- **Close.** Closes an open polyline. If necessary, it adds a segment to connect the endpoint to the start point. If the polyline is already closed, this prompt becomes Open. Open creates a break between the first and last segments of the polyline.

- **Join.** Joins touching lines, arcs, or other polylines to the polyline. The polyline must be open and the other objects need to touch the beginning or end of the polyline.

- **Width.** Enables you to specify one width for the entire polyline.

- **Edit Vertex.** Provides a set of suboptions for editing vertices. These suboptions are explained after this list.

- **Fit.** Turns the polyline into a curve that passes through the vertices.

- **Spline.** Creates a curve by using the vertices as control points. The curve does not usually pass through the vertices. This is not the mathematically exact spline that the SPLINE command produces (covered later in this chapter).
- **Decurve.** Returns a Fit or Spline curve to its original vertices.
- **Ltype gen.** Turns on continuous linetype generation for the selected polyline.
- **Reverse.** Reverses the direction of the polyline so that the starting point becomes the end point, providing more control of the display of special linetypes.
- **Undo.** Undoes the most recent edit.

TIP

You can change any line, spline, or arc into a polyline. Start PEDIT and choose a line or arc. The command responds: `Object selected is not a polyline. Do you want to turn it into one? <Y>.` Press Enter to accept the default and turn the object into a polyline. (You can change the PEDITACCEPT system variable to 1 to suppress this prompt and automatically turn non-polyline objects that you select for the PEDIT command to polylines.)

To turn a series of connected lines and arcs into a polyline, first turn one of the objects into a polyline as I just explained. Then use the Join option of the PEDIT command and select the other objects individually or by a selection window. In order to create a polyline in this way, the individual lines and arcs must connect exactly end to end. However, if you use the Multiple option, which I explain following the current list, you can join lines that aren't exactly touching.

TIP

You can convert a spline to a polyline, using the PEDIT command. When doing so, you get a prompt to enter a precision value between 0 and 99. A higher number provides a more accurate conversion. You can also change the system variable PLINECONVERTMODE to 0 to convert polylines to linear segments, or leave it at 1 (the default) to use arcs. If you want to keep the original spline along with the new polyline, change the system variable DELOBJ to 0 (off) before making the conversion.

When you choose the Edit Vertex option, you see a new set of suboptions with the `Enter a vertex editing option [Next/Previous/Break/Insert/Move/Regen/Straighten/Tangent/ Width/eXit] <N>:` prompt. You see an X at one of the vertices. This is the current vertex, which you can edit. The suboptions are as follows:

- **Next.** Moves you to the next vertex so that you can edit it.
- **Previous.** Moves you to the previous vertex.
- **Break.** Breaks the polyline. You can choose the Go suboption to break the polyline into two (although you can't see the break). You can move to another vertex by using the Next or Previous suboptions and then choosing Go. This option breaks the polyline between the original vertex and the vertex to which you moved. Use the eXit suboption to return to the previous prompt. (You can also use the BREAK command.)
- **Insert.** Inserts another vertex. At the prompt, specify its location.
- **Move.** Moves the vertex. At the prompt, specify its location.
- **Regen.** Regenerates the polyline.

- **Straighten.** Deletes vertices. This works like the Break option with the same Next, Previous, Go, and eXit suboptions. As soon as you move to a new vertex, the option draws a straight line between it and the original vertex. If you don't move to a new vertex, this option affects only an arc by changing it to a straight line segment.
- **Tangent.** Specifies a direction from the vertex. The command uses this information if you choose the Fit option.
- **Width.** Enables you to specify starting and ending widths of the segment, starting with the current vertex.
- **eXit.** Exits this group of suboptions.

CAUTION

You can make many changes during the PEDIT session. If you return to the command line and use the U or UNDO command, the entire session is undone. If you want to undo only part of the session, use the Undo option of the PEDIT command.

To edit multiple polylines at one time, follow these steps:

1. Start the PEDIT command.

2. Choose the Multiple option (type **m** ⏎ or right-click and choose Multiple from the shortcut menu) at the first prompt.

3. At the `Select objects:` prompt, select the polylines.

4. You then see the `Enter an option [Close/Open/Join/Width/Fit/Spline/ Decurve/Ltype gen/Reverse/Undo]:` prompt.

5. Choose the option that you want. For example, you can change the width of all the selected polylines or apply the Spline option to them.

You can also join two polylines that aren't touching, if you use the Multiple option first. Select the polylines and then choose the Join option. You then need to specify two suboptions:

- **Fuzz distance.** The maximum distance that the endpoints of the polylines can be from each other. In other words, in order for the join to work, the fuzz distance must be greater than the distance of the endpoints. If you want to join the endpoints regardless, type in a large number.
- **Jointype.** The method of joining polylines. You can use the Extend method, which extends (or trims) the segments to the nearest endpoints, or the Add method, which adds a straight segment between the two nearest endpoints. You can choose the Both suboption, which tries to extend or trim; if it can't, it adds a segment.

Grip editing polylines

You can also edit polylines with grips. Grips make it easy to move vertices, for example. For more information on grip editing, see Chapter 10. In addition to the primary grips at segment endpoints, polylines have secondary grips at the midpoint of each line or arc segment.

TIP

When you click a primary or secondary grip, you can press the Ctrl key repeatedly to cycle among the options.

To grip edit a polyline, select the polyline to display its primary and secondary grips. Hover the cursor over a grip to see the options, and then choose an option, as follows:

- **Stretch/Stretch Vertex.** Specify the new location for the grip.
- **Add Vertex.** Specify the location for the new vertex. You can add a vertex to both line and arc segments.
- **Convert to Arc/Line.** If the segment is a line, specify the midpoint of the arc. If the segment is an arc, it converts automatically to a line.
- **Remove Vertex.** At a vertex (but not at a secondary grip), choose this option to remove the vertex.

TIP

You can press the Ctrl key and click any segment of a polyline to select just that segment. Because polylines are one object, you cannot make many kinds of edits. For example, you can't change the layer of a segment. However, you can rotate or stretch a segment, resulting in a corresponding change in a nearby vertex.

Editing polylines with the Properties palette or Quick Properties palette

You can edit selected polylines in the Properties palette. You can choose a vertex by clicking Vertex in the Geometry section of the palette, and use the left and right arrows to move to another vertex. An X appears on the polyline to let you know which vertex you've chosen. You can then edit the vertex's coordinates by typing them in, or by clicking the Pick a Point button that appears and then picking a point in the drawing. You can change the start and ending widths and specify a global width for the entire polyline.

You can close and open a polyline in the Misc section. You can also turn on continuous linetype generation for the selected polyline by choosing Linetype Generation and then choosing Enabled from the drop-down list that appears. Of course, you can also change the layer, color, linetype, lineweight, and linetype scale.

 You can "paint" polyline properties from one polyline to another, using the MATCHPROP command. Select a polyline, choose Home tab ⇨ Clipboard panel ⇨ Match Properties, and then select the polyline that you want to edit. You can use the Settings option to refine the process.

ON THE WEB

The drawing that you need for the following exercise on editing polylines, ab16-b.dwg, is available from the Drawings download on the companion website.

STEPS: Editing Polylines

1. Open ab16-b.dwg, available from the companion website.
2. Save the file as ab16-02.dwg in your AutoCAD Bible folder. This is a topographical drawing, as shown in Figure 16.4. The contours are polylines.

3. Choose Home tab ⇨ Modify panel (expanded) ⇨ Edit Polyline to start the PEDIT command. Select the polyline at ❶, shown in Figure 16.4.

4. At the `Enter an option [Close/Join/Width/Edit vertex/Fit/Spline/Decurve/ Ltype gen/Reverse/Undo]:` prompt, choose Width. At the `Specify new width for all segments:` prompt, type **.5** ↵.

16

FIGURE 16.4

The topographical drawing's contours are polylines.

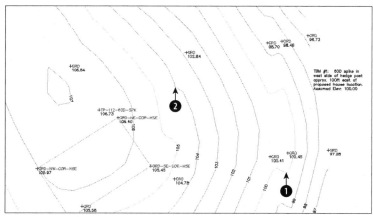

Thanks to Henry Dearborn, AIA, of Fairfield, Iowa, for this drawing.

5. Type **e** ↵ to choose the Edit vertex option. At the `Enter a vertex editing option [Next/Previous/Break/Insert/Move/Regen/Straighten/Tangent/Width/eXit] <N>:` prompt, type **n** ↵ several times until the X mark is at ❶, shown in Figure 16.4. (There are many vertices, so it's not important that you find the exact one.)

6. Type **m** ↵ to move the vertex. At the `Specify new location for marked vertex:` prompt, pick a point slightly above the existing vertex. Then type **x** ↵ to exit the Edit vertex submenu.

7. At the main PEDIT prompt, type **s** ↵. PEDIT smoothes out the polyline.

8. Press Enter to exit the PEDIT command.

9. Choose the polyline at ❷. Hover over the vertex at that point to see the options. (There are several vertices there; you can choose any one.) Choose Remove Vertex.

10. Hover over the next vertex in the area and again remove the vertex. Continue until you have straightened out the jog in the polyline.

11. Save your drawing.

Drawing and Editing Splines

The SPLINE command draws a *NURBS*, which stands for nonuniform rational B-spline. A *spline* is a smooth curve that is defined by a series of points. The SPLINE command provides a more precise representation of a spline than the Spline option of the PLINE command. By default, the curve passes through each point that you specify. Figure 16.5 shows a beanbag chair created with two splines.

FIGURE 16.5

A beanbag chair created with two splines

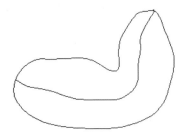

Understanding splines

By default, when you pick points to create the spline, AutoCAD stores these points as *fit points* (or data points). If the *tolerance* (how closely the spline comes to the points that you pick) is zero, the curve lies on these fit points. AutoCAD and AutoCAD LT calculate *control points* (also called control vertices) based on the fit points, and calculate the spline based on the control points, not the fit points. Most of the control points are not on the spline. When you use SPLINEDIT to edit a spline, and use the Move vertex option described later, you see the control points displayed as grips, and you can move the control points.

The top of Figure 16.6 shows a spline created by using point objects as the fit points; these are the points I picked when creating the spline. Note that the spline passes through each fit point. In the middle, you see the same spline selected with no command active. Notice that the grips are exactly on the fit points. At the bottom, you see the control points, marked by circles, which are mostly off the spline.

Because the spline is calculated based on the control points, the fit points are not necessary to generate the spline. In fact, if you move or edit a control point, only the control points are needed to generate the spline, and the fit point information is discarded so that you can no longer edit it.

You can create splines using two methods: Fit Points and Control Points (or control vertices). The default option is to use fit points. Using control points is valuable when you are drawing a spline as a basis for 3D NURBS surfaces. (See Chapter 23 for more information.) The prompts for the SPLINE command vary, based on the method you use. You can also control the method with the SPLMETHOD system variable.

FIGURE 16.6

Viewing fit points and control points for a spline

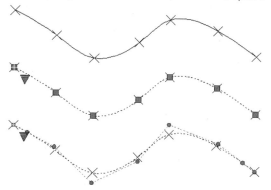

When you create a spline using the default Fit method and then select the spline, grips appear at these fit points. When you create a spline using the Control Vertices method and then select the spline, special round grips appear at the control vertices.

When you select a spline, you see a drop-down arrow that lets you choose to display fit points or control vertices. You can show the control vertices with the CVSHOW command even without selecting the spline. Use the CVHIDE command to hide them. CVSHOW and CVHIDE are in AutoCAD only.

Creating splines

 To create a spline, choose Home tab⇨Draw panel (expanded)⇨Spline Fit. Choosing Spline Fit defaults to specifying a spline with Fit points, although you can change the method. The command responds with the `Specify first point or [Method/Knots/Object]:` prompt.

Here are the options:

- **Method.** Lets you choose between Fit and CV (control vertices).

- **Knots.** Lets you choose the knot parameterization. The Knots option applies only to the Fit method. Knots control the shape of the spline as it passes through a fit point. The Chord suboption (the default) numbers edit points with decimal values representing their location on the curve. The Square Root suboption numbers edit points based on the square root of the chord length between consecutive knots. The Uniform suboption numbers edit points with consecutive integers.

- **Degree.** Lets you choose the number of directions allowed between the points you specify to define a spline. The Degree option applies only to the CV (control vertices) method. As you specify points for a spline, you define the spans of the spline. The value entered minus 1 determines the number of control points for each span. For example, a degree of 2 results in 1 control vertex between the points that define a span.

- **Object.** Converts a polyline that you've created with PEDIT's Spline option into a true spline. (It doesn't look any different, but its internal definition changes.)

When you choose a method, knot parameterization, and degree, you see the current settings displayed on the command line.

459

Drawing a spline with the Fit method

To start drawing the spline using the Fit (default) method, choose Home tab ⇨ Draw panel (expanded) ⇨ Spline Fit. At the `Specify first point or [Method/Knots/Object]:` prompt, specify the first point for the spline.

When you choose a point using the Fit method, the command displays the `Enter next point or [start Tangency/toLerance]:` prompt so that you can pick a second point. After the third point, you see the `Enter next point or [end Tangency/toLerance/Undo/Close]:` prompt, Specify the next point or use the options as follows:

- **start Tangency.** Lets you specify the direction of the start of the spline. You specify a point to indicate the direction from the start point.
- **end Tangency.** Lets you specify the direction of the end of the spline. You specify a point to indicate the direction from the last point to the end.
- **toLerance.** Specifies how closely the spline comes to the points that you pick. The default, 0, creates a spline that passes through each point. If you want the curve to have a latitude of 0.5 units from the points, set the tolerance to 0.5.
- **Undo.** Undoes that last segment of the spline that you specified.
- **Close.** Closes the spline by connecting the last point with the first point in a continuous (tangent) curve. The prompt asks for a tangent direction. You can specify a direction by picking a point (watch the spline image change as you move the cursor) or pressing Enter to accept the default tangent direction.

When you are finished specifying fit points, press Enter to end the command.

Drawing a spline with the Control Vertices method

To start drawing the spline using the CV (control vertices) method, choose Home tab ⇨ Draw panel (expanded) ⇨ Spline CV. You see the `Specify first point or [Method/Degree/Object]:` prompt. The Object option is the same as for the Fit method.

The Degree option sets the maximum number of directions you see if you draw a line between each control vertex:

- A degree 1 spline has at least two control vertices, and is always a straight line.
- A degree 2 spline has at least three control vertices, becoming a parabola.
- A degree 3 spline (the default) has at least four control vertices, making an "S" shape.

Specify the first point of the splines. At the `Enter next point or [Close/Undo]:` prompt, enter subsequent points. The Close and Undo options are the same as for the Fit method. When you are finished specifying control vertices, press Enter to end the command. Remember that the spline will not be on the control vertices.

To blend two lines or curves, go to Home tab ⇨ Modify panel ⇨ Chamfer and Fillet drop-down menu ⇨ Blend Curves. At the prompts, choose the first and second objects near the endpoint that you want to blend. You can also use the CONtinuity option to control the curvature of the connection between the objects and the spline. The two continuity suboptions are as follows:

- **Tangent.** Creates a degree 3 spline with G1 continuity.
- **Smooth.** Creates a degree 5 spline with G2 (curvature) continuity. If you use this option, do not switch from control vertices to fit points, because doing so changes that spline to degree 3 and changes the shape of the spline. See Chapter 23 for more about G1 and G2 continuity in the context of 3D surfaces.

ON THE WEB

The drawing that you need for the following exercise on drawing splines, `ab16-c.dwg`, is available from the `Drawings` download on the companion website.

STEPS: Drawing Splines

1. Open `ab16-c.dwg` from the companion website.
2. Save the file as `ab16-03.dwg` in your `AutoCAD Bible` folder. This is a topographical site map, as shown in Figure 16.7. Object Snap should be on. Set a running object snap for Insertion.

FIGURE 16.7

With a topographical site map, you can complete the gravel road based on the surveyor's data.

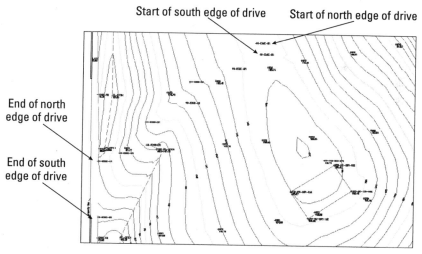

3. Use a Zoom Window to zoom in on the area near the start of the north edge of the drive. Choose Home tab ➪ Draw panel (expanded) ➪ Spline Fit.
4. Check on the command line that the current setting shows Knots=Chord. If not, use the Knots options to change the current setting.

5. At the `Specify first point or [Method/Knots/Object]:` prompt, use the Insertion object snap to pick the cross at the start of the north edge of the drive, as shown in Figure 16.7. Continue to pick the crosses marked N-EDGE-DR. Choose Pan from the Navigation bar to do a real-time pan when you reach the edge of the display. Press Esc. Continue picking points until you get to the end of the north edge of the drive, as shown in Figure 16.7. Press Enter to end point selection.

6. Press Enter to repeat the SPLINE command and pick points for the south edge of the drive, from the start of the south edge of the drive to the end, as shown in Figure 16.7. Pan as necessary. Again, press Enter to accept the default directions for the start and end tangents.

7. Select the last spline you drew. Click the down arrow near the beginning of the spline and choose Control Vertices to see the location of the control vertices. Deselect the spline.

8. If you want, Zoom Previous several times until you see the original view of the drawing. Save your drawing.

Editing splines

Like polylines, splines have their own editing command. To edit a spline, choose Home tab ⇨ Modify panel (expanded) ⇨ Edit Spline to start the SPLINEDIT command. After you select the spline, the command responds with the `Enter an option [Close/Join/Fit data/Edit vertex/convert to Polyline/Reverse/Undo/eXit]:` prompt. Here's how to use these options:

- **Close/Open.** If the spline is open, this option closes it by adding a continuous (tangent) curve from the last point to the start point. If the spline is closed, this option appears as Open. If the spline was originally closed, the Open option removes the connection between the last and first points, although the spline looks the same. If the spline was originally open and you closed it, when you use the Open option, this option erases the curve that it added when you closed it.

- **Join.** Joins selected splines, lines, and arcs to the current spline. These other objects must create a continuous object.

- **Fit Data.** Fit data means the points that you specified (if you used the Fit method of creating the spline), their tolerance, and the tangents (which specify the beginning and ending directions). This option has its own list of suboptions:

  `[Add/Close/Delete/Kink/Move/Purge/Tangents/toLerance/eXit] <eXit>:`

  - **Add.** Adds fit data points to the curve. The prompt asks you to select a point and then automatically selects the next point as well, shown with highlighted grips. At the prompt for a new point, which must be between the two highlighted points, the spline reshapes accordingly. Press Enter to exit the submenu.

  - **Open/Close.** Opens or closes the spline by using the fit points.

  - **Delete.** Deletes a selected fit point. Press Enter to exit the submenu.

  - **Kink.** Prompts you to specify a point on the spline for a new fit point that is a kink — that is, a point that does not maintain the continuity of the spline. You can then move this fit point to create a sharp corner. This option applies only to a fit point spline.

- **Move.** Moves a fit point. You can use the Next or Previous suboptions or the Select Point option to select the point that you want to move. Selected points appear as highlighted grips. You get a prompt for the new fit point location. You can also use grips to edit fit points. Use the eXit suboption to exit the submenu.
- **Purge.** Deletes fit point information. Only the control vertices remain.
- **Tangents.** Enables you to specify start and end tangents of open splines, or one tangent for closed splines. If you don't use this option, a default tangent is calculated.
- **toLerance.** Enables you to specify the tolerance, which determines how closely the spline comes to the fit points. A 0 tolerance puts the spline on the fit points.
- **eXit.** Exits the suboption menu.
- **Edit Vertex.** Displays the control vertices as round grips. This option has its own suboptions:
  - **Add.** Specify a point on the spline to add a vertex. Press Enter to exit the suboption menu.
  - **Delete.** Specify a control vertex to delete. Press Enter to exit the suboption menu.
  - **Elevate order.** Adds evenly spaced control vertices along the spline, in addition to the existing control vertices. You can specify up to 26 control vertices.
  - **Move.** Use the Next or Previous suboptions to specify which vertex you want to move, or use the Select point suboption to pick the vertex. Then specify the new location. Use the eXit suboption to exit the suboption menu.
  - **Weight.** Use the Next or Previous suboptions to specify which vertex you want to move, or use the Select point suboption to pick the vertex. Enter a new weight. A higher weight pulls the spline closer to the selected vertex. Use the eXit suboption to exit the suboption menu.
  - **eXit.** Exits the suboption menu.
- **convert to Polyline.** Changes the spline to a polyline. The prompt asks you to specify a conversion precision. Enter a value between 0 and 99. A higher value results in a more accurate polyline, but adds many more grips.
- **Reverse.** Reverses the direction of the spline so that the start point becomes the endpoint, and vice versa.
- **Undo.** Undoes the most recent edit operation.
- **eXit.** Exits the SPLINEDIT command.

NOTE

When you use the PEDIT command's Spline option on a polyline, the result is a splined polyline. The SPLINEDIT command automatically converts splined polylines to splines, even if you just select the splined polyline and exit the SPLINEDIT command.

You can edit a spline in the Properties palette or the Quick Properties palette. It works similarly to editing a polyline. The Properties palette displays the fit points or the control points so that you can change them.

Creating Regions

Regions are two-dimensional surfaces. They look like closed polylines, but your drawing can calculate more information from regions than from polylines, such as the centroid, moments of inertia, and other properties relating to mass. You can also create complex shapes by combining, subtracting, and intersecting regions. The REGION command is helpful as a preparation for 3D drawing.

You create a region from closed polylines, closed splines, circles, ellipses, and combinations of lines, arcs, and elliptical arcs that create a closed shape. The shape cannot intersect itself like a figure-8.

Figure 16.8 shows a complex region above. Although it looks like a circle with seven circles inside it, it's actually a circular surface with seven holes in it. When you select it, you can see that it's one object. The real proof is when you try to extrude it to create a 3D object out of it. You can then view it at an angle, hide background lines, and clearly see the holes, as shown below.

 To create a region, choose Home tab ⇨ Draw panel (expanded) ⇨ Region. The prompt asks you to select objects. Select all the objects and press Enter to end object selection. If all the objects create a closed, nonintersecting shape, the prompt tells you:

```
1 loop extracted.
1 Region created.
```

FIGURE 16.8

A region can be used to create a complex 3D object.

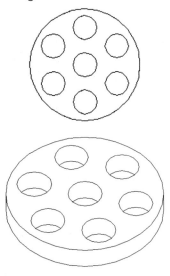

The original objects are deleted. If your objects aren't perfectly end-to-end, the prompt merely states:

```
0 loops extracted.
0 Regions created.
```

TIP

If you want to keep the original objects when converting closed shapes to a region, change the DELOBJ system variable to 0 (off) before you use the REGION command. The DELOBJ system variable determines whether objects that are used to create other objects are deleted.

The BOUNDARY command (see the next section) offers a way to create regions in situations where objects are not neatly drawn end to end.

If you had a hatch inside the objects, you lose hatch associativity. You can rehatch the region if you want.

NOTE

The XEDGES command extracts the edges of a region. For example, if you create a closed polyline of line and arc segments and make a region out of it, you can then use the XEDGES command to change the region to individual lines and arcs. (The EXPLODE command would have the same effect.) I discuss the XEDGES command more in Chapter 24, because it can also extract edges from solids.

You can combine, subtract, and intersect regions to create complex objects. The three commands to accomplish these functions are UNION, SUBTRACT, and INTERSECT. These commands are discussed in Chapter 24 because they're most common in 3D modeling.

ON THE WEB

The drawing that you need for the following exercise on creating regions, ab16-d.dwg,is available from the Drawings download on the companion website.

STEPS: Creating Regions

1. Open ab16-d.dwg, available from the companion website.

2. Save the file as ab16-04.dwg in your AutoCAD Bible folder.

 3. Choose Home tab⇨Draw panel (expanded)⇨Region. At the Select objects: prompt, use a selection window to select the entire model, as shown in Figure 16.9. Press Enter to end object selection. The prompt responds with this message:

```
7 loops extracted.
7 Regions created.
```

4. Save your drawing.

FIGURE 16.9

FIGURE 16.9

The outer profile and the six circles can all be turned into regions. The circles could then be subtracted from the outer profile to create a surface with six holes.

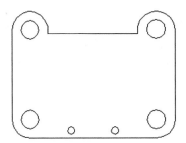

Creating Boundaries

The BOUNDARY command creates either polylines or regions from an enclosed area. This command has the capability of analyzing an area and ignoring intersecting lines that give the REGION command so much trouble. However, no spaces are allowed between objects. (Chapter 12 explains how to use the BOUNDARY command to calculate the area of a closed space.) Use the BOUNDARY command whenever you need to create a closed complex area. To create a boundary, choose Home tab ⇨ Draw panel ⇨ Hatch/Gradient/Boundary drop-down menu ⇨ Boundary to open the Boundary Creation dialog box, as shown in Figure 16.10.

FIGURE 16.10

Boundary Creation dialog box

Follow these steps:

1. If you want the command to detect internal closed areas, leave the Island Detection check box checked. Otherwise, uncheck this check box.

2. The Object Type drop-down list determines the type of object that BOUNDARY creates. Choose either Region or Polyline.

3. Choose the boundary set, which is the area to include in the analysis for the boundary. Usually, you can accept the default of Current Viewport. However, if you have a very complex drawing, choose New to temporarily return to your drawing. Specify a window around the area that you want for the boundary set. The command then returns you to the dialog box.

4. To specify the enclosed area for the boundary, choose Pick Points. You return to your drawing with the `Pick internal point:` prompt.

5. Pick any point inside the closed area that you want for your boundary. The command analyzes the area that you picked.

6. You then get a prompt for another internal point. If you want to create other boundaries, continue to pick internal points. Press Enter to end point selection.

When BOUNDARY creates a region or polyline, the original objects remain. You end up with a region or polyline on top of your original objects.

STEPS: Creating Boundaries

1. Open `ab16-e.dwg`, available from the companion website.

2. Save the file as `ab16-05.dwg` in your `AutoCAD Bible` folder. This is a bushing, as shown in Figure 16.11.

 3. Choose Home tab ⇨ Draw panel ⇨ Hatch/Gradient/Boundary drop-down menu ⇨ Boundary. In the Boundary Creation dialog box, choose Region as the Object type.

4. Choose Pick Points.

5. At the `Pick internal point:` prompt, choose ❶, shown in Figure 16.11.

6. Press Enter to end internal point selection. The prompt responds:

```
4 loops extracted.
4 Regions created.
BOUNDARY created 4 regions
```

7. To see the new region, start the MOVE command. At the `Select objects:` prompt, pick ❷. Move the region to the right; the exact distance is not important. You see both the new region and the original objects.

8. Save your drawing.

FIGURE 16.11

A bushing

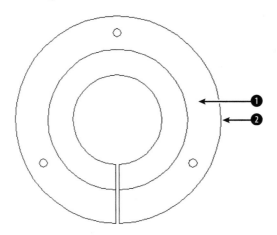

Creating Hatches

Hatches are repeating patterns of lines that fill in an area. Most types of drafting make use of hatching. In architectural drafting, hatched areas are used to indicate materials, such as insulation or grass. In mechanical drafting, hatching often indicates hidden areas or certain materials. AutoCAD and AutoCAD LT provide a large number of hatch patterns. You can create solid fills in the same way that you create hatch patterns.

 Bonus Chapter 8 explains how to create your own hatch patterns.

Figure 16.12 shows a drawing with a simple hatch pattern. Here the cross-section shows solid metal that is hatched to distinguish it from the holes.

Understanding hatch patterns

Hatch patterns have three characteristics that are similar to dimensions:

- **They are blocks.** This means that all the lines that fill in an area are one object. Blocks are covered in Chapter 18.
- **They are associative.** If you edit the object that is hatched, the hatch automatically adjusts to fit the new shape of the object.
- **They can be annotative.** If you activate the annotative property of the hatch, the hatch can automatically adjust its display scale in a viewport. (See Chapter 17 for a discussion of annotative objects and viewports.)

You can specify exactly which area you want to hatch in several ways. Often, the key to successful hatching lies in how you construct the area that you want to hatch. For example, you can use the BOUNDARY and REGION commands covered in previous sections of this chapter to create complex closed areas that you can hatch.

AutoCAD stores hatch pattern definitions in the `acad.pat` and `acadiso.pat` files. AutoCAD LT uses the `acadlt.pat` and `acadltiso.pat` files. If you create your own hatch patterns, you can put them in another file with the PAT filename extension.

FIGURE 16.12

Hatch patterns help you to distinguish different materials or textures.

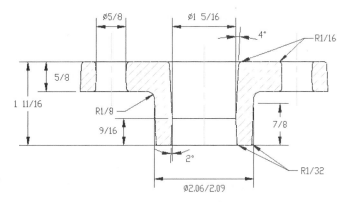

Thanks to Jerry Bottenfield of Clow Valve Company, Oskaloosa, Iowa, for this drawing.

> **TIP**
>
> Create a separate layer for hatch patterns. You may want to turn off or freeze your hatch layer to reduce visual clutter or assist in selecting objects. The hatch layer is typically a different color than the layer of the model that you're hatching.

Defining a hatch

 To hatch an area, choose Home tab ⇨ Draw panel ⇨ Hatch/Gradient/Boundary drop-down menu ⇨ Hatch. This starts the HATCH command. The Hatch Creation tab appears, as shown in Figure 16.13.

FIGURE 16.13

The Hatch Creation tab appears when you create or edit a hatch pattern.

Specifying the hatch type and pattern

In the Properties panel of the Hatch Creation tab, click the Hatch Type drop-down list, and choose one of these four options:

- **Solid.** Lets you fill an enclosed area with a solid fill (rather than a hatch pattern).
- **Gradient.** Lets you fill an enclosed area with a gradient. I cover gradients later in this chapter.
- **Pattern.** Lets you choose any of the standard hatch patterns that come with AutoCAD and AutoCAD LT.
- **User defined.** Lets you define your own hatch pattern by specifying the angle and spacing, using the current linetype.

To specify a hatch pattern, click the Hatch Pattern button in the Pattern panel. A gallery of hatch patterns opens. Scroll down to see all of the patterns. Click an image tile to choose a hatch pattern or choose the Solid tile to choose a solid fill.

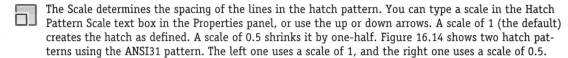

You can drag hatches from your drawing to the Tools Palette window to create hatch tools that you can then drag into your drawing. See Bonus Chapter 3 for a description of the Tools Palette window.

I explain how to create custom hatch patterns in Bonus Chapter 8. To access custom hatch patterns, choose them from the bottom of the Hatch Pattern gallery; they appear there if they are in the support file search path. To add a folder to the support file search path, start the OPTIONS command, click the Files tab, expand the Support File Search Path item, click Add, and then click Browse.

Setting the hatch angle and scale

Use the Angle text box or slider in the Properties panel of the Hatch Creation tab to rotate the angle of the hatch pattern. Watch out here, as many of the patterns are already defined at an angle. The hatch pattern in Figure 16.14 uses a 0-degree angle because the hatch pattern that was used (ANSI31) is defined as diagonal lines.

The Scale determines the spacing of the lines in the hatch pattern. You can type a scale in the Hatch Pattern Scale text box in the Properties panel, or use the up or down arrows. A scale of 1 (the default) creates the hatch as defined. A scale of 0.5 shrinks it by one-half. Figure 16.14 shows two hatch patterns using the ANSI31 pattern. The left one uses a scale of 1, and the right one uses a scale of 0.5.

If you choose User Defined from the Hatch Type drop-down list, you can create a hatch that uses the current linetype, based on the spacing and angle that you specify. To create cross-hatching, click the Double button on the expanded Properties panel. The Hatch Pattern Scale area becomes the Hatch Spacing text box, where you can define the spacing between the lines. Figure 16.15 shows a user-defined double hatch with an angle of 45 degrees and 0.1-unit spacing.

FIGURE 16.14

You can scale the hatch pattern to suit your needs.

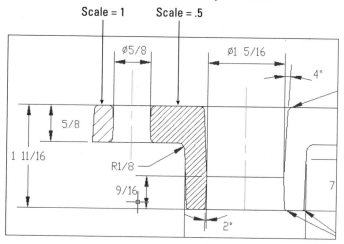

FIGURE 16.15

A user-defined hatch

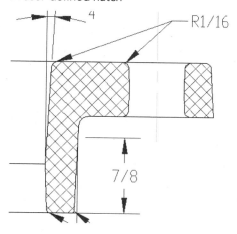

The ISO Pen Width drop-down list in the expanded Properties panel is available only for ISO predefined hatch patterns. (They all have ISO in their name.) This feature adjusts the scale of the pattern according to the pen width that you specify. When you choose a pen width from the drop-down list, the scale shown in the Hatch Pattern Scale text box automatically changes to equal the pen width. Note that you still have to separately set the width of your plotter pens when you plot your drawing.

> **AutoCAD Only**
>
> The Express Tools SUPERHATCH command creates a hatch pattern from an image, block, xref, or wipeout. Choose Express Tools tab ⇨ Draw panel ⇨ Super Hatch (or type superhatch ↵ on the command line). For information on installing Express Tools, see Bonus Chapter 15.

Setting hatch properties

Besides the pattern, angles, and scale, you can set the following properties of hatch patterns in the Properties panel of the Hatch Creation tab:

- **Hatch color.** By default, a hatch's properties are determined by its layer, but you can choose a color from the Hatch Color drop-down list.

> **Note**
>
> You can set the hatch's layer (and change the current layer) without leaving the Hatch Creation tab. Expand the Properties panel, and choose a layer from the Hatch Layer Override drop-down list.

- **Background color.** By default, a hatch has no background color, so you see the drawing area color between the lines. You can specify a background color from the Background Color drop-down list.

> **Note**
>
> You see the background color between the hatch pattern's lines. The background color doesn't have a layer. Although you would usually set the background color on the Ribbon, you can also use the HPBACKGROUNDCOLOR system variable; this system variable setting lasts through the drawing session, unless you change it.

- **Hatch Transparency.** You can make the hatch partially transparent. You would be most likely to use transparency for solid fills or gradients (rather than line patterns). You can set the transparency by layer, block, or individually for the hatch object. To set the transparency by layer or block, use the Transparency Value drop-down list to the left of the Hatch Transparency slider. To set the transparency for the object, choose Transparency Value from the drop-down list and use the Hatch Transparency slider or text box. The highest value is 90, which makes the hatch 90-percent transparent.

 For more about transparency of layers and objects, see Chapter 11.

Setting the hatch origin

The Origin panel lets you determine where the hatch pattern starts. By default, the pattern starts at the origin of the drawing, which is generally 0,0. As a result, the hatch in your object may start somewhere in the middle. This effect is very visible with certain hatch patterns, such as bricks. In Figure 16.16, you see two rectangles. The one on the left uses the default origin; the one on the right uses the lower-left corner of the rectangle as the origin.

FIGURE 16.16

You can specify where the hatch pattern starts.

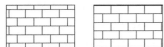

To specify the hatch origin, use the options in the Origin panel of the Hatch Creation tab. Click the Set Origin button to specify any point in your drawing. However, if you want the origin to be one of the corners or the center of the hatched boundary area, you need to expand the Origin panel and choose one of the options.

If you always want to use the same hatch origin (such as the lower-left corner of the boundary), expand the Origin panel and click the Store as Default Origin button.

Determining the hatch boundary

Hatching an entire object is the simplest way to place a hatch. However, the area that you want to hatch is often fairly complex, and the program needs to do some calculations to determine the area.

You can specify the hatch boundary in two ways: you can pick points inside an area (an internal point) and let the command try to find an enclosed boundary, or you can select objects. By default, the HATCH command prompts you to pick an internal point.

When you start the HATCH command, you see the `Pick internal point or [Select objects/seTtings]:` prompt. When you have specified the hatch pattern's properties, click the internal point that you want to specify.

> **TIP**
> When you hover the cursor over an internal point, you see a preview of the hatch. If you don't like what you see, change the hatch's properties and try again.

When you click inside a closed area, you see the following on the command line:

```
Pick internal point or [Select objects/seTtings]: Selecting
    everything...
Selecting everything visible...
Analyzing the selected data...
Analyzing internal islands...
Pick internal point or [Select objects/seTtings]:
```

The command is determining the *boundary set,* which is simply everything visible on the screen. You can continue to pick internal points to hatch adjoining areas. Each boundary is helpfully highlighted. Press Enter to place the hatch.

> **TIP**
> If you pick inside the wrong closed area, type u ↵ to remove the closed area from the current boundary set.

If you want to hatch an entire object, choose Select Boundary Objects in the Boundaries panel of the Hatch Creation tab or use the command's `Select objects` option. Select the object or objects, and press Enter to end object selection and place the hatch.

> **TIP**
>
> You can hatch outside the display on the screen. The hatch pattern extends to include the entire object or boundary that you specified.

 Sometimes you need more control over the boundary, and you also need to remove a boundary that you've selected, without starting from scratch. For example, if you have an inner island that you want to hatch, then by default, the hatch excludes the island. One way to hatch the island is to remove its boundary. To remove a boundary, click the Remove Boundary Objects button in the Boundaries panel. Select the boundaries that you want to remove.

When you pick points to determine the hatch boundary, the hatching process uses the same mechanism as the BOUNDARY command to temporarily create a boundary for hatching. To draw the boundary as a polyline or region, choose Retain Boundaries — Polyline or Retain Boundaries — Region from the Retain Boundary Objects drop-down list of the expanded Boundaries panel. Otherwise, placing the hatch discards the boundary. For more information, see the discussion of the BOUNDARY command earlier in this chapter.

When you hatch an unclosed area, sometimes picking points is more successful; other times, selecting objects works best, so try both options. You can sometimes hatch areas that are not completely closed by using the Gap Tolerance feature. In the expanded Options panel, use the Gap Tolerance text box or slider to specify a value greater than the size of the gap. You can use values from 0 to 5,000. In order to hatch an unclosed area in this way, you need to pick internal points rather than choose objects. Note that the hatch is not associative, which means that if you modify your almost-closed area, you need to rehatch. Using this feature sets subsequent hatches as nonassociative, so be sure to reclick the Associative button in the Options panel.

You may see the Hatch – Boundary Definition Error message, telling you that a closed boundary cannot be determined. Sometimes, you need to modify your objects before you can hatch.

> **NOTE**
>
> When you attempt to create a hatch boundary and are unsuccessful, occasionally the command attempts to show you where gaps are. Red circles appear around the endpoints of the boundary openings. Cancel the command and edit your objects accordingly, and then try again.

> **NOTE**
>
> To display hatches, either solid fill or lines, the FILLMODE system variable must be on, which it is by default. To turn FILLMODE off, type fillmode ↵ and 0↵. You must regenerate the drawing to see the effect.

The Hatch Creation tab has several other options:

- Click Associative in the Options panel to deselect it if you want to create a hatch that is not associated with its object. By default, hatches are associative.
- Click Annotative in the Options panel if you want to create a hatch with the ability to automatically resize its appearance according to viewport scale. (See Chapter 5 for information on using annotative scales, and see Chapter 17 for an exercise on using annotative objects.)
- Toggle Create Separate Hatches in the expanded Options panel if you are selecting several separate enclosed areas and want each area to be a separate hatch object. Otherwise, you create one hatch object that hatches these separated areas.
- Choose a draw order for hatches from the Draw Order drop-down menu on the expanded Options panel. By default, hatches display behind their boundaries, so when you pick a boundary, you select the boundary, not the hatch.

TIP

The HATCHTOBACK command sends hatches beneath all other objects.

- Choose Match Properties in the Options panel to use the hatch type, pattern, angle, scale, and/or spacing of an existing hatch. You then select a hatch pattern. You can fine-tune this process by specifying the hatch's origin. From the Match Properties drop-down menu, choose Use Current Origin to use the current origin setting, or choose Use Source Hatch Origin to use the setting of the source hatch.

Managing Islands

Islands are areas that are entirely enclosed inside a hatch boundary. Islands can make hatching more difficult because you may or may not want to hatch the inside of the island.

NOTE

Text is counted as an island, enabling you to hatch areas that contain text without hatching over the words.

How you specify the boundary can affect the results you get:

- **Picking internal points.** When you pick points, you don't need to select the islands. Hatching detects islands by default. As soon as you pick points, the Remove Boundary Objects button in the Boundaries panel of the Hatch Creation tab becomes available. You can select the islands to remove them from consideration if you want to hatch them. For example, if you remove all the islands shown in Figure 16.17, the result is the same as using the Ignore style, where everything inside the outside boundary is hatched.
- **Selecting objects.** When you select objects, you must also select the islands. If you select the entire area by window, you automatically include the internal islands. If you need to pick individual objects, you must pick the islands individually. If you later erase an island, you don't lose hatch associativity, and the hatch regenerates so that it covers the entire outer boundary.

The resulting hatch depends on the island detection setting. To specify island detection, in the expanded Options tab of the Hatch Creation tab, click the Island Detection drop-down menu and choose one of the options:

- **Normal Island Detection.** Hatches alternate areas so that the outer area is hatched, the next inner island is not hatched, the next inner island is hatched, and so on.
- **Outer Island Detection.** Hatches only the outer area and does not hatch any inner islands.
- **Ignore Island Detection.** Ignores islands and hatches everything from the outside in.
- **No Island Detection.** Uses legacy island behavior.

Figure 16.17 shows three copies of a nut hatched in the three styles. To hatch this model, I selected the entire model, except for the spout at the bottom, with a window.

FIGURE 16.17

Hatching islands using three of the boundary styles

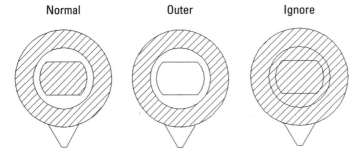

Normal   Outer   Ignore

Dragging and dropping hatch patterns

After you have spent the time creating a hatch, especially a custom hatch (as I describe in Bonus Chapter 8), you may want to use that hatch in other drawings. You can open a PAT (hatch pattern) file from the DesignCenter, preview its hatch patterns, and drag any hatch pattern into any closed object in your current drawing. Here's how to drag a hatch pattern from the DesignCenter:

1. Choose View tab ⇨ Palettes panel ⇨ DesignCenter (or press Ctrl+2) to open the DesignCenter.

2. Use the Tree view to navigate to the folder that contains your `acad.pat`, `acadlt.pat`, or other `.pat` file. If necessary, click the Desktop button and navigate from there.

> **NOTE**
> To find the location of your `.pat` files, choose Application Button ⇨ Options and click the File tab. Double-click the Support File Search Path option. One of the paths listed contains your hatch files.

3. Double-click the folder and select a hatch pattern (.pat) file. A preview of all the hatch patterns appears in the right pane.

4. From the right pane of the DesignCenter, drag the hatch pattern that you want into a closed object in your drawing (or an unclosed object with the gap tolerance value greater than the gap). If you need more options, right-click the pattern as you drag, then choose BHATCH from the shortcut menu to display the Hatch Creation tab, and then specify the hatch parameters in the usual way.

You can drag a hatch pattern to a tool palette to create a hatch with the properties of the hatch in your drawing. Then you can drag that hatch tool from the palette into any closed area in your drawing. The hatch automatically fills the area with the same properties. For more on tool palettes, see Bonus Chapter 3.

Creating gradient fills

Gradients are fills that gradually change from one color to another. You can use gradients to create presentation-quality illustrations without rendering. Because gradient fills can be partially transparent, you can use them where you need to see objects underneath.

To create a gradient:

1. Choose Home tab ⇨ Draw panel ⇨ Hatch/Gradient/Boundary drop-down menu ⇨ Gradient to display the Hatch Creation tab, with the Hatch Type drop-down list set to Gradient.

2. Specify the boundary as described in the "Determining the hatch boundary" section earlier in this chapter.

3. Choose whether you want a two-color gradient by selecting or deselecting the Gradient Colors button, to the left of the Gradient Color 2 drop-down list.

   - If you deselect the Gradient Colors button, click the Gradient Color 1 drop-down list to choose a color from the list, or choose Select Colors to open the Select Color dialog box, where you can choose the color you want. (For instructions on using this dialog box, see Chapter 11.) Click OK to close the dialog box.

> **NOTE**
>
>
>
> You can click the Gradient Tint and Shades button, and specify a tint percentage for a one-color gradient. A tint is the color mixed with white. A low tint percentage creates a gradient with the Gradient Color 1 and black (or a dark shade of the color). A high tint percentage creates a gradient with the Gradient Color 1 and white (or a light tint of the color).

   - If you select the Gradient Colors button, you can specify a color from both the Gradient Color 1 and the Gradient Color 2 drop-down lists, as just described.

4. From the Hatch Pattern drop-down list in the Pattern panel, choose one of the nine gradient styles: linear, cylinder, inverted cylinder, sphere, inverted sphere, hemisphere, inverted hemisphere, curved, and inverted curved.

5. If you want the gradient to be symmetrical, click the Centered button in the Origin panel. To create a gradient that isn't symmetrical, deselect the Centered button. When you deselect the Centered button, the gradient focus moves up and to the left. (You can change this location by changing the angle, as explained in the next step.)

6. Use the Angle slider or text box in the Properties panel to choose an angle. If your gradient is centered, the gradient rotates around its center and remains symmetrical. If your gradient is not centered, the gradient rotates around the edges. If you have already specified an internal point, you can see the change as you drag the slider.

7. Press Enter to finalize the gradient.

See Figure 16.18 for an example of some gradient fills. You could turn off the boundary's layer for a more realistic look.

FIGURE 16.18

The gradient on the left gives the illusion of light shining from the left. On the right, you see a sophisticated use of gradients to create a presentation-quality drawing.

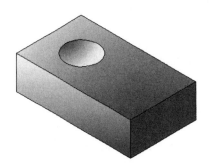 

Thanks to James Wedding for permission to use the drawing on the right from Jones & Boyd, Inc.

Editing hatches

To edit a hatch pattern, including a solid or gradient fill, choose Home tab ⇨ Modify panel (expanded) ⇨ Edit Hatch and select a hatch object to display the Hatch Edit dialog box. An easier way is to just select a hatch object. The Hatch Editor tab appears. The Hatch Editor tab is the same as the Hatch Creation tab, except that not all the options are available. You can use this tab to change any of the hatch properties.

Because hatches are associative (unless you explode them or choose to create them as nonassociative), when you edit their boundaries, they adjust to fit the new boundary. However, if the new boundary is no longer closed, the hatch may lose its associativity, and you see the `Hatch boundary associativity removed` warning message.

> **TIP**
>
> If a hatch has lost its associativity to a boundary, you can still alter its shape by using its grips to edit the hatch. Select the nonassociative hatch, select the grip, and drag.

By default, object snaps don't work with hatch lines. This prevents you from accidentally drawing to a hatch line instead of a nearby object. If you want to snap to hatch lines, choose Application Button⇨Options, click the Drafting tab, and uncheck the Ignore Hatch Objects check box. Click OK to return to your drawing.

TIP

You can obtain the area of a hatch in the Properties palette. Select a hatch and open the Properties palette. Look for the Area item in the Geometry section.

 You can re-create the boundary of any hatch as a polyline or region. Select the hatch and choose Recreate Boundary in the Boundaries panel of the Hatch Editor tab. You can use this feature to create a boundary for a hatch if you have deleted it.

You can also edit a gradient in the Properties palette; use the items in the Pattern section. You can change the colors, angle, type, and whether it is centered.

You can use the center grip of a hatch to stretch or move the hatch. If you hover the cursor over the center grip, you see options to change the origin point, hatch angle, and hatch scale. Hatches have secondary grips between the corner grips. (See the discussion on editing polylines earlier in this chapter for more information.) You can easily move vertices (with the Stretch option), add and remove vertices, and convert a straight edge to an arc.

You can trim hatches. Choose any object that crosses the hatch as the cutting edge and then select the hatch (on the side that you want to trim) as the object to trim. Chapter 10 covers trimming objects.

NOTE

The MIRRHATCH system variable determines what happens when you mirror hatches. If you set MIRRHATCH to 0 (the default), mirroring a hatch maintains the original angle; the lines of the hatch pattern don't change. If you set it to 1, mirroring a hatch mirrors the angle as well so that the lines look like a true mirror image. Compare this system variable to MIRRTEXT (which determines what happens when you mirror text). I cover MIRRTEXT in Chapter 13.

ON THE WEB

The drawing that you need for the following exercise on creating and editing hatches, `ab16-f.dwg`, is available from the `Drawings` download on the companion website.

STEPS: Creating and Editing Hatches

1. Open `ab16-f.dwg`, available from the companion website.

2. Save the file as `ab16-06.dwg` in your `AutoCAD Bible` folder.

 3. Choose Home tab⇨Draw panel⇨Hatch/Gradient/Boundary drop-down menu⇨Hatch. Click Hatch Pattern in the Pattern panel of the Hatch Creation tab that appears, and choose ANSI35 from the Pattern drop-down list.

4. Hover in the enclosed area ❶, as shown in Figure 16.19. You see a preview of the hatch. Click inside ❶ and ❷. Press Enter to create the hatch and end the HATCH command.

FIGURE 16.19

The result after placing the two hatch patterns and the solid fills

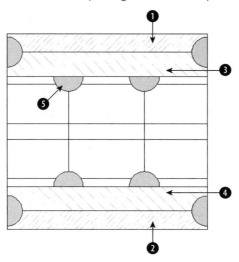

5. Start the HATCH command again. From the Hatch Type drop-down list in the Properties panel, choose User defined. In the Angle text box, type **135** ↵.In the Hatch Spacing text box, type **0.25** ↵.

6. In your drawing, pick points ❸ and ❹, shown in Figure 16.19. Press Enter to create the hatch.

7. Start the HATCH command again. From the Hatch Pattern drop-down list, choose Solid. Click inside all the semi-circle arcs and press Enter.

8. Click the circumference of the arc at ❺, making sure that you select the arc. Pick the bottom grip to make it hot, and drag downward slightly. At the Specify stretch point or [Base Point/Copy/Undo/eXit]: prompt, type **.1** ↵ to make the arc larger. Press Esc to remove the grips. The solid fills expand to fill the larger area. Click Undo on the Quick Access Toolbar to return the arc to its original size.

9. Click the hatch at ❸. Notice that this action selects the hatching in both areas (❸ and ❹) because they were created with one command. In the Properties panel of the Hatch Editor tab that opens, change the angle to 90 and the spacing to 0.15.

10. Save your drawing.

Using the SOLID command

The SOLID command creates solidly filled 2D areas. (It is not directly related to 3D solids.) In general, the HATCH command is much more flexible. Although the SOLID command is a 2D command, it's sometimes used in 3D drawing. When you create a 2D solid and give it thickness, it creates surfaces with tops and bottoms. I cover using thickness in Chapter 21.

SOLID creates straight-edged shapes. If FILLMODE is on, AutoCAD or AutoCAD LT fills in the shape with a solid fill. (That's why it's called SOLID.)

To draw a solid, type **solid** ↵. The command prompts you for first, second, third, and fourth points. You must specify these points in zigzag order (defining triangular shapes), not around the perimeter of the shape. After the fourth point, the command continues to prompt you for third and fourth points, which you can use to create new adjacent solids. Press Enter to end the command.

> **ON THE WEB**
> You can draw with sets of parallel lines, called multilines (for AutoCAD) or dlines (for AutoCAD LT). For example, you can configure two lines that represent both the inner and outer walls of a house to speed up your drawing. I cover multilines and dlines in the Chapter 16 Addendum, which is available on the companion website.

Using the SKETCH Command

The SKETCH command enables you to draw freehand. Freehand drawing is useful for contour lines in architectural or civil engineering drawings, for illustrative effects, and for when you're feeling artistic. Although you may get best results if you have a digitizer and a stylus pen, you can sketch with a mouse or puck as well. Figure 16.20 shows some contour lines created with SKETCH.

FIGURE 16.20

Contour lines drawn with SKETCH

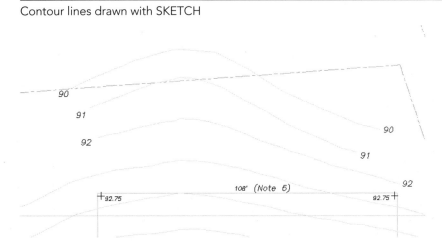

SKETCH can create lines, polylines, or splines. Start the SKETCH command by typing **sketch** ↵.

You see the following on the command line.

```
Type = Lines Increment = 0.1000 Tolerance = 0.5000:
Specify sketch or [Type/Increment/toLerance]:
```

Use the Type option to choose to draw lines, a polyline, or a spline. The Increment option defines the length of the line or polyline segment that you want to create. The Tolerance option only applies to splines and specifies how closely the curve fits to the sketch that you draw.

NOTE

If the increment is too big, small movements do not create a segment at all, and the sketch line appears jagged instead of smooth. However, you need to take into account the scale of your drawing and your zoom factor. You should also turn off Ortho Mode and Snap Mode if they're on.

To sketch, click and drag with your mouse. Sketching is like drawing. By releasing the mouse button, you can end one sketch and then start another in a new location. Press Enter to end the command.

ON THE WEB

The drawing that you need for the following exercise on sketching, ab16-h.dwg, is available from the Drawings download on the companion website.

STEPS: Sketching

1. Open ab16-h.dwg, available from the companion website.

2. Save the file as ab16-08.dwg in your AutoCAD Bible folder. It shows the front elevation of a house. You'll add the sketched path and contours, as shown in Figure 16.21.

3. Type **sketch** ↵. At the Specify sketch or [Type/Increment/toLerance]: prompt, type **t** ↵ and then type **p** ↵ to draw polylines.

4. Type **i** ↵ and then type **1** ↵ to set the increment to 1".

5. Move the cursor to ❶, shown in Figure 16.21. Click and hold the pick button, and draw the first line of the path. Release the pick button to end the sketch segment.

6. Use the same technique to draw the other lines in Figure 16.21.

7. After you're done, press Enter to end the SKETCH command.

8. Save your drawing.

ON THE WEB

You can convert paper drawings to AutoCAD or AutoCAD LT drawings by digitizing them on a tablet. I cover this feature in the Chapter 16 Addendum, which is available on the companion website.

FIGURE 16.21

A sketched path and contours

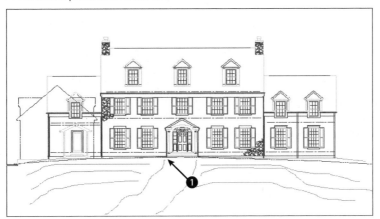

16

Summary

Several types of complex objects add greatly to the capabilities of AutoCAD and AutoCAD LT. In this chapter, you read about:

- Using polylines to combine lines, segments, and arcs of any width into one object
- Utilizing splines to draw mathematically calculated curves, fit to points that you specify
- Using regions, which are two-dimensional surfaces
- Creating regions or polylines from complex areas by using the BOUNDARY command
- Filling in an area with lines, a solid fill, or a gradient with the hatch feature
- Drawing freehand with the SKETCH command

In the next chapter, I explain how to layout and plot a drawing.

Plotting and Printing Your Drawing

IN THIS CHAPTER

Setting up a drawing for plotting or printing

Creating and annotating a layout in paper space

Assigning plot styles

Preparing to plot a drawing

Most drawing jobs are not complete until you see the final result on paper. Traditionally, drawings are plotted on a plotter. However, you can also print a drawing on a regular computer printer. Many printers and plotters can handle a wide range of drawing sizes and paper types. In this chapter, I explain the process of preparing a drawing for plotting, including laying it out in paper space, more properly known as a *layout*. Finally, I cover the actual process of creating a plot.

Preparing a Drawing for Plotting or Printing

When you complete your drawing, you often have some details to finish. If you didn't start with a title-block, you may need to insert one. Even if you have a titleblock, you may need to complete some of its annotation,such as the date that you completed the drawing. If the drawing has layers that you don't want to appear on paper, you should set their layer state to Frozen, Off, or Not Plottable.

Many architectural and mechanical drawings show several views of the model. Now is the time to check that the views are pleasingly laid out, with enough space between them for dimensions and annotation. Later in this chapter, I explain how to create viewports that lay out the drawing in various views.

Doing a draft plot

You may want to do a draft plot, either to check the drawing itself or to be sure that it will print out properly. Although you can preview the plot, sometimes the results are not what you want, and it pays to test the plot on inexpensive paper before plotting on expensive vellum. Draft plots for checking purposes can often be done on a printer. Some companies have wide-format inkjet printers that accept 17 × 22-inch paper and are used exclusively for check plots. Even if the final plot will be all in black, a color printer is a good choice for draft plots because you can easily check the layer scheme.

Plotting a drawing from model space

Model space refers to the mode in which you work when you draw and edit your model. Throughout this book, the discussions and exercises have assumed that you were in model space. After you've prepared your drawing for plotting, as just discussed, you can plot your drawing. See the discussion on plotting later in this chapter.

You can also plot entire sheet sets. For more information, see Bonus Chapter 3. The PUBLISH command, which I cover in Bonus Chapter 5, lets you plot multiple drawings. You can output your drawing to STL format, which supports 3D printing. See Chapter 22.

Creating a Layout in Paper Space

Paper space is a tool for laying out a drawing. It's analogous to creating a sheet of paper at the size on which you'll plot, and placing views on the paper. You place the views by means of *floating viewports*. Floating viewports on a paper space layout are windows into model space, through which you see your drawing.

If you're using several views of your model, you should consider creating a paper space layout. Although paper space was designed for the needs of 3D drawings, it's often used for 2D layout as well. If you want to show views of your model at different scales, paper space is indispensable. If you use a titleblock, paper space is a good choice, because the size of the titleblock needs to be appropriate for the sheet of paper on which you will plot.

A layout provides a visual environment that lets you know what your plot will look like. By creating more than one layout for a drawing, you can create more than one plot for a single drawing. For example, you can create layouts at different scales for different sheet sizes, layouts with different layer states for contractors who need to see varying aspects of a drawing, or layouts that show different sets of views of the drawing.

Entering paper space

You draw in model space. You use a paper space layout to lay out a drawing. When you're in paper space, you can view your drawing only through floating viewports.

You can easily switch from model space to paper space and back again. By default, you see tabs for model space and each of the layouts, as shown in Figure 17.1. If you don't, right-click either the Model or Layout button on the status bar, and choose Display Layout and Model Tabs. If you don't see the Model tab, right-click any layout tab and choose Activate Model Tab. To enter a paper space layout, click a layout tab.

If you see the Model and Layout buttons on the status bar, click them to switch. When the Model button is selected, you know that you're in model space.

By default, you see one floating viewport through which you can view your model. An example is shown in Figure 17.1. The paper space icon and the active layout tab confirm that you're looking at a paper space layout.

TIP

When you hover the mouse cursor over an inactive tab, you see a preview of that tab.

FIGURE 17.1

When you display a layout, the layout is automatically created, with one floating viewport through which you can see your entire drawing.

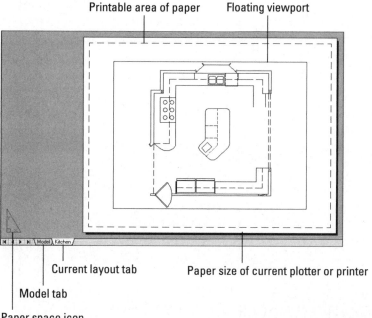

Printable area of paper   Floating viewport

Current layout tab   Paper size of current plotter or printer

Model tab

Paper space icon

 To switch back to model space, click the Model tab or button. Quick View Layouts help you switch between layouts when you have more than one. Click the Quick View Layouts button on the status bar to display a preview of the existing layouts, plus model space. Click the one you want to display. The previews disappear when you click in the drawing area. A small toolbar under the previews lets you pin the preview (so it doesn't disappear), create a new layout tab, publish the layout, or close the preview display. (I cover the PUBLISH command in Bonus Chapter 5.) You can also plot or publish by clicking the appropriate icon at the upper-left and upper-right corners of the preview, respectively.

Using the Layout Wizard

The Layout Wizard guides you through the process of laying out a drawing in paper space. Although you'll eventually want to lay out your drawings on your own, the Layout Wizard is one way to get started using a paper space layout.

To use the Layout Wizard, follow these steps:

1. Enter **layoutwizard** ↵ on the command line. You see the Begin screen, where you name the layout. This name will appear on the Quick View Layouts previews or on the layout tab at the bottom of the drawing window.

2. Type a name for the layout and click Next.

3. The second screen asks you to choose a configured plotter. This list also includes printers. For more information on configuring a plotter or printer, see Bonus Chapter 15. Click Next after you're done.

4. On the third screen, specify a paper size and drawing units, and then click Next.

5. On the next screen, specify whether you want the drawing to plot in portrait or landscape orientation. The wizard rotates a letter *A* on a sheet of paper so that you can see which way your drawing will plot. Then click Next.

6. On the Title Block screen, choose a titleblock if you want to add one. You can add it as a block, which actually inserts the titleblock (see Chapter 18), or as an *external reference,* or *xref,* which references an outside drawing of a titleblock (see Chapter 20). Choose the option you prefer in the Type section, and click Next.

> **NOTE**
>
> To add your own titleblock, first create it as a drawing (in model space) and save it in the \Template folder, or create your own folder for your templates. (To find the location of the \Template folder, choose Application Button ⇨ Options, and click the Files tab. Double-click Template Settings and then Drawing Template File Location. To use your own folder, change this location. The new location will become the default location for all of your templates. Using your own folder reduces the chance that you'll lose your templates when you reinstall or upgrade.) If you have a template that you use for a titleblock, open a new drawing using that template and save it as a drawing in the \Template folder, using the same name as the template.

7. On the Define Viewports screen, you choose from four viewport configuration options:

   - Choose None if you want to create your own floating viewports.

   - Choose Single to create one viewport.

   - Choose Std. 3D Engineering Views to create a 2 × 2 array of top, front, side, and isometric views.

   - Choose Array to specify how many views you want, in rows and columns.

   You can also set the viewport scale. If you want to set the scale of each viewport individually, leave the default Scaled to Fit option for now. Then click Next.

 For more information on scales, see Chapter 5.

8. On the Pick Location screen, click Select Location and the wizard prompts you to pick two corners to define the size of the viewport configuration that you chose. If you chose more than one viewport, these two corners define the extents of all the viewports combined, not the extents of the individual viewports. Click Next.

9. On the last screen, click Finish to close the wizard and return to your drawing.

Figure 17.2 shows the result of completing the wizard with a 2 × 1 array of viewports. Usually, you still need to pan the model and change the scale to get the view that you want in each viewport. I discuss that process later in this chapter.

FIGURE 17.2

After completing the Layout Wizard, you now see your model in the viewport(s) that you created.

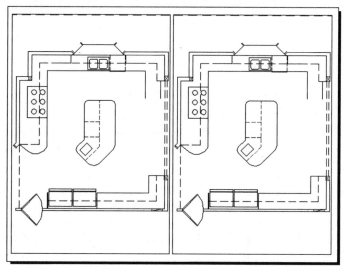

Laying out a drawing in paper space on your own

The Layout Wizard is a good way to learn, but soon you'll want to create layouts on your own. The Layout Wizard creates only the floating viewports, leaving the scaling, panning, and other tasks up to you.

Managing layouts

You can have up to 256 layouts, including the Model tab for model space. If the tabs are not displayed, click the Quick View Layouts button on the status bar. Right-click a layout tab or preview, and choose from the following options on the shortcut menu:

- **New layout.** Creates a new layout.
- **From template.** Opens the Select File dialog box in which you can choose a .dwg, .dxf, or .dwt file. Click Open. You can then choose the layout or layouts that you want from the Insert Layout(s) dialog box. When you import a template, you import everything that exists on the paper space layout, including viewports, any existing text, the titleblock, and so on. (You can then get rid of anything you don't want, if necessary.)

> If you import a layout from a drawing, any layers, linetypes, and such also come along for the ride. Use the PURGE command to get rid of anything that is not being used. See Chapter 12 for information on purging. You can also import a layout by using the DesignCenter. See Chapter 12 for details.

- **Delete.** Deletes the selected layout. A warning dialog box appears. Click OK to delete the layout.
- **Rename.** Allows you to edit the name of a layout in-place on the tab or preview. Press Enter after you are done entering a new layout name.

- **Move or Copy.** Opens the Move or Copy dialog box. To change the order of a layout, you choose the layout that you want the selected layout to be to the left of. You can also choose to move it to the end. Click Create a copy to copy the selected layout. (You can then rename it.) Click OK after you're done.

- **Select All Layouts.** Selects all layouts. You can then delete or publish them.

- **Activate Previous Layout/Activate Model Tab.** Moves you to the last layout that you had displayed or to the Model tab.
- **Page Setup Manager.** Opens the Page Setup Manager, which is discussed next.
- **Plot.** Opens the Plot dialog box, which is discussed later in this chapter.
- **Publish Selected Layouts.** If two or more layouts are selected, you can use this item to start the PUBLISH command with the selected layouts in the list of sheets to publish. For more information on the PUBLISH command, see Bonus Chapter 5.
- **Drafting Standard Setup.** Opens the Drafting Standard dialog box, which is used to create 2D drawings from 3D Inventor models. (Inventor is Autodesk software for creating 3D mechanical models. This capability is part of 2D view objects and the VIEWBASE command. I don't cover creating 2D drawings from Inventor models in this book, but I do cover 2D view objects and the VIEWBASE command in Chapter 22.
- **Import Layout as Sheet.** Imports the layout to a sheet in a sheet set. (See Bonus Chapter 3 for information on sheet sets.)
- **Export Layout to Model.** Saves the contents of the layout to a new drawing.
- **Hide Layout and Model Tabs.** Hides the layout tabs.

Using the Page Setup Manager

When you click a new (unused) layout tab, or choose it from the layout button (or a preview from Quick View Layouts) on the status bar, by default you see one floating viewport. However, you can create and save page setups that store many of the settings that were explained previously in the discussion of the Layout Wizard. The value in saving page setups is that the settings are attached to the layout. If you have more than one layout, each with its own page setup, then you can quickly switch the page settings as you move from layout to layout. After you have page setups, you can manage them in the Page Setup Manager, as shown in Figure 17.3.

 To display the Page Setup Manager, right-click the active layout tab and choose Page Setup Manager. Alternatively, choose Output tab ⇨ Plot panel ⇨ Page Setup Manager.

FIGURE 17.3

The Page Setup Manager helps you to control your page setups.

NOTE

When you check the Display When Creating a New Layout check box (at the bottom of the Page Setup Manager dialog box), the Page Setup Manager automatically appears each time you display a layout for the first time. If it does not appear, to make it display each time, right-click the current paper space layout tab (or a layout from Quick View Layouts) and choose Page Setup Manager; then check the check box. You can also specify whether you want the Page Setup Manager to appear when you click a new layout by choosing Application Button ➪ Options and clicking the Display tab. Check or uncheck the Show Page Setup Manager for New Layouts check box.

The Page Setup Manager lists your layouts and page setups. You can create a new page setup, modify an existing setup, or set a page setup current for the active layout. Click the Import button to import a page setup from another drawing.

To create a new page setup, click New. In the New Page Setup dialog box, enter a name for the page setup. Choose an existing page setup to start from so that you don't have to change all the settings, and click OK. The Page Setup dialog box appears, as shown in Figure 17.4.

FIGURE 17.4

The Page Setup dialog box

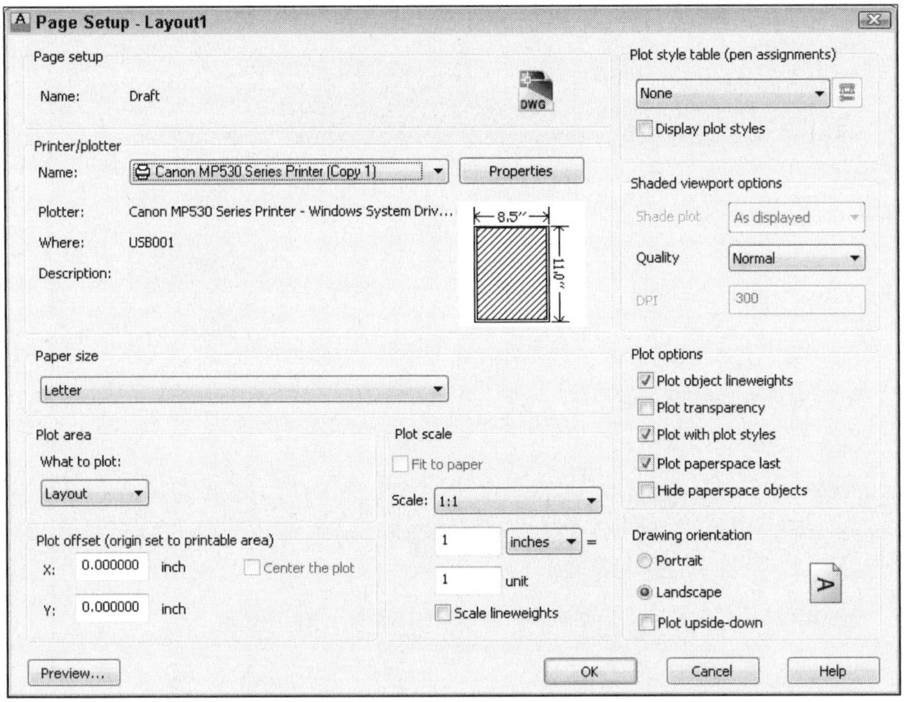

Here's how to use the Page Setup dialog box:

- **Printer/Plotter.** Choose a printer or plotter from the drop-down list. For more information, see "Specifying plot settings" later in this chapter.

- **Paper size.** Choose a paper size from the drop-down list.

- **Plot area.** By default, the plot is set to the layout. However, you can choose to plot the current display, the drawing extents, a named view, or a window that you specify; the options that are available depend on whether you're on the Model tab or a layout tab.

- **Plot offset.** You can move the plot from the lower-left corner. Specify the X and Y offset in inches. If you aren't plotting the layout, but rather some smaller area, you can check the Center the Plot check box to center the plot on the paper.

- **Plot scale.** Set the scale from the drop-down list. You can also type a scale in the text boxes. Because you scale your model in your floating viewports, you usually don't have to scale the layout as well. Therefore, you typically plot a layout in paper space at 1:1. If you're using lineweights and want to scale them, check the Scale Lineweights check box.

- **Plot style table.** Choose a plot style table if you want to use one. For more information, see the section "Working with Plot Styles" later in this chapter.

- **Shaded viewport options.** Use this feature to determine the display of the Model tab. (To set the display of a viewport on a layout, select the viewport and make the changes in the Properties palette.) With the Model tab displayed, choose one of the Shade Plot display options: As Displayed, Legacy Wireframe, Legacy Hidden, Conceptual, Hidden, Realistic, Shaded, Shaded with Edges, Shades of Gray, Sketchy, Wireframe, X-Ray, Rendered, Draft, Low, Medium, High, or Presentation. (I cover these options in the "Setting hidden and shaded views for viewports" section later in this chapter.) You can also choose a quality (resolution) — Draft, Preview, Normal, Presentation, Maximum, or Custom. If you choose the Custom quality, you can specify the dots per inch (dpi). (AutoCAD only.)

- **Plot options.** Clear the Plot Object Lineweights check box if you used lineweights but don't want the lineweights to be plotted. Check the Plot Transparency check box if you want to plot transparent objects as they appear in the drawing area. Clear the Plot with Plot Styles check box if you assigned plot styles to layers or objects but don't want to plot them. (Plot styles are discussed later in this chapter.) Clear the Plot Paperspace Last check box in order to plot objects drawn on the paper space layout first. Check the Hide Paperspace Objects check box to hide lines of 3D objects that you created *in paper space*. (Later in this chapter, I explain how to hide lines of 3D objects that were created in model space, a more common situation.)

> **NOTE**
> Plotting with transparency may take more time. See Chapter 11 for more on transparency.

- **Drawing orientation.** Choose portrait or landscape. You can also choose to plot upside down. Use these settings to rotate a drawing when you plot it.

When you've completed your settings in the dialog box, click OK to return to the Page Setup Manager. You can see the new page setup in the list. To make the page setup active, click Set Current. Then click Close to return to your drawing.

Preparing layers

If necessary, create the layers that you need. If you want to insert a titleblock, create a separate layer for it. The actual viewports should also be on their own layer, because it's common to freeze that layer or set it to non-plottable, so that the borders don't show. Even if you want to plot the viewports, making them a different color from your model helps you to easily distinguish them.

Inserting a titleblock

Insert the titleblock. You can have a file that contains just the titleblock. You can also use a block or external reference. Putting the titleblock on your layout is common because it defines the edges of your paper and is not a real-life object. These qualities make it appropriate for paper space.

Creating floating viewports

Remember that you need a floating viewport to see your model on a paper space layout. The default is one floating viewport. Floating viewports have properties that are important to understand when you're creating layouts in paper space:

- Unlike tiled viewports (which I cover in Chapter 8), floating viewports are actual objects that you can erase, move, and stretch. They can — and should — be on separate layers, so that you can control the visibility of the viewport borders when desired. They don't need to take up the entire screen. You can change their size and location freely.
- In paper space, the crosshairs are not limited to one floating viewport.
- You can separately set the visibility of the UCS icon in each floating viewport.
- You can create as many viewports as you want, but don't go overboard!
- After you create floating viewports, you can switch to model space and work on your models while still on the layout. To do so, double-click inside a viewport. You do this mostly to adjust the view of the model in the viewport. In model space, floating viewports are similar to tiled viewports in that only one can be active at a time.

Whatever you draw in paper space does not affect your models; it exists only in paper space and disappears when you click the Model tab or button.

Because viewports are created on the current layer, you need to make the desired layer current. If the default viewport appears and you don't want it, select and delete it. Then to create floating viewports, choose Layout tab ⇨ Layout Viewports panel while on a layout. Choose from the following items:

- **Rectangular** (drop-down menu). At the prompt, specify the first and then the opposite corner of the viewport, press Enter to fit the viewport to the layout, or use one of the other options.

- **Polygonal** (drop-down menu). At the `Specify start point:` prompt, pick a point. At the `Specify next point or [Arc/Length/Undo]:` prompt, continue to specify points or right-click to choose one of the options. If you choose the Arc option, you see suboptions that are just like those you see when drawing an arc in a polyline. Press Enter to use the Close option (which appears after you've specified two or more points) to complete the viewport.

- **From Object** (drop-down menu). You can create a viewport by converting an existing closed object, such as an ellipse. At the `Select object to clip viewport:` prompt, select the object.

- **Named.** If you've saved a tiled viewport configuration, choose this option to open the Viewports dialog box. On the Named Viewports tab, choose the configuration from the list and click OK. In other words, you can use a tiled viewport configuration for floating viewports. See Chapter 8 for a full discussion of saving viewport configurations.

TIP

If you have saved named views, you can immediately display them in a viewport. Click one of the viewports in the Preview pane and choose the named view from the Change View To drop-down list. At the same time, you can specify a visual style for each viewport. (I cover visual styles in Chapter 22; visual styles are available in AutoCAD only.) You can do this for each viewport that you create.

You can quickly create configurations of floating viewports using the VPORTS command, which opens the Viewports dialog box with the New Viewports tab on top, as shown in Figure 17.5. Choose the configuration you want and click OK.

As soon as you create a viewport, you see your drawing in the new viewport.

NOTE

The VPROTATEASSOC system variable controls the rotation of a view within a floating viewport. The default setting, 1, rotates the view when you rotate the viewport object. When you set this system variable to 0, the view within the viewport does not rotate when you rotate the viewport.

Returning to model space while on a layout

After creating viewports, the next step is to set the view in each viewport. To do this, you need to return to model space, while still on the layout, and make a viewport active. The active viewport shows a dark border. You can do this in two ways:

- Double-click inside the viewport that you want to become active.
- Click PAPER on the status bar. (The button then says MODEL.) Then click the viewport that you want to become active.

FIGURE 17.5

Use the Viewports dialog box to choose one of the standard configurations of floating viewports.

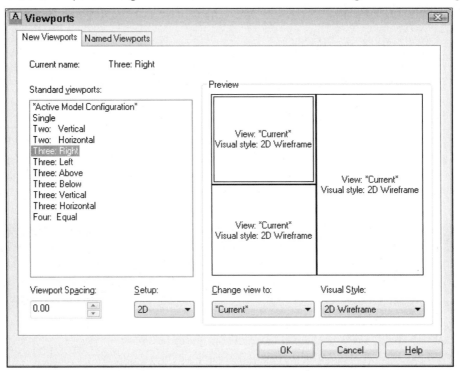

To help you work more easily in a viewport, you can maximize the viewport temporarily without leaving the layout. Just double-click the selected viewport's border. Another way to maximize a viewport is to right-click with the viewport border selected and choose Maximize Viewport. The viewport takes up the entire screen, and you see a red border around the edge. You can draw, edit, zoom, or pan in the view as you normally would in model space; however, zooming and panning have no effect on the viewport's view or scale. When you've finished making the desired changes, right-click and choose Minimize Viewport. The commands that maximize and minimize a viewport are VPMAX and VPMIN. While you're in a layout, you can use the following buttons on the status bar:

 • Maximize Viewport: Maximizes the viewport to take up the entire drawing window

 • Minimize Viewport: Returns the viewport to its original size

 • Maximize Next Viewport: Switches to the next viewport, still maximized

 • Maximize Previous Viewport: Switches to the previous viewport, still maximized

TIP

To cycle from viewport to viewport while in model space, press Ctrl+R. (This technique doesn't work if the viewport is maximized.)

Setting viewport scale

You'll probably want to set the zoom for each viewport to exact scale. Each viewport can have its own scale, and you can set the zoom in three ways:

- If you're still in paper space, select the viewport on its border. Open the Properties or Quick Properties palette. Choose Standard Scale and choose one of the standard scales from the drop-down list that appears.

- If you select the viewport, or double-click inside it to enter model space, the Viewport Scale pop-up list appears on the status bar, where you can choose a scale.

- From model space, choose Zoom Scale from the Zoom drop-down menu on the Navigation bar or choose View tab ⇨ Navigate 2D panel ⇨ Zoom drop-down menu ⇨ Scale. You need to use the inverse of the scale factor with the xp option of the ZOOM command. If you have an architectural drawing at a scale of 1:48, type **1/48xp** ↵. (The abbreviation *xp* stands for "times paper space.")

After you scale each viewport, you need to go back and pan until you see what you want in the viewport. If necessary, you can also change the size of the viewport itself.

Locking the viewport

If you remain in model space with a viewport active, and then zoom in or out, you change the displayed scale of the model. After you set the scale, you should lock it to avoid this problem. To lock a viewport, select the viewport's border (while in paper space) and display the Properties palette. Choose Display Locked and then choose Yes from the drop-down list. (You can also select the viewport, right-click, and choose Display Locked ⇨ Yes.) Now, when you zoom in and out, only paper space objects will be affected.

> **TIP**
> You can lock and unlock any selected viewport on the status bar by using the lock icon to the left of the VP Scale pop-up list, or in the Quick Properties palette.

Setting viewport size, placement, and display

To adjust the viewports themselves, return to paper space by clicking MODEL on the status bar or by double-clicking anywhere outside a viewport (but in the drawing area). You cannot access your models anymore, but you can now move, rotate, and resize the viewports if necessary. You can use grips to stretch, move, and rotate them, or use the STRETCH, MOVE, and ROTATE commands.

The VPCLIP command enables you to redefine the boundary of an existing viewport. You can delete the boundary of a clipped viewport and change it to a rectangular viewport or create a polygonal boundary just as you do when creating a polygonal viewport.

To redefine the boundary of a viewport, you must be in paper space. Choose Layout tab ⇨ Layout Viewports panel ⇨ Clip to start the VPCLIP command. Select a clipped viewport boundary from paper space. At the `Select clipping object or [Polygonal/Delete] <Polygonal>:` prompt, you can select an object to use for the new boundary or press Enter to see the same prompts that you see when you create a polygonal viewport. Right-click and choose Delete to delete the boundary of a clipped viewport (one created by choosing an object or using the Polygonal option).

You can also turn viewports on and off. When a viewport is off, it doesn't display your model. Do this when the regeneration process becomes slow as a result of a large number of viewports or a complex drawing. To turn off a viewport, select it (in paper space); then right-click and choose Display Viewport Objects ⇨ No.

Controlling scale for noncontinuous linetypes

The PSLTSCALE system variable controls linetype scaling in paper space viewports. By default, it is set to 1 so that the paper space scale controls the scale of any noncontinuous linetypes. This lets you have viewports of differing scales while displaying linetypes identically. When you set PSLTSCALE to 0, linetype scales are based on the drawing units where the object was created (in either model space or paper space). Linetypes are still scaled by the LTSCALE factor. When you either change PSLTSCALE or change the zoom scale in a viewport with PSLTSCALE set to 1, you need to do a regen to update the linetype scales in each viewport.

Setting layer visibility and properties within a viewport

If you want, you can individually set layer visibility in floating viewports. For example, you might have some text or dimensions that appear in more than one floating viewport, but you may not want to show them more than once. Or perhaps you don't want a hatch to appear in one of the viewports. You must be in model space, so double-click in any viewport. To freeze a layer in an active viewport, click the Layer drop-down list in the Home tab ⇨ Layers panel. Find the layer that you want to freeze in that viewport and click the icon in the Freeze or Thaw in Current Viewport column. Click the top of the drop-down list to close it. That layer disappears in the active viewport.

You can also freeze/thaw layers in new viewports; these are viewports that you haven't yet created. Choose Home tab ⇨ Layers panel ⇨ Layer Properties to open the Layer Properties Manager. Click the icon for the layer that you want in the New VP Freeze column, and auto-hide or close the palette.

> **TIP**
> You can freeze selected layers in all viewports except the current one or in all viewports from the right-click menu in the Layer Properties Manager. To access these options, select the layers you want to freeze in a viewport and choose In All Viewports Except Current or In All Viewports.

 Remember that layers have a plottable/not plottable state. Therefore, you can set certain layers to not plottable if you don't want them to appear on the plot. For more information, see Chapter 11.

You can change the properties of a layer ¾ color, linetype, lineweight, transparency, and plot style ¾ by viewport. For example, you could make a layer that is green in model space display as blue in one of the viewports. This feature is called *layer overrides*.

To set layer properties for individual viewports, follow these steps:

1. Display a layout and double-click the desired viewport to enter model space from that layout.

2. Open the Layer Properties Manager. You now see five new columns ¾ VP Color, VP Linetype, VP Lineweight, VP Transparency, and VP Plot Style ¾ as shown in Figure 17.6.

FIGURE 17.6

When you open the Layer Properties Manager from model space on a layout, you see
columns that let you override layer properties for the current viewport.

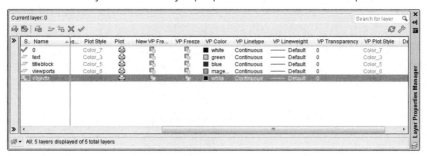

3. To override the properties of a layer for that viewport, you use the same method as for any
   other property. (See Chapter 11 for a full explanation of the Layer Properties Manager and
   layers.) For example, to override the color, click the layer's item in the VP Color column to
   open the Select Color dialog box, where you can choose a new color.

When you create a layer override, the Layer Properties Manager displays a light blue block in the column for the layer's name, the column for the property you overrode, and the VP column for that property. You see the same block for that layer in the Layer drop-down list in the Layers panel on the
Home tab. The block only appears when the affected viewport is current.

You can remove overrides in several ways, depending on whether you want to remove all of a layer's
overrides and whether you want to remove overrides in all viewports (as opposed to the current one).
To remove an override, open the Layer Properties Manager and do one of the following:

- To remove one property override (such as Color) for a layer, right-click the Color column for
  the layer containing the override and choose Remove Viewport Overrides For ➪ Color ➪ In
  Current Viewport Only or In All Viewports.

- To remove all property overrides for a layer (or all selected layers), right-click the layer and
  choose Remove Viewport Overrides For ➪ Selected Layers ➪ In Current Viewport Only or In All
  Viewports.

- To remove all property overrides, right-click any layer and choose Remove Viewport Overrides
  For ➪ All Layers ➪ In Current Viewport Only or In All Viewports.

Setting hidden and shaded views for viewports

If you have a 3D drawing, you may want to hide back lines for objects in a viewport when you plot
(similar to using the Hidden visual style on the Model tab). This procedure lets you hide lines in one
viewport but not in others. You don't see the result until you plot or display a plot preview. You can
also specify shading and rendered views for each viewport, from both model space and paper space
layouts, as shown in Figure 17.7.

FIGURE 17.7

In this drawing, one viewport displays a wireframe, one a hidden view, and one a rendered view.

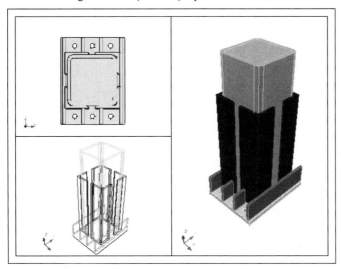

To choose the type of shaded view, select any viewport in paper space. Right-click, and choose Shade Plot. Then choose one of the following options:

- **As Displayed.** Plots the objects as they're currently displayed.
- **Wireframe.** Plots the objects in 2D wireframe display.
- **Hidden.** Plots the objects with back lines removed.
- **Conceptual.** Shades the model with flat colors on its faces (AutoCAD only).
- **Realistic.** Shades the model with a special color palette and gradients (AutoCAD only).
- **Shaded.** Displays surfaces with smooth shading in their assigned color (AutoCAD only).
- **Shaded with Edges.** Displays surfaces with smooth shading in their assigned color with visible edges (AutoCAD only).
- **Shades of Gray.** Shades the model using grayscale colors (AutoCAD only).
- **Sketchy.** Shades the model with black and white colors, but gives a hand-sketched look to the edges (AutoCAD only).
- **Wireframe.** Plots the objects in 3D wireframe display (AutoCAD only).
- **X-Ray.** Displays objects with transparency (AutoCAD only).
- **Rendered.** Plots objects using the default rendering settings. (See Bonus Chapter 2 for information on rendering. This option is not available in AutoCAD LT.) Express Tools (in AutoCAD only) include several commands for working with layouts:
    - The ALIGNSPACE command (choose Express Tools tab ➪ Layout panel ➪ Align Space) aligns objects in different viewports.
    - The VPSYNC command (choose Express Tools tab ➪ Layout panel ➪ Synchronize Viewports) changes the pan and zoom of a second viewport to match that of the first ("master") viewport that you select, so that the view of the objects is consistent (synchronized) from viewport to viewport.

- The VPSCALE command (choose Express Tools tab ⇨ Layout panel (expanded) ⇨ List Viewport Scale) displays the scale from paper space to model space of the selected viewport.

- The LAYOUTMERGE command (choose Express Tools tab ⇨ Layout panel ⇨ Merge Layout) moves all objects on one or more layouts that you specify to a single layout.

Annotating a layout

Before plotting, you may want to add notes, dimensions, and other annotations. You also need to pay attention to the scale of certain items in your viewports to make sure that they appear properly. For example, if you have one viewport at 1:1 and another at 1:4 and you show dimensions in both viewports, the dimensions will appear at different sizes in each viewport. This makes legibility difficult. Other items that may need adjustment are text, hatches, blocks, and linetypes.

You can annotate a drawing in two different ways:

- You can use *annotative objects,* which store representations at various scales and display them according to the scale of a specific viewport. They automate the process of scaling certain types of objects in viewports at various scales. You can create annotation objects for text, Mtext, dimensions, tolerances, leaders, multileaders, hatches, blocks, and block attributes. You create these objects in model space. For example, you can display objects at 1:1 in one viewport and 1:4 in another viewport, but the text will be the same size in each viewport. You can control the display of more types of objects in this way, but the process is somewhat more complex.

I discuss how to create annotative objects in the following chapters: text and Mtext in Chapter 13; dimensions, tolerances, multileaders, and leaders in Chapters 14 and 15; hatches in Chapter 16; blocks in Chapter 18; and attributes in Chapter 19.

- You can annotate in paper space, in which case you create the annotations at their desired plotting size, without scaling them. This method is fairly easy, but it doesn't allow control over drawing objects such as blocks, attributes, and hatches.

Before these methods were available, for each object, you needed to create a separate layer for each scale, calculate the appropriate size for each object, and freeze layers in the viewports where you didn't want certain objects to appear. For example, if you wanted one text object to appear at 1:1 in one viewport and another text object to appear at 1:4 in another viewport, you created them at the appropriate size on different layers. Then you froze one layer in one viewport and the other layer in the other viewport. As you can imagine, this was a complicated process.

Using annotation objects on a layout

The purpose of using annotation objects is to automate the process of scaling these objects when you display them at different scales in different viewports. To use this feature, each of the objects needs to be annotative; you add this property when you create the object or its style (such as a text style).

Follow these steps to create and use annotation objects:

1. For the following objects, first create an annotative style:

   - **Mtext.** Use the default Annotative text style or create an annotative text style by checking the Annotative check box in the Text Style dialog box. At the same time, you use the Paper Text Height text box to set the final height you want for your text when you plot it on paper. See Chapter 13 for details.

   - **Dimensions.** Use the default Annotative dimension style or create an annotative dimension style by checking the Annotative check box in the Create New Dimension Style dialog box or on the Fit tab of the New (or Modify) Dimension Style dialog box. See Chapter 15 for details. Note that you need an annotative text style for the text in your annotative dimensions.

   - **Multileaders.** Use the default Annotative multileader style or create an annotative multileader style by checking the Annotative check box in the Create New Multileader Style dialog box or on the Leader Structure tab of the Modify Multileader Style dialog box. See Chapter 14 for details. Note that you need an annotative text style for the text in your multileaders.

> **NOTE**
>
> You can also create annotative leaders by using the QLEADER command. You don't create a special style for the leader, but you need to use an annotative text style for its text. You also need an annotative text style for block attributes (covered in Chapter 19).

2. Decide which objects you will display at which scales. If you don't know this when you draw your objects, you can add scales to them later. Remember that you might have objects that you want to appear at one scale, but not at another scale; however, you might have objects that you want to appear at more than one scale. Of course, you can change the scales of your objects later. A good way to help you figure out the scales that you need is to set up your viewports before you finish drawing, including their scales.

> **NOTE**
>
> When you turn the ANNOAUTOSCALE system variable on, it automatically adds scales to annotative objects as you add annotative scales. If you have an object that you want to have only one scale, then turn off this system variable. It's off by default. Use the icon on the right side of the status bar to the right of the Annotation Visibility button to toggle ANNOAUTOSCALE on and off. When on, there's a yellow lightning bolt; when off, the lightning bolt is gray. In general, leave ANNOAUTOSCALE off unless you want to update all the annotative objects in your drawing to a new annotative scale.

3. You need to assign an annotation scale to all objects that you want to be annotative. You can do so as you draw, or afterwards. To set the annotation scale as you draw, click the Annotation Scale button at the right side of the status bar to display the scale list and choose the scale you want. For example, choose 1:4 if you plan to display the object in a viewport at the 1:4 scale.

In Chapter 5, I explain scales in general and how to edit the scale list. It's easier to work with the scale list when it doesn't include scales that you don't use. You can also change the order of the list to place scales that you use most often at the top.

4. Create the object. The Select Annotation Scale dialog box opens the first time that you create an annotation object in your session, and requests that you choose an annotation scale.

You can do so from the drop-down list in that dialog box. If you've already set the scale, just click OK. Remember that you can add and change annotation scales at any time.

5. Add other annotation scale to existing objects. You can do this in two ways:

- If ANNOAUTOSCALE is on, to add another annotation scale to existing objects, you just choose another annotation scale by clicking the Annotation Scale button on the status bar.

- If ANNOAUTOSCALE is off, you need to add annotation scales manually. Use this method if you don't want all objects to have every annotation scale that you'll be using. Select the object, right-click it, and choose Annotative Object Scale ⇨ Add/Delete Scales to open the Annotation Object Scale dialog box, as shown in Figure 17.8. You can also open the dialog box by choosing Annotate tab ⇨ Annotation Scaling panel ⇨ Add/Delete Scales, or by displaying the Properties palette, clicking the Annotative Scale item, and clicking the Ellipsis button that appears.

NOTE

When you hover the cursor over an annotation object, you see a special annotation icon near the cursor, which lets you know that the object is annotative. If an object has two or more annotation scales, you see a double annotation icon.

17

FIGURE 17.8

Use the Annotation Object Scale dialog box to add or delete annotation scales for selected objects.

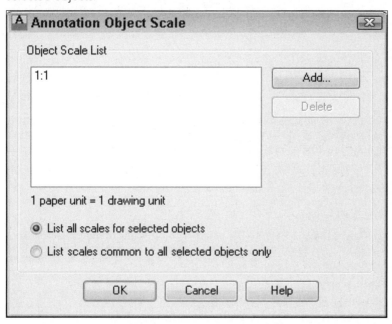

6. If you're manually adding an annotation scale, click the Add button. In the Add Scales to Object dialog box, choose the scale or scales that you want, and click OK twice to return to your drawing.

NOTE

The ANNOALLVISIBLE system variable determines whether you see all the scales for an object (On) or only the current scale (Off). Use the Annotation Visibility button on the status bar to the right of the Annotation Scale pop-up list. On the Model tab, turn this variable on to check that objects have the multiple annotation scales that you want them to have. On a layout, you usually want to keep this variable off, because seeing multiple scales is confusing.

The SELECTIONANNODISPLAY system variable specifies whether you see alternative sizes of an annotative object when you select it. The size of the object for the current annotative scale shows whether or not the object is selected, but when you select the object, you see all sizes if this system variable is set to 1, the default. However, objects at sizes for noncurrent scales are dimmed.

7. Switch to a layout and create the viewports that you need at the scales that you have chosen. Pan to get the display you want. Then lock the display, as explained earlier in this chapter.

Your annotation objects now automatically scale to match the scale of their viewport. If you don't get the results you want, you can check that the viewport scale and the annotative scale match by selecting a viewport and looking on the right side of the status bar. If they don't match, change the annotative scale from the pop-up list; your objects should now scale properly.

TIP

 To synchronize the viewport and annotative scales, click the Annotation Scale Is Not Equal to Viewport Scale button to the right of the annotative scale list on the status bar.

Adding text and dimensions in paper space

Annotation that applies to the entire drawing, such as titleblock text, can be, and often is, created on the paper space layout. You can change to a text layer and use the TEXT or MTEXT command, as usual.

Sometimes you create an object in model space — perhaps some text or a logo — and want to move it to paper space, or vice versa. For example, you may want to move a text label that you inserted in model space into your titleblock, which you inserted in paper space. The CHSPACE command makes it easy to move objects from one space to the other, without worrying about scale differences.

To move an object in either direction, follow these steps:

1. Display a layout.
2. Switch to the space where the object that you want to move resides. For example, if you want to move text from model space to paper space, double-click inside the viewport containing the text to switch to model space.
3. Choose Home tab ⇨ Modify panel (expanded) ⇨ Change Space.
4. Select the object that you want to move.
5. Make the desired viewport active and press Enter.

The command scales objects to maintain the same visual appearance. The amount of scaling depends on the scaling of the viewport. If the viewport scale is 1:1, no scaling occurs.

In Chapters 14 and 15, I discussed dimensioning in model space, but you can dimension in paper space, as well. The Trans-Spatial Dimensioning feature automatically adjusts dimensions for the scale of the viewport. These paper space dimensions are fully associative. Dimensioning in paper space has several advantages:

- You don't have to worry about the size of the individual dimension components themselves, such as the text and the arrows. If you plot from paper space, you plot at 1:1 scale.
- If you don't need to scale other objects (such as hatches and blocks), dimensioning in paper space is probably simpler than using the annotative feature.
- You can place the dimensions outside the border of the floating viewport, which may make it easier to fit the dimensions. (On the other hand, you may find it harder to fit the dimensions if you have other viewports on the layout.)
- You can easily dimension just one view of the model.

TIP

If you create dimensions in a viewport in paper space and then zoom or pan in that viewport, the objects and the dimension get out of sync. Use the DIMREGEN command on the command line to reset the dimension to match its object.

You still need to scale the size of the dimension to your viewport scale, including the text, arrows, and so on, as follows:

1. Open the Dimension Style Manager.
2. Choose the dimension style that you want to use and click Modify.
3. On the Fit tab, choose Scale Dimensions to Layout.
4. Click OK and then click Close.

When you follow this procedure, all the dimensions using the dimension style that you chose appear the same size on your final plot.

NOTE

Drawings created in earlier releases (before AutoCAD 2002 and AutoCAD LT 2002) do not automatically have the new associative dimensions. If necessary, change the DIMASSOC system variable's value to 2. Also, you usually need to use the DIMREASSOCIATE command to associate existing dimensions to their objects. See Chapter 14 for more information on associative dimensions.

Export a layout to model space of a new drawing

You can create a new drawing by exporting a layout tab. All visible layout tab objects appear in model space in the new drawing. Right-click a layout tab (or preview in Quick View Layouts) and choose Export Layout to Model (the EXPORTLAYOUT command) to open the Export Layout to Model Space Drawing dialog box. The command creates a default filename based on the current drawing and layout names. You can change the name and location. Click Save. You can then choose to open the new drawing immediately.

Saving a layout template

After you do all the work to create a layout, you can save it as a template so that you can use it in other drawings. (The template includes all objects on the layout.) Here's how:

1. Type **layout** ↵ on the command line.

2. At the prompt, right-click and choose SAveas.

3. At the `Enter layout to save to template <Layout2>:` prompt, press Enter to save the current layout, the name of which appears in brackets, or type the name of another layout.

4. The Create Drawing File dialog box opens, with the `Template` folder active. The Files of Type drop-down list shows AutoCAD (LT) Drawing Template File (`*.dwt`).Type a name for the drawing template and click Save.

To use the template to add a new layout in any drawing, right-click a layout tab (or preview in Quick View Layouts) and choose From Template, as explained earlier in this chapter.

STEPS: Laying Out a Drawing in Paper Space

1. Open `ab17-a.dwg`, available from the companion website.

2. Save the file as `ab17-01.dwg` in your `AutoCAD Bible` folder. This file already has a text style, dimension style, and multileader style that are annotative. If you do not have tabs displayed at the bottom of the drawing area, right-click the Model button on the status bar and choose Display Layout and Model Tabs.

3. Click the Layout1 tab. Right-click the tab and choose Page Setup Manager.

4. Click New. In the New Page Setup Name text box, type **PrinterDraft**. Click OK. The Page Setup dialog box opens.

5. In the Paper Size section, the paper size should be set to Letter (8.50 × 11 inches). (This enables you to plot to a printer if you don't have a plotter available.) In the Shaded Viewport Options section, choose Draft from the Quality drop-down list. Choose your printer from the Name drop-down list of the Printer/Plotter section. Click OK to return to the Page Setup Manager.

6. The `PrinterDraft` page setup should be highlighted. Click Set Current. Click Close.

7. Double-click the Layout1 tab. Type **2-view** ↵.

8. From Home tab ⇨ Layers panel, click the Layer drop-down list arrow. Choose the TB layer to make it current.

9. Choose Insert tab ⇨ Block panel ⇨ Insert to open the Insert dialog box. Click Browse. Choose `ab17-a-blk.dwg`, available from the companion website and click Open.

10. Uncheck any checked Specify On-Screen check boxes. Click OK to insert the titleblock, as shown in Figure 17.9.

FIGURE 17.9

The titleblock inserted into paper space

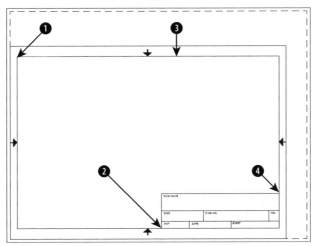

11. On the Home tab, choose the NP layer from the Layer drop-down list on the Layers panel to make it current.

12. Choose Layout tab ➪ Layout Viewports panel ➪ Viewports drop-down menu ➪ Rectangle. (If you last used another option on this drop-down list, you need to click the down arrow to find the Rectangle button.) At the first prompt, choose ❶, shown in Figure 17.9. At the second prompt, choose ❷.

13. Right-click and choose Repeat -VPORTS. At the first prompt, choose ❸. At the next prompt, choose ❹. You now see the drawing in the two viewports.

 14. Check that the ANNOAUTOSCALE button on the status bar is off. (Its tooltip reads `Automatically add scales to annotative objects when the annotation scale changes`. When the button is selected, it has a tiny yellow annotative icon.)

15. Click the border of the left viewport. Press Ctrl+1 to open the Properties palette, if it isn't already open. Choose Standard Scale from the Properties palette. Click the Standard Scale drop-down arrow and choose 1:2 from the scale list. Again in the Properties palette, click the Annotation Scale item and choose 1:2. Press Esc to deselect the left viewport.

16. Select the right viewport and set its standard scale to 1:1. Deselect the right viewport.

17. Double-click inside each viewport in turn to switch to model space, and pan until you see the view shown in Figure 17.10. It doesn't have to match exactly. Notice that the dimension text objects don't display in the left (1:2) viewport, because they only have a 1:1 scale assigned to them.

18. Click the Model tab. Change the current layer to HATCH. Choose Home tab ➪ Draw panel ➪ Hatch/Gradient/Boundary drop-down menu ➪ Hatch. You'll leave the defaults of the ANSI31 pattern, 1.0000 Scale, and 0 Angle. Choose Hatch Creation tab ➪ Options panel ➪ Annotative. At the `Pick internal point or [Select objects/seTtings]:` prompt, click inside the ellipse at the lower section of the handwheel. Press Enter to end the HATCH command.

19. Using the Annotation Scale pop-up list on the status bar, change the current scale to 1:2. You need to add this scale to the annotative objects. Select all the dimensions, except the two diameter dimensions in the lower-right quadrant of the handwheel (which read Ø 1 and Ø 7/8) and the multileader in the upper-right quadrant of the wheel (that contains the text R3/8). Also select the multileader below the handwheel and the hatch that you just drew. Choose Annotate tab ➪ Annotation Scaling panel ➪ Add Current Scale. Notice that the size of the dimensions changes.

20. On the status bar, change the annotation scale back to 1:1. The dimensions, multileaders, and hatch return to their original sizes.

21. Switch to the 2-view tab. You should see that the text of the dimensions in both viewports is the same size, as is the hatch pattern. Note that the diameter dimensions in the lower-right quadrant that don't have a 1:2 annotation scale don't appear in the left-hand viewport, which has a 1:2 annotation scale. Similarly, the multileader in the upper-right quadrant (with the text R3/8) also appears only in the right-hand 1:1 viewport because it has a 1:1 annotation scale only.

22. Double-click the right-hand viewport to enter model space from the layout with that viewport current. You'll create a layer override for the hatch. Display the Layer Properties Manager. In the VP Color column, click the HATCH row, which reads cyan. In the Select Color dialog box that opens, choose the Red swatch. The hatch now displays as red in the right viewport.

23. Double-click inside the left viewport. Go to Home tab ➪ Layers panel ➪ Layer drop-down list and click the icon in the third column (Freeze or Thaw in Current Viewport) next to the HATCH layer to freeze that layer in the viewport.

24. From the same Layer drop-down list, click the name of the Dim layer to make it current. Go to Annotate tab ➪ Dimensions panel ➪ Dimension Style drop-down list and choose STYLE1. This dimension style is set to be scaled to paper space.

25. Double-click outside a viewport, but in the drawing area, to enter paper space. Go to Annotate tab ➪ Dimensions panel ➪ Dimensions drop-down menu and choose Linear. In the left viewport, use the Quadrant object snap to create a dimension from the top quadrant to the bottom quadrant of the ellipse below the center of the handwheel. Place the dimension to the left of the ellipse. The ellipse is correctly dimensioned at ¾ unit, although it is zoomed in to a 1:2 scale. (It's too small, however.) Because you wouldn't dimension using annotative dimensions in paper space, erase the new dimension that you just created; it was just an exercise to show how dimensioning in paper space works.

26. Go to Home tab⇨Layers panel⇨Layer drop-down list and change the current layer to TEXT. Click the Layer drop-down arrow again. Click the icon in the second column (Freeze or Thaw in ALL Viewports) next to the NP layer to freeze the layer containing the viewport borders. Click the top of the drop-down list to close it.

27. Choose Annotate tab⇨Text panel⇨Text drop-down menu⇨Single Line. Complete the text in the titleblock at the default height, as shown in Figure 17.10. (You'll probably find this easier if you turn Object Snap off on the status bar.)

28. Save your drawing.

FIGURE 17.10

The completed drawing layout is now ready for plotting.

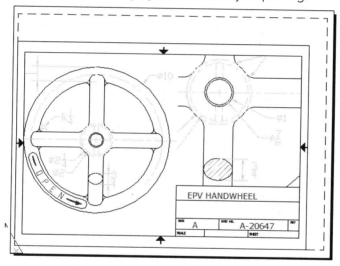

Working with Plot Styles

A *plot style* is an object property, like color, linetype, lineweight, transparency, or layer. Just as you can assign a color to an object and also to a layer, you can assign a plot style to an object and also to a layer. Because a plot style determines how an object is plotted, its function is to override the object's original properties. However, a plot style is more complex than a color or a linetype because it contains a set of properties, such as color-related properties, linetype, lineweight, and line styles. The use of plot styles is completely optional. Without plot styles, objects are simply plotted according to their properties.

You can use plot styles to create several types of plots for one drawing or layout. Plot styles also enable you to use some of the printer-like capabilities of plotters, such as screening and dithering.

Plot styles are stored in plot-style tables, which are files that you can create and edit. You generally follow these steps to use plot styles in your plots:

1. Create a plot-style table.

2. Attach a plot-style table to a layout.

3. Set the plot-style property for a layer or object.

4. Plot.

Setting the plot-style mode

Plot styles come in two types, color-dependent and named. Before you work with plot styles, you need to choose which type you want to use:

- **Color-dependent plot styles,** the default, are saved in color-dependent plot-style tables, which are files with a file extension of `.ctb`. You assign plotting properties based on object color. The disadvantage of color-dependent plot styles is that you can't assign different properties to two objects that have the same color.

- **Named plot styles** are saved in named plot-style tables, which are files with a file extension of `.stb`. Named plot styles let you assign plotting properties to objects regardless of their color. Therefore, two objects of the same color can be plotted differently.

> **NOTE**
>
> Dimensions and tables don't take full advantage of named plot styles. They support color-dependent plot styles only for their components, such as the arrows and extension lines of dimensions. Also, if you use visual styles in 3D drawings (any visual style except 2D Wireframe), plot styles are ignored. The visual style takes precedence in determining how the drawing plots. I cover visual styles in Chapter 22.

After you decide which type of plot style you want to use, you set the mode by choosing Application Button➪Options and clicking the Plot and Publish tab. Click the Plot Style Table Settings button. In the Plot Style Table Settings dialog box, choose either Use Color Dependent Plot Styles *or* Use Named Plot Styles.

In the same location, you can set the following:

- Default plot-style table (the default is `acad.stb` or `acadlt.stb` for named and `acad.ctb` or `acadlt.ctb` for color-dependent plot styles).

- Default plot style for layer 0 (the default is Normal for named plot styles and ByColor for color-dependent plot styles).

- Default plot style for objects (the default is ByLayer for named plot styles and ByColor for color-dependent plot styles).

The default plot style for objects is the current plot style for new objects, and is similar in concept to the current color or layer for new objects. After you're done, click OK.

It is important to understand that changing the plot-style mode does not affect the current drawing. To use the new setting, you must either open a new drawing or open a drawing from a previous release that has not been saved in an AutoCAD 2000/AutoCAD LT 2000 or later format. Moreover, any template that you use to open a new drawing must be set to use named plot styles. AutoCAD and AutoCAD LT come with a template called `acad -Named Plot Styles.dwt` (`acadlt -Named Plot Styles.dwt`) that you can use, or you can create your own template. Several other templates have the words "Named Plot Styles" in their title, indicating that they include the setting for named plot styles.

You can convert color-dependent plot-style tables to named plot-style tables by using the CONVERTCTB command. You can then use the CONVERTPSTYLES command to convert the drawing so that it uses named plot styles. You can also use the CONVERTPSTYLES command to convert a drawing from using named plot styles to using color-dependent plot styles.

Creating a plot-style table

Each named plot-style table comes with a default plot style called Normal. By default, the plot style for each layer in a named plot style drawing is Normal. Figure 17.11 shows the Normal plot style, shown in a plot-style table with a Style1 that you can use to create a new plot style. The Normal plot style is grayed out because you cannot change it.

The Table View tab lists your plot styles side by side. Each plot style includes settings for the various categories that are available in a plot style.

Plot-style tables are stored in the `Plot Styles` folder. The default plot-style tables are `acad.stb` or `acadlt.stb` (named plot style) and `acad.ctb` or `acadlt.ctb` (color-dependent plot style). You can store plot styles in multiple folders and reference these locations under Plot Style Table Search Path on the Files tab of the Options dialog box.

You can import plot configuration files (PCP and PC2 files) or the Release 14 configuration file (`acadr14.cfg`) to create plot-style tables or create plot-style tables from scratch.

FIGURE 17.11

The Normal plot style is the default plot style for layers.

Creating a named plot-style table

To use plot styles, you can add a plot style to an existing plot-style table or create a new plot-style table. Each plot-style table is a separate file. To create a named plot-style table, use the Add Plot Style Table Wizard. You can access this wizard by choosing Application Button⇨Print⇨Manage Plot Styles to open the \Plot Styles folder. (You may have to click the down arrow at the bottom of the Print menu to see this item.) Then double-click the Add-A-Plot Style Table Wizard icon. From this folder you can also access existing plot-style tables for editing.

To use the wizard, follow these steps:

1. The wizard opens with an explanation of plot-style tables. Choose Next.
2. On the Begin screen, shown in Figure 17.12, choose the source that you want to use for the plot-style table. You can start from scratch or use an existing plot-style table. Choose Use My R14 Plotter Configuration (CFG) to use the pen assignments from the acadr14.cfg file. If you have a PCP (Release 12/13) or PC2 (Release 14) configuration file, you can use it to import the settings from that file into the plot-style table. Then click Next.

FIGURE 17.12

Choose the source that you want to use for the new plot-style table.

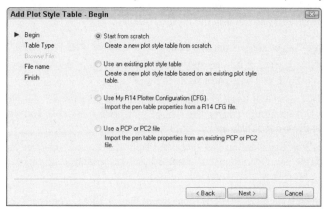

3. If you chose to start from scratch or to use R14 Plotter Configuration or PCP/PC2 files, choose whether you want color-dependent or named plot styles. If you chose to use an existing file as a basis for the plot-style table, choose the file. If you chose to use a CFG file, you must also specify the plotter, because the CFG file can contain information for more than one plotter. Click Next.

4. On the File Name screen, type a name for the plot-style table file. Click Next.

5. On the Finish screen, an option labeled Use this plot style table for new and pre-AutoCAD 2013 drawings may be available. If it is, then check this option to attach the plot-style table to all new drawings by default. You don't have to use the plot styles, but they will be available. Clear the option if you don't want to attach this plot-style table to new drawings by default. You can also click Plot Style Table Editor to edit plot styles immediately. You can edit plot styles at any time, as explained next. Click Finish.

Creating a Color-Dependent Plot-Style Table

Prior to AutoCAD and AutoCAD LT 2000, plotting was integrally related to object color. For example, you assigned pens in a pen plotter according to color. If you want to continue to create settings based on color, you can create a color-dependent plot-style table. To do this, follow the same steps for creating a named plot-style table. On the Pick Plot Style Table screen, choose Color-Dependent Plot Style Table and click Next. The rest of the steps are the same.

The result is a CTB file with 255 styles, one for each color. You cannot add, delete, or rename these styles, but you can edit their properties. For example, you can specify that objects on color 1 should be plotted with no lineweight or a specific linetype. However, be aware that color-dependent plot styles result in slower display regeneration.

In this chapter, I focus on named plot styles. However, creating color-dependent plot styles is very similar.

Editing a plot-style table

After you create a plot-style table, you can edit it by adding, naming, and deleting its plot styles (for named plot-style tables only) and, of course, creating the settings that you want for the plot styles. To open the Plot Style Table Editor, do one of the following:

A. Choose Plot Style Table Editor from the Finish screen of the Add Plot Style Table Wizard.

B. Choose Application Button ⇨ Print ⇨ Manage Plot Styles (scroll down if necessary to see this item) and double-click any existing CTB or STB file.

C. From the Page Setup dialog box (discussed earlier in this chapter) or the Plot dialog box (discussed later in this chapter), choose the named plot-style table that you want to edit from the Plot Style Table drop-down list, and click Edit.

D. From the Select Plot Style dialog box (accessed from the Layer Properties Manager after you click the Plot Style column), choose the named plot-style table that you want to edit from the Plot Style Table drop-down list and click Editor.

The Plot Style Table Editor's Table View tab was shown in Figure 17.11. The Form View tab is shown in Figure 17.13. You can edit styles by using either view tab. The Form View tab focuses on one style at a time and provides better visual confirmation of some of the choices. The Table View tab lets you compare your style to existing styles as you work.

A new Plot Style Table includes one default style, Normal. To add a style, click Add Style. Then click the style name and type a more descriptive name for the style.

> **CAUTION**
>
> You can't rename a plot style that is currently assigned to an object or layer, so it's best to name it when you create it. You can't change the names of styles in a color-dependent plot-style table.

Each plot style has a description area that you can use to provide a more detailed description of the plot style. For example, you could summarize a plot style as "color black & no lineweight."

Now go through each of the properties and make any changes that you want. In Table view, you need to click the property in the Plot Styles column for a drop-down list to appear. The properties are as follows:

- **Color.** You can specify a color other than the default, which is Object Color. For example, you might want to create a plot style that plots everything in black. Choose Select Color and define a color in the Select Color dialog box. (See Chapter 11 for an explanation of this dialog box.)

- **Dither.** Dithering uses dot patterns to approximate a greater range of colors. Not all plotters support dithering. Dithering can make thin lines and dim colors look unclear.

- **Grayscale.** Converts objects to grayscale, if supported by the plotter. You could use grayscale to de-emphasize certain layers or to print a draft plot on a black-and-white laser printer.

- **Pen # and Virtual Pen #.** These settings apply to pen plotters (a Virtual Pen # applies to non-pen plotters that simulate pen plotters) and specify the pen for the object that is assigned the plot style.

- **Screening.** Specifies the amount of ink used for a color. The range is from 0 (no ink; that is, white) to 100 (full intensity of the color). Some plotters, such as pen plotters, do not support screening. You could use a 50 percent screen to de-emphasize certain layers, such as those containing proposed changes, or to save ink.

- **Linetype.** You can specify a linetype other than the default, Object Linetype, to override the object's linetype when you plot. For example, you might want to have the option to plot certain objects that are not yet approved in a dashed or dotted linetype.

- **Adaptive.** Choose On to adapt the scale of a linetype to complete the linetype pattern on the object. Choose Off if maintaining the proper linetype scale is essential.

- **Lineweight.** You can specify a lineweight other than the default, Object Lineweight.

- **Line End Style.** When you use lineweights, you need to specify how you want to end lines. You can choose from Butt, Square, Round, and Diamond. The default is Object End Style.

- **Line Join Style.** Specifies how objects with lineweights are joined. The choices are Miter, Bevel, Round, and Diamond. The default is Object Join Style.

- **Fill Style.** You can choose from Solid, Checkerboard, Crosshatch, Diamonds, Horizontal Bars, Slant Left, Slant Right, Square Dots, and Vertical Bar. The default is Object Fill Style.

To delete a style, select it and click Delete Style. In Table view, click a style's gray column head to select it. After you're done, click the Save & Close button.

FIGURE 17.13

The Form View tab of the Plot Style Table Editor

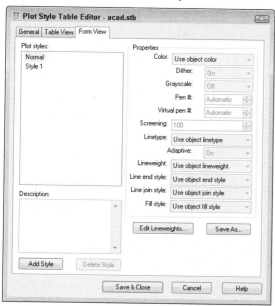

Attaching a plot-style table to a layout

As soon as you have your plot-style table and the plot styles that you want, you can start using the plot styles. The first step is to attach the table to a layout (including model space). Remember that you can attach different plot-style tables to different layouts (or the Model tab).

To attach a plot-style table to a layout or the Model tab, display the tabs if necessary (right-click the Model or Layout button on the status bar and choose Display Model and Layout tabs), and follow these steps:

1. Choose the layout or Model tab.
2. Right-click the tab and choose Page Setup Manager.
3. Choose a page setup and click Modify (or click New and create a new one).
4. In the Plot Style Table section of the Page Setup dialog box, choose a plot-style table from the Plot Style Table drop-down list.
5. If you're on the Model tab, choose Yes or No to the question asking whether you want to apply the plot-style table to the Model tab only or to all layouts. If you're on a layout tab, check the Display Plot Styles check box to see the result of the plot styles in your drawing.
6. Click OK. Then click Close to return to your drawing.

To see the result, you still need to attach a plot style to a layer or object, as I explain in the next section.

Setting the plot-style property for a layer or object

To use a plot style, you need to assign it to a layer or an object. The plot style is only applied if the plot style is first defined in the plot-style table that you've assigned to a layout (or Model tab).

To set the plot style for a layer, follow these steps:

1. Display the layout tab that you want to use, and open the Layer Properties Manager.
2. Choose the layer whose plot style you want to change, and click the Plot Style column to open the Select Plot Style dialog box.
3. Choose the plot-style table from the Active Plot Style Table list at the bottom of the dialog box.
4. Choose a plot style from the Plot Styles list.
5. Click OK to return to your drawing. If you are using the Layer Properties Manager dialog box, click OK again.

If you checked Display Plot Styles in the Page Setup dialog box, as explained in the preceding section, you should see the result of the plot style. If not, type **regenall** ↵.

To set the plot style for an object, select the object and display the Properties palette (Ctrl+1). Choose the Plot Style item, and choose a plot style from the drop-down list. You can attach a plot style to a viewport (which is an object), but the plot style doesn't affect the objects in the viewport.

You can view the effects of plot styles in two ways:

- To display plot styles in your drawing all the time, display the layout for which you want to view the plot style. Right-click the layout's tab and choose Page Setup Manager. Then select the page setup associated with the layout and click Modify. In the Page Setup dialog box, check Display Plot Styles in the Plot Style Table section. Click OK and then click Close to return to the drawing window. (You may have to use REGENALL to see the result.)

- You can also see the effects of plot styles in a preview of your plot. Choose Plot from the Quick Access Toolbar and click Preview.

ON THE WEB

The drawing that you need for the following exercise on creating and applying a plot style, ab17-b.dwg, is available from the Drawings download on the companion website.

STEPS: Creating and Applying a Plot Style

1. With any drawing open, choose Application Button⇨Options and click the Plot and Publish tab. Now click the Plot Style Table Settings button and take note of the current setting under Default Plot Style Behavior for New Drawings. Remember this setting so that you can set it back to its original setting at the end of the exercise.

2. Click Use Named Plot Styles (unless that is the current setting) and click OK twice.

3. Open ab17-b.dwg, available from the companion website.

4. Save the file as ab17-02.dwg in your AutoCAD Bible folder.

5. Choose Application Button⇨Print⇨Manage Plot Styles to open the Plot Styles window. Double-click the Add-A-Plot Style Table Wizard item. Click Next.

6. In the Begin screen, choose Start from Scratch and click Next. In the next screen, choose Named Plot Style Table (it's probably already selected) and click Next. In the File Name screen, type **ab17-02** and click Next.

7. In the Finish screen, click Finish. (Don't check Use for New and Pre-AutoCAD 2013 Drawings, because this is just an exercise.)

8. Return to the Plot Styles folder window, which should still be open on the Windows task bar. (If not, choose Application Button⇨Print⇨Manage Plot Styles.) You could have opened the new plot-style table from the wizard, but this is how you usually do it when you haven't just finished creating a table. Double-click ab17-02.stb.

9. In the Description box of the General tab, type **AutoCAD Bible Plot Style Table**.

10. Click the Table View tab. Click the Add Style button. Click the name Style1. Type **Black Color** and press Enter.

11. Click the Color row under the Black Color column, and choose Black from the drop-down list. Click Save & Close. Close the Plot Styles folder window.

12. If you don't have Model and layout tabs displayed, right-click the Model or Layout button on the status bar and choose Display Layout and Model Tabs. Select Layout1, right-click it, and then choose Page Setup Manager from the shortcut menu.

13. In the Page Setup Manager, choose New. In the New Page Setup dialog box, type **AB 2013** and click OK.

14. In the Page Setup dialog box, make sure that your printer or plotter is listed in the Printer/Plotter section. Then choose ab17-02.stb from the Plot Style Table drop-down list. Check the Display Plot Styles check box and click OK. Select AB 2013 and click Set Current. Click Close. This assigns the plot-style table to Layout1.

15. Choose Home tab ⇨ Layers panel ⇨ Layer Properties. In the Layer Properties Manager, choose A-DETL-PATT (the layer with the magenta color). Click that layer's Plot Style column to open the Select Plot Style dialog box. Choose Black Color and click OK. The Plot Style for the A-DETL-PATT layer now shows as Black Color. Click OK if you are using the Layer Properties Manager dialog box and not the palette.

16. Type **regenall** ⏎. The objects on A-DETL-PATT (the diagonal marks on the mirror) now show as black, and will plot as black.

17. Click PAPER on the status bar to switch to model space.

18. Select the bottom horizontal line of the sink cabinet.

19. Open the Properties palette (Ctrl+1). In the Properties palette, click Plot Style. From the drop-down list to the right, choose Black Color.

20. Press Esc so that the object is no longer highlighted. The line appears as black.

21. Choose Application Button ⇨ Options. On the Plot and Publish tab, click the Plot Style Table Settings button and change the Default Plot Style Behavior for New Drawings setting to what it was at the beginning of this exercise.

22. Save your drawing.

ON THE WEB
The plot style that you created, ab17-02.stb, is available from the Results download on the companion website.

Plotting a Drawing

After you lay out your drawing, you're ready to plot it. Plotting outputs your drawing onto paper (or perhaps vellum or some other medium). The first step is to check the plotter or printer. It should be on, connected to your computer, and have the appropriate paper in it.

 For more information on configuring plotters, see Bonus Chapter 15. I cover plotting electronically to a DWF file in Bonus Chapter 5.

 To start plotting, choose Output tab ⇨ Plot panel ⇨ Plot to open the Plot dialog box, as shown in Figure 17.14. As you can see, this dialog box is almost identical to the Page Setup dialog box.

NOTE
You can hide the right side of the Plot dialog box if you don't need the features there. Click the arrow at the lower-right corner of the dialog box. Click the same arrow to expand the dialog box, if necessary.

FIGURE 17.14

The Plot dialog box

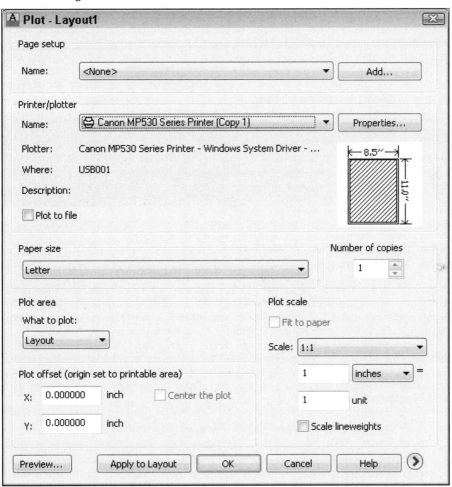

If you set the layout settings in the Page Setup dialog box as current, those settings were saved with the tab that was current at the time. You can usually just click OK in the Plot dialog box and plot immediately. Plot settings are saved in your drawing.

Specifying plot settings

If you saved a page setup, you can choose it from the drop-down list in the Page Setup section of the dialog box. See the discussion of the Page Setup dialog box earlier in this chapter for details.

To select a plotter or printer, choose from the drop-down list in the Printer/Plotter section of the dialog box. A plotter must be either a Windows system printer or a configured plotter. To add a system printer in Windows, choose Start ➪ Printers and Faxes (or Start ➪ Control Panel ➪ Hardware and Sound ➪ Printers). Click or double-click Add a Printer. (The exact instructions vary with your version of Windows.) To add a configured plotter, which has a driver specifically to optimize the functioning of that plotter, use the Add Plotter Wizard. Choose Output tab ➪ Plot panel ➪ Plotter Manager. Then double-click the Add-a-Plotter Wizard item.

TIP

To avoid inadvertently plotting to a Windows system printer when you should be plotting to a plotter, you can hide the display of Windows system printers in the Plot and Page Setup dialog boxes. Because these printers won't appear on the list of plotters, you can't plot to them. To hide system printers, choose Application Button ➪ Options and click the Plot and Publish tab. In the General Plot Options section of the dialog box, check Hide System Printers and click OK.

To choose how many copies you want to plot, change the number in the Number of Copies text box.

Check the Plot to File check box to create a plot file rather than a paper plot. When you click OK, the Browse for Plot File dialog box opens so that you can choose a name and location. Click Save.

If you want to use a plot-style table, check that it appears in the Plot Style Table drop-down list, which is in the extended portion of the dialog box, on the right. Also make sure that the Plot with Plot Styles check box is checked in the Plot Options section. In the same extended area, you can set shading options. I discuss these options in Chapter 22, because they are generally used for 3D drawings. From the Quality drop-down list, you can choose a plot quality, such as Draft, Normal, or Presentation. You can set the orientation (Portrait or Landscape) in the Drawing Orientation section.

You can merge overlapping objects so that the same area is not printed more than once. To set the Merge Overlapping property:

1. Click Properties in the Printer/Plotter section of the Plot dialog box.

2. In the Plotter Configuration Editor that opens, display the Device and Document Settings tab. Click the plus sign (+) next to Graphics. If you see Merge Control in the Graphics list that opens, you can use this feature on your printer or plotter. (For more information about the Plotter Configuration Editor, see the sidebar "Configuring your plotter.")

3. Click Merge Control. In the Merge Control area that is displayed, choose either Lines Overwrite or Lines Merge, and click OK.

4. You then have the choice of applying the change to the current plot only or making the change permanent by editing the PC3 file that contains the parameters for your plotter or printer. Choose one of the options and click OK.

Configuring Your Plotter

Most printers and plotters have settings that you can control from within AutoCAD or AutoCAD LT. You can also control how information about the drawing is sent to the printer or plotter. Configuring a plotter usually provides you with more options than if you choose the default Windows system printer settings. The settings that configure how your printer or plotter functions are in the Plotter Configuration Editor, as shown below.

To configure your plotter, choose Output tab ⇨ Plot panel ⇨ Plotter Manager to open the Plotters folder. Plotter configuration settings are stored in PC3 files. Double-click the PC3 file icon for the plotter that you want to configure to open the Plotter Configuration Editor. (You can also open the Plotter Configuration Editor from the Plot dialog box by clicking Properties in the Printer/Plotter section.) Click the Device and Document Settings tab. The top section lists the possible types of settings. To open a list with a plus sign to its left, click the plus sign; suboptions appear. As you click each item on the top, the appropriate settings appear in the lower section. To specify settings for raster and vector graphics, expand Graphics and choose a setting. Choose Custom Paper Sizes to add custom sheet sizes; these will then appear in the Page Setup and Plot dialog boxes so that you can choose them when you plot. In each case, the Editor walks you through the choices that you need to make to configure your plotter. See Bonus Chapter 15 for further information.

You can store plotter configuration settings in multiple folders and reference these locations under Printer Configuration Search Path on the Files tab of the Options dialog box. You can filter out unused paper sizes by using the Plotter Configuration Editor. However, at the end of the process, you can opt to apply the change only to the current plot. Follow these steps:

1. On the Device and Document Settings tab, choose Filter Paper Sizes.

2. In the list of paper sizes, uncheck any sizes that you don't want to display, and click OK.

3. In the Changes to a Printer Configuration File dialog box, choose to apply the changes only to the current plot or to the file. When you apply the changes to the file, they are permanent until you edit the printer configuration file again.

4. Click OK.

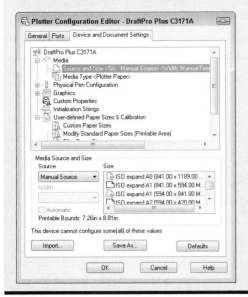

Previewing your plot

You should preview your drawing before you plot. Click the Preview button in the Plot dialog box to see exactly how your drawing will plot. You can also choose Output tab ⇨ Plot panel ⇨ Preview. Right-click to open the shortcut menu that lets you plot, zoom, pan, or exit the preview.

I cover previewing a plot last because it should be the last step before you actually plot. However, it can also be the first step to help you to determine the settings that you need.

Creating a plot stamp

The PLOTSTAMP command places text in a specified corner of the plot, such as the drawing name, layout name, date and time, and so on. To create a plot stamp, enter **-plotstamp** on the command line. Use the options to specify what you want to appear, and use the On and Off options to turn the stamp on and off. You can enter **plotstamp** to set the plotstamp in a dialog box, which is easier; however, you should then look at the Plot Options section of the extended Plot dialog box to make sure that the plot stamp is on ¾ the Plot Stamp On check box should be checked. Click the Advanced button in the Plot Stamp dialog box to specify the location, offset, and text properties of the plot stamp. (You can use fields to add information about the drawing; for more information, see Chapter 13.)

Creating the plot

To start the plotting process, simply click OK in the Plot dialog box. You can plot *in the background,* and continue to work while your drawing is plotting. By default, background plotting is off. To turn it on, choose Application Button ⇨ Options and click the Plot and Publish tab. In the Background Processing Options section, check the Plotting check box. If you're plotting in the background, you can place your cursor over the plotter icon in the status tray to view information about the status of the plot.

When the plot is finished, a notification bubble appears at the lower-right corner of your screen, as shown in Figure 17.15. You can click the link to view the Plot and Publish Details.

FIGURE 17.15

This bubble appears when your plot is done.

If you view the Plot and Publish Details, you see details for all plots that you did in the current session of AutoCAD or AutoCAD LT.

If you need to plot large numbers of drawings or multiple layouts, use the PUBLISH command, which I cover in Bonus Chapter 5.

Summary

In this chapter, you learned how to lay out and plot a drawing. You discovered how to:

- Lay out a drawing in model space
- Use a paper space layout
- Create layouts, using the Layout Wizard and using the commands individually
- Use annotative objects in a viewport
- Add text and dimensions in paper space
- Use the Page Setup dialog box to specify layout settings
- Create plot-style tables and apply plot styles
- Plot a drawing

This chapter ends Part II, "Drawing in Two Dimensions." Part III, "Working with Data," explains how to integrate your drawing with data about your objects. The following chapters cover blocks and attributes.

17

Part III

Working with Data

Working with Blocks

IN THIS CHAPTER

Merging objects into blocks

Placing blocks and files into drawings

Managing blocks and parts libraries

Building and using dynamic blocks

Insert objects without creating blocks

A s you draw, you'll find that you often need to place the same group of objects several times in a drawing. An architect needs to place windows and doors many times in a plan layout of a house. An electrical engineer places electrical symbols in a drawing again and again. A mechanical model may include nuts, bolts, and surface finish symbols many times in a drawing. *Blocks* are groups of objects that you save and name so that you can insert them in your drawing whenever you need them. A block is one object, regardless of the number of individual objects that were used to create it. If necessary, you can *explode* a block to obtain the original individual objects. Many disciplines use *parts libraries* that may consist of thousands of items. You use the block feature to save and insert these parts.

A great advantage of blocks is that by changing the block definition, you can update all the instances of that block in that drawing. Blocks also reduce the size of the drawing file. A drawing stores the definition of a block only once, along with a simple reference to the block each time it's inserted.

Dynamic blocks are blocks that contain parameters for insertion and editing. You can create a dynamic block that takes the place of numerous similar regular blocks by giving it the flexibility to take on various sizes, rotations, visibility variations, and more. Dynamic blocks support parametric constraints, which give them more intelligence. This chapter explains how to make the most of blocks.

Combining Objects into Blocks

Any object or set of objects can be saved as a block. Creating a block is easy, but a little planning makes using it much simpler. Before you create a block, you need to understand how blocks are inserted and how you want to use the specific block that you're creating.

Understanding base points and insertion points

Figure 18.1 shows the legend for a plat drawing. Each legend symbol is a block that is then inserted in the drawing as needed. A symbol has been selected, and you can see that it has one grip at the *base point*. The base point is the point that you use to insert the block. Every block must have a base point. When you insert the block, the base point is placed at the coordinate that you specify for inserting the block — the *insertion point*. All the objects of the block are then inserted in their proper place relative to that insertion point.

FIGURE 18.1

Each legend symbol is a block. Every block has a base point.

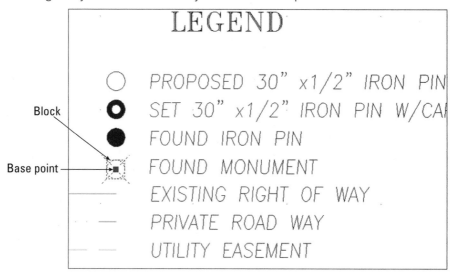

The base point does not have to be on the object, but it should be in a location that makes it easy to insert the block. Figure 18.2 shows a different sort of block, a title border/block. In this case, the base point is usually inserted at 0,0 of the drawing. By placing the base point at the lower-left corner of the border, you can easily place this block in any drawing. The base point is similar in concept to the justification point on text objects.

Creating a block

To create a block, first create the objects just as you want to save them. You may include other blocks as objects in your block. (A block within a block is called a *nested block*.)

After you've created the objects for your block, follow these steps:

1. Choose Home tab ➪ Block panel ➪ Create to start the BLOCK command and open the Block Definition dialog box, as shown in Figure 18.3. The dialog box guides you through the process of defining a block.

FIGURE 18.2

This titleblock is a block. Its base point is at the lower-left corner.

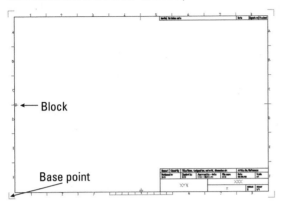

FIGURE 18.3

The Block Definition dialog box

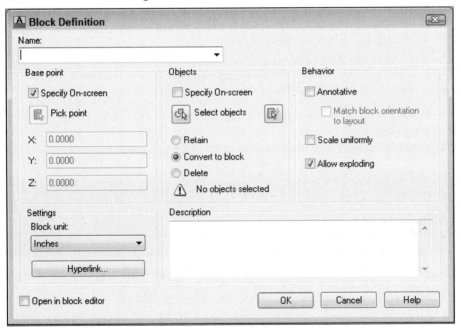

2. In the Name text box, type a name for the block. The name can be up to 255 characters, and spaces are allowed.

3. If you want to specify a base point in the dialog box, in the Base Point section, uncheck the Specify On-Screen check box. Then you can either click the Pick Point button to return to your drawing and specify a base point, or enter X, Y, and Z coordinates. Use an object snap on any of the objects in the block to place the base point somewhere on the block.

4. You can select objects for a block before starting the BLOCK command. If you have not done so, you can check the Specify On-Screen check box in the Objects section. When you click OK, you will get a prompt to select objects. Alternatively, you can click the Select Objects button, return to your drawing to select objects, and then return to the dialog box.

5. Choose how you want the objects of the block to be treated in the Objects section:

   ■ **Retain.** Keeps the objects that you selected as individual objects.

   ■ **Convert to Block.** Converts the objects to a block.

   ■ **Delete.** Deletes the objects. Use this option if you created the objects to insert them elsewhere and do not need the original objects. One advantage of deleting the objects is that their disappearance confirms that you selected the right objects.

6. Choose the insert units that you want to use when defining your block in the Settings section. (You can choose anything from microns to parsecs!) Let's say you work in kilometers and save a block with an insert unit of kilometers. When you insert a block, it will be measured in kilometers, rather than millimeters or inches. If the units aren't important to you, you can specify the units as Unitless. In the same section, you can click the Hyperlink button to add a hyperlink to the block.

7. If you want the block to be annotative, check the Annotative check box in the Behavior section of the dialog box. You can set up annotative objects to scale automatically to the scale of a viewport. When you make a block annotative, you can also check the Match Block Orientation to Layout check box to match the block's orientation to that of the paper space layout (portrait or landscape). You set a layout's orientation in the Page Setup or Plot dialog box.

 For more information on using annotative objects, see Chapter 17. I cover hyperlinks in Bonus Chapter 5.

> **CAUTION**
> You cannot put annotative blocks inside other annotative blocks. Also, you shouldn't manually scale (as with the SCALE command) blocks that contain annotative objects. When you scale an annotative block, the resulting scale includes your scale as well as the current annotation scale.

8. Check the Scale Uniformly check box to force any scaling of the block to scale at equal X and Y factors. This feature prevents distortion of the block. By default, this option is not checked. However, it's not available if you choose to make the block annotative.

9. The Allow Exploding check box lets you explode the block after you insert it. This option is checked by default.

10. If you want, enter a description for the block. The description is used by the DesignCenter.

11. Check the Open in Block Editor check box if you know that you want to create a dynamic block. (I explain dynamic blocks later in this chapter.) Then when you click OK to close the dialog box, the Block Editor immediately opens.

CAUTION

For precision, you should always use an object snap when defining the base point. If the base point that you need to use is not on any object, you can use the From object snap, object snap tracking, or some other means of specifying a precise coordinate.

---

12. Click OK to return to your drawing.

The definition of the block is now stored in the drawing, ready for you to insert as many times as needed. If you selected Delete, your objects disappeared. You can retrieve them by using the one command with a sense of humor: OOPS. The OOPS command restores the last object or set of objects that you erased. This command works whether you used the ERASE command or created a block, and even if you used some other command in the meantime. By contrast, UNDO undoes commands only in the order that you executed them.

TIP

If you create a number of block definitions that you don't end up using in the drawing, use the PURGE command to delete them. This reduces the size of the drawing file. I cover the PURGE command in Chapter 12.

ON THE WEB

The drawing that you need for the following exercise on creating a block, `ab18-a.dwg`, is available from the `Drawings` download on the companion website.

STEPS: Creating a Block

1. Open `ab18-a.dwg`, available from the companion website.
2. Save the file as `ab18-01.dwg` in your `AutoCAD Bible` folder. This is a small portion of an electrical schematic drawing, as shown in Figure 18.4. Object Snap should be on. Set running object snaps for Endpoint, Quadrant, and Intersection.

FIGURE 18.4

A portion of an electrical schematic

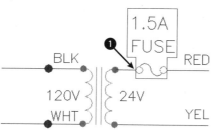

3. To make a block of the 1.5-amp fuse, choose Home tab ⇨ Block panel ⇨ Create.

4. In the Name text box of the Block Definition dialog box, type **1-5 amp fuse**.

5. In the Base Point and Objects sections, check the Specify On-screen check box.

6. In the dialog box's Objects section, choose Delete. The Insert Units should be Unitless. Leave the Description blank. The Open in Block Editor check box should not be checked.

7. Click OK.

8. In the drawing, at the `Specify insertion base point:` prompt, use the Quadrant object snap to pick ❶, shown in Figure 18.4.

9. At the `Select objects:` prompt, select the boxed objects shown in Figure 18.4 (the two lines of text, the two circles, and the two arcs). Press Enter to end selection.

10. To check that the block has been created, choose Home tab ⇨ Block panel ⇨ Create. Click the Name drop-down arrow to see your block. Click Cancel.

11. Save your drawing.

Saving blocks as files

You can use the DesignCenter (as explained later in this chapter) and Content Explorer to insert blocks from any drawing. Nevertheless, many users organize their blocks in their own files so that they can be easily stored and located. Parts and symbols libraries are made up of many individual drawing files, one for each part or symbol. These libraries are a powerful aid to drawing more efficiently.

To save a block as a file, follow these steps:

1. Go to Insert tab ⇨ Block Definition panel ⇨ Create Block drop-down list ⇨ Write Block to open the Write Block dialog box, as shown in Figure 18.5. (This starts the WBLOCK command. Writing to a file is another expression for saving to a file.)

2. In the Source section, choose how you want to create the drawing file:
   - **Block.** Use this option when you've already created the block and now want to save it as a drawing file. Choose the block from the drop-down list.
   - **Entire drawing.** Use this option to make a copy of your drawing.
   - **Objects.** Use this option to start defining the block in the same way that you define a block within a drawing, as described in the preceding section of this chapter. The Base Point and Objects sections become available.

3. Choose the location (drive and folder) for the file in the File Name and Path text box. If you're creating the file from objects, insert a name for the file in place of the default `New Block` at the end of the path.

FIGURE 18.5

Use the Write Block dialog box to save a block as a separate drawing file.

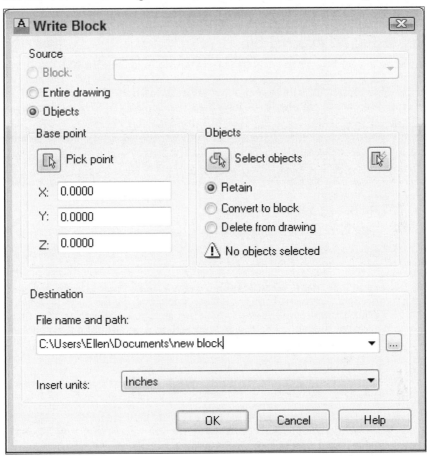

4. In the Insert Units drop-down list, choose the units that you want for your block, or choose Unitless for no units.

5. Click OK to create the drawing file.

When you save a drawing that you plan to insert as a block, use the BASE command (Home tab ⇨ Block panel [expanded] ⇨ Set Base Point) to create the insertion point. By default, the base point is 0,0,0. By setting the base point to another point in the drawing, such as an object snap on one of the objects, you can more easily control the insertion of that drawing.

> **TIP**
> If you want a drawing to act like an annotative block when you insert it, set its ANNOTATIVEDWG system variable to 1.

Replacing an existing file

If you make a mistake when selecting objects to write to a file with WBLOCK, or you want to change the objects in the file, you can replace the file. Start WBLOCK and type the name of the block file that you want to change. Be sure to choose the same file location. When you click OK, a message asks whether you want to replace the existing file. Click Replace the Existing `filename.dwg`.

> **ON THE WEB**
> The drawing that you need for the following exercise on saving a block to a file, `ab18-b.dwg`, is available from the `Drawings` download on the companion website.

STEPS: Saving a Block to a File

1. Open `ab18-b.dwg`, available from the companion website.

2. Save the file as `ab18-02.dwg` in your `AutoCAD Bible` folder. This is a large titleblock, as shown in Figure 18.6. Object Snap should be on. Set a running object snap for Endpoint.

 3. Go to Insert tab ➪ Block Definition panel ➪ Create Block drop-down menu ➪ Write Block. In the Source section of the Write Block dialog box, choose Entire Drawing. Set the File Name and Path box to `AutoCAD Bible\tb-f` by typing the path and the filename. (Alternatively, click the Ellipsis [...] button and navigate to your `AutoCAD Bible` folder. In the File Name text box, type **tb-f**. Click Save.) Click OK.

4. Press Enter to repeat the WBLOCK command.

5. In the Source section of the dialog box, choose Objects. In the Objects section, click Select Objects.

6. Use Zoom Window to zoom in on the text at the bottom-right corner of the titleblock. At the `Select objects:` prompt, select all the 90°-rotated text at ❶, shown in Figure 18.6. Press Enter to end selection.

7. In the Base Point section, click Pick Point. Use the Endpoint object snap to pick the bottom-left corner of the box containing the text that you selected. Using this base point lets you easily place the text in the box at any time.

8. In the Objects section, choose Delete from Drawing.

9. In the File Name and Path text box, type **notes-tol** after the path, which should already be set to your `AutoCAD Bible` folder. Click OK to save the block as a file.

10. Type **oops** ↲ to bring back the text.

11. Choose View tab ➪ Navigate 2D panel ➪ Zoom drop-down menu ➪ Extents, and save your drawing.

FIGURE 18.6

A titleblock can be saved as a file and inserted into any other drawing.

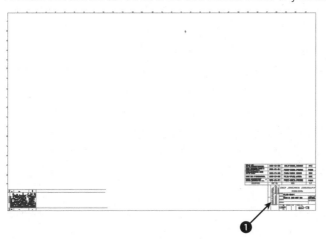

Inserting Blocks and Files into Drawings

The process for inserting blocks and separate files is the same. After you choose the location, you can change the size and rotation of the block. This capability is ideal for parts libraries. You can create parts at the size of 1 unit and then scale or rotate them as needed.

Using the Insert dialog box

To insert a block or file, follow these steps:

1. Choose Home tab ⇨ Block panel ⇨ Insert to start the INSERT command. The Insert dialog box opens, as shown in Figure 18.7.

> **NOTE**
>
> If the block is annotative, you see an annotative icon next to the block's preview.

2. You can insert a block or a file as follows:
   - To insert a block from within your drawing, click the Name drop-down list and choose one of the existing blocks.
   - To insert a file, click Browse. The Select Drawing File dialog box opens. Locate the file's drive and folder, and then choose the file. A preview appears to the right. Click Open. The Insert dialog box displays the path of the file.

FIGURE 18.7

The Insert dialog box

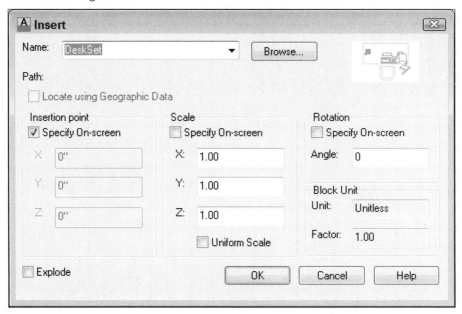

3. Uncheck Specify On-screen in the Insertion Point, Scale, and Rotation sections if you want to specify the insertion point, scale, and rotation angle in the dialog box. Then provide the requested information in the dialog box.

> **NOTE**
> The Uniform Scale check box forces scaling to be the same for the X and Y directions. The first time in each session that you insert or create an annotative object, the Select Annotation Scale dialog box opens, where you can choose the desired annotation scale from the drop-down list.

4. Check the Explode check box if you want to insert the block as individual objects rather than as one block object. The Explode check box is disabled if you did not check the Allow Exploding check box in the Block Definition dialog box when you created the block.

5. Click OK to close the Insert dialog box.

> **TIP**
> While you're dragging the block and before you specify an insertion point, if the Properties palette is open, you can change the properties of the block. For example, you can choose a layer to insert the block on a layer other than the current layer.

6. If any of the Specify On-Screen check boxes were checked, the command line prompts you for the necessary information:

■ At the `Specify insertion point:` prompt (which varies, depending on whether or not you checked the Explode check box in Step 4), specify the insertion point. You see the block with its base point at the cursor, so you can judge how it looks.

TIP

A Basepoint option appears with the `Specify insertion point:` prompt. When you use this option, you can move the insertion base point of the block to anywhere you want. Usually, you would use an object snap to specify a different point on the block.

■ At the `Enter X scale factor, specify opposite corner, or [Corner/XYZ] <1>:` prompt, press Enter to accept the default scale factor of 1, or type another scale. The Specify Opposite Corner option lets you define a square box whose side defines the scale factor. A side of 1 unit results in a scale factor of 1. If you specify the X scale factor, the command line prompts you for the Y scale factor. The default is the same scale as X, but you can specify a different one. For 3D models, use the XYZ option to specify all three scale factors. (If you checked Explode, the prompt is slightly different, and you specify the scale factor for all directions at once. If the Uniform Scale check box is checked, the prompt asks you for a scale factor.)

■ At the `Specify rotation angle <0>:` prompt, type in a rotation angle. You can also pick a point to use the angle from the insertion point to the point that you picked as the rotation angle. This technique is useful for aligning a block with an existing object.

After you provide all the necessary information, the command inserts the block or file. A negative scale factor for any of the axes creates a mirror image of the block or file. When you specify a negative X scale axis, the block is mirrored around the Y axis. When you specify a negative Y scale axis, the block is mirrored around the X axis. Figure 18.8 shows a door block inserted with positive and negative scale factors. The rotation angle of all the blocks is 0 degrees. By combining negative and positive scale factors with rotation angles, you can get any door configuration that you want. Dynamic blocks also offer a way to insert blocks at various scales and rotation angles.

When you insert a drawing file, paper space objects are not included in the block definition created in your drawing. To insert paper space objects in another drawing, open the original drawing and define the objects as a block. Then use the DesignCenter to insert that block into any other drawing.

Using the DesignCenter

 When you want to insert a block from another drawing, use the DesignCenter. The DesignCenter is the tool to use if you have a block library containing multiple blocks within one drawing. Choose View tab ⇨ Palettes panel ⇨ DesignCenter or press Ctrl+2. In the left pane, navigate to the drawing that contains the block that you want. Double-click the drawing and choose Blocks from the list that appears. In the right pane, you see a list of the blocks in that drawing. Click Preview to see a preview of each block that you select. Click Description to see a description of the block. (The description only appears if you saved one when creating the block.) You can insert the block in two ways:

● Double-click the block's icon to open the Insert dialog box so that you can specify exactly how you want to insert the block, just as I described earlier for blocks within a drawing.

● Drag the block's icon onto the drawing area to insert the block at the point where you release the mouse button, using the default scale and rotation.

FIGURE 18.8

A door block inserted at various positive and negative scale factors, creating mirror images in different directions

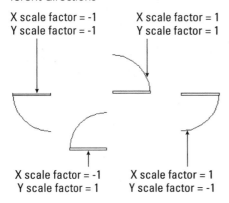

X scale factor = -1   X scale factor = 1
Y scale factor = -1   Y scale factor = 1

X scale factor = -1   X scale factor = 1
Y scale factor = 1   Y scale factor = -1

 You can use the Content Explorer or DesignCenter to insert entire drawings. They are both covered in more detail in Chapter 12. You can also insert blocks from a tool palette. Many people use tool palettes, covered in Bonus Chapter 3, as the primary way to insert blocks from a block library. You can quickly create a tool palette containing all the blocks in a folder.

ON THE WEB

The drawings that you need for the following exercise on inserting blocks, `ab14-b.dwg` and `ab18-c.dwg`, are available from the `Drawings` download on the companion website.

STEPS: Inserting Blocks

1. Open `ab18-c.dwg`, available from the companion website.

2. Save the file as `ab18-03.dwg` in your `AutoCAD Bible` folder. This is the floor plan of the first floor of a house, as shown in Figure 18.9. Many of the doors and a toilet need to be inserted. Object Snap should be on. Set running object snaps for Endpoint and Midpoint. The current layer is Door.

3. Use Zoom Window to zoom in on the left wing of the house.

4. Choose Home tab ⇨ Block panel ⇨ Insert to start the INSERT command. In the Name drop-down list of the Insert dialog box, choose DOOR (if it isn't already selected). Check all three Specify On-screen check boxes. Make sure that the Uniform Scale check box is not checked. Click OK to close the Insert dialog box.

5. As you move the cursor, you can see the dragged image of a door. This image shows you the block at an X and Y scale of 1, and a 0-degree rotation angle. Follow the prompts:

```
Specify insertion point or [Basepoint/Scale/X/Y/Z/Rotate]: Use the
    Endpoint object snap to pick ❶ in Figure 18.9.
Enter X scale factor, specify opposite corner, or [Corner/XYZ] <1>: -1 ↵
Enter Y scale factor <use X scale factor>: 1 ↵
Specify rotation angle <0>: 270 ↵ (You could also specify -90 degrees.)
```

FIGURE 18.9

The floor plan of the house needs some doors and a toilet.

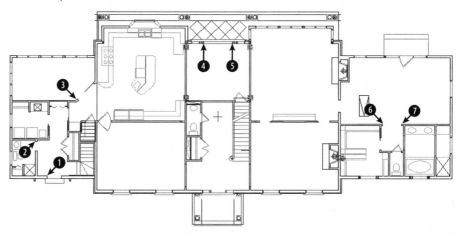

6. Repeat the INSERT command. The Insert dialog box already shows the DOOR block. Click OK. Follow the prompts. You'll probably want to zoom into the area of ❷, shown in Figure 18.9. (To do so, choose View tab ⇨ Navigate 2D panel ⇨ Zoom drop-down menu ⇨ Window.)

```
Specify insertion point or [Basepoint/Scale/X/Y/Z/Rotate]: Pick ❷ in
    Figure 18.9.
Enter X scale factor, specify opposite corner, or [Corner/XYZ]
    <1>: 2/3 ↵
Enter Y scale factor <use X scale factor>: ↵
Specify rotation angle <0>: 180 ↵
```

7. If you zoomed in for the previous step, return to the previous view by using Zoom Previous (View tab ⇨ Navigate 2D panel ⇨ Zoom drop-down menu ⇨ Previous). Zoom in to the area around ❸, shown in Figure 18.9. Choose Home tab ⇨ Block panel ⇨ Insert. Click OK. Follow the prompts:

```
Specify insertion point or [Basepoint/Scale/X/Y/Z/Rotate]: Pick ❸ in
    Figure 18.9.
Enter X scale factor or specify opposite corner, or [Corner/XYZ] <1>:
    −3/4 ↵
Enter Y scale factor <use X scale factor>: 3/4 ↵
Specify rotation angle <0>: 315 ↵
```

8. Zoom in to the area around ❹ and ❺, shown in Figure 18.9. Repeat the INSERT command. Click OK. Follow the prompts:

```
Specify insertion point or [Basepoint/Scale/X/Y/Z/Rotate]: Pick ❹ in
    Figure 18.9.
Enter X scale factor, specify opposite corner, or [Corner/XYZ] <1>: 1 ↵
Enter Y scale factor <use X scale factor>: ↵
Specify rotation angle <0>: 270 ↵
```

9. Repeat the INSERT command and click OK. Follow the prompts:

```
Specify insertion point or [Basepoint/Scale/X/Y/Z/Rotate]: Pick ❺ in
    Figure 18.9.
Enter X scale factor, specify opposite corner, or [Corner/XYZ] <1>: −1 ↵
Enter Y scale factor <use X scale factor>: 1 ↵
Specify rotation angle <0>: 90 ↵
```

10. Zoom in on the area around ❻ and ❼, shown in Figure 18.9 Start the INSERT command and click OK. Follow the prompts:

```
Specify insertion point or [Basepoint/Scale/X/Y/Z/Rotate]: Pick ❻ in
    Figure 18.9.
Enter X scale factor, specify opposite corner, or [Corner/XYZ]
    <1>: −2/3 ↵
Enter Y scale factor <use X scale factor>: 2/3 ↵
Specify rotation angle: 270 ↵
```

11. Repeat the INSERT command and click OK. Follow the prompts:

```
Specify insertion point or [Basepoint/Scale/X/Y/Z/Rotate]: Pick ❼ in
    Figure 18.9.
Enter X scale factor, specify opposite corner, or [Corner/XYZ]
    <1>: 2/3 ↵
Enter Y scale factor <use X scale factor>: ↵
Specify rotation angle: 90 ↵
```

12. Beneath the doors that you just inserted is a water closet with a toilet. Pan down to it by choosing View tab ⇨ Navigate 2D panel ⇨ Pan, and dragging. Erase the toilet, which is a block. Change the current layer to FIXTURE.

13. Choose View tab ⇨ Palettes panel ⇨ DesignCenter or press Ctrl+2. (If you don't see the two panes, click Tree View Toggle on the DesignCenter toolbar.) In the left pane, navigate to your AutoCAD Bible folder, or wherever you placed the Drawing download files from the companion website. (You may need to use the horizontal scroll bar if the left side of the list of drives and folders is not in view.) Double-click that folder, then double-click ab14-b.dwg. Click Blocks from the list of named objects below ab14-b.dwg. On the right, you see the blocks in the drawing.

14. Double-click TOILET2. You see a preview at the bottom of the DesignCenter. (If you don't, click Preview on the DesignCenter toolbar.) The Insert dialog box opens. Because you can see the preview, you know the rotation angle is correct; you can assume that the scale is correct because toilets are generally about the same size. The Insertion Point Specify On-Screen check box should be checked. The other Specify On-Screen check boxes should be unchecked. Click OK.

15. Drag the toilet into the water closet and use a Midpoint object snap to place it at the middle of the bottom wall of the water closet. If you want, close the DesignCenter by clicking its Close button.

Do a Zoom Extents and save your drawing.

The MINSERT command (AutoCAD only) lets you insert blocks (but not annotative blocks) in a rectangular array. Type **minsert** ↵. MINSERT prompts you for an insertion point, scale factors, and rotation angle using the same prompts as the INSERT command, but without the dialog box. It then starts the same prompts as the Rectangular option of the ARRAY command, asking for the number of rows and columns and the distance between them. The value of MINSERT is that it reduces the size of your drawing because the array is one block object. The disadvantage is that you can't edit the individual blocks in the array or the array as a whole in any way. If you need to edit them, erase the entire array of blocks, redefine the single block, if necessary, and start over, this time using INSERT and ARRAY separately. You cannot explode a minserted block.

Managing Blocks

Several factors require care when working with blocks. Large libraries of blocks need to be well managed so that you can find the block that you need quickly. You also need to consider the issue of which layers you use when you define your blocks so that you get the desired results when you insert them.

> **TIP**
> You can use the QSELECT command to select all instances of a block from a drop-down list. Choose Block Reference as the object type and Name as the property. From the Value drop-down list, choose the block that you want.

Working with block layers

You may want a block to take on the current layer when inserted, or to retain its original layer. You can manage block layers, along with their other properties, to obtain the desired result. A block can be defined in four ways to determine which layer, color, linetype, transparency, and lineweight properties it will use when you insert it, as shown in Table 18.1.

As Table 18.1 makes clear, two of the methods (setting the objects to ByBlock and creating them on layer 0) create chameleon blocks that take on the properties of the current layer. Use the other two methods when you want the block to retain its properties, regardless of the current layer.

Creating blocks on layer 0 is the simplest method. If you want the blocks to have a specific color and linetype, create a layer for them and switch to that layer before inserting the blocks. You can also change the layer of a block, after it's inserted, in the same way that you change the layer of any object.

TABLE 18.1 Properties of Block Component Objects and Insertion Results

Properties of Component Objects	Insertion Results
On any layer (except layer 0), with color, linetype, transparency, and lineweight set to ByLayer	The block keeps properties of that layer. If you insert a block into another drawing without that layer, the drawing creates the layer. If you insert the block into another drawing with that layer, but the layer has a different color and linetype properties, the block takes on properties of the layer that are different from those that you created it on. If you insert the block on a different layer, the block keeps the properties of the layer on which it was created, but the Properties palette reports the block as being on the layer on which it was inserted, because it reports the layer of the insertion point, not the block objects.
On any layer (including layer 0), with color, linetype, transparency, and lineweight set explicitly	The block keeps the color, linetype, transparency, and lineweight with properties that were explicitly set. If you insert the block into another drawing, the drawing creates the layer on which original objects were made.
On any layer (except layer 0), with color, linetype, transparency, and lineweight set to ByBlock	The block takes on the color of the current color setting. (If the current color is set to ByLayer, the block will take on the current layer's color.) If you insert the block into another drawing, the drawing creates the layer on which original objects were made. *Note:* If the color, linetype, transparency, and lineweight are ByBlock when you create objects for a block, the objects are always shown with black/white color, a continuous linetype, no transparency, and the default lineweight.
On layer 0 (with color, linetype, transparency, and lineweight set to ByBlock or ByLayer)	The block takes on the layer and properties of the current layer on which it's inserted. If you insert the block into another drawing, no layers are created.

ON THE WEB

The drawing that you need for the following exercise on working with blocks and layers, `ab18-d.dwg`, is available from the `Drawings` download on the companion website.

STEPS: Working with Blocks and Layers

1. Open `ab18-d.dwg`, available from the companion website.

2. Save the file as `ab18-04.dwg` in your `AutoCAD Bible` folder. This is a portion of an electrical schematic, as shown in Figure 18.10. Object Snap should be on. Set running object snaps for Endpoint, Midpoint, Quadrant, and Intersection.

3. Choose Home tab ⇨ Block panel ⇨ Create. In the Name text box of the Block Definition dialog box, type **hl switch**. Make sure that the Specify On-screen check boxes in both the Base Point and Objects sections are checked. Choose Retain in the Objects section. Click OK.

FIGURE 18.10

The electrical schematic has several symbols that would be useful as blocks.

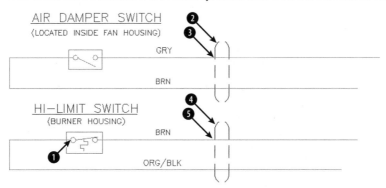

4. Use the Quadrant object snap to pick the left quadrant of the left circle in the switch, at ❶ in Figure 18.10. Use a selection window to select the entire hi-limit switch box (not including the text labels). Right-click to end selection. The objects in this block were created on the Object layer, which is red with a continuous linetype. The color, linetype, transparency, and lineweight are set to ByLayer.

5. Use a selection window to select the air damper switch. (The objects are currently on the Object layer, which is red with a continuous linetype.) Choose Home tab ⇨ Properties panel and select ByBlock from the Color drop-down list. Do the same with the Linetype and the Lineweight drop-down lists. The switch turns black (or white if you're using a black screen). The objects are still selected.

6. Choose Home tab ⇨ Block panel ⇨ Create. In the Name text box, type **ad switch**. The dialog box says 4 objects selected. Check the Specify On-screen check box in the Base Point section. Uncheck the Specify On-screen check box in the Objects section (because the objects are already selected). Check the Retain option. Click OK. Use the Quadrant object snap to pick the left quadrant of the left circle in the switch.

7. Use a selection window to select the top conduit symbol at ❷, shown in Figure 18.10 (it consists of four objects). (It is currently on the Conduit layer, which is black and has a linetype of Hidden2.) Use the Color drop-down list to set the color to Green. Use the Linetype drop-down list to set the linetype to Hidden2. Choose Home tab ⇨ Block panel ⇨ Create. In the Name text box, type **top conduit**. The dialog box tells you that four objects are selected. The Specify On-screen check box in the Base Point section should be checked. Click OK. Use the Intersection object snap to pick ❸. The conduit appears green with the Hidden2 linetype.

8. Use a selection window to select the bottom conduit at ❹. (It is currently on the Conduit layer, which is black and has a linetype of Hidden2.) Use the Layer drop-down list to set the layer to 0. Repeat the BLOCK command. In the block Name text box, type **bot conduit**. The dialog box tells you that four objects are selected. Click OK. Use the Intersection object snap to pick ❺. The conduit appears black with a continuous linetype.

18

9. Save your drawing. Choose Application Button⇨New. In the Select Template dialog box, click the down arrow next to the Open button. Choose one of the Open with No Template options. A new drawing opens with only one layer, layer 0. (You can choose Home tab⇨Layers panel⇨Layer drop-down list to check.)

10. Choose View tab⇨Palettes panel⇨DesignCenter. In the left pane, locate your AutoCAD Bible folder and then locate ab18-04.dwg. (You can also click the Open Drawings tab and find ab18-04.dwg there.) Double-click the drawing, and then click Blocks. In the right pane, double-click hl switch. In the Insert dialog box, check Specify On-screen for Insertion Point and Scale. Click OK. Follow the prompts to insert the file anywhere in the drawing, using a scale factor of 3. The block, whose objects were created on the Object layer, retained its original color (red), linetype, transparency, and lineweight but is listed as being on layer 0. Select the block and look at the Layer drop-down list to verify this.

11. Check the Layer drop-down list. A new layer, Object, is the layer that the original objects were on.

12. In the right pane of the DesignCenter, double-click top conduit. In the Insert dialog box, click OK. Follow the prompts to insert the file anywhere in the drawing, using a scale factor of 3. Again, the object retains its explicitly set properties of green color and Hidden2 linetype but is listed as being on layer 0. Click the Layer drop-down list to see that the Conduit layer has been added to the drawing.

13. Choose Home tab⇨Properties panel⇨Color, and choose Cyan from the Color drop-down list to make it the current color.

14. In the DesignCenter's right pane, double-click ad switch. In the Insert dialog box, click OK. Follow the prompts to insert the file anywhere in the drawing, using a scale factor of 3. The block (whose objects were created on the Object layer and whose properties were set to ByBlock) takes on the current color of Cyan and is listed on layer 0.

15. Choose Home tab⇨Layers panel⇨Layer Properties, and click New Layer in the Layer Properties Manager. Name the new layer **Green** and set its color to Green. Click Set Current to make it the current layer. Close or hide the Layer Properties Manager.

16. In the DesignCenter, double-click bot conduit. In the Insert dialog box, click OK. Follow the prompts to insert the file anywhere in the drawing, using a scale factor of **3**. The block, whose original objects were on layer 0, has the properties of layer Green and is listed on layer Green.

17. Click the DesignCenter's Close button to close the DesignCenter. Don't save this new drawing.

Exploding blocks

 You can explode blocks into their original objects. You may need to do this to edit a block. If you want, you can then redefine the block, as explained earlier in this chapter. To explode a block, choose Home tab⇨Modify panel⇨Explode. (You can select objects before or after choosing the EXPLODE command.) You can also explode associative arrays, polylines, dimensions, leaders, multileaders, hatches, regions, multilines, and certain 3D objects (bodies, 3D meshes, 3D solids, various types of surfaces, polyface meshes, and polygon meshes) into simpler types of objects. (Drawing in 3D is covered in Part IV.) Exploding a block with nested blocks explodes only the top-level block. You need to use the EXPLODE command again to explode the next level of blocks.

When you explode blocks that were created on layer 0 or with BYBLOCK objects, the objects return to their original status and appear black/white with a continuous linetype and default lineweight again. If you insert a block with different X and Y scales, the command does its best to create objects based on their new shapes. For example, if you have a block that includes a circle and insert it with an X scale of 1 and a Y scale of 2, you see an ellipse. Therefore, when you explode the block, you get an ellipse from what used to be a circle.

> **NOTE**
> When you explode an annotative block, you get the components of the current scale presentation only. The components are not annotative.

Using the XPLODE command

The XPLODE command is a version of the EXPLODE command that you can use to control the final layer, color, and linetype of the objects. If you select more than one object, you can set the properties for all the objects that you select at once (that is, *globally*) or for each object individually.

To xplode an object, type **xplode** ↵. (XPLODE is an AutoLISP program in AutoCAD and is built into AutoCAD LT.) At the `Select objects:` prompt, select one or more blocks. If you select more than one object, XPLODE displays the `XPlode Individually/<Globally>:` prompt. Type **i** ↵ to get prompts for each block individually. Press Enter to accept the Globally default option. If you choose the Individually option, XPLODE highlights each block in turn so that you know which block you're working on as you respond to prompts.

At the `Enter an option [All/Color/LAyer/LType/LWeight/Inherit from parent block/ Explode] <Explode>:` prompt, choose whether you want to specify color, layer, linetype, lineweight, or all four. The Inherit from Parent Block option works only for blocks created on layer 0 whose color and linetype were also set to ByBlock. These ByBlock objects then retain their color and linetype after you explode them.

Xplode cannot explode blocks whose X and Y scale factors have unequal absolute values. That means an X scale of 1 and a Y scale of –1 is okay, but not an X scale of 2 and a Y scale of –3.

> **ON THE WEB**
> The drawing that you need for the following exercise on exploding and xploding blocks, `ab18-e.dwg`, is available from the `Drawings` download on the companion website.

STEPS: Exploding and Xploding Blocks

1. Open `ab18-e.dwg`, available from the companion website.

2. Save the file as `ab18-05.dwg` in your `AutoCAD Bible` folder. This is the same electrical schematic used in the previous exercise, except that the objects are now blocks that have been inserted (see Figure 18.11). Object Snap should be on. Set running object snaps for Endpoint, Midpoint, Quadrant, and Intersection. The current layer is Object.

18

FIGURE 18.11

The electrical schematic has several blocks that have been inserted.

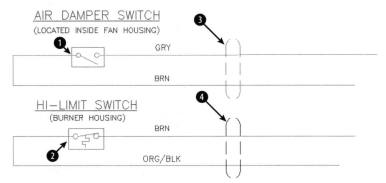

3. Choose Home tab ⇨ Modify panel ⇨ Explode. At the `Select objects:` prompt, choose the air damper switch at **❶**, shown in Figure 18.11. Press Enter to end selection. The switch turns black or white (the opposite of your screen color) because it was created from objects whose color and linetype were set to ByBlock.

4. Choose Undo from the Quick Access Toolbar.

5. Type **xplode** ↵. At the `Select objects:` prompt, choose the air damper switch again. Press Enter to end selection. At the `Enter an option [All/Color/LAyer/LType/LWeight/Inherit from parent block/Explode] <Explode>:` prompt, right-click and choose LAyer. At the `Enter new layer name for exploded objects <OBJECT>:` prompt, press Enter to accept the default of OBJECT, the current layer. The command line informs you that `Object exploded onto layer OBJECT`.

6. Choose the `hi-limit` switch at **❷**. Choose Home tab ⇨ Modify panel ⇨ Explode. The command explodes the block onto the Object layer because these objects were created on that layer with their color and linetype set to ByLayer.

7. Type **xplode** ↵. The top conduit was created from objects set explicitly to green color and Hidden2 linetype. The bottom conduit was created from objects set to layer 0. Follow the prompts:

```
Select objects: Choose the conduits at ❸ and ❹. End selection.
2 objects found.
Xplode Individually/<Globally>: ↵ to accept the default.
Enter an option [All/Color/LAyer/LType/LWeight/Inherit from parent block/
    Explode] <Explode>: Right-click and choose All.
New Color [Truecolor/Colorbook] <BYLAYER>: ↵
Enter new linetype name for exploded objects <BYLAYER>: ↵
Enter new lineweight <>: ↵
Enter new layer name for exploded objects <OBJECT>: conduit ↵
Objects exploded with color of BYLAYER, linetype of BYLAYER, and layer
    conduit.
```

8. Save your drawing.

Redefining a block

If you make a mistake, or if you want to change the block in some way, you can redefine it. If you just created the block, use UNDO and make any necessary changes. If you created the block earlier, follow these steps:

1. Insert the block and explode it. (Exploding is covered earlier in this chapter.)

2. Make the desired changes and repeat the process of defining the block, using the same name for the block.

> **CAUTION**
>
> When you specify the name of the block, you should type it, rather than choose it from the Name drop-down list. Choosing the name from the list replaces selected objects that you want to be in the new version of the block with the objects from the previous block definition, and sets the insertion point to 0,0.

3. Click Redefine (or Redefine Block) when the message asks whether you want to redefine the block.

Redefining a block that has been inserted in your drawing updates all the blocks in that drawing. This is a powerful technique to control your drawing. If you have repetitive symbols in your drawing, it's worthwhile to make blocks out of them just so that you can make this type of global change if necessary.

Editing blocks

Blocks can be complex objects. You may need to add, remove, or change a component of a block. You can also update or substitute blocks. Here are a few additional points that can help you to work with blocks.

Using the Block Editor to edit blocks

If you double-click a block, you open the Edit Block Definition dialog box. (You can also choose Home tab ⇨ Block panel ⇨ Block Editor, which executes the BEDIT command.) Choose the block from the Block to Create or Edit list and click OK. The Block Editor opens. I explain the Block Editor in detail later in this chapter in connection with dynamic blocks. However, you can use the Block Editor to edit all blocks, not just dynamic ones. Make the changes you want.

 When you're done, choose Block Editor tab ⇨ Open/Save panel ⇨ Save Block and click the Close Block Editor button in the Close panel.

 You can also use *in-place editing* to edit blocks. I cover in-place editing in Chapter 20, in the section, "Editing an Xref within Your Drawing."

Editing blocks with grips

To a certain extent, you can use grip editing with blocks. By default, when you select a block, only one grip — at the base point — is displayed. However, you can show the grips of all the objects. Choose Application Button ⇨ Options. On the Selection tab, choose Show Grips within Blocks and click OK.

As a general rule, you don't want to enable grips for blocks when working with complex blocks. However, you can turn them on to use grips to mirror, rotate, move, or scale the block if you want to use the grip of a component object as a base point for the edit.

Updating blocks

As I mentioned earlier in the chapter, when you redefine a block, all instances of that block are automatically updated. However, if you inserted a file to use as a block in a drawing and then changed that file, your current drawing has no way of knowing of the change in that drawing file. (Instead, use an external reference to solve this problem. See Chapter 20 for more on external references.)

To update a block that came from inserting an entire file, you can reinsert the file. Follow these steps:

1. Choose Home tab ⇨ Block panel ⇨ Insert.
2. Click Browse.
3. Choose the file that you've changed, and click Open. (You must locate the actual file rather than choose the block of the same name that already exists in the drawing.)
4. A message asks whether you want to redefine the block because that block already exists in the drawing. Choose Redefine Block.
5. Press Esc to avoid actually inserting a new copy of the block.

The drawing updates all the instances of the block with the new file. You can also use the DesignCenter to insert and update blocks.

> **Tip**
> You can update a block definition in your current drawing to match a block on a tool palette by right-clicking the block tool on the tool palette and clicking Redefine. All instances of the block are redefined to match the tool on the tool palette. (The block on the tool palette must be in the current drawing, not an external drawing.)

Substituting blocks

You can substitute a different file as the basis for blocks in your drawing. There are three reasons for doing this:

- If you have many instances of complex blocks, you may find that regen times are slow. You can create a simple block, WBLOCK it, and substitute it for the original blocks until plotting time.
- You can create more than one version of a drawing — for example, an office layout with various kinds of desks. You can create the drawing with one type of desk, inserting files of the desks. Substitute a file of another type of desk, and you have a new office layout design.
- Another common reason to substitute blocks is when your company switches to a different standard for a part.

To substitute blocks, follow these steps:

1. Type **-insert** ↵ on the command line.

2. Type **blockname=filename** where blockname is the name of the block and filename is the name of the file. (If the file is not in the support file search path, type the entire path.) Press Enter.

NOTE

To place a folder in the support file search path, choose Application Button ⇨ Options and click the Files tab. Double-click Support File Search Path. Click Add, and then type the path or browse to it. After you're done, click OK to close the Options dialog box.

3. A message tells you that the block with this name already exists, and asks whether you want to redefine it. Type **y** ↵.

4. Press Esc to avoid actually inserting a new copy of the new file.

The file that you inserted replaces the current blocks.

TIP

The NCOPY command (choose Home tab ⇨ Modify panel [expanded] ⇨ Copy Nested Objects) allows you to copy objects nested inside blocks or xrefs.

AUTOCAD ONLY

The Express Tools command BLOCKREPLACE (choose Express Tools tab ⇨ Blocks panel ⇨ Replace Block) is another way to substitute blocks. Another Express Tools command, XLIST (choose Express Tools tab ⇨ Blocks panel ⇨ List Properties) lists properties of nested objects within blocks. SHP2BLK (choose Express Tools tab ⇨ Modify panel [expanded] ⇨ Convert Shape to Block) converts a shape definition to a block. (I cover shape definitions in Bonus Chapter 9.)

18

Usually when you insert a file into a drawing, the block name and filename are the same. Likewise, when you WBLOCK a block, you usually name the file with the name of the block. Be aware that when you use block substitution, you have a block in your drawing that is the same as a file of a different name. For example, if you have a block in your drawing called smalldesk and substitute a file called bigdesk, you now have a block called smalldesk that is actually the same as the file bigdesk. This can become confusing, so use block substitution with care.

Creating and Using Dynamic Blocks

You probably have multiple similar blocks that you store and use on a regular basis. Moreover, you might insert these blocks at various scales and rotation angles. For example, you could have several sizes of doors that you insert at various angles, sometimes right-opening and sometimes left-opening. Dynamic blocks are blocks that contain intelligence and flexibility so that you can insert them in many variations. Thus, they can significantly reduce the number of blocks in your block library.

Dynamic blocks support both geometric and block parametric constraints. You can convert dimensional parametric constraints to block parametric constraints by choosing Block Editor tab ⇨ Dimensional panel ⇨ Convert. I cover geometric and dimensional parametric constraints in Chapter 10.

Dynamic blocks let you specify the types and amounts of variations for each block. You create (author) dynamic blocks in the Block Editor. You can use one of two systems to accomplish your goal. Each system has its strengths; use the system that most easily gives you the results you need.

> **TIP**
>
> You can control many of the colors used in the Block Editor as well as other display features. Click the dialog box launcher arrow at the right end of the Block Editor's Manage panel to open the Block Editor Settings dialog box. To change the background color of the Block Editor, choose Application Button ⇨ Options and click the Display tab. Click the Colors button. From the Context list, choose Block Editor. Then choose Uniform Background from the Interface Element list, and choose a color from the Color drop-down list. Click Apply & Close, and then click OK.

Understanding action-based parameters

This section describes action-based parameters. Action-based parameters allow for complex systems of flexibility. For a block to be dynamic, it must include at least one *parameter*. A parameter usually has an associated *action*. (I cover parametric constraints, which are different, including geometric and dimensional constraints, in Chapter 10.)

Parameters define the special properties of the dynamic block, including locations, distances, and angles. Parameters can also constrain the values within which the parameter can function. An action specifies how a block uses its associated parameter to change in some way.

For example, you may want to move one component of a block independently of the block, such as the chair in a block containing a desk and a chair. To accomplish this, you add a point parameter that specifies a point on the chair. You then add a move action that allows you to move the chair from that point. Figure 18.12 shows a desk and a chair block that includes the following dynamic components:

- The desk has a distance parameter with a stretch action. Therefore, you can stretch the desk without affecting the chair. You would use this type of action if you have several sizes of desks that you need to include in your drawing.

- The chair contains a point parameter with a move action. As a result, you can move the chair independently of the rest of the block. If you stretch the desk, you might want to move the chair so that it remains centered in front of the desk, or you might simply want to move the chair farther away from the desk.

If you open a dynamic block in a pre-2006 release of AutoCAD or AutoCAD LT, you see the last current view of the block. You cannot use the dynamic features of the block, but you can edit it as a regular block. The block is assigned a name, such as U2.

Understanding the work flow of dynamic blocks

Because defining a dynamic block takes some time — although simpler dynamic blocks are not very time-consuming to set up — the most common use for dynamic blocks is to create a block library. Normally, you define your dynamic blocks and save them for future use in your drawings. In other words, unless you need to insert a new block many times in several variations in a drawing, you won't create dynamic blocks for the current drawing on which you're working.

FIGURE 18.12

This dynamic block contains components that enable you to stretch the desk's length and move the chair.

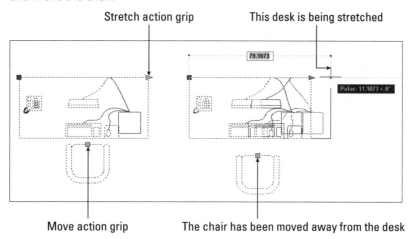

A block library can have two configurations:

- **One block per drawing.** You save each block in its own drawing. Use the BASE command to specify the origin of the drawing, which is usually on an object snap somewhere on the block. (I explain the BASE command in the "Saving blocks as files" section earlier in this chapter.) You use the INSERT command to insert the drawing, thereby inserting its block.
- **Many blocks per drawing.** You put a number of (usually) related blocks in a drawing. To insert the block, you use the DesignCenter to locate the drawing and find the individual block that you want. (See the section "Using the DesignCenter" earlier in the chapter for information on inserting blocks with the DesignCenter.)

The first part of the process of creating dynamic blocks is to define the block. I explain the details in the next few sections, but here I provide an overview of the workflow:

1. In your block library drawing or in a new drawing, create the block.
2. Choose Home tab ⇨ Block panel ⇨ Block Editor (BEDIT command). In the Edit Block Definition dialog box, choose the block, and click OK to open the Block Editor. (You can also start the BEDIT command, name the block, and create the objects in the Block Editor.) Select <Current Drawing> to work with the objects in model space if the drawing is inserted as a block in a different drawing.
3. Add parameters and associated actions, or geometric parametric constraints.
4. Save the block definition in the Block Editor.
5. Close the Block Editor.

6. If the drawing will contain just this block, use the BASE command to set the drawing origin where you want the insertion point to be, usually somewhere on the block.

7. Save the drawing.

You may want to follow this process for any number of blocks. When your blocks are defined, do the following to insert your dynamic blocks:

1. In your current drawing, either use the INSERT command to insert the drawing containing the block, or use the DesignCenter to choose the block from within the drawing.

2. Select the block to see its special grips. These grips show you where you can modify the block.

3. Usually, you click and drag a grip. Some dynamic block parameters involve choosing a visibility or option from a drop-down list or table.

Defining a dynamic block with action-based parameters

To define a dynamic block, first create the objects that you want for the block, or display an existing block. Then choose Home tab ⇨ Block panel ⇨ Block Editor to start the BEDIT command. In the Edit Block Definition dialog box, choose <Current Drawing> or the block's name and click OK. (You can also copy and paste individual objects from the drawing into the Block Editor to create a block from those objects.) The Block Editor opens, shown in Figure 18.13, and a new Block Editor tab appears on the Ribbon. At the same time, the Block Authoring Palettes window opens.

FIGURE 18.13

The Block Editor is a special window for authoring dynamic blocks.

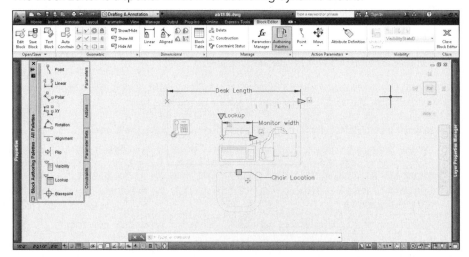

Before you start defining your block, you need to decide the types of variations that you want the block to have. You build flexibility into your blocks with a combination of parameters and actions.

Table 18.2 lists the parameters, the actions that you can add to each parameter, and a description of the uses for the parameters and actions on the specified component of the dynamic block.

TABLE 18.2   Dynamic Block Parameters and Actions

Parameter	Available Actions	Uses
Point	Move, Stretch	Move or stretch from that point (X,Y coordinate).
Linear	Move, Scale, Stretch, Array	Move, scale, stretch, or array along the line between two points.
Polar	Move, Scale, Stretch, Polar Stretch, Array	Move, scale, stretch, polar stretch at an angle, or array along the line between two points and at the specified angle.
XY	Move, Scale, Stretch, Array	Move, scale, stretch, or array at the specified X and Y distance.
Rotation	Rotate	Rotate at the specified angle.
Alignment	None	Align the entire block with other objects. You can align perpendicular or tangent to other objects. No action is required.
Flip	Flip	Flip along a *reflection line*. Flipping is like mirroring without retaining the original objects.
Visibility	None	Control the visibility of components in the block. No action is required. See the section "Adding visibility parameters" later in this chapter.
Lookup	Lookup	Choose a custom property from a list or table that you define. See the section "Adding lookup parameters and actions" later in this chapter.
Basepoint	None	Define a base point for the dynamic block.

Adding a parameter

To create a dynamic block, you start by adding a parameter. Click the parameter that you want from the Parameters tab of the Block Authoring Palettes window. Each parameter prompts you for the information it needs. For example, the Linear parameter tool responds with the `Specify start point or [Name/Label/Chain/Description/Base/Palette/Value set]:` prompt. When you specify the start point, you get a prompt for the endpoint. The flip parameter prompts you for a reflection line, which is like a mirror line.

The options for each parameter are fairly similar. Here's how to use the options:

- **Name.** You can change the name of the parameter. The name appears in the Properties palette when you select the parameter. However, you may find it confusing to change the name, because the name clearly denotes which parameter the block uses. On the other hand, if you have more than one of the same type of action, such as two stretch actions, renaming the actions to identify what they apply to can eliminate confusion. For example, you could have two Move actions, "Move table" and "Move chair."

- **Label.** The label appears in the Properties palette, but also next to the block when you have the Block Editor open. Change the label to suit your needs. For example, the linear parameter uses a label of "Distance." You might want to change that to Length, Width, or even something more specific.

- **Chain.** Sometimes, you might want one action to cause more than one change in a block. To do this, you can chain parameters. As a result, activating one parameter's actions causes the secondary parameter's action to occur. The primary parameter must have an action whose selection set includes the secondary parameter in addition to any other objects it will act on. (If the action is a stretch action, the stretch frame also needs to include the secondary parameter.) You must then set the secondary parameter's Chain Actions property to Yes.

- **Description.** You can add a description to a parameter. This description displays in the Properties palette when you select the parameter in the Block Editor.

> **NOTE**
> If you add a description, it appears as a tooltip when you select the inserted dynamic block in your drawing and hover the cursor over the parameter's grip. You could use this feature to provide a brief description of the type of parameter or instructions on how to use it.

- **Base.** Creates a base point parameter, which sets a base point for the block.

- **Palette.** By default, displays parameter labels in the Properties palette when you select the block reference in a drawing. Change to No if you don't want to display the labels.

- **Value set.** You can constrain the available values for your block's size, either as increments (for example, from 3 feet to 7 feet in 6-inch increments) or by providing a list (for example, only 36", 40", and 42"). This option prompts you to choose either the increment or the list method, and then prompts you for values. You can also specify a value set later in the Properties palette.

When you are finished using the options or have specified the necessary coordinates (such as a start point and endpoint for a linear parameter), the `Specify label location:` prompt appears. Pick a point to place the label for the parameter.

An exclamation point now appears next to the parameter. This exclamation point alerts you that you have not yet added an action to the parameter. Most parameters require an action to function properly. Figure 18.14 shows a chair with a linear parameter.

FIGURE 18.14

This chair has a linear parameter, but no action.

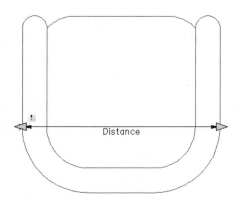

You can use the grips of the parameters as insertion points when you insert the dynamic block. During insertion, you press Ctrl to cycle among the grips if their Cycling property is set to Yes. To check, select a grip, open the Properties palette, and look for the Cycling property. You can specify the order of the cycling. Select a grip, right-click, and choose Insertion Cycling to open the Insertion Cycling Order dialog box (BCYCLEORDER command), where you can turn cycling on or off for each grip and move the grips up and down in the order of the list.

Adding an action

When you have placed a parameter, you're ready to add an associated action. Table 18.2 lists which actions you can associate with your parameter. Click the Actions tab of the Block Authoring Palettes window, as shown in Figure 18.15.

Sometimes, the parameter that you want to use has more grips than you need. For example, if you use a linear parameter, you end up with two grips, one at each end of the length that you define. However, you might want to stretch only in one direction; in this case, you need to have only one grip. To remove the extra grip, select the parameter, right-click, and choose Grip Display ⇨ 1. The other possibility is to use a point parameter with a stretch action.

> **TIP**
>
> Why would you use the linear parameter (rather than a point parameter) when you want to add a stretch action? When you stretch the inserted dynamic block, if you have Dynamic Input turned on, you see a linear tooltip that allows you to enter a total length. You can set the total length in the Properties palette, but that isn't nearly as convenient. Also, a point parameter doesn't offer the Value Set option, which lets you constrain sizes.

18

FIGURE 18.15

Use the Actions tab of the Block Authoring Palettes window to associate an action with a parameter.

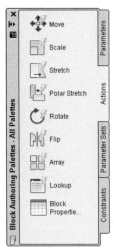

To add an action, choose an appropriate action for your parameter. At the `Select parameter:` prompt, select the parameter. Remember that you always apply an action to a parameter, rather than to an object. However, as part of the process, you specify a selection set for the action, which means selecting the object or objects. Note that you can add more than one action to a parameter.

> **CAUTION**
>
> Be sure to select the actual parameter, and not the object or the grip. An easy way to select the parameter is to click its label.

The next prompts depend on the action that you choose and on the parameter to which you're attaching the action. Table 18.3 explains some of the prompt options that you find for commonly used actions.

TABLE 18.3 Action Prompt Options

Action	Parameter	Option Responses
Move	Point	Select the objects.
Move	Linear, polar, or XY	Because you have more than one point, you need to specify which point you want to associate with the action. You can choose the point by moving the cursor over it; a red circle appears over the active point. You can also use the sTart point/Second point options. You can press Enter to use the second point (the default), and then select the objects.

Action	Parameter	Option Responses
Scale	Linear, polar, or XY	You select the objects. You can also specify a dependent base (relative to the base point of the action's parameter) or an independent base point (which you specify). If you used an XY parameter, you can also specify whether the distance is the X distance, the Y distance, or the XY distance (the default).
Stretch	Point	Select the objects.
Stretch	Linear, polar, or XY	Because you have more than one point, you need to specify which point you want to associate with the action. You can choose the point by moving the cursor over it; a red circle appears over the active point. You can also use the sTart point/Second point options or press Enter to use the second point (the default), and then select the objects. Then you specify diagonal corners of a *stretch frame* that defines the area that is included in the stretch. (You can also use a Cpolygon.) Finally, you select objects. You can continue to add or remove objects, just as you do when stretching.
Polar stretch	Polar	Identical to the prompts for the Stretch parameter. In addition, you specify objects to rotate only (but not stretch).

NOTE
Defining the stretch frame for a stretch action is similar to specifying a crossing selection window in the STRETCH command, except that you can create the stretch frame from left to right. Objects within the frame are moved, and objects that cross the frame are stretched. However, you also select objects for a stretch action. If objects are in the stretch frame, but not in the selection set, they are not stretched or moved. If objects are outside the frame, but are in the selection set, they are moved. After you select objects, you can select or deselect individual objects to add them to, or subtract them from, the selection set.

18

When you complete your answers for the prompts, AutoCAD displays an icon for the action. As you add more parameters and actions to a block, you may sometimes need to know which parameter goes with which action. To find out, hover the cursor over an action's icon to highlight its parameter.

CAUTION
If the exclamation point doesn't disappear after you add an action, the action was not successfully added! Undo the last command (BACTIONTOOL) and try again. Usually the problem involves selecting the proper parts of the parameter and correctly selecting the applicable objects. Reducing the number of grips may also solve this problem. Select the parameter, right-click, and choose Grip Display.

You can modify the action to multiply the parameter value by a factor or change the parameter angle. To do so, select the action's icon and display the Properties palette (press Ctrl+1). Then do one of the following:

- **Distance Multiplier.** Click next to the Distance Multiplier item in the Properties palette and enter another value to multiply the parameter by that factor. For example, you can multiply a stretch by a factor of .5. If you want to keep a circle centered inside a rectangle that you're moving or stretching, use a .5 multiplier so that the circle moves or stretches half of the distance of the rectangle, thereby remaining centered.

- **Angle Offset.** Click next to the Angle Offset item in the Properties palette and enter an angle to offset the parameter angle by that angle. For example, you can increase an angle by 90 degrees. This allows you to move the cursor to the right (0 degrees) and stretch an object in the 90-degree direction.

Adding visibility parameters

Visibility parameters enable you to turn the visibility of a block component on and off when you insert it. You can use visibility parameters either with other action-based parameters, or with geometric and dimension parametric constraints. You can define multiple named visibility states, thereby creating many variations of visibility or invisibility. Visibility parameters are a very powerful way to add flexibility to a block and to reduce the number of similar blocks that you store. You can add only one visibility parameter per block. You can use visibility parameters in two ways:

- **Make one component visible or invisible.** You can choose to display or not display one component. For example, if you have a telephone on a desk, you can display or not display the telephone.

- **Switch among multiple components.** You can include variations of a component, and cycle among them during insertion. For example, you can have three types of telephones (such as single-line, two-line, and multiple-line), all in the same location, with one on top of the other. When inserting the block, you can choose which telephone to display.

To add a visibility parameter, follow these steps:

1. Open the Block Editor in a drawing that contains the components that you need. If you want to switch among multiple components, place them on top of each other.

2. Choose Visibility from the Parameters tab of the Block Authoring Palettes window, and place it near the components. Before placing the parameter, you may want to use the Label option to change the label.

 3. Choose Block Editor tab ⇨ Visibility panel ⇨ Visibility States (or double-click the visibility parameter) to open the Visibility States dialog box, as shown in Figure 18.16.

4. Click the default visibility state (VisibilityState0) to select it. Enter a new name for your first state and press Enter. The name should relate to what the state will display. In the telephone example, you might use `telephone` or `single-line` as the state.

5. Click New to open the New Visibility State dialog box.

6. Enter a new visibility state name. In the telephone example, you might use `no telephone` or `two-line`. To leave the visibility of existing objects unchanged, use the default option, Leave Visibility of Existing Objects Unchanged in New State. If you want the new state to hide all objects, choose Hide All Existing Objects in New State. To display all objects, choose Show All Existing Objects in New State. Whichever option you choose, you can change the visibility of individual objects for each state afterwards. Click OK.

FIGURE 18.16

Use the Visibility States dialog box to add and name visibility states.

7. If you need more visibility states, repeat Steps 5 and 6 until you're done.

8. Click OK to close the Visibility States dialog box and return to the Block Editor.

9. Choose the first state from the Visibility States drop-down list in the Block Editor tab's Visibility panel. For that state, select all the objects that you want to make invisible, if any. Then choose Block Editor tab ⇨ Visibility panel ⇨ Make Invisible.

10. Repeat Step 9 for each state. If you chose to hide objects when you created the state, you may instead need to make certain objects visible by choosing Block Editor tab ⇨ Visibility panel ⇨ Make Visible.

NOTE

If you need to select an object that's invisible, choose Block Editor tab ⇨ Visibility panel ⇨ Visibility Mode. The object is displayed in a light gray color so that you can see and select it.

11. Check each visibility state by choosing each state in turn from the Visibility States drop-down list in the Visibility panel and making sure that each state displays what you want it to display.

When you insert the dynamic block and select it, you see a down arrow. Click the arrow to display the list of visibility states. Choose the state that you want.

Adding lookup parameters and actions

A lookup parameter/action combination creates a table that pairs labels with values. For example, you might have a desk that comes in three sizes. You can create this desk and use the Value Set option to create a list of three sizes: 4 feet, 5 feet, and 6 feet. You can then create labels that say 4' desk, 5' desk, and 6' desk. When you insert the desk, you can choose the label that you want from a drop-down list; the desk automatically stretches to the proper size. You don't need to use the Value Set option, because you specify values in the lookup table. Later in this chapter, I discuss Block Tables, which are another way to create a list of size variations. If you are using parametric constraints, you use a Block Table, rather than a lookup table.

Lookup tables are great when you want preset sizes for a block. When you insert the block, you don't even have to think about exact measurements; you just choose from a drop-down list, as shown in Figure 18.17.

FIGURE 18.17

You can specify a preset size by choosing from the drop-down list.

To create a lookup parameter and action, follow these steps:

1. In the Block Editor, add a parameter and action that you will use as the basis for the Lookup parameter and action. For example, add a linear parameter and a stretch action. If you add a value set (list or increment), the measurements will be available in advance when you create the lookup table.

2. From the Parameters tab of the Block Authoring Palettes window, add a Lookup parameter.

3. From the Actions tab, add a Lookup action. At the prompt, select the lookup parameter. The Property Lookup Table dialog box opens, as shown in Figure 18.18.

4. Click the Add Properties button, choose the parameter that you want to work with (for example, the linear parameter), and click OK. You return to the Property Lookup Table dialog box.

5. If you have values from a value set, you can see them by clicking the first row in the Input Properties side of the dialog box. A drop-down arrow appears. Choose the first value. If you don't have a value set, click the Add Properties button, choose the parameter you want, and click OK. Click on the Input Properties side, and choose a value from the drop-down list that appears. Click the same row on the Lookup Properties side of the dialog box and enter the label that corresponds with the value. Then click the next row, choose the next value, and enter the next label. Continue until you're done.

FIGURE 18.18

The Property Lookup Table dialog box enables you to associate values with labels.

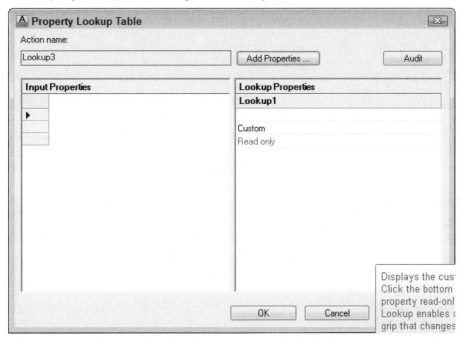

6. If the lower-right cell in the dialog box says Read Only, click it so that it changes to read Allow Reverse Lookup. (To do this, all the rows in the table must be unique.) You need to use this option in order to choose a value from a drop-down list of labels when you insert the block. Click OK.

7. Choose Block Editor tab ⇨ Close panel ⇨ Close Block Editor.

Now each value in the lookup table is associated with the labels that you entered. When you insert the dynamic block and select it, click the down arrow and choose from the options that drop down.

TIP

To edit the lookup action, right-click it and choose Display Lookup Table to open the Property Lookup Table dialog box. There you can make your changes.

Using parameter sets

The Parameter Sets tab of the Block Authoring Palettes window contains a number of ready-made parameter-action combinations that you can use. These sets are great for quick creation of dynamic blocks that are not complex. Hover the cursor over any parameter set to see a tooltip explaining the set's functioning.

When you place a parameter set, you see an exclamation point, because you have not yet selected the objects for the action. Right-click the action icon and choose Action Selection Set⇨New Selection Set to display prompts that allow you to select objects.

> **TIP**
>
> You can edit these parameter sets and create new ones. To create a new one, right-click the parameter set on the Parameter Sets tab and choose Copy. Then right-click the tab itself and choose Paste. To change a parameter set, right-click a parameter set and choose Properties. Then change the settings in the Tool Properties dialog box. To add an action, click the Actions item, and then click the Ellipsis button to open the Add Actions dialog box.

Using parametric constraints

Parametric constraints allow you to control the geometric and dimensional relationships among objects. I cover parametric constraints in full in Chapter 10. This discussion assumes that you have read that chapter.

> **AUTOCAD ONLY**
>
> You can't create parametric constraints in AutoCAD LT, but if they are in a drawing that you open, you can use them.

> **CAUTION**
>
> Dynamic block parameters and actions, just previously described, and parametric constraints have some overlap in their capabilities. In most cases, you should use one or the other, but not both, for any dynamic block. Combining the parameters-actions feature with the parametric constraints feature can create undesirable results, because constraints may prevent an action from functioning the way you want it to, or may allow a valid yet unintended result. However, visibility, alignment, and base point parameters should not cause a problem when you use them along with parametric constraints because they don't change the geometry of the block itself.

 You can apply parametric constraints to your objects in the drawing window, before creating the block and entering the Block Editor. If you don't see your constraints in the Block Editor, choose Block Editor tab⇨Geometric panel⇨Show All Geometric Constraints.

 It is important to constrain your objects as fully as possible, because the purpose of dynamic blocks is to allow for modification. Underconstrained blocks may break apart or act in other unpredictable ways. To start the process, choose Block Editor tab⇨Geometric panel⇨Auto Constrain. Then add other constraints that you think may be necessary. You can customize the auto-constraining process. Click the dialog box launcher arrow at the right end of the Geometric panel to open the Constraint Settings dialog box. For more information, see Chapter 10.

 To help create constraints, you can use click the Infer Constraints button on the status bar. For more information, see Chapter 10.

 To check the level of constraint on a block, choose Block Editor tab⇨Manage panel⇨Constraint Display Status. The objects in the block turn various colors, depending on their status. Click the button again to remove these colors. By default, the colors are as follows:

- **White.** Unconstrained
- **Blue.** Partially constrained
- **Magenta.** Fully constrained
- **Red.** Improperly constrained

To change the colors for each category, click the dialog box launcher arrow at the right end of the Manage panel to open the Block Editor Settings dialog box (the BSETTINGS command); this feature is hard to understand if the colors of your objects are the same as the default colors.

 You may find that you need to add a line or other object as a bridge between two objects, in order to set a desired distance, for example. This is called *construction geometry*. Normally, you would use a separate layer for construction geometry and then freeze or turn off that layer, or set it to Not Plottable. However, in the Block Editor, you can simply choose Block Editor tab ⇨ Manage panel ⇨ Construction Geometry and select the line or object. Press Enter to accept the default Convert option. That object then appears dashed, and does not plot.

> **TIP**
>
> You can add a Fix geometric constraint to fix the block's base point to a specific point. This ensures that the block changes relative to that fix point. Sometimes, this is all you need to add to the auto-constraining process to make a block fully constrained.

Add the geometric constraints you need from the Block Editor's Geometric panel (or the Constraints tab of the Block Authoring Palettes window), whether manually or by auto-constraining; then move on to dimensional constraints from the Dimensional panel. When you add dimensional constraints inside the Block Editor, you get a prompt for the number of grips. By including one or more grips, the dimensional constraint allows you to modify the block in your drawing, just like grips for actions (discussed earlier in this chapter). In this way, a linear constraint can replace a linear parameter/stretch action combination.

To restrict allowable values, you can add a value set to a dimensional constraint. (I cover value sets earlier in this chapter.) Select the constraint, display the Properties palette (press Ctrl+1), and use the Value Set section.

Creating a Block Table

A Block Table allows you to specify defined sizes for dimensional constraints and select those sizes from a drop-down list when you modify the dynamic block. A Block Table is similar to a lookup table, covered earlier in this chapter, but has some differences. You cannot use a Block Table with action-based parameters; instead, use a lookup table.

A dynamic block can have only one Block Table. When you use the Block Table for one dimensional constraint, it functions like a lookup table, allowing you to choose a size from the drop-down list. However, the Block Table can include more than one dimensional constraint; in this case, you can create combinations of sizes. For example, you might allow a rectangle with two dimensional constraints to be 2 x 3, 3 x 4, or 4 x 5. In this situation, you could not choose 2 x 5 from the drop-down list, because that combination is not in the Block Table. You can allow other values, but they wouldn't be available from the drop-down list.

18

To add a Block Table, first create the dimensional constraints that you need. Then choose Block Editor tab ⇨ Dimensional panel ⇨ Block Table. Follow the prompts:

```
Specify parameter location or [Palette]: Specify a location where the
     drop-down list will appear. Use the Palette option and choose Yes or
     No to specify whether you want to display the Block Table in the
     Properties palette.
Enter number of grips [0/1] <1>: Enter 1 ↵ to display a down-facing
     triangle, which will open the drop-down list of values. Enter 0 ↵ to
     hide the drop-down list.
```

The Block Properties Table dialog box opens. Click the Adds Properties, which Appear as Columns in the Table button. The Add Parameter Properties dialog box opens, listing the dimensional parameters available in the dynamic block. Choose the ones that you want to include in the Block Table, and click OK to return to the Block Properties Table dialog box. The parameters you chose are now listed as columns in the Block Table.

Enter the desired values in the cells of the table. Remember that if you chose more than one constraint, the drop-down list will only allow the combinations that you enter. Figure 18.19 shows a table with one-dimensional constraint applied to rectangle horizontal length, and three size options.

> **NOTE**
> If you created a value set for a dimensional constraint, you cannot enter values that are not specified in the value set.

FIGURE 18.19

This Block Properties Table provides three sizes for a length in a dynamic block.

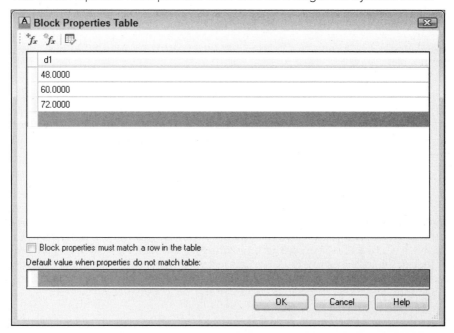

If the Block Properties Must Match a Row in the Table check box is checked, you can't modify the dynamic block to sizes not in the table. If you uncheck this check box, only sizes in the table will appear in the drop-down list, but you will be able to drag the block to sizes not listed.

 When you're done entering values in the Block Table, click the Audit the Block Property Table for Errors button. The audit process finds cells that are missing values or empty rows for values in a value set that you created, for example. After fixing any errors, click OK. Choose Block Editor tab ⇨ Open/ Save panel ⇨ Save Block to save the block.

Saving and testing dynamic blocks

 When your dynamic block is done, choose Block Editor tab ⇨ Open/Save panel ⇨ Save Block.

TIP

To make a copy of the block, choose Block Editor tab ⇨ Open/Save panel (expanded) ⇨ Save Block As. You can then modify the new block to make a variation of the original block. You can use the Save Block As button to create a duplicate of any block, not just a dynamic one.

 Before continuing, you should test the block to make sure that it works the way you want it to. To test a block, choose Block Editor tab ⇨ Open/Save panel ⇨ Test Block.

A new Test Block Window opens. Select the block and try out its dynamic features. For more information about using a dynamic block, see the "Inserting and using dynamic blocks" section later in this chapter. When you are done, click the Close Test Block Window button on the Close panel to return to the regular Block Editor window.

To close the Block Editor, choose Block Editor tab ⇨ Close panel ⇨ Close Block Editor.

If you want to put the base point for the block somewhere on the block, use the BASE command. Then save your drawing.

Inserting and using dynamic blocks

You insert a dynamic block in the same way that you insert a regular block: by using the Insert dialog box or the DesignCenter. For more information, see "Inserting Blocks and Files into Drawings" earlier in this chapter.

During insertion, you can press Ctrl to cycle among the grips if their Cycling property is set to Yes. Each time you press Ctrl, the cursor moves to another grip on the block. Also, before you specify the insertion point, you can open the Properties palette and specify values, such as the distance value of a length parameter.

To use the dynamic features of the block, first select the block. You see turquoise dynamic block grips, depending on the type of action. You click and drag these grips in the same way that you do for regular grips; the difference is that the resulting modification is controlled by the parameters-actions or the parametric constraints that you defined. If you have created a value set, you see vertical lines at the available lengths, as shown to the right of the cursor in Figure 18.20. Lookup and visibility actions, as well as Block Tables, have a down arrow so that you can open a drop-down list and choose a lookup table, visibility state, or table row, respectively.

FIGURE 18.20

This block can be a chair, loveseat, or sofa. The faint vertical lines indicate the available lengths as you drag.

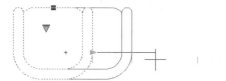

STEPS: Creating and Inserting Dynamic Blocks Using Action-Based Parameters

1. Open `ab18-f.dwg`, available on the companion website. This is a set of office furniture, as shown in Figure 18.21.

FIGURE 18.21

The office furniture is a block that can be more useful if it is dynamic.

2. Save the drawing as `ab18-06.dwg` in your `AutoCAD Bible` folder. Set an Endpoint running object snap.

3. Hover the cursor over any part of the drawing. You can see that it is all one block, called DeskSet.

4. Double-click the block. In the Edit Block Definition dialog box, choose `DeskSet` and click OK. The Block Editor opens with the desk set (including a desk, armchair, computer, monitor, and phone) displayed. Inside the Block Editor, you work with the individual components of the DeskSet block. The Block Authoring Palettes window also opens.

5. You want to be able to move the armchair separately from the rest of the block. To add a point parameter to the chair, click the Parameters tab of the Block Authoring Palettes window and choose Point.

6. Follow these prompts:

```
Specify parameter location or [Name/Label/Chain/Description/Palette]:
    Right-click and choose Label.
Enter position property label <Position>: Chair Location ↵
Specify parameter location or [Name/Label/Chain/Description/Palette]:
    Pick the endpoint at the middle of the front of the chair.
Specify label location: Pick a location for the Chair Location label.
```

7. To add a Move action to the point parameter, click the Actions tab and choose Move. Follow the prompts:

```
Select parameter: Select the point parameter by clicking its label.
Specify selection set for action. Select objects: Select all the objects
    that make up the chair. (In this instance, it doesn't make any
    difference whether or not you include the actual parameter in the
    selection set.)
Select objects: ↵
```

8. To add a linear parameter to the desk, click the Parameters tab and choose Linear. Follow the prompts:

```
Specify start point or [Name/Label/Chain/Description/Base/Palette/Value
    set]: Right-click and choose Label.
Enter distance property label <Distance>: Desk length ↵
Specify start point or [Name/Label/Chain/Description/Base/Palette/Value
    set]: Right-click and choose Value Set.
Enter distance value set type [None/List/Increment] <None> : Right-click
    and choose Increment.
Enter distance increment: 6 ↵
Enter minimum distance: 48 ↵
Enter maximum distance: 72 ↵
Specify start point or [Name/Label/Chain/Description/Base/Palette/Value
    set]: Choose the endpoint at the upper-left corner of the desk.
Specify endpoint: Choose the endpoint at the upper-right corner of the
    desk.
Specify label location: Pick a location above the desk.
```

9. We only want the right grip for the linear parameter. This makes sure that the desk can only be stretched toward the right. Select the linear parameter. Right-click and choose Grip Display ⇨ 1. The left grip disappears.

10. Click the Actions tab and choose Stretch. Follow the prompts:

```
Select parameter: Select the linear parameter by clicking its label.
Specify parameter point to associate with action or enter [sTart point/
    Second point] <Start>: Pass the cursor over the right grip and click.
Specify first corner of stretch frame or [CPolygon]: Click at ❶ in
    Figure 18.22.
Specify opposite corner: Click at ❷.
Specify objects to stretch. Select objects: Click close to but not on top
    of ❷.
Specify opposite corner: Click close to but not on top of ❶. The command
    line should show 52 found.
Select objects: ↵
```

11. The block should look like Figure 18.22.

18

FIGURE 18.22

The DeskSet block appearance after adding a move action to the armchair and a stretch action to the desk.

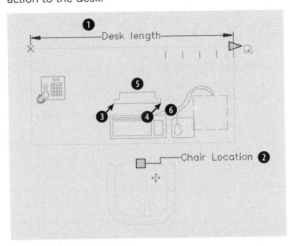

12. To allow for various sizes of monitors, click the Parameters tab and choose Linear. Right-click and choose the Label option. Type **Monitor width** ↵.

13. At the next two prompts, pick points ❸ and ❹, shown in Figure 18.22. Then place the parameter label above the monitor.

14. You can also create a value set in the Properties palette. Select the Monitor width parameter and open the Properties palette (press Ctrl+1). In the Value Set section, choose List from the Dist Type drop-down list. Next to the Dist Value List item, click the Ellipsis (...) button to open the Add Distance Value dialog box. The current width is already there. In the Distances to Add text box, type **18-1/2** ↵. The value moves below to the list box and changes to 1'-6 ½". Again in the Distances to Add text box, type **20-1/2** ↵. Click OK to close the dialog box.

15. With the linear parameter still selected, in the Properties palette, change the value of the Number of Grips item (in the Misc section) to 1. Close or minimize the Properties palette.

16. Click the Actions tab in the Block Authoring Palettes window and choose Stretch. At the Select parameter: prompt, select the linear parameter that you just created. At the next prompt, click the right parameter point. To specify the stretch frame, pick ❺ and then ❻, shown in Figure 18.22. To select objects, pick near ❻ and then near ❺. Press Enter to end selection.

17. You want to create a lookup parameter for the monitor. On the Parameters tab, choose Lookup and pick a location on the monitor. On the Actions tab, choose Lookup. Select the lookup parameter. The Property Lookup Table dialog box opens.

18. Click the Add Properties button. In the Add Parameter Properties dialog box, choose the Linear 1 parameter and click OK. Back in the Property Lookup Table dialog box, click the first row on the Input Properties side, below the Monitor width heading, and choose the first measurement from the drop-down list. In the same row on the Lookup Properties side, type **15" monitor**. (Note that monitors are measured diagonally, so the horizontal width of a 15"

monitor is not 15".) In the second row on the Input Properties side, choose the second measurement and enter **17" monitor** on the right. In the third row on the left, choose the last measurement and enter **19" monitor** on the right.

19. Click the Read Only cell; it changes to read Allow Reverse Lookup. The Property Lookup Table dialog box should have the rows shown below. Click OK.

```
1'-4 1/2"                15" monitor
1'-6 1/2"                17" monitor
1'-8 1/2"                19" monitor
```

20. Because some people may not have a land-line phone, we want to create a visibility parameter and action for the phone. On the Parameters tab, choose Visibility. Follow the prompts:

```
Specify parameter location or [Name/Label/Description/Palette]: Right-
    click and choose Label.
Enter visibility property label <Visibility>: Phone/No Phone ⏎
Specify parameter location or [Name/Label/Description/Palette]: Pick a
    location near the phone.
```

21. Choose Block Editor tab ⇨ Visibility panel ⇨ Visibility States. The Visibility States dialog box opens. Click the VisibilityState0 item and type **Has phone** ⏎. Click New. In the Visibility State Name text box of the New Visibility State dialog box, type **No phone** ⏎. Click OK twice to return to the Block Editor.

22. From the Visibility States drop-down list, make sure that No Phone is displayed; if not, choose it. Choose Block Editor tab ⇨ Visibility panel ⇨ Make Invisible. At the `Select objects:` prompt, select all the objects of the phone and press Enter to end selection. To double-check the visibility states, choose the Has Phone state and make sure that the phone appears.

23. Your block should look like Figure 18.23. Choose Block Editor tab ⇨ Open/Save panel ⇨ Save Block. Then click Close Block Editor in the Close panel. Save your drawing.

FIGURE 18.23

The completed dynamic block in the Block Editor

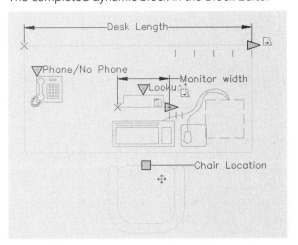

569

24. Open a new drawing based on the default template or any template that you usually use. Open the DesignCenter. In the Open Drawings pane, browse to, and double-click, `ab18-06.dwg`. Click Blocks. Drag the DeskSet block from the right side of the DesignCenter to your drawing. Close or minimize the DesignCenter.

> **NOTE**
>
> If you create a block inside a drawing and then make it dynamic, you need to use the DesignCenter to insert it. If you try to insert the entire drawing, you see only a regular block. However, if you don't create a block in the source drawing and create the dynamic block in the Block Editor without ever creating and naming a block, you can use the INSERT command to insert the entire drawing and use the dynamic features of the block.

25. Choose View tab⇨Navigation 2D panel⇨Zoom drop-down menu⇨Extents.

26. Select the DeskSet block. It should look like Figure 18.24.

FIGURE 18.24

When you select a dynamic block, you see grips for its dynamic features.

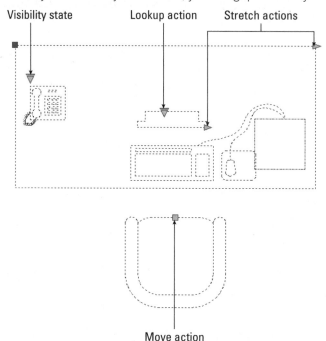

27. Click the desk's stretch grip and stretch the desk one vertical line to the left to make it 6 inches shorter. The computer moves with the desk.

28. Click the armchair's move grip and move the chair to the left so that it is still centered in front of the computer.

29. Click the monitor's lookup grip and choose `19" monitor` from the drop-down list. The monitor becomes wider.

30. Click the phone's visibility grip and choose `No phone` from the drop-down list. The phone disappears.

31. Continue to experiment with the grips to see all the possible variations. You do not need to save this drawing.

ON THE WEB

The drawing that you need for the following exercise on creating and inserting dynamic blocks using parametric constraints and a Block Table, `ab18-g.dwg`, is available from the `Drawings` download on the companion website.

STEPS: Creating and Inserting Dynamic Blocks Using Parametric Constraints and a Block Table

AUTOCAD ONLY

This exercise does not apply to AutoCAD LT.

1. Open `ab18-g.dwg`, available from the companion website. This is a sheet metal plate, similar to the one used in the Chapter 10 exercise on parametric constraints, as shown in Figure 18.25.

2. Save it as `ab18-07.dwg` in your `AutoCAD Bible` folder. Set a running object snap for Endpoint.

18

FIGURE 18.25

A sheet-metal plate that comes in several sizes

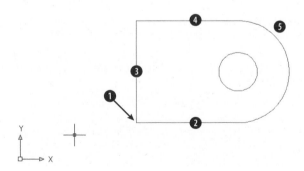

3. The goal is to create a block that can be four sizes; however, the central hole's diameter should remain unchanged. To create the block, select all the objects, and choose Home tab ⇨ Block panel ⇨ Create.

4. In the Block Definition dialog box, enter **ab18-g1** for the block name. In the Base Point section, the Specify On-Screen check box should be checked; the other Specify-On-Screen check box should not be checked. Check the Open in Block Editor check box and click OK.

5. At the `Specify insertion base point:` prompt, pick the endpoint at ❶ in Figure 18.25. The block opens in the Block Editor.

6. Choose Block Editor tab⇨Geometric panel⇨Auto Constrain. At the `Select objects or [Settings]:` prompt, type **all** ↲. Press Enter to end the command. AutoCAD adds a number of geometric constraints to the drawing — coincident, tangent, concentric, parallel, perpendicular, and horizontal.

7. As you stretch the block, the three straight sides need to remain equal. You only need to specify two of the sides. Choose Block Editor tab⇨Geometric panel⇨Equal. At the prompts, pick the bottom horizontal side at ❷ and the left vertical side at ❸.

8. As you stretch the block, you don't want the base point to move, so choose Block Editor tab⇨Geometric panel⇨Fix and choose the endpoint at ❶.

9. To keep the inner circle unchanged, add a diameter parameter. Choose Block Editor tab⇨Dimensional panel⇨Diameter. Follow the prompts:

```
Select arc or circle: Pick the inner circle.
Specify dimension line location: Pick a location to the left of the
    circle.
Enter value or name and value, and press Enter
```

10. Select the diameter parameter. Right-click and choose Grip Display⇨0. (You enter 0 because you don't need to change the diameter.)

11. To add a linear dimensional constraint, choose Block Editor tab⇨Dimensional panel⇨Linear. Follow the prompts:

```
Specify first constraint point or [Object] <Object>: ↲
Select object: Pick the top horizontal line at ❹.
Specify dimension line location: Pick a location above the line.
Enter value or name and value, and press Enter
```

12. Select the diameter parameter. Right-click and choose Grip Display⇨0. (You would need a grip if you wanted to drag the block, but you will use the Block Table feature instead.)

13. To change the name of the linear constraint, select it and open the Properties palette (press Ctrl+1). In the Constraint section, change the Name value to **length**.

14. To check that the block is fully constrained, choose Block Editor tab⇨Manage panel⇨Constraint Display Status. The entire block should be magenta. Click the same button again to turn off the display status.

15. Choose Block Editor tab⇨Dimensional panel⇨Block Table. At the `Specify parameter location or [Palette]:` prompt, pick the point at ❺. At the `Enter number of grips [0/1] <1>:` prompt, press Enter to accept the default value of 1. This grip will allow you to choose the values from the Block Table. The Block Properties Table dialog box opens.

16. Click the Adds Properties, which Appear as Columns in the Table button to open the Add Parameter Properties dialog box. Click the `length` property and click OK to return to the Block Properties Table. In the first row below the Length property, type **3**. Press Enter to go to the next row, and type **4**. In the same way, add **5** and **6**. Because these are the only allowable sizes, check the Block Properties Must Match a Row in the Table check box, and click OK.

17. Choose Block Editor tab ⇨ Open/Save panel ⇨ Save Block.

18. Choose Block Editor tab ⇨ Open/Save panel ⇨ Test Block. The Test Block Window opens. Select the block. Click the down arrow to reveal the length values you specified, as shown in Figure 18.26.

FIGURE 18.26

The metal plate has four sizes that you can choose from the Block Table's drop-down list.

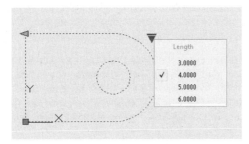

19. Choose the various sizes to see the result. The inner circle should remain concentric with the outer arc but should not change size. The three sides should always be the same length.

20. Click *Current* tab ⇨ Close panel ⇨ Close Test Block Window to return to the Block Editor.

21. Click Block Editor tab ⇨ Close panel ⇨ Close Block Editor. At the message to save, choose the option to save. You return to your drawing. If you want, you can again test the block.

22. Save your drawing.

Using Windows Features to Copy Data

You can insert objects by copying them from other drawings and pasting them into your current drawing, or using the drag-and-drop feature. You may be able to insert objects in this way without creating blocks.

Manipulating objects with the Windows Clipboard

You're probably familiar with cutting or copying data in other Windows applications and then pasting it, either within a file or from file to file. The following list compares copying, using blocks, and using the Clipboard with the CUTCLIP, COPYCLIP, and PASTECLIP commands:

- **MOVE/COPY.** Precise placement of objects; only works within a drawing.
- **BLOCK/WBLOCK/INSERT.** Precise placement of objects; can scale and rotate; creates block definition; can insert many times, even after other commands; can insert files (other drawings) that you save permanently. With the DesignCenter or Tool Palettes window, you can insert blocks from other drawings.
- **CUTCLIP/COPYCLIP/PASTECLIP.** No precise placement of objects (uses bottom-left corner of extents of object[s] that you copy); creates anonymous block in file with a name like A$CE314; can scale and rotate; can both move and copy objects; can insert (paste) many times; can copy from drawing to drawing or to other Windows applications.

In general, for one-time moving or copying with a drawing, you should use the MOVE or COPY command. If you want to copy an object several times over a period of time, use a BLOCK command. Use the Clipboard when you want to insert objects into another drawing one or more times without saving the objects. Also, the Clipboard is indispensable for copying objects to other applications.

 To place objects on the Clipboard, first select them. To move them, choose Home tab ⇨ Clipboard panel ⇨ Cut or press Ctrl+X. To copy them, choose Copy Clip in the same panel. You can paste objects that you've copied to the Clipboard into the same drawing as a block by using the PASTEBLOCK command; right-click and choose Clipboard ⇨ Paste as Block. If you want to paste the objects in another drawing, open that drawing. Choose Paste in the Clipboard panel. The command line prompts you for an insertion point.

 Chapter 9 covers the COPY command. Bonus Chapter 4 covers moving and copying objects, images, and data to and from other applications.

Using drag-and-drop

The drag-and-drop feature in Windows enables you to drag another drawing file into your drawing. Your drawing then prompts you as it would if you inserted the file by using the -INSERT command. To insert a drawing file by using drag-and-drop, follow these steps:

1. Open Windows Explorer. (Right-click the Start button and choose Explore.)
2. Navigate to the drawing file.
   - If the drawing window is visible, drag the drawing file into the AutoCAD or AutoCAD LT window.
   - If the drawing window is not visible, drag the drawing file onto the AutoCAD or AutoCAD LT button on the task bar, wait for your drawing to appear, and then drag the file into the drawing window.
3. Respond to the prompts of the -INSERT command on the command line.

When you drag the file into the drawing area, you see a plus sign at the cursor (or a rectangular cursor, depending on your operating system), indicating that you can drop the file.

To open a drawing file instead of inserting it, drag the file onto the application title bar at the very top of the application window, or simply double-click its icon in Windows Explorer. If you drag with the right-mouse button, when you release the mouse button in the drawing area, you have some additional options to create an external reference (Create Xref) or to create a hyperlink.

TIP

If you really don't know where the file is, or you're not even sure of its name, use the Windows Find feature. Choose Start ⟶ Search ⟶ For Files or Folders. (In Windows 7, choose Start and type in the Start Search text box.) On the screen that appears, set the criteria for the file. For example, you could find all drawing names that start with the letter C by typing c*.dwg in the Named text box. From the resulting list, choose the drawing that you want, and drag it onto your drawing by using the same steps listed previously.

Drag-and-drop is easy to use. You can also drag an object from one drawing to another. First open both drawings. It helps to be able to see them both at once. Choose View tab ⟶ Windows panel ⟶ Tile Vertically to see them side by side. Select the object or objects that you want to copy. Now click the object or objects again, and hold down the mouse button until the cursor displays a small rectangle. Then drag the object(s) to the other drawing.

Summary

In this chapter, I covered all the ways that you can use blocks and attributes in your drawings. You read about:

- Combining objects into blocks in your drawings so that you can edit them as a unit
- Inserting blocks at any scale and rotation
- Saving a block as a file
- Inserting blocks with the INSERT command
- Using the DesignCenter to import blocks from other drawings
- Creating dynamic blocks with action-based parameters and parametric constraints
- Using dynamic blocks
- Copying objects by using the Windows Clipboard and drag-and-drop

In the next chapter, I explain how to use attributes to label blocks.

18

Adding Attributes to Blocks

IN THIS CHAPTER

Using attributes

Creating attribute definitions

Placing blocks with attributes

Working with attributes

Y ou can attach *attributes* to blocks. Attributes are labels that are associated with blocks. Attributes have two main uses: to label objects and to create a simple database. This chapter explains how to create, use, and edit attributes.

Working with Attributes

Your drawings do not exist in a vacuum. The objects in your drawing represent real objects. These objects have characteristics that you cannot visually represent in a drawing, such as cost, manufacturer, date purchased, and so on. *Attributes* are labels that are attached to blocks. Using attributes, you can attach labels with pertinent data to blocks. You can then extract the data and import it into a database program or spreadsheet, or redisplay the data in an AutoCAD table. In AutoCAD only, you can also access data from objects that are not blocks; for more information, see the section on tables in Chapter 13.

ON THE WEB

You can access and link to outside databases from within AutoCAD (but not AutoCAD LT). See Bonus Chapter 1 on the companion website for more information on external databases.

You can also use attributes to place text relative to blocks. A common example is to use attributes for completing titleblock information, such as the drawing name, drawing number, date, scale, revision number, drafter, and so on. In this case, your plan is not to extract the data at all; you just use the attributes to help you precisely place the text in the titleblock. By inserting fields into these attributes, you can gain another benefit from attributes: automating the creation of titleblock text. For more information, see the discussion of fields in Chapter 13.

Attributes have several limitations. For example, they can only be attached to blocks (either regular or dynamic). However, you can create a dummy block that contains only attributes. The database features are also limited. Nevertheless, attributes are quite useful for simple database needs, as well as for placing text.

Defining an attribute creates a template into which you can place values when you insert the block. You define a tag that is equivalent to a field or category in a database. When you insert the block, you're prompted for the tag's value. For example, if your tag is COST, the value may be 865.79. This template is called an attribute definition.

Creating attribute definitions

The first procedure when working with attributes is to draw the individual objects that are to make up the block. If the block already exists, explode it, add the attributes, and then redefine the block.

The exception is when you want to create attributes without creating any other objects in the block. You might do this to extract attributes that apply to the drawing as a whole.

 After you have the objects, choose Home tab ⇨ Block panel (expanded) ⇨ Define Attributes to start the ATTDEF command. The Attribute Definition dialog box opens, as shown in Figure 19.1.

FIGURE 19.1

The Attribute Definition dialog box

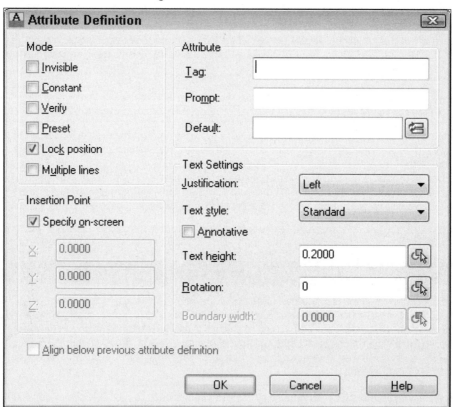

Mode section

The Mode section of the dialog box sets certain attribute properties, including visibility and default value. These properties are shown in Table 19.1.

TABLE 19.1 **Attribute Modes**

Mode	Explanation
Invisible	The attribute values that you set are not displayed in the drawing. Use this mode for attributes that you want to extract into a database but do not want to see in the drawing. Examples would be model numbers, purchase dates, cost, and so on. Of course, if you're using attributes to place text in a drawing, then you want them to be visible.
Constant	Sets a constant value for an attribute. The attribute automatically takes the attribute value that you set (in the Attribute section of the dialog box), and you do not get a prompt for a value. You might use this for the first three digits of employees' telephone numbers that have the same first three digits. You cannot edit constant attribute values.
Verify	When you insert an attribute, a prompt appears, asking you to verify the value. Use this option if you have a preset default.
Preset	Automatically inserts a default value that you specify. For example, if the most common manufacturer of a chair is American Interiors, you can specify this as a preset value. As you insert the block, this default is inserted for you, and you have to type a value only if it differs from the default. (You need to insert the attribute with the ATTDIA system variable set to 1 to get a prompt allowing you to change the value. See the explanation of ATTDIA later in this chapter.)
Lock Position	Locks the position of the attribute relative to the block. When you insert a block with attributes, locked attributes do not have their own grip and you can't move them from the block independently. Unlocked attributes have their own grip that you can use to move the attribute separately. If you want to include an attribute in the selection set of an action in a dynamic block, you must lock that attribute. You can then move it by using the –ATTEDIT command on the command line.
Multiple Lines	Allows an attribute to contain multiple lines of text. An Ellipsis button appears to the right of the Default text box, which you click to open a simplified multiline text editor. The Text Formatting toolbar appears. The text that you enter becomes the default text, but you can change it when you insert the block. You can then specify a boundary width by dragging the grips on the ruler.

TIP

Although by default you see the simplified multiline text editor, you can use the full In-Place Text Editor to format multiple line attributes. Set the ATTIPE system variable to 1. However, if you need compatibility with earlier releases of AutoCAD or AutoCAD LT, you may need to return this system variable to its default value of 0. Otherwise, earlier releases may not display the attributes properly.

19

Attribute section

In the Attribute section of the dialog box, specify the tag, which is the name of the attribute. You use this tag when you extract the attributes. A tag is equivalent to a field in a database. For example, if you import the data into a spreadsheet, the tags would be the column heads. The tag name cannot include spaces or exclamation points (!), and it is converted to uppercase letters.

The prompt is simply a plain-English version of the tag. The prompt asks you for the value of the attribute. For example, if the tag is PUR_DATE, you could define the prompt as Date Purchased.

The default is used for setting a default value. You can use this if the value is usually the same. To insert a field, click the Insert Field button and choose a field from the Field dialog box, as I explain in Chapter 13. When you insert the block and are prompted for a value, either you can use the field value or you can change it.

If you checked the Multiple Lines check box, the Default text box is not available; instead, click the Ellipsis button that appears, and enter the default value in the simplified multiline text editor.

TIP

You can use the value to clarify a format that should be followed when entering information. For example, you could set the value of a date to dd/mm/yy so that users know how to format the date.

Text Settings section

Use the Text Settings section to format the text. Choose a justification and text style from the drop-down list boxes. When you set the height, be sure to take into account the scale factor if you're not using annotative attributes. You can also set a rotation angle for the text.

Check the Annotative check box to make the attribute annotative so that it will automatically scale to match the scale of the viewport. For more information on annotative objects, see Chapter 17. I discuss annotative text, which is similar, in Chapter 13.

If you checked the Multiple Lines check box, the Boundary Width text box is available so that you can specify the width of the text. However, you can also adjust the width by dragging the arrows on the ruler of the simplified multiline text editor.

Insertion Point section

In the Insertion Point section, check the Specify On-Screen check box to specify the insertion point in your drawing. Uncheck the same check box if you want to prespecify coordinates. If you're using the attributes to place text in a schedule or titleblock, then the placement is obviously very important. If you're inserting invisible attributes, simply place them near the block. If you're creating more than one attribute for a block, place the attribute so that there is room for the other attributes underneath. When you've completed the dialog box, click OK. If you chose to specify the insertion point in the drawing, specify the point to insert the attribute.

After you define one attribute, the Align Below Previous Attribute Definition check box is active. Select this option to line up succeeding attributes under the first one.

Now is the time to confirm that the attribute definitions are the way you want them. You can edit attribute definitions before they've been placed into a block in two ways:

- Open the Properties palette (press Ctrl+1), select one attribute definition, and edit all its properties, such as the tag, value, prompt, and modes. You can also change properties such as the layer, text style, and so on.
- Double-click the attribute to start the DDEDIT command and change the tag, the prompt, and the default in the Edit Attribute Definition dialog box.

Creating the block

After you create the objects and their attribute definitions, you generally create a block. Choose Home tab ➪ Block panel ➪ Create, and select the objects and the attributes in the block.

19

Name the block and define the block's insertion point as you would normally. Generally, you want to check Delete because you don't need the block without the attribute tags in your drawing. Remember that you can make the block annotative, if you want.

Don't forget to pay attention to the layer of the attributes, just as you would the layer of the block objects. The same layer rules apply to attributes as to blocks.

After you create the block, you cannot edit the attributes in the Properties palette. I cover other techniques for editing attributes later in this chapter.

STEPS: Creating Attributes

1. Open ab19-a.dwg, available from the Drawings download on the companion website. This is a plan of an office building zoomed in to one office. A file containing one set of office furniture has been inserted, as shown in Figure 19.2.

2. Save the drawing as ab19-01.dwg in your AutoCAD Bible folder.

3. Choose Home tab⇨Modify panel⇨Explode, select the furniture in the office, and press Enter. This block has nested blocks. Choose the chair and explode it again to get its component objects.

4. Choose Home tab⇨Block panel (expanded)⇨Define Attributes. In the Attribute Definition dialog box, check Invisible in the Mode section.

5. In the Attribute section, enter the following:

   Tag: **mfr**
   Prompt: **Manufacturer**
   Default: **American Office Furniture**

6. Leave the Text Settings as they are. Make sure that the Specify On-Screen check box is checked and click OK. Pick point ❶, shown in Figure 19.2.

7. Repeat the ATTDEF command. Check the Align Below Previous Attribute Definition check box. Enter the following:

   Tag: **pur_date**
   Prompt: **Date purchased**
   Default: **3/01**

8. Click OK.

9. Choose Home tab⇨Block panel⇨Create. In the Name text box, type **armchair**. Uncheck Specify On-Screen button in the dialog box, if checked. Click Select Objects. Select the entire chair, along with the two attributes. End selection. The dialog box shows that 18 objects are selected. Click Pick Point. Use the Endpoint object snap to choose ❷ as the base point. In the dialog box, select Delete. Uncheck the Open in Block Editor check box, if checked. Click OK.

FIGURE 19.2

An office with a set of office furniture

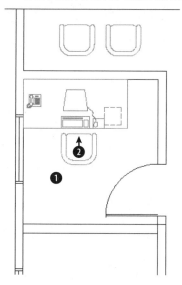

10. A message asks whether you want to redefine the block because there is already a block definition with the same name in the drawing. Choose Redefine Block.

11. Save your drawing. If you're continuing on to the next exercise, leave the drawing open.

NOTE
Redefining a block updates only block geometry, not attributes. Therefore, if you add attribute definitions to a block, only new blocks that you'll insert include the attributes. Existing blocks don't gain these new attribute definitions. To update existing blocks with their current attribute definitions, use the ATTSYNC command.

Inserting blocks with attributes

After you define a block with attributes, you insert it as you would any block. AutoCAD and AutoCAD LT automatically detect the existence of the attributes and prompt you for their values. After you enter the values, the block and its attributes appear in the drawing.

NOTE
You can insert attributes either in a dialog box or on the command line. By default, you insert them on the command line. To use a dialog box, set the ATTDIA system variable to 1. You would use the command line to automate the insertion of attributes by using an AutoLISP routine, menu item, or script file. When you use a dialog box, the Verify and Constant modes are not used. To skip all the prompts and automatically use default values that you have set, set the ATTREQ system variable to 0.

STEPS: Inserting Blocks with Attributes

1. Use `ab19-01.dwg` if you have it open from the previous exercise. Otherwise, it is available from the Results download on the companion website.

2. Save the drawing as `ab19-02.dwg` in your `AutoCAD Bible` folder.

3. Type **attdia** ⏎. If it's currently set to 0, type **1** ⏎.

4. Choose Home tab ⇨ Block panel ⇨ Insert. Choose ARMCHAIR from the Name drop-down list. Verify that the Specify On-screen option is checked only for Insertion Point, and click OK.

5. Pick a point in front of the desk (turn off Object Snap if necessary) to insert the armchair and open the Edit Attributes dialog box. The values that were entered when the attributes were defined are displayed, but you can change them.

6. The default values exist because most of the furniture was purchased at one time when the office was opened. However, let's assume that this chair was purchased later. Change the purchase date to 3/11. Click OK. Because the attributes are invisible, you see only the chair, but the values do exist in the drawing database.

7. Save the drawing.

Editing attributes

After you create the block, you can use the Block Attribute Manager. The Block Attribute Manager manages all properties of block attributes in one place. Use the Block Attribute Manager and its Edit Attribute dialog box to edit any aspect of block attributes.

Editing attribute properties with the BATTMAN command

After you insert a block and give values to its attributes, you can modify the following:

- Attribute prompt order
- Tag and prompt names
- Attribute visibility
- Text options (text style, justification, height, annotative, among others)
- Properties (layer, linetype, color, lineweight, and plot style)
- Attribute default value

After you make your changes, you can update all the blocks in your drawing to reflect the changes.

Choose Home tab ⇨ Block panel (expanded) ⇨ Attribute, Block Attribute Manager to start the BATTMAN command and open the Block Attribute Manager, as shown in Figure 19.3.

FIGURE 19.3

The Block Attribute Manager

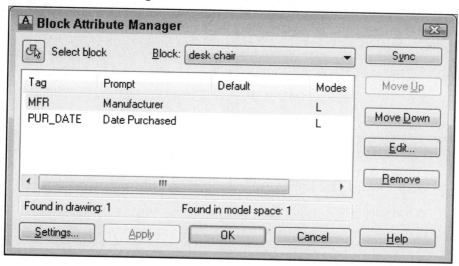

From the Block drop-down list in the Block Attribute Manager, choose the block whose attribute values you want to change. You can also click Select Block to select the block in your drawing. Use the Block Attribute Manager to:

- **Change the order of the attribute prompts when you insert a block with attributes.** Choose any attribute from the list in the Block Attribute Manager, and click Move Up or Move Down. Continue to use this procedure until you have the order that you want.

- **Delete an attribute.** Choose it and click Remove.

- **Change which attribute properties are listed in the Block Attribute Manager.** Click Settings. In the Block Attribute Settings dialog box, click all the properties that you want to see listed. For example, you can include columns for layer, style (text style), and color. Click OK.

TIP

When you add properties to the listing in the Block Attribute Manager, resize the dialog box so that you can see all the columns.

- **Edit the attributes, including prompt, default, text display, and properties.** Click Edit to open the Edit Attribute dialog box, as shown in Figure 19.4.

- **Update all the blocks in your drawing to reflect the changes that you've made.** Click Sync. Usually you do this after using the Edit Attribute dialog box. Because changes such as attribute order and mode affect only new insertions of the block, this update brings existing blocks into concordance with new blocks.

FIGURE 19.4

The Edit Attribute dialog box

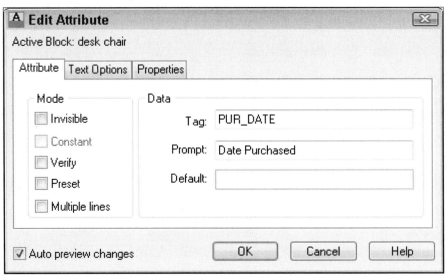

Use the Edit Attribute dialog box to edit all the properties of individual attributes. This dialog box has three tabs:

- **Attribute.** Enables you to change the mode and attribute properties. For example, in the Mode section, you can change the visibility of attributes. In the Data section, you can change the tag, prompt, and default. You can right-click the Default text box and choose Insert Field to use a field. (See Chapter 13 for a discussion of fields.)
- **Text Options.** Enable you to change text style, height, justification, and so on.
- **Properties.** Enable you to change attribute layer, color, linetype, and so on.

After you finish making changes, click OK in the Edit Attribute dialog box to return to the Block Attribute Manager. Click OK again to return to your drawing.

You may need to change the values of an attribute. Perhaps you entered the wrong purchase date or a part number has changed. Choose Home tab ⇨ Block panel ⇨ Edit Attributes drop-down menu ⇨ Single to start the EATTEDIT command, and select the block containing the attributes that you want to change. You see the Enhanced Attribute Editor, as shown in Figure 19.5.

As you can see, the Enhanced Attribute Editor is similar to the Edit Attribute dialog box. For example, it has the same three tabs. However, the Attribute tab enables you to change attribute values, something that you can't do in the Edit Attribute dialog box. To change an attribute's value, select it and type a new value in the Value text box. You can right-click the Value text box and choose Insert Field to use a field. (See Chapter 13 for more about fields.) The Text Options and Properties tabs of the Enhanced Attribute Editor are the same as in the Edit Attribute dialog box.

FIGURE 19.5

The Enhanced Attribute Editor

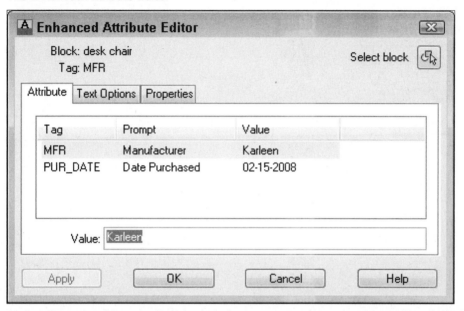

Editing attribute properties with the ATTEDIT command

You can also change attribute values by using the ATTEDIT command to open the Edit Attributes dialog box, as shown in Figure 19.6.

If a block has a number of attributes and you want to change them all in order, this dialog box makes it easy to go through all the attributes quickly. Press Tab to go to the next attribute.

One way to change attribute properties is to explode the block and double-click the attribute. This starts the DDEDIT command and opens the Edit Attribute Definition dialog box, where you can change the tag, prompt, and default value. You can then redefine the block. The preferred method though is to use the Block Attribute Manager, as explained in the previous section.

 To edit attributes on the command line, choose Home tab ⇨ Block panel ⇨ Edit Attributes drop-down menu ⇨ Multiple, or type **-attedit.** At the Edit attributes one at a time? [Yes/No] <Y>: prompt, select the Yes option. This command then prompts you for changes in attribute values and properties, such as position, text style, color, and so on.

FIGURE 19.6

The Edit Attributes dialog box

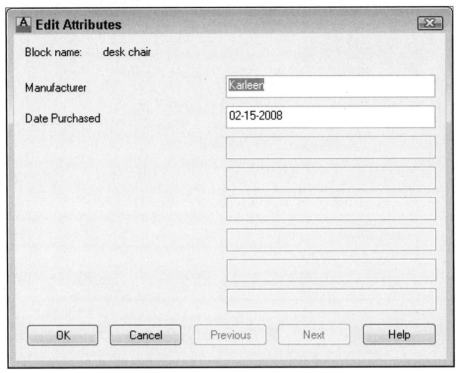

When you create invisible attributes, you can't edit them because you can't select them. The ATTDISP command controls attribute visibility globally, for all attributes in your drawing. Choose Home tab ⇨ Block panel (expanded) ⇨ Attribute Display drop-down menu, and choose one of the following options. The currently active option is checked on the menu.

- **Retain Attribute Display.** Attributes that were created as visible are visible. Attributes that were created as invisible are invisible. This is the default option.
- **Display All Attributes.** All attributes are visible.
- **Hide All Attributes.** All attributes are invisible.

Changing the current option causes your drawing to regenerate.

Making global changes in attributes

You can use the -ATTEDIT command on the command line to make global changes. If you answer No to the Edit attributes one at a time? [Yes/No] <Y>: prompt, you can make global changes to attribute values. For example, you can change all instances of A- in your part numbers to B-. You can even change invisible attribute values.

To use -ATTEDIT to make global changes, follow these steps:

1. Choose Home tab ⇨ Block panel ⇨ Edit Attributes drop-down menu ⇨ Multiple.

2. At the `Edit attributes one at a time? [Yes/No] <Y>:` prompt, type **n** ↵.

3. At the `Edit only attributes visible on screen? [Yes/No] <Y>:` prompt, answer **y** or **n** ↵, as desired. If you answer **n** to edit invisible attributes, then you must know the attribute text string that you want to change because it is invisible.

4. At the `Enter block name specification <*>:` prompt, you can type a block name to limit the changes to one block, or press Enter to include any block.

5. At the `Enter attribute tag specification <*>:` prompt, you can type a tag to limit the changes to one tag type, or press Enter to include any tag.

6. At the `Enter attribute value specification <*>:` prompt, you can type a value to limit the changes to one value, or press Enter to include any value.

7. If you chose to edit only attributes that are visible on-screen, you see the `Select Attributes:` prompt. (If not, skip to Step 8.) Pick each attribute that you want to modify, or use a window. Press Enter to end selection. If you include other objects or blocks that do not fit the block name, attribute tag, or attribute value specifications that you made, then these other objects are not selected. The command line informs you of how many attributes were selected.

8. At the `Enter string to change:` prompt, type the text string (any consecutive text) that you want to change.

9. At the `Enter new string:` prompt, type the text string that will replace the old string.

If you chose to edit attributes that are not visible on the screen, the drawing regenerates, and the command line lists the changes that it made.

Redefining attributes

You can redefine a block with attributes to include different objects and attributes, using the ATTREDEF command. Redefining a block lets you add or delete attributes or redefine a block that contains attributes. Follow these steps:

> **AutoCAD Only**
> AutoCAD LT does not include this feature. Instead, explode the block and start from scratch. You can use the DDEDIT command to change attributes after you explode a block.

1. Explode one of the blocks with attributes. If there are nested blocks that you want to change, explode them, too.

2. If you want to add attributes, define and place them. Delete unwanted attributes. Make any other changes that you want to the objects.

3. Type **attredef** ↵.

4. At the `Enter name of block you wish to redefine:` prompt, type the name of the block.

19

5. At the `Select objects for new Block...:` prompt, select the objects and the attributes that you want to include. Do not include any existing attributes that you want to delete.

6. At the `Specify insertion base point of new Block:` prompt, pick the base point for the block.

Here's how your drawing handles the changes:

- If you created new attributes, the command places them for all existing blocks and gives them their default values.

- Any attributes that you did not change retain their old values for all existing blocks.

- Any attributes that you did not include in the new block definition are deleted from existing blocks.

STEPS: Editing Attributes

1. Open `ab19-b.dwg`, available from the Drawings download on the companion website.

2. Save the file as `ab19-03.dwg` in your `AutoCAD Bible` folder. This is a portion of an office building plan layout, as shown in Figure 19.7.

3. Choose Home tab ⇨ Block panel ⇨ Edit Attributes drop-down menu ⇨ Single. At the `Select a block:` prompt, pick the chair at ❶, shown in Figure 19.7. In the Value text box of the Enhanced Attribute Editor, change the date purchased to 4/11.

   Notice that the manufacturer is American Office Furniture. Because these attributes are invisible, you can't see the result in the drawing. Click OK.

4. To see the attributes, choose Home tab ⇨ Block panel (expanded) ⇨ Attribute Display drop-down menu ⇨ Display All Attributes. You can now see the attributes for the chair, as well as nearby attributes for the desk. To turn off the attributes, repeat the process, this time choosing the Retain Attribute Display option.

5. Choose Home tab ⇨ Block panel ⇨ Edit Attributes drop-down menu ⇨ Multiple. Follow the prompts:

```
Edit attributes one at a time? [Yes/No] <Y>: n ↵
Performing global editing of attribute values.
Edit only attributes visible on screen? [Yes/No] <Y>: n ↵
Drawing must be regenerated afterwards.
Enter block name specification <*>: armchair ↵
Enter attribute tag specification <*>: ↵
Enter attribute value specification <*>: ↵
6 attributes selected.
Enter string to change: American ↵
Enter new string: Acme ↵ (Press F2 to hide the text window if it is
    open.)
```

FIGURE 19.7

An office building plan layout

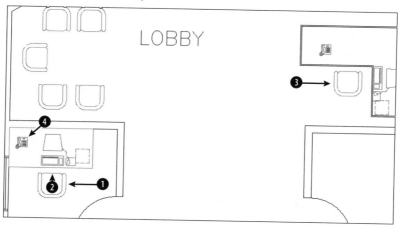

6. Choose Home tab ⇨ Modify panel ⇨ Explode and select the chair at ❶, shown in Figure 19.7. Press Enter to end selection. The attributes reappear, but without their values. Choose Home tab ⇨ Block panel (expanded) ⇨ Define Attributes. Uncheck the Multiple Lines check box in the Mode section, if checked. Create an invisible attribute with a tag and prompt of Color, and a default value of Dusty Blue. Click OK and pick an insertion point underneath the other two attributes of the armchair. (You'll need to pan down a little. Exact placement is not important.)

7. To redefine the block, do one of the following:

   If you have AutoCAD: Type **attredef** ↵. Follow the prompts:

   ```
   Enter name of Block you wish to redefine: armchair ↵
   Select objects for new Block...Select objects: Use a window to select the
        chair and the three attributes. Press Enter to end selection.
   Specify insertion base point of new Block: Use an Endpoint object snap to
        pick the endpoint at ❷.
   ```

   If you have AutoCAD LT: Choose Home tab ⇨ Block panel ⇨ Create. In the Name text box, enter **armchair**. Click the Pick Point button and use an Endpoint object snap to pick the endpoint at ❷. Click the Select Objects button and select all the objects that make up the chair, and then the three attributes. Press Enter to end selection. In the Objects section, choose the Delete option. Click OK. Click Redefine Block to redefine the block.

   The armchair block disappears.

8. Choose Home tab ⇨ Block panel ⇨ Insert. In the Insert dialog box, choose **armchair** from the Name drop-down list. With Specify On-screen checked only for Insertion Point, click OK. Insert the chair at ❷. In the Edit Attributes dialog box, click OK to accept the values, or press Enter to accept the values on the command line.

19

9. **AutoCAD only:** To verify that your drawing has redefined the block elsewhere, choose Home tab ⇨ Block panel ⇨ Edit Attributes drop-down menu ⇨ Single. Select the block at ❸. Notice that the Color tag has been added with a value of Dusty Blue. Click OK to accept the values. (In AutoCAD LT, the new attribute appears only in the block that you redefined and in new blocks that you insert.)

10. Zoom in closely to the telephone at ❹, shown in Figure 19.7. The telephone has a visible attribute of the phone number. The number is so small that it cannot usually be seen, so it does not interfere with the drawing.

11. Choose Home tab ⇨ Block panel (expanded) ⇨ Attribute, Block Attribute Manager. From the Block drop-down list, choose Phone. Click Edit. On the Attribute tab of the Edit Attribute dialog box, change the prompt to **Extension**. On the Text Options tab, choose Fit from the Justification drop-down list. On the Properties tab, choose Blue (if you're using a white background) or Cyan (if you're using a black background) from the Color drop-down list. Click OK twice to return to your drawing. The text of the phone extension is now blue and fills up the entire rectangle on the phone.

The phone number is now blue (or cyan).

12. Choose View tab ⇨ Navigate 2D panel ⇨ Zoom drop-down menu ⇨ Previous. Save the drawing.

AUTOCAD ONLY

The Express Tools command BURST (choose Express Tools tab ⇨ Blocks panel ⇨ Explode Attributes) converts attributes to text. Apply the ATTOUT and ATTIN commands (choose Express Tools tab ⇨ Blocks panel ⇨ Export Attributes, and Express Tools tab ⇨ Blocks panel ⇨ Import Attributes, respectively). Export Attribute Information and Import Attribute Information work together to enable you to edit attributes in another program. For example, ATTOUT creates a tab-delimited file that you can open in Notepad or Excel. When you use ATTIN, existing blocks are updated with the new attribute information.

ON THE WEB

Attributes contain valuable information. You can extract attributes from a drawing into a database format for use either in your drawing or in another application. The companion website contains an addendum to Chapter 19 with full coverage of how to extract a database from attributes.

Summary

In this chapter, I covered all the ways that you can use blocks and attributes in your drawings. You read about:

- Using attributes to place text and to create simple databases
- Defining attributes
- Inserting blocks with attributes and assigning values to the attributes

In the next chapter, I explain how to insert references (xrefs) to other files in your drawings.

Referencing Other Drawings

S ometimes you need to refer to another drawing without inserting it. You may want to use part of another drawing as an example for your current drawing, or to see how the model in your drawing fits in with models in other drawings. You may want the flexibility of seeing the other drawing sometimes, but not seeing it at other times. Using an external reference is like laying one drawing on top of another and being able to see both at the same time. You can easily load and unload the other drawing.

Understanding External References

External references, commonly called *xrefs*, enable you to view any drawing as a reference while in your current drawing. The external drawing is not part of your current drawing. The current drawing keeps track of the location and name of an external reference so that you can always reference it easily. As with blocks, you can snap to objects in the external reference, thereby using it as a reference for the drawing process. You can also change the visibility settings of the xref's layers.

Xrefs have several advantages over blocks:

- **Xrefs keep your drawing smaller than blocks.** The externally referenced drawing doesn't become part of your drawing. Your drawing maintains only a reference (name and location) to the other drawing.

- **You always have the most updated version of the xref.** Each time that you open a drawing, a current copy of the xref loads. By contrast, you would need to reinsert a file inserted as a block to see the most updated version.

- **In a team project, several people can use the same drawing as an xref, each having access to the latest changes.**

- **Xrefs can be attached and detached easily for maximum flexibility, loaded and unloaded to display or hide them, or overlaid for temporary use.** If you're only using the xref for reference, you may detach it before plotting.

Attaching an external reference

The first step is to attach the external reference, which is just another drawing, to your current (host) drawing. You can underlay DWF and DWFx files, which are covered in Bonue Chapter 5, DGN, and PDF files. I explain underlays at the end of this chapter.

To attach an xref of an AutoCAD or AutoCAD LT drawing, follow these steps:

1. Choose Insert tab ⇨ Reference panel ⇨ Attach to start the ATTACH command. The Select Reference File dialog box opens.

2. Select Drawing (*.dwg) from the Files of Type drop-down list. Then choose the drawing file you want to attach and click Open. The Attach External Reference dialog box (shown in Figure 20.1) opens. This dialog box displays the file that you chose, along with its path (location).

FIGURE 20.1

The Attach External Reference dialog box

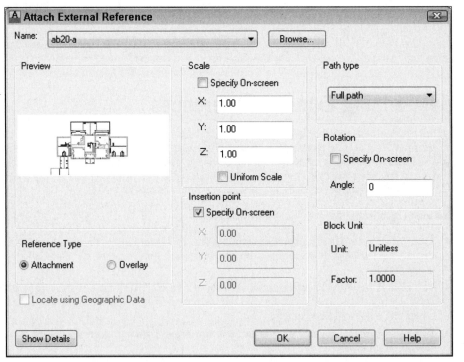

3. Choose the type of xref that you want in the Reference Type section:

   - **Attachment.** Use an attachment when you want to be sure that the xref will be displayed if someone else xrefs your current drawing. In other words, that person will see your current drawing, and your xref will be nested within it.

   - **Overlay.** Use an overlay when you're sharing drawings in a networked environment and you don't want to change your drawing by attaching an xref. If someone else attaches your drawing while you're working on it, the overlay is not displayed.

> **NOTE**
> The XREFTYPE system variable determines which of these two choices, Attachment or Overlay, is automatically chosen in the Reference Type section. The default value, 0, uses the Attachment option.

4. Choose Locate Using Geographic Data if the drawing you are attaching has a geographic location that you want to use. The check box is only enabled when the drawing has a geographic location. For more information on geographic location data, see Chapter 22.

5. From the Path Type drop-down list, choose the type of path that you want to use:

   - **Relative path.** Specifies only part of the xref drawing's path, and uses the current drive or folder. This option enables you to move a host drawing and its xrefs to a different drive that has the same folder structure.

   - **Full path.** Specifies the full path of the xref drawing, including the drive letter (such as c:).

   - **No path.** Uses the current folder of the host drawing. This option enables you to use an xref when you move the drawing; for example, when you send it to someone else with a different folder structure. To make sure that the drawing can find the xref, ensure that it is in the project files search path or in the same folder as the host drawing.

6. Use the Scale, Insertion Point, and Rotation sections of the dialog box to specify the X, Y, and Z scale factors, the insertion point, and the rotation angle, either in the dialog box or on-screen. These prompts are the same ones that you use when inserting a block or drawing file.

> **NOTE**
> A check box in the Scale section lets you specify a uniform scale, so the Y and Z values are always the same as the X value. The Block Unit section displays the units set for the referenced drawing. This is the same setting you use when you create a block and allows for the automatic scaling of the drawing. You can set this value with the INSUNITS system variable or by entering units ↵ on the command line to set it in the Drawing Units dialog box; you must do this when the drawing file is open for editing.

7. Click OK to attach the xref.

If your current view does not show the entire xref, do a Zoom Extents (choose View tab ⇨ Navigate panel ⇨ Zoom drop-down menu ⇨ Extents).

You can also attach an xref from a tool palette. For more information on tool palettes, see Bonus Chapter 3.

20

After you have the xref in your drawing, you can start to work. The xref is like a block, although you cannot explode it. However, you can use object snaps on all the objects in an xref, just as you can with blocks. This enables you to use the xref as a basis for your own drawing.

Opening an xref

Sometimes you need to open the xref to work on it directly. For example, you may see an error that you want to correct. The XOPEN command opens an xref in its own drawing window. The easiest way to use XOPEN is to click the xref to select it in your drawing, right-click, and choose Open Xref.

If you select an xref, then by default, the External Reference contextual tab appears, with tools that allow you to open and modify the selected xref.

Using the External References palette

To see what type of xrefs you have in your drawing, choose View tab ⇨ Palettes panel ⇨ External References Palette, or choose Insert tab ⇨ Reference panel and click the dialog box launcher at the right end of the panel's title bar.

> **NEW FEATURE**
> The External References palette now allows you to attach point clouds (see Chapter 21). You can also remove the path information stored with a reference or make it relative. The Found At property is now read-only, while the Saved Path is editable.

The external references are listed in the External References palette, as shown in Figure 20.2. This palette also shows the following types of references:

- **Images.** Any type of bitmap (raster) image that you can import. (See Bonus Chapter 4 for more information.)
- **DWF underlays.** DWF and DWFx files that act like xrefs. I explain how to attach DWF files at the end of this chapter, and I cover creating DWF and DWFx files in Bonus Chapter 5.
- **DGN underlays.** DGN files (MicroStation drawings) that act like xrefs. I cover DGN files at the end of this chapter.
- **PDF underlays.** PDF files that act like underlays. I explain how to attach PDF files at the end of this chapter, and I cover creating PDF files in Bonus Chapter 5.
- **Point clouds.** The point data stored in a point cloud file can be attached to a drawing. I cover point clouds in Chapter 21.

Along with the above-mentioned external reference types, the External References palette also displays data extraction tables, data links, and point clouds. For more information on data extraction and data links, see Chapter 13.

> **NOTE**
> The External References palette replaced the Xref Manager as of AutoCAD 2007 and AutoCAD LT 2007. You can open the earlier Xref Manager with the CLASSICXREF command.

FIGURE 20.2

The External References palette displays a referenced drawing, raster images, PDF file, and data extraction table.

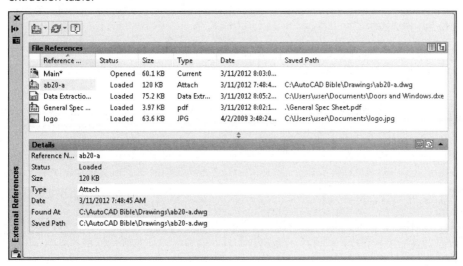

The palette lists all the referenced drawings and files. You can choose one of two views, using the buttons at the top-right corner of the palette:

- **List view** lists all the references along with their status, size, type, date and time saved, as well as the saved path, if any. Figure 20.2 shows the referenced files of Main Plan.dwg in list view.

- **Tree view** lists all the references in a graphical view that shows their relationships. This view is great for understanding nested xrefs.

> **TIP**
> You can change the width of the columns in List view by placing the cursor on a column dividing line until it changes to a two-headed arrow. Then drag in either direction. You can also double-click the dividing line between two columns to automatically resize the column to the left based on the widest value.

When you click any xref, you see a preview tooltip that shows the reference and lists its details. You can control the preview format to display the file name, a preview thumbnail, file details, or a combination. Right-click in the palette, choose Tooltip Style, and choose one of the options.

If you move or delete a referenced item, the External References palette notes that the file is not found. To troubleshoot, it helps to know where it searches for xrefs. The External References palette searches for references according to a specific order:

- **Path specified.** Locates the specified path xref.
- **Current folder.** Locates the current folder of the host drawing.

20

- **Project path.** The path for external references. To check or change the project path, choose Application Button ⇨ Options and click the Files tab. Double-click Project Files Search Path. Click Add and then click Browse to navigate to a folder where you keep drawings that you may want to use as xrefs. (AutoCAD LT doesn't offer the Project Files Search Path.)

- **Support path.** The location for support files. To check or change the support path, choose Application Button ⇨ Options and then click the Files tab. Double-click Support File Search Path. Click Add and then click Browse to navigate to a folder.

- **Start-in folder.** To find the start-in folder, right-click your AutoCAD 2013 or AutoCAD LT 2013 desktop shortcut and choose Properties.

TIP

Selecting a reference in the External References palette highlights the attached external reference in the drawing. Similarly, selecting an external reference in a drawing highlights the reference in the External References palette. You can control this behavior with the ERHIGHLIGHT system variable.

ON THE WEB

The drawings that you need for the following exercise on attaching xrefs, ab20-a.dwg and ab20-b.dwg, are available from the Drawings download on the companion website.

STEPS: Attaching Xrefs

1. Open ab20-a.dwg from the companion website. This is the floor plan for a house.

2. Open Windows Explorer (right-click Start on the task bar and choose Open Windows Explorer). Copy ab20-b.dwg from the companion website to your AutoCAD Bible folder.

3. In your drawing, choose Insert tab ⇨ Reference panel ⇨ Attach. In the Select Reference File dialog box, choose ab20-b.dwg. Click Open. You can choose Drawing (*.dwg) from the Files of Type drop-down list to filter the files displayed in the Select Reference File dialog box.

4. In the Attach External Reference dialog box, you see the filename displayed. Make sure that all Specify On-Screen check boxes are unchecked. Select Attachment from the Reference Type section, and click OK. You see ab20-b.dwg, which is a titleblock, in ab20-a.dwg.

5. Save the drawing as ab20-01.dwg in your AutoCAD Bible folder. Click the drawing's Close box to close the drawing.

6. Start a new drawing, using the acad.dwt or acadlt.dwt template. On the command line, type **units** ⏎. In the Drawing Units dialog box, choose Architectural from the Type drop-down list under the Length section. In the Units to Scale Inserted Content drop-down list, choose Inches. Click OK. Save it as ab20-02.dwg in your AutoCAD Bible folder.

7. Again choose Insert tab ⇨ Reference panel ⇨ Attach. In the Select Reference File dialog box, choose ab20-01.dwg, which you just saved in your AutoCAD Bible folder. Click Open.

8. In the Attach External Reference dialog box, you see the filename displayed. Leave the defaults and click OK. Choose View tab ⇨ Navigate 2D (or Navigate) panel ⇨ Zoom drop-down list ⇨ Extents. You see ab20-01.dwg, which includes both the titleblock and the floor plan of the house in your new drawing. The titleblock drawing (ab20-b.dwg) is a nested xref in the floor plan (ab20-01.dwg) xref. You see the following message (press F2 to open the AutoCAD Text Window so you can see the message that scrolls by):

```
Attach Xref "ab20-01": C:\AutoCAD Bible\ab20-01.dwg
"ab20-01" loaded.
Attach Xref "ab20-b": C:\AutoCAD Bible\ab20-b.dwg
"ab20-b" loaded.
```

9. To help you visualize the relationships among the three drawings, choose View tab ⇨ Palettes panel ⇨ External References Palette. The External References palette lists both drawings. Click Tree View at the top-right corner of the palette. You now see the two xrefs listed in a tree structure, showing their relationship more clearly. Close or auto-hide the palette.

10. Save your drawing. It should look like Figure 20.3.

FIGURE 20.3

The current drawing is blank but displays an xref of a house plan that has a nested xref of a titleblock. The grid was turned off in the figure for clarity.

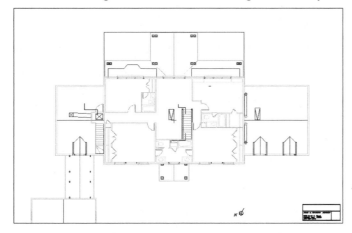

Editing an Xref within Your Drawing

While you're working in a drawing with an external reference, you may decide that the external reference needs some modification. The same may apply if you inserted a file as a block. You can make changes to the xref or block and save those changes back to the original drawing. You can even transfer objects from your drawing to the xref or block, and vice versa. This feature is called *in-place editing*.

Choosing the xref or block to edit

To start the process of in-place editing, double-click the xref that you want to edit. The Reference Edit dialog box opens, as shown in Figure 20.4. You can also choose Insert tab ⇨ Reference panel (expanded) ⇨ Edit Reference, and then select the xref that you want to edit.

FIGURE 20.4

The Reference Edit dialog box enables you to choose which reference you want to edit, including nested references.

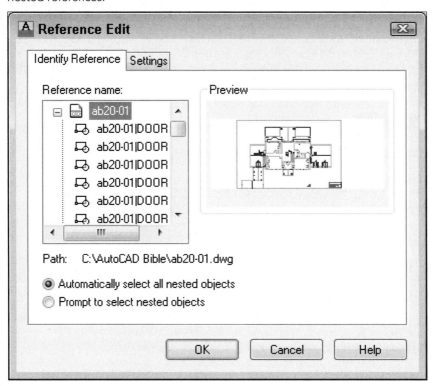

As you click each of the available references, its preview appears at the right. If the xref has nested objects, choose one of the following options (if it does not, then ignore this section of the dialog box):

- **Automatically select all nested objects.** Includes all nested objects in the editing process.
- **Prompt to select nested objects.** Prompts you to select which nested objects you want to edit.

For more control, click the Settings tab to set the following options:

- **Create unique layer, style, and block names.** Displays layer, style, and block names with a prefix of $#$, to help distinguish them from the named items in your main drawing.
- **Display attribute definitions for editing.** Enables you to edit attribute definitions of blocks with attributes. (See Chapter 18 for details on attributes.)
- **Lock objects not in working set.** Locks objects in the host drawing so that you can't accidentally modify them.

Click OK to close the Reference Edit dialog box.

> **NOTE**
>
> If the reference drawing is saved in an earlier format, you see a warning that if you save your changes back to the xref, that xref will be updated to the current file format for the release, which is the AutoCAD 2013 format.

If you checked the Prompt to Select Nested Objects option, you see a prompt to select nested objects. Complete object selection to define the working set, that is, the objects that you can edit. Other objects are faded by 50 percent (this is the default, determined by the XFADECTL system variable).

The Edit Reference panel appears on the current tab, shown in Figure 20.5, and you see the message `Use REFCLOSE or the Refedit toolbar to end reference editing session` on the command line. You're now ready to edit the xref or block.

FIGURE 20.5

The External Reference panel on the ribbon

Editing the xref

There are several types of edits that you can make on the working set of objects from the xref or block:

- If you change an object's properties, such as its layer, the object will have the new object property.

- If you erase an object, the object is deleted from the xref or block.

- If you draw a new object, the object is added to the xref or block. An exception is if you create a new object by editing objects outside the working set. For example, if you break a line (not in the working set) into two lines, then nothing is added to the working set.

- You can transfer an object from the main drawing to the xref or block. Select an object and choose <current> tab ⇨ Edit Reference panel ⇨ Add to Working Set. Remember that the working set consists of objects from the xref or block, so if you add objects to the working set, they become part of the xref or block.

- You can transfer an object from the xref or block to the host drawing. Select an object and choose <current> tab ⇨ Edit Reference panel ⇨ Remove from Working Set. The working set consists of objects from the xref or block, so if you remove objects from the working set, they're no longer part of the xref or block; instead, they become part of your main drawing.

After you finish editing the working set, if you like what you did, choose <current> tab ⇨ Edit Reference panel ⇨ Save Changes. Otherwise, choose Discard Changes.

When you save changes to a block, block definitions are redefined and all instances of the block are regenerated according to the new definition. If you gave an xref object properties that don't exist in the xref, such as a layer, the new property is copied to the xref so that the object can keep that property.

20

STEPS: Editing an Xref in Place

1. Open ab20-a.dwg, available from the companion website. Save it as ab20-03.dwg in your AutoCAD Bible folder.

2. Open ab20-b.dwg, available from the companion website. Save it as ab20-04.dwg in your AutoCAD Bible folder. Click the Close box of ab20-04.dwg to close the drawing (but not the program), leaving ab20-03.dwg on your screen.

3. Choose Insert tab ⇨ Reference panel ⇨ Attach and choose ab20-04.dwg from the AutoCAD Bible folder. Click Open. From the Attach External Reference dialog box, uncheck all the Specify On-Screen check boxes and click OK to insert the xref.

4. Double-click the titleblock (ab20-04.dwg). The Reference Edit dialog box opens. Choose ab20-04. It is displayed in the preview box. Click OK. The Edit Reference panel appears, and you can now edit the xref. Your drawing should look like Figure 20.6.

FIGURE 20.6

The titleblock is an xref in the drawing of the floor plan.

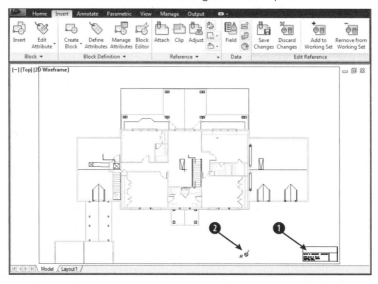

5. Select the titleblock (ab20-04.dwg) again and choose Home tab ⇨ Modify panel ⇨ Explode.

6. Choose Annotate tab ⇨ Text panel ⇨ Text drop-down menu ⇨ Single Line. At the Specify start point of text or [Justify/Style]: prompt, pick ❶, shown in Figure 20.6. Turning off Object Snap mode will make it easier to specify a point near ❶. At the Specify height <0'-0 3/16">: prompt, type **10** ↵. Press Enter again for the rotation angle.

7. Type **Davis Floor Plan** and press Enter twice to end the command.

8. Choose the text (the name and address of the architect) at the bottom of the titleblock and change its color to red to make it stand out.

9. Select the letter N and arrow symbol at ❷, shown in Figure 20.6. To transfer these objects from the xref to the floor plan drawing, choose <current> tab ⟹ Edit Reference panel ⟹ Remove from Working Set.

10. To save the changes, choose <current> tab ⟹ Edit Reference panel ⟹ Save Changes. Click OK again at the dialog box that informs you that all reference edits will be saved. You see the following information on the command line:

```
The following symbols will be permanently bound to the current drawing:
Layers: $0$TITLEBLK
Text Styles: $0$ROMANS, $0$ROMAND
Blocks: $0$KNTITL


Enter option [Save/Discard reference changes] <Save>: _sav
Regenerating model.
11 objects added to ab20-04
1 object removed from ab20-04
1 xref instance updated
```

11. Choose View tab ⟹ Palettes panel ⟹ External References Palette. In the External References palette, right-click ab20-04 and choose Detach from the shortcut menu. (Detaching xrefs is covered later in this chapter.) You can now see that ab20-03.dwg includes the letter N and arrow symbol because they were removed from the xref.

12. To see the results of the editing on the xref, open ab20-04.dwg. You can see the changes in the titleblock text and that the letter N and arrow symbol are gone.

13. Close both drawings, saving changes to ab20-03.dwg.

Controlling Xref Display

You can control the display of xref layers so that you see only those layers you need. Several features let you control the process of displaying xrefs, making it easier to see only part of an xref and speeding up the display of very large xrefs.

Working with dependent symbols in xrefs

Dependent symbols are named items in a drawing, such as layers, text styles, dimension styles, and so on. When you attach an xref, these symbols are listed in your current drawing. For example, the Layer drop-down list displays the layers of the xref. Xref symbols have the format xref_name|symbol_name. This system distinguishes xref symbols from those of your current drawing and ensures that there are no duplicate symbols.

Changing the display of layers in xrefs

You can turn on and off, or freeze and thaw, xref layers. You can also change an xref layer's properties in the Layer Properties Manager palette. By default, these changes are retained. However, you can set the VISRETAIN system variable to 0 to discard these changes. The next time you open the drawing or reload the xref, the original settings are restored.

20

Objects created on layer 0 do not take on the typical xref layer name format, but stay on layer 0. If objects in the xref are on layer 0 with the color and linetype set to ByLayer, they take on the color and linetype properties of the current layer in the current drawing. If color and linetype are set to ByBlock, then objects assume the current properties when the xref is attached. If you explicitly set color and linetype, then objects retain those settings.

Binding dependent symbols to the parent drawing

You can use the XBIND command to import only the symbols that you want from the external reference into the current drawing. This makes it easy to work with a consistent set of symbols in the current drawing and the xrefs. For example, you can choose to import the `titleblk` layer and the `kntitl` block. On the command line, type **xbind** ↵ to open the Xbind dialog box. The Xbind dialog box lists each xref in the drawing, along with its symbols in a Windows Explorer–like display, as shown in Figure 20.7.

FIGURE 20.7

Using the XBIND command to import symbols, such as layers, text styles, and so on

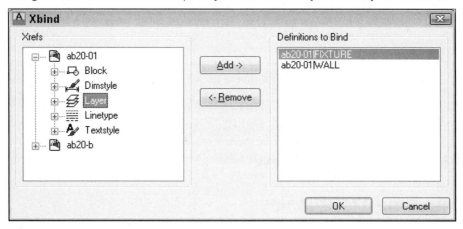

Click the plus sign next to any symbol type to open a list of symbols. Click the one you want and choose Add to add it to the Definitions to Bind list. Click OK when you're done.

Later in this chapter, I explain how you can use the DesignCenter or the Content Explorer to move xrefs and other dependent symbols from one drawing to another.

Avoiding circular references

If drawing *a* includes drawing *b* as an xref and drawing *b* includes drawing *a* as an xref, then you have a circular reference. Circular references can exist among three or more xrefs when you have nested xrefs. The program detects circular references and loads as much as it can. If you try to load an xref in such a situation, you see the following message:

```
Warning: Circular reference from XREF to current drawing.
Circular reference(s) have been found. Continue? <N> Type y to continue
    to load the xref.
Breaking circular reference from XREF to current drawing.
```

Clipping xrefs

You may want to see only part of an xref. This option is especially important when you're using very large xref drawings. The CLIP and XCLIP commands enable you to create a border in an xref, and hides any part of the xref outside the border.

 To clip an xref, choose Insert tab ⇨ Reference panel ⇨ Clip. At the prompt to select objects, pick the xref you want to clip. Note that any nested xrefs are clipped with the main xref that you select.

Table 20.1 explains the options of this command.

TABLE 20.1 XCLIP Options

Option	How to Use It
ON	Turns the clipping boundary on, displaying only the portion of the xref inside the clipping boundary. By default, the clipping boundary is on. Use this after you've turned it off to see only the clipped portion again.
OFF	Turns the clipping boundary off, displaying the entire xref. The clipping boundary is still retained. This is somewhat like turning off a layer. You may want to see the entire xref for a while (for example, while redefining the boundary). Then you can turn the boundary back on (using the ON option) when you need only the clipped portion again.
Clipdepth	This is used for 3D drawings only. After you set a clipping boundary, you can set front and back planes parallel to the boundary to display only the portion of the xref within that three-dimensional space. You create the front and back planes by specifying a distance from the clipping boundary. The Remove suboption removes the clipping planes.
Delete	Deletes the clipping boundary. The boundary is no longer retained in the drawing.
Generate polyline	Creates a polyline from the clipping boundary, using the current layer, color, and linetype. If you want to change the clipping boundary, you can edit the polyline by using PEDIT and redefine the boundary with the new polyline.
New boundary	This is the default option. Press Enter to see the suboptions, which follow.
Select polyline	Enables you to specify the clipping boundary by selecting an existing polyline. This option decurves fit-curved or arc portions of the polyline when creating the boundary.
Polygonal	Enables you to specify a polygonal area, such as a polyline with straight edges. This option creates a rubber-band line as you pick points, keeping the polygon closed. You can use this option to create an irregularly shaped area that includes only the portion of the xref that you want to see.
Rectangular	Enables you to pick two points on diagonally opposite corners of a rectangle, such as creating a selection window.
Invert clip	Enables you to hide any part of the xref inside the border. After choosing this suboption, choose one of the previous suboptions to define the clipping boundary.

TIP

In addition to clipping xrefs, the CLIP and XCLIP commands can also clip blocks.

20

To see the clipping boundary (if you haven't used an existing polyline to define it), change the value of the XCLIPFRAME system variable to 1. When you do so, you can select the boundary and modify it by using its grips. You can also click the blue arrow to invert the clip.

You can use the FRAME system variable to override the setting of the XCLIPFRAME system variable and the frame settings for all raster images and underlays in a drawing. Setting FRAME to 3 allows you to control the frame display by object type (xrefs, raster images, underlays, and point clouds) individually. The frame settings for underlays are covered later in this chapter.

Figure 20.8 shows an xref clipped with a polygonal boundary.

FIGURE 20.8

An xref clipped with a polygonal boundary

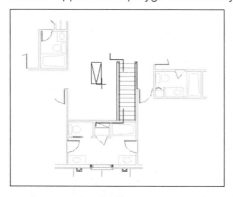

> **TIP**
>
> Select a clipped xref, raster image, or underlay to manipulate its clip boundary using grip editing. You can also invert the clipping by clicking the arrow-shaped grip.

Speeding up the display of large xrefs

In order to reduce the time needed to display large xrefs, such as those used in GIS or 3D drawings, you can use *demand loading*. This feature enables you to load only the objects necessary to display the xref in your drawing. Demand loading works together with spatial and layer indexes.

- The spatial index is created when you save a drawing. This index is used when you have enabled demand loading and attach a clipped xref that was saved with a spatial index. The index determines how much of the xref needs to be read to display it.

- The layer index is also created when you save a drawing. This index is used after you've enabled demand loading, attached an xref that was saved with a layer index, and then froze or turned off layers. The index determines how much of the xref needs to be read to display it.

To make it perfectly clear, you need all the following in order to use demand loading:

- Demand loading must be enabled in the current drawing.
- The xref must have been saved with a spatial and/or layer index.
- The xref must either be clipped (for a spatial index) or have layers that are frozen or turned off (for a layer index).

 Demand loading is similar to partial opening and loading of drawings, explained in Chapter 8.

Loading xrefs on demand

You can turn on demand loading in your current drawing. To turn on demand loading, choose Application Button⇨Options, and then click the Open and Save tab. In the Demand Load Xrefs drop-down list, choose Enabled. Others on a networked system cannot then edit the original drawing while you're referencing it. To let others edit the original drawing, choose Enabled with Copy. This option uses a copy of the referenced drawing for your xref. Click OK. You can turn on demand loading just before you attach an xref; you don't need to keep demand loading on all the time.

Using spatial indexes

You save a spatial index for a drawing that you expect to use as an xref. The saving process takes a little longer, but you save time at the other end when you load a clipped xref or clip an xref for the first time. To create a spatial index in AutoCAD, choose Application Button⇨Save As to open the Save Drawing As dialog box. From the Tools menu at the top right of the dialog box, choose Options to open the Saveas Options dialog box, shown in Figure 20.9, with the DWG Options tab on top.

FIGURE 20.9

The DWG Options tab of the Saveas Options dialog box enables you to save spatial and layer indexes.

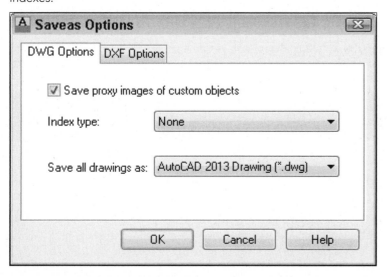

From the Index Type drop-down list, choose Spatial or Layer & Spatial. Click OK. Then click Save in the Save Drawing As dialog box. In AutoCAD LT, use the INDEXCTL system variable on the command line and set its value to 2 for just a spatial index, or to 3 for both layer and spatial indexes.

> **TIP**
> If you want to create an index for an existing drawing, click OK once to return to the Save Drawing As dialog box. Click Cancel. In other words, you don't have to actually save the drawing to set up the index, which is controlled by the INDEXCTL system variable.

After you create a spatial index, each time you save the drawing, you see the following message:

```
Updating Indexes for block *MODEL_SPACE
```

To stop saving the index each time you save in AutoCAD, choose Application Button ⇨ Save As. Choose Tools ⇨ Options. In the Saveas Options dialog box, choose None from the Index Type drop-down list. Click OK and then click Cancel. In AutoCAD LT, change the value of the INDEXCTL system variable to 0.

Using layer indexes

You save a layer index for a drawing that you expect to use as an xref to create an index of all the layers in the drawing. As with a spatial index, the saving process takes a little longer, but you save time at the other end when you load an xref with frozen or turned off layers. To create a layer index in AutoCAD, choose Application Button ⇨ Save As to open the Save Drawing As dialog box. From the Tools menu at the upper-right corner of the dialog box, choose Options to open the Saaveas Options dialog box, as shown in Figure 20.9.

From the Index Type drop-down list, choose Layer or Layer & Spatial. Click OK, and then click Cancel. In AutoCAD LT, set the INDEXCTL system variable to 1 for just a layer index, or to 3 for both layer and spatial indexes.

After you create a layer index, each time you save the drawing, you see the following message:

```
Updating Indexes for block *MODEL_SPACE
```

To stop saving the index in AutoCAD, choose Application Button ⇨ Save As. Choose Tools ⇨ Options. In the Saveas Options dialog box, choose None from the Index Type drop-down list. Click OK once and then click Cancel. In AutoCAD LT, change the value of the INDEXCTL system variable to 0.

> **ON THE WEB**
> For a step-by-step exercise on controlling xref display, see the Chapter 20 Addendum on the companion website.

Managing Xrefs

If you have many xrefs in a drawing, you need a way to keep track of them and their relationships to your drawing. You have several techniques for managing xrefs. The External References palette, DesignCenter, Content Explorer, and the xref notification feature are all tools to help you with this task.

> **TIP**
> Though it may be obvious, the first principle of managing xrefs is to keep them simple. Overly complex nested configurations are hard to manage, no matter what you do.

The External References palette is designed to let you manage xrefs (as well as DWF, DWFx, DGN, and PDF underlays, raster images, data extraction tables, data links, and point clouds) from one place. I explain the features of the External References palette in Table 20.2. You access these features by right-clicking a reference and choosing from the shortcut menu.

TABLE 20.2   External References Palette Features

Feature	What It Does
Open	Opens the selected xref in a new drawing window or the linked data source in its native program.
Attach	Opens the Attach External Reference dialog box so you can specify an xref to attach to your drawing, as explained earlier in this chapter.
Detach	Detaches an xref or data extraction table. The xref is not displayed, and the xref definition is no longer saved in the drawing. The table object linked with the data extraction file is broken, and the table no longer updates automatically.
Reload	Reloads the most recent version of the xref. Use this whenever the xref has changed during a session (because someone else on a networked system has edited the xref drawing) or after unloading an xref.
Unload	Unloads the xref without detaching it. The xref is not displayed, but the xref definition is still saved in the drawing. You can then use Reload to display the xref again.
Bind	Changes the xref to a block. Opens the Bind Xrefs/DGN Underlays dialog box, which enables you to choose to either bind or insert the xref.
Bind	When creating a block from the xref, this feature changes named layers, text styles, dimension styles, and so on (called *symbols*) from the format `reference_name|symbol_name` to `reference_name$#$symbol_name`, where # is 0 if the same name does not exist in the current drawing or 1 if it already exists. In this way, no symbol names are duplicated. This method enables you to keep track of where the symbols came from.
Insert	When creating a block from the xref, this feature removes the `reference_name|` portion of symbol names. For example, if a layer of that name already exists in your drawing, objects on that layer take on the properties of that layer, as defined in your drawing. The same applies to text styles, dimension styles, and so on. This method removes the complexity that arises with the xref naming of these symbols.
Path	Changes the stored path information for the selected external reference.
Remove Path	Removes the path information stored with an external reference. This is the same as using the None option from the Path Type drop-down list when attaching an external reference.
Make Relative	Changes the path stored with the external reference relative to the parent drawing. This is the same as using the Relative Path option from the Path Type drop-down list when attaching an external reference.
Update Data Links	Refreshes the table in the drawing associated with the referenced data source.
Update Data Extraction	Refreshes the table in the drawing using the criteria in the referenced data extraction file.

20

> **NOTE**
> You cannot bind or detach nested xrefs without binding the parent xref.

You can also click the Refresh button to reload the selected reference, or use its down button to choose Reload All References.

> **AUTOCAD ONLY**
> Express Tools offer two commands that can help you work with xrefs. Choose Express Tools tab ⇨ Blocks panel ⇨ List Xref/Block Properties to list the properties of xrefs and blocks, such as object type, layer, object, and linetype. Choose Express Tools tab ⇨ Blocks panel (expanded) ⇨ Convert Block to Xref to replace a block with an xref (that is, another drawing file).

Getting xref notification

If an xref is moved or renamed while you have it displayed in an open drawing, you need to reload it. An xref can change if someone else on your network opens and edits it while you're using it. External Reference Notification offers instant notification if an xref changes.

 When you open a drawing with an xref, the status bar displays the Manage Xrefs icon in the tray area at the right. When an xref changes, a "balloon message" or window appears to notify you, including the name of the drawing and the person who changed it. Click the link to reload the xref (or xrefs). If you want to open the External References palette, perhaps to choose which xrefs you want to reload, click the Manage Xrefs icon on the status bar. The XREFNOTIFY system variable controls the use of the xref notification balloon.

Using DesignCenter to Attach a Drawing

You can use the DesignCenter to copy named objects, including xrefs, from one drawing to another. (I cover the DesignCenter in Bonus Chapter 3.) To attach an xref from another drawing, press Ctrl+2. Navigate to the drawing and double-click it to open the list of named objects. Double-click Xrefs to see a list of xrefs in the right pane.

Double-click the xref that you want to attach. The Attach External Reference dialog box opens (refer to Figure 20.1) so that you can attach the xref. You can also right-click and choose Attach Xref, or right-click and drag a drawing from the DesignCenter into your drawing.

Attaching Xrefs and Drawings from the Content Explorer

Similar to the DesignCenter, the Content Explorer allows you to copy named objects and attach drawings as xrefs to the current drawing. To attach an xref, choose Plug-ins tab ⇨ Content panel ⇨ Explore. Navigate to the drawing that contains the xref you want to attach to a drawing. If the drawing that contains the xref is not listed, click Configure Settings at the bottom of the Content Explorer palette and specify the location of the drawing to use.

Double-click the drawing that contains the xref you want to attach and scroll to the Xrefs category. From the Xrefs category, double-click an xref and specify an insertion point in the drawing for the xref. You can also right-click an xref and choose Add, or drag and drop an xref to create a reference to the xref in a drawing. If you right-click a drawing file, not an xref under the Xrefs category, choose Attach to attach the drawing as an xref. For more information on using the Content Explorer or specifying content locations, see Bonus Chapter 3.

Creating an xref log file

If you set the XREFCTL system variable to 1 (by default, it's set to 0), a copy of all xref activity for your current drawing is saved in an ASCII text file. You can read the log to troubleshoot problems that may occur. The log file goes in the same folder as your drawing and uses your drawing name with the .xlg filename extension. This file can become long. Therefore, once in a while, you should delete all or part of the file.

AUTOCAD ONLY

The Reference Manager is a stand-alone program that manages xrefs, images, fonts, and plot configurations, which are all outside files that are referenced in your drawing. See Bonus Chapter 3 for full coverage of the Reference Manager.

ON THE WEB

The drawing that you need for the following exercise on managing xrefs, ab20-05.dwg, is available from the Results download on the companion website.

STEPS: Managing Xrefs

1. Use ab20-05.dwg from your AutoCAD Bible folder if you did the "Controlling Xref Display" exercise in this chapter's addendum from the companion website. Otherwise, open it from the Result download of the companion website.

2. Save it as ab20-06.dwg in your AutoCAD Bible folder.

3. Choose Insert tab ⇨ Reference panel ⇨ Clip. At the Select Object to clip: prompt, pick the xref anywhere. At the Enter clipping option [ON/OFF/ Clipdepth/Delete/ generate Polyline/New boundary] <New>: prompt, right-click and choose Delete to delete the clip and restore the entire view of both xrefs.

4. Choose View tab ⇨ Palettes panel ⇨ External References Palette. Click the Tree View button. Right-click ab20-b, the nested xref, and choose Unload.

5. Right-click ab20-b again. Choose Reload to reload the xref.

6. This time right-click ab20-01. Choose Bind. In the Bind Xrefs/DGN Underlays dialog box, choose Insert and click OK. This action inserts both xrefs (ab20-01 and ab20-b) as blocks. (Click the Layer drop-down list to see that there are no xref-type layer names.)

7. Save your drawing.

Working with DWF, DGN, and PDF Underlays

You can use DWF, DGN, and PDF files as underlays, which are similar to xrefs. A DWF file is an accurate, compressed vector image representation of a drawing, and I explain how to create DWF and DWFx files in Bonus Chapter 5. DGN files are drawings created with Bentley MicroStation®, another CAD program. You can produce PDF files by plotting or publishing a drawing, or by using an application such as Adobe Acrobat.

Underlays are different from xrefs in that you cannot bind them to a drawing file, with the exception of DGN underlays. The primary reason for not letting you bind DWF or PDF underlays to a drawing is because they do not contain the accuracy that DWG or DGN files have. DWF and PDF underlays are primarily used as reference documents and thereby help to protect the original owner's investment and integrity in the design or information contained in the original document.

Attaching a DWF underlay

Attaching a DWF file is similar to attaching an xref or inserting a block. To attach a DWF file, follow these steps:

1. Choose Insert tab ⇨ Reference panel ⇨ Attach (the ATTACH command), or choose Attach DWF from the Attach File drop-down list of the External References palette (the DWFATTACH command).

2. In the Select Reference File dialog box, choose the DWF or DWFx file and click Open. If needed, select DWF files (*.dwfx, *.dwf) from the Files of Type drop-down list.

3. In the Attach DWF Underlay dialog box, choose a sheet from the DWF or DWFx file, if it contains more than one. The Attach DWF Underlay dialog box is similar to the Attach External Reference dialog box shown in Figure 20.1.

4. From the Path Type drop-down list, choose the type of path you want to specify for the underlay. (See the "Attaching an external reference" section earlier in this chapter for more information.)

5. To specify the insertion point, scale, and rotation, uncheck the respective check boxes in the dialog box; otherwise, specify them on-screen.

6. Click OK to attach the DWF or DWFx file as a DWF underlay.

If your current view does not show the entire underlay, use ZOOM Extents to see it (choose View tab ⇨ Navigate 2D (or Navigate) panel ⇨ Zoom drop-down list ⇨ Extents).

Attaching a DGN underlay

To underlay a DGN file, choose Insert tab ⇨ Reference panel ⇨ Attach (the ATTACH command), or choose Attach DGN from the Attach File drop-down list of the External References palette (the DGNATTACH command). The Select Reference File dialog box opens; select a DGN file and click Open. If needed, select MicroStation DGN files (*.dgn) from the Files of Type drop-down list. The Attach DGN Underlay dialog box opens, which is similar to the Attach External Reference dialog box shown in Figure 20.1.

If the drawing has more than one model, choose the one you want to attach from the Select a Design Model from the DGN File list box. DGN files can have master units (Imperial or metric) and another set of units, called sub units. Choose which one you want to use. AutoCAD converts one unit (either master or sub) to one drawing unit. Click OK to attach the DGN underlay.

Attaching a PDF underlay

Attaching a PDF file is similar to attaching a DWF file. Choose Insert tab ⇨ Reference panel ⇨ Attach (the ATTACH command), or choose Attach PDF from the Attach File drop-down list of the External References palette (the PDFATTACH command). The Select Reference File dialog box opens; select a PDF file and click Open. If needed, select PDF files (*.pdf) from the Files of Type drop-down list. The Attach PDF Underlay dialog box opens, which is similar to the Attach External Reference dialog box shown in Figure 20.1. If the PDF file contains more than one page, choose the one you want to attach from the Select One or More Pages from the PDF File list box. Click OK to attach the PDF underlay.

Modifying an underlay

After an underlay is created, you can control its display and how you can work with the underlay's geometry by adjusting, clipping, and displaying an underlay.

Adjusting the appearance of an underlay

You can change the appearance of an underlay to make it more or less prominent, by using the ADJUST command. This command has three options:

- **Fade.** Blends the underlay more or less with the background color. You can choose a value from 0 to 100, where 100 fades the underlay completely with the background. The default value is 0 for images and PDF underlays, and 25 for DWF and DGN underlays.
- **Contrast.** Increases or decreases the contrast of the colors. The values range from 0 to 100, where 100 changes the colors to their closest primary or secondary color. The default is 50 for images, 75 for DWF and DGN underlays, and 100 for PDF underlays.
- **Monochrome.** Displays the underlay as shades of gray. Choose Yes or No.

If you selected a single underlay, the default values for Fade, Contrast, and Monochrome are the current property settings of the selected underlay. If you select multiple underlays, the default values for Fade, Contrast, and Monochrome remain as they were set the last time the command was used.

Clipping an underlay

If the underlay is large, you may not want to view all of it in your drawing. You can clip an underlay in the same way that you can clip an xref or block, by using the CLIP command. To access this command, choose Insert tab ⇨ Reference panel ⇨ Clip and then select the underlay to clip. The options are:

- **ON.** Turns on an existing clipping boundary. By default, a clipping boundary is on.
- **OFF.** Turns off an existing clipping boundary so that you can see the entire underlay.
- **Delete.** Deletes a clipping boundary.
- **New boundary.** Creates a new rectangular or polygonal clipping boundary, and allows you to create an inverted clipping boundary.

Displaying the frame of an underlay

You can turn the display of the frame for an underlay on or off. This is very similar to the frame that is displayed after clipping an xref or block. If the underlay is not clipped, the frame shows the rectangular border of the entire underlay. If you clipped the underlay, the frame shows the clipping border.

20

To display the frames for all underlays in a drawing, use the FRAME system variable and set its value to 1 (displays the frame and plots it) or 2 (displays the frame, but doesn't plot it). To turn off the display of all frames, set the value to 0. Even with the frames turned off, you can select an underlay. To change the display of the frames for underlays, choose Insert tab ⇨ Reference panel ⇨ Frame Settings drop-down list.

When FRAME is set to 3, you can control the frame display for xrefs, underlays, and raster images in the drawing by using the appropriate system variable. Use the following system variables to control the display of the frames for underlays; except for value 3, they support the same values as FRAME:

- **DWFFRAME.** Controls the frame display for DWF underlays.
- **DGNFRAME.** Controls the frame display for DGN underlays.
- **IMAGEFRAME.** Controls the frame display for raster images.
- **PDFFRAME.** Controls the frame display for PDF underlays.
- **POINTCLOUDCLIPFRAME.** Controls the frame display for point clouds.
- **XCLIPFRAME.** Controls the frame display for xrefs.

NEW FEATURE

Point clouds can now be clipped. The POINTCLOUDCLIPFRAME system variable controls the visibility of the clipping boundary for all clipped point clouds in a drawing.

Using object snaps with underlays

By default, you can use object snaps with underlays. If you need to use the object snaps of your underlay, this is the ideal setting. In PDF underlays, object snaps only work with vector-based objects; they do not work with raster-based (bitmap) objects.

However, if you don't want to use object snaps with underlays or you find yourself getting "caught" on an underlay's object snaps, you can turn object snaps off. To change the status of object snaps for underlays, choose Insert tab ⇨ Reference panel ⇨ Snap to Underlays drop-down list, and choose Snap to Underlays On or Snap to Underlays Off (the UOSNAP system variable). Note that even with UOSNAP set to 0, you can snap to the insertion point of the underlay.

You can control the use of object snaps by underlay type, using the following system variables:

- **DWFOSNAP.** Controls the use of object snapping with DWF underlays.
- **DGNOSNAP.** Controls the use of object snapping with DGN underlays.
- **PDFOSNAP.** Controls the use of object snapping with PDF underlays.

NOTE

When you set one of the underlay-specific system variables that control object snap settings to a value that is not equal to the current value of UOSNAP, UOSNAP changes to a value of 2. This value honors the underlay-specific snap settings for underlays.

Controlling the layers of an underlay

You can control the layers that are displayed for an underlay if the attached file was published with layer information. When you publish a DWF or DWFx file, you use the Publish Options dialog box to set Layer information to Include. (See Bonus Chapter 5 for more information on DWF and DWFx files.) The layers in a DGN underlay are based on the levels used in the original DGN file. PDF files can contain layer information if the application that created the PDF file saved the information during output.

Use the ULAYERS command to turn layers on or off for an underlay. To access this command, choose Insert tab ⇨ Reference panel ⇨ Underlay Layers or type **ulayers** ↵ on the command line. In the Underlay Layers dialog box, select an underlay from the Reference Name drop-down list. Click the light bulb icon next to the layers you want to turn on or off, and then click OK to apply the changes to the underlay.

Summary

In this chapter, I covered the techniques that you need to know to work with xrefs and underlays. You read about:

- Attaching and overlaying xrefs
- Opening an xref in its own window
- Editing xrefs and blocks from within the drawing in which they appear
- Setting spatial and layer indexes to speed up the display of large xrefs
- Deleting, unloading, and reloading xrefs
- Binding an xref to make it part of your drawing
- Working with DWF, DGN, and PDF underlays

This chapter ends Part III, "Working with Data." In Part IV, you start to draw in three dimensions. In the next chapter, I discuss how to specify 3D coordinates.

20

Part IV

Drawing in Three Dimensions

IN THIS PART

Specifying 3D Coordinates

IN THIS CHAPTER

Understanding 3D drawings

Working with 3D coordinates

Working with elevation and thickness

Creating a custom UCS for 3D drawings

The topics in the previous chapters have worked with X and Y axes. In this chapter, I add the Z axis. When you have a drawing with 3D objects, you can view it from any angle. The view that you've been using in 2D drawings is like looking at a house from the top, which you could call a plan view or a floor plan. From this view, even a 3D drawing looks two-dimensional. But when you look at a 3D drawing from an angle, you can see that there's more to it. Figure 21.1 shows the plan view of an office building on the left. On the right, you see the same drawing viewed in a perspective view from the front.

FIGURE 21.1

An office building in plan view (on the left) and perspective view (on the right)

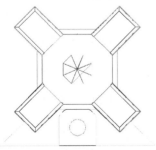

Although this drawing is quite complex, you can easily get started by working on simpler models. Three-dimensional drawing is not as difficult as it seems at first. In this chapter, I start by explaining how to work with 3D coordinates. I also cover wireframe models and 3D surfaces created with thickness and elevation. These are essentially 2D objects placed in 3D space and are therefore a good place to start when learning about drawing in 3D. Most of the features that I cover in this chapter apply to AutoCAD LT as well as to AutoCAD.

Working in a 3D Environment

AutoCAD comes with two 3D workspaces and two templates that set you up to work easily in 3D. These are not available in AutoCAD LT. To use the workspaces, choose 3D Modeling or 3D Basics from the Workspace drop-down list on the Quick Access Toolbar or the Workspace Switching button on the status bar. (I cover workspaces in detail in Bonus Chapter 15.) Use the 3D Basics workspace for simple 3D work; otherwise, use the 3D Modeling workspace.

The tabs and panels on the Ribbon change. To use a 3D template, choose Application Button⇨New. In the Select Template dialog box, choose acad3D.dwt (or acadiso3D.dwt for metric drawings), and click Open. In Figure 21.2, you see the result, with some minor changes that I made to make some elements clearer.

FIGURE 21.2

The acad3D.dwt template and the 3D Modeling workspace provide a suitable environment for working in 3D.

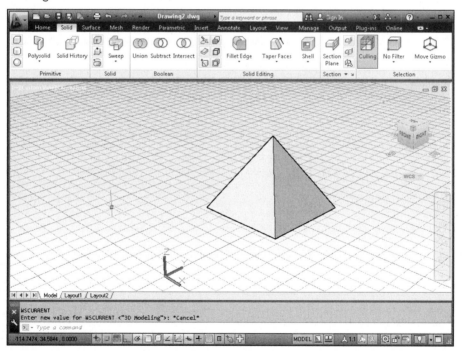

The grid is on, by default, to give you a sense of perspective and depth. The default viewpoint helps you see your 3D objects more clearly. You can change every aspect of what you see, including the colors, which palettes appear, and the viewpoint. Chapter 22 covers the ways to change the viewpoint and the visual style. Bonus Chapter 15 explains how to configure AutoCAD to look the way you want, including the colors of the grid and background.

Using 3D Coordinates

All the 2D methods of specifying coordinates have their 3D counterparts. Just as you can draw a line by specifying a start point of 3,4 and an endpoint of 5,7, you can draw a 3D line by specifying a start point of 3,4,2 and an endpoint of 5,7,6. Absolute coordinates are the same in 3D — you just add a Z coordinate. In the same way, you can specify relative coordinates. In 3D drawings, you can use two new types of coordinates that are 3D counterparts of polar coordinates, *cylindrical* and *spherical*.

Working with the User Coordinate System (UCS) is essential in 3D work. If you aren't familiar with the User Coordinate System, review the discussion in Chapter 8.

Most 2D commands accept 3D coordinates (a coordinate that includes a Z value) only on the first point. After that, you omit the Z coordinate because the Z value will be the same as that of the first point. For example, if you draw a rectangle, you can specify its first corner as 2,3,8 but the second corner must be specified without the Z value, as in 6,7. The Z value for the opposite corner is automatically 8.

The LINE command is an exception. It is a true 3D command, so you can specify X, Y, and Z values at all points.

Absolute and relative Cartesian coordinates in 3D

You don't use absolute coordinates more in 3D than you do in 2D — in fact, you may even use them less. But understanding absolute coordinates is important to understanding the Cartesian coordinate system that defines every point in your drawing. Figure 21.3 shows a wireframe model of a square and a triangle drawn with absolute coordinates, viewed from above (plan view) and from the southeast view (above, to the right, and in front). The rectangle is drawn in 2D — which means that the Z coordinates are all zero — as a reference point for visualizing the 3D points of the triangle.

You can use relative coordinates in the same way by including the change in coordinates. For example, to draw the line from (3,2,1) to (6,4,3), shown in Figure 21.3, you can start with the absolute coordinate (3,2,1) and then specify 3,2,2 because that's the difference between (3,2,1) and (6,4,3).

If you are using Dynamic Input with the default settings, specifying 3,2,2 as a second point is the same as specifying @3,2,2 with Dynamic Input off. For more information on Dynamic Input, see Chapter 4.

FIGURE 21.3

A rectangle and triangle viewed from plan view and southeast view

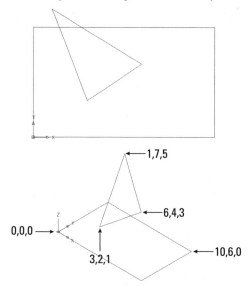

Cylindrical and spherical coordinates

Just as polar coordinates are often more useful than Cartesian coordinates in 2D, cylindrical and spherical coordinates can be more useful in 3D. Here's how they work.

Cylindrical coordinates have the format `(@)distance<angle,distance`:

- The first distance is the number of units in the XY plane from the origin (for absolute coordinates) or from your last point (for relative coordinates).
- The angle is the number of degrees from the X axis in the XY plane.
- The second distance is the number of units along the Z axis.

Cylindrical coordinates can be absolute or relative. You don't need to use the @ symbol for relative coordinates if Dynamic Input is on and set to the default option of relative coordinates. When you draw a line using cylindrical coordinates, neither distance that you specify is the length of the line. In essence, you're defining the lengths of two sides of a triangle to draw the hypotenuse. Figure 21.4 shows an example of a line drawn with cylindrical coordinates. The line was drawn from 0,0,0 to 5<30,3, which results in a line 5.8310 units long.

> **NOTE**
> You may find that cylindrical coordinates do not work very well with Dynamic Input turned on. In that case, click the Dynamic Input button on the status bar to turn off Dynamic Input.

FIGURE 21.4

A line drawn using cylindrical coordinates

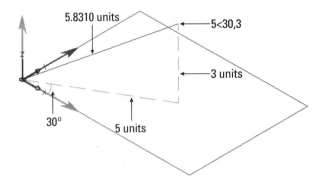

Spherical coordinates have the format distance<angle<angle:

- The distance is the total number of units from the origin (for absolute coordinates) or from your last point (for relative coordinates).
- The first angle is the number of degrees from the X axis in the XY plane.
- The second angle is the number of degrees from the XY plane in the Z direction.

Spherical coordinates can be absolute or relative. You don't need to use the @ symbol for relative coordinates if Dynamic Input is on and set to the default option of relative coordinates. When you draw a line using spherical coordinates, the distance is the actual length of the line. Figure 21.5 shows an example of a line drawn with spherical coordinates. The line was drawn from 0,0,0 to 5<15<30.

FIGURE 21.5

A line drawn using spherical coordinates

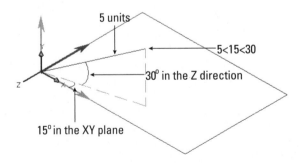

Using editing commands with 3D wireframes

Certain 2D editing commands work well in 3D. Others have special 3D versions. Because wireframes are simply 2D objects placed in 3D space, you can generally use the familiar editing commands. For example, to move an object 3 units in the positive Z axis direction, start the MOVE command and type **0,0,3** at the `Specify base point or [Displacement] <Displacement>:` prompt, and press Enter twice. You can also use the 3DMOVE command, which I cover in Chapter 24.

You need to be careful when selecting objects for editing. For example, if you draw two identically sized rectangles at different Z coordinates, when you look at them from plan view, you see only one rectangle. How do you know which rectangle you're selecting? By changing the angle from which you view your drawing (as I explain in the next chapter), you can see all the parts of the drawing and can select objects easily.

Multiple tiled viewports in which you view your drawing from different viewpoints can be very helpful in 3D drawing. For example, you can have a plan view in one viewport and a southeast view in another. Tiled viewports are covered in Chapter 8.

You can convert solids and certain surfaces to wireframes by extracting their edges with the XEDGES command. You can also use the SURFEXTRACTCURVE command to create a 2D object that follows the face of a solid or surface (AutoCAD only). I cover these commands in Chapter 23.

In the following exercise, you draw a simple wireframe piano bench and practice using 3D coordinates for both drawing and editing commands. You also view the drawing from two different angles.

STEPS: Using 3D Coordinates

1. Open `ab21-a.dwg`, available from the companion website. This exercise assumes that you have Dynamic Input turned on, set to the default of relative coordinates. The drawing uses a 2D environment.

2. Save it as `ab21-01.dwg` in your `AutoCAD Bible` folder.

3. Choose Home tab ⇨ Draw panel ⇨ Rectangle. At the `Specify first corner point or [Chamfer/Elevation/Fillet/Thickness/Width]:` prompt, type **0,0,19** ⏎. At the `Specify other corner point or [Area/Dimensions/Rotation]:` prompt, type **39,15** ⏎. This creates a rectangle 39 units long by 15 units wide that is 19 units above the XY plane. Notice that you omit the Z coordinate for the second corner.

4. Choose Home tab ⇨ Modify panel ⇨ Copy to start the COPY command. To copy the rectangle 2 units above the original rectangle, follow the prompts:

   ```
   Select objects: Pick the rectangle.
   Select objects: ⏎
   Specify base point or [Displacement/mOde] <Displacement>: 0,0,2 ⏎
   Specify second point or [Array] <use first point as displacement>: ⏎
   ```
   You now have two rectangles, but because you're looking from the top, you see only one.

5. Choose View tab ⇨ Views panel ⇨ Views drop-down list ⇨ SE Isometric. Now you can see the two rectangles, as shown in Figure 21.6.

FIGURE 21.6

The two rectangles, shown from Southeast Isometric view

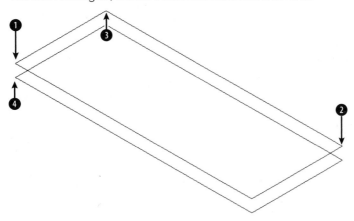

6. If Object Snap is not turned on, click the Object Snap button on the status bar. Set a running object snap for Endpoint.

7. Start the LINE command. Follow the prompts:

```
Specify first point: Pick the endpoint at ❶ in Figure 21.6.
Specify next point or [Undo]: #0,0,0 ↵ (The # symbol forces an absolute
    coordinate.)
Specify next point or [Undo]: 1,0,0 ↵
Specify next point or [Close/Undo]: 0,0,21 ↵
Specify next point or [Close/Undo]: ↵
```

8. Start the COPY command. At the Select objects: prompt, select the three lines that you just drew. End object selection. At the Specify base point or [Displacement/mOde] <Displacement>: prompt, type **38,0,0** ↵. At the Specify second point or [Array] <use first point as displacement>: prompt, press Enter to copy the three lines. Because the bench is 39 units long and the legs are 1 unit wide, copying the leg 38 units in the X direction places the copy in the right location.

9. Double-click your mouse wheel or choose View tab ⇨ Navigate panel ⇨ Zoom drop-down menu ⇨ Extents so that you can see the entire drawing.

10. Repeat the COPY command. Use two separate crossing windows to select the first leg, then the second leg. Each window should select three objects. End object selection. At the Specify base point or [Displacement/mOde] <Displacement>: prompt, type **0,15,0** ↵ to copy the legs 15 units in the Y direction. Press Enter at the Specify second point or [Array] <use first point as displacement>: prompt to copy the legs to the back of the bench.

11. To draw an open cover for the piano bench, start the LINE command. Start it at the endpoint at ❷, shown in Figure 21.6. At the `Specify next point or [Undo]:` prompt, type **15<90<45** ⏎. You know the length of the line because the cover is the same as the width of the piano bench. At the `Specify next point or [Undo]:` prompt, turn on Ortho Mode, move the cursor parallel to the length of the bench, and type **39**. At the `Specify next point or [Close/Undo]:` prompt, use the Endpoint object snap to pick ❸. End the LINE command. Zoom out and pan so that you can see the entire bench.

12. Turn Dynamic Input off by clicking the Dynamic Input button on the status bar. (Dynamic Input doesn't support cylindrical coordinates very well.) To draw some bracing inside the bench, start the LINE command again. At the `Specify first point:` prompt, choose the endpoint at ❹. At the `Specify next point or [Undo]:` prompt, type **@15<90,2** ⏎. End the LINE command. Here, cylindrical coordinates are ideal because you don't know the length of the line but you know the change in the X and Z coordinates (the width and the height of the bench's body, respectively).

13. Save your drawing. It should look like Figure 21.7.

FIGURE 21.7

The completed wireframe piano bench

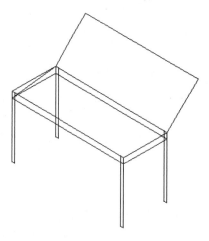

Using point filters, object snaps, object tracking, and grips in 3D

As mentioned earlier, it's often hard to tell which point you're picking in 3D. On a flat screen, you can be sure of only two dimensions. The other dimension is, so to speak, going in or out of the screen — it could be X, Y, or Z, depending on the angle that you're using to look at the drawing. That dimension is the one that's hard to pick on the screen. You use point filters, object snaps, object tracking, and grips to be sure that you have the right point in 3D drawings.

Point filters

In Chapter 4, I discuss point filters for 2D objects. They work the same way in 3D. You usually use point filters together with object snaps. For example, for the X coordinate, you might pick the endpoint of a line. Often point filters are the only way to define a 3D point that isn't on an existing object. The point filters for 3D drawings are `.xy`, `.xz`, and `.yz`. For example, if you want to pick a point 3 units in the Z direction from the endpoint of an existing line, you can use the `.xy` point filter to choose the endpoint of the line. The prompt then asks you for the Z coordinate, which you can specify as a number or by using an object snap. You can also use point filters to specify each coordinate (X, Y, and Z) separately.

Object snaps

Object snaps are essential for 3D work. Turn on Object Snap and set running object snaps. Object snaps ensure that you're specifying the point that you want. However, don't forget that in 3D drawings, you can have two lines, one on top of the other. Use a view that enables you to see the two lines separately so that you can pick the object snap that you want.

When you use an object snap in 3D, the Z value of the point comes from the Z value of the object. If you want to force a constant Z value, based on the current UCS or elevation, for a specific operation, temporarily change the OSNAPZ system variable to 1. (This system variable is not available in AutoCAD LT.) I discuss UCSs in 3D and elevation later in this chapter.

TIP

You can use point objects to help you draw in 3D. Set a visible point style (Home tab ⇨ Utilities panel [expanded] ⇨ Point Style [the DDPTYPE command]). Then place a point at a known coordinate. You can then use the Node object snap to access that point.

3D object snaps are special object snaps that apply only to 3D objects. (They're not available in AutoCAD LT.) The 3DOSMODE system variable turns 3D object snaps on and off; you can also use the 3D Object Snap tab in the Drafting Settings dialog box. Another method is to click the 3D Object Snap button on the status bar to toggle it on and off. To choose a specific object snap, right-click the button, and click the one you want to turn on or off. By default, the Vertex, Midpoint on Edge, and Center of Face object snaps are active.

Table 21.1 lists the 3D object snaps and their keyboard shortcuts.

TABLE 21.1 3D Object Snaps

3D Object Snap Name	Description	Keyboard Shortcut
Vertex	Snaps to the vertex of a 3D object	Zver
Midpoint on Edge	Snaps to the midpoint of a solid or surface face edge	Zmid
Center of Face	Snaps to the center of a solid or surface face	Zcen
Knot	Snaps to a spline knot. (I cover splines in Chapter 16.)	Zkno
Perpendicular	Snaps to a point that is perpendicular to a face	Zper
Nearest to Face	Snaps to the nearest point on a solid or surface face	Znea
None	Turns off all 3D object snaps	Znon

Object tracking

You can use object tracking in 3D as well. For example, if you want to draw a line starting from the middle of a box, you can acquire the midpoints of two sides and start the line there. (I cover object tracking in Chapter 4.) Object tracking in 3D improves the ease with which you can find the exact 3D point that you need.

Grips

You can use grips to edit 3D objects. Again, it's important to choose a view that makes the editing easy. Grip-editing wireframes is somewhat different from grip-editing solids. Chapter 24 discusses 3D editing in AutoCAD in more detail.

NOTE

Grips are shown parallel to the plane of the current User Coordinate System. When you change your viewpoint, the grips change their shape slightly to look as if they are lying on the XY plane.

ON THE WEB

The drawing that you need for the following exercise on using point filters and object snaps with 3D wireframe objects, ab21-b.dwg, is available from the Drawings download on the companion website.

STEPS: Using Point Filters, Object Tracking, and Object Snaps with 3D Wireframe Objects

1. Open ab21-b.dwg, available from the companion website.

2. Save it as ab21-02.dwg in your AutoCAD Bible folder. Object Snap should be on. Set a running object snap for Endpoint and Midpoint. Make sure that Object Snap Tracking is on. This drawing uses a 3D environment, based on acad3D.dwt. This is the same piano bench drawn in the previous exercise, but without the cover. In this exercise, you use the bench to create a chair.

3. Choose Home tab ⇨ Modify panel ⇨ Stretch. Use a crossing window to select the right side of the bench. Eight objects should be selected. End object selection. At the Specify base point or [Displacement] <Displacement>: prompt, use the Endpoint object snap to pick ❶, as shown in Figure 21.8. At the Specify second point or <use first point as displacement>: prompt, type **-15,0** ↵. (If you're not using Dynamic Input, type **@-15,0**.)

4. Pan the chair to the bottom of your screen and zoom out a little to leave room for the back of the chair, which you will draw next.

5. Start the LINE command. Follow the prompts:

   ```
   Specify first point: Choose ❷ in Figure 21.8.
   Specify next point or [Undo]: .xy ↵
   of Pick ❷.
   (need Z): 45 ↵
   Specify next point or [Undo]: Pass the cursor over the top endpoint of
       the line that you just drew, to acquire the point. Then pass the
       cursor over ❸ to acquire that point. Move the cursor to the
       approximate intersection of the two lines, until you see the
       Endpoint: -Z, Endpoint: Z tooltip, and click.
   Specify next point or [Close/Undo]: Pick ❸.
   Specify next point or [Close/Undo]: ↵
   ```

6. Repeat the LINE command. Draw a line from the midpoint of the left side of the back of the chair to the midpoint of the right side.

FIGURE 21.8

The piano bench after being shrunk with the STRETCH command

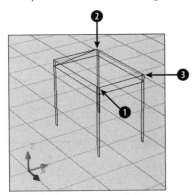

7. Choose Home tab ⇨ Modify panel ⇨ Fillet/Chamfer drop-down menu ⇨ Fillet. At the `Select first object or [Undo/Polyline/Radius/Trim/Multiple]`: prompt, right-click and choose Radius. At the `Specify fillet radius <0.0000>`: prompt, type **1** ↵.

8. At the `Select first object or [Undo/Polyline/Radius/Trim/Multiple]`: prompt, pick **①**, as shown in Figure 21.9. At the `Select second object or shift-select to apply corner or [Radius]`: prompt, pick **②**.

9. Repeat the FILLET command and pick **②** and **③** for the two lines.

10. Save the drawing. It should look like Figure 21.9.

FIGURE 21.9

A wireframe model of a chair

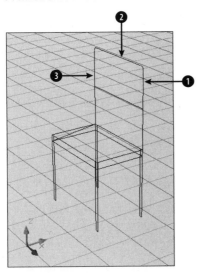

Creating 3D polylines

You've already created 3D lines by specifying 3D coordinates for the endpoints. One command that has a 3D counterpart is PLINE. The 3D command is 3DPOLY (Home tab ⇨ Draw panel ⇨ 3D Polyline in the 3D Modeling workspace or Home tab ⇨ Draw panel [expanded] ⇨ 3D Polyline in the Drafting & Annotation workspace). The 3DPOLY command is like the PLINE command with a few differences:

- You cannot draw arcs.
- You cannot give the polyline a width.
- You cannot use a noncontinuous linetype.

The 3DPOLY command can accept all 3D coordinates. You can also edit it with the PEDIT command, although there are fewer options.

> **TIP**
> If you want to create curved shapes in 3D space, you can create 2D polylines with a width and then add a thickness and an elevation. Elevation and thickness are both explained in the next section. Other options are available if you want to create surfaces (Chapter 23) or solids (Chapter 24).

Creating helixes

You can create a wireframe helix, or spiral, with the HELIX command. In the 3D Modeling or Drafting & Annotation workspace, choose Home tab ⇨ Draw panel (expanded) ⇨ Helix. (It's not available in AutoCAD LT.) When you start the command, an initial message indicates the default number of turns and the direction of the twist (clockwise or counterclockwise).

Follow the prompts:

```
Specify center point of base: Specify the center point for the base at
    the bottom of the helix.
Specify base radius or [Diameter] <default>: Enter a radius (or
    diameter) using the option. The default is the last radius you used.
Specify top radius or [Diameter] <default>: Enter a radius for the top
    of the helix.
Specify helix height or [Axis endpoint/Turns/turn Height/tWist]
    <default>: Enter a height to use the default number of turns. You
    can also use the options to change the number of turns and the
    direction of the twist. You can specify the height by specifying an
    axis endpoint (the center of the top of the helix) or the turn
    height.
```

Figure 21.10 shows a helix with five turns. You can grip-edit the helix to increase its height.

FIGURE 21.10

A helix with a small base and a larger top looks like a whirlpool.

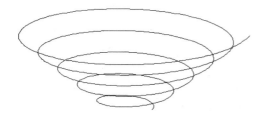

Using point clouds

Point clouds are vast collections of 3D points that represent an object or landscape. They are usually created with a 3D scanner or some other type of equipment. AutoCAD can create 3D point clouds by indexing the raw point data from a file created by a 3D scanner. (Different types of equipment create different file types.) The result is an ISD or PCG file that AutoCAD can display.

NEW FEATURE

The point cloud feature has been improved in AutoCAD 2013. You can now import scan data generated by many more industrial scanner companies, manage point clouds from the External References palette, edit more point cloud properties with the Properties palette, and clip the boundary of a point cloud like you can with other external referenced files. The Point Cloud panel on the Insert tab of the ribbon includes many of the new tools available for working with point clouds, while the Point Cloud tab contains new options for modifying a selected point cloud.

AUTOCAD ONLY

The ability to index and display point clouds is not available in AutoCAD LT.

To index point cloud data from a scan data file, and create a PCG or ISD file that can be attached to the drawing, follow these steps:

1. Choose Insert tab ⇨ Point Cloud panel ⇨ Create Point Cloud (the POINTCLOUDINDEX command) to open the Select Scan File dialog box.

2. Choose the point scan file that you want to index, and click Open.

3. In the Create Point Cloud File dialog box, under the Source Data section, specify any additional scan files to use, choose to merge all scan data files into a single point cloud data file, and set the location for the new point cloud files when created.

4. Under Settings, choose Create Autodesk Point Cloud (.pcg) or Create Ambercore Spatial Point Cloud (.isd) for the type of point cloud file you want to create. Then set the Autodesk Point Cloud format options as needed.

5. Click Create.

You then see a message appear from the AutoCAD icon tray indicating that the point cloud file is being indexed in the background. Indexing may take a while, depending on the size of the file. When complete, you see a new balloon message, Point Cloud File Indexing Complete. The point cloud file is ready to be attached. If you click the file link in the balloon, you can attach the point cloud to the drawing.

The next step is to attach the point cloud. Follow these steps:

1. Choose Insert tab ⇨ Point Cloud panel ⇨ Attach (the POINTCLOUDATTACH command) to open the Select Point Cloud File dialog box.

2. From the Files of Type drop-down list, choose the type of file you created, and click Open.

3. In the Attach Point Cloud dialog box, you can choose to specify the insertion point, scale, and rotation in the dialog box or on-screen. If you check the Lock Point Cloud check box (the POINTCLOUDLOCK system variable), you will not be able to move or rotate the point cloud. Click OK.

4. At the Specify insertion point <0,0>: prompt, specify where you want to insert the point cloud or press Enter to accept the default coordinate.

Once you have attached a point cloud file to your drawing, you may want to do a Zoom Extents to see the entire point cloud. Selecting a point cloud will display a bounding box around its extents, providing you a way to see the placement of the point cloud in your drawing. The imported points can be used to create the basis for your model. You can snap to any point using the Node object snap.

You can modify point clouds using many of the editing commands you already know. When you select an attached point cloud, you can modify its properties with the Properties palette or the Point Cloud contextual tab that is displayed. From the Point Cloud contextual tab, you can:

- Adjust the density of points displayed for all point clouds, set the color source used for the points in the selected point cloud, and toggle the automatic updating of all point clouds when a view change occurs.

- Modify the color intensity, mapping, and scheme of the point cloud based on the intensity data from the original scan file.

- Clip the boundary of the selected point cloud. Once clipped, you can toggle the display of the clipping boundary or remove the clipping boundary from the point cloud.

- Toggle the display of the bounding box for all point clouds or display the External References palette.

NOTE

Saving a drawing file that contains an attached PCG file to the AutoCAD 2010 DWG format or earlier will cause the PCG file to be re-indexed and degraded.

Because point clouds are often very large, you can adjust the percentage of points displayed for all clouds in a drawing using the Density slider (POINTCLOUDDENSITY system variable) on the Point Cloud panel. The Realtime Density slider (POINTCLOUDRTDENSITY system variable) on the Point Cloud panel controls the percentage of points that are displayed during real-time zoom, pan, and other viewing operations. To access the Density and Realtime Density sliders, you need to expand the Point Cloud panel first.

When working with a large number of points, changing views may become slow. You can choose Insert tab ⇨ Point Cloud panel ⇨ Auto Update (POINTCLOUDAUTOUPDATE system variable) to control whether AutoCAD dynamically updates a point cloud after you edit it or change the view.

Using Elevation and Thickness

Wireframes have a number of limitations. In Figure 21.11, you can see the back leg through the seat of the chair. Also, creating the detail of a real chair would be tedious if you were to use individual lines or 3D polylines. Finally, wireframes don't have any surface or solid properties. You can't display them in any realistic fashion or calculate properties, such as area, mass, and so on.

Creating surfaces with thickness

You can create simple surfaces by adding thickness to 2D objects. When you add thickness to a 2D object, the object is pushed out into the third dimension. For example, a circle becomes a cylinder and a rectangle becomes a box. Remember that you won't see the thickness if you're looking at the object from the top. Figure 21.11 shows some objects created using thickness.

Surfaces created by adding thickness are sometimes called 2½D objects. Although they have three dimensions, the third dimension can only be a straight side perpendicular to the 2D object at the base.

FIGURE 21.11

3D surfaces created by adding thickness to 2D objects

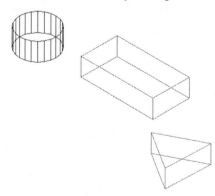

The parallel lines on the cylinder are called *tessellation lines*. These lines help you to visualize curved surfaces. They aren't actually part of the cylinder; for example, you can't use object snaps on them.

To add thickness to an existing 2D object, display the Properties palette (Ctrl+1) and select the object. (You can also select the object first.) In the palette, click the Thickness property and change the value in the text box. Press Enter.

> **NOTE**
>
> You can use the CONVTOSURFACE command to convert open polyline figures with no width, lines, and arcs to surfaces — as long as they have a thickness. You can use the CONVTOSOLID command to convert three types of closed wireframe objects with thickness to solids — polylines with a uniform width, closed polyline figures with no width, and circles. I discuss surfaces in Chapter 23 and solids in Chapter 24. These commands are not available in AutoCAD LT.

You can also change the current thickness. The current thickness affects new objects as you draw them, but does not affect existing objects. There are two ways to change the current thickness:

- With no object selected, display the Properties palette (Ctrl+1). Click the Thickness property and type a value in the text box. Press Enter.
- Use the ELEV command (which can also change the current elevation, discussed in the "Adding elevation to objects" section) by typing it on the command line. The ELEV command prompts you for the current elevation and the current thickness. At the prompt for a thickness, type a number and press Enter.

In most cases, you use a positive number, which extrudes objects in the positive direction of the Z axis. However, you can use a negative number to extrude objects in the negative direction of the Z axis. As soon as you change the current thickness, all objects that you draw have that thickness.

> **CAUTION**
>
> Because it's easy to forget the current thickness, unless you're drawing a number of objects with the same thickness, it's usually safer to draw objects with no thickness and then change the thickness. If you do change the current thickness, don't forget to change it back to zero when you're finished creating the 3D objects.

Using the HIDE command

Because objects with thickness are surfaces, not wireframes, you can use the HIDE command to hide lines that would be hidden from view in real life. AutoCAD and AutoCAD LT calculate which lines are behind surfaces from the current viewpoint, and hide them. Figure 21.12 shows the same objects as Figure 21.11 after using the HIDE command. You may notice that the cylinder has a top, but the triangular prism and the box don't. For a further explanation, see the sidebar "Do Objects with Thickness Have Tops and Bottoms?"

To return to the wireframe display, use the REGEN command. You use the HIDE command in AutoCAD LT or in a 2D environment in AutoCAD; in a 3D environment in AutoCAD, you use visual styles instead. I cover visual styles in Chapter 22.

FIGURE 21.12

3D surfaces after using the HIDE command

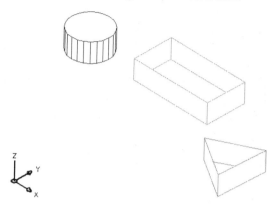

Controlling the display of hidden lines and objects

You can control the display of polylines at the face intersections of solid and surface objects, including surfaces that you create using thickness. In a 2D environment in AutoCAD, and in AutoCAD LT, you use the HLSETTINGS command to specify settings that affect the display of hidden lines. For example, instead of hiding back lines completely, you could display them as dashed lines or in a different color. In AutoCAD, this opens the Visual Styles Manager palette; in AutoCAD LT, this opens the Hidden Line Settings dialog box.

Several system variables affect the 3D display only when you use the HIDE command or the Hidden (or 3D Hidden) visual style. These system variables work on both solids and surfaces. Type **hlsettings** at the command prompt to open the Hidden Line Settings dialog box (AutoCAD LT) or Visual Styles Manager palette (AutoCAD), as shown in Figure 21.13. Note that I cover the Visual Styles Manager for other settings in Chapter 22.

Do Objects with Thickness Have Tops and Bottoms?

If you look at Figure 21.12, you see that the cylinder has a top but the triangular prism and the box don't. AutoCAD creates top and bottom surfaces on some objects with thickness but not on others. When you add a thickness to objects created with the SOLID command (a 2D command), circles, and wide polylines, they are surfaces with tops and bottoms. However, if you draw a closed polyline, for example with the RECTANG or POLYGON command, and give it a thickness, there is no top or bottom surface. The same is true for a closed figure that you draw with the LINE command. Therefore, if you want a top and bottom, use the SOLID command, draw a polyline with a width greater than zero, or draw a circle. (Hatching a closed figure with a solid fill does not have the same effect as the SOLID command.) These objects create opaque horizontal surfaces. You can see the difference when you use the HIDE command. Note that a circle doesn't display a top if you use the Hidden (or 3D Hidden in previous release) visual style. (See Chapter 22 for more on visual styles.)

FIGURE 21.13

The Visual Styles Manager allows you to control the display of back lines in AutoCAD.

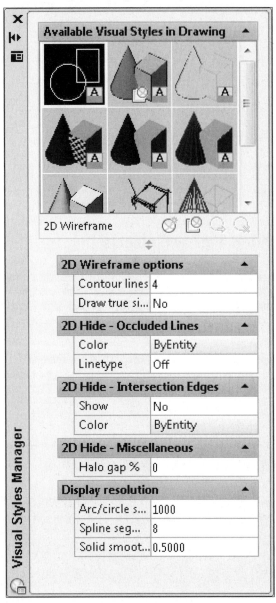

Here's how to use the Hidden Line Settings dialog box and the Visual Styles Manager palette to specify the display of hidden lines.

Use the 2D Hide - Occluded Lines section (Obscured Lines in AutoCAD LT) to choose a linetype and color for displaying hidden lines. When you choose a linetype, hidden lines are shown in the linetype that you choose. These linetypes are not affected as you zoom in or out. Choose from these linetypes:

Off (fully hides back lines)	Long Dash
Solid	Double Short Dash
Dashed	Double Medium Dash
Dotted	Double Long Dash
Short Dash	Medium Long Dash
Medium Dash	Sparse Dot

If you choose a linetype, then choose a color from the Color drop-down list. You can choose from one of the standard color index numbers (from 1 to 255). Use the 2D Hide - Intersection Edges section (Face Intersections in AutoCAD LT) to turn on the display of polylines at the intersections of 3D model faces. Then use the Color drop-down list to choose a color for the polylines.

Use the 2D Hide - Miscellaneous section (Halo Gap Percentage in AutoCAD LT) to create a gap that shortens lines at the point that they would be hidden by the HIDE command, in order to set off the lines from the unhidden portion of the model. By default, this percentage is set to 0, which creates no gap. Set the gap as a percentage of an inch. The gap doesn't change as you zoom in or out.

You can set the HIDEPRECISION system variable to 1 if you want a more exact calculation of the results from the HIDE command or Hidden wireframe. The process takes longer but yields better results in a complex drawing with many surfaces and solids. In AutoCAD, enter **hideprecision** ↵ on the command line to set its value. The default is 0. In AutoCAD LT, you can choose the option in the Hidden Line Settings dialog box.

Use the HIDETEXT system variable to hide text behind other objects (a value of On, the default). When this system variable is set to Off, text will not hide other objects, or be hidden, unless it has a thickness. In AutoCAD LT, you can choose the Include Text in HIDE Operations option from the Hidden Line Settings dialog box.

Figure 21.14 shows a model using a halo gap value of 15; a green, dashed line to display hidden lines; and face intersections displayed in red.

NOTE

The word *wireframe* is used in two ways. First, it means 3D objects that are created using only lines and 3D polylines. These objects have no surfaces or solidity. Second, it means surfaces and solids that are displayed as if they are created with lines and 3D polylines, such as the models in Figure 21.11. In this book, I usually distinguish between wireframes and wireframe display, or visual style. If the subject is surfaces and solids, the term *wireframe* generally means wireframe display.

Adding elevation to objects

Until now, I've discussed 3D objects based on 2D objects that were on the XY plane. In other words, their Z coordinate was zero. Although you generally don't want objects to float in the air, you certainly may want to place one object on top of another. To do this, you need to start the object above the XY plane (you can also place objects below the XY plane) and give an object elevation, which is its Z coordinate.

FIGURE 21.14

This model uses HALOGAP, OBSCUREDLTYPE, and OBSCUREDCOLOR to display hidden lines.

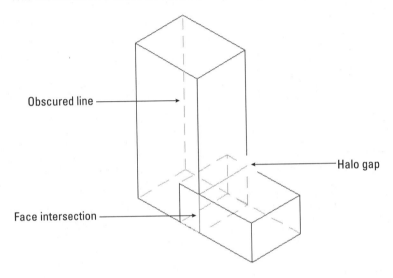

Obscured line

Halo gap

Face intersection

To give elevation to an existing object, you can use several methods:

- Select the object and display the Properties palette (Ctrl+1). Click the Elevation property, type a new elevation in the text box, and press Enter.
- Move the object(s) with the MOVE command in the Z direction.
- Use the 3DMOVE command to move the object in the Z direction. I cover this command in Chapter 24, where I discuss editing in 3D.

For new objects, change the current elevation with the ELEV command as described earlier in this chapter in the discussion on thickness.

> **NOTE**
> For some objects, you can use the Properties palette (press Ctrl+1) to change the Z coordinate. This works for circles, lines, arcs, and ellipses but not for polylines. To elevate an entire line, you need to change the Z coordinate of both the start point and the endpoint.

When you change the current elevation, all objects that you create are drawn on that elevation. Remember to change the elevation back to zero when you want to draw on the XY plane again.

CAUTION

If you specify an object snap of an object on a different elevation than your current elevation (with a different Z coordinate), AutoCAD and AutoCAD LT use the elevation of the object snap, not the current elevation. However, if you specify the first point of a 2D command, such as PLINE (to create a polyline), on the current elevation, you can use object snaps at a different elevation for subsequent points. Because the entire polyline must be on the same elevation, subsequent points follow the elevation of the first point.

STEPS: Working with Elevation, Thickness, and the HIDE Command

1. Start a new drawing by using the `acad.dwt` or `acadlt.dwt` template. The Allow/Disallow Dynamic UCS button on the status bar should be off (if you have AutoCAD). This template uses a 2D environment.

2. Save it as `ab21-03.dwg` in your `AutoCAD Bible` folder.

3. Choose Home tab ➪ Draw panel ➪ Circle drop-down menu ➪ Center, Radius to start the CIRCLE command. Specify the center as 6,6 and the radius as 18.

4. Choose View tab ➪ Views panel ➪ Views drop-down list ➪ SE Isometric to display a 3D view.

5. Select the circle. Display the Properties palette (Ctrl+1). Click the Thickness property. In the Thickness text box, type **3** ↵.

6. Type **elev** ↵. At the `Specify new default elevation <0.0000>:` prompt, type **3** ↵. Because you just changed the existing circle's thickness to 3, you set the elevation to 3 to place an object on top of the circle. At the `Specify new default thickness <0.0000>:` prompt, type **24** ↵.

7. Start the CIRCLE command again. Specify 6,6 as the center and set the radius to 3.

8. Zoom out and pan so that you can see the entire model.

9. Type **elev** ↵. At the `Specify new default elevation <3.0000>:` prompt, type **27**. At the `Specify new default thickness <24.0000>:` prompt, type **3** ↵. This places any new object on top of the two circles that you just drew.

10. Start the CIRCLE command. Specify the center as 6,6 and the radius as 18. Because you don't specify a Z coordinate, the current elevation is used. You can verify in the Dynamic Input tooltip that the Z coordinate is 27.

11. Type **hide** ↵. You can now see the cable spool clearly.

12. Save your drawing. It should look like Figure 21.15.

FIGURE 21.15

A cable spool created by drawing 2D circles with thickness and elevation

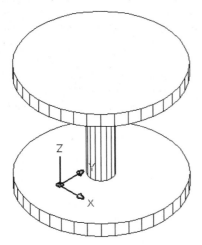

Working with the User Coordinate System

Except for certain true solids, much of 3D work starts with a 2D shape. However, the 2D drawing commands can be drawn only on, or parallel to, the XY plane. For example, the spool in Figure 21.15 consists of three circles, all parallel to the XY plane. How do you draw a circle, or any other 2D object for that matter, that is not parallel to the XY plane?

The answer is to change the User Coordinate System (UCS), thereby changing the definition of the XY plane. You can move the UCS to any location to define the XY plane in any way that you want. After you do so, you can draw a 2D object at any angle. This section offers a brief review of UCS features that are particularly useful for 3D drawing. (See Chapter 8 for complete coverage of the UCS feature.) Remember that you can save and name any UCS that you create by using the Named option of the UCS command.

 CAUTION

Although you may have found the UCS icon an annoyance in 2D work, you should display it when working in 3D. Otherwise, it's easy to lose track of which direction is which. Remember that you can choose the Origin option, which displays the UCS icon, if possible, at the origin. Choose View tab ⇨ Coordinates panel ⇨ Origin. (The Coordinates panel may not be displayed. If not, right-click anywhere on the View tab and choose Show Panels ⇨ Coordinates.)

 You can customize the look of the UCS icon. The 3D style is helpful when you're working in 3D. See Chapter 8 for details on customizing the UCS icon display.

UCSs and viewpoints

A plan view of the World UCS (the default) is different from the plan view of a UCS that you've created by rotating the UCS around the X axis, for example. The UCS defines the orientation and origin of the X, Y, and Z axes. On the other hand, the viewpoint shows your drawing from different angles without changing the orientation or origin of the axes. Understanding the difference between the UCS and viewpoints is important. The next chapter is all about viewpoints.

The UCS is important because it enables you to draw and edit at unusual angles. However, after you have a suitable UCS, you need to look at the drawing from the best viewpoint, one that displays the objects clearly with as little overlapping as possible.

If you want to change your UCS when you change your viewpoint, you can use the UCSORTHO system variable. When this variable is on and you switch to an orthographic viewpoint (top, bottom, left, right, front, or back), the UCS changes to match the viewpoint.

When the UCSFOLLOW system variable is on (set to 1), it switches you to plan view whenever you change the UCS. This means that whenever you change the UCS, you start by looking at your model from the top. You can then change the viewpoint to anything that you want.

> **NOTE**
> In 3D work, you usually use a 3D UCS icon display. However, if you use the 2D display, and choose a viewpoint that looks straight across the XY plane, you see a broken pencil icon, indicating that you're looking at the XY plane edge on.

> **AUTOCAD ONLY**
> Express Tools has a command, RTUCS, that enables you to rotate the UCS icon by dragging with the mouse. You can set an incremental angle for rotation and specify an active axis around which you rotate the UCS. Enter rtucs ↵ on the command line.

Dragging the UCS icon

To change the UCS by dragging the icon, click the icon so the grips appear at the origin and the ends of the axes.

> **NOTE**
> The UCSSELECTMODE system variable controls whether you can click the UCS icon to move or rotate it.

You can do any of the following:

- To move the origin, click the intersection of the axes (the square grip), move the cursor to the desired location and then click.
- To rotate the axes, click one of the axis grips (the circular shaped), move the cursor until the axes are at the desired angle and then click.

- To return the UCS to the World Coordinate System, click it and choose World from the menu that appears.
- To align the UCS to an object, click the icon and choose Move and Align from the menu that appears.

Using UCS options to change the UCS

To change the UCS, right-click the UCS icon and choose one of the options. The following UCS options are useful for 3D drawing:

- **Object.** You can align the UCS with any existing object. Because this option orients the UCS differently for different objects, this option can sometimes be confusing. However, to modify some objects, you must be on their XY plane — a good time to use the Object option. The overall principle is that the UCS's XY plane stays parallel to the previous UCS, except for 3Dface objects. Table 21.2 explains how the Object option aligns the UCS for various kinds of objects.

- **Face.** The Face option aligns the UCS on a face of a solid, surface, or mesh object. At the Select face of solid, surface, or mesh: prompt, click within the boundary of a face or on its edge to highlight the face, and align the X axis of the UCS with the closest edge of the first face that it finds. At the Enter an option [Next/Xflip/Yflip] <accept>: prompt, you can now refine the UCS. Right-click and choose Next to move the UCS to the adjacent face or the back face of the selected edge. Right-click and choose Xflip to rotate the UCS 180 degrees around the X axis. Right-click and choose Yflip to rotate the UCS 180 degrees around the Y axis. When you have the UCS that you want, press Enter to accept the current location of the UCS.

- **View.** The View option aligns the X and Y axes with the current view. The current origin remains the same. The View option is often used for creating text that you want to appear flat from your viewpoint of a 3D view of the drawing.

- **Origin.** The Origin option creates a UCS parallel to the current UCS, but with a new origin that you specify. You can use the Origin option for working at a new elevation, instead of changing the current elevation.

- **Z-Axis Vector.** The Z-Axis Vector option enables you to define an origin and then a point on the positive side of the Z axis. You can keep the previous origin to twist the UCS around its origin.

- **3Point.** The first point that you specify is the origin, the second point indicates the positive direction of the X axis, and the third point indicates the positive direction of the Y axis.

- **X.** The X option maintains the current origin and rotates the Y and Z axes around the current X axis at the rotation angle that you specify. The most common rotation is 90 degrees or a multiple of 90 degrees, but you can specify any angle.

- **Y.** The Y option keeps the current origin and rotates the X and Z axes around the current Y axis. You specify the angle.

- **Z.** The Z option keeps the current origin and rotates the X and Y axes around the current Z axis. You specify the angle.

- **UCS, World.** The World option returns the UCS to the World Coordinate System.

- **UCS, Previous.** The Previous option switches to the previous UCS that you used.

TABLE 21.2   UCS Orientation with the Object Option

Object	UCS Orientation
Line	The endpoint nearest your pick point is the origin. The line lies on the X axis.
2D Polyline	The endpoint of the polyline nearest your pick point is the origin. The first segment of the polyline lies on the X axis.
Dimension	Places the origin at the midpoint of the dimension text. The X axis is parallel to the X axis that you used when you created the dimension.
Text	Places the origin at the insertion point and aligns the X axis with the rotation angle of the text. The same applies to attributes.
Block	Places the origin at the insertion point and aligns the X axis with the rotation angle of the block.
Circle	The origin is at the circle's center. The X axis is aligned with your pick point.
Arc	The origin is at the arc's center. The X axis is aligned with the endpoint closest to your pick point.
Point	The origin is at the point. The X axis may be difficult to determine in advance.
Solid	Uses the first point that you specified for the origin and the first and second points to align the X axis. AutoCAD LT doesn't offer solids, but you can open AutoCAD drawings containing solids.
Surface	The origin is placed along the edge of a face. AutoCAD LT doesn't offer surfaces, but you can open AutoCAD drawings containing surfaces.
Mesh	The origin is placed at the vertex point of a face. AutoCAD LT doesn't offer meshes, but you can open AutoCAD drawings containing meshes.
3Dface	Uses the first point for the origin. The X axis is aligned with the first two points. The Y axis is aligned with the first and fourth points. The new UCS may not be parallel to the prior UCS. AutoCAD LT doesn't offer 3Dfaces, but you can open AutoCAD drawings containing 3Dfaces.

Changing the UCS dynamically

Creating a new UCS is great if you need to work in it for a while and if you want to save it for future use. However, sometimes you just want to draw one object on a certain plane of an existing solid or mesh object. For these times, you can use the dynamic UCS feature, which creates a UCS on the fly so that you can draw on any face of an object. You can also use the dynamic UCS feature to help you specify a regular UCS.

AUTOCAD ONLY
AutoCAD LT does not have the dynamic UCS feature.

The dynamic UCS feature works only on solids and meshes (both covered in Chapter 24). You turn this feature on and off by clicking the Allow/Disallow Dynamic UCS button on the status bar (or pressing F6). You can temporarily override the Dynamic UCS feature by pressing Shift+Z.

To create a temporary UCS, follow these steps:

1. Start a command. Some commands that work with the dynamic UCS feature are:
   - Commands that draw 2D geometry, text, a table, 3D solids, meshes, or a polysolid
   - The INSERT and XREF commands for inserting blocks or xrefs
   - Editing commands, such as the ROTATE, MIRROR, and ALIGN commands, and grip-editing
   - The UCS command

2. Pass the cursor over a face of a solid or mesh. A dashed border appears on the face, as shown in Figure 21.16.

3. Continue the command. For example, if you're drawing a circle, specify the center point. The UCS icon appears near the cursor in its new direction so that you can see where the XY plane is. The temporary X axis is aligned with the edge of the face and always points to the right of your screen.

NOTE

If the grid is on, it flips to match the XY plane. This can be distracting, so you may want to turn it off.

4. Finish the command. The UCS automatically returns to its previous setting.

FIGURE 21.16

When you pass the cursor over a face of a solid, the dashed border confirms the face, and you can temporarily draw on or edit that face.

ON THE WEB

The drawing used in the following exercise on creating UCSs, `ab21-c.dwg`, is available from the Drawings download on the companion website.

STEPS: Creating UCSs

1. Open `ab21-c.dwg`, available from the companion website.

2. Save it as `ab21-04.dwg` in your `AutoCAD Bible` folder. This drawing contains some centerlines based on measurements of a chair. Object Snap should be on. Set running object snaps for Endpoint, Midpoint, Center, and Quadrant. The UCS icon is set at the origin. This drawing starts in a 2D environment.

3. Choose Home tab⇨Draw panel⇨Circle drop-down menu⇨Center, Radius. Use the From object snap to specify the center at an offset from ❶ (in Figure 21.17) of @2,0. Set the radius to 0.5.

FIGURE 21.17

21

These centerlines are the basis for drawing a chair.

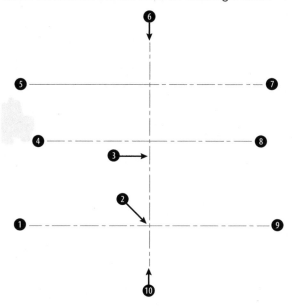

4. Display the Properties palette (Ctrl+1) and select the circle that you just drew. Change the thickness to 16. Press Enter. Close the Properties palette (or right-click its title bar and choose Auto-Hide).

5. Click Ortho Mode on the status bar to turn it on. Choose Home tab⇨Modify panel (expanded)⇨Mirror. (If you are not using the 3D Modeling workspace, you do not need to expand the Modify panel.) The circle should still be selected. (If it isn't, select it.) Specify the endpoint at ❷ for the first point of the mirror line. Specify any point vertical to ❷ for the second point of the mirror line. Choose not to delete the source object (the circle).

6. Repeat the MIRROR command. Select the two circles. Pick the midpoint of the line at ❸ for the first point of the mirror line. Pick any point horizontal to the first point for the second point of the mirror line. Press Enter. There are now four legs. Turn Ortho Mode off.

7. Type **elev** ↵. Change the elevation to 16 and the thickness to 1.

8. Choose View tab⇨Views panel⇨Views drop-down list⇨SE Isometric. You can now see the four chair legs.

9. Choose Home tab⇨Draw panel⇨Polyline. At the `Specify start point:` prompt, choose the From object snap. Use the Center object snap of the top of the circle near ❶, shown in Figure 21.17, for the base point and an offset of @–2,0. (You may have to press the Tab key until you get the Center object snap.) Continue to pick points ❹ through ❿. Notice that the Endpoint object snap symbol appears at the height of the first point. Then right-click and choose Close to close the polyline.

10. Choose Home tab⇨Modify panel (expanded)⇨Edit Polyline (or type **pedit** ↵). Select the polyline. At the prompt, right-click and choose Fit to fit the polyline. Press Enter to end the command.

11. To see the result, type **hide** ↵. Remember that the polyline has no top or bottom surface. Imagine your model as a glass-bottomed chair. It should look like Figure 21.18.

FIGURE 21.18

Part of a 3D chair

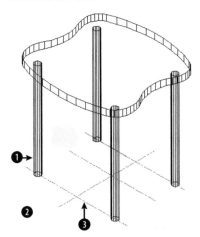

12. Select the front-left leg at ❶, shown in Figure 21.18. Use the Properties palette to verify you selected the correct circle. (If the Properties palette is not displayed, right-click and choose Properties from the menu that appears.) The center (of the circle at the bottom of the leg) is X = 3.5000, Y = –7.0000, Z = 0.0000. Press ESC to deselect the circle.

13. To see the effect of a different UCS option, right-click the UCS icon and choose Rotate Axis ⇨X. To rotate the UCS around the X axis, type **90** ↵. Again, select the same leg of the chair and display the Properties palette. Now the center is X = 3.5000, Y = 0.0000, Z = 7.0000. Look at the UCS icon (which is at 0,0,0) and try to visualize why the coordinates are the way they are listed. Press ESC to deselect the circle.

14. Because you know the center of the circle of the front leg, you can move the UCS there. Right-click the UCS icon and choose Origin. At the `Origin point <0,0,0>:` prompt, type **3.5,0,7** ↵. This places the X axis through the center of the circle.

15. Right-click the UCS icon again and choose View. The UCS is now parallel to your current view. Choose Annotate tab⇨Text panel⇨Multiline Text drop-down menu⇨Single Line Text. Start the text at ❷, shown in Figure 21.18. Set the height to 1 and the rotation to 0. Type **A glass-bottomed chair**. Press Enter twice to end the command.

16. Right-click the UCS icon and choose Object. Pick the line at ❸.

17. Right-click the UCS icon and choose Origin. Type **0,0,17** as the origin to place the UCS at the top of the seat.

18. Right-click the UCS icon and choose Rotate Axis⇨X. Type **−10** ↵ to rotate the UCS around the X axis by −10 degrees. This enables you to create the back of the chair at a 10-degree angle. Type **plan** ↵ and press Enter again to accept the default. It enables you to view your drawing from plan view (in this case, relative to the current UCS).

> **TIP**
>
> Although it's not necessary for this exercise, this would be a good UCS to save. Right-click the UCS icon and choose Named UCS ⇨ Save. Type Chair Back ↵. Now that you've gone through all these steps, it would be a shame to have to re-create the UCS again.

19. With no objects selected, display the Properties palette (Ctrl+1). Set the thickness to 16. Close the Properties palette.

20. Start the CIRCLE command. Choose the center of the lower circle of the top-left leg (it's below the chair's seat) for the center. Accept the default radius of 0.5. Use the same technique to draw a circle at the corresponding right circle.

21. Choose View tab⇨Views panel⇨Views drop-down list⇨SE Isometric to see the results. Use the Previous option of the ZOOM command to return to your previous display.

22. Change the thickness to −5. Type **hide** ↵ so that you can see the circles that you just created more clearly.

23. Start the ARC command. The start point should be at the left quadrant of the left circle that you just drew. The second point is the intersection of the vertical centerline and the top horizontal centerline. (There is an Endpoint object snap there.) The endpoint is the right quadrant of the right circle.

24. Right-click the UCS icon and choose World. Choose View tab⇨Views panel⇨Views drop-down list⇨SE Isometric. Then type **hide** ↵ to see the final result.

25. Save your drawing. The chair should look like Figure 21.19.

FIGURE 21.19

The completed glass-bottomed chair

A glass-bottomed chair

Summary

This chapter introduced you to 3D drawing. You read about:

- Understanding all the types of 3D coordinates and how to use them
- Using editing commands in 3D
- Using point filters, object snaps, and grips in 3D drawings
- Utilizing elevation and thickness
- Understanding the HIDE command and the system variables that affect the hidden display
- Working with User Coordinate Systems in 3D

In the next chapter, I explain all the ways to view 3D drawings.

22

Viewing 3D Drawings

IN THIS CHAPTER

Using the standard viewpoints

Switching your viewpoint with the ViewCube

Saving a named view with a camera

Projecting parallel and perspective views

Changing your viewpoint with 3D Orbit

Displaying shots with the ShowMotion feature

Using the Wheel to navigate

Displaying visual styles

Laying out and flattening a 3D drawing

Creating prototypes in 3D

A s soon as you start to work in three dimensions, you need to be able to see the drawing from different angles. By combining various User Coordinate Systems (UCSs) and different viewpoints, you can view and draw any object in 3D.

Unless otherwise stated, the features in this chapter apply to both AutoCAD and AutoCAD LT; however, note that many of the 3D features are for AutoCAD only. In AutoCAD, you'll find 3D viewing tools easier to find if you use the 3D Modeling workspace; this workspace is not available in AutoCAD LT. (To switch workspaces, choose from the Workspace drop-down list on the Quick Access Toolbar, or click the Workspace Switching button on the right side of the status bar.) Therefore, this chapter assumes that you're using the 3D Modeling workspace if you have AutoCAD.

Your basic point of reference is plan view in the World Coordinate System (WCS). This is the view that you use in 2D, so it's familiar. Plan view is the view from the top (although which side is the top is not always obvious). Figure 22.1 shows a plan view of a 3D model on the left. On the right, you see a 3D view of the same model, which lets you visualize the three dimensions much more clearly.

FIGURE 22.1

The left image is the plan view; the right image is a 3D view.

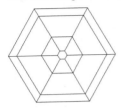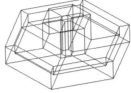

When working in 3D, you can use many of the familiar 2D techniques for viewing your drawing:

- Use ZOOM Previous to display the previous viewpoint.
- Save views so that you can easily return to them.
- Use real-time zoom and pan as well as all the other zoom options.
- Create tiled viewports to display more than one view at a time.

 You can save drawings in the 3D DWF format (in AutoCAD only) for viewing on the web or sending to people. For more information, see Bonus Chapter 5.

This chapter also explains how to save 3D views, create presentations from saved views, walk through a 3D model, create visual styles that control how your models look, lay out 3D drawings in 2D paper space for plotting, and print in 3D.

Working with the Standard Viewpoints

AutoCAD and AutoCAD LT offer 10 standard viewpoints. These viewpoints are useful — and easy to use. They are relative only to the World Coordinate System (WCS), not the current User Coordinate System (UCS). Therefore, they're most useful when you're using the WCS.

To use a preset viewpoint, choose View tab ⇨ Views panel ⇨ Views drop-down list, and choose the view-point that you want from the list. Each of the preset viewpoints automatically does a Zoom Extents. In AutoCAD only, in the 3D Modeling workspace, you can also choose Home tab ⇨ View panel ⇨ Views (3D Navigation) drop-down list, and choose one of the viewpoints.

Using the VPOINT command

The VPOINT command was the original, command-line method of setting viewpoints. Now it's generally used for scripts and AutoLISP routines when you need a way to set a viewpoint from the command line. (AutoCAD LT does not support AutoLISP routines.)

The VPOINT command defines a viewpoint using X, Y, and Z vectors. The vectors for the standard view-points are based on a maximum of 1 unit. Imagine a model of the three axes floating out in space. You're a superhero and can fly around the model from any angle. When you're over the Z axis, you can define the Z vector from 0,0,0 to your position as 1. The other vectors are 0 (zero) because you're right over them, so that 0,0,1 defines the top, or plan, view. The next section shows the vector equiv-alents for the standard viewpoints to give you a feel for the vector system. I explain the VPOINT com-mand's compass and tripod later in this chapter.

Looking at a drawing from the standard viewpoints

Showing the viewpoints is easier than describing them. In Table 22.1, I show a simple 3D house from all ten standard viewpoints. Although the front of the house faces east, that is particular to this house. From your drawing's point of view, east is 0 degrees when looking from the top view, and 0 degrees faces to the right.

> **NOTE**
> A system variable, UCSORTHO, automatically changes the UCS to match the viewpoint when you switch to one of the orthographic (top, bottom, left, right, front, and back) viewpoints. In order to distinguish between the viewpoints and UCSs, I turned UCSORTHO off for the following section.

TABLE 22.1   Standard Viewpoints

Viewpoint	Description	Example
Top (see Note after table)	The top view is the plan view. You're looking at the model from a bird's-eye perspective, suspended over the model. VPOINT equivalent: 0,0,1.	
Bottom	The bottom view is the plan view for groundhogs. It's not very useful for buildings, but it may be useful for 3D mechanical drawings. Notice the direction of the UCS icon. If you're using the 2D UCS icon, you'll notice that the square is missing at the axis intersection, indicating that you're viewing from the negative Z direction, or from "underneath." VPOINT equivalent: 0,0,–1.	
Left	The left view shows you your model from the left side, of course. In architecture, it would be one of the elevation views. Notice that the text appears backward. This is because the text was drawn from the right view. VPOINT equivalent: –1,0,0.	
Right	The right view shows you your model from the right side. Like the left view, the right view is an elevation view. Notice that the text now appears correctly because it was drawn from this view. VPOINT equivalent: 1,0,0.	
Front	The front view, another elevation view, shows your model from the front. The text, stating that the front faces the east, doesn't represent any rule in AutoCAD or AutoCAD LT. I simply use it to help you to see the differences in the sides of the house. VPOINT equivalent: 0,–1,0.	
Back	The back view, another elevation view, shows your model from the back. Here you see the text of the front of the house, shown backward. VPOINT equivalent: 0,1,0.	

continued

TABLE 22.1 *(continued)*

Viewpoint	Description	Example
Southwest	The SW (southwest) isometric view shows you your model from a diagonal viewpoint in all three dimensions. Notice how one corner of the house is closest to you (the corner between the left and front views), and how you're also looking at the house from a view halfway between a side view and the top view. The isometric views are excellent for viewing all the 3D objects in a drawing. As you can see, many more objects are visible than with the top view or any of the side views. VPOINT equivalent: –1,–1,1.	
Southeast	The SE (southeast) isometric view also shows your model from a diagonal viewpoint in all three dimensions. Here you're looking at the house at the corner between the right and front views, as well as halfway between a side view and the top view. You see the same objects as you do in SW isometric view. However, in a drawing not as symmetrical as the house, one view may bring certain objects to the front so that you can select them. VPOINT equivalent: 1,–1,1.	
Northeast	The NE (northeast) isometric view shows your model from the corner between the right and the back views, as well as halfway between a side view and the top view. VPOINT equivalent: 1,1,1.	
Northwest	The NW (northwest) isometric view shows your model from the corner between the left and the back views, as well as halfway between a side view and the top view. VPOINT equivalent: –1,1,1.	

> **NOTE**
> You can also access the top view by typing plan on the command line. Note that the PLAN command does not change the UCS, even though you choose to see the plan view of a different UCS. This actually makes it very flexible because you can see what your drawing looks like from a different UCS without actually changing the UCS. The PLAN command is explained later in this chapter.

Note that the terms Northeast, Southwest, and so on are not related to any real directions. However, you can specify a North direction for your model. You would generally do this in an architectural or civil engineering drawing. To do so, choose Render tab ➪ Sun & Location panel ➪ Set Location (in AutoCAD only). If you are using AutoCAD LT, enter **geographiclocation** (the command name) on the command line.

You can then choose to specify the geographic information by importing a KML or KMZ file, by importing information from Google Earth, or by manually entering location values. KML and KMZ files are Google Earth file formats. For the Google Earth option to work, you need to install Google Earth (at http://earth.google.com). If you choose to enter location values, the Geographic Location dialog box opens. Here you can enter latitude and longitude measurements manually, or use a map. You specify which hemisphere (North/South and East/West) you're in. You can also set the time zone, North direction, and up direction (Z axis), and specify an elevation for a specific coordinate.

If you start the GEOGRAPHICLOCATION command in a drawing that already has a location, you get a choice to edit the current location, redefine it (start from scratch), or remove it.

Using DDVPOINT

If the standard views aren't sufficient for your needs, DDVPOINT can give you both flexibility and precision. To use this command, enter **ddvpoint** ↵ on the command line to open the Viewpoint Presets dialog box, as shown in Figure 22.2. This dialog box enables you to set the view to a great degree of accuracy.

FIGURE 22.2

The Viewpoint Presets dialog box

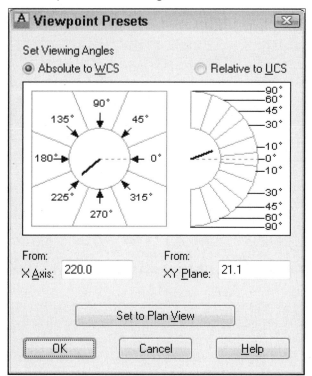

The left side of the dialog box determines the angle from the X axis in the XY plane. These angles work as follows:

270	Front view
0	Right view
90	Back view
180	Left view

Other angles result in viewpoints between these views. For example, an angle of 315 degrees enables you to look at your drawing from a view between front and right. This is similar to the SE isometric view.

The right side of the dialog box determines the angle from the XY plane, in the Z direction. A 0-degree angle enables you to look at your drawing from the front, back, or one side (elevation views), depending on the setting on the left part of the dialog box. Often you want to look at your drawing from above. A 90-degree angle shows you the plan view. An angle between 0 and 90 gives you a slanted view from the top, such as for one of the isometric standard views. (The isometric views set the angle from the XY plane to 35.3 degrees.)

> **TIP**
>
> There's an art to using the two dials to set the view angle that you want. If you click the inside border of either one, close to the indicator needle, you set the angle based on exactly where you clicked. This results in uneven degrees, such as 47.6. However, if you click the outside border of either image, or the numbers themselves, the angle is rounded to the value in the segment.

When you open the dialog box, the black needles indicate the angles for the current view. When you change the angles, the black (or white) needles move to the new angle, but the original needle remains to indicate the current angle. This enables you to constantly see the current angles for reference. Beneath the dials are text boxes that reflect your choices. You can simply type the angles that you want in the text boxes. A very handy Set to Plan View button is at the bottom of the dialog box. This enables you to quickly return to plan view when you become a little dizzy from flying around your model.

The default is to view the drawing based on the WCS. However, sometimes you need to see your drawing relative to a UCS that you've created. To do so, click Relative to UCS. Click OK after you finish making your changes.

> **TIP**
>
> Keep the number of UCSs to the minimum necessary and save them. When possible, use a new viewpoint instead of creating a new UCS. The Dynamic UCS feature (available in AutoCAD only) creates temporary UCSs; I discuss this feature in Chapter 21.

Using the ViewCube to View Your Drawing

The ViewCube is a quick, visual way to switch your viewpoint. You can think of the preset viewpoints as sides, edges, or corners of a cube. The ViewCube is semitransparent until you hover the cursor over it. To display a viewpoint, click the side, edge, or corner that you want. You can also drag the

ViewCube to interactively change your viewpoint. In this way, you can easily make small adjustments as you work. This is very similar to using 3D Orbit, which I discuss later in this chapter. Figure 22.3 shows the ViewCube.

FIGURE 22.3

The ViewCube is an easy way to change the viewpoint of your 3D model.

AutoCAD Only
The ViewCube (NAVVCUBE command) is not available in AutoCAD LT.

22

The ViewCube has some additional features:

- **UCS menu.** Below the ViewCube is a list of saved and default UCSs. You can switch UCSs and create a new UCS.
- **Compass.** You see the four directions marked around the ViewCube. The directions are based on the settings for the GEOGRAPHICLOCATION command, discussed earlier in this chapter. You can click one of the directions, or the arrow next to it, to view the model from that direction.
- **Home.** Click the Home button at the top-left corner of the ViewCube area (only visible when you hover the cursor over it) to display the model at its default viewpoint, which is either the extents of the drawing (for preexisting models), or a top/left/front view. You can specify the definition of the Home view. To do so, set the view the way you want it, right-click the ViewCube, and choose Set Current View as Home.

You can right-click the ViewCube and choose the type of projection: parallel or perspective. I discuss these projections later in this chapter.

Choose View tab ➪ Windows panel ➪ User Interface drop-down menu ➪ ViewCube (the NAVVCUBE command) to turn the display of the ViewCube on and off. You can also toggle the display of the ViewCube by clicking the Viewport Controls, located in the upper-left corner of the drawing area, and then choosing ViewCube. To specify display settings, right-click the ViewCube and choose ViewCube Settings. When you choose the Settings option, the ViewCube Settings dialog box opens, where you can do the following:

- Specify in which corner of the screen the ViewCube appears
- Set the ViewCube size
- Set the ViewCube opacity when inactive
- Display or hide the UCS menu
- Snap to the closest view when dragging. If you want to make small adjustments by dragging, uncheck this check box.
- Zoom to extents after a view change

- Use view transitions when switching views to create a smooth, animated change
- Orient ViewCube to the current UCS
- Keep the scene upright. You can make sure that you can't turn the model upside-down.
- Show or hide the compass
- Restore default settings

Compare the ViewCube with the 3D Orbit feature, covered later in this chapter. Then you can choose the feature that will provide you with better control or quicker results.

Creating a Named View with a Camera

A camera is a way to define and save a 3D view. When you save a named view by using the VIEW command, you display the view that you want and then save it. When you use a camera, you define a location and a target to define the view. AutoCAD places a camera glyph (visual representation) in the drawing to represent the view. You can select the camera glyph and edit its properties by using its grips. You can also edit the camera's properties in the Properties palette. By default, the camera glyph does not plot. Cameras are listed in the View Manager dialog box, along with other named views.

Creating a camera

 To create a view with a camera, choose Render tab ⇨ Camera panel ⇨ Create Camera to start the CAMERA command. At the `Specify camera location:` prompt, specify a coordinate for the camera. You can place the coordinate on the XY plane and change the height later, using the Height option. At the `Specify target location:` prompt, specify the target, which is what the camera is looking at.

Note
The Camera panel is not displayed by default. To display it, right-click any area on the Render tab and choose Show Panels ⇨ Camera.

The next prompt offers the following options:

- **?.** Displays the `Enter camera name(s) to list <*>:` prompt. Press Enter to list all current camera names and other named views in the drawing.
- **Name.** Lets you name the camera. If you don't use this option, the command assigns a default camera name, starting with Camera1 and so on.
- **LOcation.** Use this option to change the camera location.
- **Height.** Sets the camera height. You can use this to change the Z value of the camera after specifying its location on the XY plane.
- **Target.** Use this option to change the camera's target.

- **LEns.** Defines the field (width) of view in degrees, using a camera lens length in millimeters. Table 22.2 describes the relationship between lens length and field of view.
- **Clipping.** Creates front and back clipping planes for the view.
- **View.** You can use this option to make the camera's view current. Use the Yes suboption. This ends the command.
- **eXit.** Exits the command.

TABLE 22.2   Lens Length and Field-of-View Equivalents

Lens Length	Field of View (in Degrees)
15 mm	100
20 mm	84
24 mm	74
28 mm	65
35 mm	54
50 mm	40
85 mm	24
135 mm	15
200 mm	10

You can also create a camera from the Tool Palette window. Display the Cameras tool palette tab. Choose one of the three cameras (Normal, Wide-angle, or Extreme Wide-angle) and drag it onto the drawing area. Release the mouse button. Then click to place the camera and click again to specify the target.

When you create the camera, you can set its view to current by using the View option. After you change the view, you can get back to the view by choosing it in the View Manager and setting it to current. You can also select the camera, right-click, and choose Set Camera View.

Editing a camera

When you edit a camera, the Camera Preview window opens to show you a preview of the camera's view, as shown in Figure 22.4. You can change the visual style within the Camera Preview window, using the Visual Style drop-down list. (This doesn't change the visual style in the main drawing area.)

To edit a camera, select it and use its grips to change the camera location, target location, and lens length (field of view), as shown in Figure 22.5. Each grip has a tooltip to tell you its purpose. When you select a grip to make it hot, you can enter a new coordinate in the Dynamic Input tooltip. You can also edit the properties of a selected camera in the Properties palette.

FIGURE 22.4

The Camera Preview window shows you what the camera's view will look like.

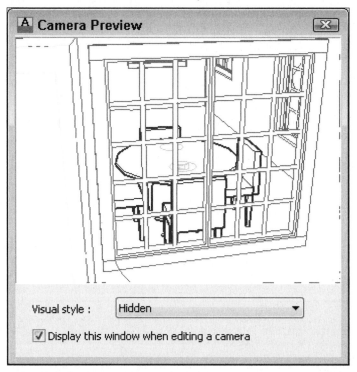

ON THE WEB
The drawing that you need for the following exercise on using standard viewpoints, CAMERA, the ViewCube, and DDVPOINT, ab22-a.dwg, is available from the Drawings download on the companion website.

STEPS: Using Standard Viewpoints, CAMERA, the ViewCube, and DDVPOINT

1. Open ab22-a.dwg available from the Drawings download on the companion website.

2. Save it as ab22-01.dwg in your AutoCAD Bible folder. It shows the same house used in Table 22.1, from the SE isometric view.

3. Type **ucsortho** ⏎ **0** ⏎ to turn off the UCSORTHO system variable. Turning off UCSORTHO prevents the UCS from changing whenever you switch to one of the six orthogonal viewpoints.

 4. Choose View tab ⇨ Views panel ⇨ Views drop-down list ⇨ Top.

5. From the Viewport Control at the upper-left corner of the drawing area, click Viewport Controls (the middle of the three controls) and choose Bottom, or choose View tab⇨Views panel⇨Views drop-down list⇨Bottom.

6. Choose Front from the same menu. You see the front of the house with the trees.

7. Choose Right from the same menu. You see the text North side.

8. Choose NW Isometric from the same menu. You're looking at the back of the house.

9. Choose SW Isometric from the same menu. You're looking at the front of the house. If you want, try the rest of the standard viewpoints.

10. Choose Top again.

11. If you have AutoCAD, click the bottom-right corner of the ViewCube's central square. Because this corner is between the South and East directions, as shown by the compass, you now see the SE Isometric view.

12. Click Top in the ViewCube to see the top of the house.

13. To see the front view of the house, click the S in the compass, or the arrow just above the S.

22

FIGURE 22.5

Grip-editing a camera

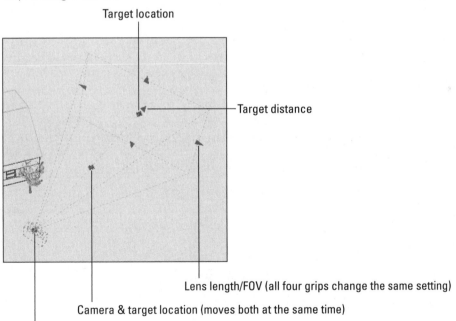

Target location

Target distance

Lens length/FOV (all four grips change the same setting)

Camera & target location (moves both at the same time)

Camera location

14. If you are using AutoCAD, choose Render tab ⇨ Camera panel ⇨ Create Camera. (If you are using AutoCAD LT, skip to the next step.) If you don't see the Camera panel, right-click any blank area on the Render tab and choose Show Panels ⇨ Camera. Follow the prompts:

```
Current camera settings: Height=0" Lens Length=50.0000 mm
Specify camera location: 27',-15' ↵
Specify target location: 15',20' ↵
Enter an option [?/Name/LOcation/Height/Target/LEns/Clipping/View/
    eXit]<eXit>: n ↵
Enter name for new camera <Camera1>: thruFrontDoor ↵
Enter an option [?/Name/LOcation/Height/Target/LEns/Clipping/View/
    eXit]<eXit>: h ↵
Specify camera height <14'>: 5' ↵
Enter an option [?/Name/LOcation/Height/Target/LEns/Clipping/View/
    eXit]<eXit>: le ↵
Specify lens length in mm <35.0000>: 28 ↵
Enter an option [?/Name/LOcation/Height/Target/LEns/Clipping/View/
    eXit]<eXit>: v ↵
Switch to camera view? [Yes/No] <No>: y ↵
```

15. Type **ddvpoint** ↵ on the command line to open the Viewpoint Presets dialog box. Set the left dial (angle from X axis) to 315 degrees by clicking the number 315. Set the right dial (angle from XY plane) to 60 degrees by clicking the second-from-the-top segment pointed to by the number 60. Click OK. You see a view somewhat like the SE isometric view, but from much higher up.

16. Repeat the DDVPOINT command. In the X Axis text box, type **240**. In the XY Plane text box, type **5**. Click OK. You view the house from slightly off the ground, much as you might see it if you were walking up to the house.

17. If you have AutoCAD, choose View tab ⇨ Visual Styles panel ⇨ Visual Styles drop-down list ⇨ Hidden. If you have AutoCAD LT, type **hide** ↵ on the command line. Notice that you can see the windows on the far side through the windows on your side of the house.

18. Choose View tab ⇨ Views panel ⇨ View Manager. Click the New button. In the New View/Shot Properties (or New View in AutoCAD LT) dialog box, type the name of the view, **walk up**. Click OK twice to return to your drawing. It should look like Figure 22.6.

FIGURE 22.6

The final view of the house

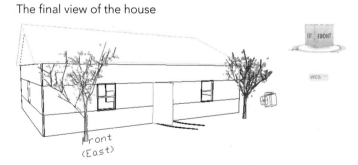

19. If you're working on someone else's computer or want UCSORTHO on, type **ucsortho** ↵ **1** ↵ to turn it back on.

20. Save the drawing.

> **NOTE**
>
> In AutoCAD, when you save the view, by default you save it with the current visual style. Therefore, if you change the visual style and restore the view, the visual style changes back to the one you used when you saved the view. If you don't want to save the visual style, choose <None> from the Visual Style drop-down list in the New View/Shot Properties dialog box.

Adding a Background to a Named View

When you save a named view in the View Manager, you can add a background. I discussed the View Manager in Chapter 8, but here I explain how to add a background. Backgrounds only apply to 3D views. They are not available in AutoCAD LT.

You can add a solid, gradient, or image background to a named view. Whenever you display that view, the background appears if the current visual style has backgrounds turned on (the VSBACKGROUNDS system variable). Backgrounds, especially image backgrounds, are usually used in the context of rendering, and I include an exercise on adding a background in Bonus Chapter 2.

To create a view with a background, choose View tab ⇨ Views panel ⇨ View Manager. In the View Manager, click the New button to define the new view. At the bottom of the New View/Shot Properties dialog box, choose Solid, Gradient, or Image from the drop-down list.

> **NOTE**
>
> You can specify lighting in real-world units. To turn on this feature, you set the LIGHTINGUNITS system variable to 1 or 2. By default, this feature is on (set to 2). When photometry is on, you have an additional background option, Sun & Sky. If you choose this option, the Adjust Sun & Sky Background dialog box opens. The settings in this dialog box are the same for creating sunlight when photometry is on. I explain this feature, called *photometry*, in Bonus Chapter 2 where I discuss lights.

The Background dialog box opens, shown in Figure 22.7, after choosing the Image option and clicking Browse to choose an image file.

> **NOTE**
>
> You can open the Background dialog box directly by using the BACKGROUND command.

FIGURE 22.7

The Background dialog box enables you to display a background while you work.

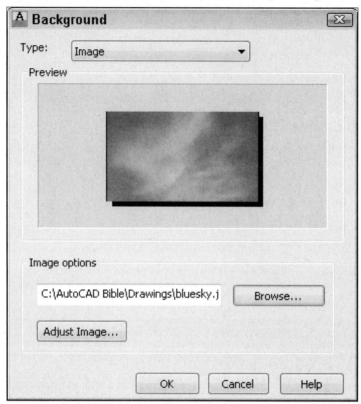

In the Background dialog box, you again have the opportunity to choose one of three options. To specify the background, choose one of the following:

- **Solid background.** Choose Solid (the default) from the Type drop-down list. Click the color swatch in the Color section. In the Select Color dialog box that opens, choose a color.
- **Gradient background.** Choose Gradient from the Type drop-down list. For a two-color gradient, uncheck the Three Color check box. Click in each color swatch to open the Select Color dialog box and choose a color. To rotate the gradient, enter a rotation angle in the Rotation text box or use the arrows to change the value.
- **Image background.** Choose Image from the Type drop-down list. Click the Browse button to choose an image file (in BMP, JPEG, TIF, PNG, TGA, GIF, or PCX format), and click Open. To adjust the position, scale, or offset of the image, click the Adjust Image button. In the Adjust Background Image dialog box, you can choose a position (Center, Stretch, or Tile) to specify how the image fits the viewport. You can also click the Offset or Scale option button and use

the sliders to change the offset or scale of the image. Click OK when you're done. You can see an example of an image background near the end of Bonus Chapter 2.

When you specify the background, click OK to return to the View Manager, and click OK again to return to your drawing.

To edit a background, choose the view from the View Manager, click the Background Override item in the General category, click the down arrow, and choose Edit. You can also choose <None> to remove the image.

> **NOTE**
>
> The New View/Shot Properties dialog box lets you define shot properties. I discuss shot properties and the related ShowMotion feature later in this chapter.

Displaying a Quick Plan View

The PLAN command is a quick way to return to plan view. Type **plan** ↵. This command has three options:

- **Current Ucs.** This is the default. You see the plan view of the current UCS.
- **Ucs.** The UCS option enables you to choose a named UCS. Type **?** ↵ to see a list of the named UCSs. Otherwise, type the name of a UCS.
- **World.** This option gives you the plan view of the WCS. If your current UCS is the WCS, there is no difference between this option and the Current UCS option.

> **AUTOCAD ONLY**
>
> The Express Tools' extended PLAN command, EXPLAN, prompts you to select objects so that you can see the plan view zoomed in on those objects. Choose Express Tools tab ⇨ Tools panel (expanded) ⇨ Extended Plan. For information about installing Express Tools, see Bonus Chapter 15.

Returning to Plan View When You Change the UCS

If you like plan views, you'll love UCSFOLLOW. UCSFOLLOW is a system variable that returns you to plan view whenever you change the UCS. It's for those who like to find their bearings in plan view first, before going on to change the viewpoint in another UCS.

The default value is 0 (off), which means that your drawing does not return to plan view. In other words, your display remains unchanged when you change the UCS. Type **ucsfollow** and change the value to 1 to turn UCSFOLLOW on. From then on, your drawing automatically displays the plan view when you change the UCS.

Displaying Parallel and Perspective Projections

You may have noticed when you open AutoCAD with the default 3D environment that the grid lines look like they're receding into the distance. That's because AutoCAD is displaying a *perspective* view, which makes parallel lines converge as they get farther away. Because this is how parallel lines look in real life (try looking down a road into the distance), a perspective view looks more realistic than a parallel view that keeps lines parallel, regardless of their distance. However, when you zoom in, objects may appear distorted. Use a perspective view when you want to convey a realistic sense of depth. In general, perspective view is most useful in architectural settings. AutoCAD LT doesn't include perspective projections, but displays a perspective view if perspective projection is set using AutoCAD. The PERSPECTIVE system variable controls the current view. A value of 0 turns off perspective view; 1 turns it on.

Using 3D Orbit

The 3D Orbit feature is a fully interactive way to change your viewpoint in real-time. Using 3D Orbit is like orbiting the earth to view any continent or ocean below. When you enter 3D Orbit mode, you cannot use other commands. In this regard, 3D Orbit is like Realtime Pan and Realtime Zoom. Similarly, you can press Esc or Enter to exit 3D Orbit mode. You access the 3D Orbit options by right-clicking in the drawing area to display the 3D Orbit shortcut menu.

> **AUTOCAD ONLY**
> 3D Orbit is not available in AutoCAD LT. This entire section, including the exercise, is for AutoCAD only.

Use 3D Orbit for fine control over the viewpoint. To quickly change the viewpoint to one of the preset views, you can use the ViewCube, covered earlier in this chapter. (You can also drag the ViewCube, which then functions similarly to 3D Orbit.)

Starting 3D Orbit

 To start the 3DORBIT command, choose View tab ⇨ Navigate panel ⇨ Orbit drop-down menu ⇨ Orbit. If another mode of 3D Orbit is active, right-click and choose Other Navigation Modes ⇨ Constrained Orbit or type **1**. You enter 3D Orbit mode, and AutoCAD displays the 3D Orbit cursor, as shown in Figure 22.8. The term *constrained* means that the orbit is restricted to either the XY plane or the Z direction (but not both at once).

> **TIP**
> You can use 3D Orbit transparently, that is, in the middle of another command. Just press and hold Shift and your mouse's wheel (using it like a button), rotate your model as you want, and release the buttons. You then continue the command in progress. This way of using the 3DORBIT command without actually executing the command makes it very easy to navigate your model. You can also use 3D Orbit in the Block Editor when editing 3D blocks.

The 3D Orbit mode includes the ability to zoom and pan. Therefore, you can use this command for more than just orbiting.

FIGURE 22.8

3D Orbit mode allows you to change the viewpoint of your drawing in real-time.

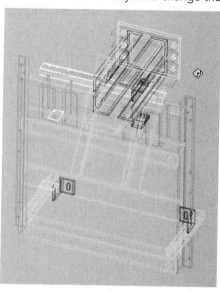

TIP

For faster performance, select only the objects that you want to view with 3D Orbit before starting the command. Objects that you did not select disappear while you're in 3D Orbit mode. They reappear as soon as you leave 3D Orbit mode.

Navigating with 3D Orbit

The default 3D Orbit mode is Constrained Orbit. Drag to the left or right to rotate the model around on the XY plane, and drag up or down to rotate the model along the Z axis. You can't rotate the model upside down in Constrained Orbit mode. Drag diagonally to create isometric views.

If you need more freedom, you can use Free Orbit mode. Choose View tab ⇨ Navigate panel ⇨ Orbit drop-down menu ⇨ Free Orbit. If another mode of 3D Orbit is active, right-click and choose Other Navigation Modes ⇨ Free Orbit or type **2**. In Free Orbit mode, you have less control but more options.

Free Orbit mode displays an *arcball* and has four cursors that affect how your model rotates. Each cursor is location based. As you move your cursor to a new location, the cursor shape changes, and the type of rotation changes. The arcball is shown in Figure 22.9.

FIGURE 22.9

3D Orbit's Free mode uses an arcball.

Arcball

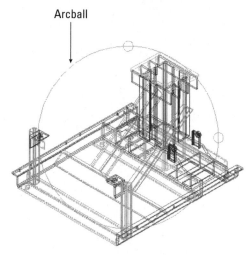

You use the arcball in the following ways:

 • **Rolling with the circular arrow cursor.** When you place your cursor outside the arcball, it takes the shape of a circular arrow. As you click and drag around the outside of the arcball, your model turns around an imaginary axis that extends from the center of the arcball outward and perpendicular to the screen — that is, pointing at you. This type of rotation is called a *roll.*

 • **Rotating freely with the sphere and lines cursor.** As soon as you move your cursor within the arcball, it takes the shape of a small sphere encircled by two lines. As you click and drag within the arcball, your model moves around the center of the arcball in the direction that you drag. Imagine that your model is encased in a transparent sphere, similar to a gerbil or hamster ball. As you drag the cursor, you're rotating the sphere around its center point. If you drag from one edge of the arcball to its opposite edge, you can release the mouse, move back to your starting point, and then click and drag again in the same direction. When you do this a few times, you rotate your model 360 degrees. You achieve the best results by dragging in a line in any direction, rather than around and around.

 • **Rotating around the vertical axis with the horizontal ellipse cursor.** When you move your cursor over either the left or right quadrant circle on the arcball, it becomes a horizontal ellipse. As you click and drag from either quadrant, your model rotates around the arcball's vertical axis, which extends from the top quadrant to the bottom quadrant. Although your cursor enters the arcball, it retains its horizontal ellipse form until you release the mouse button. You can drag from one quadrant to its opposite quadrant, release the mouse button, move back to your starting point, and then click and drag again in the same direction. When you do this a few times, you rotate your model 360 degrees.

- **Rotating around the horizontal axis with the vertical ellipse cursor.** When you move your cursor over either the top or bottom quadrant circle on the arcball, it becomes a vertical ellipse. As you click and drag from either quadrant, your model rotates around the arcball's horizontal axis, which extends from the left quadrant to the right quadrant. You can drag from one quadrant to its opposite quadrant, release the mouse button, move back to your starting point, and then click and drag again in the same direction. When you do this a few times, you rotate your model 360 degrees.

Using the 3D Orbit visual aids

3D Orbit includes three visual aids that can help you find your bearings:

- **Compass.** Displays a sphere that is made up of three dashed lines labeled as the X, Y, and Z axes. The lines look like the threads of a baseball.
- **Grid.** Displays a grid of lines representing the XY plane. The Z coordinate of the grid is equal to the value of the ELEVATION system variable, which is set to 0 (zero) by default. You can specify the structure of the grid with the GRIDUNIT system variable. You can set this value by right-clicking the Grid Display button on the status bar and choosing Settings before you use this visual aid.
- **UCS icon.** Displays a shaded, three-dimensional 3D UCS icon. The X axis is red, the Y axis is green, and the Z axis is blue.

You would rarely want to use all three visual aids. The compass and grid can both interfere with viewing your model, so use them temporarily when needed.

To display the visual aids, right-click while in 3D Orbit mode and choose Visual Aids from the shortcut menu. Then choose the aid that you want from the submenu. To turn off the visual aids, follow the same procedure — the submenu items toggle the visual aids on and off when you click them.

> **NOTE**
> If you choose a visual style (other than the default 2D wireframe), the visual aids remain active after you exit 3D Orbit. You can switch to the 2D wireframe visual style, as explained earlier in this chapter, or you can re-enter 3D Orbit and turn off the visual aids.

Creating a continuous orbit

Absolutely the coolest feature of 3D Orbit — and one of the coolest features of AutoCAD as a whole — is continuous orbit. Continuous orbit enables you to choose a direction of rotation and then let go. 3D Orbit automatically continues the rotation in the same direction and continues it until you change or stop it. With continuous orbit, who needs screensavers? Here's how it works:

1. Choose View tab ⇨ Navigate panel ⇨ Orbit drop-down menu ⇨ Continuous Orbit. If 3D Orbit mode is active, right-click and choose Other Navigation Modes ⇨ Continuous Orbit or type **3**.

2. Click and drag in the direction of rotation that you want to create. The faster you drag, the faster the resulting orbit.

3. Release your mouse button. Your model continues to rotate in the same direction. All you do is watch.

Continuous orbit is an ideal way to view your model. As your model rotates, you can pick out any errors and then stop continuous orbit to fix them. You can change the direction of your continuous orbit at any time by clicking and dragging in a new direction and then releasing the mouse button. To stop continuous orbit, choose any other 3D Orbit mode or click in the drawing area.

Resetting the view

You can end up with some strange views of your model when using 3D Orbit, so AutoCAD provides a way to reset your view to the view that was current when you first started 3D Orbit. With any 3D Orbit mode active, right-click and choose Reset View from the shortcut menu.

Refining your 3D Orbit view

3D Orbit offers many options for refining your view so that you see just the view that you want. You can pan and zoom, adjust the camera distance, create parallel and perspective views, set clipping planes, or display a preset view. You can also start Walk or Fly mode, as discussed in the Chapter 22 Addendum, available on the companion website.

Because you cannot use other commands while in 3D Orbit mode, you access most of these options by right-clicking in the drawing area to access the 3D Orbit shortcut menu.

Panning in 3D Orbit

To pan in 3D Orbit mode, right-click and choose Other Navigation Modes ⇨ Pan from the 3D Orbit shortcut menu or type **9**. You see the familiar hand cursor. Click and drag to pan, in the same way that you normally pan in real-time. To stop panning, right-click and choose another mode.

Zooming in 3D Orbit

To zoom in 3D Orbit, right-click and choose Other Navigation Modes ⇨ Zoom from the 3D Orbit shortcut menu or type **8**. You see the familiar magnifying glass cursor with a plus (+) and a minus (–) sign. Click and drag in the direction of the plus sign (toward the top of your screen) to zoom in; click and drag in the direction of the minus sign (toward the bottom of your screen) to zoom out, just as you do when you normally use zoom in real-time. To stop zooming, switch to any other mode.

Using Zoom options in 3D Orbit

To zoom to a window in 3D Orbit, right-click and choose Zoom Window from the shortcut menu. Your cursor displays a small rectangle. Click and drag, and then release the mouse button to define the two corners of the window.

To zoom to drawing extents in 3D Orbit, right-click and choose Zoom Extents. To return to the previous view, right-click and choose Zoom Previous.

Adjusting the camera distance

You can adjust the distance between the viewer, called the *camera,* and the target, which by default is set to the center of the 3D view (this view may be different from the center of your model). Changing this camera distance is equivalent to zooming in and out.

To adjust the camera distance in 3D Orbit, right-click and choose Other Navigation Modes ⇨ Adjust Distance from the shortcut menu or type **4**. The cursor changes to a horizontal line with a double-headed arrow pointing up and down. Click and drag toward the top of your screen to move the camera closer to your objects — similar to zooming in. Click and drag toward the bottom of your screen to move the camera away from your objects — similar to zooming out.

Controlling view properties

When you use 3D Orbit, the Properties palette displays special properties that relate to 3D Orbit features, as follows:

- **View Height** is a way to specify the distance of the imaginary camera. In other words, you can use this property to zoom in and out on your model. A larger number makes your model look smaller because the distance (or height) of the camera from the model increases.

- **View Width** is another way to zoom in and out. Here you specify the width of the view of the imaginary camera. A larger number makes your model look smaller because the view encompasses a larger area (and your model is a smaller part of that area).

- **Lens Length** and **Field of View** define the angle of the view. I discuss these concepts in the section "Creating a Named View with a Camera" earlier in this chapter.

22

To change one of these properties, click its row in the Properties palette. Type a new value and press Enter.

Creating parallel and perspective views

To create a perspective view in 3D Orbit, right-click and choose Perspective. To return to parallel view, choose Parallel. For more information on perspective views, see the section "Displaying Parallel and Perspective Projections" earlier in this chapter.

Using a preset view

After you use 3D Orbit a few times, your model may appear askew, with no indication of how to return it to a viewpoint that you can comprehend. You can switch to any of the preset views discussed at the beginning of this chapter. From 3D Orbit, right-click and choose Preset Views from the shortcut menu. Then choose one of the standard viewpoints on the submenu list.

ON THE WEB

The drawing that you need for the following exercise on working in 3D Orbit, ab22-b.dwg, is available from the Drawings download on the companion website.

STEPS: Working in 3D Orbit

1. Open ab22-b.dwg available from the Drawings download on the companion website. This is a 3D chair shown from a Northeast isometric view.

2. Choose View tab ⇨ Navigate panel ⇨ Orbit drop-down menu ⇨ Orbit.

3. Place the mouse cursor to the right of the chair in the middle (vertically) of the screen. Drag to the left twice until the chair turns around completely and is back to approximately its original position.

4. Place the cursor below the chair and drag up until it stops. Drag down until the chair is in its original position. Place the cursor above the chair and drag down until it stops. Return the chair to its original position again.

5. Place the cursor above the chair until you are looking down at it — a Top view. The chair is still rotated. Drag from the left to the right until the chair's bottom is horizontal on the screen.

6. Right-click and choose Other Navigation Modes ⇨ Free Orbit. Place the cursor inside the arcball and drag in various directions to see that you now have more freedom to tumble the chair upside down.

7. Right-click and choose Zoom Previous to return to the Top view.

8. Type **1** to return to Constrained Orbit mode. The arcball disappears.

9. Right-click and choose Other Navigation Modes ⇨ Continuous Orbit. Click and drag with the cursor, making a small movement from right to left, and then release the mouse button. You may need to try this a couple of times to find a continuous orbit that you like. Try clicking and dragging in a different direction to change the direction of the continuous orbit, and then release the mouse button.

10. Type **1** to stop the continuous orbit.

11. Right-click and choose Reset View to re-display the chair exactly in its original view.

12. Type **9** (pan). Pan the chair to the right a little.

13. Right-click and choose Other Navigation Modes ⇨ Zoom. Drag upward to zoom the chair in slightly.

14. Right-click and choose Preset Views ⇨ NW Isometric.

15. Press Esc to exit 3D Orbit mode.

Don't save your drawing.

Using ShowMotion to Cycle Through Views

To show a drawing to others, or better visualize multiple angles of a model, you can create named views called *shots*, and then use the ShowMotion feature to display them one after another as a presentation. You can add motion and animation to your shots.

AutoCAD Only
The ShowMotion feature is not available in AutoCAD LT.

Creating shots

You start by creating the shots that you want. You may want to plan these in advance, by creating a storyboard to lay out the shots in the desired order. To create a shot, display the desired view, including the viewpoint, zoom, and visual style. (I discuss visual styles later in this chapter.) Then click the ShowMotion button on the Navigation bar to display the ShowMotion toolbar at the bottom of your screen. If you do not see the ShowMotion button on the Navigation bar, click the Customize button at the bottom or on the right side of the Navigation bar and choose ShowMotion.

From the ShowMotion toolbar, choose New Shot (the NEWSHOT command) to open the New View/Shot Properties dialog box, with the Shot Properties tab on top, as shown in Figure 22.10. Alternatively, you can choose View tab ⇨ Views panel ⇨ View Manager, click New, and click the Shot Properties tab.

FIGURE 22.10

Use the Shot Properties tab of the New View/Shot Properties dialog box to specify the properties of a shot.

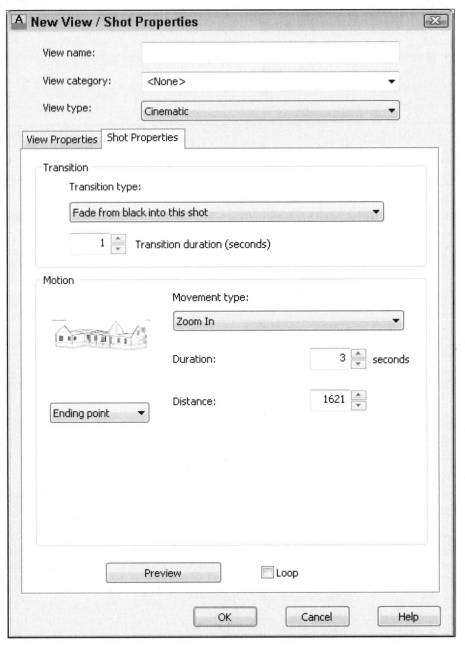

In the View Name text box, enter a name for the shot. You can create view categories, which are groups of shots. Use categories to help you organize many shots into sections. To create a view category, enter a name in the View Category text box. After you create a view category, you can choose it for subsequent shots from the View Category drop-down list.

From the View Type drop-down list, you can create three types of shots:

- **Still.** A single camera position (For more information on cameras, see "Creating a Named View with a Camera" earlier in this chapter.)
- **Cinematic.** A single camera position, plus camera movement
- **Recorded Walk.** Animation along a path

In the Transition section, choose a transition type from the drop-down list. The transition occurs between the display of the previous shot and the current shot that you are defining. You have three choices:

- **Fade from black into this shot.** Creates a fade transition to the shot from a black screen. Use this option when you want the fade effect and have a black background.
- **Fade from white into this shot.** Creates a fade transition to the shot from a white screen. Use this option when you want the fade effect and have a white background.
- **Cut to shot.** Immediately switches to the new shot.

Then choose the duration of the transition in seconds by entering a value or clicking the up or down arrow.

The bottom part of the dialog box changes, depending on the view type. For a still shot, you simply choose the duration, in seconds. For a cinematic shot, you start by choosing one of eight movement types. For example, you can zoom in or out. For a recorded walk, you return to your drawing and drag in the direction of the walk. Release the mouse button to stop recording. (See the section "Walking through a Model" in the Chapter 22 Addendum for another way to record a walk through your drawing.) You can preview the results by clicking the Preview button. You can also loop the entire presentation by clicking the Loop check box at the bottom. When you're done, click OK.

Continue to create new shots until you have the ones that you want. To modify any shot, right-click its thumbnail and choose Properties. Make your changes in the dialog box and click OK.

Displaying shots

To display the shots in order, use the NAVSMOTION command. Type **navsmotion** on the command line to display the ShowMotion toolbar at the bottom of your screen, as shown in Figure 22.11.

The ShowMotion feature displays two levels of thumbnails. The bottom level shows either the first of a set of shots or the first view in a view category. The upper level shows all the shots, organized by view categories, if any. As you pass your cursor over a thumbnail, it enlarges. When you hover the cursor over each thumbnail, two buttons appear — one to play or display the shot or view category, and the other to go to the beginning of that shot or view category.

FIGURE 22.11

The ShowMotion toolbar lets you control your presentation.

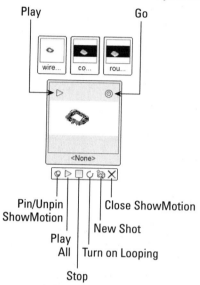

Play   Go

Pin/Unpin ShowMotion

Play All

Stop

Close ShowMotion

New Shot

Turn on Looping

The ShowMotion toolbar contains buttons that enable you to pin or unpin the ShowMotion interface, play the entire set of shots, stop the display, loop the display, create a new shot, and close the interface.

When you click the Play button on either a thumbnail or the toolbar, it becomes a Pause button that you can click to pause the display.

ON THE WEB

You can "walk" or "fly" through a model to see more clearly what it looks like and as a tool for showing your model to clients. You can also record a video. I cover these features in the Chapter 22 Addendum, available on the companion website.

Navigating with the SteeringWheels

The *SteeringWheel*, or *wheel* for short, is a navigation and viewing tool that combines several features in one place. The wheel appears at your cursor and comes in several variations, as shown in Figure 22.12.

FIGURE 22.12

The SteeringWheel has several variations, all of which help you navigate and view your drawing.

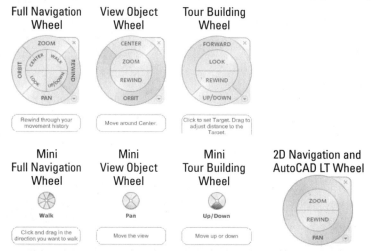

> **NOTE**
>
> The 2D Navigation and AutoCAD LT wheel doesn't offer any variations or settings. I cover the SteeringWheel for 2D navigation in Chapter 8. Here I explain the 3D navigation features, which are available in AutoCAD only.

 To display the wheel, choose View tab ⇨ Navigate panel ⇨ SteeringWheels (choose one from the drop-down list), or click the SteeringWheels button on the Navigation bar. If you are on a layout, or in AutoCAD LT, you see the 2D Navigation wheel.

To use any wheel, you place the cursor over the desired tool on the wheel, then click and drag. Each tool is in a section called a *wedge*. The default wheel in AutoCAD is shown at the top left in Figure 22.12 and includes the following tools:

- **Zoom.** Performs a real-time zoom.
- **Rewind.** Displays previous views in thumbnails. You can revert to any previous view by clicking its thumbnail.
- **Pan.** Pans the view.
- **Orbit.** Functions like the 3D Orbit feature, orbiting around a pivot point.
- **Center.** Defines the pivot point for orbiting. Press Ctrl as you zoom (or use the View Objects wheel) to provide a center point for zooming.
- **Walk.** Lets you walk through your drawing.
- **Look.** Swivels the view.
- **Up/Down.** Moves the view along the Z axis, like going up or down in an elevator. You drag along a Top-Bottom slider.

As you can see in Figure 22.12, the View Object and Tour Building wheels contain subsets of the tools in the default wheel. The mini wheels provide the same tools as their full counterparts, but they are smaller and don't contain the full labeling. All the wheels provide tooltips and brief instructional messages when you hover the cursor over a wedge.

To specify settings for the wheel (AutoCAD only), right-click it and choose SteeringWheel Settings to open the SteeringWheels Settings dialog box, where you can do the following:

- Set the wheel size and opacity.
- Specify if you want to see tooltips and messages.
- Specify if you want to see the wheel when you open AutoCAD.
- Specify settings for the Look, Orbit, Walk, Rewind, and Zoom tools.

When you're done with the wheel, press Esc or Enter. You can also click the wheel's X button (for the full-size version), or right-click and choose Close Wheel.

ON THE WEB

The original command for defining perspective views was DVIEW. Most people use the newer 3DORBIT now, but you may still find DVIEW helpful for its precise ways of defining a view. DVIEW is also useful if you want to create 3D views by using AutoLISP. The DVIEW command is not available in AutoCAD LT. I cover the DVIEW command in the Chapter 22 Addendum, available on the companion website.

Working with Visual Styles

Sometimes, you want to see the wireframes; other times, all the lines make visualizing your drawing difficult or you may want a more realistic look. Visual styles allow you to display your drawing in different ways, depending on your needs. Visual styles are very flexible, because you can create your own styles.

NOTE

Visual styles take the place of shading and the SHADEMODE command of earlier releases in AutoCAD. Visual styles are not available in AutoCAD LT. See the "Using the shading options in AutoCAD LT" section for more information about shading in AutoCAD LT.

Displaying visual styles in AutoCAD

To display a visual style in AutoCAD, choose View tab ⇨ Visual Styles panel ⇨ Visual Styles drop-down list. You have the following preset options:

- **2D Wireframe.** Displays objects in the familiar wireframe display, with no shading and the 2D UCS icon. It uses the 2D model space background (black by default) and offers only 2D options.
- **Conceptual.** Shades the objects, using the *Gooch* face style, which uses a gradation of cool and warm colors. The effect is somewhat cartoonlike, but can make details of your objects easier to see.

- **Hidden.** Hides the display of back edges and faces.
- **Realistic.** Shades the objects. This option displays materials that you have attached to the objects if materials are turned on. (You turn materials and textures on and off in the Materials panel of the Ribbon. I discuss materials in detail in Bonus Chapter 2.) If you are not working with materials, you'll get the clearest display with objects that are not black/white.
- **Shaded.** Shades objects, like the Realistic visual style, but shows only materials, not textures. This style doesn't show edges.
- **Shaded with Edges.** Like Shaded, but without edges.
- **Shades of Gray.** Shades objects with variations of gray.
- **Sketchy.** Adds a jitter edge. For an explanation, see the next section.
- **Wireframe.** A 3D version of 2D wireframe, with more options. Displays objects in wireframe, along with a shaded UCS icon. It uses the 3D parallel or perspective background, which by default is gray or shades of gray. (I explain these backgrounds later in this chapter.)
- **X-Ray.** Sets the opacity of faces to 50 percent.

Creating custom visual styles

The full power of visual styles is apparent when you create your own. To create your own visual style, choose View tab ⇨ Visual Styles panel ⇨ Visual Styles drop-down list ⇨ Visual Styles Manager to open the Visual Styles Manager palette, as shown in Figure 22.13.

To create a new visual style, click the Create New Visual Style button in the Visual Styles Manager to start from default settings. To use the settings of an existing style as a basis, select the visual style that most resembles the style that you want to create, right-click it, and choose Copy. Then right-click in the Visual Styles Manager and choose Paste. Then change the settings. The settings in the Visual Styles Manager fall into three groups: Face, Environment, and Edge.

Face settings determine how the faces of 3D objects look. You can set the following options:

- **Face Style.** You can set the face style to None (like 3D Wireframe or 3D Hidden), Gooch (used by Conceptual), or Realistic (used by Realistic).
- **Lighting Quality.** By default, the lighting is smoothed over curved objects. You can turn this off for a faceted look. The Smoothest option provides better results.
- **Highlight Intensity.** Controls the size of highlights created by lighting on objects without materials. The default is –30 and the value can range from –100 to 100. Larger numbers result in larger highlights. A negative number turns off highlights.
- **Opacity.** Sets the opacity of the faces.

Environment settings affect the display of shadows and backgrounds. You can turn these on or off. You add a background by using the VIEW command, as I explained earlier in this chapter.

Edge settings affect how the edges of your 3D models look. Edges are the lines or curves that border the faces. You can choose from three edge modes: Facet Edges, Isolines, or None. The Wireframe (3D) visual style uses isolines to give you a better sense of curves. The Hidden visual style uses facet edges to show just the edges and to provide a cleaner look. If you use isolines, you can choose the number of lines (the ISOLINES system variable). You can also decide if the isolines are always on top, which provides edges even to shaded objects.

FIGURE 22.13

The Visual Styles Manager enables you to create and save custom visual styles.

Export Selected Visual Style to Tool Palette

Apply Selected Visual Style to Current Viewport

Create New Visual Style

Delete Selected Visual Style

Visual Style swatches

Opacity

Highlight intensity

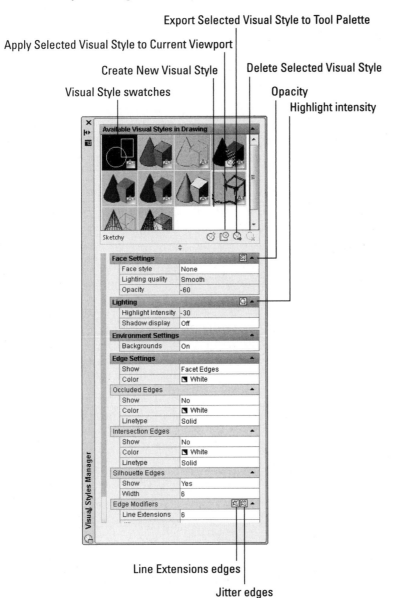

Line Extensions edges

Jitter edges

Two edge modifiers, line extension and jitter, help to provide a hand-drawn look. Jitter adds additional lines, as if you're sketching. Line extension extends lines past their ends, as shown in Figure 22.14.

FIGURE 22.14

You can get a hand-drawn look with the jitter and line extension features.

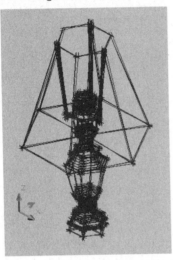

 To set overhang, display the Visual Styles Manager, click the Line Extensions Edges button in the Edge Modifiers section, and change the Line Extensions value.

 To set jitter, display the Visual Styles Manager, click Jitter Edges in the Edge Modifiers section, and change the Jitter value.

Fast silhouette edges are the lines or curves around the edge of a model. The Hidden and Conceptual visual styles use fast silhouette edges, and you can increase their width for a bolder look. In the Visual Styles Manager, change the settings under the Silhouette Edges section.

Intersection edges display lines where solids intersect. Figure 22.15 shows a model with a smaller box intersecting with a larger box. The left side does not display an intersection edge between the two boxes; the right side does.

When you're done designing your visual style, you can use the Apply Selected Visual Style to Current Viewport button to apply the visual style. The visual style also appears in the drop-down lists on the Home tab's View panel and the View tab's Visual Styles panel, so you can choose it from either location. You can also use the Delete the Selected Visual Style button to delete your visual styles; however, you can't delete the styles that come with AutoCAD.

FIGURE 22.15

You can choose to display edges where solids intersect.

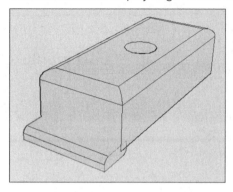 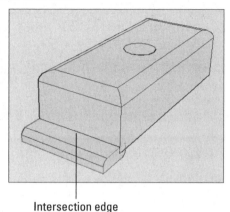

Intersection edge

Using the shading options in AutoCAD LT

The SHADEMODE command in AutoCAD LT has only two options, 2D Wireframe and Hidden. The 2D Wireframe option allows you to turn off the shading that was set for one of the options available only in AutoCAD; you can use this when you open a drawing that was created in AutoCAD. However, AutoCAD LT has a SHADE command that provides the following options:

- **256 Color (0).** Displays shaded faces. Shading is flat, but curved faces give the impression of gradual shading because they're broken up into many faces, each a slightly different color.

- **256 Color Edge Highlight (1).** Similar to 256 Color, but highlights edges using the same color as your drawing background.

- **16 Color Hidden Line (2).** Looks like a hidden display. The non-hidden edges are in the object's color, and the faces are the color of the background of the drawing area.

- **16 Color Filled (3).** The reverse of 16 Color Hidden Line so that the faces are in the object's color, and non-hidden edges are the background color.

You control which shading method the SHADE command uses by changing the value of the SHADEDGE system variable. Type **shadedge** ↵ on the command line and then enter the number to the right of the shading method above. After setting the shading method, type **shade** ↵ on the command line.

In AutoCAD LT, you cannot edit your objects in Shaded mode, which is a better-looking version of the HIDE command. If you regenerate the drawing, the shading goes away.

Display materials, textures, and lights as you work

Materials, textures, and lights are used in rendering, which is covered in Bonus Chapter 2. You can display materials and textures that you've attached to objects, even as you work, although doing so may slow down performance. You can also display lights. To display these features, you need to use the Realistic visual style, or a visual style that uses the Real face style.

AutoCAD Only

This section applies to AutoCAD only. AutoCAD LT does not include materials, textures, or lights, which is part of the rendering capability of AutoCAD.

 To display materials and textures, choose Render tab ⇨ Materials panel ⇨ Materials and Textures drop-down menu ⇨ Materials / Textures On.

 To display lights that you have created, choose Render tab ⇨ Lights panel (expanded) ⇨ Default Lighting so that the button is selected. You can adjust the brightness and contrast of lighting by expanding the Lights panel; drag the Brightness and Contrast sliders.

 If you don't see lights or materials, they may be off due to Adaptive Degradation. AutoCAD automatically turns off certain features, based on the capability of your graphics card and overall computer system. For more information, see Bonus Chapter 15.

On the Web

The drawing that you need for the following exercise on using and creating visual styles in a drawing, ab22-c.dwg, is available from the Drawings download on the companion website. This exercise is for AutoCAD only. AutoCAD LT doesn't offer these shading options.

STEPS: Using and Creating Visual Styles

1. Open ab22-c.dwg available from the Drawings download on the companion website.

2. Save it as ab22-02.dwg in your AutoCAD Bible folder. This drawing should display the 3D Wireframe visual style.

3. Choose View tab ⇨ Visual Styles panel ⇨ Visual Styles drop-down list ⇨ 2D Wireframe. The background color and the UCS icon change.

4. This time, choose Hidden. Back lines disappear and the background is the same as for Wireframe.

5. Choose the Conceptual visual style. The colors of the model change to blue and green.

6. Choose the Realistic visual style. This time, if your computer system can support it, you see the bronze satin material that I attached to the drawing.

7. On the View tab ⇨ Visual Styles panel, click the dialog box launcher at the right side of the panel's title bar to open the Visual Styles Manager.

8. Click the Create New Visual Style button below the list of visual styles in the Visual Styles Manager palette. In the Create New Visual Style dialog box, enter **MyRealistic** in the Name text box. In the Description text box, enter **No edges;silhouette**. You want to create a visual style that doesn't show edges within the model but displays a thick silhouette around its outside. Click OK.

9. Change the following settings:

    ```
    Face Settings-Material display: Material and textures
    Edge Settings-Show: None
    Silhouette Edges-Show: Yes
    Silhouette Edges-Width: 9
    ```

10. Click the Apply Selected Visual Style to Current Viewport button. You see the change in the model. The internal edges disappear, but there's a thicker edge around the outside.

11. Close or hide the Visual Styles Manager. Choose View tab ⇨ Visual Styles panel ⇨ Visual Styles drop-down list ⇨ Realistic. Then choose the MyRealistic visual style to see the difference. Your model should look like Figure 22.16.

FIGURE 22.16

The model with the MyRealistic custom visual style

Laying Out 3D Drawings

Laying out a 3D drawing on a layout tab is an important aspect of viewing a 3D drawing, because the layout determines the final output of the drawing. (Chapter 17 explains layouts.) AutoCAD offers several commands that help you lay out your 3D drawing in paper space layouts or create 2D representations of 3D drawings:

- FLATSHOT
- SOLVIEW, SOLDRAW, and SOLPROF
- VIEWBASE and VIEWPROJ

AUTOCAD ONLY
These commands are available only in AutoCAD.

Flattening 3D drawings

You may want to create a 2D representation of a 3D drawing. Some reasons to do this are for technical illustrations and to keep the core models of a drawing confidential. The FLATSHOT command takes all 3D objects in a drawing and makes 2D blocks from them. You can put objects that you don't want to include on off or frozen layers.

 Before you start, display your drawing in the desired view. If necessary, switch to parallel projection; the FLATSHOT command does not work reliably in perspective projection. (An easy way to do so is to right-click the ViewCube and choose Parallel.) Then choose Home tab⇨Section panel (expanded)⇨ Flatshot. The Flatshot dialog box opens, as shown in Figure 22.17, where you can specify settings.

In the Destination section, you decide where the 2D objects will go. You can insert them in the current drawing as a new block, replace an existing block, or export them to a new drawing. In the Foreground Lines section, you choose the color of the lines of the objects. Foreground lines are those that would not be hidden in Hidden visual style. In the Obscured Lines section, you decide how to treat lines that would be hidden in Hidden visual style. You can choose not to display them, for a hidden look, or use a different color or linetype. Click Create when you're done.

If you chose to insert a new block, place the block. If you chose to export to a new file, open that file. You will probably have to Zoom to Extents to see the block. Switch to Top viewpoint to see the 2D representation the way it looked in 3D. Figure 22.18 shows the results, both with and without obscured lines.

FIGURE 22.17

Use the Flatshot dialog box to specify how the FLATSHOT command works.

FIGURE 22.18

Flatshot can create a 2D representation of 3D objects with or without hidden lines.

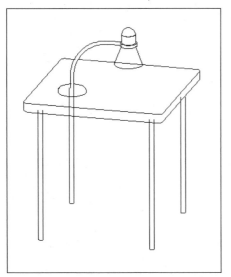 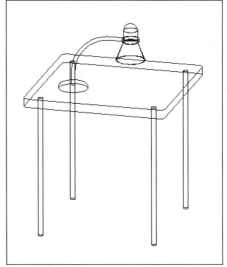

AUTOCAD ONLY

The FLATTEN command is an Express Tools command that also creates 2D representations of 3D objects. In addition, it reduces elevation and thickness to 0. It is available on the Modify panel (expanded) or by typing FLATTEN at the command line.

Creating 2D view objects

2D view objects are a 2D snapshot of a 3D model. You use the VIEWBASE command to create the snapshots on a paper space layout.

AUTOCAD ONLY

This section covers tools only available in AutoCAD and not AutoCAD LT.

NEW FEATURE

You can now create section and detail views from a base or projected view, and the view representations can be automatically updated when the source 3D model changes. New commands for this feature are VIEWCOMPONENT, VIEWDETAIL, VIEWDETAILSTYLE, VIEWSECTION, VIEWSECTIONSTYLE, VIEWSKETCHCLOSE, and VIEWSYMBOLSKETCH. In addition to new commands, the CVIEWSTYLE, CVIEWSECTIONSTYLE, VIEWSKETCHMODE, and VIEWUPDATEAUTO system variables were added.

A 2D view object looks similar to a viewport, because you see it on a paper space layout, but it isn't a viewport into model space. The 2D view object is a representation of your 3D model and contains all visible 3D surfaces. When you change your model and return to the layout, you see a notification that your model has changed and one or more drawing views are no longer up to date. A link lets you update the drawing views; this executes the VIEWUPDATE command. You can also start the VIEWUPDATE command; choose Layout tab ⇨ Update panel ⇨ Update View. If the VIEWUPDATEAUTO system variable is set to 1, 2D view objects are updated automatically when the source 3D model is changed.

The VIEWBASE and VIEWPROJ commands create orthogonal views and isometric views, so you can use these commands as a substitute for creating several viewports showing a variety of viewpoints. The first view you create is called a base view; views based on that view are called projected views.

> **NOTE**
> You can use the VIEWBASE command on objects imported from Autodesk Inventor. Many of the options vary when you use the command on Autodesk Inventor files. I don't cover these options in this book.

To create a 2D view object with several viewpoints, follow these steps:

1. Click a layout tab to make it current.

2. To make sure that you are in paper space, double-click outside the layout area. Delete the viewport that appears on the layout; click it and press the DEL key. If you use VIEWBASE from model space, you will be prompted to specify an existing layout to use or to create a new layout.

3. Choose Layout tab ⇨ Create View panel ⇨ Base drop-down menu ⇨ From Model Space to start the VIEWBASE command.

4. At the `Specify location of base view or [Type/Representation/Orientation/ Hidden lines/Scale/Visibility] <Type>:` prompt, click to place the view object. You can move it later. The `Select option [Representation/Orientation/Hidden lines/Scale/Visibility/Move/eXit] <eXit>:` prompt appears.

   - To change the base (initial) view, go to Drawing View Creation tab ⇨ Orientation panel ⇨ View drop-down list, and choose one of the views from the list.

   - To change the scale, go to Drawing View Creation tab ⇨ Appearance panel ⇨ Scale drop-down list and choose a scale.

   - To change the view style, which is like a shading style, go to Drawing View Creation tab ⇨ Appearance panel ⇨ Hidden Lines drop-down list and choose a style. Your choices are Visible Lines, Visible and Hidden Lines, Shaded with Visible Lines, and Shaded with Visible and Hidden Lines.

5. Press Enter to exit the second prompt and display the `Specify location of projected view or [Undo/eXit] <eXit>:` prompt.

6. Click in a new location to display a second (projected) view.

7. Continue to click in new locations to display the desired projected views, as shown in Figure 22.19.

8. Press Enter to exit the command.

FIGURE 22.19

A lamp shown in four views

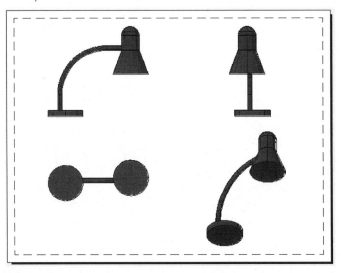

> **NOTE**
> The Object Visibility drop-down list in the Appearance panel lets you fine-tune some display settings. The dialog box launcher button on the Appearance panel opens the View Options dialog box, where you can specify a fixed or centered justification.

To change a view object, select a view and right-click. Choose Edit View. This starts the VIEWEDIT command and displays the Drawing View Editor tab. To move a view object, you can either use the Move button in the Modify panel or right-click and choose Move.

To add additional views, use the VIEWPROJ command. At the Select parent view: prompt, select the base view and then specify the location of the additional views.

The VIEWSTD command lets you set defaults for future 2D view objects, but doesn't affect existing view objects.

After you place a base or projected view on a paper space layout, you can create section and detail views to display additional information about the source 3D model. You can then annotate these views using dimensions and leaders. Follow these steps:

1. Choose Layout tab ➪ Create View panel ➪ Section drop-down menu (the VIEWSECTION command) and choose the style of section line you want to create from the Section drop-down menu.

2. Choose the view you want to create a section view from.

3. Specify the points to define the section view.

4. Drag the cursor away from the parent view and click to place the section view.

You can use the VIEWDETAIL command to define a circular or rectangular detail view. Follow these steps to create a detail view:

1. Choose Layout tab ⇨ Create View panel ⇨ Detail drop-down menu and choose a boundary style for the detail view.

2. Choose the view you want to detail.

3. Specify a center point and size for the detail boundary.

4. Drag the cursor away from the parent view and click to place the detail view.

Section lines or detail boundaries are associated with their parent view, but you can adjust their placement and size independently. You can modify section lines and detail boundaries using methods you are already familiar with, such as grips, the ribbon, and the Properties palette. You can also use constraints to control the placement and size of section lines and detail boundaries. Use the VIEWSYMBOLSKETCH (choose Layout tab ⇨ Modify View panel ⇨ Symbol Sketch) and VIEWSKETCHCLOSE commands to enter and exit Symbol Sketch mode where you can apply constraints to section lines and detail boundaries.

You control the appearance of section lines and views, as well as detail boundaries and views, through section and detail view styles. You can apply existing section and view styles, or you can create your own custom styles like text and dimension styles. Use the controls on the Styles and Standards panel of the Layout tab to set the current section or detail view style to use when creating a new view, or manage the styles in the current drawing. The VIEWDETAILSTYLE and VIEWSECTIONSTYLE commands allow you to create, modify, and manage section and detail view styles.

Using SOLVIEW to lay out paper space viewports

 SOLVIEW automates the process of creating floating viewports and orthogonal views (views at right angles from each other). To start SOLVIEW, choose Home tab ⇨ Modeling panel (expanded) ⇨ Solid View. AutoCAD immediately switches you to a layout tab. SOLVIEW has four options:

- **UCS** enables you to choose the UCS to work from, as well as set the scale, center, and clipping corners of a floating viewport. Use this option first. After you choose a UCS, type in a scale. You can change this later if you want. SOLVIEW then prompts you for the center of the view. Pick a point and wait until the 3D model regenerates. SOLVIEW continues to prompt you for a view center, letting you pick points until you like what you see. Press Enter to continue the prompts. Specify the diagonally opposite corners of the viewport. At the Enter view name: prompt, type a name that describes the view, such as Top, Side, or East Elevation. This helps you when you start creating orthogonal views. SOLVIEW creates the first viewport. You can continue with the Ortho and other options, but it helps to exit the command here to see the first viewport. Double-click inside the viewport and do a Zoom Extents to see the model in the viewport.

- **Ortho** creates orthogonal views. Once you have your first viewport, restart the SOLVIEW command and use this option. At the Specify side of viewport to project: prompt, pick one of the edges of the first viewport. Choose a view center inside the first viewport and specify the corners for the new viewport. Type a name for this new view.

    If you don't see the model properly when you pick the view center, continue with the prompts, picking corners where you want them. To see the results, double-click inside the viewport and do a Zoom Extents. You can then pan and zoom as you want.

- **Auxiliary** creates inclined views. At the `Specify first point of inclined plane:` prompt, pick a point in one of the viewports. At the `Specify second point of inclined plane:` prompt, pick another point in the same viewport. The two points are usually at an angle to create the inclined view. At the `Specify side to view from:` prompt, pick a point. You then pick a view center and corners, and then specify a view name.
- **Section** creates cross-sections. At the `Specify first point of cutting plane:` prompt, pick a point in a viewport. At the `Specify second point of cutting plane:` prompt, pick a point on the opposite side of the model to create a cross-section. You then pick a side to view from, and enter the view scale, a view center, viewport corners, and a view name.

Figure 22.20 shows an example with a top view, an auxiliary view, and a section.

FIGURE 22.20

An example of using SOLVIEW

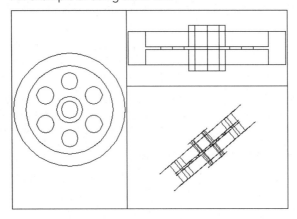

Using SOLDRAW to create hidden lines and hatching

 SOLDRAW uses the views created by SOLVIEW, and creates 2D profiles that include solid and hidden lines to represent the profiles and hatching for sectional views. You must use SOLVIEW before using SOLDRAW.

To use SOLDRAW, choose Home tab ⇨ Modeling panel (expanded) ⇨ Solid Drawing. SOLDRAW puts you into a paper space layout and prompts you to select objects, which means floating viewports. You can select all of them if you want. SOLDRAW then proceeds to automatically create the profile views. Figure 22.21 shows an example of the hatching created for a sectional view.

SOLDRAW uses hatch pattern defaults to define the hatch. You may have to change these settings by using HATCHEDIT.

FIGURE 22.21

The result of using SOLDRAW on a sectional view

> **NOTE**
>
> SOLVIEW creates a whole set of new layers in your drawing. SOLDRAW freezes your original layers, leaving visible only the layers that are needed to display the profile in that paper space viewport. SOLVIEW creates a special layer that you can use for dimensioning — one for each view that you create. For a view named front, the layer is named front-dim. You can use these dimensioning layers to create dimensions in paper space.

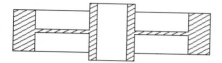

Using SOLPROF to create profiles

The SOLPROF command creates profiles like SOLDRAW, but you don't need to use SOLVIEW first. In addition, SOLPROF is more interactive than SOLDRAW. To start the command, choose Home tab ➪ Modeling panel (expanded) ➪ Solid Profile. SOLPROF prompts you to select objects.

> **NOTE**
>
> When you start SOLPROF, you must have already created a floating viewport, and you must be in model space. Double-click inside any viewport to enter model space.

At the Display hidden profile lines on separate layer? [Yes/No] <Y>: prompt, type **Y** or **N** ↵. By specifying Yes, you give yourself the capability of freezing or turning off the layer that contains hidden parts of the model. You can also hide other 3D objects behind the one that you're profiling.

At the Project profile lines onto a plane? [Yes/No] <Y>: prompt, type **Y** or **N** ↵. If you choose Yes, SOLPROF creates 2D objects. If you choose No, SOLPROF creates 3D objects.

At the Delete tangential edges? [Yes/No] <Y>: prompt, type **Y** or **N** ↵. A tangential edge is the meeting of two contiguous faces. Most drafting applications don't require you to show tangential edges.

Figure 22.22 on the left shows the result of SOLPROF after freezing the layer that contains the original object; you need to freeze this layer to see your profile! SOLPROF creates its own layers for the profile. Figure 22.22 on the right shows the result of SOLPROF after also freezing the layer that SOLPROF created, which contains the hidden parts of the model. In this case, the layer was named PH-159. Look for the *H* in the layer name, which stands for hidden. The last part of the layer name is the handle of the object that you're profiling, so it differs for each object.

FIGURE 22.22

A profile created with SOLPROF, before and after freezing the layer that contains the hidden parts of the model.

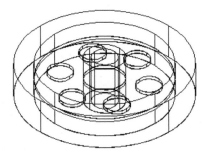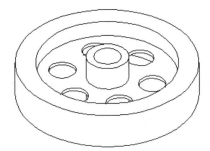

You can combine viewports created with SOLPROF and viewports created with SOLVIEW and SOLDRAW. For example, you can create two orthogonal views with SOLVIEW and SOLDRAW, and then add a viewport and use SOLPROF to create another view.

> **TIP**
>
> When you have a separate layer for the hidden portion of the model, you can modify that layer's color and/or linetype to show the hidden lines in a contrasting color or linetype.

Printing in 3D

Stereolithography, or 3D printing, is a way of quickly creating prototypes. A 3D printer uses information from a drawing to deposit layer upon layer of a plastic, metal, or composite material, until the model is completed. Models can even be functional objects. In this way, 3D printing can allow you to see and test your 3D model. Figure 22.23 shows a 3D printer and a sample model.

FIGURE 22.23

A 3D printer and a sample 3D model created with the 3D printing process.

Thanks to Z Corporation for this photo.

A 3D printer works from an STL file, which translates the drawing information into a format that the printer can understand. In order to export a model to an STL file, it must be completely in the positive range of the X, Y, and Z axes.

To export a model to an STL file, choose Application Button ⇨ Export ⇨ Other Formats. In the Export Data dialog box, choose Lithography (*.stl) from the Files of Type drop-down list. Name the file and click Save. At the `Select solids or watertight meshes:` prompt, select the objects that you want to include in the STL file and end selection to complete the export. However, you get additional options if you choose Application Button ⇨ Publish ⇨ Send to 3D Print Service. From there, you can get to a list of 3D printing services to print your model.

Summary

In this chapter, I covered all the ways to view your 3D drawing. You read about:

- Using the standard viewpoints, DDVPOINT, and the ViewCube to change viewpoints.
- Creating a named 3D view with a camera and adding a background to a named view.
- Using the PLAN command to quickly return you to plan view.
- Displaying parallel and perspective projections.
- Applying 3D Orbit to view your model from any position.
- Using ShowMotion to cycle through views.
- Using the SteeringWheel to navigate in your drawing
- Using and creating visual styles and the shading options in AutoCAD LT.
- Using the FLATSHOT command, which creates 2D blocks from 3D objects.
- Employing SOLVIEW, SOLDRAW, and SOLPROF to lay out views of a 3D drawing.
- Using VIEWBASE and VIEWPROJ to create 2D layouts from 3D objects.
- Exporting to STL format for 3D printing.

In the next chapter, I explain how to create 3D surfaces.

Creating 3D Surfaces

I n this chapter, you learn to create all types of surfaces. In AutoCAD, you can draw four types of surfaces:

- **Polygonal meshes.** These surfaces use triangles and other polygons to define the surface and have been available for a long time. They are not the same as the newer mesh objects (smooth surfaces). See the Chapter 23 Addendum on the companion website for more information.

- **Smooth mesh surfaces.** These are also polygonal meshes, but the polygons are smaller, making the surface smoother and more flexible.

- **Procedural surfaces.** Procedural surfaces maintain properties based on how you created them. For example, if you use a spline as the basis for a surface, then editing the spline edits the surface accordingly.

- **NURBS (non-uniform ration b-spline) surfaces.** You can edit NURBS surfaces by moving and stretching their vertices.

ON THE WEB

The Chapter 23 Addendum, which you can download from the companion website, contains information about creating surfaces with the 3DFACE and PFACE commands, and creating 3D polygon meshes.

Surfaces have a great advantage over 3D wireframe models because you can hide back surfaces and create shaded images for easier visualization of your models. Surfaces also enable you to create unusual shapes, such as topological maps or free-form objects. You cannot obtain information about physical properties — such as mass, center of gravity, and so on — from surfaces. Such information can be obtained only from 3D solids, which are covered in the next chapter.

NOTE

This chapter assumes that you are using the 3D Modeling Workspace.

AUTOCAD ONLY

This entire chapter applies to AutoCAD only. For information on surfaces that AutoCAD LT can create, see Chapter 21.

Drawing Procedural and NURBS Surfaces

Procedural surfaces (sometimes called analytic or explicit surfaces) contain analytic and history information, enabling them to be associative. As a result, when you edit a procedural surface, you can edit the basis of the surface, such as a spline, and the surface adjusts accordingly. For example, if you extrude an arc, you can edit the arc to change the surface.

By contrast, NURBS (non-uniform rational b-spline) surfaces are not associative. Instead, you edit them by moving or stretching their vertices. The vertices are defined in the U and V directions. (U and V are like X and Y, but don't have to match the XY directions of the User Coordinate System.)

The SURFACEMODELINGMODE system variable determines which type of surface you create. When off (0, the default), you create a procedural surface. When on (1), you create a NURBS surface.

The SURFACEASSOCIATIVITY system variable toggles associativity. With this system variable on (set to 1), surfaces retain their connection to their source objects. The source objects are retained, regardless of the DELOBJ system variable's setting.

 To create a procedural surface, go to Surface tab ⇨ Create panel and make sure that the NURBS Creation button is not selected. In addition, select the Surface Associativity button in the same location. To create a NURBS surface, choose Surface tab ⇨ Create panel ⇨ NURBS Creation to turn on NURBS creation. (NURBS surfaces cannot be associative.)

Then use one of the following commands:

PLANESURF	SURFNETWORK
REVOLVE	SURFBLEND
EXTRUDE	SURFPATCH
SWEEP	SURFOFFSET
LOFT	

These commands are covered over the next few sections of this chapter, along with other commands that create smooth mesh surfaces.

Creating Planar Surfaces

You can use the PLANESURF command to create a surface that is on the XY plane, and bounded by points that you specify. Choose Surface tab ⇨ Create panel ⇨ Planar. You can specify two diagonal points that define a rectangle, or select a closed object (or multiple objects, end to end, that define a closed area). Figure 23.1 shows a planar surface, representing a lake, defined by several arcs.

FIGURE 23.1

A planar surface bounded by arcs

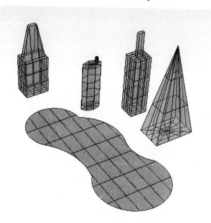

The number of isolines on the surface depends on the values of the SURFU and SURFV system variables. The default value for both is 6. You can use the Object option to turn closed 2D objects into a planar surface.

If the NURBS Creation button (Surface tab ⇨ Create panel) is off and the Surface Associativity button is on (same location), you create a procedural surface. You can then modify the source objects — as long as they still create a closed area and are still end to end. If the NURBS Creation button is on, you create a NURBS surface.

> **TIP**
> You can perform editing operations, such as union, subtraction, interference, intersection, and imprinting, on planar surfaces, as well as surfaces created with the REVOLVE, EXTRUDE, SWEEP, and LOFT commands. These last four commands are covered later in this chapter. I cover 3D editing in Chapter 24.

Revolved surfaces

A common way to define a surface is to revolve an outline around an axis. You can create some very complex surfaces in this way. AutoCAD offers two commands to create surfaces from the revolution of an outline — REVSURF and REVOLVE.

Using the REVSURF command

The REVSURF command takes an object that defines an outline or profile — AutoCAD also calls it a *path curve* — and revolves it around an axis. The REVSURF command creates a smooth mesh object by default. Figure 23.2 shows two examples of revolved surfaces.

> **NOTE**
> You can create the older polygon mesh surface type, instead of a full-featured mesh object, by setting the MESHTYPE system variable's value to 0. Mesh objects are covered fully in Chapter 24.

The path curve must be one object — a line, arc, circle, polyline, ellipse, or elliptical arc. It can be open, like the path curves shown in Figure 23.2, or closed.

FIGURE 23.2

Two revolved surfaces

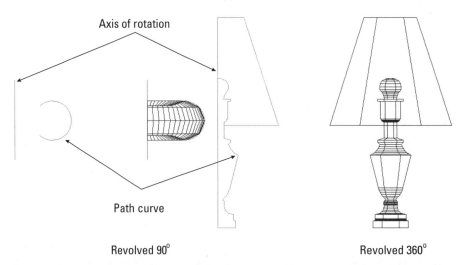

> **TIP**
> If you have several adjoining objects that you'd like to use as one path curve, you can use the PEDIT command to change lines and arcs to polylines and join them together. For more information, see Chapter 16. You can also use the JOIN command, which I cover in Chapter 10.

You can start the angle of rotation at any angle; it doesn't have to start on the plane of the path curve. You can rotate the path curve to any angle. Rotating the path curve 360 degrees closes the model.

When you rotate the path curve less than 360 degrees, you need to know which way to rotate. You can specify a positive (counterclockwise) or negative (clockwise) angle.

The point at which you pick the axis of rotation object affects the positive direction of rotation. Then you use the right-hand rule to determine which way the path curve will rotate around the axis. To do this, point your right thumb along the axis in the opposite direction from the endpoint closest to where you pick the axis. The direction in which your other fingers curl is the positive direction of rotation. Figure 23.3 shows the same model revolved in different directions. In the left model, the line of the axis was picked near the bottom endpoint. In the right model, the line of the axis was picked near the top endpoint.

FIGURE 23.3

From the viewer's point of view, the left revolved surface was rotated back 125 degrees, and the right revolved surface was rotated forward 125 degrees.

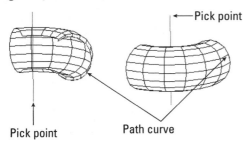

You use the SURFTAB1 and SURFTAB2 system variables to determine how AutoCAD creates the mesh. AutoCAD calls this the *wireframe density*.

- SURFTAB1 affects how the M direction — the direction of revolution — is displayed.
- SURFTAB2 affects how the N direction — the path curve — is displayed.

The higher the setting, the more lines AutoCAD uses to display the model. However, if the path curve is a polyline with straight segments, AutoCAD just displays one line at each segment vertex.

In Figure 23.11, SURFTAB1 is 6 and SURFTAB2 is 12. To set these system variables, type them on the command line and specify the new value that you want.

> **NOTE**
>
> Although you count M and N mesh sizes by vertices, you specify SURFTAB1 and SURFTAB2 by the number of surface areas that you want to see.

To create a revolved surface, follow these steps:

1. First create the path curve, which must be one object.

2. Draw the axis of revolution, usually a line.

 3. Choose Mesh tab ➪ Primitives panel ➪ Modeling, Meshes, Revolved Surface to start the REVSURF command.

4. At the `Select object to revolve:` prompt, select the path curve object.

5. At the `Select object that defines the axis of revolution:` prompt, select the axis of revolution object.

6. At the `Specify start angle <0>:` prompt, press Enter to accept the default of 0 (zero) or type a start angle.

7. At the `Specify included angle (+=ccw, -=cw) <360>:` prompt, press Enter to revolve the surface 360 degrees or type a positive or negative angle.

You need to create the path curve and the axis in a different plane than the one you use when revolving them. You can draw the path curve and axis in one UCS and use REVSURF in another. If the object doesn't come out in the right direction, you can rotate the entire object when completed. Rotating objects in 3D is covered in the next chapter.

REVSURF retains the original path curve and axis objects. It helps to draw them in a different layer and color so that you can easily erase them afterward; otherwise, they're hard to distinguish from the revolved surface. Having the original objects on a separate layer also helps if you need to redo the revolved surface — you can more easily avoid erasing them when you erase the revolved surface.

ON THE WEB

The drawing that you need for the following exercise on drawing revolved surfaces, ab23-a.dwg, is available from the Drawings download on the companion website.

STEPS: Drawing Revolved Surfaces

1. Open ab23-a.dwg from the Drawings download on the companion website.

2. Save it as ab23-01.dwg in your AutoCAD Bible folder. The path curve and axis are already drawn. This drawing was saved in the Conceptual visual style.

 3. Choose Mesh tab ➪ Primitives panel ➪ Modeling, Meshes, Revolved Surface.

4. At the `Select object to revolve:` prompt, select the polyline to the right.

5. At the `Select object that defines the axis of revolution:` prompt, select the line.

6. At the `Specify start angle <0>:` prompt, press Enter.

7. At the `Specify included angle (+=ccw, -=cw) <360>:` prompt, press Enter to revolve the path curve in a full circle.

8. Save your drawing. It should look like Figure 23.4.

FIGURE 23.4

The revolved surface

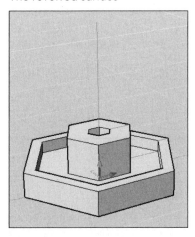

Using the REVOLVE command

The REVOLVE command allows you to select more than one object to revolve, something that you can't do with the REVSURF command. The prompts of the two commands ask for the same information, a profile and an axis, but in a slightly different way.

The REVOLVE command can create either a solid or a surface, based on the setting of the Closed Profiles Creation Mode. If you type the command on the command line, the mode is listed as either Solid or Surface and you can use the Mode option to change the setting. If you start the command from the Surface tab, you get a surface. If you start the command from the command line or the Solid tab, by default you get a solid — if a solid is possible. For a solid to be possible, the profile must be closed or the profile must be in one plane.

To use the REVOLVE command to create a surface, choose Surface tab ➪ Create panel ➪ Revolve. To create a procedural surface that maintains associativity, go to Surface tab ➪ Create panel and make sure that the NURBS Creation button is off and the Surface Associativity button is on. I cover the REVOLVE command more fully in Chapter 24.

Figure 23.5 shows two examples of the REVOLVE command, one that creates a surface and the other that creates a solid. The arc is revolved around the line in each case, but when the line and the arc create a closed figure, the result can be a solid.

FIGURE 23.5

When the axis does not touch the arc, the REVOLVE command creates a surface. When the axis and the arc together create a closed figure, the command creates a solid.

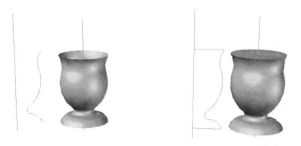

STEPS: Drawing Procedural Surfaces with the REVOLVE command

1. Open `ab23-a.dwg` available from the Drawings download on the companion website. This is the same drawing used in the previous exercise.

2. Save it as `ab23-02.dwg` in your `AutoCAD Bible` folder. The path curve and axis are already drawn. This drawing was saved in the Conceptual visual style.

3. On the Surface tab, in the Create panel, make sure that the NURBS Creation button is deselected. At the same time, select the Surface Associativity button to the left.

4. Choose Surface tab ⇨ Create panel ⇨ Revolve. On the command line, check the Closed profiles creation mode; just above the prompt, you should see `_su` (for SURface). If not, use the MOde option to choose the SUrface setting.

5. At the `Select objects to revolve or [MOde]:` prompt, select the polyline to the right. Press Enter to end object selection.

6. At the `Specify axis start point or define axis by [Object/X/Y/Z] <Object>` prompt, press Enter to specify the Object option.

7. At the `Select an object:` prompt, select the red line.

8. At the `Specify angle of revolution or [STart angle/Reverse/EXpression] <360>:` prompt, press Enter to revolve the path curve in a full circle.

9. Save your drawing. It should look like Figure 23.6.

10. Select the red line that you used as an axis and click its middle grip to make it hot. Move your cursor to the left; because the model is a procedural surface, the hole at the center of the model gets larger. Move the cursor to the right slightly; the hole gets smaller. Press Esc to leave the model as is.

FIGURE 23.6

The procedural revolved surface

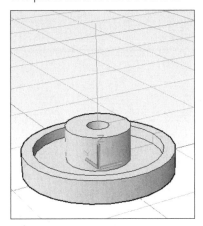

Drawing an Extruded Surface

A simple way to create a 3D object is to start with a 2D object and *extrude* it (thrust it out). In AutoCAD, extruding refers to creating a 3D object from a 2D object. Three commands, TABSURF, EXTRUDE, and SWEEP, allow you to extrude 2D objects to create surfaces.

Working with the TABSURF command

The TABSURF command takes an outline, or profile, called a *path curve,* and extrudes it along a vector that defines the direction and distance of the extrusion. The TABSURF command creates a smooth mesh object by default. Figure 23.7 shows two examples of extruded surfaces.

> **NOTE**
>
> You can create a polygon mesh surface, instead of a full-featured mesh object, by setting the MESHTYPE system variable's value to 0. Mesh objects are covered fully in Chapter 24.

FIGURE 23.7

Two extruded surfaces created by using TABSURF

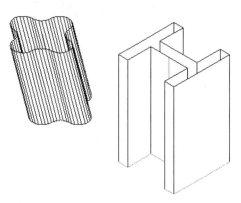

For the I-beam, you could have simply given the 2D polyline profile a thickness and achieved a similar result. However, you could not have done so with the extruded surface on the left, because the extrusion is not perpendicular to the XY plane that contains the 2D polyline profile. TABSURF can extrude a shape in any direction. When you select the vector object, your pick point determines the direction of the extrusion. AutoCAD starts the extrusion from the end of the vector closest to the pick point. Use a non-planar view when using TABSURF to check that you've accurately defined the extrusion vector into the third dimension. Any of the preset isometric views are helpful.

You use the SURFTAB1 system variable to control the number of lines AutoCAD uses to display the curve. If the curve is made up of polyline segments, AutoCAD displays one line at each segment vertex.

> **CAUTION**
>
> Note the I-beam in Figure 23.7. If you create an object by mirroring, stretching, and so on, you'll see extra tabulation lines at the separate segments in the polyline definition. If you want a clean look, you need to draw clean. You could use the original shape as a guide to draw a new polyline on top of the old one, and then erase the original.

To draw a tabulated surface, follow these steps:

1. Draw the object to extrude — a line, arc, circle, polyline, ellipse, or elliptical arc. This is the path curve.

2. Draw the vector, usually a line. If you use a 2D or 3D polyline, AutoCAD uses an imaginary line from the start point to the endpoint to determine the vector.

 3. Choose Mesh tab ⇨ Primitives panel ⇨ Modeling, Meshes, Tabulated Surface.

4. At the `Select object for path curve:` prompt, select the path curve object.

5. At the `Select object for direction vector:` prompt, select the line that you're using for the vector.

STEPS: Drawing Tabulated Surfaces

1. Open ab23-b.dwg available from the Drawings download on the companion website.

2. Save it as ab23-03.dwg in your AutoCAD Bible folder. You see a tabletop. Its bottom is at a Z height of 30. The current elevation is 30. You're looking at the table from the SE isometric view. Object Snap should be on. Set running object snaps for Endpoint, Midpoint, and Center. Disable Dynamic UCS on the status bar (or press F6), and enable Dynamic Input on the status bar (or press F12). The current layer is Const. The drawing is shown in Figure 23.8.

3. Start the CIRCLE command. Follow the prompts:

   ```
   Specify center point for circle or [3P/2P/Ttr (tan tan radius)]: Choose
       the From object snap.
   _from Base point: Pick the endpoint at ❶ in Figure 23.8.
   <Offset>: @-1,3 ↵
   Specify radius of circle or [Diameter]: .75 ↵
   ```

4. Start the LINE command. At the Specify first point: prompt, choose the Center object snap of the circle that you just drew. At the Specify next point or [Undo]: prompt, type 3,-3,-30 ↵ to draw a line flaring out from the circle and going down to the floor. End the LINE command.

FIGURE 23.8

The tabletop

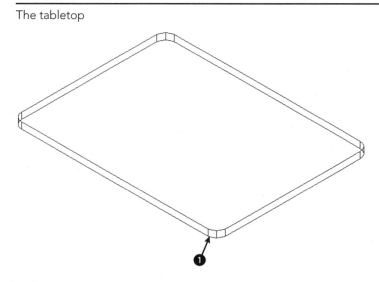

5. Choose Mesh tab ⇨ Primitives panel ⇨ Modeling, Meshes, Tabulated Surface. At the `Select object for path curve:` prompt, select the circle. At the `Select object for direction vector:` prompt, select the line. (You can see only the top part of the line, but that's the part that you need to pick.) AutoCAD creates the tabulated surface.

6. Start the MIRROR command. Select the entire leg. Choose the Midpoint of the bottom edge of both long sides of the table for the two points of the mirror line.

7. Repeat the MIRROR line and select both legs. Mirror them by using the Midpoints of the bottom edge of the short sides of the table for the two points of the mirror line.

8. Do a Zoom Extents to see the entire table.

9. Save your drawing. It should look like Figure 23.9.

FIGURE 23.9

The completed table

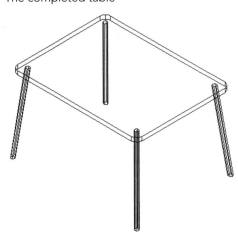

Working with the EXTRUDE command

The EXTRUDE command is similar to the TABSURF command, but offers more options. The EXTRUDE command can create either a solid or a surface, based on the setting of the Closed Profiles Creation Mode. If you type the command on the command line, the mode lists either Solid or Surface and you can use the MOde option to change the setting. If you start the command from the Surface tab, you get a surface. If you start the command from the command line or the Solid tab, you get a solid — if a solid is possible. For a solid to be possible, the profile must be closed or the profile must be in one plane.

To create a procedural surface that maintains associativity, go to Surface tab ⇨ Create panel and make sure that the NURBS Creation button is off and the Surface Associativity button is on.

To start the EXTRUDE command to create a surface, choose Surface tab ⇨ Create panel ⇨ Extrude. I discuss the EXTRUDE command more fully in Chapter 24.

Figure 23.10 shows an open 2D figure (an arc) and a closed figure (a line and an arc), and the results after using the EXTRUDE command.

FIGURE 23.10

On the left, the EXTRUDE command creates a surface from an arc. On the right, the command creates a solid from the closed figure of a line and an arc.

ON THE WEB

The drawing that you need for the following exercise on drawing NURBS surfaces with the EXTRUDE command, ab23-c.dwg, is available from the Drawings download on the companion website.

STEPS: Drawing NURBS Surfaces with the EXTRUDE Command

1. Open ab23-c.dwg available from the Drawings download on the companion website.

2. Save it as ab23-04.dwg in your AutoCAD Bible folder. You see a red keyhole shape, the base for a model. Object Snap should be on. Set running object snaps for Endpoint.

3. On the Surface tab, in the Create panel, make sure that the NURBS Creation button is on and the Surface Associativity button is off.

 4. Choose Surface tab ⇨ Create panel ⇨ Extrude. On the command line, check the Closed profiles creation mode; just above the prompt, you should see _su (for SUrface). If not, use the MOde option to choose the SUrface setting.

5. At the Select objects to extrude or [MOde]: prompt, select the red base, which is a polyline, and press Enter to end selection.

6. At the Specify height of extrusion or [Direction/Path/Taper angle]: prompt, drag the cursor up and type **8** ↵. The model should look like Figure 23.11.

7. Select the face closest to you, at ❶ in Figure 23.11. Click the central grip to make it hot. At the prompt for a stretch point, type **@5,0** ↵.

 8. To extend the rest of the model, choose Surface tab ⇨ Edit panel ⇨ Extend. At the Select surface edges to extend: prompt, select the end edges at ❷ and ❸ in Figure 23.11. Press Enter to end selection. (I cover this command later in this chapter.)

9. At the Specify extend distance or [Modes]: prompt, enter **m** ↵ to specify the extension mode.

10. At the `Extension mode [Extend/Stretch] <Extend>:` prompt, enter **s** ↵ to stretch the selected edges.

11. At the `Creation type [Merge/Append]:` prompt, enter **m** ↵ to extend the existing surface without creating a new one.

12. At the `Specify extend distance or [Modes]:` prompt, enter **@5,0** ↵. AutoCAD extends the edges to meet the new location of the end surface.

13. Save your drawing.

FIGURE 23.11

The extruded NURBS surface

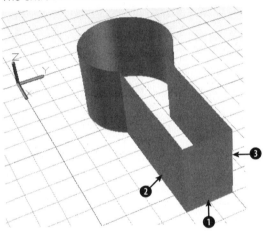

Sweeping objects along a path

Sweeping is similar to extruding, but you have more options. Like the EXTRUDE command, the SWEEP command can create both surfaces and solids, based on the setting of the Closed Profiles Creation Mode. If you type the command on the command line, the mode lists either Solid or Surface and you can use the MOde option to change the setting. If you start the command from the Surface tab, you get a surface. If you start the command from the command line or the Solid tab, you get a solid — if a solid is possible.

To create a procedural surface that maintains associativity, go to Surface tab ➪ Create panel and make sure that the NURBS Creation button is off and the Surface Associativity button is on.

To start the SWEEP command to create a surface, choose Surface tab ➪ Create panel ➪ Sweep. I discuss the SWEEP command more fully in Chapter 24.

Figure 23.12 shows two sweeps. On the left, an arc is swept along a helix, creating a surface. On the right, a circle is swept along the helix, creating a solid. You can scale the profile and twist it to create some very interesting models. To start the SWEEP command to create a surface, choose Surface tab⇨ Create panel⇨Sweep. I cover the SWEEP command fully in the next chapter, where I discuss solids.

FIGURE 23.12

You can create interesting surfaces and solids by using the SWEEP command.

Drawing Surfaces Between Objects

If you have two or more existing objects, you may want to define the surface that would extend between these objects. Or, you may want to extrapolate a surface along two or more objects. You can use several commands to create these surfaces.

Creating ruled surfaces

Use the RULESURF command to create a surface that extends between two 2D objects. The objects can be lines, polylines (2D or 3D), circles, ellipses, elliptical arcs, splines, points, or helixes. The two objects must be either both open or both closed. Only one of the two can be a point.

Use the SURFTAB1 system variable to control the number of lines that AutoCAD uses to display the surface. Figure 23.13 shows some ruled surfaces.

> **NOTE**
>
> The RULESURF command creates a smooth mesh object by default. You can create a polyface or polygon mesh surface, instead of a full-featured mesh object, by setting the MESHTYPE system variable's value to 0. Mesh objects are covered fully in Chapter 24.
>
> The pick points of the two objects affect the resulting curve. If you pick them both on the same side, you get the type of curves shown on the left in Figure 23.13. If you pick them on opposite sides, the curve intersects itself, as shown on the right in Figure 23.13.

FIGURE 23.13

A variety of ruled surfaces

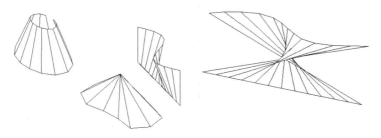

Follow these steps to draw a ruled surface:

1. Draw the two objects for the ruled surface.
2. Choose Mesh tab ⇨ Primitives panel ⇨ Modeling, Meshes, Ruled Surface.
3. At the `Select first defining curve:` prompt, choose the first object.
4. At the `Select second defining curve:` prompt, choose the second object.

ON THE WEB

The drawing that you need for the following exercise on drawing ruled surfaces, `ab23-d.dwg`, is available from the Drawings download on the companion website.

STEPS: Drawing Ruled Surfaces

1. Open `ab23-d.dwg` available from the Drawings download on the companion website.
2. Save it as `ab23-05.dwg` in your `AutoCAD Bible` folder. You see a spline, as shown in Figure 23.14. In this exercise, you use the spline to draw some drapes.
3. Mirror the spline. For the mirror line, turn on Ortho Mode and use ❶ and ❷, as shown in Figure 23.14. Don't delete the original spline.

FIGURE 23.14

A spline

4. Start the COPY command and select both splines. At the `Specify base point or [Displacement/mOde] <Displacement>:` prompt, type **0,0,73** ↵ to copy the splines 73 units in the positive Z direction. Press Enter at the `Specify second point or [Array] <use first point as displacement>:` prompt.

5. Choose View tab ⇨ Views panel ⇨ Views drop-down list ⇨ SE Isometric.

 6. Choose Mesh tab ⇨ Primitives panel ⇨ Modeling, Meshes, Ruled Surface. At the `Select first defining curve:` prompt, choose the top-right spline near its right endpoint. At the `Select second defining curve:` prompt, choose the bottom-right spline near its right endpoint.

7. Repeat the RULESURF command. At the `Select first defining curve:` prompt, choose the top-left spline near its left endpoint. At the `Select second defining curve:` prompt, choose the bottom-left spline near its left endpoint.

8. Save your drawing. It should look like Figure 23.15.

FIGURE 23.15

The completed drapes

Lofting objects

The LOFT command lets you choose two or more 2D objects and creates a new surface or solid by interpolating through them. As you select the cross sections to define the lofted surface or solid, a preview of the object to be created is displayed. The transparency level of the preview is controlled with the PREVIEWCREATIONTRANSPARENCY system variable.

You can create both surfaces and solids based on the setting of the Closed Profiles Creation Mode of the LOFT command. If you type the command on the command line, the mode lists either Solid or Surface and you can use the MOde option to change the setting. If you start the command from the Surface tab, you get a surface. If you start the command from the command line or the Solid tab, you get a solid — if a solid is possible.

To create a procedural surface that maintains associativity, go to Surface tab ⇨ Create panel and make sure that the NURBS Creation button is off and the Surface Associativity button is on.

 Figure 23.16 shows two lofts. On the left is a surface created from four arcs. On the right is a solid created from four circles. To start the LOFT command to create a surface, choose Surface tab ⇨ Create panel ⇨ Loft. The LOFT command has a number of parameters that you need to set. I cover this command in detail in Chapter 24.

FIGURE 23.16

You can create either a surface or a solid with the LOFT command.

Using the EDGESURF command

For the EDGESURF command, you need four touching objects. The objects can be lines, arcs, splines, or polylines (2D or 3D). EDGESURF creates a smooth mesh that approximates a *Coon's surface patch mesh* — a surface defined by four edges. Figure 23.17 shows an edge surface.

> **NOTE**
> You can create a polygon mesh surface, instead of a full-featured mesh object, by setting the MESHTYPE system variable's value to 0. Mesh objects are covered fully in Chapter 24.

Use the SURFTAB1 and SURFTAB2 system variables to vary the displayed lines in each direction.

Follow these steps to create an edge surface:

1. Draw the four objects to create a boundary for the surface. They must touch, so use Endpoint object snaps to create them or to move them into place.
2. Choose Mesh tab ⇨ Primitives panel ⇨ Modeling, Meshes, Edge Surface.
3. AutoCAD prompts you to select edges 1 through 4. You can select them in any order.

FIGURE 23.17

An edge surface created with the EDGESURF command.

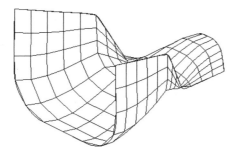

Creating the four edges involves moving from one UCS to another UCS because they're all in 3D. It helps to create a bounding box for your object by using the BOX command. You can then use the dynamic UCS feature to temporarily change UCSs for each edge.

23

STEPS: Drawing Edge Surfaces

1. Open `ab23-e.dwg` available from the Drawings download on the companion website.

2. Save it as `ab23-06.dwg` in your `AutoCAD Bible` folder. You see four curves in a bounding box, as shown in Figure 23.18. In this exercise, you use the curves to draw a dustpan.

3. Freeze the `Const` layer.

 4. Choose Mesh tab ⇨ Primitives panel ⇨ Modeling, Meshes, Edge Surface. At the prompts, select ❶, ❷, ❸, and ❹, shown in Figure 23.19.

5. Choose View tab ⇨ Visual Styles panel ⇨ Visual Styles drop-down list ⇨ Hidden to see the result.

6. Save your drawing. It should look like Figure 23.19. It's either a dustpan or a starship — your choice.

FIGURE 23.18

The four curves are the basis for creating an edge surface.

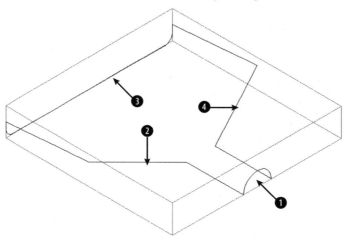

FIGURE 23.19

The completed dustpan — or starship

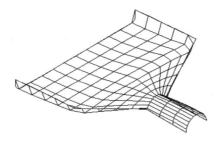

Using the SURFNETWORK command

The SURFNETWORK command creates a surface between a number of curves or the edges of surfaces or solids in two directions, called U and V. (U and V are like X and Y, but can be in any direction; they don't have to match the UCS.) Figure 23.20 shows some splines on the left, which were used to create the surface below.

FIGURE 23.20

The three splines in the U direction and two splines in the V direction create the network surface below.

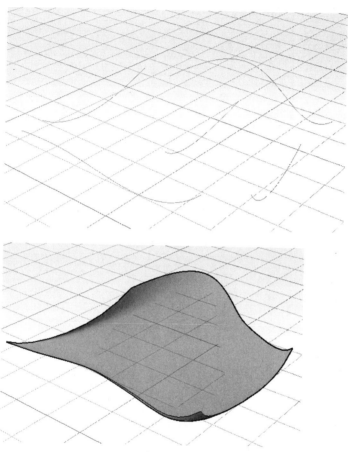

To create a procedural surface that maintains associativity, go to Surface tab ⇨ Create panel and make sure that the NURBS Creation button is off and the Surface Associativity button is on. To create a NURBS surface, the NURBS Creation button should be on and the Surface Associativity button off.

To create a surface using the SURFNETWORK command, follow these steps:

1. Create at least two curves or edges in one direction (the U direction) and then at least two perpendicular to the first (the V direction).

 2. Choose Surface tab ⇨ Create panel ⇨ Network.

3. At the `Select curves or surface edges in the first direction:` prompt, select the edges. Press Enter to end selection.

4. At the `Select curves or surface edges in second direction:` prompt, select the edges. Press Enter to end selection.

ON THE WEB
The drawing that you need for the following exercise on drawing network surfaces, `ab23-f.dwg`, is available from the Drawings download on the companion website.

STEPS: Drawing Network Surfaces

1. Open `ab23-f.dwg` available from the Drawings download on the companion website.

2. Save it as `ab23-07.dwg` in your `AutoCAD Bible` folder. You see three splines in one direction and two in a perpendicular direction.

3. Choose Surface tab ⇨ Create panel ⇨ Surface Associativity. The NURBS Creation button to the right should not be selected. This will create a procedural surface.

4. Choose Surface tab ⇨ Create panel ⇨ Network.

5. At the `Select curves or surface edges in the first direction:` prompt, select the three edges that run approximately parallel to each other. Press Enter to end selection.

6. At the `Select curves or surface edges in second direction:` prompt, select the other two edges. Press Enter to end selection.

7. AutoCAD creates the network surface. Your drawing should look like Figure 23.21.

FIGURE 23.21

The network surface, shown in the Conceptual visual style

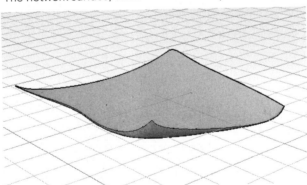

Connecting surfaces with the SURFBLEND command

The SURFBLEND command connects edges of two surfaces or surfaces and solids, and gives you options to specify the properties of the blend. As you select the surfaces to blend, a preview of the surface to be created is displayed. The transparency level of the preview is controlled with the PREVIEWCREATION-TRANSPARENCY system variable. You can control the following properties for each blend:

- **Continuity.** Specifies how the two surfaces meet. You can choose G0 (Position, usually the sharpest edge), G1 (Tangent), or G2 (Curvature, a curved blend). The default is G0. Figure 23.22 shows a blend surface using each of these choices.
- **Bulge.** Determines the roundness of the blend. You can specify values from 0 to 1. The default is .5. Bulge only applies to blends that have G1 or G2 continuity.

Not all edges can be connected with a blend surface. The problem is usually the spatial relationship between the edges that you select.

To create a procedural surface that maintains associativity, go to Surface tab ⇨ Create panel and make sure that the NURBS Creation button is off and the Surface Associativity button is on. To create a NURBS surface, the NURBS Creation button should be on and the Surface Associativity button off. Figure 23.22 shows three blend surfaces with continuity of G0, G1, and G2.

FIGURE 23.22

The blend surface connects the holes in the two flat surfaces.

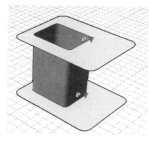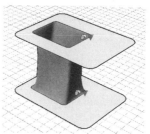

To draw a blend surface, follow these steps:

1. Create at least two curves or edges in one direction (the U direction) and then at least two perpendicular to the first (the V direction).
2. Choose Surface tab ⇨ Create panel ⇨ Blend.
3. At the `Select first surface edges to blend or [CHain]:` prompt, select the edges. Use the Chain option to select contiguous edges. Press Enter to end selection.
4. At the `Select second surface edges to blend or [Chain]:` prompt, select the edges. Press Enter to end selection.

5. At the `Press Enter to accept the blend surface or [CONtinuity/Bulge magni-tude]:` prompt, use the drop-down grip or the CONtinuity option to specify G0, G1, or G2. Using the drop-down grips at both ends of the connection, you can choose a continuity for each point; if you use the prompt, you get a prompt for each edge. Use the Bulge magnitude option to determine the roundness of the connection. Press Enter to accept the blend and end the command.

ON THE WEB

The drawing that you need for the following exercise on drawing blend surfaces, `ab23-g.dwg`, is available from the Drawings download on the companion website.

STEPS: Drawing Blend Surfaces

1. Open `ab23-g.dwg` available from the Drawings download on the companion website.
2. Save it as `ab23-08.dwg` in your `AutoCAD Bible` folder. You see two curved surfaces.
3. Choose Surface tab ⇨ Create panel ⇨ Surface Associativity. The NURBS Creation button to the right should not be selected. This will create a procedural surface.
4. Choose Surface tab ⇨ Create panel ⇨ Blend.
5. At the `Select first surface edges to blend or [CHain]:` prompt, select the upper edge of the leftmost surface. Press Enter to end selection.
6. At the `Select second surface edges to blend or [Chain]:` prompt, select the lower edge of the rightmost surface. Press Enter to end selection.
7. At the `Press Enter to accept the blend surface or [CONtinuity/Bulge magni-tude]:` prompt, use the drop-down grips to change both edges to G2. Notice the difference in the curvature.
8. Type **b** ↵ to use the Bulge Magnitude option. Enter **1** ↵ twice to set each edge's bulge magnitude to 1. Notice how the bulge increases.
9. Press Enter to accept the surface and end the command. Your drawing should look like Figure 23.23.

FIGURE 23.23

The blend surface

Patching holes with the SURFPATCH command

The SURFPATCH command patches holes. You can think of SURFPATCH as a way to put a roof over a closed surface with a hole in its middle. As you select the surface edges to patch, a preview of the surface to be created is displayed. The transparency level of the preview is controlled with the PREVIEWCREATIONTRANSPARENCY system variable.

You can also use it to create a surface from a closed 2D object, such as a polyline, ellipse, circle, or spline; in this case, the result is similar to using the PLANESURF command with the Object option.Like the SURFBLEND command, you can specify continuity and bulge. In addition, you can constrain the patch with curves or points, as shown on the right side of Figure 23.24.

To create a procedural surface that maintains associativity, go to Surface tab ⇨ Create panel and make sure that the NURBS Creation button is off and the Surface Associativity button is on. To create a NURBS surface, the NURBS Creation button should be on and the Surface Associativity button off.

To create a patch surface, follow these steps:

1. Draw surfaces that form a closed loop, such as the one shown on the left in Figure 23.24, which was created by drawing a rectangle, filleting its corners, and extruding. If you want to constrain the patch with curves or points, draw them as well.

2. Choose Surface tab ⇨ Create panel ⇨ Patch.

3. At the `Select surface edges to patch or [CHain/CUrves] <CUrves>:` prompt, select the surface edges. (In Figure 23.24, the surface has eight edges — four sides and four filleted corners.) Press Enter to end selection. To create a surface from a closed 2D object, use the Curves option and select the object. To quickly select contiguous edges, use the Chain option.

4. At the `Press Enter to accept the patch surface or [CONtinuity/Bulge magnitude/ Guides]:` prompt, press Enter to place the patch surface and end the command. Use the CONtinuity or Bulge Magnitude option, as explained previously for the SURFBLEND command. If you use the Constrain Geometry Guides option, select the curves or points that you drew.

FIGURE 23.24

A closed loop surface, before and after patching. The patch uses G2 continuity to create a domed effect. On the bottom, the surface was constrained by a spline.

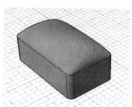

STEPS: Drawing Patch Surfaces

1. Open ab23-h.dwg available from the Drawings download on the companion website.

2. Save it as ab23-09.dwg in your AutoCAD Bible folder. You see a desk lamp. The top cylinder is a surface, which needs a cap that will be the on-off switch.

3. Choose Surface tab ⇨ Create panel ⇨ Surface Associativity. This will create a procedural surface. The NURBS Creation button to the right should not be selected.

4. Choose Surface tab ⇨ Create panel ⇨ Patch.

5. At the Select surface edges to patch or [Chain/CUrves] <CUrves>: prompt, select the upper edge of the cylinder surface. Press Enter to end selection.

6. At the Press Enter to accept the patch surface or [CONtinuity/Bulge magnitude/Guides]: prompt, click the drop-down grip and choose Curvature (G2).

7. At the Press Enter to accept the patch surface or [CONtinuity/Bulge magnitude/Guides]: prompt, type **b** ↵ for the Bulge Magnitude option. Type **.75** ↵ to make the bulge higher.

8. Press Enter to accept the surface and end the command. Your drawing should look like Figure 23.25.

FIGURE 23.25

The patch surface at the top represents the lamp's on-off switch.

Editing and Analyzing Surfaces

How you edit a surface depends on the type of surface you created. The following lists the newer surfaces and their basic editing process:

- **Smooth meshes.** Use the editing tools on the Mesh tab (which I cover in Chapter 24). For example, you can smooth and crease meshes, as well as extrude, split, and merge faces.
- **Procedural surfaces.** Edit the objects you used to create the surface, and the surface adjusts. For example, if you extruded a spline, you can edit the spline to change the extruded surface.
- **NURBS surfaces.** Edit the vertices of the surface, using grip editing techniques. To display the vertices, choose Surface tab ⇨ Control Vertices panel ⇨ Show CV. In the same panel, you can hide, remove, add, and rebuild vertices.

> **TIP**
> You can turn procedural surfaces into NURBS surfaces, but not vice versa. So it makes sense to start out creating a procedural surface, do any necessary editing, and then convert to a NURBS surface. Use the CONVTONURBS command (Surface tab ⇨ Control Vertices panel ⇨ Convert to NURBS).

Creating surfaces with the SURFOFFSET command

You can consider the SURFOFFSET command both a surface creation and editing command, because it creates new surfaces from existing ones. It's very much like the 2D OFFSET command (which is usually considered an editing command). You can also offset regions. (I cover regions in Chapter 16.)

To offset surfaces or regions, follow these steps:

1. Choose Surface tab ⇨ Create panel ⇨ Offset.
2. At the `Select surfaces or regions to offset:` prompt, select the surfaces or regions you want and press Enter to end selection. You see sets of arrows indicating the current direction of the offset.
3. At the `Specify offset distance or [Flip direction/Both sides/Solid/ Connect/Expression] <0.0000>:` prompt, enter an offset distance or use one of the options:
   - **Flip direction.** Switches the direction of the offset
   - **Both sides.** Offsets on both sides of the selected objects
   - **Solid.** Creates a solid from the original objects and their respective offsets, similar to the THICKEN command (covered later in this chapter).
   - **Connect.** Connects multiple offset surfaces, if they are connected. For example, if you have four lines that make up a rectangle (four separate objects) and extrude them, the SURFOFFSET command creates four separated surfaces without this option. Using the option extends the offset objects' edges to meet.
   - **Expression.** Lets you enter a formula or equation to specify the offset distance. A simple example is =4+10 to offset a distance of 14 units.

AutoCAD offsets the selected objects. Figure 23.26 shows an offset surface.

FIGURE 23.26

FIGURE 23.26

An offset surface

 The SURFSCULPT command creates a solid from surfaces that enclose an area with no gaps. I cover this command in Chapter 24.

Trimming and extending surfaces

The SURFTRIM command is like a 3D TRIM command, trimming surfaces (or regions) that extend beyond another surface or object. It's a great clean-up tool. You can also use SURFUNTRIM to undo trims. The SURFEXTEND command is similar to the 2D LENGTHEN command, but is for surfaces.

To trim a surface, follow these steps:

1. Choose Surface tab ⇨ Edit panel ⇨ Trim.

2. At the `Select surfaces or regions to trim or [Extend/PROjection direc-tion]:` prompt, select the surface. Press Enter to end object selection.

   - Use the Extend option (which defaults to Yes) to specify whether the cutting edge can be extended for the purpose of the trim. If you set this option to No, the cutting edge must actually meet the surface you are trimming.

   - The PROjection direction option projects the cutting edge onto the surface, allowing you to trim objects that only appear to have a cutting edge. The default suboption, Automatic, trims as you would expect in 2D, but also extends in the Z direction. Use the View subop-tion to trim objects that appear to have a cutting edge from the current viewpoint. Use the Ucs suboption to project the cutting edge onto the XY plane of the current UCS. Use the None suboption to ensure trimming only when the cutting edge is on the surface you are trimming.

3. At the `Select cutting curves, surfaces or regions:` prompt, select the object that meets the first surface where you want to trim it. Press Enter to end selection.

4. At the `Select area to trim [Undo]:` prompt, pick the first surface (the one you want to trim) in the area that you want to trim (rather than the area that you want to keep).

   Figure 23.27 shows the process of trimming a surface with SURFTRIM.

FIGURE 23.27

Trimming a surface

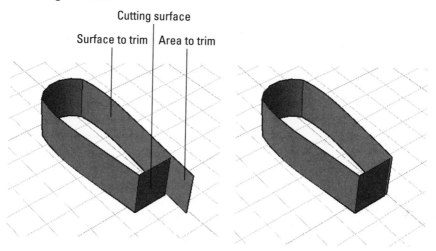

The SURFEXTEND command is like the 2D LENGTHEN command (which I cover in Chapter 10). However, you can choose to extend the existing surface or create a new surface that is appended to the original one. To extend a surface, follow these steps:

1. Choose Surface tab ⇨ Edit panel ⇨ Extend. You see the current Mode and Creation settings.

2. At the `Select surface edges to extend:` prompt, select a surface edge. You cannot select a surface; you must select just its edge. Press Enter to end object selection.

3. At the `Specify extend distance [Expression/Modes]:` prompt, enter a distance. You can use the Expression option to enter an equation or formula. Use the Modes option to specify one of two suboptions (or to access the Creation type option):
   - **Extend:** Extends the surface to continue its shape and direction
   - **Stretch:** Stretches the surface without continuing its shape and direction

4. At the `Creation type [Merge/Append] <Append>:` prompt, choose one of the two options:
   - **Merge:** Extends the surface so that the original surface is longer
   - **Append:** Adds a new surface adjacent to the original one

   AutoCAD extends the surface using the options you specified.

Filleting surfaces with the SURFFILLET command

Filleting surfaces is similar to filleting in 2D (which I cover in Chapter 10). You can also fillet two regions. As you select the surfaces or regions to fillet, a preview of the fillet to be created is displayed. The transparency level of the preview is controlled with the PREVIEWCREATIONTRANSPARENCY system variable.

To fillet a surface, follow these steps:

1. Choose Surface tab ⇨ Edit panel ⇨ Fillet. You see the current Radius and Trim Surface settings.

2. At the `Select first surface or region to fillet or [Radius/Trim surface]:` prompt, select the first surface or region, or use one of the suboptions:
   - Use the Radius suboption to set the radius of the fillet.
   - Use the Trim surface suboption to specify whether edges of the surface are trimmed. By default, they are trimmed.

3. At the `Select second surface or region to fillet or [Radius/Trim surface]:` prompt, select the second surface or region.

4. At the `Press Enter to accept the fillet surface or [Radius/Trim surfaces]:` prompt, press Enter to fillet the surfaces or regions and end the command. Figure 23.28 shows surfaces before and after filleting.

FIGURE 23.28

The surfaces were filleted in two places.

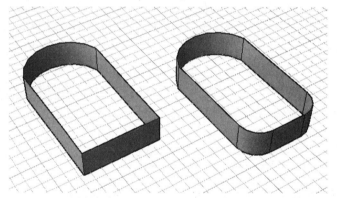

STEPS: Editing Surfaces

1. Open `ab23-i.dwg` available from the Drawings download on the companion website.

2. Save it as `ab23-10.dwg` in your `AutoCAD Bible` folder. You see some construction lines that will be the basis for your model. Set a running object snap for Endpoint.

3. Choose Surface tab ⇨ Create panel ⇨ Extrude. At the `Select objects to extrude or [MOde]:` prompt, select all of the lines and press Enter to end selection.

4. At the next prompt, move the cursor up and type **6** ↵. You can see the result on the left side of Figure 23.29.

5. Choose Surface tab ⇨ Edit panel ⇨ Extend. At the `Select surface edges to extend:` prompt, pick the edge at ❶ in Figure 23.29. Press Enter to end selection.

6. At the `Specify extend distance [Expression/Modes]:` prompt, type **m** ↵. Press Enter again to accept the current mode.

7. At the `Creation type [Merge/Append] <Append>:` prompt, type **m** ↵ to extend the original surface rather than add a new one.

8. At the `Specify extend distance [Expression/Modes]:` prompt, pick the endpoint at ❷.

9. Choose Surface tab ⇨ Edit panel ⇨ Trim.

10. At the `Select surfaces or regions to trim or [Extend/PROjection direction]:` prompt, select the surface at ❸. Press Enter to end selection.

11. At the `Select cutting curves, surfaces or regions:` prompt, select the surface at ❹ and press Enter to end selection.

12. At the `Select area to trim [Undo]:` prompt, select the first surface at ❺. Press Enter to end the command.

13. Choose Surface tab ⇨ Edit panel ⇨ Fillet. At the `Select first surface or region to fillet or [Radius/Trim surface]:` prompt, type **r** ↵ to set the radius. Type **3**↵.

14. At the `Select first surface or region to fillet or [Radius/Trim surface]:` prompt, pick the surface at ❸. At the `Select second surface or region to fillet or [Radius/Trim surface]:` prompt, pick the surface at ❹. Press Enter to accept the fillet and end the command.

15. Repeat the SURFFILLET command and fillet the surfaces at ❻ and ❼.

16. Choose Surface tab ⇨ Create panel ⇨ Offset. At the `Select surfaces or regions to offset:` prompt, select all of the surfaces, including the fillets, for a total of six objects. Press Enter to end selection.

17. At the `Specify offset distance or [Flip direction/Both sides/Solid/ Connect/Expression] <0.0000>:` prompt, type **f** ↵ to move the direction arrows to the inside of the closed model.

18. The prompt repeats. Type **2** ↵ to offset the model by 2 units.

19. Choose View tab ⇨ Visual Styles panel ⇨ Visual Styles drop-down list ⇨ Conceptual. Your model should look like Figure 23.29.

23

FIGURE 23.29

The model shows the result after being extruded, extended, trimmed, filleted, and off-set.

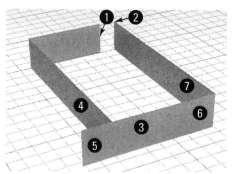 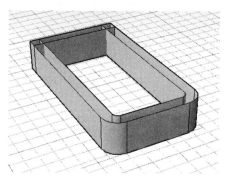

Projecting objects onto surfaces

The PROJECTGEOMETRY command projects 2D objects (points, lines, or curves) as well as 3D polylines and helixes onto a 3D solid or surface. It's similar to the IMPRINT command, which I cover in Chapter 24, but actually creates a surface on the face of the solid or surface. The object you project must be on or above the solid or surface. By setting the SURFACEAUTOTRIM system variable to 1, you can use the command as a way of trimming the 3D object.

To start the PROJECTGEOMETRY command, choose Surface tab ⇨ Project Geometry panel and choose one of the following options:

- **Surface Projection UCS.** Projects the object along the Z axis of the current UCS. The object you are projecting must be directly above or below the receiving object.
- **Surface Projection View.** Projects the object along the line of the current viewpoint. The object you are projecting must look like it is above or below the receiving object.
- **Surface Projection Vector.** Projects the object along a line that you specify with two points. The object you are projecting must be in line with the two points and the receiving object.

Figure 23.30 shows an example of projecting a circle onto a surface, with the SURFACEAUTOTRIM system variable set to 1 (on). The example on the left used the UCS option; the example on the right used the View option.

Analyzing surfaces

You can use surface analysis tools to check continuity, curvature, and draft angles of surfaces. These tools are helpful to make sure there are no unseen problems before going to the manufacturing stage.

FIGURE 23.30

Two examples of projecting geometry onto a surface — the UCS and the View options

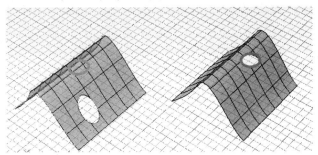

AutoCAD offers three analysis tools:

- **Analysis Zebra.** Analyzes continuity by displaying parallel lines on the model.
- **Analysis Curvature.** Finds areas of high and low curvature by displaying a color gradient.
- **Analysis Draft.** Analyzes draft angle changes within a range that you specify by displaying a range of colors. Draft analysis is important for parts that are molded, to allow for easier removal from the mold.

To analyze surfaces, choose Surface tab ⇨ Analysis panel and choose one of the analysis types. For a more detailed configuration, choose Surface tab ⇨ Analysis panel ⇨ Analysis Options to open the Analysis Options dialog box, which contains a tab for each type of analysis. You can specify colors, ranges, and other settings.

Working with Multiple Types of Objects

Several commands convert one type of object to another or allow you to use multiple types of objects together. For example, you can convert 2D objects to surfaces and surfaces to solids.

Converting 2D objects to surfaces

Perhaps the simplest way to create a surface is to convert an existing object to a surface. The CONVTOSURFACE command allows you to do just that. You can convert the following objects to surfaces:

- 2D objects created with the SOLID command
- Regions
- Zero-width polylines with thickness and that don't create a closed figure
- Lines and arcs with thickness (covered in Chapter 21)

> **CAUTION**
>
> By default, the original objects are deleted. You can control this by using the DELOBJ system variable, which determines whether objects that are used to create other objects are deleted. To keep the original objects, change the value of DELOBJ to 0 (zero). (The default value is 3, which deletes the objects.) You can set the value to –3 to prompt you and allow you to decide if you want to delete the original objects.

 To convert one of the supported objects to a surface, choose Mesh tab ⇨ Convert Mesh panel ⇨ Convert to Surface to start the CONVTOSURFACE command. Then select the object or objects that you want to convert.

Converting meshes to smooth surfaces

Objects that you create by using the PLANESURF, REVOLVE, EXTRUDE, SWEEP, and LOFT commands are called *smooth* surfaces to distinguish them from the older polygon or polyface mesh surfaces. You can control how mesh objects are converted to solids and smooth surfaces by using the SMOOTHMESH-CONVERT variable. To set the system variable, choose Mesh tab ⇨ Convert Mesh panel ⇨ Smooth/Faceted drop-down list and choose one of the options. You can choose to create smoothed or flattened faces, and choose whether or not to merge coplanar faces. Then choose Mesh tab ⇨ Convert Mesh panel ⇨ Convert to Surface.

Thickening a surface into a solid

The THICKEN command allows you to add thickness to a surface and thereby turn it into a solid. You can only use it on surfaces created with the PLANESURF, EXTRUDE, SWEEP, LOFT, or REVOLVE command. However, you can start with a region, line, or arc — using CONVTOSURFACE, for example, to create a surface — and then use THICKEN to turn it into a solid.

To thicken a surface to a solid, follow these steps:

1. Choose Solid tab ⇨ Solid Editing panel ⇨ Thicken.

2. Select the surface or surfaces that you want to thicken.

3. At the `Specify thickness <0.0000>:` prompt, enter a thickness. A positive number thickens in the positive direction of the axes; a negative number thickens in the negative direction.

Sculpting surfaces to create a solid

The SURFSCULPT command converts surfaces that create a completely enclosed volume and turn it into a solid. You can also use the command with solids and mesh objects (which I cover in Chapter 24).

 To create a solid from surfaces that are enclosed, choose Surface tab ⇨ Edit panel ⇨ Surface Sculpt. At the `Select surfaces or solids to sculpt into a solid:` prompt, use a crossing window to select all of the surfaces. Press Enter to end selection. AutoCAD creates the solid.

> **NOTE**
>
> SURFSCULPT doesn't work with surfaces that have G1 or G2 continuity. For more information, see the earlier discussion on the SURFBLEND command.

Extracting edges and isolines from a surface, solid, or a region

You can turn a surface, solid, or a region into a wireframe object by extracting its edges. To extract an edge, choose Solid tab ⇨ Solid Editing panel ⇨ Extract Edges. The XEDGES command works with 3D solids, mesh objects, regions, surfaces, and subobjects (edges and faces). You cannot convert polygon or polyface meshes. Figure 23.31 shows edges extracted from a lofted surface.

FIGURE 23.31

The XEDGES command can extract edges from a surface.

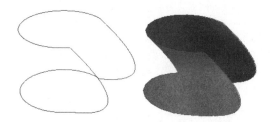

You can also select individual edges or faces to extract by pressing the Ctrl key and clicking the edges or faces that you want. Then use the XEDGES command to extract them.

> **NEW FEATURE**
>
> When working with complex 3D objects, extracting just the visible edges of an object might not be enough. AutoCAD 2013 lets you extract the curvature of a surface in the U or V direction. The extracted curves are generated as lines, arcs, polylines, and splines. To extract the curvature of a surface or face on a solid, choose Surface tab ⇨ Curves panel ⇨ Extract Isolines. Then select the surface or solid to work with, and drag the cursor over the surface or face to extract a curve from. Figure 23.32 shows the extraction of a curve from a face on a lofted 3D solid.

FIGURE 23.32

An extracted curve from the face of a lofted 3D solid using the SURFEXTRACTCURVE command

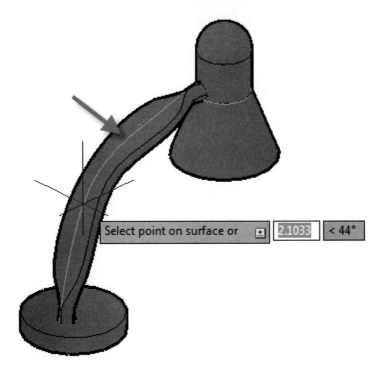

Select point on surface or   2.1033   < 44°

Summary

In this chapter, you read all about 3D surfaces. You read about:

- Creating plane surfaces
- Drawing surfaces with 3D polygon meshes, including the basic shapes — box, wedge, pyramid, cone, sphere, dome, dish, and torus
- Making a surface by revolving a profile around an axis
- Extruding and sweeping a curve
- Creating a surface between two curves
- Making an edge surface from four curves
- Creating procedural and NURBS surfaces
- Editing and analyzing procedural and NURBS surfaces
- Working with multiple types of objects
- Extracting the edges and isolines of surfaces, solids, and regions

In the next chapter, you discover how to create true solids and meshes (well, true electronic ones, at least) as well as how to edit in 3D.

Creating Solids and Editing in 3D

IN THIS CHAPTER

Creating basic geometrical shapes

Drawing extruded, swept, revolved, lofted, and polyline solids

Manipulating solids directly

Creating mesh shapes

Building complex solids

Create cross-section views of your 3D models

Working with editing commands in 3D

Editing solids in 3D

Determining solid properties

Although you can create great-looking models with surfaces, if you want truly realistic models, you need to create solids. After all, in real life, objects have solidity. Even a thin object such as a wastepaper basket or a drape has some thickness. Solids enable you to create more realistic models than surfaces. AutoCAD offers two types of solids: smooth and mesh. You can also combine or subtract solids and get information about their physical properties. Figure 24.1 shows a complex model created using solids.

> **AutoCAD Only**
> AutoCAD LT doesn't draw solids. For the 3D capabilities of AutoCAD LT, see Chapters 21 and 22.

As I explain in Chapter 21, when working in 3D, you should use a 3D environment, including the 3D Modeling workspace and the `acad3d.dwt` (or similar) template.

FIGURE 24.1

You can create complex and realistic models using solids.

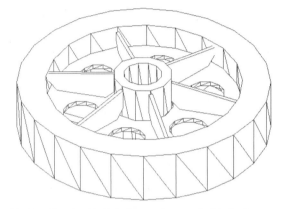

Thanks to Hans-Joachim Fach, Bremen, Germany, for this drawing.

Drawing Basic Smooth Solids

AutoCAD makes it easy to create most basic geometrical shapes. These shapes are easy to draw because you can dynamically see the result as you draw.

Drawing a box

The box is one of the most commonly used 3D objects and is often the basis for more complex models. Figure 24.2 shows a solid box shown with the 3D Hidden visual style.

FIGURE 24.2

A solid box

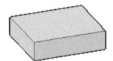

To draw a box, follow these steps:

1. Choose Home tab ⇨ Modeling panel ⇨ 3D Solid drop-down menu ⇨ Box.

2. At the `Specify first corner or [Center]:` prompt, specify any corner of the box, or right-click and choose Center to specify the 3D center of the box (not the center of the base).

3. If you specify the corner (the default), you then see the `Specify other corner or [Cube/Length]:` prompt.

   The default is to pick the opposite corner in the XY plane. This defines the base of the box. You can define the base just like you define any rectangle, by dragging and picking the opposite corner or by entering coordinates. At the `Specify height or [2Point]:` prompt, drag in the Z direction and pick a height or enter a height value. You can also pick two points to specify the height. This completes the box.

   If you use the Length option, AutoCAD asks you for a width and a height. If you use the Cube option, AutoCAD asks for one length and completes the box.

4. If you specify the center at the first prompt, you see the `Specify center:` prompt. Specify the center of the box. The `Specify corner or [Cube/Length]:` prompt appears.

   If you pick the corner of the box, AutoCAD then asks you for the height to complete the box.

   If you specify the length, AutoCAD then asks for a width and a height. If you use the Cube option, AutoCAD asks for a length and completes the box.

You can specify a negative length, width, or height to build the box in the negative direction. If you specify the center of the cube, don't forget that the center's Z coordinate is different from the corner's Z coordinate. AutoCAD always creates the box parallel to the XY plane.

Drawing a wedge

A wedge is a box sliced diagonally in half. The prompts are virtually the same as for the Box command. Figure 24.3 shows two wedges.

FIGURE 24.3

Two solid wedges

To create a wedge, follow these steps:

1. Choose Home tab ⇨ Modeling panel ⇨ 3D Solid drop-down menu ⇨ Wedge.

2. At the `Specify first corner or [Center]:` prompt, specify any corner of the wedge or use the Center option to specify the 3D center of the wedge.

3. If you specify the corner (the default), you then see the `Specify other corner or [Cube/Length]:` prompt.

   The default is to pick the opposite corner in the XY plane — you can also define it by using coordinates. The command then asks you for the height in the Z direction. This completes the wedge.

   If you use the Length option, AutoCAD asks you for a width and a height.

   If you use the Cube option, AutoCAD asks for one length and completes the wedge. For positive lengths, the wedge slopes downward in the positive X direction. (However, if you have Dynamic Input on, the slope will follow the direction of the cursor.)

4. If you specify the center, you see the `Specify center:` prompt. Specify the center point. The `Specify corner or [Cube/Length]:` prompt displays.

   If you pick the corner of the wedge, the command asks for a height.

   If you specify the length, AutoCAD then asks for a width and a height. If you use the Cube option, AutoCAD asks for a length and completes the wedge.

Drawing a cone

You can draw cones with circular or elliptical bases. By specifying a negative height, you can create an inverted cone (like an ice-cream cone). By specifying the Axis endpoint (the apex), you can draw cones on an angle from the XY plane. You can also specify a top radius to create a truncated cone (sometimes called a frustum cone). Figure 24.4 shows some cones.

FIGURE 24.4

Cones with varying heights and bases

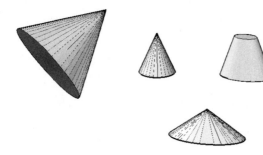

Follow these steps to draw a cone:

1. Choose Home tab ⇨ Modeling panel ⇨ 3D Solid drop-down menu ⇨ Cone.

2. At the `Specify center point of base or [3P/2P/Ttr/Elliptical]:` prompt, specify the center of the base if you want a circular cone. Otherwise, use the 3P, 2P, or Ttr options to define a circular base. Use the Elliptical option to define an elliptical base.

    If you specified a center point, at the `Specify base radius or [Diameter]:` prompt, specify a radius or use the Diameter option to specify the diameter.

    If you chose the Elliptical option, use the prompts to define the elliptical base. These prompts are like the prompts for the ELLIPSE command.

3. At the `Specify height or [2Point/Axis endpoint/Top radius]:` prompt, specify the height by dragging or entering a value. Use the 2Point option to specify the height by picking two points. The Axis endpoint option is another way to specify the height, and enables you to create an angled cone. (By default, the Axis endpoint is a relative coordinate, based on the center of the base.) The Top radius option creates a truncated cone.

Drawing a sphere

Spheres are not used very often alone, but they can be the basis for more complex models — they certainly look pretty! Figure 24.5 shows two solid spheres. The left sphere uses the default ISOLINE value of 4. The right sphere uses an ISOLINE value of 8.

FIGURE 24.5

Two solid spheres, with ISOLINES set at 4 (left) and 8 (right)

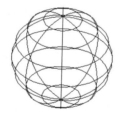

24

To draw a sphere, follow these steps:

1. Choose Home tab ⇨ Modeling panel ⇨ 3D Solid drop-down menu ⇨ Sphere.

2. At the `Specify center point or [3P/2P/Ttr]:` prompt, specify the center of the sphere. If you want the sphere to lie on the XY plane, the Z coordinate of the center should be equal to the radius of the sphere. Use the 3P, 2P, or Ttr option to define a circle at the center of the sphere.

3. At the `Specify radius or [Diameter]:` prompt, drag and pick a point on the surface of the sphere or enter a value for the radius. You can use the Diameter option to specify the diameter.

Drawing a cylinder

Cylinders are very common in 3D drawing, both for building models and creating holes. Figure 24.6 shows three solid cylinders. The grid helps you to visualize the XY plane. You can draw cylinders with circular or elliptical bases. By specifying the center of the top of the cylinder separately, you can draw it at an angle.

FIGURE 24.6

Some solid cylinders

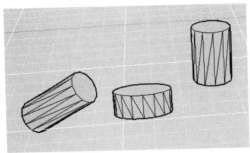

Follow these steps to draw a cylinder:

1. Choose Home tab ⇨ Modeling panel ⇨ 3D Solid drop-down menu ⇨ Cylinder.

2. At the `Specify center point of base or [3P/2P/Ttr/Elliptical]:` prompt, specify the center point for a circular cylinder or define the circle by using the 3P, 2P, or Ttr option. You can also choose the Elliptical option to define an ellipse as a base.

   If you specified a center point, then at the `Specify base radius or [Diameter]:` prompt, specify a radius or use the Diameter option to specify the diameter.

   If you chose the Elliptical option, use the prompts to define the elliptical base.

3. At the `Specify height or [2Point/Axis endpoint]:` prompt, specify the height by dragging, entering a value, or using the 2Point option. You can create a tilted cylinder by using the Axis endpoint option to specify the center of the other end of the cylinder. (By default, the Axis endpoint is a relative coordinate, based on the center of the base.)

Drawing a torus

A *torus* is a solid 3D donut. Figure 24.7 shows some examples with the parts of the torus labeled. You can make some unusual shapes by varying the torus and tube radii. If the torus radius is negative and the tube radius is larger than the absolute value of the torus radius (for example, −2 and 3), you create a lemon (or football) shape. If the tube radius is larger than the torus radius, you create a puckered ball (or apple) shape.

FIGURE 24.7

Varieties of the torus

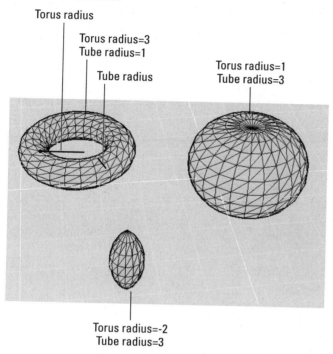

Torus radius

Torus radius=3
Tube radius=1

Tube radius

Torus radius=1
Tube radius=3

Torus radius=-2
Tube radius=3

To create a torus, follow these steps:

1. Choose Home tab ⇨ Modeling panel ⇨ 3D Solid drop-down menu ⇨ Torus.

2. At the `Specify center point or [3P/2P/Ttr]`: prompt, specify the center of the torus (the center of the hole). You can also use the 3P, 2P, or Ttr option to define a circle as the basis for the torus.

3. At the `Specify radius or [Diameter]`: prompt, specify the radius of the entire torus or use the Diameter option to specify the diameter.

4. At the `Specify tube radius or [2Point/Diameter]`: prompt, specify the radius of just the tube or use the Diameter option to specify the tube's diameter. You can use the 2Point option to pick two points that define the tube radius.

24

Drawing a pyramid

You can draw pyramids with a base of 3 to 32 sides. The prompts for the base are similar to the prompts for the POLYGON command. (For more information on the POLYGON command, see Chapter 6.) A pyramid can come to a point, or you can truncate it. You can also tilt the pyramid. Figure 24.8 shows three variations on the pyramid.

FIGURE 24.8

You can draw several types of pyramids.

Follow these steps to draw a pyramid:

1. Choose Home tab ⇨ Modeling panel ⇨ 3D Solid drop-down menu ⇨ Pyramid. The default number of sides is listed, as well as whether the base will be inscribed or circumscribed.

2. At the `Specify center point of base or [Edge/Sides]:` prompt, specify the center of the base. You can use the Edge option to define an edge, or the Sides option to specify the number of sides.

3. At the `Specify base radius or [Inscribed]:` prompt, drag to specify the radius or enter a value. You can use the Inscribed (or Circumscribed) option to change whether the radius is inscribed (based on the base points) or circumscribed (based on the base side mid-points).

4. At the `Specify height or [2Point/Axis endpoint/Top radius]:` prompt, drag to specify the height or enter a value. Use the 2Point option to specify the height by picking two points. Use the Axis endpoint to specify the tip. If it isn't directly over the base's center, you tilt the pyramid. Use the Top radius to truncate the pyramid; drag or enter a value for the top's radius and then enter the height of the pyramid.

ON THE WEB

The drawing that you need for the following exercise on drawing basic 3D solids, `ab24-a.dwg`, is available from the Drawings download on the companion website.

STEPS: Drawing Basic 3D Solids

1. Open `ab24-a.dwg`, available from the companion website.

2. Save the file as `ab24-01.dwg` in your `AutoCAD Bible` folder. Turn on Object Snap. Set running object snaps for Quadrant and Center. In this exercise, I assume that you have dynamic input on, set to the default of relative coordinates.

3. Choose Home tab ⇨ Modeling panel ⇨ 3D Solid drop-down menu ⇨ Cylinder. Follow the prompts:

   ```
   Specify center point of base or [3P/2P/Ttr/Elliptical]: 7,6.5 ↵
   Specify base radius or [Diameter] <3.0000>: 3 ↵
   Specify height or [2Point/Axis endpoint] <1.0000>: Move the cursor upward
       and enter 1 ↵
   ```

4. Repeat the CYLINDER command. Zoom closer to the top end of the lamp's arm and change the viewpoint so that you can see the end circle more clearly. Follow the prompts:

   ```
   Specify center point of base or [3P/2P/Ttr/Elliptical]: 2p ↵
   Specify first end point of diameter: Choose the bottom quadrant of the
       top end of the lamp's arm.
   Specify second end point of diameter: 3,0 ↵
   Specify height or [2Point/Axis endpoint] <17.2980>: Move the cursor
       upward and enter 2.5 ↵.
   ```

5. Choose Home tab ⇨ Modeling panel ⇨ 3D Solid drop-down menu ⇨ Sphere. Follow the prompts:

   ```
   Specify center point or [3P/2P/Ttr]: 2p ↵
   Specify first end point of diameter: Pick the left quadrant of the top of
       the cylinder that you just drew.
   Specify second end point of diameter: Pick the right quadrant of the top
       of the cylinder that you just drew.
   ```

6. Choose Home tab ⇨ Modeling panel ⇨ 3D Solid drop-down menu ⇨ Cone. Follow the prompts:

   ```
   Specify center point of base or [3P/2P/Ttr/Elliptical]: Pick the center
       of the bottom of the cylinder.
   Specify base radius or [Diameter] <1.5000>: Pick any quadrant on the edge
       of the cylinder's bottom edge.
   Specify height or [2Point/Axis endpoint/Top radius] <4.0000>: t ↵
   Specify top radius <3.0000>: 3 ↵
   Specify height or [2Point/Axis endpoint] <4.0000>: Move the cursor
       downward and enter 4 ↵.
   ```

7. Choose View tab ⇨ Navigate panel ⇨ Zoom drop-down menu ⇨ Extents.

8. Choose View tab ⇨ Visual Styles panel ⇨ Visual Styles drop-down list ⇨ Conceptual.

9. Save your drawing. It should look like Figure 24.9.

24

FIGURE 24.9

The desk lamp

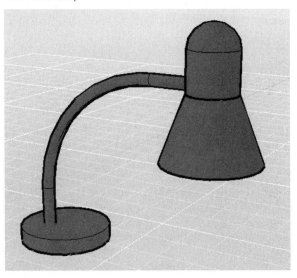

Creating Extruded Solids

The EXTRUDE command is similar to adding thickness to a 2D object (discussed in Chapter 21) or using the TABSURF command (see Chapter 23). You can also extrude the face of an existing solid, as I explain later in this chapter. You can extrude lines, arcs, elliptical arcs, 2D polylines, circles, ellipses, splines, 2D solids, planar surfaces, and regions. You can use the REGION command to create one object from several objects for this purpose. You can select several objects and extrude them at one time. Figure 24.10 shows several extruded solids.

The EXTRUDE command can create either a solid or a surface, based on the setting of the Closed Profiles Creation Mode. If you type the command on the command line, the mode is listed as either Solid or Surface, and you can use the MOde option to change the setting. If you start the command from the Surface tab, you get a surface. If you start the command from the command line or the Solid tab, you get a solid. When using the solid mode, you get a solid — if a solid is possible. For a solid to be possible, the profile must be closed or the profile must be in one plane.

Managing objects used to make other objects

When you extrude a circle to make a cylinder, for example, what should happen to the circle? Do you want to delete it because you want to turn it into a cylinder, or do you want to keep it in case your cylinder isn't just right and you need to use the circle again? The DELOBJ system variable determines whether objects used by the EXTRUDE command (as well as REVOLVE, LOFT, SWEEP, and others) to make other objects are retained. By default, certain source objects are deleted. Therefore, when you use a 2D object to make a solid, the 2D object is deleted.

FIGURE 24.10

Some extruded solids

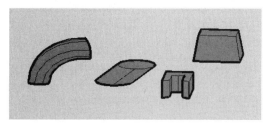

The DELOBJ system variable has the following options:

- **0:** Retains all source objects.
- **1:** Deletes profile curves. For example, if you use a circle to create a cylinder, the circle is deleted. Cross-sections and guides used with the SWEEP command are also deleted. However, if you extrude along a path, the path is not deleted. This is the default option.
- **2:** Deletes all defining objects, including paths and guide curves.
- **3:** Deletes all defining objects, including paths and guide curves only if a solid is created.
- **-1:** Prompts to delete profile curves. This is like 1, but you get a prompt so you can choose.
- **-2:** Prompts to delete all defining objects. This is like 2, but you get a prompt.
- **-3:** Prompts to delete all defining objects if the result is a surface, but not if the result is a solid.

> **TIP**
>
> Put source objects on a separate layer. Set DELOBJ to 0 (zero) to keep objects used to create other objects, or to -2 to be prompted whenever a choice is possible. When you're done, turn off the layer containing your source objects.

Using the EXTRUDE command

When you extrude an object, by default you extrude it perpendicular to the object. However, you can also taper the extrusion, as in the extruded rectangle on the right in Figure 24.10. A positive angle tapers the object inward. A negative angle tapers the object outward so it gets wider in the direction of the extrusion.

> **NOTE**
>
> Don't taper the object too much. If the taper angle results in the object coming to a point before its full height, AutoCAD cannot create the solid.

You can extrude the object by specifying a height of extrude, a direction by specifying two points, or along a path. A path can be a line, circle, arc, ellipse, elliptical arc, polyline, spline, or even a helix. The path object must be in a different plane than the original object. Not all paths are suitable for extruding objects. In the following situations, the extrusion may not work. The path should not be:

24

- Too close to the original object's plane
- Too complex
- Too tightly curved or bent for the size of the original object

Here are the steps for creating an extruded solid:

1. Draw the object that you want to extrude. If you want to extrude along a path, draw the path object in a different plane from the source object.

 2. Choose Home tab ⇨ Modeling panel ⇨ Solid Creation drop-down menu ⇨ Extrude.

3. Select the object or objects to extrude.

4. At the `Specify height of extrusion or [Direction/Path/Taper angle/ Expression] <3.5226>:` prompt, specify the height of the extrusion (drag or enter a value). Use the Path option to extrude along a path object; just select the path object. The Direction option is similar to the Path option, except that you specify two points to indicate the path. Use the Taper angle option to enter a taper angle. Use the Expression option to help calculate the height of the extrusion.

> **NOTE**
>
> You can select an edge or other subobject as the path. Also, the path does not have to be in one plane.

> **ON THE WEB**
>
> The drawing that you need for the following exercise on creating extruded solids, ab24-b.dwg, is available from the Drawings download on the companion website.

STEPS: Creating Extruded Solids

1. Open `ab24-b.dwg`, available from the companion website.

2. Save the file as `ab24-02.dwg` in your `AutoCAD Bible` folder. Make sure that Object Snap is on. Set running object snaps for Endpoint and Midpoint. This is a small mounting angle, shown in an edge view.

 3. The angle is made up of lines and arcs. To extrude it, you need to change it into a polyline or region. To change it into a polyline, choose Home tab ⇨ Modify panel (expanded) ⇨ Join. Follow the prompts:

```
Select source object or multiple objects to join at once: Use a window to
    select all the objects in the mounting angle.
Select objects to join: ↵
```

 4. Choose Home tab ⇨ Modeling panel ⇨ Solid Creation drop-down menu ⇨ Extrude. The Closed Profiles Creation Mode should be set to Solid. (If not, use the MOde option and the SOlid suboption.) Select the mounting angle, and then press Enter to end object selection. At the `Specify height of extrusion or [Direction/Path/Taper angle/Expression] <-1.0800>:` prompt, move the cursor up and type **3** ↵.

5. Choose View tab ⇨ Visual Styles panel ⇨ Visual Styles drop-down list ⇨ Conceptual.
6. Save your drawing. It should look like Figure 24.11.

FIGURE 24.11

The completed mounting angle

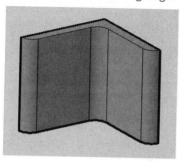

The mounting angle should have two holes in it. You would create the holes by using the SUBTRACT command, which I cover later in this chapter.

Drawing Swept Solids

The SWEEP command is similar to the EXTRUDE command, but it concentrates on using paths to define the direction of the extrusion.

The SWEEP command has some great tricks up its sleeve:

1. You can draw the source object on the same plane as the path. You don't even have to place the source object on the path. The SWEEP command figures out the center of the source object. (You can use the Base point option to specify the base point for the source object.)
2. You can twist the object along the path.
3. You can scale the source object.
4. If the source object is a closed object, like a circle, you get a solid; if it's open, you get a swept surface.

The DELOBJ system variable determines what happens to the original objects; for more information, see the explanation in the previous section. Figure 24.12 shows some swept solids.

24

FIGURE 24.12

You can create very interesting shapes by using the SWEEP command.

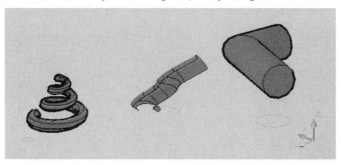

To create a swept solid or surface, follow these steps:

1. Draw the path that you want to sweep along.

2. In the same plane as the path, draw the object or objects that you want to sweep.

 3. Choose Home tab ⇨ Modeling panel ⇨ Solid Creation drop-down menu ⇨ Sweep.

> **NOTE**
>
> The SWEEP command can create either a solid or a surface, based on the setting of the Closed Profiles Creation Mode. For more information, see the explanation in the section on the EXTRUDE command. Also, the path can be an edge or other subobject.

4. At the `Select objects to sweep or [MOde]:` prompt, select the object or objects that you drew.

5. At the `Select sweep path or [Alignment/Base point/Scale/Twist]:` prompt, select the path.

   - Use the Alignment option if you don't want to align the object perpendicular to the path. By default, the SWEEP does so; for this reason, you don't have to set up the path and the object in different planes.

   - Use the Base Point option to specify a base point on the objects to be swept, to determine the point on that object that actually lies along the path.

   - Use the Scale option to scale the object before sweeping it.

   - Use the Twist option to twist the object along the path. For example, if you specify 180°, the object twists that much from the beginning to the end of the path. This option has a suboption, Bank, that allows you to specify if you want the object to also rotate in the 3D direction when you use a 3D sweep path (a 3D polyline, 3D spline, or helix).

> **ON THE WEB**
>
> The drawing that you need for the following exercise on creating swept solids, `ab24-c.dwg`, is available from the Drawings download on the companion website.

STEPS: Creating Swept Solids

1. Open `ab24-c.dwg`, available from the companion website. This is the same drawing that was used for the exercise on drawing basic shapes; however, this time the desk lamp is missing its arm. A path is already drawn on the `const` layer.

2. Save the file as `ab24-03.dwg` in your `AutoCAD Bible` folder. If necessary, change the visual style to 3D Wireframe (choose View tab ⇨ Visual Styles panel ⇨ Visual Styles drop-down list ⇨ Wireframe).

3. Make the `const` layer current. Draw a circle anywhere with a radius of 0.375 (a diameter of 0.75).

4. Switch to the `object` layer.

5. Choose Home tab ⇨ 3D Modeling panel ⇨ Solid Creation drop-down menu ⇨ Sweep. The Closed Profiles Creation Mode should be set to Solid. (If not, use the MOde option and the SOlid sub-option.) Follow these prompts to sweep the circle along the arm (a polyline):

   ```
   Select objects to sweep: Select the circle.
   Select objects to sweep: ↵
   Select sweep path or [Alignment/Base point/Scale/Twist]: Select the arm
        (the polyline).
   ```

6. Save your drawing. Look back to Figure 24.9 to see what the lamp looks like.

Drawing Revolved Solids

The REVOLVE command revolves a profile around an axis. You can revolve lines, arcs, elliptical arcs, 2D polylines, circles, ellipses, splines, 2D solids, planar faces, and regions.

The DELOBJ system variable affects whether the original objects are deleted. See the discussion on this system variable earlier in this chapter in the section "Managing objects used to make other objects."

The REVOLVE command can create either a solid or a surface, based on the setting of the Closed Profiles Creation Mode. For more information, see the explanation in the section on the EXTRUDE command. The path can be an edge or other subobject and the path does not have to be in one plane. Additionally, you can use the Reverse option to change the direction of the revolution and the EXpression option to enter a formula or equation to calculate the angle of revolution. 1.5708 * (180 / PI) is an example of an expression.

Figure 24.13 shows a solid created by revolving a rectangle around a line. (You can also create this solid by drawing two circles, extruding them into cylinders, and then subtracting the smaller cylinder from the larger one — it just depends on which technique you're more comfortable with.)

FIGURE 24.13

A solid created by revolving a rectangle around a line.

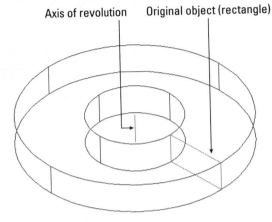

To create a revolved solid, follow these steps:

1. Choose Home tab ⇨ Modeling panel ⇨ Solid Creation drop-down menu ⇨ Revolve.

2. At the `Select objects to revolve or [MOde]:` prompt, select one or more objects.

3. At the `Specify axis start point or define axis by [Object/X/Y/Z] <Object>:` prompt, you can pick two points to create an axis of revolution. You can also select an object as an axis. Use the X, Y, or Z option to revolve the object around the respective axis.

4. At the `Specify angle of revolution or [STart angle/Reverse/EXpression]` `<360>:` prompt, press Enter to revolve the object 360 degrees or type an angle, either positive or negative. You can use the STart angle option to specify a start and end angle; for example, you can start at 45 degrees and end at 90 degrees. Use the Reverse option to reverse the angle of revolution. The Expression option lets you calculate the angle of revolution based on a formula or equation.

You need to determine the positive direction of rotation if you're revolving less than 360 degrees. (Of course, it may be quicker to try one way and just do it the other way if it doesn't turn out right.) Here's how to figure it out:

1. First determine the positive direction of the axis. If you specify start and endpoints, the positive axis direction goes from the start point to the endpoint. If you pick an object, the positive axis direction goes from the pick point to the other endpoint. If you choose the X, Y, or Z axis, the positive direction is obvious.

2. Point your right thumb in the positive direction of the axis.

3. Look at the curl of your fingers on that hand. That's the positive direction of rotation.

Drawing Lofted Solids

The LOFT command creates a solid or surface that is interpolated from a series of profiles, or cross-sections. Figure 24.14 shows some lofted solids.

FIGURE 24.14

Two solid and two surface lofted objects. On one of the surfaces, you can see the source cross-sections (splines).

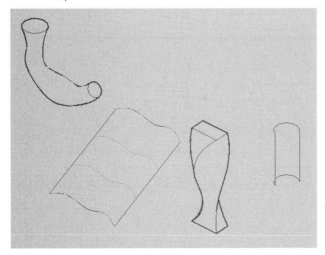

The difficult part of lofting is drawing and placing the source cross-sections to get the result that you want. As you select cross-sections, you see a preview of how the new object will look. The transparency level of the preview is controlled with the PREVIEWCREATIONTRANSPARENCY system variable. To create a lofted surface or solid, follow these steps:

1. Draw a series of closed or open profiles. You can start with one and then copy it to nearby locations on the path that will run centrally along the lofted object. You can then modify the copies as necessary. These cross-sections become the basis for the lofted object. You need at least two cross-sections.

   - If you want to control the sides of the loft (generally for surfaces), draw guides on each side of your cross-sections. Guides must start at the first cross-section, end at the last cross-section, and intersect each cross-section.

   - If you want to specify a path through the middle of the loft, draw a path object. The path must intersect the plane of each cross-section. The resulting lofted model runs the length of the path.

2. Choose Home tab ⇨ Modeling panel ⇨ Solid Creation drop-down menu ⇨ Loft.

3. At the `Select cross-sections in lofting order or [POint/Join multiple edges/MOde]:` prompt, choose each cross-section in order, and then end selection.

4. At the `Enter an option [Guides/Path/Cross sections only/Settings] <Cross sections only>:` prompt, press Enter to accept the default, which uses the cross-sections only to define the loft. Use the Guides option to select guides you have drawn. Use the Path option to select a path you have drawn. Choose Settings to display the Loft Settings dialog box. You use this dialog box to fine-tune the definition of the loft and specifically to control how the loft is curved at its cross-sections.

   - **Ruled.** Creates a straight (ruled) solid or surface between the cross-sections and sharp edges at the cross-sections.

   - **Smooth Fit.** Creates a smooth solid or surface between the cross-sections and sharp edges at the first and last cross-sections.

   - **Normal to.** Defines which cross-sections the solid or surface is perpendicular (normal) to — the start, end, both start and end, or all cross-sections.

   - **Draft Angles.** Controls the draft angle (the beginning and ending angles) at the first and last cross-sections. This is similar to specifying start and end tangents on a spline. A 0° angle is the default: normal to the cross-section's plane in the direction of the next cross-section. A 180° angle goes outward, away from the cross-section. You also define a magnitude, which is the relative distance that the solid or surface goes before bending to the next cross-section. In other words, if you use a 180° angle, a large magnitude creates a large bulge.

   - **Close Surface or Solid.** Closes the model.

   - **Periodic (smooth ends).** Creates a smooth closed surface when you choose Ruled or Smooth Fit.

With all these options, you may need to experiment a little. Drag the Loft Settings dialog box to the side, and watch what happens as you change the settings. After you create a loft, you can select it and make changes in the Properties palette; again, you can see the results of your changes immediately.

STEPS: Creating Lofted Solids

1. Open `ab24-d.dwg`, available from the companion website. This is the same drawing that was used for the exercise on drawing swept solids; again, the desk lamp's arm is missing, but it

has some cross-sections (on the `const` layer) that you can use to create a lofted solid. The `object` layer should be current.

2. Save the file as `ab24-04.dwg` in your `AutoCAD Bible` folder. If necessary, change the visual style to 3D Wireframe (choose Home tab ⇨ View panel ⇨ Visual Styles drop-down list ⇨ 3D Wireframe).

3. Choose Home tab ⇨ Modeling panel ⇨ Solid Creation drop-down menu ⇨ Loft. The Closed Profiles Creation Mode should be set to Solid. (If not, use the MOde option and the SOlid sub-option.) Follow these prompts to loft the cross-sections along the arm:

```
Select cross sections in lofting order or [POint/Join multiple edges/
    MOde]: Select the bottom-most cross-section (a circle).
Select cross sections in lofting order or [POint/Join multiple edges/
    MOde]: Continue to select all the other cross-sections, one at a
    time, moving upward until you select the circle closest to the head
    of the lamp. Press Enter to end selection.
Enter an option [Guides/Path/Cross sections only/Settings] <Cross
    sections only>: c ⏎
```

4. Turn off the `const` layer.

5. Change the visual style to Conceptual (choose View tab ⇨ Visual Styles panel ⇨ Visual Styles drop-down list ⇨ Conceptual).

6. Save your drawing. Use the 3D Orbit override (Shift+mouse wheel) to change to a view that shows the arm more clearly. It should look like Figure 24.15.

FIGURE 24.15

The completed lamp with a lofted arm

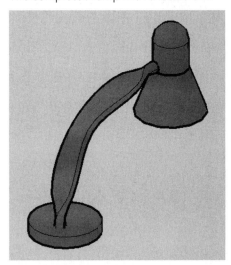

Drawing Polyline-Like Solids

The POLYSOLID command is helpful to architects who want to draw walls in 3D. Using POLYSOLID is like drawing a polyline with a width, or a multiline. You simply draw in plan view from point to point, but the result is a swept solid, using the width and height you specify. You can also convert existing 2D objects — lines, arcs, 2D polylines, and circles — into polysolids.

Figure 24.16 shows a simple layout, drawn by using polysolids.

FIGURE 24.16

You can draw walls by using the POLYSOLID command.

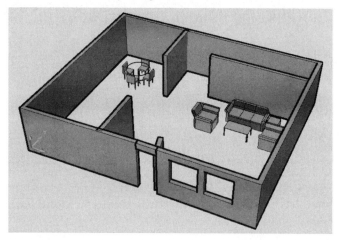

Follow these steps to draw a polysolid:

1. If you want to convert a 2D object, draw the object or open a drawing containing an existing 2D object.

 2. Choose Home tab ⇨ Modeling panel ⇨ Polysolid.

3. At the `Specify start point or [Object/Height/Width/Justify] <Object>:` prompt, start by choosing the Height option.

4. At the `Specify height <8'-0">:` prompt, enter a height.

5. The original prompt returns. Choose the Width option. At the `Specify width <0'-6">:` prompt, enter a width.

6. Again the original prompt returns.

   - If you want to convert an existing object, choose the Object option (you can just press Enter because it's the default option). At the `Select object:` option, select the 2D object to complete the polysolid.

- If you want to draw a new polysolid, specify the start point and continue to specify segments as you would for a polyline. After you specify the first point, you can use the Arc option to create arcs. The prompts are like those for the PLINE command, but you have fewer options. The arc starts tangent to the previous segment. You can specify the direction or the second point for more control.

You can use the Close option to close the polysolid. You can also use the Justify option to determine whether the polysolid is centered around the points you specify (the default), left-justified (your points are to the left side if you're drawing upward), or right-justified.

On the Web

The drawing that you need for the following exercise on creating polysolids, `ab24-e.dwg`, is available from the Drawings download on the companion website.

STEPS: Creating Polysolids

1. Open `ab24-e.dwg`, available from the companion website. This drawing contains two polylines — one to turn into a polysolid and one to create a door gap.

2. Save the file as `ab24-05.dwg` in your `AutoCAD Bible` folder. If necessary, change the visual style to 3D Wireframe (choose View tab ⇨ Visual Styles panel ⇨ Visual Styles drop-down list ⇨ 3D Wireframe). The current layer should be `Walls`.

3. Set the value of the DELOBJ system variable to 0 (zero) so that you don't delete the source object.

4. Choose Home tab ⇨ Modeling panel ⇨ Polysolid. Follow the prompts:

```
Specify start point or [Object/Height/Width/Justify] <Object>: h ↵
Specify height <0'-4">: 8' ↵
Specify start point or [Object/Height/Width/Justify] <Object>: w ↵
Specify width <0'-0 1/4">: 6 ↵
Specify start point or [Object/Height/Width/Justify] <Object>: ↵ to
    choose the Object option.
Select object: Select the larger polyline.
```

5. Select the new polysolid and change its layer to `Walls`.

6. Zoom into the gap for the door. Repeat the POLYSOLID command. Follow the prompts:

```
Specify start point or [Object/Height/Width/Justify] <Object>: j ↵
Enter justification [Left/Center/Right] <Right>: r ↵
Specify start point or [Object/Height/Width/Justify] <Object>: h ↵
Specify height <8'-0">: 7' ↵
Specify start point or [Object/Height/Width/Justify] <Object>: Pick the
    front endpoint on the left side of the gap.
Specify next point or [Arc/Undo]: Pick the front endpoint on the right
    side of the gap.
Specify next point or [Arc/Undo]: ↵
```

24

7. To create a gap for a side door, you need to create a surface and slice the solid with the surface. (I discuss slicing later in this chapter.) Switch to the 2D layer. Choose Home tab⇨Modeling panel⇨Solid Creation drop-down menu⇨Extrude. Select the smaller polyline, end selection, and drag it so that it's higher than the polysolid wall you just created. This creates an extruded surface.

8. Choose Home tab⇨Solid Editing panel⇨Slice to start the SLICE command. (I discuss this command later in this chapter.) Follow the prompts:

```
Select objects to slice: Select the first polysolid that you created.
Select objects to slice: ↵
Specify start point of slicing plane or [planar
Object/Surface/Zaxis/View/XY/YZ/ZX/3points] <3points>: s ↵
Select a surface: Select the extruded surface.
Select solid to keep or [keep Both sides] <Both>: Pick anywhere on the
    main portion of the polysolid wall.
```

> **NOTE**
> If you find that this step doesn't work properly, undo it and redo the step, this time choosing the Both option. Then erase the smaller section of the polysolid in the door opening.

9. Make the `Walls` layer current. Turn off the 2D layer.

10. Save your drawing. It should look like Figure 24.17. If you want, add a polysolid over the front door and rotate the front door to open it. You should also change the DELOBJ system variable back to its original value.

FIGURE 24.17

The polysolid walls with a door and a gap

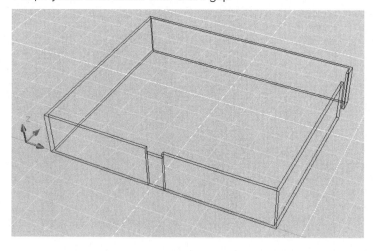

Manipulating Solids

You can directly manipulate solids and meshes (discussed later in this chapter) in several ways that don't involve executing a command. These methods are grip-editing, selecting subobjects (faces, edges, and vertices), and using the Move, Rotate, and Scale tools (called *gizmos*).

Grip-editing solids

You can grip-edit solids in several ways. When you select them, they show grips that allow you to stretch them in all directions. Figure 24.18 shows the grips for a solid box. The triangular grips stretch objects in the direction of the arrow. The square grips also stretch objects, usually at a corner. One grip at the center just moves the object.

 You can also use grips to move, rotate, scale, and mirror solids. I cover grip-editing in Chapter 10 for 2D drawings; the same principles apply for 3D drawings.

FIGURE 24.18

You can stretch a 3D solid box in many directions.

Stretch up to increase height

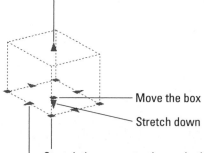

Move the box

Stretch down

Stretch the corner to change both the width and length

Stretch one side in the direction of the arrow

Selecting subobjects

You can select *subobjects* and edit them. A subobject is the face, edge, or vertex of a solid. A subcomponent of a composite solid — one that you used UNION, SUBTRACT on — is also a subobject. You can select more than one subobject, whether on one solid or several solids.

To grip-edit a subobject, follow these steps:

1. Press Ctrl.
2. Pass the cursor over a face, edge, or vertex. Faces and edges highlight, but vertices don't.
3. Click the grip that appears, or hover the cursor over a grip and choose an option.
4. Drag the grip to grip-edit the solid.

You can press Ctrl and click to select a subobject when you select objects for the MOVE, ROTATE, SCALE, or ERASE command. You can press Ctrl and drag a selection or crossing window to select multiple subobjects.

If you want to select the back face of a solid, you can cycle through the faces by pressing and holding Ctrl and repeatedly pressing the Spacebar. Just as you can press Shift and pick to remove any object from a selection set, you can remove a subobject from a selection set by pressing and holding Ctrl and pressing Shift while you pick a subobject (see Figure 24.19).

NOTE

To help make selecting subobjects easier, you can create a filter that specifies which type of subobject you want to select: face, edge, or vertex. Click Home tab ⇨ Selection panel ⇨ Subobject Filter drop-down menu and choose one of the options. You can also right-click before selecting any object and choose Subobject Selection Filter from the shortcut menu.

TIP

The LEGACYCTRLPICK system variable lets you return to the older use of Ctrl+click, which was to cycle through overlapping objects for easier selection. By default, this system variable is set to 0, which allows you to select subobjects on 3D solids. Change its value to 1 to use Ctrl+click to cycle through objects. When set to 1, you can't use Ctrl+click to select subobjects.

FIGURE 24.19

You can select subobjects and edit them separately from the solid.

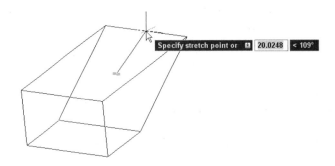

Moving, rotating, and scaling with the gizmos

When moving, rotating, and scaling in 3D, it's often hard to visualize the direction in which you want the object to go. Three tools (called *gizmos*) help with these tasks.

Using the Move gizmo and the 3DMOVE command

You can use the regular MOVE command to move objects in any direction, X, Y, or Z, but entering the coordinates can be awkward. Instead, you can use the Move gizmo, with or without executing the 3DMOVE command, to interactively move objects in 3D space. Figure 24.20 shows the Move gizmo.

To use the Move gizmo by itself, follow these steps:

1. Select an object, with no command active. If you have a 3D visual style active (anything except 2D Wireframe), the Move gizmo automatically appears. (By default, the Quick Properties palette appears nearby; close it if it interferes with your view.)

> **NOTE**
>
> The DEFAULTGIZMO system variable determines which gizmo appears by default. You can set this system variable by choosing Home tab ➪ Selection panel ➪ Subobject Gizmo drop-down menu, and choosing one of the gizmos. If one of the other gizmos appears, right-click the gizmo and choose Move from the shortcut menu. You can now use gizmos with subobjects. If you don't want the Move gizmo to display automatically, set the GTAUTO system variable to 0 (zero).

FIGURE 24.20

Use the Move gizmo to interactively move objects.

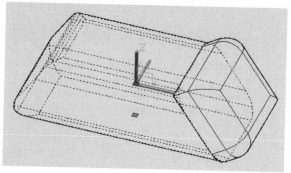

2. Pass the cursor over any grip (but not an arrow); the Move gizmo jumps to that grip. This temporarily places the origin of the UCS at that point and sets the base point for the move operation.

> **NOTE**
>
> In any 3D visual style, the X axis of the UCS icon is red, the Y axis is green, and the Z axis is blue. The Move gizmo uses the same colors to indicate the same directions.

24

3. You can now choose one of three setups to move the selected object:

   - **To move the selected object in any direction.** Drag on the grip itself. This is no different from dragging without the Move gizmo.

   - **To constrain the selected object along one axis.** Pass the cursor over that axis until it turns yellow and you see a line extending to the edge of the screen on either side, as shown in Figure 24.20. Click that axis; now you can move the object only along that axis line. Drag the object in the positive or negative direction along the line. You can use direct distance entry to move the object a specific distance, or just click where you want the grip to be.

- **To constrain the selected object along one plane.** Pass the cursor over the right-angle indicator at the intersection of any two axes, until it turns yellow. Click that right-angle indicator; now you can move the object only in that plane. Move the object in the desired direction. You can enter a relative coordinate or click where you want the grip to be.

TIP

Once you constrain the move, you can press the Spacebar to cycle among the three gizmos, retaining the directional constraint you specified.

 The 3DMOVE command also uses the Move gizmo, but adds prompts similar to the MOVE command. Follow these steps:

1. Choose Home tab ⇨ Modify panel ⇨ 3D Move and select objects, or select objects first and then start the command.

NOTE

If you're using the 2D Wireframe visual style, the command switches you temporarily to the 3D Wireframe visual style. When you're done, the 2D Wireframe visual style returns.

2. At the `Specify base point or [Displacement] <Displacement>:` prompt, the Move gizmo appears.
   - To use the **base point/second point method**, specify a base point. You can now constrain movement to an axis or plane as described just previously in this section. Then specify a second point to move the object.
   - To use the **displacement method**, enter a displacement as an X,Y or polar coordinate. At the `Specify displacement <0.0000, 0.0000, 0.0000 >:` prompt, press Enter to move the object and end the command. In this situation, you don't use the Move gizmo because you are specifying the movement by entering coordinates.

You have a chance to use the 3DMOVE command later in this chapter in the exercise on Extending Objects in 3D.

Using the Rotate gizmo and the 3DROTATE command

The Rotate gizmo lets you interactively rotate in 3D. You can rotate freely or constrain rotation around one axis. You can use it with or without the 3DROTATE command. To use it alone, follow these steps:

1. Select an object, with no command active. If you have a 3D visual style active (anything except 2D Wireframe), the Rotate gizmo automatically appears. (By default, the Quick Properties palette appears nearby; close it if it interferes with your view.)

TIP

If one of the other gizmos appears, right-click the gizmo and choose Rotate from the shortcut menu. In the previous explanation of the Move gizmo, I explain how to specify which gizmo appears by default.

2. Pass the cursor over any grip (but not an arrow); the Rotate gizmo jumps to that grip. This temporarily places the origin of the UCS at that point and sets the base point for the move operation.

3. To constrain the selected object along one axis, pass the cursor over that axis's handle (a circle) until it turns yellow and you see a line extending to the edge of the screen on either side, as shown in Figure 24.21. Click that axis; now you can rotate the object only along that axis. Drag the object along the circle. You can enter a value to rotate the object a specific angle, or just click when the object is at the desired angle.

TIP

After you constrain the rotation, you can press the Spacebar to cycle among the three gizmos, retaining the directional constraint you specified.

FIGURE 24.21

The Rotate gizmo lets you constrain rotation to any axis in 3D space.

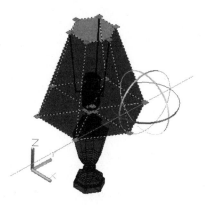

You can also use the 3DROTATE command. Follow these steps:

 1. Start the 3DROTATE command by choosing Home tab ⇨ Modify panel ⇨ 3D Rotate.

NOTE

If you are in 2D Wireframe visual style, this command temporarily changes you to 3D Wireframe. You need to be in a nonorthogonal view to use 3DROTATE.

2. Select objects. The Rotate gizmo appears, as shown in Figure 24.21.
3. At the `Specify base point:` prompt, specify the base point for the rotation. The Rotate gizmo jumps to the base point.
4. At the `Pick a rotation axis:` prompt, hover the cursor over the ribbon that matches the axis around which you want to rotate. It turns yellow and you see an axis line, as shown in Figure 24.21. Click the yellow ribbon.
5. At the `Specify angle start point or type an angle:` prompt, you can simply enter the rotation angle that you want, or pick two points to specify the angle.

I discuss another way to rotate, the ROTATE3D command, later in this chapter. There you'll find an exercise that uses the Rotate gizmo.

Using the Scale gizmo and the 3DSCALE command

The Scale gizmo, shown in Figure 24.22, lets you interactively scale in 3D. Most 3D objects you can scale uniformly along all three axes; however, you can scale meshes along one axis or a plane that you choose. I discuss meshes later in this chapter.

FIGURE 24.22

You can scale 3D objects with the Scale gizmo.

You can use the Scale gizmo with or without the 3DSCALE command. To use it alone, follow these steps:

1. Select an object, with no command active. If you have a 3D visual style active (anything except 2D Wireframe), the Scale gizmo automatically appears. (By default, the Quick Properties palette appears nearby; close it if it interferes with your view.)

NOTE

If one of the other gizmos appears, right-click the gizmo and choose Scale from the shortcut menu. In the previous explanation of the Move gizmo, I explain how to specify which gizmo appears by default.

2. Pass the cursor over any grip (but not an arrow); the Scale gizmo jumps to that grip. This temporarily places the origin of the UCS at that point and sets the base point for the move operation. (Meshes only have one grip.)

TIP

To move the Scale gizmo to a location not on a grip, right-click and choose Relocate Gizmo. You can then use an object snap to specify any other location.

3. For meshes only, you can constrain the scale along an axis or plane. Do one of the following:
   - **To constrain the selected object along one axis.** Pass the cursor over that axis until it turns yellow and you see a line extending to the edge of the screen on either side. Click that axis; now you can scale the object only along that axis. Drag the object along the axis and click when the object is at the desired size or enter a scale factor.

- **To constrain the selected object along a plane.** Pass the cursor over one of the lines that join the axes. For example, to scale along the XY plane, pass the cursor over the line that runs from the X axis to the Y axis. The line turns yellow as do the axis names. Click that line; now you can scale the object only along the specified plane. Drag in the direction you want to scale or enter a scale factor.

> **NOTE**
>
> Once you constrain the scale, you can press the Spacebar to cycle among the three gizmos, retaining the directional constraint you specified.

> **TIP**
>
> It can be hard to see the lines between the planes if the axes are facing away from you. If so, you can press Shift and drag with the mouse wheel to change the 3D view.

You can also use the 3DSCALE command. Follow these steps:

    1. Start the 3DSCALE command by choosing Home tab ⇨ Modify panel ⇨ 3D Scale.

> **NOTE**
>
> If you are in 2D Wireframe visual style, this command temporarily changes you to 3D Wireframe. You need to be in a nonorthogonal view to use 3DSCALE.

2. Select objects. The Scale gizmo appears, as shown in Figure 24.22.

3. At the `Specify base point:` prompt, specify the base point for the scale operation.

4. At the `Pick a scale axis or plane:` prompt, click an axis or plane line. Remember that you can only pick a scale axis or plane for mesh objects; you can only scale other 3D objects uniformly.

5. At the `Specify scale factor or [Copy/Reference]:` prompt, enter a scale factor or drag to the desired scale.

Working with Mesh Shapes

Meshes are 3D shapes that allow you to create *organic,* flexible models. Meshes contain divisions that tile the mesh into faces. This division of the model into tiles is called *tessellation.* The tessellation divisions bound the edges of each face. You have detailed control over each face, edge, and vertex in the mesh. Figure 24.23 shows a closed mesh.

Creating meshes

Just as you can create basic smooth solids, called *primitives,* you can create mesh primitives. The same shapes are available and the prompts are almost identical. To create a mesh primitive, choose Mesh tab ⇨ Primitives panel ⇨ Mesh Creation drop-down menu and choose one of the primitives. Then follow the prompts to complete the object. For more information on these prompts, see the "Drawing Basic Smooth Solids" section earlier in this chapter.

24

FIGURE 24.23

A closed mesh after moving and rotating some of the edges and faces

By default, the REVSURF, RULESURF, EDGESURF, and TABSURF commands (covered in Chapter 23) create meshes. These commands are also available in the Primitives panel of the Mesh tab.

Editing meshes

The power of meshes becomes apparent when you edit them; the editing tools allow you to mold shapes in ways that you can't with surfaces or smooth solids. The following sections explain how to edit meshes.

Using grips and gizmos to edit meshes

When you select a mesh, you see only one grip. However, by selecting subobjects, you can easily use grips to stretch, move, rotate, scale, or mirror parts of the mesh. (See the "Selecting subobjects" section earlier in this chapter for more information.) In this way, you can edit one or more faces, edges, and vertices. In the same way, you can use the Move, Rotate, and Scale gizmos to edit entire meshes or portions of them.

Adjusting mesh smoothness

 You can apply a smoothness value to a mesh to round its edges (the MESHSMOOTHMORE command). By default, you create a mesh with no smoothness and then add smoothness, if desired. Four levels of smoothness are available. To add smoothness, choose Mesh tab ⇨ Mesh panel ⇨ Smooth More. You can use this command until you get a message saying that you can't smooth the mesh any more. You can see a mesh's current Smooth level, and edit that level, in the Quick Properties palette or the Properties palette.

Figure 24.24 shows a mesh box in its original state and at Smooth levels 1 through 4.

 Conversely, you can make a smoothed mesh less smooth (the MESHSMOOTHLESS command), but not less than its original shape. To unsmooth a mesh, choose Mesh tab ⇨ Mesh panel ⇨ Smooth Less. You can do this repeatedly until you see a message that you can't unsmooth the mesh any further.

FIGURE 24.24

You can smooth a mesh to create a molded look.

Refining a mesh

When you *refine* a mesh, you increase the number of faces and, therefore, tessellations that the mesh contains. At the same time, each face becomes smaller, allowing you to make more localized changes to the mesh. You can refine an entire mesh or even an individual face. When you refine an individual face, you divide it into multiple faces. In order to refine a mesh, it must have a smoothness level of 1 or higher.

Refining an object resets its smoothness level to 0, but doesn't change its shape. Therefore, the object continues to look rounded, but you can't reduce its smoothness.

Refining an individual face subdivides the face into new faces, but does not reset the base level of smoothness. This method confines the changes to a smaller area and preserves system resources.

You can specify the number of tessellations that a mesh primitive has before you create it. To do so, go to Mesh tab ⇨ Primitives panel, and click the dialog box launcher arrow at the right end of the panel's title bar to open the Mesh Primitive Options dialog box (the MESHPRIMITIVEOPTIONS command). Choose the type of primitive from the list in the Mesh box and then enter the number of tessellation divisions for the length, height, and base. In the Preview box at the right, you can choose a smoothness level to see how that primitive will look at each level. It's easier to specify the tessellations that you need in advance than to change them later, and you don't need to smooth the model first.

Extruding a face

 You can extrude an individual face. Select the face and choose Mesh tab ⇨ Mesh Edit panel ⇨ Extrude Face. At the `Specify height of extrusion or [Direction/Path/Taper angle] <2.0000>:` prompt, enter an extrusion height, or use one of the options. These are the same options used for the EXTRUDE command, which I cover earlier in this chapter.

Splitting a face

 You can split a face into two parts, specifying the split path with object snaps or any other method of specifying coordinates. Split a face when you want to modify just part of it. To split a face, choose Mesh tab ⇨ Mesh Edit panel ⇨ Split Face. Then press Ctrl and select the face you want to split. Setting the filter in the Selection panel's Subobject Filter drop-down menu to Face can help you select the face more easily. Then specify the first and second split points. Specifying these points can be difficult, and you may have to try a few times to get the points you want.

24

Creasing a mesh

After smoothing a mesh, you may realize that you want part of the mesh to remain sharp, or *creased*. You can crease a face, edge, or vertex. To crease a subobject, set the filter in the Subobject panel of the Mesh tab for that subobject type. Then choose Mesh tab ⇨ Mesh panel ⇨ Add Crease (the MESHCREASE command). At the prompt, select the subobjects that you want to crease.

At the `Specify crease value [Always] <Always>:` prompt, press Enter to always crease the subobject. If you want the crease to apply only at lower smoothing levels, specify a level from 1 to 4. Then the subobject loses its crease if you smooth above that level. You can select the subobject and modify the crease value in the Properties palette.

Figure 24.25 on the left shows a mesh primitive box with the top face extruded. In the middle, you see the result after two smoothing operations. On the right, you see the result after creasing the top face of the extrusion.

FIGURE 24.25

To retain a face's sharpness after smoothing a mesh, you can add a crease to the face.

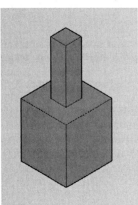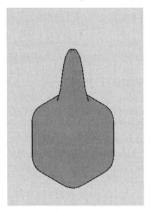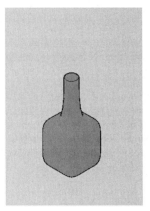

 You can uncrease a subobject; choose Mesh tab ⇨ Mesh panel ⇨ Remove Crease. You can also set the Crease value to 0 on the command line or None in the Properties palette.

Closing a hole

You can create a mesh by selecting edges of a mesh that are on the same plane surrounding a hole. For example, if you extrude a mesh face inward — or delete it — you can cover up the resulting hole. You do this with the MESHGAP command. Choose Mesh tab ⇨ Mesh Edit panel ⇨ Close Hole. Then select the edges of the hole. You can use the Chain option to select consecutive edges.

Converting solids and meshes

You can convert smooth surfaces and solids to meshes, and vice versa. Each type of object has its own capabilities and you can take advantage of both by converting from one to the other. Previous sections have described how you can edit meshes. The following sections describe how you can edit smooth solids.

Converting smooth solids and surfaces to meshes

You can convert existing 3D solids, 3D surfaces, 3D faces, polygon meshes, polyface meshes, regions, and closed polylines to mesh objects by using the Smooth Object tool (MESHSMOOTH command). But before you do so, you should set options for the conversion. Choose Mesh tab ⇨ Mesh panel, and click the dialog box launcher arrow to the right of the panel's name to open the Mesh Tessellation Options dialog box, as shown in Figure 24.26. You can also use this dialog box to actually convert objects.

If you want to convert an object right away, click the Select Objects to Tessellate button to return to the drawing. Select the objects.

FIGURE 24.26

The Mesh Tessellation Options dialog box controls the results when you convert 3D solids and surfaces to meshes.

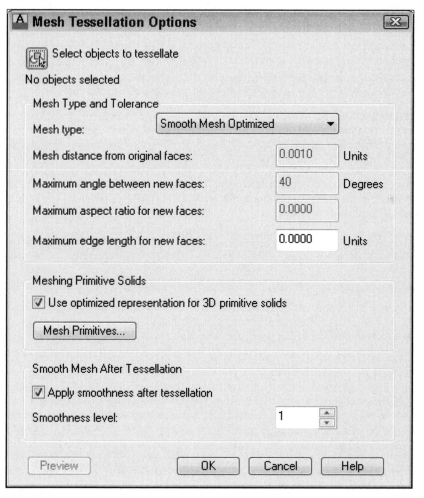

24

In the Mesh Type and Tolerance section, you have the following settings:

- **Mesh Type.** Choose a mesh type from the Mesh Type drop-down list. The default, Smooth Mesh Optimized, shapes the faces according to the shape of the mesh object. You can also specify mostly quadrilateral or triangle shapes. The latter two choices don't allow you to apply smoothness during conversion.

- **Mesh Distance from Original Faces.** Sets the maximum deviation of the faces from the shape of the original object. Smaller values result in a more accurate shape, but create more faces. This may slow down performance. The default value is 0.001.

- **Maximum Angle Between New Faces.** Sets the maximum angle between adjacent faces. If you increase the angle, you increase the density of mesh faces in high-curvature areas, and decrease the density in flatter areas. Increase the value if you need to create small details in your model. The default value is 40° and you can set values between 0 and 180.

- **Maximum Aspect Ratio for New Faces.** Sets the maximum height/width ratio for mesh faces. Use this feature to avoid long, skinny faces. The default value, 0, does not limit the aspect ratio. Values greater than 1 specify the maximum ratio that the height can exceed the width. Values less than 1 specify the maximum ratio that the width can exceed the height. A value of 1 creates faces that have the same height and width.

- **Maximum Edge Length for New Faces.** Sets the maximum length of a face's edge. The default value, 0, lets the size of the model determine the size of the faces.

You can check the Use Optimized Representation for 3D Primitive Solids check box to use the values in the Mesh Primitive Options dialog box, discussed in the "Refining a mesh" section earlier in this chapter. Click the Mesh Primitives button to open the Mesh Primitive Options dialog box and make changes there.

You can apply a smoothness level during conversion to a mesh. To do so, check the Apply Smoothness after Tessellation check box and specify the Smoothness Level. The default value is 1, which applies one level of smoothness.

> **TIP**
>
> For the most accurate results when converting, change the Smoothness Level value to 0. You can smooth the object afterwards if you want.

Click OK to close the dialog box and specify the settings. If you selected an object, the conversion takes place. Otherwise, choose Mesh tab ⇨ Mesh panel ⇨ Smooth Object and select the object to convert that object according to the settings in the dialog box.

Converting meshes to smooth solids

After creating and editing meshes, you may want to convert them to smooth solids. As I explain in the next section, you can combine (union), subtract, intersect, and fillet smooth solids, something that you cannot do with meshes. To use these editing commands on meshes, you need to convert them.

 To convert a mesh to a solid, choose Mesh tab ⇨ Convert Mesh panel ⇨ Convert to Solid (the CONVTOSOLID command). Select the object or objects to execute the conversion.

> **NOTE**
>
> Choose Mesh tab ⇨ Convert Mesh ⇨ SmoothMeshConvert drop-down menu (SMOOTHMESHCONVERT system variable) to specify whether you want smoothed or faceted solids and whether you want to optimize (merge) coplanar faces. The default option, Smooth, Optimized (0), creates a smooth model and optimizes coplanar faces. The Smooth, Not Optimized (1) option creates a smooth model but doesn't optimize faces. The Faceted, Optimized (2) option creates flattened faces and optimizes coplanar faces. The Faceted, Not Optimized (3) option creates flattened faces and does not optimize coplanar faces.

> **TIP**
>
> You can use the DELOBJ system variable (set it to 0) to retain the original mesh, in case you need to redo the operation later. By default, the value is 1, which deletes the original object. I describe all of the available DELOBJ values earlier in this chapter.

STEPS: Creating and Editing Meshes

1. Open a new drawing based on the `acad3d.dwt` template. If you're not in the 3D Modeling workspace, click the Workspace drop-down list on the Quick Access Toolbar and choose 3D Modeling. Switch to the Conceptual visual style. This exercise assumes that Dynamic Input settings are set to the default of relative coordinates. (For more information, see Chapter 4.)

2. Save it as `ab24-06.dwg` in your `AutoCAD Bible` folder.

3. Go to Mesh tab ⇨ Primitives panel and click the dialog box launcher arrow at the right end of the panel's title bar to open the Mesh Primitive Options dialog box. In the Tessellation Divisions section, select Box from the Mesh Primitive tree and change the Length value to **5**. Click OK.

4. Choose Mesh tab ⇨ Primitives panel ⇨ Primitives drop-down menu ⇨ Mesh Box. Follow these prompts:

   ```
   Specify first corner or [Center]: 5,5 ↵
   Specify other corner or [Cube/Length]: 85,25 ↵
   Specify height or [2Point] <28.9633>: 60 ↵
   ```

5. Choose View tab ⇨ Views panel ⇨ Views drop-down list ⇨ SE Isometric. The box, shown in Figure 24.27, will become a camera. The units are in millimeters.

6. Go to Mesh tab ⇨ Selection panel ⇨ Subobject Filter drop-down menu ⇨ Face. Then choose Move Gizmo from the Default Gizmo drop-down menu on the Subobject panel. These choices will help you edit the box.

7. Click the faces at ❶, ❷, and ❸. You should see a red dot in each face and the Move gizmo should appear. Move the cursor over ❷ and the Move gizmo jumps to that point.

8. Move the cursor over the blue Z axis of the Move gizmo until it becomes yellow, and click. Drag upward a little, and then type **10** ↵. Press Esc to deselect the faces.

24

FIGURE 24.27

This mesh box will become a camera.

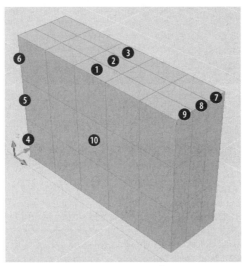

Thanks to Heidi Hewett and Guilermo Melantoni of Autodesk for the original concept of this camera and its modeling.

9. From the Subobject Filter drop-down menu, choose Edge. Then select the three edges at ❹, ❺, and ❻. Move the cursor over the green Y axis of the gizmo until it turns yellow, and click. Drag outward from the camera body a little and then type **20** ↵ to create a grip for the camera. Press Esc to deselect the edges.

10. Select the three edges at ❼, ❽, and ❾. Move the cursor over the blue Z axis until it turns yellow, and click. Then drag downward a little, and type **7** ↵. Press Esc to deselect the edges.

11. From the Subobject Filter drop-down menu, choose No Filter. Click anywhere on the camera to select it. To round the model, choose Mesh tab ⇨ Mesh panel ⇨ Smooth More. Repeat to smooth the camera a second time. Press Esc to deselect the model.

12. Choose Face from the Subobject Filter drop-down menu. Choose the face at ❿, which will be the lens. When the gizmo appears, right-click it and choose Scale to switch to the Scale gizmo. You want to scale the ZX plane. Place the cursor between the X and Z axes until they turn yellow, and click. It can be difficult to get the right plane; if so, right-click, and choose Set Constraint ⇨ ZX. At the prompt to specify the scale factor, type **1.5** ↵.

13. With the face still selected, pass the cursor over the Z axis until it turns yellow, and click. Then type **1.5** ↵ to scale in the Z direction.

14. To move the lens upwards, right-click the Scale gizmo and choose Move from the shortcut menu. Pass the cursor over the Z axis until it turns yellow, and click. Then drag upwards a little. Type **8** ↵.

15. To extrude the lens, with the lens face still selected, choose Mesh tab ⇨ Mesh Edit panel ⇨ Extrude Face. At the prompt, drag outward from the camera's body a little, and enter **5** ↵.

16. To work on the eyepiece at the back of the camera, choose View tab ⇨ Views panel ⇨ Views drop-down list ⇨ NW Isometric.

17. Click the top-center face on the back of the camera, where the eyepiece would be, to select that face.

18. Right-click the Move gizmo, and choose Scale. You want to scale this face in the ZX plane. Place the cursor between the X and Z axes on the gizmo to turn both axes yellow, and click; if this is hard, right-click and choose Set Constraint ⇨ ZX. At the prompt for a scale factor, enter **.5** ↵ to reduce the size of the face.

19.  To create an inner face for the eyepiece, with the face still selected, choose Mesh tab ⇨ Mesh Edit panel ⇨ Extrude Face. At the prompt, drag outward from the camera's body a little, and type **2** ↵.

20. The extrusion creates a new, inner face. To push that new face out, select the innermost face and again extrude it outward, this time with a value of **1**.

21. To make the eyepiece itself flat, you can crease it to remove its roundness. With the same inner face selected, choose Mesh tab ⇨ Mesh panel ⇨ Add Crease. At the prompt, press Enter to accept the Always option.

22. To make the eyepiece smaller, again select the inner face. If the Scale gizmo does not appear, right-click and choose Scale. As you did previously, select the ZX plane. At the prompt, enter **.7** ↵.

23. To push the eyepiece inward, right-click the Scale gizmo and choose Move to display the Move gizmo. Highlight the green Y axis (it becomes yellow) and click. Drag inward and enter **2** ↵. Press Esc to deselect the face and see the result.

24. You might want to work further on the camera in ways that require a smooth solid. For example, adding a hole for a strap would require the SUBTRACT command (explained in the next section of this chapter). First, from the Subobject Filter drop-down menu, choose No Filter. Then go to Mesh tab ⇨ Convert Mesh ⇨ Smooth Mesh Convert drop-down menu, and check that the Smooth, Optimized option (the default) is selected. To convert the mesh to a smooth solid, choose Mesh tab ⇨ Convert Mesh panel ⇨ Convert to Solid. Select the camera and press Enter to end selection. Wait while AutoCAD executes the conversion. The final result should look like Figure 24.28.

FIGURE 24.28

The camera is now a smooth solid, ready for further editing.

Creating Complex Solids

To create realistic objects, you usually need to edit the simple shapes that I have discussed in this chapter. You can create complex solids by adding them, subtracting them, or intersecting them. These processes are called *Boolean operations,* which in this context means using logical functions, such as addition or subtraction, on objects. You cannot perform Boolean operations on meshes; to do so, first convert them to smooth solids, as described in the previous section of this chapter.

Combining solids

You use the UNION command to add two solids together, making one solid. If the solids are touching, you get a new, unified solid. If the solids are not touching, but rather are completely separate, using UNION is similar to grouping, because you select them as one object. Figure 24.29 shows the union of two solids showing in the Hidden visual style.

> **TIP**
> You can also use the UNION command with 2D regions, either for 2D drawings or as a basis for a 3D model.

 To start the UNION command, choose Home tab ⇨ Solid Editing panel ⇨ Solid, Union. At the `Select objects:` prompt, select the objects that you want to unite.

FIGURE 24.29

The results of UNION on two solids

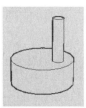

> **CAUTION**
> When you create complex solids, the original solids are not retained. Setting the DELOBJ system variable to 0 (zero) doesn't work because the original solids have been changed. If you want, you can copy the original objects to another location in the drawing, in case you need to use them again. You can also use UNDO if the result is not what you expected.

Subtracting solids

You use the SUBTRACT command to subtract one solid from another. This command is most commonly used to create holes. Figure 24.30 shows the result of subtracting a small cylinder from a larger one.

FIGURE 24.30

You can create holes by using the SUBTRACT command.

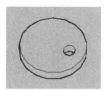

To subtract solids, follow these steps:

1. Choose Home tab ⇨ Solid Editing panel ⇨ Solid, Subtract.

2. At the following prompt, choose the solid (or region) that you want to subtract from (the one you want to keep):

   ```
   Select solids, surfaces, and regions to subtract from...
   Select objects:
   ```

3. At the following prompt, choose the solid (or region) that you want to subtract (the one you want to get rid of):

   ```
   Select solids, surfaces, and regions to subtract...
   Select objects:
   ```

Creating a solid from the intersection of two solids

You can also create a solid from the volume that two solids have in common. This volume is called their intersection. Figure 24.31 shows two solids before and after using the INTERSECT command. As you can see, you can create some very unusual models this way.

FIGURE 24.31

A box and a sphere before and after using the INTERSECT command.

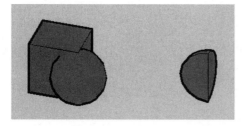

 To use the INTERSECT command, choose Home tab ⇨ Solid Editing panel ⇨ Solid, Intersect. Just select the objects in any order. AutoCAD creates the new solid. As explained for the UNION command, the command does not save your original objects.

Creating a solid from surfaces that enclose a volume

You can create a solid from surfaces that completely enclose a volume, creating an unbroken space, with the SURFSCULPT command. To create the solid, first draw solids that completely enclose a space on all sides. For example, you could draw a rectangle, then choose Surface tab ⇨ Create panel ⇨ Extrude and extrude the rectangle. Then you could choose Surface tab ⇨ Create panel ⇨ Planar Surface to create a surface at the bottom of the extruded rectangle and again at the top. These surfaces would enclose a volume on all six sides. Then choose Surface tab ⇨ Edit panel ⇨ Surface Sculpt and select the surfaces to create the solid.

Creating a new solid by using INTERFERE

INTERFERE is similar to INTERSECT, except that the original solids remain. AutoCAD creates a third solid from the volume that the two solids have in common. You can also use the INTERFERE command to highlight the common volume of several pairs of solids.

Figure 24.32 shows a solid that was created by using INTERFERE, as well as the Interference Checking dialog box, which opens after you select objects.

FIGURE 24.32

When you use INTERFERE, the original solids remain intact.

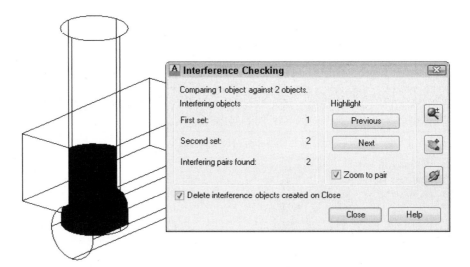

INTERFERE is useful when you have a number of interfering solids. This command enables you to divide the selection set of solids into two sets so that you can compare one against the other. For example, you can compare a box with three other solids by putting the box in one set and the other three solids in the other set.

> **TIP**
>
> You can use INTERFERE for troubleshooting and visualizing a complex drawing. For example, you can use INTERFERE to determine which solids need to be subtracted from other solids. The new objects are created on the current layer. You can change the current layer before using INTERFERE to help you more clearly distinguish the new solid that you create.

To use INTERFERE, follow these steps:

1. Choose Home tab ⇨ Solid Editing panel ⇨ Interfere.

2. At the `Select first set of objects or [Nested selection/Settings]:` prompt, select objects. If you want to compare only two objects, you can put them both in the first set. Otherwise, select solids for the first set and press Enter to end object selection.

3. At the `Select second set of objects or [Nested selection/checK first set] <checK>:` prompt, select the second set of objects and press Enter to end object selection. If you don't want a second set, press Enter to check the solids. The Interference Checking dialog box opens and the display zooms in to the model, shading the interference and showing the rest of the model in wireframe, as shown in Figure 24.32.

4. If you have more than one interference, click the Next button to display the next one. You can use the Zoom Realtime, Pan Realtime, and 3D Orbit buttons to adjust your display. Then press Esc to return to the dialog box.

5. If you want to keep the interference solid after you close the dialog box, uncheck the Delete Interference Objects Created on Close check box.

6. Click Close when you're done.

> **ON THE WEB**
>
> The drawing used in the following exercise on creating complex solids, `ab24-f.dwg`, is available from the Drawings download on the companion website.

STEPS: Creating Complex Solids

1. Open `ab24-f.dwg`, available from the companion website.

2. Save the file as `ab24-07.dwg` in your `AutoCAD Bible` folder. Make sure that Object Snap is on. Set running object snaps for Endpoint, Midpoint, and Center. This drawing is measured in millimeters. The solids have been created by drawing circles, using EXTRUDE, and moving the solids to the proper Z coordinate. The result is shown in Figure 24.33.

3. To create the six holes arrayed around the center plate, choose Home tab ⇨ Solid Editing panel ⇨ Solid, Subtract. Follow the prompts:

```
Select solids, surfaces, and regions to subtract from...
Select objects: Select the central plate at ❶ in Figure 24.33.
Select objects: Right-click.
Select solids, surfaces, and regions to subtract...
Select objects: Select the six circles arrayed around the plate. Right-
    click to end selection.
```

24

FIGURE 24.33

These solids are the basis for the model.

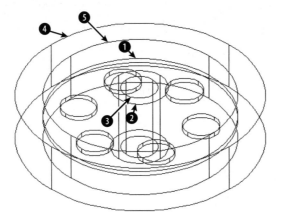

4. To create the central tube, repeat the SUBTRACT command. Follow the prompts:

   ```
   Select solids, surfaces, and regions to subtract from...
   Select objects: Select the outer tube at ❷.
   Select objects: Right-click.
   Select solids, surfaces, and regions to subtract...
   Select objects: Select the inner tube at ❸. Right-click to end
      selection.
   ```

5. To "carve out" the central disk, again repeat the SUBTRACT command. Follow the prompts:

   ```
   Select solids, surfaces, and regions to subtract from...
   Select objects: Select the outer circle at ❹.
   Select objects: Right-click.
   Select solids, surfaces, and regions to subtract...
   Select objects: Select the inner circle at ❺. Right-click to end
      selection.
   ```

6. Change the visual style to Hidden (choose View tab ⇨ Visual Styles panel ⇨ Visual Styles drop-down list ⇨ Hidden). This enables you to check the effects of the subtraction operations. Your drawing should look like Figure 24.34.

7. Choose Home tab ⇨ Solid Editing panel ⇨ Solid, Union. Select the three solids at ❶, ❷, and ❸, shown in Figure 24.34, and right-click to end selection.

8. Save your drawing.

FIGURE 24.34

The result of three subtraction operations

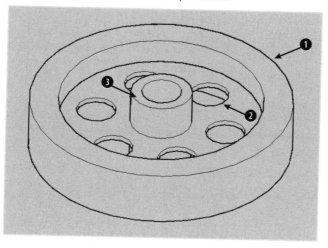

Pressing or pulling a region

The PRESSPULL command finds closed areas, creates a region, and then lets you extrude or "press" a hole in that region. You can also press/pull segmented faces of 3D solids, and extrude 2D and 3D open objects to create surfaces. For example, in Figure 24.35, you can press/pull the following:

- All the enclosed objects, such as the closed spline, the circle, and the rectangles.
- Most open 2D and 3D objects, such as lines, polylines, splines, and 3D polylines.
- The area enclosed by the overlapping rectangles.
- The triangular area on the box created by drawing a line across the top face.
- The space in the middle of the four touching smooth solid (but not mesh) boxes, which does not contain any objects.

You can use the PRESSPULL command on any face of a solid. To use the command on a 2D object, you need to move the UCS to the plane of the boundary, as if you were hatching the area.

NEW FEATURE

The PRESSPULL command allows you to select multiple objects using either the Multiple option or by holding Shift while selecting objects to press/pull. You can also select open 2D and 3D objects in addition to clicking inside an enclosed boundary.

24

FIGURE 24.35

You can press or pull many types of enclosed areas.

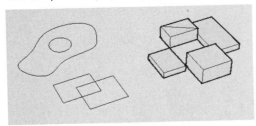

 To press/pull an open object or closed area, choose Home tab⇨Modeling panel⇨Presspull. At the `Select object or bounded area.` prompt, select an object or click inside an enclosed area.

You can now move the cursor up or down in either direction to press or pull the new object. You can click when you like what you see, or enter a value for the height. (You can usually click and drag in one action, but sometimes AutoCAD takes some time to calculate the new object; in that case, click, wait a second, and then move the cursor up or down.) Use the Multiple option to select additional objects to press or pull.

Using solid history

Because AutoCAD doesn't retain source objects when you use the UNION, SUBTRACT, or INTERSECT command, it would be nice to have a way to modify the original objects separately. Solid history does just that.

> **NOTE**
> The SOLIDHIST system variable controls whether the history is maintained in the drawing. By default, this system variable is off (set to 0). To retain solid history, set SOLIDHIST to 1.

You can also display the object's history by selecting the object and setting the Show History item in the Properties palette to Yes. For example, if you used a cylinder to make a hole in a box by using the SUBTRACT command, when you show the history, you see the original cylinder again. This display lasts even when you deselect the object, until you change the setting in the Properties palette.

More important, you can use solid history to edit components of a complex solid. For example, you can move or resize a hole or one part of two objects that you combined. To work with one component of a complex solid, press the Ctrl key as you pass the cursor over the object. The individual component is highlighted. Click to display grips for grip-editing. I explain how to select individual components *(subobjects)* and grip-edit solids earlier in this chapter.

The BREP command converts 3D solids into boundary representation (BREP) solids. This process deletes a solid's history and you can no longer grip-edit the solid or change its properties in the Properties palette. BREP is available on the command line only.

> **ON THE WEB**
> The drawing used in the following exercise on using PRESSPULL and solid history, `ab24-g.dwg`, is available from the Drawings download on the companion website.

STEPS: Using PRESSPULL and Solid History

1. Open `ab24-g.dwg`, available from the companion website.

2. Save the file as `ab24-08.dwg` in your `AutoCAD Bible` folder. This is the base of the lamp that was used for several exercises earlier in this chapter. There is a circle on the `const` layer at the top of the base. If necessary, change the visual style to Wireframe (choose View tab ⇨ Visual Styles panel ⇨ Visual Styles drop-down list ⇨ Wireframe).

3. Choose Home tab ⇨ Modeling panel ⇨ Presspull. At the `Select object or bounded area.` prompt, move the cursor inside the small circle until you see that it is highlighted. Click and drag downward through the thickness of the base (until you see it below the base — make it long) and then click. The cylinder jumps to the thickness of the base. You now have a hole in the base (for the arm). Press Enter to exit the command.

4. Turn off the `const` layer.

5. Choose Home tab ⇨ Selection panel ⇨ Subobject Filter drop-down menu ⇨ Solid History. The Solid History option allows you to select the objects that were recorded when a solid was edited.

6. Press the Ctrl key and pass the cursor over the center of the new hole. When you see the long cylinder that you originally pressed, click it. You now see some grips.

7. Click the grip at ❶, shown in Figure 24.36, and drag the hole to any new location. Then click.

8. Deselect the object.

9. Save your drawing.

FIGURE 24.36

You can drag a hole to another location because composite objects retain a record of their history.

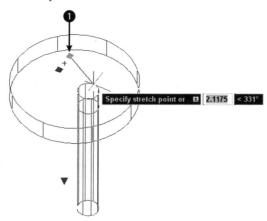

24

Sectioning and Slicing Solids

In many drawings, you need to show a cross-section of your models. A cross-section displays the inside of a 3D object. The SECTION, SECTIONPLANE, and SLICE commands create cross-section views of your 3D models.

Using the SECTION command

The SECTION command creates a 2D region from a cross-section of a 3D model along a plane that you specify. The original objects are left untouched. Figure 24.37 shows a region created by using the SECTION command.

FIGURE 24.37

The region created by using SECTION is shown with a dashed line.

Region created using SECTION

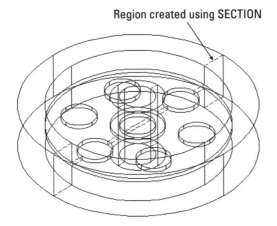

> **TIP**
> The SECTION command creates the region on the current layer. Switch to a layer with a contrasting color from the object's layer so that the region is clearly visible.

To use the SECTION command, enter **section** on the command line. Select the object that you want to section. AutoCAD displays the `Specify first point on Section plane by [Object/Zaxis/View/XY/YZ/ZX/3points] <3points>:` prompt. Use these options to define the plane of the cross-section. Table 24.1 explains how to use the options.

TABLE 24.1   SECTION Options

Option	Description
Object	Enables you to choose a circle, ellipse, arc, spline, or 2D polyline.
Zaxis	Defines the plane by defining a Z axis. The sectioning plane is then the XY plane perpendicular to the Z axis that you defined. You define the Z axis by first specifying a point on the sectioning plane. This point is the 0,0,0 point (for purposes of this command only) where the sectioning plane and the Z axis meet. Then you pick a point on the Z axis.
View	Defines the section plane parallel to the current view at the intersection of a point that you specify.
XY	Defines the section plane parallel to the XY plane at the intersection of a point that you specify.
YZ	Defines the section plane parallel to the YZ plane at the intersection of a point that you specify.
ZX	Defines the section plane parallel to the ZX plane at the intersection of a point that you specify.
3points	This is the default. Specify three points to define the section plane. Using object snaps is a good idea.

You can move the region that you create and view it separately to spot errors in your models.

Creating an interactive section object

The SECTIONPLANE command creates a movable section object that displays the inside of a 3D model. When you turn *live sectioning* on, you can see the resulting cross-section in real-time as you move the section plane. You can flip the section plane to show the other half of the model. Figure 24.38 shows a section object.

To create a section plane, follow these steps:

1. Choose Mesh tab ➪ Section panel ➪ Section Plane.
2. At the `Select face or any point to locate section line or [Draw section/Orthographic]:` prompt, do one of the following:

   - Pick a face of a 3D solid. Live sectioning is turned on.
   - Pick the first point of a section line. Then specify a second point at the `Specify through point:` prompt.
   - Use the Draw Section option to pick several points to create a section with corners (jogs). Live sectioning is turned off.
   - Use the Orthographic option to choose one of the orthographic directions. This creates a plane that applies to all 3D objects in your drawing. Live sectioning is turned on.

24

FIGURE 24.38

You can use the SECTIONPLANE command to see various sections of a model in real-time.

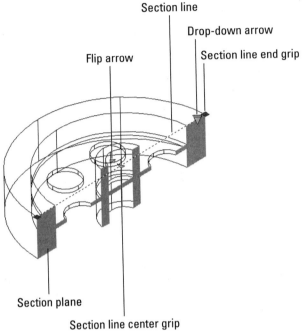

Section line

Drop-down arrow

Flip arrow

Section line end grip

Section plane

Section line center grip

3. If Live sectioning is not on, you see just the section object's line. Select the section line, right-click, and choose Activate Live Sectioning.

4. Use the centerline end and center grips to move the section plane and adjust the sectioning of the object in real-time. You can use the flip arrow to view the other side of the object. Click the drop-down arrow to display a section boundary or section volume.

You can click the live section line and right-click to access section settings. To continue working, deactivate live sectioning and deselect the section plane line, which is quite unobtrusive.

The drop-down arrow lets you choose a section boundary or volume. The section boundary defines a plane perpendicular to the section option, underlying the visible part of the 3D model. The section volume defines a box encompassing the visible part of the model.

To specify settings for section planes, click the dialog box launcher arrow at the right end of the Section panel's title bar to open the Section Settings dialog box. Here you can activate live sectioning and specify how the intersection of the object and the section looks.

Using the SLICE command

The SLICE command slices a solid (but not a mesh) into two parts along a plane or surface. The original solids are modified but can be reunited with UNION. You can delete either part or keep both. Figure 24.39 shows the result of slicing a model, after one half of the model has been deleted. This can help you to identify problems in the construction of the model. For example, this slice reveals a fault with the model — the flat disk continues through the central tube — not the desired result. However, you can also use the SLICE command to construct your models. For example, in the exercise on drawing basic solids, the lamp top was a sphere. You could slice this sphere, because the lamp should only have a top half of the sphere.

FIGURE 24.39

The result of slicing a solid and retaining one of the resulting pieces

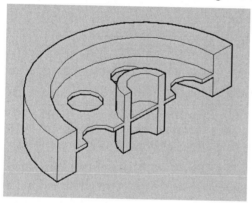

 To use the SLICE command, choose Home tab ⇨ Solid Editing panel ⇨ Slice. Select the object that you want to slice. AutoCAD displays the `Specify start point of slicing plane or [planar Object/Surface/Zaxis/View/XY/YZ/ZX/3points] <3points>:` prompt. Use these options to define the plane of the cross-section. The options are the same as for the SECTION command, except for the Surface option, and are explained in Table 24.1. (The Planar Object option is the same as the Object option in the SECTION command.)

The Surface option enables you to cut any lofted, extruded, swept, or revolved surface out of the solid. You can create some interesting shapes this way.

ON THE WEB

The drawing used in the following exercise on slicing solids, ab24-07.dwg, is available from the Result download on the companion website.

24

STEPS: Slicing Solids

1. If you did the exercise on creating complex solids, open `ab24-07.dwg`, available from your AutoCAD Bible folder; otherwise, open it from the Result download on the companion website. If necessary, change the visual style to Wireframe. Object Snap should be on, with running object snaps for Endpoint, Midpoint, Center, and Quadrant. The drawing is shown in Figure 24.40.

FIGURE 24.40

The 3D model for slicing

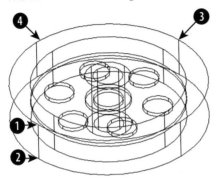

2. Save your drawing as `ab24-09.dwg` in your AutoCAD Bible folder.

3. Choose Home tab ⇨ Solid Editing panel ⇨ Slice. Follow the prompts:

```
Select objects: Select the solid model.
Select objects: Right-click.
Specify start point of slicing plane or [planar
Object/Surface/Zaxis/View/XY/YZ/ZX/3points] <3points>: ↵
Specify first point on plane: Pick the quadrant at ❶ in Figure 24.40.
Specify second point on plane: Pick the quadrant at ❷.
Specify third point on plane: Pick the quadrant at ❸.
Specify a point on desired side of the plane or [keep Both sides]: Pick
      the model at ❹.
```

4. As mentioned earlier, the slicing reveals an error — the disk cuts through the central tube, as shown in Figure 24.41. To fix the error, zoom in so that the model takes up the entire screen.

5. Start the CYLINDER command. Follow the prompts:

```
Specify center point of base or [3P/2P/Ttr/Elliptical]: Pick the midpoint
      at ❶ in Figure 24.41.
Specify base radius or [Diameter] <3.2605>: Pick the endpoint at ❷.
Specify height or [2Point/Axis endpoint] <9.2711>: Move the cursor upward
      and type 16 ↵.
```

FIGURE 24.41

The solid after slicing and deleting one half

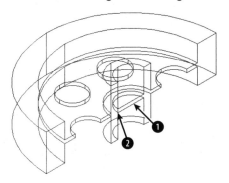

6. Choose Home tab ⇨ Solid Editing panel ⇨ Solid, Subtract. At the `Select solids, sur-faces, and regions to subtract from... Select objects:` prompt, select the large solid and right-click to end object selection. At the `Select solids, surfaces, and regions to subtract... Select objects:` prompt, select the new cylinder that you just drew and right-click. AutoCAD subtracts the cylinder from the larger model.

7. Change the visual style to Hidden (choose View tab ⇨ Visual Styles panel ⇨ Visual Styles drop-down list ⇨ Hidden). Return to your previous view.

8. Save your drawing. If you're continuing on to the next exercise, keep the drawing open.

> **NOTE**
> To correct the model, you could subtract out the circle as you just did in the exercise, mirror the entire model, and use UNION to make the two halves whole. Mirroring in 3D is covered in the next section. You could also undo the slice as soon as you saw the error and make the correction on the entire model.

Using Editing Commands in 3D

When you draw in 3D, you need to edit your models either to make corrections or as part of the construction process. A number of editing commands are exclusively for 3D or have special 3D options. In this section, you explore these special commands and options. Table 24.2 lists most of the 2D editing commands and how they're used in 3D drawings.

TABLE 24.2   Editing Commands in 3D

Command	Use in 3D Drawings
ERASE	Same as for 2D.
COPY	Same as for 2D.
MIRROR	Can be used on 3D objects as long as the mirror line is in the XY plane, including using grips. Otherwise, use MIRROR3D.
OFFSET	Can be used in 3D space, but only on 2D objects. You can also use the SURFOFFSET command with 3D surfaces or the OFFSETEDGE command with faces on 3D solids.
ARRAY	Can be used on 3D objects in the XY plane and Z direction. You can also use 3DARRAY.
MOVE	Same as for 2D; can also use the 3DMOVE command and the Move gizmo.
ROTATE	Can be used on 3D objects in the XY plane. Otherwise, use ROTATE3D, or 3DROTATE. You can use the Rotate gizmo.
SCALE	Can be used on 3D objects. Scales in all three dimensions. You can use the 3DSCALE and the Scale gizmo. For meshes, you can choose the plane or axis to scale.
STRETCH	Can be used in 3D space, but only on 2D objects, wireframes, and surfaces. The results may not be what you expect because it is hard to visualize the direction of the stretch. You can stretch 3D objects with grips.
LENGTHEN	Can be used in 3D space, but only on 2D objects.
TRIM	Has special options for 3D, but works only on 2D objects, such as lines. You can also use the SURFTRIM and SURFUNTRIM commands with 3D surfaces.
EXTEND	Has special options for 3D, but works only on 2D objects, such as lines. You can also use the SURFEXTEND command with 3D surfaces.
BREAK	Can be used in 3D space, but only on 2D objects.
CHAMFER	Has special options for 3D. You can also use the CHAMFEREDGE command on 3D solids.
FILLET	Has special options for 3D. You can also use the FILLETEDGE command on 3D solids or the SURFFILLET command on 3D surfaces.
EXPLODE	Works on 3D objects — solids explode to surfaces, and surfaces explode to wireframes. Sometimes, you get regions. You can explode blocks containing 3D objects.
ALIGN	Works on 3D objects. You can also use the 3DALIGN command.

Mirroring in 3D

If the mirror line is on the XY plane, you can mirror any 3D object with the regular MIRROR command. If you want to mirror in any other plane, use MIRROR3D.

To use MIRROR3D, follow these steps:

1. Choose Home tab ⇨ Modify panel ⇨ 3D Mirror.
2. Select the object or objects that you want to mirror.

3. At the `Specify first point of mirror plane (3 points) or [Object/Last/Zaxis/View/XY/YZ/ZX/3points] <3points>:` prompt, choose one of the options to define the mirroring plane. These are the same options described in Table 24.1 for the SECTION command. The only additional option is Last, which uses the last defined mirroring plane.

4. At the `Delete source objects? [Yes/No] <N>:` prompt, press Enter to keep the original objects, or right-click and choose Yes to delete them.

STEPS: Mirroring in 3D

1. If you have `ab24-09.dwg` open from the previous exercise, use this drawing. If you don't have it open, open it from your `AutoCAD Bible` folder or from the Results download on the companion website. If necessary, change the visual style to Wireframe. Make sure that Object Snap is on, and set a running object snap for Endpoint. The drawing is shown in Figure 24.42.

FIGURE 24.42

This 3D model was sliced and can now be mirrored.

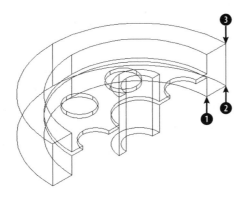

2. Save your drawing as `ab24-10.dwg` in your `AutoCAD Bible` folder.

3. Choose Home tab ⇨ Modify panel ⇨ 3D Mirror. Follow the prompts:

```
Select objects: Select the solid. Right-click to end object selection.
Specify first point of mirror plane (3 points) or
[Object/Last/Zaxis/View/XY/YZ/ZX/3points] <3points>: Pick ❶ in Figure
    24.42.
Specify second point on mirror plane: Pick ❷.
Specify third point on mirror plane: Pick ❸.
Delete source objects? [Yes/No] <N>: Right-click and choose Enter.
```

4. Choose Home tab ⇨ Solid Editing panel ⇨ Solid, Union. Select both solids. Right-click to end object selection. AutoCAD unites them.

5. Save your drawing.

Arraying in 3D

You can array any 3D object by using the ARRAY command. You can create rectangular, polar, and path arrays.

Creating 3D rectangular arrays

A 3D rectangular array has rows, columns, and levels. To create a 3D rectangular array, follow these steps:

1. Choose Home tab ⇨ Modify panel ⇨ Array drop-down menu ⇨ Rectangular Array to start the ARRAYRECT command.

2. Select the objects that you want to array.

3. At the `Select grip to edit array or [ASociative/Base point/COUnt/Spacing/COLumns/Rows/Levels/eXit] <eXit>:` prompt, enter an option and change its value at the command prompt or specify values on the ribbon to define the array. For a 3D array, change the value in the Levels text box on the ribbon or the Levels option at the command prompt.

4. Press Enter or click Close Array to complete the array.

STEPS: Creating a Rectangular Array in 3D

1. Open `ab24-h.dwg`, available from the companion website.

2. Save the file as `ab24-11.dwg` in your `AutoCAD Bible` folder. This is a drawing showing a sphere, a bead-like shape sometimes used for table legs. In this exercise, you create a 3D rectangular array to create four table legs.

3. Choose Home tab ⇨ Modify panel ⇨ Array drop-down menu ⇨ Rectangular Array. Follow the prompts:

   `Select objects:` *Select the bead. Press Enter to end object selection.*

4. From the Array Creation tab on the ribbon, do the following:
   - Columns panel, enter **2** in the Columns text box and enter **36** in the Between text box.
   - Rows panel, enter **2** in the Rows text box and enter **26** in the Between text box.

- Levels panel, enter **20** in the Levels text box and enter **1.5** in the Between text box.
- Close panel, click Close Array.

5. Do a Zoom Extents to see the result. (Now you would create the tabletop.)
6. Save your drawing. It should look like Figure 24.43.

FIGURE 24.43

The four legs of a table, created by using a rectangular array

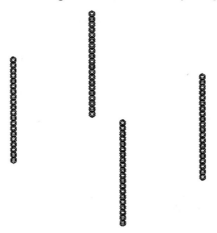

Creating 3D polar arrays

Instead of using a center point as you do in a 2D polar array, you define a center axis. Draw the center axis before creating the array. To create a 3D polar array, follow these steps:

1. Choose Home tab ⇨ Modify panel ⇨ Array drop-down menu ⇨ Polar Array to start the ARRAYPOLAR command.
2. Select the objects that you want to array and press Enter to end selection.
3. At the `Specify center point of array or [Base point/Axis of rotation]:` prompt, specify a base point or right-click and choose Axis of Rotation.
4. When defining an axis of rotation, specify the two ends of the center axis.
5. Enter an option and change its value at the command prompt or specify values on the ribbon to define the array. For a 3D array, change the value in the Levels text box on the ribbon or the Levels option at the command prompt.
6. Press Enter or click Close Array to complete the array.

If you rotate less than a full circle, you need to determine the positive angle of rotation. The positive direction of the axis goes from the first point that you specify (the center point) to the second point. Point your right thumb in the positive direction and follow the curl of the fingers of that hand to determine the positive angle of rotation.

24

STEPS: Creating 3D Polar Arrays

1. Open `ab24-i.dwg`, available from the companion website.

2. Save the file as `ab24-12.dwg` in your `AutoCAD Bible` folder. You see part of a lamp, as shown in Figure 24.44. Make sure that Object Snap is on. Set a running object snap for Endpoint.

FIGURE 24.44

A partially completed lamp

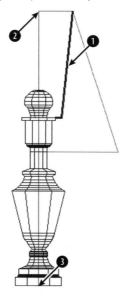

3. To array the bracket that supports the lampshade, choose Home tab ⇨ Modify panel ⇨ Array drop-down menu ⇨ Polar Array. Follow the prompts:

```
Select objects: Select the support at ❶ in Figure 24.44.
Select objects: ↵
Specify center point of array or [Base point/Axis of rotation]: a ↵
Specify first point on axis of rotation: Pick the endpoint at ❷.
Specify second point on axis of rotation: Pick the endpoint at ❸.
```

4. From the Array Creation tab on the ribbon, do the following:

   ▪ Items panel, enter **3** in the Items text box and enter **360** in the Fill text box.

   ▪ Close panel, click Close Array.

5. One of the three supports cannot be seen in this view. To see all three, press Shift+mouse wheel to enter transparent 3D Orbit mode, and drag diagonally a bit until you can see all three supports.

6. Choose View tab ⇨ Views panel ⇨ Views drop-down list ⇨ Top or click the top of the ViewCube to return to plan view, and save your drawing.

Creating path arrays

You can also create path arrays in 3D. The only difference between a 3D and a 2D path array is that in 3D the path can be off the XY plane. To create a path array, choose Home tab ⇨ Modify panel ⇨ Array drop-down menu ⇨ Path Array. For more information on path arrays, see Chapter 10.

Rotating in 3D

You can rotate 3D objects in the XY plane with the ROTATE command. Use ROTATE3D when you need to rotate objects in any other plane. (The 3DROTATE command, which I discussed earlier in this chapter, offers interactive rotating in 3D.) When you use the ROTATE3D command, you need to specify the axis of rotation. The ROTATE3D options are shown in Table 24.3.

Table 24.3 ROTATE3D Options

Option	Description
Object	Enables you to choose a line, circle, arc, or 2D polyline. If you choose a circle or arc, AutoCAD rotates around a line that starts at the object's center and extends perpendicular to the object's plane.
Last	Uses the last defined axis of rotation.
View	Defines the axis of rotation parallel to the current view at the intersection of a point that you specify.
Xaxis	The axis of rotation is parallel to the X axis and passes through a point that you specify.
Yaxis	The axis of rotation is parallel to the Y axis and passes through a point that you specify.
Zaxis	The axis of rotation is parallel to the Z axis and passes through a point that you specify.
2points	This is the default. Specify two points to define the axis. It's a good idea to use object snaps.

TIP

Sometimes creating an object in the XY plane and then rotating it afterward is easier. In other words, you may create an object in the wrong plane on purpose and use ROTATE3D or 3DROTATE later to properly place it.

To use ROTATE3D, follow these steps:

1. Enter **rotate3d** ↵ on the command line.

2. Select the object or objects that you want to rotate.

3. At the `Specify first point on axis or define axis by [Object/Last/View/Xaxis/Yaxis/Zaxis/2points]`: prompt, select one of the options explained in Table 24.3, and define the axis according to the option prompts.

4. At the `Specify rotation angle or [Reference]`: prompt, specify a positive or negative rotation angle or choose the Reference option. (The Reference option works like the Reference option for ROTATE. See Chapter 9.)

You need to determine the positive direction of rotation. Point your right thumb in the positive direction of the axis and follow the curl of your fingers. If you pick two points, the positive direction of the axis goes from the first pick point to the second pick point.

ON THE WEB

The drawing used in the following exercise on rotating in 3D, `ab24-j.dwg`, is available from the Drawings download on the companion website.

STEPS: Rotating in 3D

1. Open `ab24-j.dwg`, available from the companion website.

2. Save the file as `ab24-13.dwg` in your `AutoCAD Bible` folder. You see the same lamp used in the previous exercise, but it has now been completed.

3. To insert the lamp in a plan view drawing of a house, you need to see it in plan view from the WCS. In other words, you should be looking down at the lamp. To do this, you need to rotate the lamp around the X axis. To visualize this, look at the UCS icon and imagine rotating the top of the lamp toward you around the horizontal (X) axis. To rotate the lamp, enter **rotate3d** ↵ on the command line. Follow the prompts:

   ```
   Select objects: Start a crossing window to select the entire lamp.
   Select objects: Right-click to end selection.
   Specify first point on axis or define axis by [Object/Last/View/Xaxis/
       Yaxis/Zaxis/2points]: Right-click and choose Xaxis.
   Specify a point on the X axis <0,0,0>: Right-click.
   Specify rotation angle or [Reference]: 90 ↵
   ```

4. Zoom to the extents of the drawing to see the entire lamp. The lamp is now rotated 90 degrees around the X axis in relation to the UCS, and you're looking at it from the top.

5. To get a better view, choose View tab ➪ Views panel ➪ Views drop-down list ➪ SE Isometric. Change the visual style to Hidden (choose View tab ➪ Visual Styles panel ➪ Visual Styles drop-down list ➪ Hidden). The lamp should look like Figure 24.45.

6. Save your drawing.

7. To try the same rotation by using the 3DROTATE command, re-open `ab24-j.dwg`. You can save it again as `ab24-13.dwg`, because the result will be the same, or save it as `ab24-13-1.dwg`.

FIGURE 24.45

The lamp is now ready to place in a 3D drawing of a house.

8. Change the visual style to Wireframe. Press Shift+mouse wheel and change the viewpoint so that you can see all three axes on the UCS icon.

9. Choose Home tab ⇨ Modify panel ⇨ 3D Rotate. At the `Select objects:` prompt, select the entire lamp and end selection.

10. At the `Specify base point:` prompt, specify the bottom corner of the lamp, using an Endpoint object snap.

11. At the `Pick a rotation axis:` prompt, hover over the red (X axis) ribbon until it turns yellow, and click.

12. At the `Specify angle start point or type an angle:` prompt, enter **90 ⏎**.

13. Save your drawing.

Aligning in 3D

I have already covered the ALIGN and the 3DALIGN commands in Chapter 10. When you work in 3D, you can use these commands to move, rotate in the XY plane, and rotate in the Z direction — all in one command. In this exercise, you use the 3DALIGN command.

On the Web

The drawing used in the following exercise on aligning in 3D, `ab24-k.dwg`, is available from the Drawings download on the companion website.

24

STEPS: Aligning in 3D

1. Open `ab24-k.dwg`, available from the companion website.

2. Save the file as `ab24-14.dwg` in your `AutoCAD Bible` folder. You see part of the base assembly for an industrial washer, as shown in Figure 24.46. One sidebar needs to be moved and rotated into place. Make sure that Object Snap is on; set a running object snap for Endpoint.

FIGURE 24.46

Part of a base assembly for an industrial washer with a sidebar that needs to be moved and rotated into place

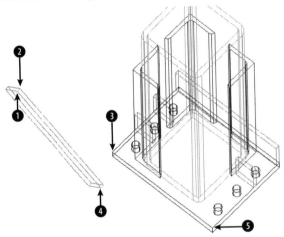

Thanks to Robert Mack of the Dexter Company, Fairfield, Iowa, for this drawing.

3. Notice that it's hard to tell which way the sidebar is facing because it's displayed in wireframe. Change the visual style to Hidden (choose View tab ⇨ Visual Styles panel ⇨ Visual Styles drop-down list ⇨ Hidden). You can now see that ❶, shown in Figure 24.46, is facing away from you. Switch back to the Wireframe visual style.

4. Choose Home tab ⇨ Modify panel ⇨ 3D Align. Follow the prompts:

```
Select objects: Select the sidebar.
Select objects: Right-click.
Specify base point or [Copy]: Pick ❶ in Figure 24.46.
Specify second point or [Continue] <C>: Pick ❹.
Specify third point or [Continue] <C>: Pick ❷.
Specify first destination point: Pick ❸.
Specify second destination point or [eXit] <X>: Pick ❺.
Specify third destination point or [eXit] <X>: Pick any point further
     back than ❸ on the plate.
```

The smaller bars (shown in red in the drawing) provide several endpoints that you can easily locate.

5. AutoCAD aligns the sidebar. Save your drawing. It should look like Figure 24.47.

FIGURE 24.47

The sidebar has been aligned with the rest of the model.

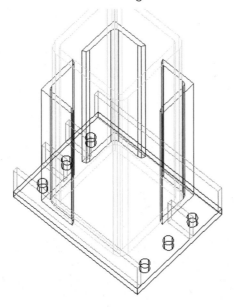

Trimming and extending in 3D

You can use the TRIM and EXTEND commands to trim or extend 2D objects in 3D space. (I cover these commands for 2D drawing in Chapter 10.) AutoCAD provides the Project option for working in 3D space. The Project option has three sub-options:

- **None.** AutoCAD trims or extends only objects that actually intersect or can intersect in 3D space.
- **UCS.** This is the default. AutoCAD projects objects onto the XY plane of the current UCS. Therefore, if two lines are on different Z coordinates, you can trim and extend one of them with reference to the other, even though they do not and cannot actually meet in 3D space.
- **View.** This projects objects parallel to the current view. Objects are trimmed or extended, based on the way they look on the screen. They need not (and probably won't) actually meet in 3D space.

You can also use the Extend option to trim or extend to implied intersections, as explained in Chapter 10.

Filleting in 3D

You can fillet solids (but not meshes) with the FILLETEDGE command. (In Chapter 23, I cover the SURFFILLET command, which fillets surfaces.) If you create a 3D object from lines, you can fillet the lines.

To use the FILLETEDGE command for solids, follow these steps:

1. Choose Solid tab ⇨ Solid Editing panel ⇨ Fillet/Chamfer Edge drop-down menu ⇨ Fillet Edge. You see the current radius on the command line.

2. At the `Select an edge or [Chain/Loop/Radius]:` prompt, use the Radius option to specify a radius, or select the edges of the solid that you want to fillet. Press Enter to end selection. You cannot deselect edges that you have already selected. AutoCAD displays the result using the current radius.

   - To specify adjacent (tangent) edges, use the Chain option and specify the edges.

   - To specify a loop of edges, use the Loop option. For any edge, there are two possible loops, so when you select a loop edge, you need to accept the current selection or choose the Next loop.

3. At the `Press Enter to accept the fillet or [Radius]:` prompt, press Enter to complete the command. You can also change the radius at this prompt by either using the Radius option or dragging on the fillet grip, which looks like an arrow. If you drag the grip, you need to click to finalize the result.

ON THE WEB

The drawing used in the following exercise on filleting solids, `ab24-1.dwg`, is available from the Drawings download on the companion website.

STEPS: Filleting Solids

1. Open `ab24-1.dwg`, available from the companion website.

2. Save the file as `ab24-15.dwg` in your `AutoCAD Bible` folder. This is a solid model of a mounting angle, as shown in Figure 24.48. It needs to be filleted. Turn Object Snap off.

3. Choose Solid tab ⇨ Solid Editing panel ⇨ Fillet/Chamfer Edge drop-down menu ⇨ Fillet Edge.

4. At the `Select an edge or [Chain/Loop/Radius]:` prompt, type **r** ↵ to set the radius. Then type **.25** ↵.

5. At the `Select an edge or [Chain/Loop/Radius]:` prompt, pick ❶, ❷, and ❸. Press Enter to end selection. If you want, drag the fillet grip to adjust the fillet radius and click to finalize the result.

6. Press Enter to accept the fillet and end the command.

7. Save your drawing. It should look like Figure 24.49.

FIGURE 24.48

The mounting angle needs filleting.

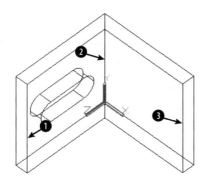

FIGURE 24.49

The filleted mounting angle

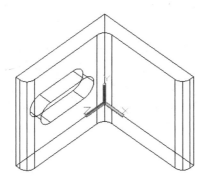

Chamfering in 3D

You can chamfer solids, but not meshes or surfaces. If you create a 3D object from lines, you can chamfer the lines. I cover the CHAMFER command in Chapter 10.

To chamfer a solid, follow these steps:

1. Choose Solid tab ⇨ Solid Editing panel ⇨ Fillet/Chamfer drop-down menu ⇨ Chamfer Edge. You see the Distance1 and Distance2 values on the command line.

2. At the `Select an edge or [Loop/Distance]:` prompt, use the Distance option to specify the two distances or select an edge that you want to chamfer.

3. At the `Select another edge on the same face or [Loop/Distance]:` prompt, you can select additional edges around the same face as your first edge. Press Enter to end selection.

4. You can drag the chamfer grips (one for each distance) and then click to make adjustments. Press Enter to accept the chamfer when you're finished.

Exploding and converting 3D objects

The EXPLODE command has a particular effect that varies according to the type of 3D object. Table 24.4 lists the effects of exploding 3D objects.

TABLE 24.4 Using EXPLODE on 3D Objects

Object	Result
Smooth solids	Flat surfaces become regions; curved surfaces become surfaces.
Mesh solids	3D faces.
Swept, lofted, extruded, or rotated surfaces	These surfaces become 2D objects or other surfaces that you can explode again to 2D objects.
Polyface meshes	3D faces.
Polygon meshes	3D faces.
Polylines with thickness	Lines.

 You can use the XEDGES command to convert smooth solids, mesh solids, surfaces, and regions to 2D wireframe objects. This is another kind of exploding. To use XEDGES, choose Solid tab ⇨ Solid Editing panel ⇨ Extract Edges. Then select objects. You can subselect faces and edges, as described earlier in this chapter, and use XEDGES on them. In addition to the XEDGES command, you can also use one of the following commands:

- **OFFSETEDGE.** Creates a closed polyline or spline that is an offset from the edges of a solid or surface face. By specifying the distance, you specify the size of the polyline or spline. Choose Solid tab ⇨ Solid Editing panel ⇨ Offset Edge.

- **SURFEXTRACTCURVE.** Extracts the curvature of a surface in the U or V direction instead of just the edges of a surface. Choose Surface tab ⇨ Curves panel ⇨ Extract Isolines.

NEW FEATURE
The SURFEXTRACTCURVE is new in AutoCAD 2013.

 The CONVTOSOLID command, discussed earlier in this chapter in the context of converting meshes to smooth solids, also converts polylines with a uniform width, closed polylines with zero-width, and circles to solids if they have a thickness. These are all objects that look like solids anyway. Choose Home tab ⇨ Solid Editing panel (expanded) ⇨ Convert to Solid and select the objects. (I discuss the CONVTOSURFACE command in Chapter 23.)

The Express Tools' FLATTEN command converts a 3D drawing into a 2D drawing, and changes the thickness and elevation of objects to zero. Choose Express Tools ⇨ Modify panel (expanded) ⇨ Flatten Objects and select objects.

Using the SOLIDEDIT Command

The SOLIDEDIT command offers options to edit faces, edges, and complete smooth solids in specific ways. This command has so many options that it might as well be several commands. Many of the options are now out of date because of the methods of direct manipulation of solids introduced in AutoCAD 2007. However, the command still has value because it offers some options that are available nowhere else, or it makes certain edits easier. SOLIDEDIT doesn't work on meshes.

SOLIDEDIT offers three major types of solid editing:

- **Faces.** A number of options enable you to edit the faces of solids. You can extrude, move, rotate, offset, taper, delete, copy, and color (assign a color to) faces.
- **Edges.** You can color and copy edges.
- **Bodies.** The body options apply to solids as a whole. You can imprint, separate, shell, clean, and check solids.

The next three sections explain how to edit faces, edges, and bodies.

Editing faces

A face is a surface on a solid. A face can be either flat or curved. For example, a hole in a block is a face, and many of the face-editing operations work well to modify holes. Of course, you can edit an outer face of a surface as well. The SOLIDEDIT command supports several methods of selecting a face or faces:

- You can select subobjects by using the Ctrl key, as described earlier in this chapter.
- You can click within the boundary of a face. AutoCAD selects the front-most face.
- You can click an edge to select its adjoining faces.

To make selecting the subobject you want easier, choose Home tab ⇨ Selection panel ⇨ Subobject Filter drop-down menu, and choose the type of subobject that you want. If you don't get the face that you want at first, at the `Select faces or [Undo/Remove]:` prompt, right-click and choose Undo to undo your last selection operation. Right-click and choose Remove to select a face to remove from the selection set. (You can also press Shift and pick a face to remove it.) The prompt then includes an Add option that you can use to start adding faces again. Then press Enter to end face selection.

You may want to perform more than one operation on a face. After you complete an operation, you can right-click to open the shortcut menu and choose another operation. To exit the command, right-click and choose Exit twice or press Enter twice.

24

Extruding faces

Extruding a face is like extruding a 2D object. Instead, you can select a face (as described earlier in this chapter) and use the EXTRUDE command; the prompts are similar. If you just want to extrude a face, without tapering it, you can grip-edit the solid.

 To extrude a face by using SOLIDEDIT, choose Home tab ⇨ Solid Editing panel ⇨ Faces drop-down menu ⇨ Extrude Faces. Then follow the prompts to specify a height and a taper. You can also use the Path option to extrude along an object. When you're done, press Enter twice to exit the command. For more information, see the "Using the EXTRUDE command" section earlier in this chapter.

AutoCAD extrudes the face. As you exit, AutoCAD performs a validation of the solid to make sure that the solid is a valid solid if the SOLIDCHECK system variable is on. By default, SOLIDCHECK is on (set to 1) and automatically checks solids when you edit them.

Moving faces

You can move a face when a solid is complex enough to have at least two separate elements — for example, a plate with a hole in it. You can then move the hole around wherever you want. You can also subselect the hole and move it by using its grips or the Move gizmo.

 To move a face, choose Home tab ⇨ Solid Editing panel ⇨ Faces drop-down menu ⇨ Move Faces. Then follow the prompts as you would with the MOVE command. Press Enter twice to exit the command.

If you choose a face that cannot be moved, AutoCAD displays the `Modeling Operation Error: No solution for an edge` message.

Offsetting faces

You can offset a face when a solid has two separate elements, such as a wall with a window cut out of it. You can then resize the window by offsetting it. Offsetting a face increases all parts of the face equally by a distance that you specify.

Use a positive offset value to increase the volume of the solid. If your face is a solid axle in the middle of a disk, for example, and you offset the axle with a positive value, the axle gets bigger. However, if your face is a hole in the middle of a disk, a positive offset value makes the hole smaller because that makes the resulting solid bigger.

Use a negative offset value to decrease the volume of the solid. Using the same example, a negative offset value would make the axle smaller, but it would make the hole bigger.

To offset a face, follow these steps:

1. Choose Home tab ⇨ Solid Editing panel ⇨ Faces drop-down menu ⇨ Offset Faces.
2. Select the face or faces that you want to offset and press Enter to end face selection.
3. At the `Specify the offset distance:` prompt, type a positive or negative distance. You can also pick two points to specify a positive offset.
4. Press Enter twice to exit the command.

AutoCAD offsets the face. If there is no room for the offset, AutoCAD displays the message `Modeling Operation Error` on the command line.

Deleting faces

You can delete a face of a solid. This is a great way to instantly get rid of a hole, axle, or window within a solid. You can delete faces to undo the effects of both the UNION and SUBTRACT commands. You can also remove filleted and chamfered faces. AutoCAD won't delete every face; for example, you can't turn a box into a tetrahedron by deleting the box's top face. Note that you can also subselect the face and press the Delete (Del) key.

 To delete a face or faces, choose Home tab ⇨ Solid Editing panel ⇨ Faces drop-down menu ⇨ Delete Faces. Select the face or faces and press Enter. AutoCAD deletes the face or faces that you selected. If your face(s) can't be deleted, you see the message `Modeling Operation Error` on the command line.

Rotating faces

You can rotate a face when a solid is complex enough to have at least two separate elements — for example, a box with a hole in it. The prompts for rotating are very similar to those for ROTATE3D, covered earlier in this chapter; you can select a subobject and use that command, or the Rotate gizmo. To rotate a face by using SOLIDEDIT, choose Home tab ⇨ Solid Editing panel ⇨ Faces drop-down menu ⇨ Rotate Faces. Select the face or faces that you want to rotate, using the selection method(s) described earlier. Follow the prompts, which are similar to those of the 3DROTATE command. Press Enter twice to exit the command.

If you choose a face that cannot be rotated, or if there isn't room on the solid for the rotation, AutoCAD lets you know with the message `Modeling Operation Error` on the command line. Note that you can also subselect the face and rotate it by using grip-editing.

Tapering faces

You can taper an entire simple solid, such as a box, or you can taper a face that is an element within a complex solid, such as a hole or an extruded face. Tapering angles the sides of the face. To determine the direction of the taper, that is, which end gets tapered, you specify a base point and a second point. The base point side of the solid is not tapered, and AutoCAD tapers the face in the direction from the base point toward the second point. You also specify the angle of the taper. A positive taper angle tapers the face inward; a hole is tapered outward. A negative taper angle tapers the face outward; a hole is tapered inward. In general, you should use small tapering angles. If the face tapers to a point before it reaches its existing height, then AutoCAD cannot complete the taper.

To taper a face, follow these steps:

1. Choose Home tab ⇨ Solid Editing panel ⇨ Faces drop-down menu ⇨ Taper Faces. AutoCAD starts the SOLIDEDIT command and automatically enters the first two prompts of the command for you.

2. Select the face(s) that you want to taper. Press Enter to end face selection.

3. At the `Specify the base point:` prompt, pick the base point for the taper direction. Object snaps are a good idea.

4. At the `Specify another point along the axis of tapering:` prompt, specify a second point to indicate the direction of the taper. Again, use an object snap.

5. At the `Specify the taper angle:` prompt, specify an angle between –90° and +90°.

6. Press Enter twice to exit the command.

If AutoCAD can't taper the face, you see the message `Modeling Operation Error` on the command line.

Copying faces

You can copy any face, including a hole. AutoCAD creates regions or surfaces out of the face. However, if you copy a complex face, such as a hole that may consist of several regions, you can't turn it back into a solid again.

To copy a face, follow these steps:

1. Choose Home tab ⇨ Solid Editing panel ⇨ Faces drop-down menu ⇨ Copy Faces.

2. Select the face(s) that you want to copy. Press Enter to end face selection.

3. At the `Specify a base point or displacement:` prompt, specify a base point. Object snaps are helpful.

4. At the `Specify a second point of displacement:` prompt, specify a second point to indicate the direction and distance for the copy.

5. Press Enter twice to exit the command.

Coloring faces

You can assign a color to a face of an object. You might want to color a face to make it easier to see. The color overrides the color setting for the solid's layer.

> **NOTE**
>
> When an object is assigned more than one material, priority goes to attachment by object, then by color, and finally by layer. If you attach a material to a solid by layer, and then attach a material to one of its faces (that you have colored) by color, both the solid and the face display their materials. For more information, see Bonus Chapter 2.

To color a face, follow these steps:

1. Choose Home tab ⇨ Solid Editing panel ⇨ Faces drop-down menu ⇨ Color Faces.

2. Select the face or faces that you want to color. Press Enter to end face selection.

3. AutoCAD opens the Select Color dialog box. Choose a color and click OK.

4. Press Enter twice to exit the command.

Attaching a material to a face

You can assign a material to a face of an object. You would do this for the purpose of displaying the object with that material in your drawing, or for rendering. For more information on materials and how to add them to your drawing, see Bonus Chapter 2.

To add a material to a face, first add the material to the drawing (as I explain in Bonus Chapter 2). Then follow these steps:

1. Start the SOLIDEDIT command. Choose the Face option, then choose the mAterial option.

2. Select the face or faces that you want to use. Press Enter to end face selection.

3. At the `Enter new material name <ByLayer>:` prompt, type the name of the material as it appears in the Materials palette.

4. Press Enter twice to exit the command.

Editing edges

The two-dimensional place where two faces meet is an edge. You can perform only two editing operations on edges: You can copy them and color them.

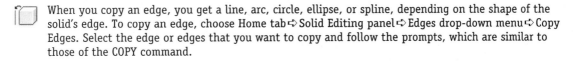 When you copy an edge, you get a line, arc, circle, ellipse, or spline, depending on the shape of the solid's edge. To copy an edge, choose Home tab ➪ Solid Editing panel ➪ Edges drop-down menu ➪ Copy Edges. Select the edge or edges that you want to copy and follow the prompts, which are similar to those of the COPY command.

You can color an edge to make it more visible. The color overrides the color setting for the solid's layer. To color an edge, choose Home tab ➪ Solid Editing panel ➪ Edges drop-down menu ➪ Color Edges. Select the edge or edges that you want to color, and choose the color that you want.

Editing bodies

Several of the SOLIDEDIT options apply to solids as a whole. The operations available are imprinting, cleaning, separating, shelling, and checking. These operations are discussed in the following sections.

Imprinting solids

You can imprint an arc, circle, line, 2D polyline or 3D polyline, ellipse, spline, region, or 3D solid on a solid. The object that you're imprinting must intersect a face on the solid. The shape made by the intersection of the object is left on the solid, as if you put ink on the edges of the object and stamped it on the solid. Figure 24.50 shows an example of imprinting.

FIGURE 24.50

The ellipse was drawn on the top of the solid. After imprinting and deleting the ellipse, the shape of half of the ellipse remains on the solid.

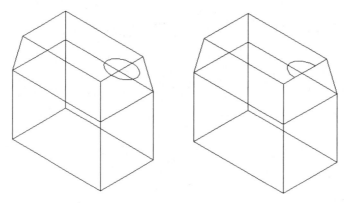

 In Chapter 23, I cover the **PROJECTGEOMETRY** command, which is somewhat similar.

To imprint a solid, follow these steps:

1. First create one of the stampable objects previously listed so that it intersects with a solid. If you draw in top view, check in an isometric view to make sure that the intersection is where you want it.

 2. Choose Home tab ➪ Solid Editing panel ➪ Edges drop-down menu ➪ Imprint.

3. At the `Select a 3D solid or surface:` prompt, select a solid. You can select only one.

4. At the `Select an object to imprint:` prompt, select the object that you want to imprint.

5. At the `Delete the source object [Yes/No] <N>:` prompt, type **y** ↵ or press Enter to indicate No.

6. AutoCAD repeats the `Select an object to imprint:` prompt. You can continue the command in the same way or press Enter if you're done.

7. Press Enter to exit the command.

AutoCAD imprints the solid or curface. If you didn't delete the source object, you'll need to move it to see the result. You can subselect an imprint and delete it or edit it in any other way. You can also use an imprint to divide a face, and then use the PRESSPULL command to extrude or press that portion of the face.

Cleaning solids

After all the editing, you can end up with some pretty strange solids. Cleaning solids removes adjacent faces that share the same surface and other duplicate or unused edges, vertices, and geometry. Cleaning does not remove imprints.

To clean a solid, choose Home tab ➪ Solid Editing panel ➪ Body drop-down menu ➪ Clean. At the `Select a 3D solid:` prompt, select a solid. AutoCAD cleans it.

Separating solids

You can separate a solid that is made up of nontouching sections. You would generally create such a solid from separate, nontouching solids, using the UNION command. The Separate option undoes the effect of the UNION command so that the solids become separate again.

 To separate a solid, choose Home tab ➪ Solid Editing panel ➪ Body drop-down menu ➪ Separate. At the `Select a 3D solid:` prompt, select the solid by picking any of its sections. AutoCAD separates the solids.

If your solid sections are even just touching, you get one of the odder AutoCAD messages: `The selected solid does not have multiple lumps.`

Shelling solids

When you shell a solid, you hollow out its inside, leaving a thin wall. Think of making a drinking glass from a truncated cone (or tapered cylinder) or a room from a solid box. To shell a solid, follow these steps:

1. Choose Home tab ➪ Solid Editing panel ➪ Body drop-down menu ➪ Shell.
2. At the `Select a 3D solid:` prompt, select a solid.
3. At the `Remove faces or [Undo/Add/ALL]:` prompt, remove any face or faces that you don't want to shell. For example, if you're making a drinking glass from a truncated cone, you want to remove the larger circular face (the one you would drink out of) so that it will remain open. Otherwise, you end up with an enclosed solid that has a hollow interior. After you finish removing faces, press Enter. (The command line confirms `1 face found, 1 removed`, but there is no visual confirmation that AutoCAD has removed the correct face.)
4. At the `Enter the shell offset distance:` prompt, type the width of the wall that you want to create. A positive value creates a shell to the inside of the current solid. A negative value creates a shell to the outside of the current solid.
5. Press Enter twice to shell the solid and exit the command.

Checking solids

Checking ensures that your solid is a valid 3D solid object so that you can edit it without getting ACIS failure error messages. This might be a useful feature to put into an AutoLISP or VBA program, to make sure that it doesn't fail because of invalid solids.

 To check a solid, choose Home tab ➪ Solid Editing panel ➪ Body drop-down menu ➪ Check. At the `Select a 3D solid:` prompt, select a solid. Usually, AutoCAD replies with the message: `This object is a valid ShapeManager solid.`

ON THE WEB

The drawing used in the following exercise on editing solid bodies, `ab24-m.dwg`, is available from the Drawings download on the companion website.

2 4

STEPS: Editing Solid Bodies

1. Open `ab24-m.dwg`, available from the companion website.

2. Save the file as `ab24-16.dwg` in your `AutoCAD Bible` folder. This is a simple solid box with an ellipse drawn on part of its top face.

3. Choose Home tab⇨Solid Editing panel⇨Edges drop-down menu⇨Imprint. Follow the prompts:

    ```
    Select a 3D solid or surface: Select the box.
    Select an object to imprint: Select the ellipse.
    Delete the source object [Yes/No] <N>: y ↵
    Select an object to imprint: Right-click to complete the imprint and end
        the command.
    ```

4. Choose Home tab⇨Modeling panel⇨Presspull. Click inside the remaining part of the ellipse that was imprinted on the 3D solid. Move the cursor up. Type **.2** ↵ on the command line or Dynamic Input tooltip. Press Enter to end the command.

5. Choose Home tab⇨Solid Editing panel⇨Body drop-down menu⇨Shell. Follow the prompts:

    ```
    Select a 3D Solid: Select the box.
    Remove faces or [Undo/Add/ALL]: Pick anywhere inside the top face.
    Remove faces or [Undo/Add/ALL]: Right-click and choose Enter.
    Enter the shell offset distance: .1 ↵
    ```

6. Press Enter twice to exit the command.

7. Choose View tab⇨Visual Styles panel⇨Visual Styles drop-down list⇨Hidden. You can now see the result of the shell operation.

8. Save your drawing. It should look like Figure 24.51.

FIGURE 24.51

The shelled box

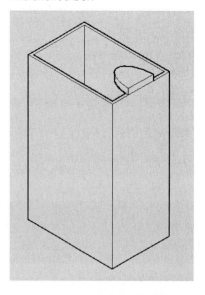

Listing Solid Properties

The MASSPROP command provides information about regions and solids that is useful for engineering applications. The bounding box, for example, is an imaginary box that contains the solid. The calculations are based on the relationship of the solid to the UCS. If you rotate the solid or change the UCS, you get different results. For example, after running MASSPROP to find the center of gravity (centroid) and axes of your model, move the UCS to the centroid and then run MASSPROP again to identify the moments of inertia.

For 2D regions, the area moment of inertia that MASSPROP generates can be used to calculate bending and twisting stresses. You could generate a 2D region of a solid model by using the SECTION command and then use the UCS command with the OBJECT option to set the UCS coplanar to the region. The MASSPROP command would then report the area moment of inertia.

AutoCAD assumes a density of 1 for all solids. You can then apply material density multipliers on the values that get reported.

To list a solid's properties, type **massprop** ↵ on the command line. Select the object that you want to list. AutoCAD opens the Text Window to display the calculations. At the `Write analysis to a file? [Yes/No] <N>:` prompt, press Enter to accept the No default, or right-click and choose Yes. AutoCAD prompts you for a filename and copies the data to that file.

> **NOTE**
> You can use the MEASUREGEOM command to get the volume of a 3D model. Enter measuregeom ↵ on the command line and use the Object option to select one or more objects. AutoCAD displays the volume. Use the eXit option (or type x ↵) to end the command.

Summary

In this chapter, you learned how to create and edit solids. You read about:

- Drawing basic shapes
- Creating extruded, swept, revolved, and lofted solids from 2D profiles
- Drawing polysolids
- Manipulating solids by grip-editing, selecting subobjects, and using the Move, Rotate, and Scale gizmos
- Creating and editing mesh solids
- Using UNION, SUBTRACT, and INTERSECT to create more-complex shapes
- Using the INTERFERE command to see the volume of interference between solids
- Pressing or pulling a solid
- Utilizing the SECTION, SLICE, and SECTIONPLANE commands to visualize and reshape solids
- Using the move grip tool and the 3DMOVE command
- Using MIRROR3D, ARRAY, and ROTATE3D for 3D editing
- Using the 3DALIGN, TRIM, EXTEND, FILLETEDGE, and CHAMFEREDGE commands for 3D editing

24

- Exploding into surfaces and solids into 2D objects
- Using the SOLIDEDIT and IMPRINT command to edit faces, edges, and bodies
- Calculating a number of engineering functions and values for solids by using the MASSPROP and MEASUREGEOM commands

In Bonus Chapter 2 on the companion website, I cover rendering 3D models.

A Final Word

AutoCAD offers almost unlimited potential for the design and drawing of real-world objects. I hope that this book helps you to understand the world of AutoCAD and makes it easier for you to create the professional drawings that you need to redesign the world and make it a better place.

As a reminder, there is much more to this book than what you see printed between its covers. You can find 15 bonus chapters, several chapter addendums, and additional content by visiting the www. wiley.com/go/autocad2013bible or www.ellenfinkelstein.com/autocad2013bible/ websites.

Although I cannot provide technical support for my readers, I would be happy to hear your comments and suggestions at http://ellen@ellenfinkelstein.com. Best wishes and enjoy!

Part V

Appendixes

IN THIS PART

Appendix A
AutoCAD and AutoCAD LT Resources

Appendix B
What's on the Companion Website?

AutoCAD and AutoCAD LT Resources

IN THIS APPENDIX

Learning AutoCAD or AutoCAD LT

Accessing technical support

Joining Autodesk user groups

Finding Internet resources

A side from this book, you have many other resources for learning about AutoCAD. These resources range from the AutoCAD Welcome Screen to websites, and include everything else in between.

ON THE WEB
On the companion website, you can find a document containing clickable links for the Internet resources in this appendix. Look for the Links download.

Learning AutoCAD and AutoCAD LT

AutoCAD and AutoCAD LT are not programs that you can easily pick up as you work with them. You'll need some formal education, whether by using this book, taking a course, or using a combination of methods.

Using AutoCAD and AutoCAD LT Help resources

AutoCAD's own Help resources are a good place to start when you have a question. In Chapter 3, I explain how to use Help. Also, in the Welcome Screen that appears when you launch AutoCAD, click the What's New in 2013 button for information on new features. You can access the Welcome Screen at any time by clicking the Help (?) button's down arrow and choosing Welcome Screen.

Learning from your reseller

You're supposed to learn AutoCAD from your reseller. Most resellers offer some training when you purchase AutoCAD. However, the amount of training and follow-up support varies greatly, and so does the price. If you have more than one AutoCAD reseller nearby, check not only the cost of AutoCAD but also the cost of training.

Unlike AutoCAD, AutoCAD LT is often sold online without any training. Keep in mind that AutoCAD LT is not a simple program either, and some training will definitely help you get more out of the program.

Resellers usually offer upgrade seminars and courses when you upgrade. If you're already using AutoCAD or AutoCAD LT, you may be able to take a course that focuses on the new features.

If you're going to use third-party applications that work with AutoCAD or other Autodesk products, check how much experience the reseller has with these products and what kind of support the reseller offers.

Autodesk has an Autodesk Training Center program that certifies trainers. Your reseller may or may not be an Autodesk Training Center; remember to ask. Premier Training Centers offer additional training in certain disciplines, thus offering solutions that are more specialized to their customers.

Taking a course

You may be able to take a course in AutoCAD at a local college or Autodesk Training Center. Many universities and community colleges offer courses in AutoCAD. Such courses may fit your schedule because they're often offered in the evening, over a period of several weeks. Of course, that may not work if you need to get up and running very quickly. AutoCAD LT courses are less common. However, a course on AutoCAD would certainly help you to learn AutoCAD LT.

Autodesk holds a once-a-year conference, called Autodesk University, which offers classes that are taught by top AutoCAD experts. For more information, go to au.autodesk.com.

Autodesk sells short, self-paced courses on both AutoCAD and AutoCAD LT. From the Autodesk home page (www.autodesk.com), hover over Support, and then choose Courseware from the menu. You can find other training-related links under the same menu.

Learning from other users

If you work in an office with several AutoCAD or AutoCAD LT users, you'll find that they're usually happy to share information and tips with you. This won't generally get you started from scratch, but it's great for rounding out your knowledge.

Reading magazines and newsletters

Cadalyst (www.cadalyst.com) covers AutoCAD as well as other CAD programs. It is published in both print and web versions, and includes many helpful articles. In addition, *Cadalyst* has an extensive website that I discuss later in this appendix.

AUGI has a couple of great publications, including *AUGIWorld* magazine. You can find out more at www.augi.com. A free registration is required. Then click the AUGIWorld link.

If you're interested in the CAD industry in general, try Ralph Grabowski's weekly *upFront.eZine*, which you can subscribe to by sending the e-mail message "subscribe upfront" to `http://editor@xyz-press.com`.

I offer an e-mail newsletter, *AutoCAD Tips Newsletter*. It contains tips, tutorials, and techniques. I invite you to sign up at `www.ellenfinkelstein.com/acad_submit.html`.

Accessing Technical Support

Autodesk has always referred customers to their reseller for technical support. As with training, you should check out the provisions of the technical support. Some resellers charge for each phone call, while others provide free support to all customers for as long as Autodesk supports the product.

However, Autodesk offers its own support. For an overview of support options, hover over Support and choose Support & Documentation from the Autodesk home page (`www.autodesk.com`), then select one of the links to the right of AutoCAD or AutoCAD LT. The Knowledge Base link allows you to access a large number of technical documents that answer many common questions. You can also access additional documentation and the product's online help.

The Autodesk website offers discussion groups. From Autodesk's home page, hover over Support, choose Discussion Groups, and then choose AutoCAD or AutoCAD LT. You can ask questions and receive answers from other users as well as from Autodesk employees.

Autodesk User Groups

Autodesk User Groups (AUGs) meet regularly, offer courses and seminars, bring in speakers, and generally offer the types of resources that all AutoCAD users need. Go to the AUGI website at `www.augi.com` to see if there is a group in your area.

AUGI also offers its own technical support and training. You can find a lot of information and educational resources there, as well as AutoCAD and AutoCAD LT forums, which have their own easy entrance via the AutoCAD Community at `www.augi.com/communities/ACAD-Community/`.

Internet Resources

The companion website to this book contains several valuable resources:

- Approximately 400 pages of additional content, including 15 bonus chapters and several chapter addenda.
- The drawings for the many exercises are in the Drawings download.
- 3 video tutorials
- A hyperlinked list of Internet resources from this appendix.

A

You can find these resources in two locations:

- The publisher, Wiley, maintains the official companion website at www.wiley.com/go/autocad2013bible.

- I have the same content on my website. The only difference is that, when you sign up for my free AutoCAD Tips Newsletter, you'll get a free ebook, "25 Productivity Tips Every AutoCAD User Should Know," additional video tutorials, and a collection of software for AutoCAD. Go to www.ellenfinkelstein.com/autocadbible/.

The Internet sports hundreds of CAD-related websites. Here are some of the most prominent:

- **The Autodesk** website, at www.autodesk.com, contains a lot of product and support resources on AutoCAD and other Autodesk products. At www.autodesk.com/autocad, AutoCAD's home page, you can find a great deal of information about AutoCAD, including training and upgrade information. For information on AutoCAD LT, go to www.autodesk.com/autocadlt.

- **The *Cadalyst*** website, at www.cadalyst.com, is another important resource. Here you can find news, events, links, products, downloads, and so on. The *Cadalyst* files, at cadtips.cadalyst.com, offer all the AutoLISP code that the magazine has published since 1993.

- **TenLinks.com**, at www.tenlinks.com, is a wide-ranging directory and news source, with a daily e-mail newsletter.

- **CAD2Design's AutoCAD channel**, at http://autocad.cad2design.com/news, aggregates blog posts (including mine) from around the Internet. The web has many more AutoCAD sites, but most of them are more specialized. Table A.1 lists some useful sites. If you don't have this list when you access the Internet, just type **AutoCAD** into any major search engine. One website will lead to another until you find what you need. Enjoy!

TABLE A.1   Useful AutoCAD Websites

Name	URL	Description
AUGI	www.augi.com	AutoCAD User Group International. This site includes a lot of information on AutoCAD, connections to local groups, and a newsletter.
Better Than Nothing AutoLISP	http://home.pacifier.com/~nemi	Leonid Nemirovsky's AutoLISP routines are useful and are free to download. I put several of them on the companion website of this book. Leonid wrote two (lt.lsp and ldt.lsp) at my request, for which I'm grateful.
CAD Forum	www.cadforum.cz/cadforum_en/	This site offers loads of tips on both AutoCAD and AutoCAD LT, and a popular forum.
CAD-Notes	www.cad-notes.com	This website contains many AutoCAD tips and articles. Click the AutoCAD Articles link.

Name	URL	Description
CADTutor	`www.cadtutor.net`	Free tutorials and articles on AutoCAD.
Dotsoft	`www.dotsoft.com`	Terry Dotson's site offers AutoCAD-related software for sale, along with a lot of freebies and tips.
EllenFinkelstein.com	`www.ellenfinkelstein.com`	My site contains AutoCAD tips, tutorials, and techniques. You can sign up for the AutoCAD Tips Newsletter or read my AutoCAD Tips Blog.
HyperPics	`www.hyperpics.com`	Lee Ambrosius' site offers AutoCAD and AutoCAD LT tips and tricks, with a lot of information on customization.
ManuSoft	`www.manusoft.com`	This site offers a good collection of software for AutoCAD — some for free, others to buy.
upfront.eZine	`www.upfrontezine.com`	You can find the archives of Ralph Grabowski's ezine, and purchase his eBooks.

A number of AutoCAD blogs have sprung up — and more keep coming. Some of these blogs are full-fledged websites, containing dozens or even hundreds of tips and tutorials. If you want the latest news, tips, and information, try one of these:

- **AutoCAD Tips Blog** (my own) at `www.ellenfinkelstein.com/acadblog`
- **Between the Lines** by Autodesk employee Shaan Hurley at `http://autodesk.blogs.com/between_the_lines`
- **RobiNZ CAD Blog** by Robin Capper at `http://rcd.typepad.com/rcd`
- **Beyond the UI** by Lee Ambrosius (contributor and technical editor of this book) at `http://hyperpics.blogs.com/beyond_the_ui`
- **Lynn Allen's Blog** by Autodesk employee Lynn Allen at `http://blogs.autodesk.com/lynn`
- **AutoCAD Insider** by Autodesk employee Heidi Hewitt at `http://blogs.autodesk.com/autocadinsider`
- **Beth's CAD Blog** by Beth Powell at `http://bethscadblog.blogspot.com`
- **CAD Panacea** by R.K. McSwain at `www.cadpanacea.com`
- **CAD-a-Blog** by Brian Benton at `http://cadablog.blogspot.com`
- **JTB World Blog** by Jimmy Bergmark at `http://jtbworld.blogspot.com`
- **Mistress of the Dorkness** by Melanie (Stone) Perry (who helped me update some of the chapters of this book) at `http://mistressofthedorkness.blogspot.com`
- **CADman-Do** by David Cohn at `http://cadman-do.blogspot.com`
- **The Lazy Drafter** by Todd Shakelford at `http://lazydrafter.blogspot.com`

A

- **blog nauseam** by Steve Johnson at `www.blog.cadnauseam.com`
- **LT Unlimited** by Autodesk employee Kate Morrical at `http://blogs.autodesk.com/ltunlimited`
- **The LT Side of Things** by Erik Deyo at `http://ltsideofthings.blogspot.com`
- **It's Alive in the Lab** by Scott Sheppard at `http://blogs.autodesk.com/labs`
- **BLAUGI** by Autodesk User Group International at `http://augi.typepad.com`
- **Through the Interface** by Autodesk employee Kean Walmsley at `http://blogs.autodesk.com/through-the-interface`

What's on the Companion Website

IN THIS APPENDIX

Checking your system requirements

Using the companion website

Accessing the software

Troubleshooting tips

The *AutoCAD 2013 and AutoCAD LT 2013 Bible* companion website contains all the drawings and files that you need to do the exercises in the book, as well as the results of those exercises. It also contains over 500 pages of additional content that were previously in the printed book. In addition, I've created several video tutorials based on content in this book. Finally, you can find a document of links to Internet resources on AutoCAD and AutoCAD LT. I hope that you find this companion website a valuable addition to your AutoCAD arsenal.

You can access content on the companion website in two locations:

- **Official Wiley website.** The publisher of this book maintains a companion website at www. wiley.com/go/autocad2013bible. Click the Downloads link to access the files, and then choose the download you want. The files available for download are listed later in this appendix.

- **Author's website:** I have the same content available on my own website at www.ellen finkelstein.com/autocad2013bible, when you sign up for my free AutoCAD Tips Newsletter. You'll also get a free copy of my ebook, "Top 25 AutoCAD Productivity Tips Every AutoCAD User Should Know," additional video tutorials, and a collection of software for AutoCAD.

In the rest of this appendix, I'll cover the following topics:

- Using the downloads with Microsoft Windows and your browser
- What's on the companion website
- Troubleshooting
- Customer Care

Using the Downloads with Microsoft Windows and Your Browser

Both companion website locations offer a list of downloads. All are in ZIP format. The ZIP format is useful because it combines many files into one and compresses them at the same time. You will need to extract (unzip) these files to access their contents. Follow these steps to download and extract the files:

1. Click the file that you want to download.

2. If you have an option to Run or Save, choose Save. If you have an option to choose a location, choose the AutoCAD Bible folder that you created. (For instructions, see the Quick Start Chapter and Chapter 1.) If you don't have an option to choose a location, then to find the downloaded file, you need to know your browser's setting for saving downloads.

3. Windows 7 can extract the files from the ZIP file. Do either of the following:
   - To extract a single file or folder, double-click the compressed folder to open it. Then, drag the file or folder from the compressed folder to a new location.
   - To extract the entire contents of the compressed folder, right-click the folder, click Extract All, and then follow the instructions.

4. Move the extracted file or files to your AutoCAD Bible folder, as described in Chapter 1.

> **NOTE**
> You can also use a third-party extraction program, such as WinZip or 7-Zip.

What's on the Companion Website

The following list provides a summary of the drawings and other materials that you'll find on the companion website:

- **Drawings download.** I've placed all the files that you need for the exercises in the Drawings download, named Drawings.zip. Almost all these files are named using the format ab15-a.dwg, ab15-b.dwg, ab15-c.dwg, and so on. In these examples, the number 15 corresponds to the chapter number, and the letters correspond to the first, second, and third drawings that you need to open. A few files have other names, such as bluesky.jpg and others. In each case, I provide you with the name of the file to open in the exercise's steps.

- **Results download.** The Results download, in a file named Results.zip, offers you the results of all the exercises. You may want to check your work in the exercises against these results. You may also sometimes use the result of one exercise as the basis for a second exercise. In this situation, if you haven't done the previous exercise, you can access the resulting file from the Results download and use it for the exercise.

- **Links document.** Appendix A contains numerous links to AutoCAD resources. The Links document (Links.zip) contains these resources as live links to make it easy for you to navigate to them with a single click.

- **Video download.** I have created a few video tutorials for you, to help you visualize some of the more difficult concepts, including the entire Quick Start chapter, because I know that beginners use this chapter. I hope that these videos will help you learn some of AutoCAD's features more quickly.

- **Bonus chapters.** Due to space constraints and to save printing costs, I have put 15 chapters of the book on the companion website as well as seven parts of chapters (called addenda). All in all, you will find about 400 pages of extra content! Table B-1 lists this content.

> **NOTE**
> Trial versions of the current release are available from Autodesk's website. For AutoCAD, go to www.autodesk.com/autocad-trial. For AutoCAD LT, go to www.autodesk.com/autocadlt-trial.

Finding Bonus Chapter and Addendum Content

Table B.1 lists all the bonus chapters and addenda on the companion website.

TABLE B.1   The Companion Website Bonus Chapter and Addendum Content

Chapter or Addendum Number	Chapter or Addendum Name
Bonus Chapter 1	Working with External Databases
Bonus Chapter 2	Rendering in 3D
Bonus Chapter 3	Keeping Control of Your Drawings
Bonus Chapter 4	Working with Other Applications
Bonus Chapter 5	Creating Electronic Output
Bonus Chapter 6	Customizing Commands, Toolbars, and Tool Palettes
Bonus Chapter 7	Creating Macros and Slide Shows
Bonus Chapter 8	Creating Your Own Linetypes and Hatch Patterns
Bonus Chapter 9	Creating Shapes and Fonts
Bonus Chapter 10	Customizing the Ribbon and Menus
Bonus Chapter 11	Understanding AutoLISP and VisualLISP Basics
Bonus Chapter 12	Exploring AutoLISP Further
Bonus Chapter 13	Exploring Advanced AutoLISP Topics
Bonus Chapter 14	Programming with .NET
Bonus Chapter 15	Installing and Configuring AutoCAD and AutoCAD LT
Chapter 10 Addendum	Using Parametric Constraints, Filters, and Groups
Chapter 12 Addendum	Using AutoCAD's Calculator
Chapter 16 Addendum	Creating Multilines and Dlines, and Digitizing Paper Drawings
Chapter 19 Addendum	Extracting Attribute Data
Chapter 20 Addendum	Controlling the Display of External References
Chapter 22 Addendum	Creating Walk-throughs and Perspective Views
Chapter 23 Addendum	Creating 3D Surfaces with Older AutoCAD Commands

Troubleshooting

If you have difficulty downloading or opening any of the materials on the companion website, try the following solutions:

- **Make sure your firewall isn't blocking the download.** Check if you can download files from other websites or ask your IT person for help.
- **Try the download again.** Sometimes, a download (especially a large one) is interrupted and gets corrupted. Trying a second time often helps.

Customer Care

If you have trouble with the Wiley companion website downloads, please call the Wiley Product Technical Support at 877-762-2974. Outside the United States, call 1-317-572-3993 or fax 317-572-4002. You can also contact Wiley Product Technical Support at www.wiley.com/techsupport. John Wiley & Sons will provide technical support only for installation and other general quality control items. For technical support on the applications themselves, consult the program's vendor or author.

To place additional orders or to request information about other Wiley products, please call 877-762-2974.

Index

Symbols and Numerics

Index

Index